The Internationalisation of Criminal Evidence

Beyond the Common Law and Civil Law Traditions

Although there are many texts on the law of evidence, surprisingly few are devoted specifically to the comparative and international aspects of the subject. The traditional view that the law of evidence belongs within the common law tradition has obscured the reality that a genuinely cosmopolitan law of evidence is being developed in criminal cases across the common law and civil law traditions.

By considering the extent to which a coherent body of common evidentiary standards is being developed in both domestic and international jurisprudence, John Jackson and Sarah Summers chart this development with particular reference to the jurisprudence on the right to a fair trial that has emerged from the European Court of Human Rights and to the attempts in the new international criminal tribunals to fashion agreed approaches towards the regulation of evidence.

John D. Jackson is a barrister at law and Professor of Criminal Law at the School of Law, University College Dublin.

Sarah J. Summers is currently Oberassistentin in criminal law and criminal procedure at the Law School in the University of Zurich, Switzerland, and a researcher at the Max Planck Institute for Foreign and International Law, Freiburg in Breisgau, Germany.

The Law in Context Series

Editors: William Twining (University College London), Christopher McCrudden (Lincoln College, Oxford) and Bronwen Morgan (University of Bristol).

Since 1970 the Law in Context series has been in the forefront of the movement to broaden the study of law. It has been a vehicle for the publication of innovative scholarly books that treat law and legal phenomena critically in their social, political and economic contexts from a variety of perspectives. The series particularly aims to publish scholarly legal writing that brings fresh perspectives to bear on new and existing areas of law taught in universities. A contextual approach involves treating legal subjects broadly, using materials from other social sciences, and from any other discipline that helps to explain the operation in practice of the subject under discussion. It is hoped that this orientation is at once more stimulating and more realistic than the bare exposition of legal rules. The series includes original books that have a different emphasis from traditional legal textbooks, while maintaining the same high standards of scholarship. They are written primarily for undergraduate and graduate students of law and of other disciplines, but most also appeal to a wider readership. In the past, most books in the series have focused on English law, but recent publications include books on European law, globalisation, transnational legal processes and comparative law.

Books in the Series
Anderson, Schum & Twining: *Analysis of Evidence*
Ashworth: *Sentencing and Criminal Justice*
Barton & Douglas: *Law and Parenthood*
Beecher-Monas: *Evaluating Scientific Evidence: An Interdisciplinary Framework for Intellectual Due Process*
Bell: *French Legal Cultures*
Bercusson: *European Labour Law*
Birkinshaw: *European Public Law*
Birkinshaw: *Freedom of Information: The Law, the Practice and the Ideal*
Cane: *Atiyah's Accidents, Compensation and the Law*
Clarke & Kohler: *Property Law: Commentary and Materials*
Collins: *The Law of Contract*
Cowan: *Housing Law and Policy*
Cranston: *Legal Foundations of the Welfare State*
Dauvergne: *Making People Illegal: What Globalisation Means for Immigration and Law*
Davies: *Perspectives on Labour Law*
Dembour: *Who Believes in Human Rights?: The European Convention in Question*
de Sousa Santos: *Toward a New Legal Common Sense*
Diduck: *Law's Families*
Fortin: *Children's Rights and the Developing Law*
Glover-Thomas: *Reconstructing Mental Health Law and Policy*
Gobert & Punch: *Rethinking Corporate Crime*

Goldman: *Globalisation and the Western Legal Tradition: Recurring Patterns of Law and Authority*
Harlow & Rawlings: *Law and Administration*
Harris: *An Introduction to Law*
Harris, Campbell & Halson: *Remedies in Contract and Tort*
Harvey: *Seeking Asylum in the UK: Problems and Prospects*
Hervey & McHale: *Health Law and the European Union*
Holder & Lee: *Environmental Protection, Law and Policy*
Jackson and Summers: *The Internationalisation of Criminal Evidence*
Kostakopoulou: *The Future Governance of Citizenship*
Lewis: *Choice and the Legal Order: Rising above Politics*
Likosky: *Transnational Legal Processes*
Likosky: *Law, Infrastructure and Human Rights*
Maughan & Webb: *Lawyering Skills and the Legal Process*
McGlynn: *Families and the European Union: Law, Politics and Pluralism*
Moffat: *Trusts Law: Text and Materials*
Monti: *EC Competition Law*
Morgan & Yeung: *An Introduction to Law and Regulation: Text and Materials*
Norrie: *Crime, Reason and History*
O'Dair: *Legal Ethics*
Oliver: *Common Values and the Public–Private Divide*
Oliver & Drewry: *The Law and Parliament*
Picciotto: *International Business Taxation*
Reed: *Internet Law: Text and Materials*
Richardson: *Law, Process and Custody*
Roberts & Palmer: *Dispute Processes: ADR and the Primary Forms of Decision-Making*
Rowbottom: *Democracy Distorted: Wealth, Influence and Democratic Politics*
Scott & Black: *Cranston's Consumers and the Law*
Seneviratne: *Ombudsmen: Public Services and Administrative Justice*
Stapleton: *Product Liability*
Stewart: *Gender, Law and Justice in a Global Market*
Tamanaha: *Law as a Means to an End: Threat to the Rule of Law*
Turpin and Tomkins: *British Government and the Constitution: Text and Materials*
Twining: *Globalisation and Legal Theory*
Twining: *Rethinking Evidence*
Twining: *General Jurisprudence: Understanding Law from a Global Perspective*
Twining: *Human Rights, Southern Voices: Francis Deng, Abdullahi An-Na'im, Yash Ghai and Upendra Baxi*
Twining & Miers: *How to Do Things with Rules*
Ward: *A Critical Introduction to European Law*
Ward: *Law, Text, Terror*
Ward: *Shakespeare and Legal Imagination*
Wells & Quick: *Lacey, Wells and Quick: Reconstructing Criminal Law*
Zander: *Cases and Materials on the English Legal System*
Zander: *The Law-Making Process*

The Internationalisation of Criminal Evidence

Beyond the Common Law and Civil Law Traditions

JOHN D. JACKSON AND SARAH J. SUMMERS

CAMBRIDGE UNIVERSITY PRESS
Cambridge, New York, Melbourne, Madrid, Cape Town,
Singapore, São Paulo, Delhi, Tokyo, Mexico City

Cambridge University Press
The Edinburgh Building, Cambridge CB2 8RU, UK

Published in the United States of America by Cambridge University Press, New York

www.cambridge.org
Information on this title: www.cambridge.org/9780521688475

© John D. Jackson and Sarah J. Summers 2012

This publication is in copyright. Subject to statutory exception
and to the provisions of relevant collective licensing agreements,
no reproduction of any part may take place without the written
permission of Cambridge University Press.

First published 2012

Printed in the United Kingdom at the University Press, Cambridge

A catalogue record for this publication is available from the British Library

Library of Congress Cataloguing in Publication data
Jackson, John D., 1955–
The internationalisation of criminal evidence : beyond the common law and civil law
traditions / John D. Jackson, Sarah J. Summers.
   p. cm. – (Law in context)
ISBN 978-1-107-01865-5 (hardback)
1. Evidence, Criminal. I. Summers, Sarah J. II. Title.
K5465.J33 2012
345'.06 – dc23   2011039976

ISBN 978-1-107-01865-5 Hardback
ISBN 978-0-521-68847-5 Paperback

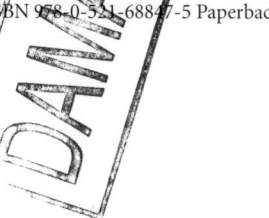

Cambridge University Press has no responsibility for the persistence or
accuracy of URLs for external or third-party internet websites referred to
in this publication, and does not guarantee that any content on such
websites is, or will remain, accurate or appropriate.

For my mother and father, Kathy, Jane and Alex (John Jackson)

For my family and for Sararard Arquint (Sarah Summers)

Contents

Foreword	*page* xiv
Preface and acknowledgements	xvi
Abbreviations	xix
Table of international cases	xxii

Part I Evidentiary contexts — 1

1 Evidence across traditions — 3
1.1 Introduction: the convergence debate — 3
1.2 Comparative evidence scholarship — 9
1.3 The rationalist tradition and the rights tradition — 14
1.4 Towards shared evidentiary principles — 19
1.5 Beyond the common and civil law traditions — 27

2 The common law tradition — 30
2.1 Introduction: free proof and the common law — 30
2.2 Common law conceptions of the law of evidence — 34
2.3 Evidence law adrift? — 38
2.4 Challenges to free proof — 40
    2.4.1 The epistemic challenge — 41
    2.4.2 The scientific challenge — 45
    2.4.3 The constitutional challenge — 50
2.5 Conclusion — 55

3 Evidential traditions in continental European jurisdictions — 57
3.1 Introduction — 57
3.2 The development of criminal evidence law and the movement towards 'freedom of proof' — 58
3.3 The importance of the nineteenth-century procedural reforms — 66
3.4 Freedom of proof and restrictions on the doctrine in modern evidence law — 69
3.5 Excluding or prohibiting the use of evidence — 72

		3.6	Recent developments in evidence law	74
		3.7	Conclusion	76

4	The international human rights context			77
	4.1	Introduction		77
	4.2	The evolution of evidentiary human rights norms		79
		4.2.1	The right to a fair trial	79
		4.2.2	The equality of arms principle	83
		4.2.3	The right to an adversarial trial	86
	4.3	The process of proof and the regulation of the investigation/pre-trial phase		95
		4.3.1	Defence rights and the importance of the procedural environment	97
		4.3.2	Potential for pre-trial activities to impinge on defence rights	99
	4.4	Towards convergence or realignment?		101
	4.5	Conclusion		106

5	Evidence in the international criminal tribunals			108
	5.1	Towards an international system of justice		108
	5.2	Problems of legitimacy		110
		5.2.1	Function and purpose of international criminal trials	111
		5.2.2	The evidentiary context	112
		5.2.3	Reaching agreed rules of procedure and evidence	115
	5.3	Common law foundations		116
	5.4	The ad hoc tribunals		119
	5.5	Rubbing points between the common law and the civil law		124
	5.6	The need for realignment		131
		5.6.1	The right to equality of arms	133
		5.6.2	The right to an adversarial trial	136
	5.7	Towards the future and the International Criminal Court		140
	5.8	Conclusion		145

Part II	Evidentiary rights			149

6	Fair trials and the use of improperly obtained evidence			151
	6.1	Introduction		151
	6.2	Theories explaining the exclusion of improperly obtained evidence		153
	6.3	Evidence obtained by way of torture, inhuman or degrading treatment		158
		6.3.1	Evidence obtained by way of torture	160
		6.3.2	Evidence obtained by way of inhuman or degrading treatment	163

		6.3.3	Fairness and evidence obtained by recourse to torture or ill-treatment	166
	6.4	Deception, coercion, traps and tricks		169
		6.4.1	Wiretapping and covert surveillance	171
		6.4.2	De facto 'interrogation' of suspects in custody	175
		6.4.3	De facto 'questioning' of suspects not in custody	179
		6.4.4	Fairness and the use of evidence obtained by deception and coercion	181
	6.5	Entrapment		188
	6.6	Fruit of the poisonous tree		191
	6.7	Conclusion: improperly obtained evidence, fairness and the under-regulated pre-trial/investigative process		194

7 The presumption of innocence 199

	7.1	Introduction		199
	7.2	The meaning of the presumption of innocence		200
		7.2.1	The presumption as an evidentiary protection	200
		7.2.2	Treating defendants as innocent	205
		7.2.3	Substantive innocence	208
	7.3	The presumption of innocence and the rationalist tradition		211
	7.4	The presumption and fair trial standards		215
	7.5	The scope of the presumption of innocence under human rights law		217
	7.6	Reversal of the burden of proof		221
	7.7	Avoiding prejudice		228
		7.7.1	An independent and impartial tribunal	229
		7.7.2	Participatory rights	233
		7.7.3	The right to a reasoned judgment	237
	7.8	Conclusion		239

8 Silence and the privilege against self-incrimination 241

	8.1	The historical and transnational importance of the right of silence		241
	8.2	The scope of the privilege in international law		246
		8.2.1	The international instruments	246
		8.2.2	*Funke* v. *France*	248
		8.2.3	Charged with a criminal offence	250
		8.2.4	Incrimination	251
		8.2.5	Compulsion	252
		8.2.6	Defiance of the will of the suspect	253
	8.3	Exception to the rights against self-incrimination and of silence		256
		8.3.1	The public interest	256
		8.3.2	Other factors	258
		8.3.3	Inferences from silence	260

8.4	Rationale of the privilege and the right of silence	266
8.5	The right of silence as a necessary condition for active defence participation	273
8.6	Incorporating fair trials standards from the point of being called to account	277
8.7	Conclusion	283

9 Defence participation 285

9.1	Introduction: legal representation and self-representation	285
9.2	The right to effective legal assistance	289
	9.2.1 Early legal assistance	289
	9.2.2 Communication with counsel	289
	9.2.3 Right to private communication and legal professional privilege	291
	9.2.4 Balancing away the privilege	293
9.3	The right to full disclosure of evidence	295
	9.3.1 The case against the accused	295
	9.3.2 The scope of the right to disclosure: *Jespers* and *Edwards*	297
	9.3.3 Uncertainties as to scope	301
	9.3.4 An absolute right?	304
9.4	Common law shortcomings	307
9.5	Beyond disclosure: access to evidence outside the possession of the prosecution	310
	9.5.1 Defence investigations	310
	9.5.2 Application to the court	312
9.6	Public interest immunity	316
	9.6.1 The principle of judicial scrutiny	317
	9.6.2 Adversarial argument	319
9.7	Conclusion	323

10 Challenging witness evidence 325

10.1	Introduction	325
10.2	Justifying the right to challenge incriminatory witness evidence	327
10.3	The regulation of the right to challenge witness evidence: the human rights perspective	334
	10.3.1 The importance of the witness evidence: the sole or decisive test	338
	10.3.2 An adequate and proper opportunity to challenge the witness	342
	10.3.2.1 The significance of the procedural environment: principal versus preliminary proceedings	342

		10.3.2.2	The circumstances of witness hearing: the importance of an impartial judge and the right to counsel	345
		10.3.2.3	Obligation to organise the witness examination hearing	349
		10.3.2.4	Restrictions on the defence's opportunity to challenge the witness	351
		10.3.2.5	The substantive sufficiency of the opportunity to challenge the witness	356
	10.3.3	Defence obligations, waiver and forfeiture		359
	10.3.4	Challenging expert witnesses		361
10.4	Conclusion			362

11 Towards a theory of evidentiary defence rights — 367
11.1 Beyond tradition — 367
11.2 Prospects for evidentiary defence rights — 371
11.3 Victims' rights and participation — 372
11.4 State security and terrorism — 380
11.5 Cost and expedition — 384
11.6 Legal culture and tradition — 387

Index — 392

Foreword

Prior to the middle of the twentieth century, criminal procedure was essentially a branch of national law. It had developed into two systems regarded as fundamentally different: the 'sport-match model' of the common law which was party-driven and where the judge's role was akin to that of an umpire; and the 'drill model' of the civil law whereby the judge was responsible for finding the true facts. As far as evidence was concerned, the common law was characterised by detailed regulations and exclusionary rules, whereas the continental system adhered more strongly to the principle of free proof. These systems appeared to be irreconcilably opposed to each other, which is one of the reasons why it proved extremely difficult to pass treaties on mutual assistance in criminal matters between the United States and European states – Switzerland managed to conclude such a treaty in 1975, while it took until 2003 for Germany to achieve the same result.

Two developments in particular led to this branch of the law assuming importance at an international level: the emergence of international criminal proceedings, starting with the Nuremberg and Tokyo trials and culminating in the establishment of a permanent International Criminal Court on the one hand, and the development of a regional and international case law on the basis of human rights' instruments on the other. Regarding international criminal tribunals, it was necessary to find solutions which would be truly international and could find acceptance both in countries adhering to the common law system and those following the European continental tradition. In the area of human rights, it was initially the European Commission and Court of Human Rights which were faced with the challenge of applying fair trial standards in a way that would make sense in the United Kingdom, Ireland and Malta, as well as in France, Germany and Italy.

This book dares to take up the formidable task of providing a theoretical foundation for this development, focusing on the law of evidence. John Jackson and Sarah Summers approach the task with awe-inspiring thoroughness and profound depth. They begin by analysing the current state of criminal proceedings in a historical and comparative perspective and go on to analyse the possibilities of an international law of evidence which exists between the two poles: 'a new framework is being built across the different legal cultures [which] is not rooted in one more than the other'. Rather than sticking to traditional concepts they find the solution in the respect for fairness, that is, the active participation of the defence in the proceedings as a whole. While this approach is generally shared by the European Court of Human Rights, they uncover a surprising amount of inherent contradictions and other shortcomings in its case law.

This book provides a rare insight into the workings of criminal proceedings, the interests and values involved and their interplay. It will set a foundation for further studies both in the area of criminal procedure, international as well as domestic, but also in the field of internationally binding rules of fundamental rights. No scholar undertaking research in these matters can ignore this monumental work.

Judge Stefan Trechsel
The Hague, January 2011

Preface and acknowledgements

Although the law of evidence has traditionally been treated as a common law subject confined to national borders, there has been a growing awareness across the common law and civil law world about the need for different systems to adopt common approaches towards criminal evidence as national systems cooperate with each other to combat transnational crime. The subject is also attracting growing recognition in international human rights law as bodies such as the European Court of Human Rights (ECtHR) have begun to develop common evidentiary standards to be applied across national boundaries. At the same time, the conflicts that led to grave crimes against humanity in the Balkans, Rwanda and other conflict zones have compelled the international community to bring those responsible to justice by developing systems of procedure and evidence that are acceptable across different legal traditions.

This book examines these attempts to find common approaches towards issues of criminal evidence across different national boundaries and legal traditions. Each of us has been following these developments for some time. As a teacher of the law of evidence at Queen's University Belfast John Jackson became interested in them as he witnessed the impact that the ECtHR was having on common law systems of evidence. Sarah Summers began to become interested in criminal evidence when she was working on her published doctoral thesis on the development of fair trials rights in Europe. Although originally from Scotland, she presently teaches criminal law and procedure at the University of Zurich. We decided to bring our experience of common law and civil law jurisdictions together to examine the evolution of common evidentiary standards in Europe and in the international criminal tribunals. We have tried to reflect case law and other legal developments up to the end of December 2010.

John would like to thank the British Academy for the award of a two-year research leave fellowship from 2006 to 2008 which enabled much of the work to be carried out and to thank the School of Law at University College Dublin for enabling him to continue the work through to its final stages. He would also like to thank Laura McMahon for research assistance, Jill Hunter and her colleagues in the University of New South Wales School of Law for all their hospitality while he held a professorial visiting fellowship there in February and March 2007 and Giovanni Sartor, Ana Vrdoljak and other colleagues in the Department of Law at the European University Institute for their hospitality while he was a senior Fernand Braudel fellow there from September 2007 to June 2008.

Sarah would like to thank the School of Law at the University of Zurich for enabling her to work on this project and Andreas Donatsch and Christian Schwarzenegger in particular for their support.

Thanks are due to Mirjan Damaška, William Twining and Stefan Trechsel for providing inspiration for the project. We owe debts to many scholars whose work and comments provided us with important insights as our work progressed. It would be difficult to name all of them, but we are particularly grateful to: Ron Allen, Sararard Arquint, Gideon Boas, Rosemary Byrne, Craig Callen, Antonio Cassese, Mirielle Delmas-Marty, Gary Edmond, Lindsay Farmer, Richard Friedman, Mark Findlay, Hock Lai Ho, Jill Hunter, Máximo Langer, Robin Lööf, Jim Murdoch, Andrew Paizes, Hannah Quirk, Mike Redmayne, Michael Risinger, Andrew Roberts, Paul Roberts, P. J. Schwikkard, Chris Taylor, Peter Tillers and John Spencer.

We would like to thank Jean Allain for introducing us to a number of practitioners at the international criminal tribunals and Michael O'Boyle for facilitating John's visit to the European Court of Human Rights in April 2008. A number of practitioners and judges gave up their time to talk to us about the approaches of different international courts and tribunals. We would like to thank particularly Graham Blewitt, Nicolas Bratza, Teresa Doherty, Norman Farrell, Fabricio Guerglia, David Hunt, Gabrielle MacIntyre, Catherine Marchi-Uhel, Peter Murphy, Egbert Myjer, Geoffrey Nice, Michael O'Boyle, Kate O'Regan, Eugene O'Sullivan, Alphons Orie, Navaneethem Pillay, Ken Roberts, Phillip Weiner, Stefan Trechsel and Boštjan Zupančič.

We were able to air ideas emerging from our work on a number of occasions and we would like to thank all those who participated in workshops and seminars at the Schools of Law at the University of Aberdeen, the University of Cape Town, University College Dublin, the University of New South Wales, Nottingham Trent University, Queen's University Belfast and the National University of Singapore, at the Department of Law at the EUI and at the Dutch Supreme Court. As our work began to take shape a number of scholars generously gave up their time to comment on draft chapters. Robert Bloom, Sean Doran, Fiona de Londras, Ed Imwinkelried, Máximo Langer, Yassin M'Boge, Hannah Quirk, Paul Roberts and Chris Taylor read one or more chapters and the book has benefited from their assistance.

We would also like to thank the staff at Cambridge University Press, and in particular Sinead Moloney, for their patience as we broke a number of deadlines in trying to complete the work and for working so hard to ensure the book was published. Finally, we would like to thank our partners and families for showing remarkable forbearance as the project ate up more time than we ever imagined.

John D. Jackson
University College Dublin
Sarah J. Summers
University of Zurich

Abbreviations

AC	Appeal Cases
ACHR	American Convention on Human Rights
ACtHR	American Court of Human Rights
AJ	Alberta Judgments (Canada)
All ER	All England Law Reports
BCLR	Butterworths Constitutional Law Reports (South Africa)
BGE	Decisions of the Federal Court (Switzerland)
BGH	Federal Court (Germany)
BGHSt	Federal Criminal Court (Germany)
BHRC	Butterworths Human Rights Cases
BVerfG	Federal Constitutional Court (Germany)
CC	Criminal Code
CCC	Canadian Criminal Cases
CCP	Code of Criminal Procedure
CD	Collection of Decisions of the European Commission of Human Rights
Ch	Chapter
CJ	Chief Justice
CLR	Commonwealth Law Reports
Cox CC	Cox's Criminal Cases
CR	Criminal Reports (Canada)
Cr App R	Criminal Appeal Reports
Crim LR	Criminal Law Review
dec.	decision
DLR	Dominion Law Reports (Canada)
DPP	Director of Public Prosecutions
DR	Decisions and Reports of the European Commission of Human Rights
ECHR	European Convention for the Protection of Human Rights and Fundamental Freedoms
ECommHR	European Commission of Human Rights
ECR	European Case Reports

ECtHR	European Court of Human Rights
EHRR	European Human Rights Reports
EIO	European Investigation Order
EU	European Union
EUI	European University Institute
EWCA	Court of Appeal of England and Wales
EWHC	High Court of England and Wales Decisions
GC	Grand Chamber, ECtHR
HCJAC	High Court of Justiciary, Appeal Court (Scotland)
HM Advocate	Her Majesty's Advocate, His Majesty's Advocate
HMSO	Her Majesty's Stationery Office
HRC	Human Rights Committee, United Nations
IACtHR	Inter-American Court of Human Rights
ICC	International Criminal Court
ICCPR	International Covenant on Civil and Political Rights
ICTR	International Criminal Tribunal for Rwanda
ICTY	International Criminal Tribunal for the Former Yugoslavia
ILRM	Irish Law Reports Monthly
IR	Irish Reports
LJ	Lord Justice
NICC	Northern Ireland Crown Court
NStZ	Neue Zeitschrift für Strafrecht
OJ	Official Journal of the European Union
OTP	Office of the Prosecutor, ICTY
PACE	Police and Criminal Evidence Act 1984
QB	Queen's Bench Division, Law Reports
R	Regina
RPE	Rules of Procedure and Evidence, ICTY
SCC	Supreme Court of Canada
SCCR	Scottish Criminal Case Reports
SCR	Supreme Court Reports (Canada)
SCSL	Special Court for Sierra Leone
SCt	Supreme Court Reporter
SLT	Scots Law Times
TFEU	Treaty on the Functioning of the European Union
UK	United Kingdom
UKHL	House of Lords, United Kingdom
UKPC	UK Privy Council Decisions
UKSC	UK Supreme Court
UN	United Nations
UNCAT	UN Convention against Torture and Other Cruel, Inhuman or Degrading Treatment
US	United States

Abbreviations

USA	United States of America
USSC	US Supreme Court
WLR	Weekly Law Reports
YB	Yearbook of the European Convention on Human Rights

Table of international cases

A and others v. *United Kingdom* [GC], no. 3455/05, 19 February 2009   297
Abas v. *Netherlands* (dec.), no. 27943/95, 26 February 1997   250, 251
AG v. *Malta* (dec.), no. 16641/90, 10 December 1991   224
AH v. *Finland*, no. 46602/99, 10 May 2007   340
Airey v. *Ireland*, 9 Oct. 1979, Series A no. 32   184
AL v. *Finland*, no. 23220/04, 27 January 2009   340
Alban-Cornejo v. *Ecuador*, 22 November 2007, Series C no. 171   380
Aliev v. *Ukraine*, no. 781/1997, 7 August 2003, UN Doc. CCPR/C/78/D/781/1997   277
Al-Khawaja and Tahery v. *United Kingdom*, nos. 26766/05 and 22228/06, 20 January 2009   92, 95, 330, 336, 337, 339, 345, 354, 360
Allan v. *United Kingdom*, no. 48539/99, ECHR 2002-IX   175, 176, 177, 178, 179, 183, 255, 256, 258, 266
Allen v. *United Kingdom* (dec.), no. 76574/01, ECHR 2002-VIII   251
AM v. *Italy*, no. 37019/97, ECHR 1999-IX   340, 353
Ambrosini, de Massera and Massera v. *Uruguay*, no. R.1/5, 15 August 1979, Doc. A/34/40, 124   219
Amutgan v. *Turkey*, no. 5138/04, 3 February 2009   281
AP, MP and TP v. *Switzerland*, 29 August 1997, Reports 1997-V, 1477   210, 220
Arenz v. *Germany*, No. 1138/2002, 24 March 2004, UN Doc. CCPR/C/80/D/1138/2002 (2004)   82
Artico v. *Italy*, 13 May 1980, Series A no. 37   359
Artner v. *Austria*, 28 August 1992, Series A no. 242-A   87, 89, 90, 338
Arutyunyan v. *Uzbekistan*, no. 917/2000, 29 March 2004, UN Doc. CCPR/C/80/D/917/2000 (2004)   82
AS v. *Finland*, no. 40156/07, 28 September 2010   340, 354
AS v. *Poland* (dec.), no. 39510/98, 9 October 2003   349
Asch v. *Austria*, 26 April 1991, Series A no. 203   87, 89, 90, 338, 340
Atlan v. *United Kingdom*, no. 36533/97, 19 June 2001   85, 300, 304
Austria v. *Italy (Pfunders Case)* (report), no. 788/60, 30 March 1963, (1963) 6 YB 740   218, 234, 235
Averill v. *United Kingdom*, no. 36408/97, ECHR 2000-VI   362

B v. *Austria*, 28 March 1990, Series A no. 175   96
Baegen v. *Netherlands* (report), attached to the judgment of 27 October 1995, Series A no. 327-B   351, 352
Barberà, Messegué and Jabardo v. *Spain*, 6 December 1988, Series A no. 146   82, 86, 218, 219, 343, 369
Bates v. *United Kingdom* (dec.), no. 26280/95, 16 January 1996   224
Bayer v. *Austria* (dec.), no. 13866/88, 2 April 1990   357
Beckles v. *United Kingdom*, no. 44652/98, 8 October 2002   262
Berhani v. *Albania*, no. 845/05, 27 May 2010   82
Berry v. *Jamaica*, no. 330/1988, 7 April 1994, UN Doc. CCPR/C/50/D/330/1988 (1994)   159, 247
Blastland v. *United Kingdom* (dec.), no. 12045/86, (1987) 52 DR 273   340
Bleier v. *Uruguay*, no. 30/1978, 29 March 1982, UN Doc. CCPR/C/OP/2, 138 (1990)   160
Bochaton v. *France*, No. 1084/2002, 1 April 2004, UN Doc. CCPR/C/80/D/1084/2002 (2004)   82
Bocos-Cuesta v. *Netherlands*, no. 54789/00, 10 November 2005   335, 353
Boddaert v. *Belgium*, 12 October 1992, Series A no. 235-D   96
Bonev v. *Bulgaria*, no. 60018/00, 8 June 2006   349
Bönisch v. *Austria*, 6 May 1985, Series A no. 92   74, 84, 232
Borgers v. *Belgium*, 30 October 1991, Series A no. 214-B   84
Brandstetter v. *Austria*, 28 August 1991, Series A no. 211   74, 84, 86
Brennan v. *United Kingdom*, no. 39846/98, ECHR 2001-X   103, 280, 291, 292
Bricmont v. *Belgium*, 7 July 1989, Series A no. 158   234
Brozicek v. *Italy*, 19 December 1989, Series A no. 167   297
Brusco v. *France*, no. 1466/07, 14 October 2010   297
Buck v. *Germany*, no. 41604/98, 28 April 2005   185
Bulacio v. *Argentina*, 18 September 2003, Series C no. 100   380
Bykov v. *Russia* [GC], no. 4378/02, 10 March 2009   170, 171, 179, 180, 181, 182, 183, 256
Cabal v. *Australia*, no. 1020/2001, 7 August 2003, UN Doc. CCPR/C/78/D/1020/2001 (2003)   219
Caka v. *Albania*, no. 44023/02, 8 December 2009   335
Caldas v. *Uruguay*, no. 43/1979, 21 July 1983, UN Doc. Supp no. 40 (A/38/40) at 192 (1983)   290
Camilleri v. *Malta* (dec.), no. 51760/99, 16 March 2000   82, 358
Campbell and Fell v. *United Kingdom*, 28 June 1984, Series A no. 80   292
Can v. *Austria* (report), 12 July 1984, Series B no. 79   290, 291
Cantoral-Benavides v. *Peru*, 18 August 2000, Series C no. 69   247
Cardot v. *France* (report), attached to the judgment of 19 March 1991, Series A no. 200   346
Castillo Petruzzi and others v. *Peru*, 17 September 1997, Series C no. 33   290
Castillo Petruzzi and others v. *Peru*, 30 May 1999, Series C no. 52   248

CG v. *United Kingdom*, no. 43373/98, 19 December 2001   349
Chadwick v. *United Kingdom*, no. 54109/00, 18 November 2003   367
Chahal v. *United Kingdom*, 15 November 1996, Reports 1996-V, 1831   161, 321
Chalkley v. *United Kingdom*, no. 63831/00, 12 June 2003   173
Chappell v. *United Kingdom*, 30 March 1989, Series A no. 152-A   185
Cimen v. *Turkey*, no. 19582/02, 3 February 2009   281
Colozza v. *Italy*, 12 February 1985, Series A no. 89   296
Compass v. *Jamaica*, no. 375/1989, 19 October 1993, UN Doc. CCPR/C/49/D/375/1989   336
Condron v. *United Kingdom*, no. 35718/97, ECHR 2000-V   238, 262
Constantin and Stoian v. *Romania*, nos. 23782/06 and 46629/06, 29 September 2009   170
Conteris v. *Uruguay*, no. 139/1983, 17 July 1985, UN Doc. Supp. No. 40 (A/40/40) 196 (1985)   160, 290
CPH v. *Sweden* (dec.), no. 20959/92, 2 September 1994   352
Croissant v. *Germany*, 25 September 1992, Series A no. 237-B   288
Cuartero Casado v. *Spain*, nos. 1399/2005, 25 July 2005, UN Doc. CCPR/C/84/D/1399/2005 (2005)   82
Cuscani v. *United Kingdom*, no. 32771.96, 24 September 2002   90, 361, 367
Dankovsky v. *Germany* (dec.), no. 36689/97, 29 June 2000   348, 352
De Cubber v. *Belgium*, 26 October 1984, Series A no. 86   230
Delcourt v. *Belgium*, 17 January 1970, Series A no. 11   81, 84
Delta v. *France*, 19 December 1990, Series A no. 191-A   82, 87, 137, 229, 343
Deweer v. *Belgium*, 27 February 1980, Series A no. 35   83, 96, 219, 279
Dikme v. *Turkey* no. 20869/92, ECHR 2000-VIII   187
Dombo Beeher BV v. *Netherlands*, 27 October 1993, Series A no. 274   84
Doorson v. *Netherlands*, 26 March 1996, Reports 1996-II, 446   91, 337, 351, 355, 356, 358, 361, 376
Dudko v. *Australia*, no. 1347/2005, 29 August 2007, UN Doc. CCPR/C/90/D/1347/2005 (2007)   84
Eckle v. *Germany*, 15 July 1982, Series A no. 51   96, 279
Edwards and Lewis v. *United Kingdom* [GC], nos. 39647/98 and 40461/98, ECHR 2004-X   85, 190, 319, 321
Edwards v. *United Kingdom*, 16 December 1992, Series A no. 247-B   85, 135, 152, 228, 300, 302
Engel and others v. *Netherlands*, 8 June 1976, Series A no. 22   82, 210, 229, 234
Errol Simms v. *Jamaica*, no. 541/1993, 3 April 1995, UN Doc. CCPR/C/53/D/541/1993 (1995)   82
Eurofinacom v. *France* (dec.), no. 58753/00, 7 September 2004   189, 190
Fayed v. *United Kingdom*, 21 September 1994, Series A no. 294-B   250
Feldbrugge v. *Netherlands*, 29 May 1986, Series A no. 99   86

Ferrantelli and Santangelo v. *Italy*, 7 August 1996, Reports 1996-III, 937   230, 335, 350
Fitt v. *United Kingdom* [GC], no. 29777/96, ECHR 2000-II   304, 319, 320
FK v. *Austria* (dec.), no. 16925/90, 11 May 1994   357
Foucher v. *France*, 18 March 1997, Reports 1997-II, 452   83
Fox, Campbell and Hartley v. *United Kingdom*, 30 August 1990, Series A no. 182   185, 381
Fuenzalida v. *Ecuador*, no. 480/1991, UN Doc. CCPR/C/57/D/480/1991 (1996)   313
Funke v. *France*, 25 February 1993, Series A no. 256-A   83, 103, 241, 248, 249, 250, 251, 253, 255, 266
Gäfgen v. *Germany*, no. 22978/05, 30 June 2008   158, 192
Gäfgen v. *Germany* [GC], no. 22978/05, 1 June 2010   158, 192, 193
Ganga v. *Guyana*, no. 912/2000, 1 November 2004, ICCPR, A/60/40 vol. II   247
García Ruiz v. *Spain* [GC], no. 30544/96, ECHR 1999-I   152
Garner v. *United Kingdom* (dec.), no. 38330/97, 26 January 1999   335, 349, 350
Georgios Papageorgiou v. *Greece*, no. 59506/00, ECHR 2003-VI   313
Gladyshev v. *Russia*, no. 2807/04, 30 July 2009   165, 166
Glover v. *United Kingdom* (dec.), no. 39835/03, 23 November 2004   301
Göcmen v. *Turkey*, no 72000/01, 17 October 2006   165
Goodwin v. *United Kingdom*, 27 March 1996, Reports 1996-II   305
Gordon v. *Jamaica*, no. 237/1987, UN Doc. CCPR/C/46/D/237/1987 (1992)   234, 313
Gossa v. *Poland*, no. 47986/99, 9 January 2007   337
Grant v. *Jamaica*, no. 353/1988, UN Doc. CCPR/50/D/353/1988 (1994)   313
Gregory v. *United Kingdom*, 25 February 1997, Reports 1997-I, 296   231, 232
Guesdon v. *France*, no. 219/1986, 25 July 1990, No. 219/1986, UN Doc. CCPR/C/39/D/219/1986 (1990)   83
H v. *France*, 24 October 1989, Series A no. 162-A   361
H v. *United Kingdom* (dec.), no. 15023/89, 4 April 1990   226
Haas v. *Germany* (dec.), no. 73047/01, 17 November 2005   349
Haci Özen v. *Turkey*, no. 46286/99, 12 April 2007   165, 166, 186, 187, 198
Hadjianastassiou v. *Greece*, 16 December 1992, Series A no. 252   82, 104, 237
Håkan Wester v. *Sweden* (dec.), no. 31074/96, 14 January 1998   335, 343, 349, 358
Halford v. *United Kingdom*, 25 June 1997, Reports 1997-III, 1004   171
Hardy v. *Ireland* (dec.), no. 23456/94, 29 June 1994   226
Harutyunyan v. *Armenia*, no. 36549/03, 28 June 2007   161, 163, 167, 198
Hauschildt v. *Denmark*, 24 May 1989, Series A no. 154   230

Hayward v. *Sweden* (dec.), no. 14106/88, 6 December 1991   340
Heaney and McGuinness v. *Ireland*, no. 34720/97, ECHR 2000-XII   250, 251, 252, 257, 258, 261
Heglas v. *Czech Republic*, no. 5935/02, 1 March 2007   171, 180, 183
Hiro Balani v. *Spain*, 9 December 1994, Series A no. 303-B   238
HK v. *Netherlands* (dec.), no. 20341/92, 6 January 1993   335, 349, 350
Holm v. *Sweden*, 25 November 1993, Series A no. 279-A   231
Hols v. *Netherlands* (dec.), no. 25206/94, 19 October 1995   253
Hopia v. *Finland* (dec.), no. 30632/96, 25 November 1999   358
Howarth v. *United Kingdom*, no. 38081/97, 21 September 2000   279
Huikko v. *Finland* (dec.), no. 30505/96, 11 May 1999   358
Hulki Günes v. *Turkey*, no. 28490/95, ECHR 2003-VII   187
I v. *Switzerland*, no. 13972/88 (dec.), 31 May 1991   351
İçöz v. *Turkey* (dec.), no. 54919/00, 9 January 2003   158
IJL, GMR and AKP v. *United Kingdom*, nos. 29522/95, 30056/96 and 30574/96, ECHR 2000-IX   250, 251
Imbrioscia v. *Switzerland*, 24 November 1993, Series A no. 275   96, 100, 196, 279
Incal v. *Turkey*, 9 June 1998, Reports 1998-IV, 1547   230, 381
Ireland v. *United Kingdom*, 18 January 1978, Series A no. 25   159, 160
Isgrò v. *Italy*, 19 February 1991, Series A no. 194-A   347, 348
Jalloh v. *Germany* [GC], no. 54810/00, ECHR 2006-IX   158, 161, 162, 163, 164, 165, 166, 167, 186, 194, 197, 198, 254, 255, 257, 258, 259, 260, 266, 269, 341
Janosevic v. *Sweden*, No. 34619/97, ECHR 2002-VII   224, 225, 227
Jasper v. *United Kingdom* [GC], no. 27052/95, 16 February 2000   190, 304, 319, 320
JB v. *Switzerland*, no. 31827/96, ECHR 2001-III   251, 252, 254, 266
Jespers v. *Belgium* (report), no. 8403/78, 14 December 1981, (1981) 27 DR 61   85, 135, 297, 298, 299, 300, 302, 303, 304, 312, 314
John Murray v. *United Kingdom* [GC], 8 February 1996, Reports 1996-I, 30   96, 103, 237, 239, 253, 260, 264, 266, 279, 280, 282, 381
Juan Santaella Telleria and others v. *Venezuela*, nos. 448/01 and 666/01, 12 October 2005, Report No. 47/05, Ser.L/V/II.124 Doc. 5   82
K v. *Austria*, 2 June 1993, Series A no. 255-B   249
Kamasinski v. *Austria*, 19 December 1989, Series A no. 168   334
Kaufman v. *Belgium* (dec.), no. 10938, 9 December 1986, (1986) 50 DR 98   83, 369
Kavanagh v. *Ireland*, no. 819/1998, 4 April 2001, UN Doc. CCPR/C/71/D/819/1998 (2001)   98
Kemmache v. *France (No. 3)*, 24 November 1994, Series A no. 296-C   82
K-F v. *Germany*, 27 November 1997, Reports 1997-VII, 2657   185
Khamidov v. *Russia*, no. 72118/01, 15 November 2007   82

Table of international cases

Khan v. *United Kingdom*, no. 35394/97, ECHR 2000-V 152, 164, 167, 169, 171, 172, 173, 174, 175, 178, 179, 182, 183, 184, 185, 186, 187, 341, 364
Khudobin v. *Russia*, no. 59696/00, ECHR 2006-XII 189, 190
King v. *United Kingdom (No. 2)* (dec.), no. 13881/02, 17 February 2004 252
KJ v. *Denmark* (dec.), no. 18425/91, 31 March 1993 350
Klimentyev v. *Russia*, no. 46503/99, 16 November 2006 335
Koç v. *Turkey* (dec.), no. 32580/96, 23 September 2003 158
Kok v. *Netherlands* (dec.), no. 43149/98, 4 July 2000 355
Kokkinakas v. *Greece*, 25 May 1993, Series A no. 260-A 202
Kopp v. *Switzerland*, 25 March 1998, Reports 1998-II 292
Kostovski v. *Netherlands*, 20 November 1989, Series A no. 166 87, 88, 90, 97, 137, 140, 234, 243, 355
Krasnikiu v. *Czech Republic*, no. 51277/99, 28 February 2006 336
Kyprianou v. *Cyprus*, no. 73797/01, ECHR 2005-VIII 230
Labita v. *Italy* [GC], no. 26772/95, ECHR 2000-IV 160
Lagerblom v. *Sweden*, no. 26891/95, 14 January 2003 288
Lamy v. *Belgium*, 30 March 1989, Series A no. 151 303
Lanza and Perdomo v. *Uruguay*, no. R.2/8, Doc. A/35/40, 111 219
Lavents v. *Latvia*, no. 58442/00, 22 November 2002 229
Le Compte, Van Leuven and De Meyere v. *Belgium*, 23 June 1981, Series A no. 43 230
Lee Davies v. *Belgium*, no. 18704/05, 28 July 2009 185, 368
Levinta v. *Moldova*, no. 17332/03, 16 December 2008 161, 162, 194
Lindqvist v. *Sweden* (dec.), no. 26304/95, 22 October 1997 360
Little v. *Jamaica*, no. 283/1988, 1 November 1991, UN Doc. CCPR/C/43/D/283/l988 (1991) 290
Lluberas v. *Uruguay*, no. 123/1982, 25 March 1983, UN Doc. Supp no. 40 (A/39/40) at 175 (1984) 290
Loayza Tamayo Case v. *Peru*, 17 September 1997, Series C no. 33 220
Lucà v. *Italy*, no. 33345/96, ECHR 2001-II 91, 336, 338
Lückhof and Spanner v. *Austria*, nos. 58452/00 and 61920/00, 10 January 2008 252
Lüdi v. *Switzerland*, 15 June 1992, Series A no. 238 87, 188, 355
M v. *Norway* (dec.), no. 14483/88, 10 February 1992 360
MA and BS v. *Norway* (dec.), no. 29185/95, 22 October 1997 340
Magee v. *United Kingdom*, no. 28135/95, ECHR 2000-VI 280, 281, 282
Malone v. *United Kingdom*, 2 August 1984, Series A no. 82 171
Mamaç and others v. *Turkey*, nos. 29486/95, 29487/95 and 29853/96, 20 April 2004 280
Mantovanelli v. *France*, 18 March 1997, Reports 1997-II, 424 74
Marais v. *Madagascar*, no. 49/1979, 24 March 1983, UN Doc. Supp no. 40 (A/38/40) at 141 (1983) 290
Martínez Muñoz v. *Spain*, no. 1006/2001, 30 October 2003, UN Doc. CCPR/C/79/D/1006/2001 (2001) 82

Mayali v. *France*, no. 69116/01, 14 June 2005   349
MC v. *Bulgaria*, no. 39272/98, 4 December 2003   210
Mellors v. *United Kingdom* (dec.), no. 57836/00, 30 January 2003   343
Michael and Brian Hill v. *Spain*, no. 526/1993, 2 April 1997, UN Doc. CCPR/C/59/D/526/1993   288
Mild and Virtanen v. *Finland*, nos. 39481/98 and 40227/98, 26 July 2005   350
Minelli v. *Switzerland*, 25 March 1983, Series A no. 62   219, 220
Mirilashvili v. *Russia*, no. 6293/04, 11 December 2008   335, 338, 349, 361, 362
MK v. *Austria* (dec.), no. 21155/93, 2 September 1994   340
Monnell and Morris v. *United Kingdom*, 2 March 1987, Series A no. 115   86
Moreira de Azevedo v. *Portugal*, 23 October 1990, Series A no. 189   81
Mulai v. *Republic of Guyana*, no. 811/1998, 20 July 2004, UN Doc. CCPR/C/81/D/811/1998 (2004)   82
Murray v. *United Kingdom*, 28 October 1994, Series A no. 300-A   185
Nallaratnam v. *Sri Lanka*, no. 1033/2001, 21 July 2004, UN Doc. CCPR/C/81/D/1033/2001 (2004)   247
Narinen v. *Finland*, no. 45027/98, 1 June 2004   185
NC v. *Italy*, no. 24952/94, 11 January 2001   185
Nemet v. *Sweden* (dec.), no. 17168/90, 7 October 1991   350
Ng v. *Canada*, no. 469/1991, 5 November 1993, UN Doc. CCPR/C/49/D/469/1991 (1994)   371
Nielsen v. *Denmark* (report), no. 343/57, 15 March 1961, 4 YB 494   82
Niemietz v. *Germany*, 16 December 1992, Series A no. 251-B   292, 294
O and T v. *Netherlands* (dec.), nos. 17631/91 and 17632/91, 2 September 1992   360
O'Halloran and Francis v. *United Kingdom*, nos. 15809/02 and 25624/02, 29 June 2007   256, 259
Öcalan v. *Turkey*, no. 46221/99, 12 March 2003   290, 291
Öcalan v. *Turkey* [GC], no. 46221/99, ECHR 2005-IV   103, 280, 290
Örs and others v. *Turkey*, no. 46213/99, 20 June 2006   165
Ozerov v. *Russia*, no. 64962/01, 18 May 2010   84, 98, 230
P, RH and LL v. *Austria* (dec.), no. 15776/89, 5 December 1989   218
Panovits v. *Cyprus*, no. 4268/04, 11 December 2008   106, 282, 345
Papon v. *France* (dec.), no. 54210/00, ECHR 2001-XII   70
Pavletić v. *Slovakia* (dec.), no. 39359/98, 13 May 2003   349, 355
Peltonen v. *Finland* (dec.), no. 30409/96, 11 May 1999   357, 358
Perdomo v. *Uruguay*, (R.2/8) ICCPR, UN Doc. Supp no. 40 (A/35/40) at 111 (1980)   219, 290
Petri Sallinen and others v. *Finland*, no. 50882/99, 27 September 2005   185
PG and JH v. *United Kingdom*, no. 44787/98, ECHR 2001-IX   152, 169, 171, 174, 182, 183
Pham Hoang v. *France*, 25 September 1992, Series A no. 243   224

Phillip v. *Trinidad and Tobago*, no. 594/1992, 20 October 1998, UN Doc. CCPR/C/64/D/594/1992   290

Piersack v. *Belgium*, 1 October 1982, Series A no. 53   230, 231

Pishchalnikov v. *Russia*, no. 7025/04, 24 September 2009   283

PK v. *Finland* (dec.) no. 37442/97, 9 July 2002   343

Pobozny v. *Slovak Republic* (dec.), no. 32110/96, 16 April 1998   349

Portmann v. *Switzerland* (dec.), no. 1356/04, 22 April 2008   177, 183

Pratt and Morgan v. *Jamaica*, nos. 210/1986 and 225/1987, 6 April 1989, UN Doc. Supp. No. 40 (A/44/40) 222   359

Prosecutor v. *Akayesu*, Case No. ICTR-96–4-T, 28 January 1997, Trial Chamber, Decision by the Tribunal on its Request to the Prosecutor to Submit the Written Witness Statements   125

Prosecutor v. *Akayesu*, Case No. ICTR-96–4–T, 2 September 1998, Trial Chamber, Judgment   113

Prosecutor v. *Bagosora*, Case No. ICTR-98–41-T, 14 October 2004, Trial Chamber, Decision on the Prosecutor's Motion for the Admission of Certain Materials under Rule 89(C)   278

Prosecutor v. *Barayagwiza*, Case No. ICTR-97–19-T, 2 November 2000, Trial Chamber, Decision on Defence Counsel Motion to Withdraw   130

Prosecutor v. *Blagojević*, Case No. IT-02–60-PT, T. Ch., 12 December 2002, Trial Chamber, Joint Decision on Motions Related to Production of Evidence   135

Prosecutor v. *Blaškić*, Case No. IT-95–14-AR108bis, 29 October 1997, Judgment on the Request of the Republic of Croatia for Review of the Decision of Trial Chamber II of 18 July 1997, Appeals Chamber   114

Prosecutor v. *Blaškić*, Case No. IT-95–14-T, 29 April 1998, Trial Chamber, Decision on the Defence Motion for Sanctions for the Prosecutor's Repeated Violations of Rule 68 of the Rules of Evidence and Procedure   127, 135

Prosecutor v. *Bralo*, Case No. IT-95–17-A, 30 August 2006, Appeals Chamber, Decision on Motions for Access to Ex Parte Portions of the Records on Appeal and for Disclosure of Mitigating Material   134, 135, 136

Prosecutor v. *Brdjanin and Talić*, Case No. IT-99–36, 15 February 2002, Trial Chamber, Order on the Standards Governing the Admission of Evidence   125

Prosecutor v. *Brdjanin and Talić*, Case No. IT-99–36-AR73.9, 11 December 2002, Appeals Chamber, Decision on Interlocutory Appeal   305

Prosecutor v. *Brdjanin*, Case No. IT-99–36-A, 24 July 2006, Trial Chamber, Orders to File Table   202

Prosecutor v. *Brima*, Case No. SCSL-2004–16-AR73, 26 May 2006, Appeals Chamber, Decision on Prosecution Appeal Against Decision on Oral Application for Witness TF1–150 to Testify Without Being Compelled to Answer Questions on Grounds of Confidentiality   305, 306

Prosecutor v. *Delalić*, Case No. IT-96–21, 2 September 1997, Trial Chamber, Decision on Mucić's Motion for the Exclusion of Evidence   278

Prosecutor v. *Delalić*, Case No. IT-96–21, 22 April 1999, Trial Chamber, Separate Opinion of Judge David Hunt on motion by Esad Landzo to Preserve and Provide Evidence   315

Prosecutor v. *Dokmanović*, Case No. IT-95–13a-PT, Trial Chamber, Order of 28 November 1997   125, 130

Prosecutor v. *Erdemović*, Case No. T-96–22-A, 7 October 1997, Appeals Chamber, Judgment   131

Prosecutor v. *Galić*, Case No. IT-98–29-A, 7 June 2002, Appeals Chamber, Decision on Interlocutory Appeal Concerning Rule 92bis (C)   137, 138

Prosecutor v. *Haradinaj and others*, Case No. IT-04-84-PT, 22 November 2006, Trial Chamber, Decision on Second Haradinaj Motion to Lift Redactions of Prosecution Witness Statements   377

Prosecutor v. *Jokic*, Case No. IT-01–42-PT and IT-01–46-PT, 20 February 2002, Trial Chamber, Orders on Motions for Provisional Release   276

Prosecutor v. *Karadžić*, Case No. IT-95–5/18-PT, 12 December 2009, Trial Chamber, Decision on Accused's Application for Certification to Appeal Decision on Rule 70(B)   318

Prosecutor v. *Karemera*, Case No. ICTR-98–44-T, 15 December 2006, Trial Chamber, Decision on Defence Motions to Prohibit Witness Proofing   142

Prosecutor v. *Karemera*, Case No. ICTR-98–44-T, 25 October 2007, Trial Chamber, Decision on Joseph Nzirorera's Notices of Rule 68 Violations and motions for Remedial and Punitive Measures   135

Prosecutor v. *Katanga and Ngudjolo Chui, Situation in the DRC*, Case No. ICC-01/04–01/07–474, PTC I, 13 May 2008, Decision on the Set of Procedural Rights Attached to Procedural Status of Victim at the Pre-Trial Stage of the Case   378

Prosecutor v. *Kordić and Čerkez*, Case No. IT-95–14/2-A, 2 July 2001, Appeals Chamber, Decision on Second Motions to Extend Time For Filing Appellants Brief   135

Prosecutor v. *Krajišnik*, Case No. IT-00–39-PT, 28 February 2003, Trial Chamber, Decision on Prosecution Motions for Judicial Notice of Adjudicated Facts and for Admission of Written Statements by Witnesses Pursuant to Rule 92*bis*   125

Prosecutor v. *Kupreškić*, Case No. IT-95–16-T, 21 September 1998, Trial Chamber, Decision on Communication Between Parties and Their Witnesses   135

Prosecutor v. *Kupreškić*, Case No. IT-95–16-AR73.3, 15 July 1999, Appeals Chamber, Decision on Appeal by Dragan Papić Against Ruling to Proceed by Deposition   124

Prosecutor v. *Limaj*, Case No. IT-03–66-T, 10 December 2004, Trial Chamber, Decision on Defence Motion on Prosecution Practice of 'Proofing' Witnesses   142

Prosecutor v. *Lubanga Dyilo*, Case No. ICC-01/04–01/06, 15 May 2006, Pre-Trial Chamber, Decision on the Final System of Disclosure and the Establishment of a Timetable   145

Prosecutor v. *Lubanga Dyilo*, *Situation in the DRC*, Case No. ICC-01/04–01/06–679, 8 November 2006, Pre-Trial Chamber, Decision on the Practice of Witness Familiarisation and Witness Proofing   141

Prosecutor v. *Lubanga Dyilo*, Case No. ICC-01/04–01/06, 17 November 2006, Pre-Trial Chamber, Decision on Defence Requests for Disclosure of Materials   144

Prosecutor v. *Lubanga Dyilo*, *Situation in the DRC*, Case No. ICC-01/04–01/06–925, 13 June 2007, Appeals Chamber, Decision of the Appeals Chamber on the Joint Application of Victims a/0001/06 to a/0003/06 and a/0005/06 concerning the 'Directions and Decision of the Appeal Chamber' of 2 February 2007   379

Prosecutor v. *Lubanga Dyilo*, Case No. ICC-01/04–01/06, 9 November 2007, Trial Chamber, Decision Regarding the Timing and Manner of Disclosure and the Date of Trial   318

Prosecutor v. *Lubanga Dyilo*, *Situation in the DRC*, Case No. ICC-01/04–01/06–1049, 30 November 2007, Trial Chamber, Decision Regarding the Practices Used to Prepare and Familiarise Witnesses for Giving Testimony at Trial   142

Prosecutor v. *Lubanga Dyilo*, *Situation in the DRC*, Case No. ICC-01/04–01/06–1119, 18 January 2008, Trial Chamber, Decision on victims' participation   378

Prosecutor v. *Lubanga Dyilo*, Case No. ICC-01/04–01/06–1401, 13 June 2008, Trial Chamber, Decision on the consequences of non-disclosure of exculpatory materials covered by Art. 54(3)(e) agreements and the application to stay the prosecution of the accused, together with certain other issues raised at the Status Conference on 10 June 2008   318

Prosecutor v. *Martić*, Case No. IT-95–11-T, 19 January 2006, Trial Chamber, Decision Adopting Guidelines on the Standards Governing the Admission of Evidence   125

Prosecutor v. *Milošević*, Case No. IT-02–54-AR73.4, 21 October 2003, Appeals Chamber, Dissenting Opinion of Judge David Hunt on Admissibility of Evidence in Chief in the form of Written Statements   139

Prosecutor v. *Milošević*, Case No. IT-02–54-T, 22 September 2004, Trial Chamber, Reasons for Decision on Assignment of Defence Counsel   130

Prosecutor v. *Milošević*, Case No. IT-02–54-AR73.7, 1 November 2004, Appeals Chamber, Decision on Interlocutory Appeal of the Trial Chamber's Decision on the Assignment of Defence Counsel   130

Prosecutor v. *Milutinovic*, Case No. IT-05–87-T, 12 December 2006, Trial Chamber, Decision on Ojdanic Motion to Prohibit Witness Proofing   142

Prosecutor v. *Naletilić and Martinović*, Case No. IT-98–34-PT, 10 November 2000, Trial Chamber, Decision on Prosecutor's Motion to Take Depositions for Use at Trial   125

Prosecutor v. *Niyitegeka*, Case No. ICTR-96–14-T, 16 May 2003, Trial Chamber, Judgment and Sentence   264

Prosecutor v. *Norman*, Case No. SCSL-04–14-T, 8 June 2004, Trial Chamber, Decision on the Application of Samuel Hinga Norman for Self-Representation under Art. 17(4)(d) of the Statute of the Special Court   130

Prosecutor v. *Ntagerura*, Case No. ICTR-99–46-A, 7 July 2006, Appeals Chamber, Judgment   202, 239

Prosecutor v. *Orić*, Case No. IT-03–68-AR 72.2, 20 July 2005, Appeals Chamber, Interlocutory Decision on Length of Defence Case   133

Prosecutor v. *Sesay*, Case No. SCSL-04–15-T, 26 October 2005, Trial Chamber, Decision on the Gbao and Sesay Joint Application for the Exclusion of the Testimony of Witness TF1–141   142

Prosecutor v. *Sesay*, Case No. SCSL-04–15-T-1188, 30 June 2008, Trial Chamber   204

Prosecutor v. *Simić and others*, Case No. IT-95–9, 27 July 1999, Trial Chamber, [Public version] Ex Parte Confidential Decision on the Prosecution Motion under Rule 73 for a Ruling Covering the Testimony of a Witness   305

Prosecutor v. *Stakic*, Case No. IT-97–24-A, 22 March 2006, Appeals Chamber, Judgment   200, 305

Prosecutor v. *Tadić*, Case No. IT-94–1-Y, 10 August 1995, Trial Chamber, Decision on the Prosecutor's Motion Requesting Protective Measures for Victims and Witnesses   131, 132

Prosecutor v. *Tadić*, Case No. IT-94–1, 5 August 1996, Trial Chamber, Decision on Defence Motion on Hearsay   124

Prosecutor v. *Tadić*, Case No. IT-94–1-A, 15 July 1999, Appeals Chamber, Judgment   133, 134

PS v. *Germany*, no. 33900/96, 20 December 2001   340, 353

Pullar v. *United Kingdom*, 10 June 1996, Reports 1996-III, 794   230, 231

PV v. *Germany* (dec.), no. 11853/85, 13 July 1987   344, 348

Quaranta v. *Switzerland*, 24 May 1991, Series A no. 205   279, 289

Quinn v. *Ireland*, no. 36887/97, 21 December 2000   266, 279

Rachdad v. *France*, no. 71846/01, 13 November 2003   349

RAG v. *Netherlands* (dec.), no. 21921/93, 5 July 1994   361

Ramanauskas v. *Lithuania* [GC], no. 74420/01, 5 February 2008   170, 190

Ramil Rayos v. *The Philippines*, no. 1167/2003, 24 March 2003, UN Doc. CCPR/C/81/D/1167/2003 (2004)   82

Remli v. *France*, 23 April 1996, Reports 1996-II, 571   231

Riedl-Riedenstein and others v. *Germany*, no. 1188/2003, 2 November 2004, UN Doc. CCPR/C/82/D/1188/2003 (2004)   82

Ringeisen v. *Austria*, 16 July 1971, Series A no. 13   96

Robert and Gerhard Lorich v. *Austria* (dec.), nos. 20953/92 and 21049/92, 11 January 1995   340
Robinson v. *Jamaica* no 223/1987, 30 March 1989, UN Doc. Supp no. 40 (A/44/40) at 241 (1989)   83
Robinson v. *United Kingdom* (dec.), no. 20858/92, 5 May 1993   226
Roche v. *United Kingdom*, no. 32555/96, ECHR 2005-X   210
Romero v. *Uruguay*, no. 85/1981, 29 Mar. 1984, UN Doc. CCPR/C/OP/2, 116 (1990)   160
Rowe and Davis v. *United Kingdom*, no. 28901/95, ECHR 2000-II   85, 86, 304
Ruiz Torija v. *Spain*, 9 December 1994, Series A no. 303-A   238
Ruiz-Mateos v. *Spain*, 23 June 1993, Series A no. 262   84
S v. *Switzerland*, 28 November 1991, Series A no. 220   291
Sadak and others v. *Turkey*, nos. 29900/96, 29901/96, 29902/96 and 29903/96, ECHR 2001-VIII   349
Sahadeo v. *Republic of Guyana*, no. 728/1996, 1 November 2001, UN Doc. CCPR/C/73/D/728/1996 (2001)   159
Saïdi v. *France*, 20 September 1993, Series A no. 261-C   90, 335, 338
Salabiaku v. *France*, 7 October 1998, Series A no. 141-A   220, 221, 222, 223, 224, 225
Salduz v. *Turkey* [GC], no. 36391/02, 27 November 2008   96, 100, 103, 280, 281, 282, 289, 345, 385
Sander v. *United Kingdom*, no. 34129/96, ECHR 2000-V   230, 231
Saric v. *Denmark* (dec.), no. 31913/96, 2 February 1999   104, 238
Sarikaya v. *Turkey*, no. 36115/97, 22 April 2004   280
Saunders v. *United Kingdom* [GC], 17 December 1996, Reports 1996-VI, 2044   151, 196, 242, 250, 251, 252, 253, 254, 255, 256, 258, 259, 266, 268, 270, 274, 276
SC v. *United Kingdom*, no. 60958/00, ECHR 2004-IV   106
Schenk v. *Switzerland*, 12 July 1988, Series A no. 140   82, 151, 157, 171, 172, 173, 174, 175, 182, 229
Schonenberger and Durmaz v. *Switzerland*, 20 June 1988, Series A no. 137   292
SE v. *Switzerland* (dec.), no. 28994/95, 4 March 1998   351, 355
Sekanina v. *Austria*, 25 August 1993, Series A no. 266-A   218
Selmouni v. *France* [GC], no. 25803/94, ECHR 1999-V   159, 161
Sequeira v. *Portugal* (dec.), no. 73557/01, ECHR 2003-VI   190
Serguey Romanov v. *Ukraine*, no. 842/1998, 30 October 2003, UN Doc. CCPR/C/79/D/842/1998 (2003)   82
Serves v. *France*, 20 October 1997, Reports 1997-VI, 2159   249, 266
Shannon v. *United Kingdom*, no. 6563/03, 4 October 2005   250
Sheper v. *Netherlands* (dec.), no. 39209/02, 5 April 2005   249
Simpson v. *Jamaica*, no. 695/1996, 31 October 2001, UN Doc. CCPR/C/73/D/695/1996   347

Slobodan v. *Netherlands* (dec.), no. 29838/96, 15 January 1997   360, 361
Smartt v. *Republic of Guyana*, no. 867/1999, 6 July 2004, UN Doc. CCPR/C/81/D/867/1999 (2004)   82
Smith v. *Jamaica*, no. 355/1989, UN Doc. CCPR/C/47D/282/1988 (1993)   290
SN v. *Sweden*, no. 34209/96, ECHR 2002-V   338, 349, 352, 353, 360
Soering v. *United Kingdom*, 7 July 1989, Series A no. 161   371
Sofri and others v. *Italy*, no. 37235/97, ECHR 2003-VIII   313
Solakov v. *Former Yugoslav Republic of Macedonia*, no. 47023/99, ECHR 2001-X   335, 336, 338, 348
Söylemez v. *Turkey*, no. 46661/99, 21 September 2006   165
Stanford v. *United Kingdom*, 23 February 1994, Series A no. 282-A   87
Stoimenov v. *Former Yugoslav Republic of Macedonia*, no. 17995/02, 5 April 2007   361
Svetik v. *Belarus*, no. 927/2000, 8 July 2004, UN Doc. CCPR/C/81/D/927/2000 (2004)   82
T and V v. *United Kingdom*, nos. 24724/94 and 24888/94, 16 December 1999   105
Tagac and others v. *Turkey*, no. 71864/01, 7 July 2009   281
Taxquet v. *Belgium*, no. 926/05, 13 January 2009   70, 238, 335
Teixeira de Castro v. *Portugal*, 9 June 1998, Reports 1998-IV, 1451   188, 189, 190
Telfner v. *Austria*, no. 33501/96, 20 March 2001   271
Tengerakis v. *Cyprus*, no. 35698/03, 9 November 2006   152
The Greek Case (report), nos. 3321/67, 3322/67, 3323/67 and 3344/67, 18 November 1969, (1969) 12 YB 1   159
Thomas v. *Jamaica*, no. 272/1988, 31 March 1992, UN Doc. A/47/40   290
Thorgeirson v. *Iceland*, 25 June 1992, Series A no. 239   231
Timergaliyev v. *Russia*, no. 40631/02, 14 October 2008   367
Tirado Ortiz and Lozano Martin v. *Spain*, no. 43486/98, ECHR 1999–V   258
Tourón v. *Uruguay*, no. R.7/32, 31 March 1981 UN Doc. Supp no. 40 (A/36/40) at 120 (1981)   290
Trivedi v. *United Kingdom* (dec.), no. 31700/96, 27 May 1997   340
Tyrer v. *United Kingdom*, 25 April 1978, Series A no. 26   83
Unterguggenberger v. *Austria* (dec.), no. 34941/97, 25 September 2001   344
Unterpertinger v. *Austria* (report), no. 9120/80, 11 October 1984, Series B no. 93   344
Unterpertinger v. *Austria*, 24 November 1986, Series A no. 110   87, 88, 137, 344
V v. *Finland*, no. 40412/98, 24 April 2007   189
Van de Hurk v. *Netherlands*, 19 April 1994, Series A no. 288   238
Van Mechelen and others v. *Netherlands*, 23 April 1997, Reports 1997-III, 691   83, 89, 228, 337, 351, 355, 356, 376
Verdam v. *Netherlands* (dec.), no. 35353/97, 31 August 1999   348, 350

Veznedaroglu v. *Turkey*, no. 32357/96, 11 April 2000   160
Vidal v. *Belgium*, 22 April 1992, Series A no. 235-B   234, 235
Vilhunen v. *Finland* (dec.), no. 30509/96, 25 November 1999   358
Visser v. *Netherlands*, no 26668/95, 14 February 2002   339, 351
W v. *Finland*, no. 14151/02, 24 April 2007   340
Weh v. *Austria*, no. 38544/97, 8 April 2004   251, 252, 269, 274
Weinberger v. *Uruguay*, no. R.7/28, 29 October 1980, UN Doc. Supp no. 40 (A/36/40) at 114 (1981)   290
Windisch v. *Austria*, 27 September 1990, Series A no. 186   87, 137
X v. *Austria* (dec.), no. 753/60, (1960) 3 YB 310   234
X v. *Austria* (dec.), no. 2676/65, 3 April 1967, 23 CD 31   229
X v. *Austria* (dec.), no. 4428/70, 1 June 1972, 40 CD 1   344
X v. *Austria* (dec.), no. 9295/81, 6 October 1982, DR 30, 227   218
X v. *Belgium* (dec.), no. 7450/76, 28 February 1977, DR 9, 109   219
X v. *Belgium* (dec.), no. 8417/78, 4 May 1979, 16 DR 200   344
X v. *Belgium* (dec.), no. 8876/80, 16 October 1980, DR 23, 235   229
X v. *Denmark* (dec.), no. 2518/65, 14 December 1965, 18 CD 44   133
X v. *FRG* (dec.), no. 254/57, 16 December 1957, 1 YB 150, 152   82, 84
X v. *FRG* (dec.), no. 1035/61, 17 January 1963   237
X v. *Germany* (dec.), no. 4119/69, 21 July 1970, CD 35, 127   234
X v. *Germany* (dec.), no. 5620/72, 18 July 1974, 46 CD 110   229
X v. *United Kingdom* (dec.), no. 5124/71 (1975) 42 CD 135   221, 225, 298
Y v. *Norway*, no. 56568/00, ECHR 2003-II   220
Z and others v. *United Kingdom* [GC], no. 29392/95 ECHR 2001-V   210
Zarouali v. *Belgium* (dec.), no. 20664/92, 29 June 1994, 78-B DR 97   70

Part I
Evidentiary contexts

1

Evidence across traditions

1.1 Introduction: the convergence debate

Within the last 30 years there has been a renewal of interest among teachers and students in comparative criminal justice as a field of study.[1] With growing pressure on legal systems to respond to the demands of globalisation and cosmopolitanism,[2] penal law has become one of a growing number of areas of law that is engaging with comparative legal studies.[3] Much of the debate has centred on whether or not these demands are driving legal systems towards convergence. A combination of pressures would seem to be supporting the convergence thesis within criminal justice.[4] National legal systems plagued by common problems of rising crime, concern for victims and the growing cost and delay in processing cases through the courts would seem to have led to a willingness to seek 'foreign' solutions to similar problems. In addition to these internal pressures, there have been external pressures on states to find common transnational solutions to deal with the problems of organised crime and drug trafficking.

In addition to this, international terrorism and the growing ethnic and religious conflicts around the world pose a particular challenge for international law as to whether these problems can be resolved by international legal cooperation or whether as protagonists of the 'war on terror' would have it they are better met through the exercise of hegemonic power with international law

---

[1] See, e.g. R. S. Frase, 'Main-Streaming Comparative Criminal Justice: How to Incorporate Comparative and International Concepts and Materials into Basic Criminal Law and Procedure Courses' (1998) 100 *West Virginia Law Review* 773; and D. Nelken, *Comparative Criminal Justice: Making Sense of Difference* (London: Sage, 2010).

[2] On the effects of globalisation, see W. Twining, *Globalisation and Legal Theory* (London: Butterworths, 2000). On cosmopolitanism, see P. Roberts, 'Rethinking the Law of Evidence: A Twenty-First Century Agenda for Teaching and Research' (2002) 55 *Current Legal Problems* 297.

[3] See P. Roberts, 'On Method: The Ascent of Comparative Criminal Justice' (2002) 22 *Oxford Journal of Legal Studies* 539.

[4] On the convergence thesis generally, see B. S. Markesinis (ed.), *The Gradual Convergence* (Oxford: Clarendon Press, 1994) 30. Others have been equally adamant that convergence is not taking place. See P. Legrand, 'European Legal Systems Are Not Converging' (1996) 45 *International & Comparative Legal Quarterly* 52.

being reduced to accommodate the demands of the most powerful states.[5] Those who would seek to deal with these problems through international law need to develop common legal solutions. An example of this is the effort made by the international legal community to deal with those who have committed war crimes and crimes against humanity through international criminal tribunals applying international criminal law.[6] But if this new international regime is to work successfully, there needs to be a consensus on the appropriate rules of evidence and procedure for holding such trials.[7]

It is at this point of reaching consensus on issues of evidence and procedure that there continues to be considerable suspicion of other systems and where the convergence thesis begins to unravel. To be sure, the success achieved by the international community in agreeing rules for trying those charged with war crimes and crimes against humanity in the ad hoc tribunals in The Hague and Arusha and, more recently, before the permanent International Criminal Court may be counted as a victory for convergence, although the delays in bringing those charged to justice is causing some to question whether the existing processes are not undermining the whole enterprise of international criminal justice.[8] But when national systems are asked to change their own laws of evidence and procedure or subject their citizens to those of others, there is often fierce loyalty displayed towards local traditions and a fierce resistance to change.

A good example is to be seen in Europe, where the existence of a single market within the European Union would seem to lead logically to close cooperation in criminal justice and a realignment of national systems of evidence and procedure, but where progress has been slow. Within the last decade there has been recognition that the traditional means of dealing with transnational crime through mutual assistance has been cumbersome and that there needs to be closer cooperation between enforcement agencies.[9] EU competence has been declared in the area of criminal justice,[10] giving recognition to two bodies:

---

[5] This age-old controversy as to whether international law is simply a disguise for international power politics has been given a new lease of life since the events of 9/11 and the invasion of Iraq. See, e.g. P. B. Heymann, *Terrorism, Freedom and Security* (Boston: MIT Press, 2003); and P. W. Kahn, *Sacred Violence: Torture, Terror and Sovereignty* (Ann Arbor: University of Michigan Press, 2008). For a discussion of how this debate relates to transitional justice discourses, see C. Bell, C. Campbell and F. Ni Aoláin, 'The Battle For Transitional Justice: Hegemony, Iraq and International Law', in J. Morison, K. McEvoy and G. Anthony (eds.), *Judge, Transition and Human Rights: Essays in Memory of Stephen Livingstone* (Oxford University Press, 2007).

[6] See generally G. Robertson, *Crimes against Humanity: The Struggle for Global Justice* (London: Penguin, 2002).

[7] See R. May and M. Wierda, 'Trends in International Criminal Evidence: Nuremberg, Tokyo, The Hague, Arusha' (1999) 37 *Columbia Journal of Transnational Law* 725; and G. Boas, 'Creating Laws of Evidence for International Criminal Law: The ICTY and the Principle of Flexibility' (2001) 12 *Criminal Law Forum* 41.

[8] R. Zacklin, 'The Failings of the Ad Hoc International Tribunals' (2004) 2 *Journal of International Criminal Justice* 541–5.

[9] See, e.g. Council of Europe Convention on Mutual Assistance in Criminal Matters (1959), EU Convention on Mutual Assistance in Criminal Matters (2000).

[10] See Art. 83(2) of the Treaty on the Functioning of the European Union (TFEU), [2010] OJ C83.

Europol, which has the power to request national police forces to commence investigations and participate in joint investigation teams; and Eurojust, to facilitate coordination of prosecutions where there is a cross-border element.[11] The EU has also begun to replace the principle of mutual assistance with the principle of mutual recognition, whereby decisions taken in one member state are accepted as valid in other member states and are acted on accordingly.[12] This stops short of requiring convergence between systems as it tolerates a degree of diversity, but it does require there to be an element of trust in each others' systems as a judicial decision issued in one member state must be recognised and executed in the requested member state. Although the first steps in this direction to establish a common arrest warrant and the mutual recognition of orders freezing property or evidence were limited in nature,[13] the European Evidence Warrant is much broader, requiring the mutual recognition of orders for obtaining objects, documents and data for use in criminal proceedings in the issuing state.[14] As yet, however, the proposal for an evidence warrant falls short of providing for the mutual admissibility of evidence in the courts of the member states, although there is an aspiration that this should occur.[15]

It is not surprising that an area of law long confined within the nation state should be so closely identified with the state and that resistance is met when attempts are made to modify features that are closely associated with national systems. Nor indeed should there be an uncritical eye cast towards such attempts. Issues of evidence in particular are not confined to the technical nuts and bolts of making a system run more smoothly, but go to the heart of the rights of individuals. If a person has no means to challenge the evidence against him or her, for example, that is not a 'mere' matter of procedure, but a matter of substance affecting the fundamental relationship between the state and the individual when the individual is charged with a criminal offence. What is perhaps surprising, however, is that instead of addressing such fundamental

---

[11] Europol was formally established through the Europol Convention 1995. Eurojust was established by a Council decision in 2002: see 2002/187/JHA OJ.

[12] At the Tampere European Council in October 1999, the principle of mutual recognition was highlighted as the 'cornerstone' of judicial cooperation in both criminal and civil matters. On the notion of mutual recognition in the light of the Treaty of Lisbon, see V. Mitsilegas, *EU Criminal Law* (Oxford: Hart Publishing, 2009) 156 ff. See also S. Peers, 'EU Criminal Law and the Treaty of Lisbon' (2008) 33 *European Law Review* 507.

[13] See Council Framework Decision on the European arrest warrant ([2002] OJ L190) and Council Framework Decision on the execution in the EU of orders freezing property or evidence ([2003] OJ L196) respectively.

[14] See Council Framework Decision 2008/978/JHA, 18 December 2008 on the European evidence warrant for the purpose of obtaining objects, documents and data for the use in proceedings in criminal matters. See further S. Gless, *Beweisrechtsgrundsätze einer grenzüberschreitenden Strafverfolgung* (Baden Baden: Nomos, 2007); and J. A. E. Vervaele (ed.), *European Evidence Warrant: Transnational Judicial Inquiries in the EU* (Antwerpen: Intersentia, 2005).

[15] Compare the Green Paper produced by the Commission, COM (2009) 624 final (which includes the 'mutual admissibility' element) with the Draft Directive regarding the EIO in criminal matters proposed by a group of Member States, 29 April 2010, Interinstitutional File 2010/0817 (COD), which does not.

matters of substance, comparative scholarship in the field has tended to reinforce the nationalist tendency of states to differentiate themselves from others by classifying systems of evidence and procedure into two discrete categories: one defined as 'adversarial' or 'accusatorial' and the other as 'non-adversarial' or 'inquisitorial'. This typology has enjoyed such a strikingly long lease of life that it is unusual even today for any work of comparative criminal evidence and procedure to eschew reference to these terms. Acknowledging that such systems are ideal types, scholars have proceeded to examine how 'adversarial' or 'non-adversarial' particular systems are and whether or not such systems are converging by reference to this dichotomy. It is widely assumed that this approach is not only a valuable heuristic tool for theorising about different influences at play in Anglo-American and continental processes, but that it also provides a useful independent standard for comparing different systems and determining how convergent or divergent they are.[16]

The convergence debate has therefore become fixated on whether systems are moving in an 'inquisitorial' or 'adversarial' direction, with little clarification of what these terms actually mean. Some commentators have detected a slow, gradual convergence in the evidentiary processes of common law and civil law systems towards a 'middle position' as the respective oral 'adversary' and written 'inquisitorial' traditions within each system are borrowed from each other.[17] The trends that have been identified in civil law countries include an increasing prominence given to parties and their lawyers, the diminishing authority of professional judges, a shift from pre-trial to trial phases of adjudication which has led to greater importance given to oral evidence and the right to confrontation, with less reliance on the accused as a source of testimonial evidence, and, finally, greater pressures to find 'consensual' alternatives to traditional trial processes.[18] Trends away from adversary excesses in certain common law countries, on the other hand, have been said to include greater judicial management over the

---

[16] For defences of the use of adversarial and inquisitorial models in order to analyse criminal procedure systems, see N. Jörg, S. Field and C. Brants, 'Are Inquisitorial and Adversarial Systems Converging?', in P. Fennell, C. Harding, N. Jörg and B. Swart (eds.), *Criminal Justice in Europe: A Comparative Study* (Oxford University Press, 1995) 41; L. Ellison, *The Adversarial Process and the Vulnerable Witness* (Oxford: Clarendon Press, 2001) 142; M. Langer, 'From Legal Transplants to Legal Translations: The Globalisation of Plea Bargaining and the Americanization Thesis in Criminal Processes' (2004) 45 *Harvard International Law Journal* 1; and P. Duff, 'Changing Conceptions of the Scottish Criminal Trial: The Duty to Agree Uncontroversial Evidence', in A. Duff, L. Farmer, S. Marshall and V. Tadros (eds.), *The Trial on Trial (1): Truth and Due Process* (Oxford: Hart, 2004) 31.

[17] Markesinis, *The Gradual Convergence*, 30. See, e.g. C. Bradley, *Criminal Procedure: A Worldwide Study* (Durham: Carolina Academic Press, 1998) xxi; and G. Van Kessel, 'European Trends Towards Adversary Styles in Procedure and Evidence', in M. Feeley and S. Miyazawa (eds.), *The Japanese Adversary System in Context* (Basingstoke: Macmillan, 2002) 225.

[18] Van Kessel, 'European Trends', 227. These trends are by no means self-evident in the practices of all civil law countries. A counter-tendency to the shift from pre-trial to trial phases of adjudication, for example, is that the police have been gaining additional powers in certain jurisdictions at the expense of judicial authorities. See E. Mathias, 'The Balance of Power between the Police and the Public Prosecutor', in M. Delmas-Marty and J. Spencer (eds.), *European Criminal Procedures* (Cambridge University Press, 2002) 459, 481.

criminal process, greater disclosure requirements on prosecution and defence, in some cases a curtailing of the right of silence and greater reliance on pre-trial evidence for vulnerable witnesses.[19]

While these developments would appear to lend credence to the convergence thesis, others have pointed to counter-influences at work that are actually moving the systems further away from each other. Sceptics of convergence point to the unintended effects of 'transplanting' processes and procedures from one national and legal culture into another.[20] Institutional and cultural resistance within the receiving system sometimes proves too strong to achieve the impact intended, with the result that the character of the imported practice or procedure is altered in the new procedural environment. As Damaška has put it, 'the music of the law changes, so to speak, when the musical instruments and the players are no longer the same'.[21] Italy is often used as an example where a new criminal procedure code was drafted along 'adversarial' lines, but where this transplant has been met with a number of institutional obstacles.[22] But it is not merely the institutional context in which a transplant is introduced that determines its success: it is also the willingness with which the actors involved are prepared to embrace it. Consequently, it has been argued that the procedures that operate in common law and civil law systems may be understood not only as two ways of arranging legal procedure, but also as two different procedural cultures reflecting normative conceptions of how proceedings *should* be organised.[23] Attempts to import 'foreign' solutions often lead to practices being 'translated' in a different way and this can lead to fragmentation and divergence rather than convergence within the systems concerned.

Thanks to Damaška's influence, comparativists no longer look simply at rules of evidence and procedure in order to determine whether systems are converging. The analysis has become a deeper inquiry into the influence of

---

[19] Van Kessel, 'European Trends', 227; J. McEwan, 'Cooperative Justice and the Adversarial Criminal Trial: Lessons from the Woolf Report', in S. Doran and J. Jackson (eds.), *The Judicial Role in Criminal Proceedings* (Oxford: Hart, 2000) 171; J. Jackson, 'The Adversary Trial and Trial by Judge Alone', in M. McConville and G. Wilson (eds.), *The Handbook of the Criminal Justice Process* (Oxford University Press, 2002) 335; A. T. H. Smith, 'Criminal Law – The Future' [2004] *Criminal Law Review* 971, 972–3. Not all common law countries have been so susceptible to such changes, however. For the limited impact of continental-inspired reforms on the US criminal justice system, see J. H. Langbein, 'The Influence of Comparative Procedure in the United States' (1995) 43 *American Journal of Comparative Law* 545.

[20] On the notion of 'transplants' from one legal system to another, see A. Watson, *Legal Transplants: An Approach to Comparative Law*, 2nd edn (Athens: University of Georgia Press, 1993). For sceptical views, see, e.g. N. Boari, 'On the Efficiency of Penal Systems: Several Lessons from the Italian Experience' (1997) 17 *International Review of Law and Economics* 115; and G. Teubner, 'Legal Irritants: Good Faith in British Law or How Unifying Law Ends Up in New Divergences' (1998) 61 *Modern Law Review* 11.

[21] M. Damaška, 'The Uncertain Fate of Evidentiary Transplants: Anglo-American and Continental Experiments' (1997) 45 *American Journal of Comparative Law* 839, 840.

[22] See, e.g. W. T. Pizzi and M. Montagna, 'The Battle to Establish an Adversarial Trial System in Italy' (2004) 25 *Michigan Journal of International Law* 429; and E. Grande, 'Italian Criminal Justice: Borrowing and Resistance' (2000) 48 *American Journal of Comparative Law* 227, 232.

[23] Langer, 'From Legal Transplants'.

institutional and cultural factors.[24] But scholars have still continued to use the adversarial/inquisitorial dichotomy to guide their analysis. To borrow Damaška's metaphor, the musical instruments may have become more refined and the players more sophisticated, but the musical score remains the same. This is not to say that it is possible, or even desirable, to outlaw the terms altogether from the comparativist's lexicon. They are such a familiar part of this lexicon that it is exceedingly difficult to maintain any comparative study without some reference to them even if we wanted to.[25] We also do not seek to deny that these terms may be useful for identifying different procedural traditions within common law and civil law systems. As the terms are broadened out to include different political structures of authority and different legal cultures, they can be viewed as encompassing different normative expressions of how to conduct legal proceedings.[26] They may therefore retain some use historically as an expression of the two different procedural traditions systems that have dominated the common law and civil law world and as descriptions of how actors perceive their practices.

But we would argue that the dichotomy is increasingly unhelpful in describing actual systems of justice and as a heuristic tool for gauging whether or not systems are converging as the 'ideal-types' increasingly diverge from real-life processes.[27] It is commonly assumed that the essence of the contrast lies in arranging proceedings around the notion of a dispute or contest between two sides – prosecution and defence – in a position of theoretical equality before a court which must decide on the outcome and arranging them around the notion of an official and thorough inquiry driven by court officials.[28] The difficulty here is that as procedures have been changing within the last 30 years, it is becoming increasingly doubtful whether this essential contrast still has much explanatory force within different common law and civil law systems. If we take as an example the Swiss system, which is commonly perceived to fall within the inquest model, in common with a number of other new procedural codes on the Continent,[29] Swiss judicial authorities no longer take centre stage in

---

[24] See in particular M. Damaška, *The Faces of Justice and State Authority* (New Haven: Yale University Press, 1986).

[25] The authors owe this thought to Paul Roberts.

[26] See S. Field, 'Fair Trials and Procedural Tradition in Europe' (2009) 29 *Oxford Journal of Legal Studies* 365, 372.

[27] See the analysis in J. Jackson, 'The Effect of Human Rights on Criminal Evidentiary Processes: Towards Convergence, Divergence or Realignment' (2005) 68 *Modern Law Review* 737, 740–7.

[28] See, e.g. M. Damaška, 'Evidentiary Barriers to Conviction and Two Models of Criminal Procedure: A Comparative Study' (1973) 121 *University of Pennsylvania Law Review* 506, 563–5; and P. Roberts and A. Zuckerman, *Criminal Evidence*, 2nd edn (Oxford University Press, 2010) 49.

[29] See J. R. Spencer, 'Evidence', in Delmas-Marty and Spencer, *European Criminal Procedures*, 625, discussing France and Belgium. For an overview of the criminal procedural reforms in Austria, see R. Moos, 'Die Reform des Vorverfahrens im österreichischen Strafverfahren', in H. Müller-Dietz, E. Müller, K.-L. Kunz, H. Radtke, G. Britz, C. Momsen and H. Koriath (eds.), *Festschrift für Heike Jung zum 65. Geburtstag* (Baden-Baden: Nomos, 2007) 590.

the handling of evidence. In Switzerland, the investigating judge is now the prosecutor and, in common with a number of other continental systems, the position of the investigating judge has been abolished altogether.[30] In the pre-trial process, the prosecutor now arranges the confrontation hearings and is responsible for conducting them.[31] There is no impartial third party present, just the prosecution and defence, and the defence has the chance to question the witnesses. Indeed, a novel feature in a number of so-called 'inquisitorial' systems now is that the prosecution and defence may reach an agreement over the outcome of the case, with the result that the court no longer plays any meaningful role in fact-finding at all.[32] This is not to say that there are not still quite considerable differences between common law and civil law systems. One difference that is still significant is that for all the possibilities for plea bargaining, the trial is still generally the only forum in common law systems where evidence can be effectively challenged by the defence. Within civil law systems, the defence has the opportunity and is expected to challenge evidence before trial in the various pre-trial phases, even though in many instances there may not be a judge present to oversee fairness in the process. This suggests that the contrast between the systems is better found in the stage at which 'adversarial' testing takes place than in any fundamental difference between 'adversarial' and 'inquisitorial' proceedings.

1.2 Comparative evidence scholarship

The adversarial/inquisitorial dichotomy has had a particularly baneful effect on evidence scholarship. Evidence scholarship has enjoyed something of a renaissance within the last 30 years, taking an 'interdisciplinary turn' away from purely doctrinal scholarship towards inquiries into the psychology of witnesses and fact-finders, forensic science and theories of probability and proof, taking in new perspectives from the domains of feminist theory and law and economics.[33]

---

[30] E.g. in Germany, Portugal and Italy, see C. Van Den Wyngaert, *Criminal Procedure Systems in the European Community* (London: Butterworths, 1992). On the decline of the investigating judge, see H. Jung, 'Der Untersuchungsrichter – ein Nachruf?', in R. Moss, U. Jesionek and O. F. Müller, *Strafprozessrecht im Wandel: Festschrift für Roland Miklau zum 65. Geburtstag* (Innsbruck: Studienverlag, 2006).

[31] Art. 147 Swiss Code of Criminal Procedure: see W. Wohlers, 'Art 147', in A. Donastch, T. Hansjakob and V. Lieber (eds.), *Kommentar zur Schweizerischen Strafprozessordnung (StPO)* (Zurich: Schulthess, 2010). For criticism, see P. Albrecht, 'Was bleibt von der Unmittelbarkeit?' (2010) 128 *Schweizerische Zeitschrift für Strafrecht* 180 ff; and S. Arquint and S. Summers, 'Konfrontationen nur vor dem Gericht' (2008) 2 *Plädoyer* 38 ff.

[32] See, e.g. T. Weigend, 'The Decay of the Inquisitorial Ideal: Plea Bargaining Invades German Criminal Procedure', in J. Jackson, M. Langer and P. Tillers (eds.), *Crime, Procedure and Evidence in a Comparative and International Context: Essays in Honour of Mirjan Damaška* (Oxford: Hart, 2008), 39. See also G. Gilléron, *Strafbefehl und plea bargaining als Quelle von Fehlurteilen* (Zurich: Schulthess, 2010).

[33] M. Saks and R. C. Park, 'Evidence Scholarship Reconsidered: Results of the Interdisciplinary Turn' (2006) 47 *Boston College Law Review* 1. For further analyses of modern evidence scholarship, see W. Twining, *Rethinking Evidence: Exploratory Essays*, 2nd edn (Cambridge

When it comes to comparative law, however, evidence has been largely neglected. When comparative issues of evidence are debated, they tend to revolve around the old debate as to whether adversarial or inquisitorial systems are better at finding the truth. Some contributors have brought the insights of modern psychology and economics to bear on this debate, with the result that defects have been detected with each system.[34] On one view, 'adversarial' systems are deeply flawed because the parties responsible for gathering and presenting the evidence are deeply partisan, with the result that the informational sources used are highly selective and become distorted. This partisan manner of collecting evidence is carried into the trial where the process of examination and cross-examination imposed upon witnesses results in a highly skewed picture of reality being conveyed to the triers of fact. The winner in such a contest is not the party with the most truth on his side, but the side that has the most wealth to marshal the best legal resources.[35] The triers of fact, meanwhile, are forced to maintain a position of neutral passivity in such a contest and are unable to harness the contest towards the kind of active inquiry that would be required to make the enterprise a serious truth-finding endeavour. In another vivid metaphor, Damaška has compared the limited vision that this whole process sheds upon the facts in dispute to a car driving at night, with two narrow beams illuminating the world presented to the adjudicator from the beginning until the end of trial.[36] But Damaška has also been critical of certain aspects of continental procedure, particularly the risk in judge-driven procedures that triers of fact will form hypotheses too early.[37] Other critics have pointed out that although 'inquisitorial' fact-finders have the freedom to mount their own inquiries, there are insufficient incentives for fact-finders to generate a sufficiently strong evidential base for making accurate judgments, with the result once more that hypotheses might be formed too early.[38]

Although the insights of cognitive science and economics can do much to enlighten debates on different fact-finding modes, rigorous empirical and

University Press, 2006); R. Park, 'Evidence Scholarship: Old and New' (1991) 75 *Minnesota Law Review* 849; J. Jackson, 'Analysing the New Evidence Scholarship: Towards a New Conception of the Law of Evidence' (1996) 16 *Oxford Journal of Legal Studies* 309; Symposium, 'New Perspectives on Evidence' (2001) 87 *Virginia Law Review* 1491–2081; J. D. Jackson, 'Modern Trends in Evidence Scholarship: Is All Rosy in the Garden?' (2003) 21 *Quinnipiac Law Review* 893; and P. Roberts and M. Redmayne (eds.), *Innovations in Evidence and Proof* (Oxford: Hart, 2007).

[34] For economic approaches, see G. Tillock, *Trials on Trial: The Pure Theory of Legal Procedure* (New York: Columbia University Press, 1980); and R. Posner, 'An Economic Approach to the Law of Evidence' (1999) 51 *Stanford Law Review* 1477. For cognitive approaches, see C. Callen, 'Cognitive Strategies and Models of Fact-Finding', in Jackson, Langer and Tillers, *Crime, Procedure and Evidence*, 165.

[35] For trenchant critiques of adversary procedure, see J. Langbein, 'The German Advantage in Civil Procedure' (1985) 52 *University of Chicago Law Review* 823; and J. Langbein, *The Origins of the Adversary Criminal Trial* (Oxford University Press, 2003).

[36] M. Damaška, *Evidence Law Adrift* (New Haven: Yale University Press, 1997) 92.

[37] Damaška, *Evidence Law Adrift*, 95–6.

[38] R. A. Posner, *Frontiers of Legal Theory* (Cambridge, MA: Harvard University Press, 2001) 340–1.

conceptual inquiries are required in order to reach definitive conclusions as to which model is better suited for truth discovery.[39] Too often, however, the debate has tended to degenerate into highly partisan views as to the merits of one mode of proof over the other, with little common ground as to whether the supposed models actually translate into the reality of real-life processes.[40] Much of the debate, moreover, has focused on civil procedure and there has been little examination as to whether the models that are used for the purpose of comparison reflect real-life criminal processes. It is questionable as we have seen whether the differences lie any longer in some essential contrast between party-dominated or judge-dominated procedures.

Beyond this debate, the adversarial/inquisitorial dichotomy would seem to have encouraged the view among evidence scholars that the gulf between the common and civil law systems is simply too great to admit any serious study. Within 'adversarial' systems, the law of evidence is viewed as a highly regulated system of rules for the admission of evidence at the contested trial. By contrast, civil law systems operating under a court-dominated inquiry are assumed not to have a law of evidence at all.[41] We shall see that these simple assumptions are a distortion of the way in which evidence has evolved in common law and civil law systems. For now, it is important to see that this narrow view of the law of evidence obscures two important truths about any system of adjudication which subscribes to the importance of evidence and proof. Firstly, any system which gives triers of fact the task of evaluating evidence must subscribe to some extent to a doctrine of 'free proof'; and, secondly, any adjudicative system must have *some* rules of evidence and proof. Taking the first point, historical analysis is now showing that even the highly regulated systems of evidence such as the old Roman canon systems were limited in their capacity to interfere with 'natural' processes of reasoning of fact-finders.[42] By the same token, those averse to regulation, like Jeremy Bentham, who have called for a 'natural' as opposed to a technical system of proof, still must subscribe to certain rules of evidence in order for a system of adjudication to function at all.[43] Indeed, any fact-finding enterprise has to have rules and procedures for carrying out its

---

[39] See M. Damaška, 'Presentation of Evidence and Factfinding Precision' (1975) 123 *University of Pennsylvania Law Review* 1083; and P. Tillers, 'The Fabrication of Facts in Investigation and Adjudication' (2006), available at http://ssrn.com/abstract=962241. For an economic approach, see Tillock, *Trials on Trial*.

[40] See the acrimonious exchange between R. Allen, S. Kock, K. Riecherberg and D. T. Rosen, 'The German Advantage in Civil Procedure: A Plea for More Details and Fewer Generalities in Comparative Scholarship' (1988) 82 *Northwestern University Law Review* 705; and J. H. Langbein, 'Trashing the German Advantage' (1988) 82 *Northwestern University Law Review* 763.

[41] For a recent statement of this view, see South African Law Commission, *Sexual Offences: Process and Procedure* (2002) Discussion paper 102 (Project 107), para. 12.11.3.1.4.

[42] See, e.g. M. Damaška, 'The Death of Legal Torture' (1987) 87 *Yale Law Journal* 860; and M. Damaška, 'Rational and Irrational Proof Revisited' (1997) 5 *Cardozo Journal of International and Comparative Law* 25.

[43] For discussion of Bentham's 'anti-nomian' thesis, see W. Twining, *Theories of Evidence: Bentham and Wigmore* (London: Weidenfeld & Nicolson, 1985).

inquiry.[44] Every fact-finding enterprise which requires a decision to be reached, for example, must adopt certain rules for specifying the degree of certainty required for a decision. In legal systems, this involves making an essentially moral and political judgement concerning the extent to which the various parties should be exposed to the risk of error. The standards of proof are conventionally different in civil and criminal cases. In civil litigation, an assumption of equality is made between the parties as it has been considered wrong to favour one party over another and the standard has thus been guided by the principle that the risk of errors should be allocated as evenly as possible between the parties. In criminal cases, on the other hand, it is considered preferable to allocate the risk of error asymmetrically in favour of the defendant, because the risk of a person being wrongly convicted is considered much graver than the risk of a person being wrongly acquitted.

As well as rules specifying *when* the facts are to be considered proved, any system of adjudication must have rules to determine *how* evidence is to be obtained and facts are to be proved. Within the common law world, a distinction tends to be made between the law of evidence, which is concerned mainly with rules addressed to decision-makers determining what is to count as evidence and proof – how evidence is to be applied – and rules of procedure addressed to investigators, determining how evidence is obtained in the first place.[45] But rules determining how evidence is to be obtained are no less rules of 'evidence' than rules of procedure. The question that we have seen has dominated much of the literature on comparative procedure as to whether the task of obtaining evidence should be put in the hands of the parties to a dispute as in so-called 'adversarial' systems or in the hands of the courts as in so-called 'inquisitorial' systems is self-evidently a matter of evidence as much as a question of procedure. The question may not be determined solely on the basis of epistemic considerations. Much may depend on what are considered to be the ultimate goals to be served and the importance attached to other values in the process. But to say that rules about obtaining evidence are not rules of evidence would seem to amount to an artificial narrowing of the subject. To mount an artificial chasm between rules on how evidence is to be applied and how it is obtained also obscures the obvious relationship between the two. Assuming that we wish to enhance the reliability of decisions, the way in which evidence is obtained may have a considerable effect upon the way in which we want that evidence to be assessed. In particular, we may wish to put limits on the admissibility or use of evidence obtained by unreliable means. Alternatively, however reliable the evidence is, we may nevertheless wish to limit its admission or use because it was obtained by morally repugnant means. We shall see, for example, that most modern adjudication systems now forbid the use of evidence obtained by torture. In regulating what may be counted and used as evidence, legal

---

[44] A. A. S. Zuckerman, *The Principles of Criminal Evidence* (Oxford: Clarendon, 1989) 1–2.
[45] See M. Redmayne, 'The Structure of Evidence Law' (2006) 26 *Oxford Journal of Legal Studies* 805, 805–6.

systems send out strong messages as to what safeguards need to be put in place for obtaining certain kinds of evidence and which methods of obtaining evidence are acceptable and which are not.

Adopting a wider definition of the law of evidence than is commonly adopted in common law systems, this book aims to examine the ways in which evidence is regulated across common law and civil law systems. Instead of using the adversarial/inquisitorial dichotomy in order to do this, however, in the commonly accepted methodology of most comparative scholarship on evidence and procedure which sets up the systems in opposition to each other, the book aims to consider what values the systems share and whether there are commonly accepted principles that can be drawn upon to build a system of evidence that commands consensus across the different legal traditions. Not only, however, do we seek to avoid the common methodology used for describing different systems, we also seek to move beyond the debate as to whether systems are converging or diverging to the more normative question of whether we can find common principles of evidence on which to build consensus. Following Schwikkard, we aim to identify values shaping evidence rules that have the 'potential to inform assessments of the extent of convergence in national and international evidence law, as well as providing a basis for evaluating the merits of importing or exporting rules between jurisdictions'.[46] The aim is not to erect a common code of evidence which should be adopted by different systems. We do not seek to deny that there are important institutional and cultural differences between the common law and civil law traditions. But if we can find a 'common grammar' for building consensus, we may be able to promote change and improvements in a manner which does not invite the cry that 'foreign' implants are being imposed upon native soil.[47]

It will be argued that within the criminal evidentiary domain there are two relevant traditions which common law and civil law systems share in common – what after Twining may be called a 'rationalist tradition' of adjudication and evidence and what may be called a tradition of individual rights which in recent years has been translated into human rights. Each of these traditions is historically grounded. The rationalist tradition can be traced back to the empiricist philosophy of Bacon, Locke and Hume which took hold in England and also had a strong influence on French Enlightenment thinkers. The tradition of individual rights can be traced back to social contract theorists such as Hobbes, Locke, Rousseau, Montesquieu, Kant and Beccaria and the French Enlightenment.

Although these are well-established traditions in European philosophical discourse, they have tended to be divorced from the legal discourse of procedural design.[48] Hence it has tended to be assumed that the rationalist tradition can

---

[46] P. J. Schwikkard, 'Convergence, Appropriate Fit and Values in Criminal Process', in Roberts and Redmayne, *Innovations in Evidence and Proof*, 331, 332.
[47] M. Delmas-Marty, 'The "Hybridisation" of Criminal Procedure', in Jackson, Langer and Tillers, *Crime, Procedure and Evidence*, 251, 258.
[48] Ashworth and Redmayne, for example, make a distinction between 'internal values' and 'external values'. Truth and fairness are considered internal values and 'adversarialism' an

encompass the widely divergent adversarial and inquisitorial models of criminal procedure.[49] Similarly, it has tended to be assumed that individual rights can be secured adequately within either of these models.[50] Our argument, however, is that far from the rationalist and individual rights traditions being disconnected from procedural design, they have, on the contrary, enabled a common set of evidentiary principles to be developed across the common law/civil law divide. It is not suggested that there have not been tensions in the development of these principles. The rationalist tradition with its emphasis on truth finding can at times conflict with a pure human rights emphasis on the rights of the individual. Bentham, an arch exponent of the rationalist tradition, famously likened rights to 'nonsense on stilts'.[51] Nor will it be denied that there are significant differences in the manner in which common law and civil law systems continue to organise their evidentiary processes. But it will be argued that an undue emphasis on legal cultural traditions has obscured the influence that shared epistemological, moral and political traditions can have on these systems. In particular, it will be argued that certain common criminal evidentiary principles can be seen in the work of the European jurists of the nineteenth century and more latterly in the jurisprudence of the human rights bodies tasked with interpreting the human rights treaties after the Second World War, principally the Human Rights Committee of the UN and the European Court of Human Rights. As pressures mount to develop common policies to deal with transnational and international problems of crime, these principles can be drawn upon to provide fair and acceptable evidentiary and procedural solutions. Before coming to these principles, let us probe more closely their epistemological and moral foundations.

1.3 The rationalist tradition and the rights tradition

In his ground-breaking work on the intellectual history of common law evidence scholarship, Twining identified a number of basic assumptions that were shared by almost all specialist writings on the common law of evidence and which he associated with a 'rationalist tradition'.[52] He divided these assumptions into sets of ideas: first those relating to the aims and nature of 'rational' adjudication; and

---

external value. See A. Ashworth and M. Redmayne, *The Criminal Process*, 4th edn (Oxford University Press, 2010) 26–8.

[49] Twining considered that the rationalist model fits civilian discourse as well if not even better than Anglo-American: see Twining, *Rethinking Evidence*, 97.

[50] Not always: there is a 'lengthy tradition in American law [which] looks to the Continental, inquisitorial system of criminal adjudication for negative guidance about our own ideals', see D. A. Sklansky, 'Anti-Inquisitorialism' (2009) 122 *Harvard Law Review* 1634, 1636.

[51] J. Bentham, 'An Examination of the Declaration of the Rights of Man and the Citizen Decreed by the Constituent Assembly in France', in J. Bentham, *Selected Writings on Utilitarianism* (Ware: Wordsworth, 2000) 405.

[52] See W. Twining, 'The Rationalist Tradition of Evidence Scholarship', in Twining, *Rethinking Evidence*, 35.

secondly those concerning how matters of fact are proved by rational means. According to the first set of ideals, the essential purpose of adjudication is 'rectitude of decision', the correct application of substantive laws (deemed to be consonant with utility) to facts proved on the basis of relevant evidence presented to the court. This is a model that owes much to Bentham's utilitarian philosophy, but Twining adapted it to make 'rectitude of decision' the main objective. According to the second set of ideas, epistemology is cognitivist, rather than sceptical and a correspondence theory of truth is to be preferred to a coherence theory of truth. The theory postulates that events and states of affairs occur and have an existence which is independent of human observation and that true statements correspond with these facts. Present knowledge about facts, which is what much adjudication is concerned with, is possible, but because it is based on incomplete knowledge, evidence establishing the truth about the past is typically a matter of probabilities. The characteristic mode of reasoning is inductive, by which one starts with certain basic data and moves by way of inductive generalisation towards a probable conclusion.

Although Twining uses the term 'rationalist' to describe these views, in truth they have little to do with the rationalist theories of knowledge associated with Plato and Descartes and much more with Newtonian science and the empiricist philosophy of Bacon, Locke and Hume. Observation and memory supply the basic data for reasoning. We can only go beyond the data of our senses and memory by relying on general principles of cause and effect which are known entirely from experience when we find that particular objects or events are associated with other objects or events. These principles are arrived at by what Hume called 'experimental inference' or what is now called 'inductive generalisation'.[53] This is known as the scientific method and although it owed its origins to English empiricism, it had a strong influence on French Enlightenment thinkers such as Voltaire and Montesquieu and came to be widely adopted and developed in both the natural and social sciences across the European continent.[54]

In Chapters 2 and 3 we trace the influence of the rationalist theory of evidence on the respective common law and civil law traditions. For now it is sufficient to note that although Twining himself conceded that there is room for differences of perspective and we shall see that the tradition itself has come under some degree of reinterpretation in the post-modern world of the twentieth century, the core tenets at the heart of the tradition – a belief in the importance of truth, reason and justice – have remained relatively unchallenged. From this broad perspective, the tradition has been able to expose deficiencies in both the traditional adversarial and inquisitorial systems. The key tenet of the rationalist tradition that truth finding is about probabilities

---

[53] B. Aune, *Rationalism, Empiricism and Pragmatism: An Introduction* (New York: Random House, 1970) 57.
[54] See, e.g. M. R. Cohen and E. Nagel, *An Introduction to Logic and Scientific Method* (New York: Harcourt, Brace, 1934); and E. Durkheim, *The Rules of the Sociological Method*, trans. W. D. Halls (New York: The Free Press, 1982).

and that fact-finders must apply their own inductive method to the evidence in order to arrive at a conclusion was able to find its way into Anglo-Saxon tradition more easily than in the continental tradition, where the rules of canon law prescribed their own value to particular types of evidence. Empiricists like Locke who developed criteria for evaluating testimony based on the number of witnesses, inner integrity and agreement with other evidence had a strong influence on the English treatise writers who were grappling with how juries should evaluate evidence when they no longer had first-hand knowledge of the events in question and had to rely upon witnesses.[55] But the lack of any machinery for investigating cases before trial exposed a serious truth deficit in the party-oriented nature of eighteenth-century English criminal trial proceedings. In one of the trials described by Langbein,[56] prosecution witnesses testified that they were certain of their identification of two defendants charged with a night-time highway robbery because the night was bright and starlit, whereas each of the defendants who were unrepresented claimed that it was rainy and dark. The court ignored the suggestion of one of the defendants that it look into whether or not it did rain on the night in question and the jurors were left to decide the issue and chose to convict the accused. Across the English Channel, however, the alternative system of inquisitorial justice did not fare much better by the standards of the emerging rationalist tradition. Here, Roman-canon procedure used in the European states placed the responsibility of truth finding on judges, who were in turn required to follow strict rules of proof which were an anathema to the rationalist tradition. The rigidity of the canon law requirement of two eyewitnesses or a confession meant that judicial torture continued to be used well into the eighteenth century in many jurisdictions.[57]

The rationalist tradition thus exposed the truth deficiencies of the adversarial and inquisitorial systems. The latter came under the particular scrutiny of Enlightenment criticism. In his *On Crimes and Punishments*, Beccaria launched an attack on the system of legal proofs and developed instead a theory of moral proof by which the weight of the evidence is assessed not by the number of proofs available, but by the number of independent proofs that could be obtained.[58] But if Enlightenment thinkers were considerably influenced by the scientific method of inferring general principles from observations, they also began to mount a critique of criminal justice systems based upon the fundamental premise that the individual was no longer a mere object of state authority, but was instead the reason for statehood and needed to be treated accordingly

---

[55] See B. J. Shapiro, *Beyond Reasonable Doubt and Probable Cause* (Berkeley: University of California Press, 1991) 8.
[56] Langbein, *Origins of the Adversary Criminal Trial*, 338.
[57] J. H. Langbein, *Torture and the Law of Proof: Europe and England in the Ancien Régime* (Chicago University Press, 1977).
[58] See C. Beccaria, *On Crimes and Punishments and Other Writings*, ed. R. Bellamy, trans. R. Davies (Cambridge University Press, 1995).

as a subject rather than an object of state power.[59] In his *De l'Esprit des Lois*, Montesquieu used the methods of observation and induction to demonstrate that in a society which valued the individual freedom of its citizens, there was a need to separate governmental powers.[60] Beccaria's work was more explicitly addressed to criminal justice. Although it is famous for adopting a utilitarian approach to punishment which was to influence Jeremy Bentham, his justification for the criminal law was based upon the social contract theories of Hobbes, Locke and Rousseau. According to such theories, the agreement to obey the law involves a trade-off whereby individuals sacrifice their freedom in the 'state of nature' to preserve the greatest possible liberty over all. In return for allegiance to society, the individual is granted protection from the freedom-restricting acts of others and also from the arbitrary power of the sovereign state brought into being by the contract.

Beccaria derived three consequences arising out of the social contract.[61] The first was that laws alone can decree punishments for crimes; this authority rests only with the legislator who represents the whole of society united by the social contract. Secondly, however, the sovereign as the representative of society may only frame laws in general and may not rule on whether an individual has violated the social contract, for that would mean that the sovereign would be a judge in its own cause. There was therefore a need for a third party to judge the truth of the matter. Thirdly, once a breach of the social contract was declared, there had to be some proportionality in the punishment. Further principles were developed by Beccaria to protect accused persons during the trial, including the need for strong evidence of guilt such as to amount to a moral certainty, the right to be treated with respect, without being subject to violence, or to unnecessary invasions of privacy or violations of their autonomy throughout the process and the right to be allowed time and the means to clear themselves if innocent. A further feature of proceedings was that there should be some participation by the public in the hearing and verdicts and the proof of guilt should be public so that the public can see the protections offered by the social contract.

These ideas had a considerable influence on modern-day principles of criminal justice and they reached their apex in the American Bill of Rights and the French *Déclaration des Droits de L'Homme et du Citoyen*. They are also almost all reflected in the human rights documents that were agreed after the Second World War and in Chapter 4 we consider how they have been interpreted by the international legal community. For now, it is sufficient to note that the

---

[59] C. J. Safferling, *Towards an International Criminal Procedure* (Oxford University Press, 2001) 21.

[60] M. De Montesquieu, *The Spirit of Laws*, trans. T. Nugent (London: Collingwood and Clarke, 1823). '... constant experience shews us, that every man invested with power is apt to abuse it; and to carry his authority as far as it will go... To prevent this abuse, it is necessary from the very nature of things, power should be a check to power.' Book XI, ch. 4, 151.

[61] Beccaria, *On Crimes and Punishments*, ch. 3.

traditional adversarial and inquisitorial criminal justice systems fell far short of realising these norms. Although some features such as publicity and the presence of the jury were evident in the eighteenth-century criminal trial in England, defendants suffered considerable disadvantages by being subjected in most cases to questioning in a trial by 'altercation' without any legal representation.[62] The position for defendants in continental trials was even worse. The law of torture was as we have seen a continuing stain on the procedure and the accused was the mere object of the inquiry. Trials were secret and written and only the pronouncement of the judgment was public.

It is no exaggeration therefore to say that at the dawning of the French Revolution, both systems were suffering from a lack of legitimacy both in terms of their ability to reach reliable results and in terms of how individuals should be treated by the state. The great challenge for proceduralists after the Revolution was to devise a system more in tune with the emerging rationalist and individual rights traditions of the time. There was no longer confidence in an inquisitorial judge dominating the process. As a consequence of the shift in perception whereby parties were considered subjects instead of mere objects of the process, the criminal process had to be re-conceptualised away from a purely policy-implementing model towards one that was more concerned with conflict resolution when the defendant denied the charges that were brought against him.[63] In short, although the ultimate goal of the criminal process may be the implementation of the criminal law or, more broadly, to implement the objectives of state policy on crime whether these be retribution, crime prevention or whatever,[64] when an allegation is made of criminal conduct, that allegation or charge had to be determined in a manner that paid due respect to the interests of the accused. There could be scope for argument according to legal tradition as to how much emphasis was to be given to these interests. It is commonly considered that the civil law systems have remained more committed to a search for 'substantial' truth, while common law systems aim more for the 'procedural' truth that arises from the contest between the parties.[65] But the point to be made is that within the broad consensus that emerged as to how criminal proceedings should be conceptualised in the nineteenth century, truth finding or rectitude of decision was not the only objective to be pursued and it had to be constrained by taking into account the interests of the accused.

---

[62] Langbein, *Origins of the Adversary Criminal Trial*, 13–16.
[63] The distinction between conflict-resolution and policy-implementing models of justice is to be seen in Damaška, *Faces of Justice*, 62 and 73.
[64] Debates on the objectives of criminal process have raged for 'millennia', according to Roberts. See P. Roberts, 'Subjects, Objects and Values in Criminal Adjudication', in A. Duff, L. Farmer, S. Marshall and V. Tadros, *The Trial on Trial (2): Judgment and Calling to Account* (Oxford: Hart, 2006) 37, 50.
[65] T. Weigend, 'Is the Criminal Process about Truth: A German Perspective?' (2003) 26 *Harvard Journal of Law & Public Policy* 157, 168. E. Grande, 'Dances of Criminal Justice: Thoughts on Systemic Differences and the Search for the Truth', in Jackson, Langer and Tillers, *Crime, Procedure and Evidence*, 145.

Conversely, however, as far as individual rights are concerned, it would be impossible to construct a system that was devoted entirely to respecting the rights of the individual accused, as this would defeat the instrumental objectives of the criminal process.[66] It is not plausible that we entered society in order to have rights of the accused; they are obviously instrumental to something else.[67] Allen takes the example of the privilege against self-incrimination whereby suspects may want to exercise this privilege, but such an exercise of will is detrimental to civil society and the effort to construct a criminal process dedicated to convicting the guilty. Interestingly, social contract theorists were divided on the importance that should be attached to the privilege against self-incrimination. While Hobbes considered that 'no man . . . can be obliged by Covenant to accuse himselfe',[68] Beccaria considered that those under examination who refused to answer questions put to them deserved a severe penalty in order to prevent accused persons avoiding their public duty in this way.[69] For Beccaria, the contract is not entered into for the purposes of protecting the individual accused, but by being 'wearied by living in an unending state of war and by a freedom rendered useless by the uncertainty of retaining it', we sacrifice 'a part of that freedom in order to enjoy what remains in security and calm'.[70] But it was not enough to create a sovereign in order to achieve security; it was also necessary to create a system of procedures and punishments in order to protect it from the private usurpations of individuals. Criminal procedure was necessary to prevent a slide back to rampant individualism. However, for Beccaria, it was vital in framing rules of procedure and punishment that a principle of proportionality was kept in mind so that individuals were not subjected to needless deprivation of liberty and suffering. The notion of proportionality was also given a central place in the social contractarian theories that undergirded the work of leading German jurists who were beginning in the late eighteenth century to outline the degree of state intervention that could be justified in the conflict between private autonomy and public good.[71]

1.4 Towards shared evidentiary principles

What became clear across Europe in the nineteenth century was that if criminal processes were to achieve the necessary acceptance across society, they would need to encapsulate key elements of the rationalist and individual rights traditions. Although truth finding may not be the end of criminal procedure, it

---

[66] Roberts, 'Subjects, Objects and Values'.
[67] R. J. Allen, 'The Simpson Affair, Reform of the Criminal Justice Process and Magic Bullets' (1996) 67 *University of Colorado Law Review* 989, 1021.
[68] T. Hobbes, *Leviathan* (Harmondsworth: Penguin, 1651, 1968) ch. XXI, 269.
[69] Beccaria, *On Crimes and Punishments*, ch. 38, 98.
[70] Beccaria, *On Crimes and Punishments*, ch. 1, 9.
[71] See A. Stone Sweet and J. Mathews, 'Proportionality Balancing and Global Constitutionalism' (2008) 47 *Columbia Journal of Transnational Law* 73.

had to play a central role in resolving the disputes that arose over the guilt of the accused or there could not be public acceptance of the verdict. Moreover, the truth-finding process had to reflect the dominant empiricist epistemology which assigned freedom for individual fact-finders to draw their own conclusion from evidence. Similarly, although the safeguarding of individual rights of the accused could not be the end of the process, there had to be some role built into the process which respected the individual accused. The different legal traditions may again be said to have placed a different emphasis on these new emerging values, with the civil law emphasising the need for officials to be given the scope to make accurate determinations of guilt and the common law emphasising more the rights of the individual. But a shared set of evidentiary principles nevertheless began to emerge which was able to give some weight to both of these traditions.

Firstly, in accordance with empiricist philosophy, individuals have to be given the scope to arrive at their own conclusions on the basis of all the relevant evidence that is available. This argues against imposing rules of weight and rules of exclusion on fact-finders. Secondly, however, in accordance with social contract theory, individuals accused of breaching the contract are entitled to the highest level of proof being mounted against them before they are convicted. Allegiance to the social contract is predicated on a bargain whereby individuals agree to obey the laws deemed necessary by the sovereign for security and liberty provided they themselves are not punished for breach in the absence of strong proof. Thirdly, fact-finders have to operate in an independent and impartial environment. To support this principle certain procedural requirements are necessary. The functions of bringing accusations and determining guilt have to be separated and in order for there to be an assurance that the verdict of the court is independently and impartially arrived at, the prosecution and the defence have to be given an opportunity to put their case to the court. Finally, the value of individual autonomy has to be respected within the evidentiary process. Some forms of conduct are absolutely prohibited, such as obtaining evidence by means of torture or coercion. Other interferences with autonomy, such as the requirement to submit to examinations and answer questions, can only be justified on a strict proportionality basis.

The first step taken in the continental systems towards the realisation of these principles was to abolish the system of legal proofs that provided such a challenge to the rationalist tradition and to the principle of individual dignity. Although there had been mounting criticism of this system by Enlightenment thinkers up to the Revolution and indeed a number of reforms were forthcoming, most notably the abolition of torture to extract proof of offences in France in 1780, it was not until the revolutionary era itself that the entire system of Roman-canon evidentiary regulation was abolished.[72] The

---

[72] See A. Esmein, *A History of Continental Criminal Procedure: With Special Reference to France*, trans. J. Simpson (Boston: Little, Brown, 1913) 383–4.

idea that the law should not assign probative value to items of evidence is now widely accepted as one of the cornerstones of enlightened fact-finding in adjudication.

If legal rules mandating how evidence should be weighted declined, this is not to say that the evidentiary framework that came to be advanced across the common law/civil law world in criminal processes was freed completely from regulation. We have seen that any system has to have certain decision rules allocating the burden and standard of proof. By the mid nineteenth century, there was a consensus that the legitimacy of the process meant that every effort had to be made to avoid wrongful convictions. High standards of proof, burdens of proof, cautionary rules and directions and reasoned judgments began to be adopted, although in Chapter 7 we shall see that it was not until the early twentieth century that they began to be articulated fully and there is still some fluidity about the concepts. Different strategies came to be developed within each legal tradition. The presence of the jury in common law processes enabled greater use of exclusionary rules and direction. Ironically, just at the time that this new doctrine of 'free proof' was being advanced by Enlightenment thinkers, judges in English criminal trials were beginning to develop certain exclusionary rules of criminal evidence as a means of safeguarding the position of the accused within the developing adversarial trial.[73] These new rules of evidence, however, were very different from the old ones. Whereas the old rules of proof stipulated what should count as the basis for a conviction, the new exclusionary rules preventing, for example, the admission of evidence of an accused's bad character stipulated instead what should *not* count as evidence. Instead of developing such rules, civil law countries required judges to give reasoned judgments for decisions. Although some of these devices such as the use of exclusionary rules could be said to undermine the 'rationalist' search for truth, they were often justified, as we shall see, by the need to avoid the graver error of convicting the innocent and consequently could at least be justified within the broad rationalist framework of truth finding. The greater tolerance which Anglo-American systems are said to have for evidentiary barriers to conviction, for example, may be justified by the excessively 'adversarial' framework in which participatory fact-finding is set with much greater resources given to the prosecution than the defence.[74]

The next step that was required in order to implement the new evidentiary principles was the need for party participation in the criminal process. This entailed a major change to traditional continental criminal procedure as it was practised before the nineteenth century.[75] Instead of the criminal justice system being dominated by a single entity – the judge who performed the roles of prosecution, defence and judge – the Napoleonic *Code d'instruction*

---

[73] Langbein, *Origins of the Adversary Criminal Trial*, ch. 4. [74] Damaška, 'Evidentiary Barriers'.
[75] S. J. Summers, *Fair Trials: The European Criminal Procedural Tradition and the European Court of Human Rights* (Oxford: Hart, 2007) ch. 2.

criminelle of 1808 sowed the seeds for a new 'accusatorial trinity', as it was later called,[76] whereby the criminal justice system would be dominated by three separate entities: prosecution, defence and judge. In France it is true that an investigating judge unfettered by the doctrine of legal proofs was free to conduct an active inquiry and evaluate the evidence freely according to his conviction. But there was then a public trial at which the interests of the prosecution and defence were represented. This could be seen as a victory for the accusatorial tradition which operated around the notion of a contest where the claimant and the accused were responsible for collecting their own evidence. But this tradition flew in the face of rationalist tradition in so far as a lack of resources could leave the parties unable to embark on an effective fact-finding endeavour. The absence of counsel at the trial meant that the judge could also end up playing the roles of both prosecution and defence.[77] Gradually, throughout the nineteenth century, counsel came to represent prosecution and defence in English 'adversary' procedure, but it took much longer before a public prosecution system emerged with responsibility or control over pre-trial investigation as well as trial presentation.[78] Within continental procedure, by contrast, it has taken longer for the defence to be given an effective role, with the ability not only to advance arguments against the prosecution, but to take an effective role in investigation.[79] But what has emerged is a consensus across the common and civil law traditions that we cannot leave fact-finding exclusively in the hands of one judicial figure when there are competing claims between complainants and defendants over events.

This emphasis on the participation of the parties could be represented as compromising the ideals of the rationalist tradition, subverting the notion of officials dedicated to determining the guilt of the accused in the interests of the autonomy rights of the accused. It is certainly arguable that the development of a role for legal counsel can help to protect the accused against abuse during the criminal process and enable arguments to be advanced effectively in favour of the defendant. But it would be a mistake to see these changes as motivated purely by the principle of individual dignity, as they can also be justified as necessary to further the cause of rationalist truth finding. The rationalist tradition itself requires that there be as full an informational base of relevant evidence as possible before judgments can be made on whether charges should be brought

---

[76] The term can be traced to the Austrian jurist Vargha. See J. Vargha, *Die Verteidigung in Strafsachen* (Vienna: Manz'sche k. u. k. Hof-Verlag und Univ Buchhandlung, 1879). For a comprehensive discussion of the work of the European jurists who developed this new European criminal procedural tradition, see Summers, *Fair Trials*.

[77] Summers, *Fair Trials*, 35.

[78] Although a Crown Prosecution Service was established in England and Wales in 1985, investigation has been left in the hands of the police with prosecutors dependent on the police file for making decisions to prosecute. See B. Hancock and J. Jackson, *Standards for Prosecutors: An Analysis of the National United Kingdom Prosecuting Agencies* (Nijmegen: Wolf, 2006).

[79] For a recent survey, see E. Cape, J. Hodgson, T. Prakken and T. Spronken (eds.), *Suspects in Europe* (Antwerp: Intersentia, 2007).

or guilt decided and this is arguably better provided by an investigating and prosecuting authority and by an effective defence than by a single inquisitorial judge. Where there is a prosecuting agency able to mount an effective investigation and an effective defence able to pursue or suggest its own inquiries and challenge the product of what the prosecution chooses to rely upon, this can in theory help to expand the range of relevant evidence and help to scrutinise its weight. The difficulty is that this participatory 'dialectic' theory of evidence, as one of us has called it,[80] is one that we shall see is far from being realised even today, particularly in the important pre-trial phases of procedure. The danger as we shall see within civilian systems is that the strong inquisitorial culture that can still prevail prevents the defence ever being given an effective participatory role in the proceedings and the danger in common law systems is that party participation becomes traduced into 'adversarial' fact-finding, with prosecutors refusing to share information with the defence and the defence refusing to cooperate in the fact-finding endeavour.

When it comes to the inferential task of reaching conclusions from the evidence, again, the separation of the roles of prosecution, defence and trier of fact can be justified in the interests of rationalist fact-finding, ensuring that the fact-finder, be it judge or jury, is as impartial as possible in reaching decisions on guilt or innocence. Jurists on both sides of the common law and civil law tradition have recognised the difficulties of maintaining impartiality during investigations. In a landmark article published in 1889, von Kries exposed the myth of impartiality by showing that the tasks of the German *Untersuchungerichter* to investigate criminal offences and detect the perpetrators made it more important for him to find the guilty than to prove the innocence of those who were wrongly accused.[81] Later, in 1935, von Ploskowe commented that in expecting the French *juge d'instruction* to perform the three incompatible roles of prosecution, defence and judge, continental procedure had created a vice that could not be corrected by reform. We shall see that the ideal of the 'passive' 'impartial' judge or jury has itself come under scrutiny, however, in the twentieth century as demands are made for fact-finders to be made accountable for their decisions.[82]

On this view then the participatory rights that emerged from the separation of the roles of prosecution, defence and judge are not necessarily subversive of the rationalist endeavour. From the point of view of social contract theory also, these rights are indeed not independent of the truth-finding process, but are seen as vital for ensuring that accused persons are not falsely found in breach of the social contract and are fundamentally linked to the presumption of innocence. It is true that other justifications have been made for participatory

---

[80] J. D. Jackson, 'Theories of Truth Finding in Criminal Procedure: An Evolutionary Approach' (1988) 10 *Cardozo Law Review* 475, 522.
[81] J. Von Kries, 'Vorverfahren und Hauptverfahren' (1889) *Zeitschrift fur die gesamte Strafrechtswissenschaft* 1.
[82] J. D. Jackson, 'Making Juries Accountable' (2002) 50 *American Journal of Comparative Law* 477.

rights which are independent of the truth-finding endeavour. One of these can be traced back to the Kantian notion that individuals should not be treated as a means, but as an end.[83] Tribe has postulated that the right to be heard and the right to be told why are analytically separate from the right to secure a different outcome.[84] On this view, before actions are taken against individuals, for example that they are declared guilty, they have a right to be consulted about what is to be done to them irrespective of whether or not their input is likely to affect the outcome. Certain features of the criminal process such as the right to cross-examine witnesses which are now widely accepted in state constitutions and human rights treaties may be explained not on the ground that they avoid errors, but on the ground that they give the accused an opportunity to confront the accusations against him before they may be accepted.[85] The difficulty with viewing participation rights independently from outcome, however, is that they cease to have value once it is admitted that they would fail to have any effect on the outcome. Kaplow has asked whether participants would see any value in a procedure where they were told in advance that their participation would be ignored and could have no effect on the outcome. A meaningful right to be heard, in other words, requires that the decision-maker listens and takes account of the participants.[86]

Another argument that can be made for participation rights is from the literature on procedural justice, which has shown that procedures which delegate significant control over the process to the parties themselves are seen as fairer by the parties irrespective of whether they have won or lost than procedures in which the decision-maker retains control.[87] Leaving aside the difficulties that the laboratory conditions in which these procedures have been tested have tended to be divorced from real-life settings such as a criminal trial,[88] the point can be made that if we want defendants to accept verdicts against them, we should maximise their participation in procedures whether or not these assist in the truth discovery process.[89] This would seem to provide an independent instrumental ground for participation rights. But again the satisfaction felt by

---

[83] See I. Kant, *The Metaphysics of Morals* (Cambridge University Press, 1996).
[84] L. Tribe, *American Constitutional Law*, 2nd edn (New York: Foundation Press, 1988) 666–7. See also R. Summers, 'Evaluating and Improving Legal Process – A Plea for "Process Values"' (1974) 60 *Cornell Law Review* 1; M. D. Bayles, 'Principles for Legal Procedure' (1986) 5 *Law & Philosophy* 33; M. D. Dubber, 'The Criminal Trial and the Legitimation of Punishment', in Duff et al., *Trial on Trial (1)*. Cf. D. Galligan, *Discretionary Powers: A Study of Legal Decision Making* (Oxford University Press, 1986); and A. Stein, *Foundations of Evidence Law* (Oxford University Press, 2005) 31–3.
[85] Stein, *Foundations of Evidence Law*, 31.
[86] See L. Kaplow, 'The Value of Accuracy in Adjudication: An Economic Analysis' (1994) 23 *Journal of Legal Studies* 307.
[87] See J. Thibaut and L. Walker, *Procedural Justice: A Psychological Analysis* (Hillsdale, NJ: Lawrence Erlbaum, 1975).
[88] But see J. D. Casper, T. R. Tyler et al., 'Procedural Justice in Felony Cases' (1988) 22 *Law and Society Review* 483.
[89] See T. R. Tyler, *Why People Obey the Law* (New Haven: Yale University Press, 1990).

defendants seems to rest on the basis that the triers of fact actually listened and took into account the arguments of the defence. If again they were told that this was not so, the satisfaction levels might have been considerably reduced, thus revealing again the necessary link between participation and outcome. To say, however, that there is a link between participation and an accurate outcome is not to say that participation can be reduced simply to the need for accuracy. We have seen that the rationalist tradition of truth finding cannot guarantee accurate verdicts. Mistakes cannot be avoided in an imperfect procedural system and when defendants are wrongly convicted, they may be more inclined to accept the verdict where they have been given some meaningful participation in the process that led to their conviction.[90]

Finally, and most recently, Duff et al. have made a substantial argument for participation based less on the importance of participation rights than on the fact that the defendant's participation is required in order to do justice to the normative functions of the criminal trial.[91] In their view, the trial is not just a forum for determining whether the defendant committed an offence in order to identify accurately those who are to be subjected to punishment, but is a process whereby the defendant is invited (but not required) to participate as part of the process of calling the defendant to account before it is decided whether she should be condemned for wrongdoing.[92] It is impossible to do justice here to the sophistication of all the arguments made. To the extent that they do not deny that, nevertheless, many features of the trial can be explained and rationalised 'either in instrumental terms as means to truth, or in terms of values that set side-constraints on this pursuit', they do not depart from the evidential tradition we have identified.[93] In particular, they emphasise the importance of triers of fact coming to knowledge of the defendant's guilt before condemning her for it in order to comply with the presumption of innocence and they concede that certain features of the trial such as the right of silence might be explained on what they call 'rule of law' reasons to do with protecting citizens against the state's oppressive power.[94] In the historical section at the beginning of their book, they also acknowledge that the social contract conception of the political subject as an individual who has entered into a compact with the state and who has to be protected against the arbitrary use of state power was influential in shaping the development of the English criminal trial.[95]

Where there may be a parting of company is in the view that irrespective of the right of silence, there is a normative expectation in the very structure of the trial that the defendant should take part in a process of judgment before there has been a formal finding of guilt against her.[96] Hence it is claimed that there are two stages in the trial: first, the prosecution must prove that 'the

---

[90] L. B. Solum, 'Procedural Justice' (2004) 78 *University of Southern California Law Review* 181.
[91] A. Duff, L. Farmer, S. Marshall and V. Tadros, *The Trial on Trial (3): Towards a Normative Theory of the Criminal Trial* (Oxford: Hart, 2007).
[92] Ibid., 119.   [93] Ibid., 119, n. 71.   [94] Ibid., 89 and 101.   [95] Ibid., 39–40.
[96] Ibid., 83 and 139.

defendant committed the offence charged'; and if this task is discharged the defendant must then 'answer for that crime, whether by offering a defence or by accepting her guilt'.[97] This second stage of calling the defendant to answer for a crime that has not yet been formally proved risks blurring the line between the factual (trial) question of whether the defendant is guilty of the offence and the normative (post-trial) question of whether the defendant should be punished for it. In other words, a defendant should only be held responsible for a crime that has been proved against her *after* the trial.[98]

On a social contract vision of participation, defendants should indeed be entitled and even encouraged to respond to charges brought against them, but only by way of answering the factual/legal question of whether they are guilty of the offence charged. Only after they have been shown to have breached the social contract should there be any question of them answering for what they have done. Their presence is required at the trial not in order to answer for the crime and not even in order to give evidence concerning the offence, but in order to assist the defence of the case so that the best possible answer is given to the charge. In this scenario, the trial is not about calling the defendant *as a citizen* to account for criminal wrongdoing, but about calling the defence *as a party*, including the defendant, his counsel and any witnesses on his behalf, to account for the case against him. This explains why it is so important that the defendant is represented by a defence counsel as only a skilled forensic examination and presentation of the defence case can make an effective challenge to the prosecution case which is also, of course, presented by counsel. Duff et al. argue that on their theory of defence participation, the fact that counsel speaks for the defendant need not fundamentally reduce the degree to which she explains herself to the court and indeed in some circumstances the explanation may be enhanced by being communicated through counsel. On their theory, however, which they admit is inadequately realised in practice, counsel should only make participatory interventions under the defendant's control.[99] But to suggest that the defence counsel be limited to acting broadly under the defendant's control while prosecution counsel is left to manage its case as it wishes, within the

---

[97] Ibid., 147.
[98] See H. L. Ho, 'Book Review: Duff, Farmer, Marshall and Tadros, Trial on Trial (vol. 3): Towards a Normative Theory of the Criminal Trial' (2008) 6 *International Commentary on Evidence* Issue 1, Art. 3. Duff et al. also appear to risk being over-inclusive in the number of defendants they would subject to this process by suggesting that prosecutors may proceed against them when there is a sufficient case to answer (ibid., 185). The authors recognise that there is a difference between a test for prosecution which is based upon whether the fact-finder *could* reasonably convict on the evidence (a case to answer) and the present test in England and Wales based upon whether there is a realistic prospect that a reasonable jury *would* convict on the evidence; yet they blur the distinction by suggesting, on the one hand, that there must be at least a case to answer and, on the other hand, that there may be reasons not to proceed when there is not a realistic prospect of conviction.
[99] Duff et al., *Trial on Trial (3)*, 211 and 213.

boundary of whatever ethical rules exist, would seem to open up a significant inequality of arms between the two sides to the contest. By contrast, it may be argued that the defendant should be able to call upon counsel to manage his case on his behalf subject to the ethical requirement that counsel does not act contrary to the instructions given. This is why on this theory it may be more apt to consider defence rights of participation as 'institutional' rights for the defence,[100] rather than as individual rights for the accused. Later, we shall review these rights, which include the provision of confidential legal advice and assistance, disclosure and access to relevant evidence in order to participate in the fact-finding process.

The need for 'institutional' rights does not deny the need to recognise the importance of individual dignity in evidentiary processes. In order to safeguard this principle, there is a prohibition on certain kinds of evidence that have been obtained by coercive means. There would seem to be a clear conflict here with the rationalist tradition of truth finding. But it depends again on how this prohibition is characterised. On one view, certain gross violations such as subjection to violence and intrusive invasions of privacy are such an infringement on the autonomy of the accused that it is necessary to exclude any evidence obtained by reliance on such means even if damage is thereby done to the fact-finding enterprise. This exclusion acts as a clear side-constraint on the aim of truth finding. From a social contract point of view, when the sovereign obtains evidence by illegal acts that fall so far outside the bounds of the social contract, the use of such evidence would be in breach of the contract. Duff et al. argue that in these circumstances the state no longer has the moral standing to call the defendant to account for wrongdoing. But while they argue against the use of the evidence on apparently moral grounds, social contract theory arguably views its use as a fundamental breach of the social contract which de-legitimises the whole enterprise of the trial. In such circumstances damage is not so much done to the fact-finding enterprise: the entire fact-finding enterprise of proving the case against the accused cannot legitimately continue until the breach is corrected, the evidence is withdrawn and the enterprise can resume. Other less intrusive actions which violate the autonomy of the individual, however, may cause a different judgment to be made when tested against the benefits of obtaining the evidence. One example we shall discuss is the privilege against self-incrimination, which is difficult to justify as an absolute principle except within the context of particular coercive situations.

1.5 Beyond the common and civil law traditions

This book argues that we are witnessing the emergence of a common set of evidentiary principles across the common law/civil law divide, which is rooted

---

[100] Summers, *Fair Trials*, 61.

in the Enlightenment 'rationalist' and 'social contract' traditions that developed in the eighteenth century. Although the rationalist tradition clings strongly to the Enlightenment belief that fact finding requires that triers of fact be given the freedom to draw their own inferences from evidence without the imposition of artificial rules of weight, the recognition that the criminal process is about reaching decisions under conditions of uncertainty by means that are acceptable to the accused and society means that the evidentiary framework needs to be carefully regulated to allow for the exercise of protective and participatory rights. In this sense, the book argues against the dichotomy commonly invoked by evidence scholars between the adversary system of 'exclusionary rules' and the inquisitorial system of 'free proof'.

The argument for the emergence of shared evidentiary principles has both empirical and normative aspects. On the empirical side, the book attempts to show in different contexts how this common evidentiary framework is emerging. It is not suggested that the transition has been an easy path, nor that the common law and civil law cultures do not present formidable obstacles to its emergence, nor indeed that the international bodies charged with applying common norms and solutions across national boundaries have always provided a coherent approach towards issues of evidence. It is claimed, however, that a new framework is being built across the different legal cultures and is not rooted in one more than the other. The book also argues normatively that the framework steers a viable route through the competing claims made for the criminal process that, on the one hand, it must provide effective means of truth finding, and on the other a means of protecting individual rights. The tensions between the rationalist and social contract traditions can be resolved by 'translating' the rationalist tradition into a 'dialectic' theory of proof and the theory of individual rights into 'institutional' rights for the defence.

The book does not argue for some neat procedural design that can be applied evenly across the different contexts of national criminal processes and international criminal tribunals. Roberts has argued that developing a system of evidentiary rules to govern the admissibility and presentation of evidence at trial is 'more akin to an on-going project of construction, refinement and maintenance – a juridical Forth Bridge – than a one-off design challenge to produce a definitively timeless procedural classic'.[101] The process of developing an evidentiary system cannot be immune to different contexts in which fact finding takes place, ranging from petty criminality to organised transnational crimes to the special context of compiling evidence of war crimes. Nor can it be immune to the different legal and political traditions that exercise a strong influence over professional actors, nor indeed to the pressures for convergence to which these traditions must adapt. One of the more sweeping changes that has taken place within the last 30 years across the common law and civil law traditions has been the substitution of new processes of negotiated justice for the notion

---

[101] Roberts, 'Subjects, Objects and Values', 38.

of the oral public trial that became the norm in nineteenth-century procedural design.[102] The reasons for this are complex, but are commonly attributed to the pressures for criminal justice systems to reduce cost and increase system efficiency. Truth finding and fairness would seem to be joint casualties in this move towards system efficiency. Our argument, however, is that the core values of the new evidentiary framework – 'dialectic' fact-finding and 'institutional' defence rights – can be brought to bear in a variety of different contexts, including the pre-trial environment, where there are pressures to abandon trials altogether. It will be argued that these values can be used not to impose a common mode of process irrespective of the particular context of each proceeding, but more as a means of promoting a common discourse across boundaries and increasing trust across different legal traditions.

The first part of the book looks at how a common evidentiary framework is emerging in different contexts. In Chapters 2 and 3, we explore in more detail how the key tenets of the rationalist tradition of evidence have been adapted across the common law and civil law traditions and how misconceptions about the common law system of exclusionary rules of evidence and the civil system of 'free proof' have obscured the manner in which this tradition of rationalism has shaped both systems. Chapter 4 then examines how the individual rights manifested in the international instruments agreed after the Second World War have been developed by international institutions to fashion common evidentiary standards around the notions of 'equality of arms' and 'adversarial rights'. Chapter 5 proceeds to examine how the international community has managed to agree a common evidentiary framework within the international criminal tribunals that have emerged to deal with international crimes. After examining these different contexts, we turn in the second part of the book to examine how specific rights are being interpreted to fashion common evidentiary standards, in particular the right to a fair trial (Chapter 6), the presumption of innocence (Chapter 7), the privilege against self-incrimination (Chapter 8), the right to legal assistance and disclosure (Chapter 9) and the right to cross-examination (Chapter 10). Chapter 11 draws conclusions and considers the prospects for developing a common theory of evidentiary defence rights across the common law and civil law traditions.

[102] T. Weigend, 'Why have a Trial when you can have a Bargain?', in Duff et al., *Trial on Trial (2)*, 207; and S. Thaman, 'Plea-Bargaining, Negotiated Confessions and Consensual Resolution of Criminal Cases', in K. Boele-Woelki and S. van Erp (eds.), *General Reports of the XVII Congress of the International Academy of Comparative Law* (Utrecht: Eleven International, 2007).

2

The common law tradition

2.1 Introduction: free proof and the common law

One of the enduring myths in discourse about the law of evidence is that it is a peculiar characteristic of the common law and that there is no such thing as a 'law of evidence' in continental Europe.[1] The technical rules of evidence that are a product of the common law system are contrasted with the principle of 'free proof' that dominates continental processes of proof. Although we shall see that it is important to understand that there are fundamental differences in the way in which evidence is regulated between the two traditions, it is misleading to characterise the two systems in this manner. For one thing, there is often a lack of clarity about what is meant by 'free proof' and depending on each layer of meaning it is by no means always self-evident that common law systems are necessarily less 'free' than continental processes.[2]

At one level the term may simply mean an absence of rules of evidence altogether. As we saw in the last chapter, any adjudicative system must have *some* rules of evidence and proof for determining when facts are considered to be proved and how they are to be proved. When the task of obtaining and adducing evidence is put in the hands of the parties, there is inevitably a need for more rules to regulate the handling of evidence than when a system puts the task of evidence management in the hands of a court. Even Bentham, who argued for a natural as opposed to a technical system of adjudication, accepted that there was a need for adjudicators to exclude evidence where it was irrelevant or superfluous or its production would involve preponderant vexation, expense or delay in the individual case.[3]

---

[1] According to Thayer, 'English speaking countries have what we call a "Law of Evidence;" but no other country has it.' See J. B. Thayer, *A Preliminary Treatise on Evidence at the Common Law* (Boston: Little, Brown, 1898) 2. This statement needs to qualified, however, as in the preceding passage he makes it clear that he is referring specifically to exclusionary rules of evidence. For a recent statement of this view, see South African Law Commission, *Sexual Offences: Process and Procedure* (2002) Discussion Paper 102 (Project 107), para. 12.11.3.1.4.
[2] For discussion of the different meanings that can be attached to 'free proof', see W. Twining, 'Freedom of Proof and the Reform of Criminal Evidence' (1997) 31 *Israel Law Review* 439; and D. Dwyer, 'What Does it Mean to be Free? The Concept of "Free Proof" in the Western Legal Tradition' (2006) 3 *International Commentary on Evidence*, Issue 1, Art. 6.
[3] J. Bentham, *A Treatise on Judicial Evidence* (London: Paget, 1825) 229–30. See W. Twining, *Theories of Evidence: Bentham and Wigmore* (London: Weidenfeld & Nicolson, 1985) 68.

Freedom of proof, however, is not commonly characterised as a complete absence of rules of evidence. More commonly, it is associated with the idea that triers of fact should be free to evaluate the evidence in any manner they choose without 'legal chains'.[4] From the continental law perspective, this was a reaction against the ills of the old canon law system that compelled fact-finders to assign weight to particular classes of evidence although the effect of these rules as an irrational constraint on the trier of fact has been considerably exaggerated.[5] We shall examine continental views of free proof in the next chapter. The point to be made here is that once again it is hard to find a system of adjudication without any rules or standards on how evidence should be evaluated. We need to be cautious about assuming that common law systems impose much greater fetters on fact-finders than modern continental systems. The common law was never as strict in classifying the weight to be given to particular kinds of evidence as the old canon law. Indeed, to this day one of the characteristics of the jury system is the freedom it has to evaluate evidence in the manner it chooses, deliberating as it does in secret, and the lack of appellate scrutiny that is given to its verdicts.[6] Conversely, as we shall see, continental systems as well as common law systems now employ a variety of rules to constrain the fact-finder's freedom to use certain evidence. Some of these rules may be motivated by policy concerns that have little to do with fact-finding. Even Bentham was prepared to concede that protection should be given to certain limited classes of evidence.[7] Today, as we shall see, the individual rights tradition has impelled most jurisdictions to refuse to use evidence to ground convictions that have been obtained in breach of certain constitutional or human rights. Other rules are more explicitly designed to promote the accuracy of fact-finding by preventing reliance on particular kinds of 'suspect' evidence.

It is also important to see that these rules of proof can take different forms ranging within a spectrum with the most mandatory rules at one extreme and the least mandatory at the other. At the most mandatory extreme, they can take the form of the old canonical rules directing triers of fact on what weight to give evidence, or they may require triers of fact to presume certain facts from other facts that are proved. In a less positive manner, they can forbid triers of fact from resorting to certain kinds of reasoning.[8] Within the common law, jurors may be told to ignore certain evidence that has been improperly admitted or they may be instructed to use the evidence for one purpose but not for another. Less

---

[4] M. Damaška, 'Free Proof and its Detractors' (1995) 43 *American Journal of Comparative Law* 343.
[5] Damaška, 'Free Proof', 344.
[6] J. D. Jackson, 'Making Juries Accountable' (2002) 50 *American Journal of Comparative Law* 477.
[7] He would have given privileged status to confessions to Catholic priests and state secrets: see Twining, *Theories of Evidence*, 99.
[8] A good example of a 'forbidden chain of reasoning' is the rule that the prosecution are not permitted to argue that evidence of an accused's previous criminal acts show he has a propensity to commit offences of the type charged: see *DPP* v. *Boardman* [1975] AC 421, 453, per Lord Hailsham. For a similar approach in continental law, see Damaška, 'Free Proof'.

peremptorily still, triers of fact may be given warnings or advice on how to treat certain kinds of evidence in their fact-finding endeavour or they may be told that they may infer certain facts from other facts. At the least coercive end of the spectrum, triers of fact may be simply required to act reasonably or rationally according to the tenets of the rationalist tradition in reaching their decisions. It is difficult to find any legal system that does not impose any constraints on fact-finders, at least to the extent of quashing unreasonable or irrational decisions. Bentham disapproved strongly of man-made regulations which are 'peremptory', 'inflexible', 'rigid' or 'unbending' – or formal rules addressed to the will of the judge – but it was appropriate for the legislator to provide 'cautionary instructions', 'guiding principles', 'admonitory maxims' addressed to the understanding of the judge.[9] The latter were not truly constraints on free proof in terms of imposing constraints on the natural reasoning processes of triers of fact – they were merely assisting triers in their rationalist endeavours. Therefore, Bentham's notion of free proof is not the freedom to reason in any manner that the trier of fact chooses, but the freedom to apply the ordinary processes of cognition in pursuit of the rationalist endeavour. On this view rules which constrain triers of fact to act rationally are not fetters on 'free proof': they are assisting in the exercise of free proof. Rules which interfere with natural reasoning processes, on the other hand, would be fetters on this principle.

One way of effectively enforcing rules that forbid triers of fact to use evidence in certain ways is to exclude them from hearing it in the first place and it is this exclusionary aspect of the law of evidence that is most commonly associated with the common law, made possible by means of its traditionally bifurcated process of decision-making, with a judge screening evidence from a jury. According to Thayer, who we shall see has exercised a profound influence over the characterisation of the common law rules of evidence as exclusionary rules, the Anglo-American system is 'radically peculiar' because 'a great mass of evidentiary matter, logically important and probative, is shut out from the view of the judicial tribunals by an imperative rule, while the same matter is not thus excluded anywhere else'.[10] It is important to see, however, that exclusionary rules not only constrain the use that is made of certain evidence. They go one step further in impeding the trier of fact's freedom to pursue what lines of inquiry she might wish to make. Again, the institutional environment of the common law which has assigned a passive role to juries in the proceedings, at least in modern times, makes this possible. By contrast, the continental outlook looks askance at attempts to curtail the trier of fact's freedom of inquiry. It is this exclusionary aspect of the common law approach to evidence that can be most evidently used to make contrasts with continental processes. But it is also this feature of the common law system that has generated most controversy *within*

---

[9] Bentham, *Treatise on Judicial Evidence*, 180 and vol. IV, 151 ff; and J. Bentham, *Rationale of Judicial Evidence*, ed. J. S. Mill (London: Hunt & Clark, 1827), vol. 1, 44, vol. 3, 219 ff, vol. 4, 477 ff.

[10] Thayer, *Preliminary Treatise on Evidence*, 1–2.

common law discourse. On the one hand, there is the Benthamite view that 'to exclude evidence is to exclude justice', as you may exclude much information that is reliable.[11] Conversely, however, there is a view that it may be necessary to exclude kinds of prejudicial albeit relevant evidence, bad character evidence for example, in order to guard against the undue weight that may be given to it by decision-makers. We shall see that both points of view can be sustained within the rationalist tradition, although 'optimistic' rationalists tend to favour the free admission of relevant evidence, while 'pessimistic' rationalists tend to take a more restrictive approach.[12]

Seen in this light, the controversy may seem to be resolvable by means of empirical inquiry.[13] We can agree that there should be a presumption in favour of free proof – permitting triers of fact to receive any relevant evidence and use their natural reasoning processes in evaluating it. In relation to a specific piece of evidence, however, where there is evidence that may be over-valued by fact-finders, it should be excluded. But the controversy also goes beyond empirical dispute and extends into the moral and political realm.[14] On one view, rules of proof are needed in order to satisfy the goals that the law of evidence should serve: minimising errors, reducing costs and allocating the risk of errors.[15] These goals are not merely epistemological, but also moral. The rationalist tradition as we have seen accepts that fact-finders form probabilistic judgments that do not reach the level of certainty. Given that mistakes will inevitably occur in the forensic context, the law must allocate the risk of errors in a morally acceptable way and, in order to do this, effectively exclusionary rules governing hearsay and character are needed as well as decision rules on the burden and standard of proof. From another perspective, rules of evidence should not just be viewed functionally from an 'external' point of view in terms of the degree to which they advance certain ends, but should also be evaluated morally from an 'internal' point of view which focuses on the responsibilities of the fact-finder.[16] On this conception many of the traditional common law exclusionary rules proscribing hearsay and bad character, for example, may be justified not just in terms of promoting accuracy, but in terms of embodying values intrinsic to both the rationality and justice of deliberation.

---

[11] Bentham, *Rationale of Judicial Evidence*, vol. 4, 490. See also vol. 5, 1.
[12] For the view that nearly all of the specialist writings on evidence are generally optimistic, see W. Twining, 'The Rationalist Tradition of Evidence Scholarship', in W. Twining, *Rethinking Evidence: Exploratory Essays* (Cambridge University Press, 2006) 35, 79.
[13] Twining, *Theories of Evidence*, 71–2. See also R. Allen, 'The Narrative Fallacy, the Relative Plausibility Theory and a Theory of the Trial' (2005) 3 *International Commentary on Evidence*, Issue 1, Art. 5, 5: 'it is indeed an empirical question whether more or less information best serves the goals of trials'.
[14] M. Pardo, 'The Political Morality of Evidence Law' (2007) 5 *International Commentary on Evidence*, Issue 2.
[15] A. Stein, *Foundations of Evidence Law* (Oxford University Press, 2005) 11–12.
[16] H. L. Ho, *A Philosophy of Evidence Law* (Oxford University Press, 2008) 48–9.

2.2 Common law conceptions of the law of evidence

In order to see how the common law came to be associated with exclusionary rules and how these have been developed in modern times, we need to take a look at the way in which common law conceptions of the law of evidence developed. For long periods of European history, lawsuits were designed to resolve disputes on the basis of the party which had right or God on its side rather than on the basis of substantive law.[17] Germanic and Anglo-Saxon trials prescribed certain authorised and widely accepted methods of proof through which God revealed the truth and parties able to pass through the appropriate proof unscathed succeeded in their claims.[18] When the Lateran Council abolished trial by ordeal in 1215 and Roman law systems of proof were developed to enforce the law, this still rested on a belief much in accordance with the popular epistemology of the time,[19] that knowledge of facts rested on authority – whether of the Church, the early scholastic writers or the Bible. When it came to legal proof, a claim to knowledge could be defended by appealing to the rules of proof authorised by the legal system or to the oaths of witnesses or jurors. It required an epistemological leap before it could become accepted that triers of fact were able to estimate for themselves the probative value of the facts sworn by the witnesses. This came when the scientific theories of Copernicus, Kepler and Galileo suggested that individuals could make their own inquiries about the nature of the world. This view was reflected in the writings of philosophers as diverse as Descartes, Leibniz, Spinoza, Bacon and Locke.[20]

The shift in Anglo-Saxon and continental procedure towards a reliance on the beliefs of triers of fact did not, however, lead to an end to rules of proof. The legal treatise writers of eighteenth-century England were heavily influenced by the works of John Locke which emphasised the need for a satisfied conscience, but that did not mean that the law should give up in its quest to guide and at times mandate how this conscience should be satisfied. Throughout the sixteenth and seventeenth centuries, certain categories of witness were considered incompetent and unable to testify. On top of this, certain types of evidence came to be privileged over others. In one of the first English legal treatises devoted exclusively to evidence published in 1754, Geoffrey Gilbert, the Lord Chief Baron of Exchequer from 1722 to 1726, organised various types of evidence in a hierarchical fashion around a best evidence principle under which pieces of evidence were categorised with various degrees of weight in advance of the trial. Official records under seal were classified at the top of the tree, followed by public records such as affidavits and depositions, then private documents such

---

[17] H. Berman, *Law and Revolution: The Formation of the Western Legal Tradition* (Cambridge, MA: Harvard University Press, 1983) 57–60.
[18] W. Holdsworth, *A History of English Law*, 3rd edn (London: Methuen, 1922), vol. 1, 305–11.
[19] L. J. Cohen, 'Freedom of Proof', in W. Twining (ed.), *Facts in Law* (Wiesbaden: ARSP Beiheft, 1983) 1, 6–9.
[20] Cohen, 'Freedom of Proof', 10–11.

as deeds. Unwritten evidence came a poor second in this hierarchy of evidence because witnesses who testified orally were subject to failures of memory and partiality, while documents were the 'most sedate and deliberate Acts of the Mind'.[21] In terms reminiscent of the numerical Roman canon system, Gilbert relied on the number of witnesses who gave evidence under oath rather than on the probative force of each witness's evidence. Finally, considerable weight was placed on the use of presumptions to make up for the absence of definitive written evidence.

It is easy to find fault with Gilbert's scheme of classification. Bentham ridiculed the view that written evidence should be ranked over oral evidence because many written documents can be clearly unreliable. More generally, the best evidence principle flew in the face of his 'anti-nomian' thesis by attempting to regulate judgments of probability by formal rules. But the idea that there were certain categories of evidence that were better than others did have an explanatory appeal for a number of textbook writers who were concerned to categorize the existing rules of evidence, and it influenced much of the exposition of the law of evidence throughout the nineteenth century. Indeed, it has been argued that it still provides a rationale for many of the rules of evidence.[22] Perhaps the best example of a rule which is clearly influenced by the need to adduce the best evidence is the so-called 'best evidence' rule itself, according to which parties must produce an original document to prove its contents rather than some copy of the original. Although this rule is no longer as strictly complied with as in the past,[23] it can be argued that a number of other rules of evidence which are still in existence are explicable on the basis of the best evidence principle, for example, the rule that requires witnesses to take an oath, the rule requiring witnesses to submit to cross-examination, the hearsay evidence rule and the rule against lay opinions.

Furthermore, although it is easy to criticize the idea that certain kinds of evidence are to be preferred over others on the ground that they are necessarily of greater probative value, it is not so irrational for certain kinds of evidence to be preferred on the ground that they are easier to evaluate or that they increase the flow of relevant information concerning events in issue. When rules forbidding hearsay evidence or opinion evidence are applied rigidly, they are prone to the Benthamite criticism that they may result in the exclusion of reliable information and they can act therefore as a fetter on common-sense reasoning. But when applied more flexibly as rules excluding 'inferior' evidence only when other, 'better', evidence is available, they may be viewed less as exclusionary rules designed to decrease the flow of relevant information and more as inclusionary rules designed to increase the flow of relevant available

[21] G. Gilbert, *The Law of Evidence*, 1st edn (Dublin: S. Cotter, 1754) 5.
[22] D. Nance, 'The Best Evidence Principle' (1988) 13 *Iowa Law Review* 227.
[23] R. Pattenden, 'Authenticating "Things" in English Law: Principles for Adducing Tangible Evidence in Common Law Jury Trials' (2008) 12 *International Journal of Evidence & Proof* 273.

information. The hearsay rule, for example, may be viewed as a rule which encourages parties to produce first-hand information rather than second-hand information. On this view, the rules of evidence are primarily aimed at the parties rather than at the triers of fact, as they operate to educate and discipline the parties in their presentation of evidence. They are essentially the result of the adversarial presentation of evidence, whereby it is left mainly to the parties to adduce evidence. Their effect in individual cases may be to prevent the trier of fact hearing certain relevant information, but this is because the parties have not adduced 'better' evidence reasonably available to them, and not because it is considered that the trier of fact is incapable of dealing with the evidence.

Although it has been argued that the best evidence principle accounts even today for many of the rules of evidence, it has been more common at least since the late nineteenth century to view the law of evidence as directed more at triers of fact and to view it in a rather negative way as imposing constraints on the natural reasoning processes of triers of fact. This conception of the law of evidence owes much to Bentham's anti-nomian thesis. Whereas the best evidence principle proceeds from the assumption that the process of legal proof needs rules in order to increase the flow of information, the anti-nomian thesis proceeds on the basis of a presumption against rules, certainly against rules of exclusion and rules of weight which give priority to certain kinds of evidence. Instead of the law of evidence being viewed as an all-embracing set of rules for the regulation of proof in legal procedure, it came to be viewed as a series of disparate exceptions to the Benthamite principle of free proof, whereby there should be no interference with free inquiry and natural or common-sense reasoning. The great American evidence scholar James B. Thayer did most to rationalize the law of evidence along these lines.[24] Like Gilbert, he was concerned to systematise and rationalise existing rules of evidence rather than to attack them as Bentham had done. But while Gilbert sought to give an expansionary role to the law of evidence by increasing the evidentiary package beyond what the parties might otherwise be prepared to adduce in court, Thayer's concept of the law of evidence was essentially limiting and exclusionary in nature, putting constraints on the admission of evidence at trial, rather than seeking to widen the ambit of the evidence.

Thayer based the law of evidence on two strikingly simple principles: that nothing is to be received which is not logically probative of some matter requiring to be proved, and that everything which is probative should be received unless a clear ground of policy or law excludes it. Twining has pointed out that the first principle, although exclusionary in nature, is not strictly speaking part of the law of evidence at all.[25] For according to Thayer, whether certain evidence is logically probative or relevant to some matter requiring to be proved is not a matter for law, but is a matter of logic and common sense. This leaves the

---

[24] See Thayer, *Preliminary Treatise on Evidence*, 266 and 509.
[25] Twining, *Rethinking Evidence*, 190.

inclusionary principle that everything which is probative or relevant should be received unless forbidden by some rule of evidence. Twining has argued that this Thayerite conception of the law of evidence dominated Anglo-American evidence scholarship throughout the twentieth century, although there have been a number of refinements. Further distinctions were made by Thayer's pupil, John H. Wigmore, between relevancy and legal relevancy, the latter denoting 'something more than a minimum probative value', and between what he called 'rules of extrinsic policy' and 'rules of auxiliary probative policy'.[26] The former imposed side-constraints on the pursuit of rectitude in order to promote values extrinsic to the forensic process, such as confidentiality, the unity of marriage, national security or the protection of the accused. The latter were designed to promote rectitude of decision and were concerned therefore with what have been called issues internal to proof.[27] Others have distinguished these two categories of rules by referring to the former category as absolute rules of exclusion which require relevant evidence to be rejected in the public interest and to the latter category as rules of 'use' rather than rules of 'exclusion', since they restrict the use to be made of evidence by the trier of fact and they only require exclusion of such evidence where the evidence is to be used solely for a purpose prohibited by law.[28] So, for example, the hearsay rule operates to exclude out of court statements when these are introduced to prove the truth of what they contain, but it does not operate to exclude out of court statements when they are to be used to prove something else, for example to prove that the words were spoken. Many of these so-called exclusionary rules are rules which impose fetters on the tribunal of fact as well as on the judge, as they require the tribunal of fact to use evidence in a certain way even if it is admitted by the judge. They intrude severely on the principle of free proof when so viewed and go directly against the anti-nomian thesis.

A number of comments may be made about this dominant conception of the law of evidence as a series of constraints on common-sense reasoning. Firstly, it has a strikingly narrow focus. It is confined to processes at court and more particularly to the kind of evidence that may be presented to the tribunal of fact as legal evidence in court. Concepts such as materiality, relevance and admissibility have been developed to give expression to the Thayerite principles mentioned above, but only the concept of admissibility is truly governed by the law of evidence, as it is this concept which requires judges to consider whether there is any rule or policy requiring the exclusion of otherwise relevant evidence. Secondly, Thayer's conception of law of evidence is a very negative one. Even on the broader view that there are rules of use as well as pure exclusion which will require a judge to direct the tribunal of fact on how to use various kinds of evidence,

[26] J. H. Wigmore, *A Treatise on the Anglo-American System of Evidence in Trials at Common Law* (Boston: Little, Brown, 1983) rev. P. Tillers, vol. 1A, § 28, 964 and § 11, 689.
[27] D. Galligan, 'More Scepticism about Scepticism' (1988) 8 *Oxford Journal of Legal Studies* 249.
[28] P. McNamara, 'The Canons of Evidence – Rules of Exclusion or Rules of Use?' (1986) 10 *Adelaide Law Review* 341.

the conception operates as a restraint on triers of fact rather than as offering any positive guidance on how to evaluate evidence. Thirdly, it would appear to be based on a rather limited faith in the ability of the jury to process evidence properly. Thayer accepted that certain principles of exclusion forbidding the reception of misleading evidence, hearsay, opinion and bad character evidence could be justified largely because of the jury. But he was anxious to move the law of evidence away from a system of mandatory rules of exclusion and exceptions to rules. Instead, he advocated resort to general principles and flexible standards through a broadening of judicial discretion, giving trial judges greater freedom to admit or exclude relevant evidence through consideration of its probative value rather than through the application of rigid and categorical rules.

Increasingly, the principles of exclusion have been applied in a flexible manner to admit ever more relevant evidence. Across the common law world, there has been a tendency for the principles of exclusion to be given lesser importance and to be substituted by a general judicial discretion to exclude relevant evidence in certain situations. The English courts have come to permit judges to exclude evidence in criminal cases where the probative value of the evidence is outweighed by its prejudicial effect.[29] Even the hearsay rule, often regarded as the 'centrepiece' of modern evidence law, has disappeared altogether as an exclusionary concept in civil cases and while retaining its exclusionary form in criminal cases has come to embrace an inclusionary discretion permitting judges to admit hearsay in the interests of justice.[30] In the United States, the Federal Rules of Evidence have given judges an explicit discretion to exclude evidence if probative value is substantially outweighed by the danger of undue prejudice, confusion of the issues, or misleading the jury, or by considerations of undue delay, waste of time, or needless presentation of cumulative evidence.[31] Writing in the context of the law of evidence in the United States, Eleanor Swift has concluded that Thayer's call for the extension of judicial discretion has triumphed.[32]

2.3 Evidence law adrift?

Two theories have dominated attempts to explain and justify the common law rules of evidence – the jury control theory and the adversary control theory.[33]

---

[29] For classic formulations of this principle, see *R* v. *Christie* [1914] AC 545, 564–5; and *R* v. *Sang* [1979] AC 402, 434.
[30] See Civil Evidence Act 1995; s. 114 of the Criminal Justice Act 2003. For detailed analysis of this section, see J. Spencer, *Hearsay Evidence in Criminal Proceedings*, 2nd edn (Oxford: Hart, 2008). See also the structured discretionary approach in South Africa under s. 3(1)(c) of the Law of Evidence Amendment 45 of 1988.
[31] Federal Rules of Evidence 403.
[32] E. Swift, 'One Hundred Years of Evidence Law Reform: Thayer's Triumph' (2000) 88 *California Law Review* 2439.
[33] For a third theory arguing that a concern about witness perjury is the best explanatory hypothesis for the logical structure of evidence law, see E. J. Imwinkelried, 'The Worst Evidence

Thayer's own view that the law of evidence 'is the child of the jury'[34] came to dominate twentieth-century evidence scholarship.[35] The argument here is that judges needed to develop exclusionary rules to prevent juries placing more weight on certain kinds of evidence than was really merited. A jury may give undue weight, for example, to hearsay evidence or character evidence. Before the onslaught of lawyer-controlled proceedings, judges used to make their views on the evidence very clear. As proceedings became dominated by lawyers, more formal controls had to be instituted. One of these was the exclusion of evidence, but as well judges came to direct juries formally on the burden and standard of proof and on how to approach the evidence that was admitted. Many have been critical of the technical directions which these rules have entailed and questioned whether juries are able to follow them or even understand them. But in the absence of a reasoned decision by juries setting out the grounds for their decision, detailed and sometimes technical directions on how a jury *ought* to ground their decision are the best the system can do.[36]

During the course of the century, a rival theory was developed to explain the rules of evidence, which holds that the contested nature of the adversary trial requires special quality controls to be put upon the admission of evidence. When the proof process is dominated by the evidence which the parties have gathered and collected, there is a particular need to be sceptical about the nature of this information and a need to impose rigorous testing devices and foundational requirements.[37] The right to cross-examination becomes particularly important in this context, as parties must be given the opportunity to challenge the sources of information presented by their opponents and the hearsay rule provides an important means of ensuring that the evidentiary sources of a party's case can be tested. But as Damaška has argued, it is not only party control which raises doubts about the quality of the evidence presented in the adversary system. Another feature of the system is the importance placed upon the concentrated trial where the parties are given their day in court.[38] As a result of this procedural arrangement, there is a need for evidentiary regulation both to prevent information overload and to avoid unfair surprise by one party preventing the other from testing the evidentiary sources of its case. The jury system also plays a significant part in supporting these rules, however, as it

---

Principle: The Best Hypothesis as to the Logical Structure of Evidence Law' (1992) 46 *University of Miami Law Review* 1069.

[34] Thayer, *Preliminary Treatise on Evidence*, 47.
[35] Nance, 'The Best Evidence Principle', 279. Cogent criticism of the theory is to be found, however, in E. Morgan, 'The Jury and the Exclusionary Rules of Evidence' (1937) 4 *University of Chicago Law Review* 247.
[36] See M. Seigel, 'A Pragmatic Critique of Modern Evidence Scholarship' (1994) 88 *Northwestern University Law Review* 995, 1022: 'admonitions are best viewed as a part of the ritual associated with the trial process... An admonition brings closure, a sense that the system has done its best to make things right'.
[37] M. Damaška, *Evidence Law Adrift* (New Haven: Yale University Press, 1997) ch. 4.
[38] Damaška, *Evidence Law Adrift*, ch. 3.

enables the trial court to filter out inadmissible evidence from the hearing of the tribunal of fact. It is difficult in a unitary trial where judges act both as the tribunal of law and of fact to expect them to put evidence ruled as inadmissible out of their minds and consequently to 'unbite the apple of knowledge'.[39]

In his book *Evidence Law Adrift*, Damaška argues that during the course of the twentieth century the three pillars that have sustained the institutional environment of common law litigation – the jury system, party control and the concentration of trial proceedings – have all been eroded and that the entire evidentiary edifice of the common law has come under threat.[40] The decline in the use of the jury over the century and the increasing shift towards unitary courts made it impossible to exclude evidence from judicial triers of fact. Over the course of the century, common law proceedings became more episodic as pre-trial evidentiary procedures such as discovery assumed greater significance, with the consequence that sources of information could be checked at procedural stages before the trial and there was consequently less need for rigorous evidentiary controls at trial. Finally, the growth in judicial activism prompted by the withdrawal of the jury and the increasing complexity of litigation and need for trial management put greater pressure on parties to agree evidence and rely less on exclusionary rules of evidence.[41]

2.4 Challenges to free proof

Damaška's thesis has received a mixed response.[42] On the one hand, there would certainly seem to be some justificatory force in the association that is made between the three pillars that have sustained the institutional environment of common law litigation and the exclusionary rules of evidence. On the other hand, some have questioned the causal connection between the two by pointing out that many of the common law rules such as hearsay and bad character had begun to unravel well before the erosion of the three pillars that provided for their support.[43] Others have questioned whether the degree to which the pillars that purportedly provide the function for the rules have been in such decline. In particular, it has been argued that the adversarial culture has shown no signs

---

[39] Damaška, 'Free Proof', 352.   [40] Damaška, 'Free Proof', 352.
[41] The effect of the withdrawal of the jury in criminal trials has been empirically monitored in J. Jackson and S. Doran, *Judge without Jury: Diplock Trials in the Adversary System* (Oxford: Clarendon, 1995). The classic article on managerial judging is J. Resnik, 'Managerial Judges' (1982) 96 *Harvard Law Review* 376. See also M. Langer, 'The Rise of Managerial Judging in International Criminal Law' (2004) 53 *American Journal of Comparative Law* 835.
[42] See generally 'Symposium Issue: Truth & Its Rivals: Evidence Reform and the Goals of Evidence Law, Panel 2 – Evidence Law Adrift' (1997) 49 *Hastings Law Journal* 359–401; P. Roberts, '*Faces of Justice* Adrift? Damaška's Comparative Method and the Future of Common Law Evidence', in J. Jackson, M. Langer and P. Tillers (eds.), *Crime, Procedure and Evidence in a Comparative and International Context: Essays in honour of Professor Mirjan Damaška* (Oxford: Hart, 2008) 295; and R. J. Allen and G. N. Alexakis, 'Utility and Truth in the Scholarship of Mirjan Damaška', in ibid., 329.
[43] Allen and Alexakis, 'Utility and Truth'.

of abating in certain common law countries.[44] Indeed, as Damaška himself seemed to recognise,[45] the decline in concentrated trial proceedings would seem to have extended adversarial styles of litigation into the pre-trial process through increasing resort to negotiated settlements and plea bargaining.

While many of the common law exclusionary rules have undoubtedly been in decline throughout the twentieth century, it would seem too early yet to write their obituary. Reform of some of the rules has been a slow and tortuous business in certain common law jurisdictions. The common law system of evidence is a 'grown' order, not a 'made' order and as such is susceptible to slow, evolutionary change rather than 'magic bullets'.[46] Law reform commissions have recommended changes, but conservative forces within legal professions have been reluctant to slaughter old 'sacred cows'.[47] Although these forces may be viewed as no more than vested interests designed to ward off the day when freedom of proof inevitably triumphs, it is possible to identify certain counter-tendencies that may not only explain but also justify the continued use of exclusionary rules in the common law context. We will call these each in turn – the epistemic challenge, the scientific challenge and the constitutional rights challenge.

2.4.1 The epistemic challenge

Evidence scholarship has traditionally paid little attention to the processes of reasoning by which inferences should be drawn from a mass of evidence. We have seen that the rationalist tradition to which evidence scholars have subscribed has assumed that the mode of reasoning is inductive rather than deductive, but only more recently have they turned attention towards the processes of reasoning about evidence and considerable debate has been generated between advocates of various theories of probability.[48] When we consider the implications of this work for the debate on freedom of proof, much depends on the particular perspectives and theories being adopted. As regards probability theory, those who prefer a classic Bayesian approach towards legal fact finding would seem to be cautious about the merits of using evidentiary rules to regulate reasoning processes.[49] We have seen that exclusionary rules may be used where it is considered that the trier of fact may give mistaken weight to certain evidence, or

---

[44] Roberts, '*Faces of Justice* Adrift?'.   [45] Damaška, *Evidence Law Adrift*, 138.
[46] R. J. Allen, 'The Simpson Affair, Reform of the Criminal Justice Process and Magic Bullets' (1996) 67 *University of Colorado Law Review* 989.
[47] See, e.g. R. Cross, 'The Right to Silence and the Presumption of Innocence – Sacred Cows or Safeguards of Liberty?' (1970) 11 *Journal of the Society of Public Teachers of Law* (NS) 66; and J. Jackson, 'Hearsay: The Sacred Cow That Won't Be Slaughtered?' (1998) 2 *International Journal of Evidence & Proof* 166.
[48] R. Lempert, 'The New Evidence Scholarship: Analysing the Process of Proof' (1986) 66 *Boston University Law Review* 439; and J. Jackson, 'Analysing the New Evidence Scholarship: Towards a New Conception of the Law of Evidence' (1996) 16 *Oxford Journal of Legal Studies* 309.
[49] See Redmayne, 'The Structure of Evidence Law'.

in Bayesian parlance may miscalculate the likelihood ratio in terms of whether a material fact to be proved is more or less likely given the truth of certain evidence as compared with its falsity. Where there is a large gap between the true likelihood ratio and the likelihood ratio that a jury may be prone to estimate, that might indicate a reason for exclusion of the evidence on the ground that the jury is likely to fall into error. The difficulty is that in order to make that calculation, we need to know what the likelihood ratio is and what estimate a jury is likely to make.[50] Even if we could reach a reasonable conclusion about these matters, any error would seem to have to be very considerable in order to justify exclusion. For the relevant question is not whether there is likely to be an error in the estimation or whether it is likely to vary considerably from the true likelihood ratio, but whether the error is so great that the costs of admitting the evidence in terms of mis-calculation are going to outweigh the costs of not allowing the jury to hear the relevant evidence at all. This suggests that it would be preferable to adopt the Benthamite strategy of warning the jury about the kind of mistakes they might make in estimating the likelihood ratio rather than excluding evidence altogether.

Much may depend, however, on the kind of evidence that is the subject of these calculations. A distinction has been made in some of the literature between 'reasoning prejudice', which occurs when juries make mistakes of reasoning when estimating the probabilities of events, and 'moral prejudice', which occurs when the nature of the evidence itself causes the jury to abandon the reasoning process and to decide the case on grounds other than the probative force of the evidence.[51] There is some data to suggest, for example, that when a defendant has a previous conviction for indecent assault on a child, juries may be predisposed towards conviction whatever the evidence against him.[52] Juries are not supposed to act in this way and it might be hoped that sufficient warnings might suffice to prevent them doing so without the need to resort to exclusion.

Leaving aside the extreme case where jurors blatantly act in defiance of the evidence, however, other jury research indicates that prejudice can play a more insidious role in the reasoning process as juries try to make sense of the evidence. More generally, cognitive psychology has questioned whether juries reason by revising estimated probabilities according to each new piece of evidence they receive.[53] Instead of this atomistic approach, they approach evidence much

---

[50] A. Goldman, *Knowledge in a Social World* (Oxford University Press, 1999) 294.

[51] See, e.g. A. A. S. Zuckerman, *The Principles of Criminal Evidence* (Oxford: Clarendon, 1989) 233; Law Commission, *Evidence in Criminal Proceedings: Previous Misconduct of a Defendant* (London: HMSO, 1996), CP 141, para. 7.2; Law Commission, *Evidence of Bad Character in Criminal Proceedings* (London: HMSO, 2001), No. 273, Cm. 5257, para. 5.18; and P. Roberts and A. Zuckerman, *Criminal Evidence*, 2nd edn (Oxford University Press, 2010) 590–5.

[52] S. Lloyd Bostock, 'The Effects on Juries of Hearing about the Defendant's Previous Criminal Record: A Simulation Study' [2000] *Criminal Law Review* 734.

[53] See, e.g. C. Callen, 'Notes on a Grand Illusion: Some Limits on the Use of a Bayesian Theory in Evidence Law' (1982) 57 *Indiana Law Journal* 1; and R. J. Allen, 'The Nature of Juridical Proof' (1991) 13 *Cardozo Law Review* 373.

more holistically by organising their perceptions around schemas or stories or scripts which represent their social knowledge of the world.[54] These help to fill in gaps to provide a single interpretation and once this is done there is a strong tendency to fit new information into the existing pattern rather than revise or change the original pattern adopted. When it comes to trial fact-finding, Pennington and Hastie have developed a story model of decision-making according to which jurors engage in an active and constructive comprehension process in which evidence is organised, elaborated and interpreted during the course of the trial into a narrative form.[55] Litigants and attorneys also on this theory enjoy considerable freedom in the way in which to shape evidence. Furthermore, it is questioned whether juries will all reach the same conclusion on the presentation of the same evidence. When we test evidence, we do not test it against a universally available stock of knowledge about the common course of events, but by reference to particular schemas or stories that form the basis of our knowledge structures.[56] Evidence is not merely constituted by the information which emerges in the course of an investigation and is presented to a court, but consists of an interaction between information and the theories and background assumptions of investigators and triers of fact.

Some of these ideas would seem to challenge the more comfortable assumptions of the rationalist tradition. Rationalist theory as we have seen saw a considerable role for 'inductive generalisations' in reaching conclusions of fact. These may vary, of course, from one individual trier to another, but the rationalist tradition has assumed that a large degree of cognitive consensus can be reached on the basis of these common-sense generalisations. As one of the leading modern exponents of the rationalist tradition put it, the kinds of generalisations that we use in everyday life are for the most part too essential a part of our culture for there to be any serious disagreement about them.[57] This was perhaps true when we lived in homogeneous cultures and shared similar understandings. But it is not so true in multi-ethnic communities that make up many of today's societies. Apart from demonstrating how cultural biases can infiltrate our construction of the stories we use in order to organise and evaluate evidence, cognitive science has brought to light other biases that come into play as triers of fact develop strategies to make sense of evidence.[58] For example, we form beliefs at an early stage in the search for information which

---

[54] For early discussion of holistic approaches, see Wigmore, *Treatise on Evidence*, vol. 1, § 37.7, 1082; A. Hareira, 'An Early Holistic Conception of Judicial Fact-Finding' [1986–7] *Juridical Review* 79. The importance of narrative in proof was recognised by the USSC in *Old Chief* v. *United States*, 519 US 172 (1997).

[55] N. Pennington and R. Hastie, 'A Cognitive Theory of Juror Decision Making: The Story Model' (1991) 13 *Cardozo Law Review* 519.

[56] See M. MacCrimmon, 'Developments in the Law of Evidence: The 1988–89 Term – The Process of Proof: Schematic Constraints' [1990] 1 *Supreme Court Law Review (2d)* 345.

[57] L. J. Cohen, *The Probable and the Provable* (Oxford: Clarendon, 1977) 275–6.

[58] See generally D. Kahneman, P. Slovic and A. Tversky (eds.), *Judgment under Uncertainty: Heuristics and Biases* (Cambridge University Press, 1982).

are cognitively difficult to reverse once they are accepted and when we are given evidence we tend to believe that we are given it for good reason and to give it greater probative value than it is worth.[59]

It is unclear how far these ideas challenge the fundamental assumptions of the rationalist tradition.[60] The emphasis on the dependence of theory on empirical data would seem to mark a shift away from the empiricist tradition of Bacon, Locke, Bentham and Mill towards the more idealist tradition of Kant, Hegel, Collingwood and Polanyi, which emphasises the shaping of experience by reason. But this need not necessitate any fundamental threat to the rationalist adherence to the key beliefs in truth, reason and justice. On one view, theoretical structures are as much dependent on facts and evidence as acts and evidence are dependent on theoretical constructs.[61] The implications of these ideas for the anti-nomian thesis associated with the rationalist tradition are, however, more stark. The thesis assumes that because every normal and unbiased person will come to the same conclusion about evidence, there is little need to regulate the proof process. If one has faith in the ability of triers of fact to find facts, then one does not need rules of evidence to regulate the evaluation of evidence. But if, on the contrary, human beings are likely to bring their own biases into the process of investigating and evaluating facts, then we need to regulate the proof process to guard against the risk of error.

There has been some debate as to whether or not the biases that are the consequence of the cognitive strategies we adopt to reach conclusions of fact should be regulated by exclusionary rules. Much may depend again on the institutional environment in which proof processes operate. A bifurcated system of judge and jury is more conducive to screening out evidence than a unitary trial.[62] Beyond the institutional environment, some have argued that rules are needed to offset cultural biases and protect marginalised groups, including defendants against narratives and generalisations based on the dominant stories of communities.[63] Rules prohibiting evidence of the bad character of the accused and preventing triers of fact resorting to rape myths concerning consent to sexual intercourse are examples of this kind.[64] From another view, however, the 'less information one has, the more dominant social stereotypes, biases and over-generalisations are likely to be' and '[o]ne of the advantages of a system closer to free proof is that it permits the parties to respond to what

---

[59] C. Callen, 'Cognitive Strategies and Models of Fact-Finding', in Jackson, Langer and Tillers, *Crime, Procedure and Evidence*, 165.

[60] See W. Twining, 'Some Scepticism About Some Scepticisms', in Twining, *Rethinking Evidence*, 99; and J. D. Jackson, 'Modern Trends In Evidence Scholarship: Is All Rosy in the Garden?' (2003) 21 *Quinnipiac Law Review* 893.

[61] P. Tillers, 'Mapping Inferential Domains' (1986) 66 *Boston University Law Review* 883, 903.

[62] Callen, 'Cognitive Strategies'.

[63] D. Menashe and M. E. Shamash, 'The Narrative Fallacy' (2005) 3 *International Commentary on Evidence*, Issue 1, Art. 3.

[64] See, e.g. *R v. Seaboyer* (1991) 83 DLR (4th) 193, 258, 278; and *R v. A (No. 2)* [2001] 2 Cr App R 351, 360.

they fear will be the generalisations already possessed by fact finders, and to try to disabuse them of their preconceptions'.[65] This suggests that we need to regulate evidentiary processes in an inclusionary rather than an exclusionary manner, constructing processes that generate evidence from as many relevant standpoints as possible. Some may view the traditional adversary procedures as doing precisely this and rights such as cross-examination associated with them can help to challenge flaws in party-driven evidence. But these procedures may need to be supplemented by certain exclusionary rules. We have seen that one of the original rationales for some of the common law rules of evidence was to provide incentives to parties to provide the best evidence. Beyond this, if the outcomes at trial depend as much on the hidden social knowledge of triers of fact as on the evidence elicited in the courtroom, we may need to be more prepared than many systems have been to admit expert evidence that can inform triers of fact of the discriminatory tendencies of certain kinds of evidence.[66] This takes us to a further challenge which is whether a system of free proof can cope satisfactorily with the increasing resort to scientific and expert evidence in the courts.

2.4.2 The scientific challenge

The rise in the use of technical experts in legal proceedings has led to a growing literature on science and the law.[67] Within the evidentiary domain, scholars have commented on how many issues of fact are increasingly coming within the domain of expert or scientific evidence.[68] This would seem to pose a challenge to the rationalist tradition and the notion of free proof within legal processes. Although the method of inductive proof was first put into practice by scientists before it came to influence philosophers, historians and lawyers,[69] an ever-increasing number of facts of importance for the legal process are founded

---

[65] Allen, 'The Narrative Fallacy'. See also R. Burn, 'Fallacies on Fallacies: A Reply' (2005) 3 *International Commentary on Evidence*, Issue 1, Art. 4.

[66] See, e.g. M. MacCrimmon, 'Developments in the Law of Evidence: The 1989–90 Term – Evidence in Context' [1991] *Supreme Court Law Review (2d)* 385 and 'Developments in the Law of Evidence: The 1991–92 Term – Truth, Fairness and Equality' [1993] *Supreme Court Law Review (2d)* 122; R. J. Currie, 'The Contextualised Court: Litigating "Culture" in Canada' (2005) 9 *International Journal of Evidence & Proof* 73; and C. Boyle, 'Finding Facts Fairly in Roberts and Zuckerman's *Criminal Evidence*' (2005) 2 *International Commentary on Evidence*, Issue 2, Art. 3.

[67] A classic text is S. Jasanoff, *Science at the Bar: Law, Science, and Technology in America* (Cambridge, MA: Harvard University Press, 1995).

[68] See M. Redmayne, *Expert Evidence and Criminal Justice* (Oxford: Clarendon, 2001). The increasing use of scientific and medical evidence in criminal trials can be traced back to the nineteenth century: see A. Duff, L. Farmer, S. Marshall and V. Tadros, *The Trial on Trial (3): Towards a Normative Theory of the Criminal Trial* (Oxford: Hart, 2007) 49.

[69] See B. Shapiro, *Probability and Certainty in Seventeenth Century England: A Study of the Relationships between Natural Science, Religion, History, Law and Literature* (Princeton University Press, 1983); and J. D. Jackson, 'Two Methods of Proof in Criminal Procedure' (1988) 51 *Modern Law Review* 549.

upon sophisticated technical instruments or upon scientific data beyond the scope of our natural human senses and experience.[70] Just as significant has been the growth in the sciences of the mind which has had the effect of leading to new forms of psychological evidence such as post-traumatic stress disorder, battered women's syndrome, rape trauma syndrome, recovered memory syndrome and the like.[71] Even the task of assessing the credibility of witnesses which has been considered best left to the common sense of the lay jury has now been challenged by the growth of experts willing to testify on witness credibility and by such 'scientific' techniques as polygraph evidence.

This can conjure up a somewhat apocalyptic vision of legal fact-finding processes being replaced altogether by scientists and experts. There are certainly instances where challenges have been made to traditional common law processes. Challenges to the traditional common law methods of eliciting testimony by means of examination and cross-examination were to be seen in the work of early twentieth-century experimental psychologists.[72] Although this did not prompt any fundamental review of legal procedures,[73] the legal system has had to refine its approach towards certain kinds of witness testimony such as the evidence of children and other vulnerable witnesses in a number of ways.[74] In more recent years, psychologists have challenged common-sense attitudes towards the weight to be attached to certain kinds of evidence, such as eyewitness identification.[75] The growth in forensic science has also exposed the weaknesses of other traditional categories of evidence, such as confessions and informer evidence, as DNA testing has shown a number of convictions based on such evidence to be false.[76] These examples may be viewed, however, as assisting in the task of improving legal processes and the quality of decision-making within the rationalist tradition rather than as undermining it.

More critically, as DNA testing has come to be adopted as a kind of 'ultimate' court of appeal in such cases, it may be asked whether we still need courts to determine issues of guilt and innocence. The answer is suggested, however, by the fact that for all its successes, poor DNA analysis can itself become the source of injustice, as recent controversy over the use of a new kind of

---

[70] Damaška, *Evidence Law Adrift*, 143–4.
[71] E. Beecher-Monas, *Evaluating Scientific Evidence* (Cambridge University Press, 2007) ch. 10.
[72] The early classic text is H. Muensterberg, *On the Witness Stand: Essays on Psychology and Crime* (New York: Doubleday, 1908).
[73] For an account of the fierce debate engendered by the work of experimental psychologists, see D. S. Greer, 'Anything but the Truth? The Reliability of Testimony in Criminal Trials' (1971) 11 *British Journal of Criminology* 131.
[74] See, e.g. Youth Justice and Criminal Evidence Act 1999 (England & Wales). For an account of these special provisions, see J. Spencer and R. Flin, *Children's Evidence* (London: Blackstone, 1992); and L. Ellison, *The Adversarial Process and the Vulnerable Witness* (Oxford: Clarendon, 2001).
[75] E. Loftus, *Eyewitness Testimony* (Cambridge, MA: Harvard University Press, 1979) is the classic text.
[76] See B. Scheck, P. Neufeld and J. Dwyer, *Actual Innocence: When Justice Goes Wrong and How to Make it Right* (New York: Random House, 2000). See also www.innocenceproject.org.

DNA examination, known as 'Low Copy Number', has shown.[77] The history of miscarriages of justice in the United Kingdom has shown that forensic scientists may become partisan and that, as one appeal court judge has put it, the 'image of a man in a white coat working in a laboratory approaching his task with cold neutrality and dedicated only to the pursuit of truth' is sometimes far removed from reality.[78] The image of the neutral disinterested scientist is being shed as a growing literature is examining the increasingly influential role of scientists in society.[79] It may be tempting to see science as the new saviour, with verdicts being based on hard evidence and models of formal reasoning rather than on the frailties of common-sense reasoning. The difficulty, as sociologists of science have been saying for some time, is that scientists can disagree among themselves as much as other witnesses and reach differing interpretations of reality.[80] Leaving aside any biases they may have, it has been argued that it is in the nature of scientific endeavour constantly to seek better evidence, to be prepared to revise even the most entrenched claim in the face of unfavourable evidence.[81] This spirit of inquiry is incompatible with the constraints of legal inquiry where decisions have to be reached in the interest of finality. Apart from the difficulty in reaching scientific consensus, society's attitudes towards science and technology are deeply ambivalent and the need for public acceptance of verdicts suggests that it will be some time before 'men and women in white coats' replace jury verdicts.[82]

If evidentiary matters cannot be handed over entirely to scientists, however, the question arises as to how non-scientists are to handle scientific evidence on which they have no expertise. Allen and Miller have argued that a choice must be made between whether we gravitate towards a system of deference to experts which would result in a reduction of rationality or towards a system of education which would result in helping fact-finders to understand the scientific evidence so that they make a rational decision.[83] According to Allen, there are

---

[77] The dangers of reliance on such evidence were exposed in the Northern Ireland Omagh bomb trial: see *R* v. *Sean Hoey* [2007] NICC 49.

[78] *R* v. *Ward* [1993] 1 WLR 619, 674, per Glidewell LJ.

[79] See, e.g. S. Jasanoff (ed.), *Handbook on Science and Technology Studies*, 3rd edn (Boston: MIT Press, 2008).

[80] See, e.g. B. Barnes, D. Bloor and J. Henry, *Scientific Knowledge: A Sociological Analysis* (Chicago University Press, 1996). This has led to a growing literature which looks at the role of science and technology in society.

[81] See S. Haack, 'Inquiry and Advocacy, Fallibilism and Finality: Culture and Inference in Science and the Law' (2003) 2 *Journal of Law, Probability and Risk* 205. For the different values within law and science, see S. Goldberg, *Culture Clash: Law and Science in America* (Cambridge, MA: Harvard University Press, 1994); and P. H. Schuck, 'Multi-Culturalism Redux: Science, Law and Politics' (1993) 11 *Yale Law & Policy Review* 1.

[82] Roberts, '*Faces of Justice* Adrift?', 295. See also P. Roberts, 'The Science of Proof: Forensic Science Evidence in English Criminal Trials', in J. Fraser and R. Williams (eds.), *Handbook of Forensic Science* (Cullompton, Devon: Willan, 2008).

[83] See R. J. Allen and J. Miller, 'The Common Law Theory of Experts: Deference or Education' (1993) 87 *Northwestern University Law Review* 1131; and R. J. Allen, 'Expertise and the *Daubert* Decision' (1994) 84 *Journal of Criminal Law & Criminology* 1157.

no cases that defy the ability of fact-finders to understand them, no matter how scientific or technical the issues raised. The deficits of the juridical fact-finder, he claims, are 'not cognitive; they are informational'.[84] Judges and juries lack knowledge about various branches of human inquiry, as we all do, but in his view there is little reason to believe that, with instruction, they could not master the relevant fields. The real objection, he claims, to educating jurors in relevant fields of inquiry is that it would be costly and within the common law system of adjudication the costs would skew the decision towards those with greater resources. But many have expressed doubts as to whether a lay jury can be expected to draw the correct inferences from scientific evidence, especially when they are presented with 'junk science' led by the parties.[85] As Goldman has said, 'perhaps *some* jurors, *some* of the time, draw correct probabilistic conclusions from the mass of scientific statements produced by both sides. But it is unlikely that lay jurors can generally be expected to make suitable inferences on arcane and sophisticated topics when even substantial education and training do not always suffice to produce understanding.'[86]

Faced with these difficulties, common law courts have adopted various evidentiary strategies towards expert evidence which have not always been consistent or coherent.[87] The traditional English approach has tended to defer to experts by allowing them to express expert opinions provided the subject matter of the opinion is beyond the knowledge, skill or experience of the tribunal of fact, and the expert has sufficient expertise in the field.[88] Although the position may now be changing, English law has traditionally not required any specific threshold to be met to ensure the reliability of expert evidence.[89] In 1923, in *Frye v. US*,[90] a US Federal Court of Appeals appeared to impose stricter gate-keeping responsibilities on judges when it agreed that the trial court had been correct to exclude a polygraph technique because it had not achieved general acceptance in the relevant scientific community. This seemed to put a reliability threshold on the evidence by deferring to expertise in the relevant field. A majority of courts in the United States applied this standard and it appeared to creep into other jurisdictions as well.[91] The difficulty with this approach was that it led to uneven application as courts applied varying degrees of rigour to the standard

---

[84] Allen, 'Expertise and the *Daubert* Decision', 1159.
[85] See P. W. Huber, *Galileo's Revenge: Junk Science in the Courtroom* (New York: Basic Books, 1991). For discussion of the selection of expert witnesses by the parties, see Redmayne, *Expert Evidence and Criminal Justice*, 201–2.
[86] Goldman, *Knowledge in a Social World*, 308.
[87] For a critique of the English approach, see A. Roberts, 'Drawing on Expertise: Legal Decision-Making and the Reception of Expert Evidence' [2008] *Criminal Law Review* 443.
[88] For discussion, see Redmayne, *Expert Evidence and Criminal Justice*. Other rules such as the ultimate issue rule forbidding an expert expressing an opinion on the ultimate issue are arguably redundant: see J. Jackson, 'The Ultimate Issue Rule: One Rule Too Many' [1984] *Criminal Law Review* 75.
[89] I. Dennis, *The Law of Evidence*, 4th edn (London: Sweet & Maxwell, 2010) 895.
[90] (1923) 293 F. 1013.
[91] See, e.g. in Australia *R* v. *Bonython* (1984) 38 SASR 45; and *R* v. *Parenzee* [2007] SASC 143.

which gave little indication as to which facts of the expert testimony had to be generally accepted and how widely or narrowly the relevant scientific community was to be defined.[92] In *Daubert* v. *Merrell Dow Pharmaceuticals, Inc*,[93] the US Supreme Court considered that the *Frye* test had been superseded by the Federal Rules of Evidence in 1975, which made no mention of the *Frye* test, but required judges to ensure that any and all scientific testimony or evidence admitted is not only relevant but reliable. According to *Daubert*, the reliability test involved a consideration of four factors: (1) whether a theory or technique can be (and has been) tested; (2) whether the theory or technique has been subjected to peer review and publication; (3) the known or potential rate of error; and (4) general acceptance in the scientific community.[94]

Although the scope and application of the *Daubert* criteria have been clarified in later Supreme Court decisions,[95] *Daubert* remains the leading case and is now applied in federal courts in the United States, although the *Frye* test continues to be applied in a significant minority of US states.[96] It has also been cited with approval in certain other jurisdictions outside the United States.[97] There is some doubt about the impact it has had. Although the test would seem to put explicit responsibilities on judges to test the validity of scientific evidence, it has been claimed that within the realm of forensic science the courts have continued in some jurisdictions to admit bite-mark analysis, microscopic hair analysis, voiceprint evidence and handwriting analysis despite the lack of a theoretical basis, population databases, standardised methodology or empirical data on error rates for these kinds of evidence.[98] This suggests that much

[92] See Redmayne, *Expert Evidence and Criminal Justice*, 113; and A. Ligertwood and G. Edmond, *Australian Evidence*, 5th edn (Chatswood: LexisNexis, 2010) paras 7.51–2.
[93] 509 US 579 (1993).
[94] *US* v. *Jones* 107 F.3d 1147 (6th Cir. 1997). It has been argued that this over-simplifies the position as some of these factors can be separated out – e.g. there is a difference between whether a claim can be tested and the degree to which it has been tested – and there is overlap between others – e.g. 'general acceptance' is the product of 'peer review'. See M. P. Denveaux and D. M. Risinger, 'Kumho Tire and Expert Reliability: How the Question You Ask Gives the Answer You Get' (2003) 34 *Seton Hall Law Review* 15, 32.
[95] See, e.g. *General Electric Co.* v. *Joiner*, 522 US 136 (1997) (denying the need to distinguish between methodology and conclusions in assessing reliability); and *Kumho Tire Co.* v. *Carmichael* 526 US 137 (1999) (holding that the need for reliability in expertise applied with equal force to all 'knowledge' and not just 'scientific knowledge').
[96] e.g. in jurisdictions such as California, Florida, Illinois, New York, Pennsylvania and Washington.
[97] See, e.g. in Canada *R* v. *Mohan* [1994] 2 SCR 9, *R* v. *J (J-L)* [2000] 2 SCR 600; and in New Zealand *R* v. *Calder* NZHC 12 April 1995. Its influence is also to be seen in the England and Wales Law Commission report, *The Admissibility in Criminal Proceedings in England and Wales: A New Approach towards Evidentiary Reliability* (London: HMSO, 2009) Consultation Paper 109.
[98] Beecher-Monas, *Evaluating Scientific Evidence*, 95–6. See in relation to handwriting, J. Mnookin, 'Scripting Expertise: The History of Handwriting Identification Evidence and the Judicial Construction of Expertise' (2001) 87 *Virginia Law Review* 1723; and D. M. Risinger, 'Goodbye to All That, or A Fool's Errand, By One of the Fools: How I Stopped Worrying About Court Responses to Handwriting Identification (and "Forensic Science" in General) and

criminal identification evidence that is admitted in the courts cannot possibly meet *Daubert* standards. One of the difficulties is that a considerable burden is put on trial judges to be educated properly in the relevant theories or techniques because they cannot make proper reliability assessments without an understanding of the science.[99] Judges are not helped in this endeavour by criminal defence lawyers who rarely have any background in the area of expertise in issue and by prosecutors who have little responsibility in an adversary system to vouch for the reliability of the evidence they adduce.[100]

Scepticism about the ability to educate judges and juries in making proper reliability assessments is causing some jurisdictions to consider adopting approaches that are favoured in non-common law systems.[101] Suggestions have been made for some degree of direct intervention by court-appointed experts in applying *Daubert*-like standards of admissibility.[102] Others have gone further and called for greater use of court-appointed experts in assisting the ultimate tribunal of fact by testifying at trial.[103] The danger with this is that an 'official' perspective can result in certain opinions going unchallenged.[104] It would seem sensible to explore any changes that will help judges and juries to make rational and accurate decisions, but if the rationalist tradition is to be preserved, it would seem necessary to ensure that they are given sufficient autonomy to exercise their own reasoning powers in relation to all of the expert evidence that they are given, whether the experts are called by the parties or are appointed to advise the court.

2.4.3 The constitutional challenge

Thus far, we have been discussing common law conceptions of evidence in a unified manner, applicable equally in civil and criminal proceedings, but within the last 20 years evidence scholars have tended to make a distinction between criminal and civil evidence and a number of texts are devoted exclusively to

---

Learned to Love Misinterpretations of *Kumho Tire v. Carmichael*' (2007) 43 *Tulsa Law Review* 447.

[99] Certain Supreme Court justices have raised doubts about whether judges can achieve this: see, e.g. Justice Rehnquist in *Daubert*, Justice Brennan in *General Electric Co. v. Joiner*, 522 US 136, 148 (1997).

[100] Risinger, 'Goodbye to All That', 473; and P. C. Giannelli and K. C. McMunigal, 'Prosecutors, Ethics and Expert Witnesses' (2007) 75 *Fordham Law Review* 1493.

[101] For continental approaches, see, e.g. O. Leclerc, *Le Juge et l'Expert: Contribution à l'Etude des Rapports entre le Droit et la Science* (Paris: Librarie Générale de Droit et de Jurisprudence, 2005); and P. T. C. Van Kampen, *Expert Evidence Compared: Rules and Practices in the Dutch and American Criminal Justice System* (Antwerpen and Groningen: Intersentia Rechswetenschappen, 1998).

[102] See, e.g. the procedures approved in *Joiner*. See also House of Commons Science and Technology Committee, *Forensic Science on Trial*, Seventh report of Session 2004–5, HC 96-I.

[103] Goldman, *Knowledge in a Social World*, 309–10; cf. S. Haack, 'Truth and Justice, Inquiry and Advocacy, Science and Law' (2004) 17 *Ratio Juris* 15.

[104] See, e.g. J. F. Nijboer, 'Forensic Expertise in Dutch Criminal Procedure' (1991) 14 *Cardozo Law Review* 165.

criminal evidence.[105] On one view this may be attributed to the continuing narrow preoccupation of common law evidence with exclusionary rules of evidence. In a number of jurisdictions exclusionary rules have declined markedly in civil cases, particularly it would seem as a result of the erosion of institutional pillars such as the withdrawal of juries in all but the rarest of cases.[106] With a decline in the use of exclusionary rules in civil cases, the bulk of the law of evidence came to be focused mainly on the criminal sphere.[107] But the continuing viability of the rules in criminal cases also led to an increasing recognition of the importance of examining the rules of evidence within their procedural context and a new preoccupation with their moral and political foundations. Thus, the author of one of the founding texts specifically devoted to criminal evidence, Adrian Zuckerman, has claimed that 'as soon as we inquire about the aims and principles of the legal process of finding, we find that there is not just one legal procedure for determining facts but many'.[108] So far as criminal proceedings are concerned, there are extensive differences in the underlying concerns and the law governing civil and criminal cases. To be sure, one principle that they both hold in common – rectitude of outcome and how this is to be secured in adjudication – has, as we have seen, been one of the major preoccupations of the common law of evidence. But as we saw in the previous chapter, another concern that has been given particular prominence in criminal proceedings has been the need for individual rights and the law of criminal evidence has been given a special role in protecting them.

Since the Second World War, there has been a particular tendency in both common law and civil law jurisdictions to enshrine constitutional rights within their domestic law and for them to accede to international human rights treaties.[109] From a common law perspective, however, it is important to note that these rights have not been viewed as some constitutional 'add-on' to existing common law protections, but rather in many instances as solidifying existing common law principles. The confrontation right in the US Sixth Amendment and the right to present full answer and defence under section 7 of the Canadian Charter of Rights and Freedoms would seem to entrench the principle of adversary litigation. Others enshrine basic principles that have long been

---

[105] Texts specifically devoted to criminal evidence include Zuckerman, *Principles of Criminal Evidence*; Roberts and Zuckerman, *Criminal Evidence*; R. May, *Criminal Evidence*, 3rd edn (London: Sweet & Maxwell, 1995); J. C. Smith, *Criminal Evidence* (London: Sweet & Maxwell, 1995); and J. Doak and C. McGourlay, *Criminal Evidence in Context* (Exeter: Law Matters, 2005). See also R. May and M. Wierda, *International Criminal Evidence* (Ardsley: Transnational Publishers, 2001) and K. Khan, C. Buisman and C. Gosnell (eds.), *Principles of Evidence in International Criminal Justice* (Oxford University Press, 2010).

[106] For the decline of the jury in civil cases in England, see S. Lloyd-Bostock and C. Thomas, 'The Decline of the "Little Parliament": Juries and Jury Reform in England and Wales', in N. Vidmar (ed.), *World Jury Systems* (Oxford University Press, 2000).

[107] According to one estimation, the modern subject is at least four-fifths criminal evidence: P. Roberts, 'Rethinking the Law of Evidence: A Twenty-First Century Agenda for Teaching and Research' (2002) 55 *Current Legal Problems* 297, 317–18.

[108] Zuckerman, *Principles of Criminal Evidence*, 2.

[109] M. Cappelletti, *The Judicial Process in Comparative Perspective* (Oxford University Press, 1989).

practised at common law. The right to a fair trial, for example, is now to be found in the constitutions of a number of Commonwealth jurisdictions, it has been recognized as implicit in the Irish Constitution and has been incorporated into the domestic law of the United Kingdom under the Human Rights Act 1998.[110] But before this the common law courts had themselves developed a right to a fair trial. Some of the basic principles of fairness contained in Article 6 of the ECHR, such as the right to an independent and impartial tribunal and the right to be heard, derive from the common law principles of natural justice.[111] Others such as the presumption of innocence and the privilege against self-incrimination have also been hallmarks of the common law criminal trial.[112]

This does not mean that there is no significance in the attachment of constitutional status to individual rights. When rights are enshrined in a constitutional manner, they give expressive significance as part of the constitutional settlement embedded in the social contract and even if they are not enshrined as some kind of 'higher' law, courts are likely to give them 'added value'.[113] Within the United Kingdom, the incorporation of the rights in the ECHR has been embraced by the judiciary and had a profound effect on 'rights' discourse.[114] As well as invigorating existing rights, constitutionalisation can also act as a break on any movement to diminish their force and to dismantle the institutional supports and procedural or evidentiary rules that sustain them. Thus, two of the three pillars of common law litigation considered by Damaška to be in decline during the course of the twentieth century are in fact sustained by constitutional provisions.[115] The right to a jury enshrined in a number of common law jurisdictions helps to preserve the bifurcated nature of legal proceedings which makes enforcement of exclusionary rules effective and the

---

[110] In Ireland, e.g. the requirement in Art. 38 of the Constitution that 'no person shall be tried on any criminal charge save in due course of law' has been held by the Irish courts to enshrine a variety of fair trial rights, including the presumption of innocence: see *O'Leary* v. *AG* [1995] 1 IR 254.

[111] 'The common law principles of natural justice anticipated by many years the concept of a fair trial which has been elaborated by the ECtHR under art 6(1) of the ECHR': *Bow Spring (owners)* v. *Manzanilli II (owners)* (2004) EWCA Civ 1007, para. 57.

[112] In Ireland, 'the presumption of innocence is not only a right in itself; it is the basis of other aspects of a trial in the course of law at common law': *People (DPP)* v. *DO'T* [2003] IR 286, 290, per Hardiman J. English lawyers and judges have tended, however, to avoid explicit mention of the presumption of innocence, referring instead to the more 'prosaic' rules of evidence such as the burden of proof is on the prosecution to prove the accused's guilt: Roberts and Zuckerman, *Criminal Evidence*, 221. They have similarly tended to view the privilege against self-incrimination as expressing a number of distinct though connected rights: *R* v. *Director of Fraud Office ex p. Smith* [1993] AC 1, 30–1, per Lord Mustill.

[113] *Mohammed* v. *The State* [1999] 2 AC 111, 123.

[114] See, e.g. M. Loughlin, *Sword and Scales: An Examination of the Relationship between Law and Politics* (Oxford: Hart, 2000). For a critical perspective, see S. Halliday and P. Schmidt, *Human Rights Brought Home: Socio-Legal Perspectives on Human Rights in the National Context* (Oxford: Hart, 2004).

[115] J. Jackson, 'Adrift but Still Clinging to the Wreckage: A Comment on Damaška's *Evidence Law Adrift*' (1998) 49 *Hastings Law Journal* 377, 380–1.

rights to confrontation and cross-examination help to sustain classic adversary litigation.

Of course, those who are unpersuaded by Damaška's thesis may consider that the rationalist tradition's drive towards free proof is relentless whatever the procedural environment mandated by these constitutional provisions. But some of the procedural and substantive rights that are enshrined as constitutional rights would seem to support exclusionary rules more directly. If, as we shall argue, the presumption of innocence is founded upon the need to protect defendants from being wrongly convicted, this may entail not only a rule requiring the prosecution to prove the defendant's guilt beyond reasonable doubt, but also certain rules which operate to exclude evidence such as evidence of bad character which may create unfair prejudice against the accused.[116] In view of the number of wrongful convictions based upon eyewitness identifications, confessions and informer evidence in the United States, there have been recent calls for these kinds of evidence to be excluded at least in death penalty cases.[117] The privilege against self-incrimination may also be seen to encourage the exclusion of relevant evidence being advanced by witnesses and defendants when it may expose their guilt. In addition, some of the substantive rights to be found in constitutional and human rights provisions such as the right not to be subjected to torture, inhuman or degrading treatment or the right to privacy may require evidence obtained in breach of these rights to be excluded if the moral and political legitimacy of the criminal trial is to be upheld.[118] Under the Canadian Charter of Rights and Freedoms, for example, which has had a profound effect upon the law of evidence in Canada, evidence may be excluded if its admission would tend to bring the administration of justice into disrepute.

In another respect, however, a number of the fair trial rights would seem to point the other way towards the inclusion of relevant evidence rather than exclusion of such evidence. The rights enumerated in Article 6(3) of the ECHR, for example, which we will examine in detail later – to be informed of the nature and cause of the accusation against one, to have adequate time and facilities for the preparation of one's defence, to defend oneself through legal assistance, to examine or have examined witnesses and to have the free assistance of an interpreter – all encourage the defence to participate positively in the trial by putting forward a rival case to the prosecution. One of the reasons why the US Supreme Court held that the military tribunals designed to hear the cases of detainees in Guantánamo Bay were not an adequate substitute for the constitutional right to habeas corpus was because the hearings cut back on participatory due process rights such as the right to counsel and to

---

[116] Zuckerman, *Principles of Criminal Evidence*, 7.
[117] See R. Little, 'Addressing the Evidentiary Sources of Wrongful Convictions: Categorical Exclusion of Evidence in Capital Statutes' (2008) 37 *Southwestern University Law Review* 965.
[118] Dennis, *Law of Evidence*, para. 2.25, 53–4.

find or present evidence to challenge the government's case.[119] Constitutional rights such as the US Sixth Amendment compulsory process guarantee can give accused persons the right to present evidence which might otherwise be barred.[120] Some systems have gone further and begun to constitutionalise pre-trial rights to enable the defence to mount an effective defence before trial. After the passage of legislation in the United Kingdom which did much to regulate suspects' rights in the pre-trial process, the judiciary held that a suspect's right of access to legal advice was a fundamental right.[121] It is true that in order to make some of these participatory rights meaningful, exclusionary rules can come into play. The right to confrontation or cross-examination may require the exclusion of hearsay evidence as a means of requiring declarants to give oral testimony under cross-examination if their evidence is to be acted upon. The recognition of the constitutional right of a suspect to be provided with access to legal advice before being questioned may lead to the exclusion of evidence obtained from suspects when they have been denied such access.[122] But these rights are primarily aimed at giving the accused person an opportunity to exercise his or her rights to participate in the generation of relevant evidence under conditions of fairness rather than cutting back on the use of relevant information.[123]

Constitutional rights do not compel the need for exclusionary rules of evidence of the common law kind. As we shall see civil law systems which have embraced constitutional rights just as whole-heartedly are averse to exclusionary principles. But they do appear to require a system of regulated rather than free proof in so far as convictions will lack legitimacy where they are grounded on evidence obtained in violation of fundamental rights. As we saw in the last chapter, however, this should not be seen as any abandonment of the rationalist tradition. It is true that the need to protect substantive rights may constrain the fact-finding enterprise, but the whole enterprise is predicated on certain values being preserved within what may be called the constitutional social contract. We want the fact-finding enterprise to produce as accurate an outcome as possible, but if in the process certain fundamental rights such as the right not to be subjected to torture, inhuman or degrading treatment are undermined in order to obtain evidence, any reliance on such evidence is likely to taint the entire proceedings. Similarly, the right to a fair trial and the procedural values associated with it should not be seen as somehow divorced from the substantive need to reach an accurate outcome. The right to cross-examination, for example, may help to ensure evidence is properly tested and the right to an

---

[119] *Boumediene and others v. Bush, President of the United States and others*, 553 US 723 (2008).
[120] See, e.g. *Washington v. Texas*, 388 US 14 (1967); and *Chambers v. Mississippi*, 410 US 284 (1973).
[121] *R v. Samuel* [1988] QB 615. This right was also given constitutional status in Ireland in *People (DPP) v. Healy* [1990] 2 IR 73.
[122] See *R v. Samuel* [1988] QB 615; cf. *R v. Alladice* (1988) 87 Cr App R 380; cf. *People (DPP) v. Buck* [2002] 2 IR 268.
[123] See *People (DPP) v. Healy* [1990] 2 IR 73, 81, per Finlay CJ.

impartial tribunal may help to ensure accurate verdicts. It is true that if these rights are seen through the lens of protecting the accused's individual autonomy to do anything he or she pleases, come what may, including a right to subject witnesses to personal humiliation during cross-examination or a right to disrupt proceedings or refuse to participate in the proceedings, then accuracy may become subverted. But this is not, by and large, the way in which they have been interpreted within the common law and we shall see that it is not the way in which they have been interpreted within the human rights regimes that straddle the common law and civil law systems.

2.5 Conclusion

We began by arguing that although it is misleading to think that any legal system can be regulated without rules of evidence, common law systems have been differentiated from others through their development of a set of rules blocking out otherwise relevant evidence from the trier of fact. Although the procedural pillars that support these exclusionary mechanisms have been in some decline in many common law systems, notably the system of jury trial, this is still the dominant conception of the law of evidence. The Benthamite vision of free proof in the sense that the trier of fact should be free to pursue any relevant evidence and evaluate it according to his or her common sense has been halted by a realisation that triers of fact may need to be freed from their own prejudices, by concerns over the rising tide of scientific evidence and by constitutional fetters upon the use of evidence. These may not dictate the need for strict exclusionary rules, but within the common law procedural context they are likely to mean that judges will maintain at least some exclusionary discretion over the admissibility of evidence.

While the challenges to free proof provide grounds for restricting the freedom of the trier of fact, they are also providing grounds for adopting a more inclusionary approach towards evidence. The growing emphasis on fair trial standards may lead to a more expansive notion of the law of evidence as more attention is directed towards regulating the way in which evidence should be received both before and at trial in order to maximise the pool of relevant evidence under conditions of fairness. This is reminiscent of the old 'best evidence' conception of evidence that we have seen was espoused a long time ago by Gilbert. Some have detected signs of the 'adversarial' common law criminal trial moving beyond the 'reconstructive' phase which it assumed in the nineteenth century, whereby the purpose was to test the prosecution case 'reconstructed' by professional police officers, experts and lawyers.[124] The new 'fair' trial is one in which the defence is protected by fair trial standards, but is also expected to play

---

[124] L. Farmer, 'Responsibility and the Proof of Guilt', in M. D. Dubber and L. Farmer (eds.), *Modern Histories of Crime and Punishment* (Stanford University Press, 2007); and Duff et al., *Trial on Trial (3)*, 46–53.

a positive role by providing its own narrative of the evidence. In later chapters we shall examine these fair trial standards in greater detail and consider how common law and civil law systems are adapting to this challenge. But first we must consider the manner in which proof has been regulated within the civil law tradition.

3

Evidential traditions in continental European jurisdictions

3.1 Introduction

In the last chapter we saw that there is a common view that the legal systems influenced by the continental tradition do not have rules of criminal evidence. Occasionally this general notion is expressed more precisely as reflecting the fact that such systems lack exclusionary evidential rules[1] or in the notion that exclusionary rules are unique to the common law[2] or even US law.[3] These claims are based on quite a particular understanding of both evidence law and of the differences between the common law and civilian traditions and merit closer examination. In order to understand better the principles underpinning modern criminal evidence law and to consider the relationship between the evidential traditions, it is useful to examine the development of the principles of criminal evidence in some of those legal systems influenced by the civilian legal tradition. The aim here is not to conduct a comparison of the various rules of evidence and procedure in the various European legal systems, but rather to consider broad themes which have been, and which continue to be, of relevance in the majority of continental European jurisdictions in the context of the regulation of the decision-making process in criminal cases. In this context it makes sense to consider countries like Austria, Belgium, France, Germany and Switzerland together, not because their modern laws of evidence are the same (because they quite clearly are not), but because in the development of the laws of criminal evidence, fashioned as they are by reciprocal influences, the countries share something of a common history. The primary focus of this chapter is the development of evidential principles in the two largest and most influential legal systems, namely France and Germany, but reference will also be made to other European jurisdictions.

---

[1] J. Langbein, *Comparative Criminal Procedure: Germany* (St Paul: West Publishing Co, 1977) 69: 'The constitutional exclusionary rules are for the most part an American peculiarity. Illegally obtained evidence is generally admitted not only in Germany and other continental legal systems, but also in England and the Commonwealth legal systems.'

[2] J. B. Thayer, *A Preliminary Treatise on Evidence at the Common Law* (Boston: Little, Brown, 1898) 2.

[3] *Bivens* v. *Six Unknown Agents of Federal Bureau of Narcotics*, 403 US 388, 415 (1971), Burger CJ (dissenting), referring to the fact that exclusionary rules are 'unique to American jurisprudence'.

The examination of the development of the evidential principles applied in continental European jurisdictions demonstrates the importance of the nineteenth century in relation to both the laws of evidence and procedure. This was an immensely important period for the laws of evidence and procedure, as the effects of the French Revolution were felt across the continent. There was considerable interest in comparative law as the jurists of the time sought to analyse the procedural laws of various jurisdictions in order to provide inspiration for their own procedural codes. While the dominant influences on the criminal laws of continental Europe between the fifteenth and eighteenth centuries were the Roman and canon laws, the modern laws of criminal evidence and procedure bear very little resemblance to the pre-nineteenth-century laws. They have their origins instead in the substantial reforms instituted in the period following the French Revolution. As Eisenberg notes:

> The applicable principles regulating the assessment of evidence developed following the abolition in the nineteenth century of the strict statutory laws of evidence of German customary criminal procedure law.[4]

Paradoxically, the nineteenth century has been somewhat neglected by common law scholars who have tended to focus on the seventeenth- and eighteenth-century works of the major English jurists on which the modern common law is based. This tendency has been exacerbated by the American scholarship, which has understandably had a tendency to compare the pre-independence law of England with that of the same period in the jurisdictions of continental Europe. This chapter sets out to challenge some of the assumptions commonly made by common-law-educated lawyers about the law of evidence in continental European jurisdictions. Particular attention will be paid in this regard to the perceived relationship between the doctrine of free proof and inquisitorial procedural systems and to the notion that there are no constraints on judicial decision-making in the various continental European legal systems.

3.2 The development of criminal evidence law and the movement towards 'freedom of proof'

The evidential principles applied by continental European jurisdictions during the Middle Ages were closely linked to the procedural systems of the time and have little in common with the modern laws of evidence and procedure. There is little trace now for instance of the old Germanic trial by battle or trial by ordeal.[5]

---

[4] See, e.g. U. Eisenberg, *Beweisrecht der StPO: Spezialkommentar*, 6th edn (Munich: Beck, 2008), para. 88: 'Die geltenden Grundsätze der Beweiswürdigung haben sich entwickelt, seitdem im Laufe des 19.Jh das formale, gesetzlich fixierten Regeln unterworfene Beweisrecht des gemeinen deutschen Strafprozesses abgelöst wurde.'

[5] For a useful overview of early forms of proceedings, including proof by battle, in France, see A. Esmein, *History of Continental Criminal Procedure: With Special Reference to France*, trans. J. Simpson (Boston: Little, Brown, 1913) 59 ff.

The development of criminal evidence law

Until the sixteenth century, witness testimony and statements of the accused were of minor importance and the onus was on the accused to prove his or her innocence. By the sixteenth century, however, there was a growing awareness across the continent of the deficiencies of the law of evidence and a desire to try and reduce the uncertainty associated with the system.[6] The notion that the judge should only be bound by oaths, honour and conscience was rejected in favour of principles adopted from Roman law. The dual influences of Roman and canon law had a considerable impact around this time on the evidential and procedural laws of the various continental European jurisdictions. The laws of evidence and proof, which stemmed from Roman law, developed alongside – and indeed as something of an antidote to – the procedures of the inquisitorial systems, which were heavily influenced by the canon law.[7]

From the sixteenth until the nineteenth centuries, the majority of 'continental' European legal systems were greatly influenced by the principles of Roman law. The law of evidence was defined by fixed strict statutory rules.[8] These strict rules comprised what was known as a positive theory of evidence and left little room for judicial discretion in the determination of the guilt or innocence of the accused – the judgment had to be rendered 'secundum allegata et probata'.[9] The system was based on the belief that it was possible to establish objective truth and legal certainty and thus avoid simple reliance on subjective beliefs and probabilities.[10]

These rules not only dictated which evidence was admissible or usable in the determination of the charge, through the imposition of evidential hierarchies, they actually required the judge to convict the accused if the evidential rules were satisfied, irrespective of whether or not the judge believed that the accused had committed the crime.[11] The value of the evidence was determined according to these pre-determined principles. In France, until the eighteenth century, there

---

[6] According to C. G. von Wächter, *Beiträge zur Deutschen Geschichte insbesondere zur Geschichte des Deutschen Strafrechts* (Tübingen: Ludwig Friedrich Fues, 1845) 74: 'No one would want to defend the evidential rules of the middle ages. They endangered the innocent and favoured the guilty.'

[7] For a general overview of these developments, see Wächter, *Beiträge zur Deutschen Geschichte*.

[8] See, e.g. J. Glaser, *Beiträge zur Lehre vom Beweis im Strafprozess* (Leipzig: Duncker & Humblot, 1883) 6 ff.

[9] See Esmein, *History of Continental Criminal Procedure*, 251, citing Constantin, Comment de l'Ord. de 1539, 238: 'It is not enough that the judge is as thoroughly convinced as any reasonable man could be by a collection of presumptions and facts leading to presumption. This is a most erroneous way of judging....'.

[10] J. F. H. Abegg, *Lehrbuch des gemeinen Criminalprozesses mit besonderer Berücksichtigung des preußischen Rechts* (Königsberg: Gebrüder Bornträger, 1833) 141; Glaser, *Beiträge zur Lehre vom Beweis*, 5; C. A. Mittermaier, *Theorie des Beweises im Peinlichen Prozesse nach den gemeinen positiven Gesetzen und den Bestimmungen der französischen Criminalgesetzgebung* (Darmstadt: Johan Wilhelm Heyer, 1821) 47.

[11] In France, for instance, such rules stated that witness testimony could be rejected inter alia on the grounds of affection, fear, mortal enmity, weakness from age and weakness of intellect, infamy, personal interest, relationship and if it was given by paupers and beggars: P.-F. Muyart de Vouglans, *Institutes au Droit Criminel* (Paris: Le Breton, 1757) 322.

were three categories of proof: complete proofs (*la preuve pleine*), proximate presumptions (*semi pleine*) and remote presumptions. Only complete proofs, such as some forms of written proof, various presumptions[12] or the testimony of two eyewitnesses (in accordance with the principle of *testis unus, testis nullus*) were deemed sufficient to justify a capital sentence.[13] This categorisation of evidence was also found in German law,[14] where the evidence was divided into complete and incomplete proofs. Incomplete proofs were further divided into half proofs (*halben Beweis*), proofs deemed to be more than half proofs (*mehr als halben Beweis*) and proofs deemed to be less than half proofs (*weniger als halben Beweis*).[15] While those proofs which constituted less than a half proof could never ground a conviction, proof deemed to be more than a half proof was sufficient, and it seems that while half proofs such as the testimony of one witness were initially deemed to be inadequate, it later became acceptable to convict on the basis of a half proof.[16] As in France, the main types of evidence were the confession of the accused and witness testimony – all other types of circumstantial evidence were rejected.[17] In the event that sufficient evidence existed, the judge was required to convict, irrespective of factors such as whether or not he or she believed the witnesses' testimony to be truthful. The main effect of these rules was to reduce the judge's discretion by governing not only what evidence could be used, but also *how* the evidence was to be assessed.

The consequence of the insistence on the application of these strict rules was the development of evidential principles which were too strict to apply in practice. In those cases, for instance, in which there was neither a confession nor the testimony of two witnesses, it was necessary to acquit the accused, as any other available evidence was deemed to provide an insufficient basis for the conviction. As Glaser points out, had these rules functioned as they were intended to, it is likely that they would have led to greater certainty that innocent persons were not convicted, albeit at the expense of public order. In reality, this bias in favour of the accused proved unworkable and in cases where such evidence was not available other methods of securing sufficient evidence were developed, such as by torturing the accused or a witness in order to secure a confession or incriminating testimony.[18] The value of a confession depended on the seriousness of the crime and potential sentence: the lesser the crime the more willing the authorities were to accept the confession as the sole evidence

---

[12] See Muyart de Vouglans, *Institutes au Droit Criminel*, 261.
[13] See, e.g. F. Hélie, *Traité de L'Instruction Criminelle*, 2nd edn (Paris: Henri Plon, 1866), vol. IV, para. 1766, 335.
[14] The formal unification of Germany occurred in 1871 and the Federal Criminal Procedure Code was enacted in 1877. Until this time each of the various states had its own laws and criminal procedure code.
[15] See Mittermaier, *Theorie des Beweises*, 124.
[16] This seems to have occurred during the period when the use of torture became unacceptable and it became increasingly difficult to establish full proof: see below. See Mittermaier, *Theorie des Beweises*, 124.
[17] Mittermaier, *Theorie des Beweises*, 90.   [18] Glaser, *Beiträge zur Lehre vom Beweis*, 6.

of guilt. In the absence of complete proofs it was not possible to convict, and so it was essential to augment the existing evidence with a confession – irrespective of how this was obtained. It is rather ironic that the reliance on methods such as torture by water, pelote and courtepointe[19] stemmed from the conviction that only very clear and unambiguous proof of guilt was sufficient to justify a conviction. Thus, while it was unacceptable to hang a man who had not confessed, it was nonetheless quite justifiable to torture him to obtain this confession and then to hang him.[20]

While the strict hierarchical evidential rules were developed in order to counter the authoritarian procedural system, their application in practice led to greater not lesser burdens on accused persons. As Esmein puts it:

> This tyranny of proof was invoked as a necessary counterbalance to the inquisitorial and secret character of the procedure, and it would appear as though such proof 'clearer than the sun at noonday,' was required in the interests of the defence. But, on the other hand, the theory of legal proofs bound still more firmly the fetters of the criminal procedure by rendering the conviction of the guilty person more difficult to obtain; the double movement led inevitably in the same direction.[21]

Instead of offsetting the injustices of the procedural system, the fixing of strict evidential rules significantly restricted judicial discretion. It thereby compounded and even legitimised the oppression and torture of suspects and accused persons, while simultaneously devaluing the guarantee of a safe conviction. It is of little surprise therefore that the setting of concrete rules of evidence became closely associated with the tyranny of the 'inquisitorial' pre-nineteenth-century procedural law. Their subsequent abolition can thus be at least partly understood in the context of the general movement of reform, which was driven by the desire to reduce the oppressiveness of the criminal process.

Many influential writers, including Beccaria,[22] Montesquieu and Voltaire, argued strongly against the system of proofs that had taken hold in Germany, France and Italy, while campaigning simultaneously for the abolition of torture. The decision to abolish the use of torture,[23] however, inevitably led to a crisis in the various criminal justice systems, as the main method of securing 'full proofs' was no longer available. The period in the wake of these fundamental changes was unsurprisingly a time of considerable uncertainty and change as the various jurisdictions sought to introduce other means on which to base a

---

[19] Mittermaier, *Theorie des Beweises*, 137. [20] Mittermaier, *Theorie des Beweises*, 111.
[21] Esmein, *History of Continental Criminal Procedure*, 251.
[22] C. Beccaria, *On Crimes and Punishments and Other Writings*, ed. R. Bellamy, trans. R. Davies (Cambridge University Press, 1995) ch. 16.
[23] Torture was finally abolished in Prussia in 1754, in Baden in 1767, in Meklenburg in 1769, in Sachsen in 1770, in Bayern in 1807, in Württemberg in 1809 and in Hannover in 1818: Wächter, *Beiträge zur Deutschen Geschichte*, 78. It was abolished in France in 1788 and in Spain in 1820: see T. Volkmann-Schluck, 'Continental European Criminal Procedures: True or Illusive Model?' (1981) 9 *American Journal of Criminal Law* 2.

conviction and thus to mitigate the strict rules of evidence. In France, which was engaged around this time in major reforms of its entire criminal justice system, the issue was the subject of considerable debate. It was decided that the principle that the decision-maker be personally convinced of the guilt of the accused (*le principe de la preuve morale*) should be applied in relation to the newly created jury trials. The principal reason for the introduction of this method seems to have been the belief that the strict system of proofs was too difficult for a jury to use and thus incompatible with trial by jury.[24] The jury were to be led by their moral conviction. According to the Law of 16 to 29 September 1791:

> It is especially on the basis of evidence and the debates which take place in their presence, that the jurors must establish their personal certainty; because it is their personal certainty that is at issue here; it is this which the law demands that they express, it is this which society and the accused relies upon.[25]

This rule was subsequently adopted in Article 342 of the *Code d'instruction criminelle* of 1808, but again it only applied to jury trials.[26] There seems to have been some hesitancy before this notion of '*intime conviction*' was extended to trials determined by a judge sitting without a jury. Although several jurists, including Mittermaier and Carmignani,[27] argued against this movement, the principle was later extended to include trials which were presided over by a judge sitting alone. Helié explained the development in the following way:

> There are not two forms of certainty, one for juries and another for judges. Moral certainty is, for both, the criteria of the truth and must consequently be the only ground on which they base their sentence.[28]

Although there is no express mention of the notion in the relevant provisions of the *Code d'instruction criminelle*, they nevertheless contain an implicit assumption that both the judges of the *tribunaux de police* and the *police correctionnelle* were to determine the charge in accordance with their discretion.[29] This discretion did not extend to determining which mode of proof to apply. Helié cites several cases where appeals were allowed where a judge had applied the old rules of proof. These old rules were deemed to be incompatible with the principles of the new criminal law.[30]

---

[24] See the debates referred to by Helié, *Traité de L'Instruction Criminelle*, vol. IV, 339.
[25] Art. 24 of Title VI of the Law of 16–29 September 1791.
[26] See Helié, *Traité de L'Instruction Criminelle*, vol. IV, 340; See also J. A. Roux, *Cours de Droit Pénal et de Procéedure Pénal* (Paris: Contant-Laguerre, 1920) 685.
[27] See Helié, *Traité de L'Instruction Criminelle*, vol. IV, 345.
[28] Helié, *Traité de L'Instruction Criminelle*, vol. IV, 349.
[29] Helié, *Traité de L'Instruction Criminelle*, vol. IV, 351, with reference to Arts. 154 and 189 of *le Code d'instruction criminelle* 1808. This was also the case in Belgium, which also applied the Code of 1808: see A. Braas, *Précis d'Instruction Criminelle ou Procéedure Pénale* (Brussels: Émile Bruylant, 1932) 289.
[30] e.g. Arr. Cass. 29 juin 1848 (Bull. no. 193): see Helié, *Traité de L'Instruction Criminelle*, vol. IV, 352.

In Germany, the development towards this notion of the personal conviction of the judge was more prolonged. In south Germany, for instance, laws were introduced which stated that circumstantial evidence was to be treated in the same way as witness testimony[31] and was thus sufficient, except in capital cases, to form the basis of a conviction. According to Glaser: 'The artificiality increased instead of decreasing.'[32] The creation of such artificial constructions served to erode further the legal certainty that was supposed to be achieved through the application of the strict evidential rules.

The consequence of such developments was that reliance on the statutory rules of evidence as a guarantee of the certainty of the conviction became almost impossible to maintain. Commentators began to write in support of a system in which the moral conviction of the judge corresponded to the statutory norms and rules of evidence. And thus the nineteenth century saw the gradual introduction in Germany of a 'negative' theory of evidence. The distinction between the 'positive' and 'negative' theories of evidence can best be demonstrated by way of an example. Under the positive theory of evidence, the judge was bound by the incriminating testimony of two witnesses to convict the accused. According to the negative theory, on the other hand, no one could be convicted, even in spite of the testimony of two witnesses, if the judge had reason to doubt the guilt of the accused. It was therefore no longer possible simply to state that the 'truth' could be confirmed through evidence of a certain quality; instead it was necessary to add that this would only suffice 'provided that the judge does not find, in spite of this evidence, a reason for doubting this truth'.[33] These developments meant that the judge could not simply rely on the nature of the evidence (for example, the statements of two witnesses), but had also to assess the value of this evidence (that is, whether the witnesses and their testimony could be seen to be credible).

There was no single defining moment in which this transformation occurred; rather Glaser describes a gradual shift whereby the evidential provisions began to be expressed in the form of 'negative' rather than 'positive' rules. By the middle of the nineteenth century, some of the German procedural codes (which were still determined on a regional and not federal level) began to apply broadly 'negative' theories of evidence. These provisions went further than those which simply included a provision leaving the judge the freedom to acquit in cases where he or she was not convinced of the guilt of the accused, in that they tried to regulate how the judge was to determine the evidence. The Prussian criminal code, for example, stated in relation to determining the credibility of witnesses,

---

[31] Wächter, *Beiträge zur Deutschen Geschichte*, 78; P. J. A. von Feuerbach, 'Die Aufhebung der Folter in Baiern', in P. J. A. von Feuerbach, *Themis oder Beiträge zur Gesetzgebung* (Landshut: Krüll, 1812) 239, 267.
[32] Glaser, *Beiträge zur Lehre vom Beweis*, 10: 'Die Künstelei stieg, statt abzunehmen.' See too Wächter, *Beiträge zur Deutschen Geschichte*, 79.
[33] Glaser, *Beiträge zur Lehre vom Beweis*, 15.

that this was to depend 'on their character, on the completeness, certainty and inner probability of the statements themselves'.[34]

As Glaser notes, the development of a negative theory of evidence alongside the retention of the strict rules of proof proved inherently, and insolvably, contradictory. On the one hand, it promoted the theory that it was possible and necessary to regulate, by way of abstract rules, not just the quality of the evidence, but also the value of the evidence. This suggested that the system put its faith in the ability of these rules, rather than the judge, to ensure that the correct result was achieved. On the other hand, there seems to be, in the endorsement of the need for judicial discretion in the determination of the evidence, doubt as to the ability of these abstract rules to provide sufficient guarantees.[35]

A variety of different approaches were adopted by the various German jurisdictions in an attempt to surmount not only evidential problems, but also to address the growing disquiet as to the legitimacy of the procedural rules. According to Kries, as soon as the attempts to integrate a negative theory of proof failed, the movement switched towards the introduction of the principles of immediacy, orality and, as in France, reliance on the judge's ability to determine the charge correctly.[36] Although these developments took place in stages and at different speeds throughout Germany and indeed throughout the various continental European jurisdictions, they indicate that there was some awareness of the close relationship between the principles of procedure and evidence and that the effectiveness of evidential rules regulating the determination and sufficiency of the proof of guilt could be affected by rules regulating how the proceedings should take place.

The Kingdom of Sachsen was the first jurisdiction in Germany to seek, in spite of retaining the written procedural system, to free the judge from the binding laws of evidence in its criminal code of 1843.[37] The procedural code of Baden of 1845 on the other hand retained the strict rules of evidence, while at the same time adopting the principle of oral proceedings.[38] The Prussian procedural code of 1846 differed from both of these by introducing the principle of oral proceedings, while at the same time essentially abolishing the strict rules of evidence, which bound the judge in determining the charge.[39] A number of evidential laws were retained, such as those governing how the evidence was

---

[34] Glaser, *Beiträge zur Lehre vom Beweis*, 11, citing para. 359 of the Prussian Criminal Code.
[35] Glaser, *Beiträge zur Lehre vom Beweis*, 15.
[36] A. von Kries, *Lehrbuch des Deutschen Strafprozeßrechts* (Freiburg i B: GM Wagner, 1892); see also E. Rupp, *Der Beweis im Strafverfahren: Ein Beitrag zur wissenschaftlichen Darstellung des deutschen Prozessrechts* (Freiburg i.B. and Tübingen: Mohr, 1884).
[37] See H. A. Zachariae, *Handbuch des Deutschen Strafprocesses: Systematische Darstellung des auf den Quellen des gemeinen Rechts und der neuern deutschen Gesetzgebung beruhenden Criminal-Verfahrens* (Göttingen: Verlag der Dieterichschen Buchhandlung, 1868) 407 and the comments of Wächter, *Beiträge zur Deutschen Geschichte*, 80.
[38] Bädische Strafproc. Ordn. v. 1845, Lit IV, von Beweis Arts. 284–339.
[39] Das Preussische Gesetz v. 17 Juli 1846, para. 19.

to be taken and regulating who could act as a witness and which witnesses were not to be examined on oath.[40] By 1848, the majority of German states, irrespective of whether or not they had adopted the new criminal procedure laws, had abolished the fixed rules of evidence in favour of ensuring that judges (and indeed in some cases the jury) were free in assessing the sufficiency of the evidence.

The commentators of this time were practically unanimous in their belief that the freedom of the judge to determine the case was not unrestricted. 'The emancipation from the rules of evidence', wrote Schwarze, 'has neither freed judges from the obligation to examine the evidence in accordance with the rules of logic and with experience, nor has it given them the authority to decide the charge, without examining the evidence, and on the basis of an uncertain and weak general impression'.[41] A similar position was taken by Walther, who states that the freedom of conviction must not be taken to be identical to 'whims and arbitrariness'.[42] 'The conflict is not between the notions of reason and arbitrariness', he writes, but rather 'between general, abstract and legally binding rules of proof and the principle of judicial freedom to determine the charge which, while not tied to fixed rules, lets itself be determined through logic and experience'.[43] In the absence of fixed statutory rules binding the judge or the jury in the assessment of the evidence, many jurisdictions introduced the requirement that the judge (or in some countries the jury[44]) give reasons for the verdict as a way of controlling the judge's discretion.[45] A good example of the combination of the principle that the judge be responsible for the determination of the charge and the requirement that the verdict be justified by way of a reasoned judgment is to be found in the Prussian criminal code of 1849:

> The prevailing statutory rules concerning the procedure governing the hearing of evidence and in particular governing the persons permitted to appear and give evidence under oath as witnesses continue to apply. On the other hand, the positive rules as to the effects of evidence which have applied until now, will no longer apply. The judge with the responsibility for determining the charge must determine from now on following a careful examination of all evidence for the prosecution and the defence and in accordance with his free conviction determined on the basis of the evidence from the hearings which took place before him, whether the accused is guilty or not guilty. He is however obliged to state in the judgment the reasons which led him to this decision.[46]

[40] Zachariae, *Handbuch des Deutschen Strafprocesses*, vol. II, para. 138, 409.
[41] F. O. Schwarze, 'Die gesetzliche Beweistheorie, mit besonderer Rücksicht auf die Beweisregeln des Englischen Strafverfahrens' (1858) 6 *Goltdammer's Archiv für Preußisches Strafrecht* 721, 726.
[42] F. Walther, *Lehrbuch des bayerischen Strafprozessrechts* (Munich: Literar.-artist. Anst., 1859) 324: 'Laune und Willkür'.
[43] Walther, *Lehrbuch des bayerischen Strafprozessrechts*, 324.
[44] e.g. France – for the procedure in relation to jury trials, where the jury were required to answer a number of questions: see Roux, *Cours de droit pénal*, 703.
[45] See Glaser, *Beiträge zur Lehre vom Beweis*, 31.   [46] Para. 22 V v. 3 Jan. 1849.

The fundamental shift across the continent can be seen as a movement in the direction of a 'rationalist' theory of evidence – away from the fixed rules of evidence, which compelled the judge to convict or acquit the accused, towards less concrete rules which were intended to assist and lead the judge in determining the charge. The judge was not permitted to determine the charge on the basis of a personal feeling or from extra-judicial sources, but was only to rely on the evidence raised during the proceedings. This did not mean that judges were entirely free and a number of restrictions on judicial freedom were either created or retained. The principal restrictions took one of two forms: limitations stemming from procedural rules governing the manner in which the evidence was to be taken or witness privileges. In Belgium, for example, the judges of the *tribunaux* were not allowed to base their decision on illegal investigations or searches.[47] They were also cautioned to take special care with regard to witness testimony, which was deemed to be weak, difficult to manage and dangerous,[48] and special rules were created in relation to children and those under a professional duty of secrecy.[49] A variety of similar restrictions were enforced in France both in relation to jury trials and in those trials which were conducted by a judge sitting alone.[50] In Germany, evidential prohibitions were placed on the use of various categories of evidence, thereby underlining the importance of adherence to criminal procedural rules.[51] The categories included the prohibition on the use of evidence in the interests of the state; privileges afforded to heads of state and their families; prohibitions based on the importance of protecting the privacy of individuals (including the right of the accused to refuse to participate, his or her right to remain silent and restrictions on medical intervention); witness privileges based on relationship to the accused person; duties of confidentiality, particularly in the context of lawyers, doctors and members of the clergy; and prohibitions designed to protect private property interests.[52]

3.3 The importance of the nineteenth-century procedural reforms

Although the evidential reforms of this period seem to have gained the support of the vast majority of commentators, many felt that there was still some way to go in relation to reforming the procedural laws. Writing approvingly of the reform of evidence law in Sachsen, Wächter, for instance, expresses a note of caution:

> It grants the judge the right to convict provided that he is convinced, from the contents of the files, of the accused's guilt. This is a notable step in the right

---

[47] Braas, *Précis d'Instruction Criminelle*, 291, citing Liège, 28 Mai 1910, B.J. 1910, 733.
[48] Braas, *Précis d'Instruction Criminelle*, 293: 'fragile, difficile à manier et dangereuse'.
[49] Braas, *Précis d'Instruction Criminelle*, 294.   [50] e.g. Roux, *Cours de droit pénal*, 696 ff.
[51] e.g. E. Beling, *Die Beweisverbote als Grenzen der Wahrheitsforschung im Strafprozess* (Breslau: Schletter'sch Buchhandlung, 1903) 3–5.
[52] Beling, *Die Beweisverbote als Grenzen*, 6–24.

direction; but it is only one step – the second remains to be taken. This one step is, as an isolated action, hugely endangered by our written procedure.

As long as we have our secret and written procedure, then we are still far away from the ultimate goal. Only the introduction of two things will lead us in the right direction: conviction on the basis of the belief of an independent, experienced and permanent judge, and a public and oral hearing before the judge who is to determine the charge.[53]

It is no coincidence that, around this time, several renowned jurists were urging the adoption of considerable procedural reforms. The nineteenth century was a time of considerable procedural change and the developments in the law of evidence must be seen in the context of the wide-ranging reforms of the continental European criminal justice systems in the aftermath of the French Revolution. These reforms were influenced by and critically assessed in the works of several notable jurists, whose interest in legal systems of other European countries is clearly evident. Mittermaier, for instance, examines the procedural laws of Austria, England, France, Scotland and Switzerland before going on to develop his own critique of German criminal procedure law.[54] There is a distinct sense in many of the works of this time that the European procedural systems were developing according to common principles. Esmein writes that '[t]he trend of the trial procedure, in the various European countries, is shown rather by common characteristics than by essential differences'.[55]

German jurists such as Feuerbach and Mittermaier were broadly critical of the French system (and in particular the emphasis which it placed on the preliminary phases of the proceedings) and, influenced by English law, were strong advocates of adherence to the principles of oral and immediate proceedings.[56] There is evidence in the works of the French jurists which points towards firm recognition of the importance of oral and public trial hearings,[57] albeit with the important caveat that they had considerably less enthusiasm for the principle of immediacy – the need for the evidence to be presented directly to the judge or fact-finder – and favoured instead an approach which placed more emphasis on the investigating authorities. Other countries adopted a variety of other approaches, which can be seen to be a mixture of these systems. In view of the emphasis on judicial responsibility as a guarantee of the accurate determination

---

[53] Wächter, *Beiträge zur Deutschen Geschichte*, 80.
[54] C. J. A. Mittermaier, *Die Mündlichkeit, das Anklageprinzip, die Öffentlichkeit und das Geschworenengericht in ihrer Durchführung in den verschiedenen Gesetzgebungen: dargestellt und nach den Forderungen des Rechts und der Zweckmäßigkeit mit Rücksicht auf die Erfahrungen der verschiedenen Länder* (Stuttgart: Cotta, 1845). See further S. J. Summers, *Fair Trials: The European Criminal Procedural Tradition and the European Court of Human Rights* (Oxford: Hart, 2007) ch. 2.
[55] Esmein, *History of Continental Criminal Procedure*, 604 (commenting on: (i) the separation of courts and procedures on the basis of the different offences; (ii) the introduction of lay decision-makers; and (iii) publicity, confrontation and oral testimony).
[56] Mittermaier, *Die Mündlichkeit*, 212 ff.
[57] Especially in relation to the jury trials: see, e.g. Roux, *Cours de droit pénal*, 684.

of the charge, it might have been expected that the procedural reforms would have advanced in a similar direction, by requiring that the evidence be presented directly to the judge. Yet while the decision to free the judiciary from the strict rules of proof was followed practically unanimously across continental Europe, the principle of immediacy did not meet with the same uniform acceptance.

The predominant difference that remained therefore was, and indeed still is, the regulation of how the evidence was to be conveyed to the decision-maker. By 1868, Zachariäe insisted that the long-discussed argument in Germany as to whether the trial should be conducted orally or in writing could be regarded as settled.[58] In his opinion it was generally accepted that the oral, immediate procedure was the most fundamental and irrefutable guarantee for the establishment of the material truth.[59] The reform movement of the nineteenth century culminated in Germany in 1877 with the enactment of the first federal criminal code of procedure, marking a movement away from the old procedural rules of the inquisition and a firm recognition of the importance of oral, immediate and public trials.[60] Other jurisdictions, however, such as France (with the exception of the jury trials), Austria and many of the Swiss Cantons remained unconvinced of the benefits of immediate procedure and resisted these developments.

In spite of this the procedural systems developed during the nineteenth century a great many similarities. The various jurisdictions all moved towards a system of public trials in which the investigating authorities had the primary responsibility for gathering all of the evidence relevant to the determination of the charge and for prosecuting in the case. All of the systems required that the judge be independent. As regards the manner in which the evidence was to be conveyed to the judge, the legal systems were unanimous (irrespective of whether or not the immediacy principle had been adopted) in requiring that all evidence, whether it be for or against the accused, be passed to the judge. The solution to the two main causes of concern of the nineteenth-century reformers – the taking place of trials in secret and the inflexible rules of proof which unacceptably restricted judicial discretion – led, on the one hand, to the placing of greater responsibility on the judge and, on the other, to a movement away from written proceedings in favour of oral hearings. Both developments represented in some sense the 'subjectivisation' of criminal proceedings, allowing for the individualisation of and differentiation between cases.[61] In order to prevent future miscarriages of justice, the judge was to have

---

[58] Zachariäe, *Handbuch des deutschen Strafprocesses*, 50.

[59] A view shared in relation to civil procedure law by R. von Canstein, *Die rationellen Grundlagen des Civilprocesses* (Vienna: Manz, 1877) 78 and 96. S. Maas, *Der Grundsatz der Unmittelbarkeit in der Reichsstrafprozeßordnung* (Breslau: Schletter, 1907) 29 seems to disagree, however, that this matter was settled.

[60] For a brief summary which also examines the influence of the French Revolution on the German procedural reforms, see C. Roxin, *Strafverfahrensrecht*, 24th edn (Munich: C. H. Beck, 1995) 481 ff, § 70.

[61] See further R. Stichweh, 'Zur Subjektivierung der Entscheidungsfindung im deutschen Strafprozess des 19. Jahrhunderts: Aspekte der Ausdifferenzierung des Rechtssystems', in

control over the proceedings and complete personal and moral responsibility for assessing the evidence and determining the charge.

3.4 Freedom of proof and restrictions on the doctrine in modern evidence law

The principle of free proof continues to be one of the most important principles, albeit to differing degrees,[62] in the majority of the continental European legal systems.[63] This principle requires the judge to take all available evidence into consideration in determining the guilt or innocence of the accused. The doctrine is, however, less controversial and less absolute than its reputation would suggest. It is important to distinguish the freedom of the judge to consider the available evidence from general notions of judicial discretion.[64] The doctrine of free proof should be understood in its historical context, not so much as allowing judges to determine freely the charge without regard to other principles or values, but rather in terms of freeing them from the strict hierarchical principles and restrictions on their assessment of the weight of the evidence.[65] This notion of free proof is closely associated with another rule, namely that in the determination of the charge judges should only be bound by their 'inner conviction' (*richterliche Überzeugung*; *l'intime conviction*). The emphasis on the importance of the judge's personal conviction as a means for ensuring that the correct decision is reached is an important rule in the regulation of the assessment of evidence in criminal cases. Although this principle has an inherent subjective element, it should not be misunderstood as requiring

---

A. Gouron et al. (eds.), *Subjektivierung des justiziellen Beweisverfahrens: Beiträge zum Zeugenbeweis in Europa und den USA, 18–20. Jahrhundert* (Frankfurt: Klostermann, 1994) 292 ff.

[62] See J. Pradel, 'Criminal Evidence', in J. F. Nijboer and W. J. J. M. Sprangers (eds.), *Harmonisation in Forensic Expertise: An Inquiry into the Desirability of and Opportunities for International Standards* (Leiden: Thela, 2000).

[63] e.g. Art. 427 of the French Code of Criminal Procedure: for discussion, see H. LeClerc, 'Les Limites de la Liberté de la Preuve – Apscets Actuels en France' (1992) *Revue de science criminelle et droit pénal comparé* 17. On the application of the principle in Germany, see, e.g. G. Willms, 'Wesen und Grenzen des Freibeweises', in R. Glanzmann (ed.), *Ehrengabe für Bruno Heusinger* (Munich: C. H. Beck 1968) 393; and Eisenberg, *Beweisrecht*, paras. 88 ff. In relation to Switzerland, see BGE 115, 1989, IV 259, E.9; see also Art. 10(2) of the Swiss Criminal Procedure Code; A. Donatsch, T. Hansjakob and V. Lieber (eds.), *Kommentar zur Schweizerischen Strafprozessordnung* (Zurich: Schulthess, 2010); N. Schmid, *Handbuch des schweizerischen Strafprozessrechts* (Zurich: Dike Verlag, 2009) para. 225; Austria, EvBl 1975/180; S. Seiler, *Strafprozessrecht*, 10th edn (Vienna: WUV Universitätsverlag, 2009) N 431; Portugal, Art. 125 of the Code of Criminal Procedure; and Belgium, Art. 154 of the Code of Criminal Procedure.

[64] See J. F. Nijboer, 'Methods of Investigation and Exclusion of Evidence', in Nijboer and Sprangers, *Harmonisation in Forensic Expertise*, 431, 440.

[65] See also M. Damaška, 'The Jury and the Law of Evidence: Real and Imagined Interconnections' (2006) 5 *Law Probability and Risk* 255, 263; W. Küper, 'Historische Bemerkungen zur "freien Beweiswürdigung" im Strafprozeß', in K. Wasserburg and W. Haddenhorst (eds.), *Wahrheit und Gerechtigkeit im Strafverfahren: Festgabe für Karl Peters aus Anlaß seines 80. Geburtstages* (Heidelberg: C. F. Müller, 1984).

simply that the judge have an intuitive feeling for the truth. The conviction must be based on logical, comprehensible reasons,[66] an obligation bolstered by the requirement found in many legal systems that reasons be provided for the judgment.[67] Whereas in earlier times judges would have been compelled, even against their better judgment, by the appearance of two witnesses with incriminating testimony to convict the accused, the principles of free proof and inner conviction provided judges in a similar position with the opportunity of acquitting the accused. The principles can therefore be seen as representing similar concerns as, and playing a similar role to that of, the common law notion of proof 'beyond reasonable doubt' which requires that the accused be acquitted if there are lingering doubts about the sufficiency of the evidence.[68]

Were these principles to be applied absolutely, there would be no room for notions of procedural fairness in the regulation of the decision-making process. The only issue would be whether the decision could be said to be substantively correct. It is important to bear in mind, however, that the doctrine of free proof is not absolute. In each of the jurisdictions there are a variety of rules which prohibit the judge from using certain evidence to substantiate the conviction – either because of the nature of the evidence itself, or because of the way in which it was obtained.[69] It is useful here to distinguish between intrinsic and extrinsic exclusionary rules.[70] Extrinsic exclusionary rules, designed to protect other values not necessarily (or primarily) connected to the pursuit of truth, are quite common in continental legal systems.[71] Typical examples include rules proscribing the use of evidence which was obtained in violation of procedural requirements such as where a witness is not informed of his or her right to refuse to give a witness statement[72] or which was improperly obtained. The use

---

[66] Küper, 'Historische Bemerkungen', 45.
[67] The requirement that reasons be provided is found in Germany, Switzerland and the Netherlands. It is less strictly observed in France and Belgium: see, e.g. J. F. Nijboer, 'Current Issues in Evidence and Procedure: Comparative Comments from a Continental Perspective' (2009) *International Commentary on Evidence*, Issue 2, Art. 7, 15. The right to a reasoned judgment has been read into Art. 6(1) ECHR by the Strasbourg organs: see S. Trechsel, *Human Rights in Criminal Proceedings* (Oxford University Press, 2005) 102. See further ch. 4. On problems posed by the jury system and the lack of reasons in France and Belgium, see, e.g. *Zarouali* v. *Belgium* (dec.); and *Papon* v. *France* (dec.). In *Taxquet* v. *Belgium*, para. 48, the court held that the questions to the jury were formulated and answered in such a 'vague and general' way that the applicant could legitimately complain that he did not know why he had been found guilty. The case was referred to the Grand Chamber on 5 June 2009.
[68] S. Maffei, *The European Right to Confrontation in Criminal Proceedings: Absent, Anonymous and Vulnerable Witnesses* (Groningen: Europa Law Publishing, 2006) 136–7.
[69] C. Jäger, 'Beweiserhebungs- und Beweisverwertungsverbote als prozessuale Regelungsinstrumente im strafverfolgenden Rechtsstaat' [2008] *Goltdammer's Archiv für Strafrecht* 473.
[70] See, e.g. M. Damaška, *Evidence Law Adrift* (New Haven: Yale University Press, 1997) 12–17. See too Wigmore's distinction between rules of extrinsic policy and rules of auxiliary probative policy discussed in Ch. 2.2.
[71] See, e.g. C. Bradley, 'The Exclusionary Rule in Germany' (1983) 96 *Harvard Law Review* 1032.
[72] e.g. §§ 52–5 of the German criminal procedure code: the courts have ruled that evidence obtained in contravention of these provisions cannot be used in support of a conviction – see,

of statements made by an accused under duress is expressly prohibited by the German procedural code[73] and the principle is replicated in various procedural laws across the continent.[74] Another broad category of evidence which cannot be relied upon is made up of the various testimonial privileges, including the evidence of those bound by a legal duty of confidentiality, such as ministers, doctors and lawyers,[75] and the accused's family members. In Germany, for instance, the witness privilege extends to partners, parents, children, grandparents, grandchildren, siblings, nieces, nephews, aunts, uncles, parents-in-law, sisters- and brothers-in-law and grandparents-in-law.[76]

Intrinsic exclusionary rules, which exist primarily to enhance the accuracy of fact finding, are not however commonly found in continental legal systems. Rules such as those found in most common law systems regulating the use of character or propensity evidence are extremely rare.[77] It is equally difficult to find rules equivalent to those regulating derivative proof such as the common law notion of hearsay. The lack of such rules can be attributed in part to the 'unitary' character of the decision-making body in continental European jurisdictions, as opposed to the (mainly, but not solely) bifurcated structure of the courts in most common law systems. This makes it difficult to conceive of a role for concepts such as admissibility. The absence of intrinsic rules can also be explained by the fact that such rules, while 'theoretically reconcilable with the ideal of free proof... could still offend that ideal in practice'.[78] In view of the fact that it would be impossible to prevent exposure to the derivative evidence, the only solution would be to require the judges to disregard the evidence, even if they considered it to be important and convincing, thereby reintroducing rules restricting judges in their evaluation of the evidence. Consequently, while primary evidence was consistently preferred over secondary sources, derivative evidence could still be considered.

---

e.g. BGH 29, 244; BGH NstZ 90, 348 and BGH 37, 30. German procedure law makes a distinction between such rules which fall within the *Beweiserhebungsverbote* and the *Beweisverwertungsverbote*, which is expressly set out in some provisions such as in § 136a.

[73] Para. 136a. See also E. Weßlau, 'Zwang, Täuschung und Heimlichkeit im Strafverfahren' (1998) 110 *Zeitschrift für die gesamte Strafrechtswissenschaft* 1 ff.

[74] See, e.g. Art. 140 of the Swiss Federal Code of Criminal Procedure. See also J. Gauthier, 'Quelques remarques sur la liberté des preuves et ses limites en procédure pénale' (1990) 107 *Revue Pénal Suisse* 184, 185; and H. Walder, 'Rechtswidrig erlangte Beweismittel im Strafprozess' (1966) 82 *Schweizerische Zeitschrift für Strafrecht* 36.

[75] Paras. 53 and 53a of the German Criminal Procedure Code: see further Eisenberg, *Beweisrecht*, 387; Switzerland – see Art. 171 Swiss Federal Criminal Procedure Code, for commentary see A. Donatsch, Art. 171, in Donatsch, Hansjakob and Lieber, *Kommentar*, 787.

[76] Para. 52(1)(3) of the Criminal Procedure Code: see further Eisenberg, *Beweisrecht*, 379. See also, e.g. Art. 168 of the Swiss Federal Criminal Procedure Code, which is similarly broad.

[77] See further M. Damaška, 'Propensity Evidence in Continental Legal Systems' (1994) 70 *Chicago-Kent Law Review* 55; according to Pradel, character evidence may only be used in Portugal if 'it is strictly necessary to prove the components of the crime and in particular the guilt of the accused or for the application of the hereditary guarantee': see Pradel, 'Criminal Evidence', 411 and 418.

[78] M. Damaška, 'Of Hearsay and Its Analogues' (1992) 76 *Minnesota Law Review* 425, 434.

3.5 Excluding or prohibiting the use of evidence

Some of the rules restricting the use of evidence may look similar to equivalent common law rules of evidence; nevertheless, the manner in which they are applied and the way in which they influence the decision-making process differ substantially. It is important to recognise this in order to understand the scope of other evidential principles. Most continental European jurisdictions provide for a unitary trial structure, which means that the same judge is responsible for determining both whether the evidence can be used and for determining the criminal charge. It is true that trial by jury is practised in some legal systems in the context of some serious crimes. However, jury trials are sufficiently rare to be considered an exception to the general rule and even in such cases it is quite common for the judge to join the jury in deliberations.[79] Also of importance is the fact that the evidence is not, or not exclusively, presented directly at trial. Much of the evidence is heard and challenged during the investigation and is then recorded in the file, which is passed onto the judge or judges. The structure of the criminal proceedings means therefore that there is little room in the continental European context for notions of admissibility or for exclusionary rules in the sense that they are understood in common law countries. It is doubtful whether it is constructive to refer to 'exclusionary rules' in the context of systems in which all of the evidence must be heard by the judge or the fact-finder.[80] There can be little room for notions of admissibility if there is no separation between the judging and fact-finding roles.[81]

The exclusion of certain pieces of evidence suggests more than simply the fact that the evidence cannot be used. It implies further that the decision-maker does not know of the substance or content of the evidence. In a trial involving a judge and jury, the judge determines whether or not the evidence goes before the jury. If he or she decides that it is inadmissible, the jury will not be made aware of the content of the evidence. This not knowing is the essence of 'admissibility' and of 'exclusion'. As soon as the decision-maker knows the content of the evidence, these aspects are lost. The difference between knowing and not knowing the content of the evidence has been the subject of empirical research and there has been some suggestion that knowledge of the evidence which is to be excluded means that the judge will inevitably take this into account in the decision-making process. In one well-known study, Schünemann set out to assess whether the opportunity to view the files in advance of the trial had a substantial effect on the outcome of the case. Half of the judges in the study were

---

[79] E.g. in jury trials in the Canton of Zurich, prior to the introduction of the new Swiss Federal Code of Criminal Procedure, the jury deliberated together with the judge: see A. Donatsch and N. Schmid, *Kommentar zur Strafprozessordnung des Kantons Zürich* (Zurich: Schulthess, 2000) Arts. 198 ff.
[80] But see Bradley, 'The Exclusionary Rule'.
[81] See too Nijboer, 'Methods of Investigation', 434: 'I feel that admissibility is a concept that does not fit well in civil law systems.'

provided both with the file of the investigation phase and with the opportunity to conduct a trial hearing, while the other half could only rely on the trial hearing and did not receive the file. All seventeen judges who had received the file and had the chance to conduct a trial hearing convicted the accused, compared with just eight out of eighteen judges who had had to decide on the sole basis of the trial hearing.[82]

In view of such research, it is legitimate to question whether judges can really be expected to ignore evidence which they have already seen. It is also debatable whether the duty to provide a reasoned verdict can really be said to restrict a judge's discretion.[83] Although it enables scrutiny of the reasons for the judgement, and thus of the evidence that was relevant to the conviction, there is nevertheless the possibility that judges could disguise, be it knowingly or subconsciously, their reliance on evidence that they were not supposed to use. It is important to bear in mind, however, that this distinction is not just of relevance in relation to proceedings in continental European jurisdictions.[84] Even in common law legal systems, a considerable number of cases are disposed of by way of a judge sitting alone without a jury, although it may be the case that such judges consider their role to be that of a juror rather than, for instance, to ensure the accuracy of the verdict.[85]

In spite of this, it would be misleading merely to criticise the structure of the proceedings without recognising the importance attached to the role of the judge as a means of guaranteeing the accuracy of the verdict.[86] The rules aim to regulate the decision itself rather than the presentation of the evidence. In particular, they are specifically designed to restrict judicial discretion, while at the same time leaving judges with enough freedom to fulfil their role in personally overseeing and guaranteeing the determination of the charge.

In view of the importance of the principle that the judge be provided with all of the information relevant to the charge before making his or her decision, the fact that the judge knows of the evidence which he or she is not permitted

---

[82] B. Schünemann, 'Der Richter im Strafverfahren als manipulierter Dritter? Zur empirischen Bestätigung von Perseveranz- und Schulterschlusseffekt' (2000) 3 *Strafverteidiger* 159–65. See also C. Roxin and B. Schünemann, *Strafverfahrensrecht*, 26th edn (Munich: C. H. Beck, 2009) § 69 N 2. Some have also suggested that professional judges are more likely to convict more often than juries: see J. R. Spencer, 'Evidence', in M. Delmas Marty and J. R. Spencer (eds.), *European Criminal Procedures* (Cambridge University Press, 2002) 594.

[83] See, e.g. Bradley, 'The Exclusionary Rule', 1063.

[84] See, e.g. I. Dennis, *The Law of Evidence*, 4th edn (London: Sweet & Maxwell, 2010) para 1.19, who refers to the 'multiplicity of styles of legal proceedings'.

[85] See J. Jackson and S. Doran, *Judge without Jury: Diplock Trials in the Adversary System* (Oxford: Clarendon Press, 1995).

[86] See, e.g. Bradley, 'The Exclusionary Rule', 1064: 'If... the suppressed evidence is not obviously necessary to support a finding of guilt but is in reality the dispositive factor in the minds of the fact finders... defendants who should have been acquitted may be convicted nonetheless. This weakness is not a function of the exclusionary rules themselves, however, but rather of the structure of the trial process in Germany.'

to use need not only be seen as a 'weakness' of the process. It could equally be characterised as both deliberate and in keeping with the notion that judicial knowledge of all of the facts serves as a means of guaranteeing the accuracy of the conviction. An obvious consequence of the requirement that the judge be convinced of the guilt of the accused is that the judge is provided with all of the available evidence. The withholding of evidence from the judge would constitute an unacceptable interference with his or her discretion and would necessarily compromise the application of the principle. It would be difficult to see how the judge could take full personal and moral responsibility for a verdict when he or she was aware of the existence of other evidence which he or she had not received. The consequence of the rule requiring that the judge does not receive particular pieces of evidence would necessarily mean that this important decision as to the usability of the evidence would be taken by someone other than the judge. It is difficult to see how such a system could be reconciled with the notion that the judge be personally convinced of the accused person's guilt.

3.6 Recent developments in evidence law

In recent times, the importance of the judge's role in evaluating the evidence has been subject to several challenges, of which two in particular deserve special consideration. Firstly, the increasing use and significance of scientific and forensic expertise has given rise to questions about the ability of judges to deal with such evidence. This issue is of particular importance in many European jurisdictions, where the systemic bias in favour of court-appointed experts focuses attention on the dependence of the judge on expert witnesses. In most continental European legal systems, the investigating or prosecuting authorities are responsible for commissioning forensic expertise. In some legal systems, such as that of the Netherlands, government forensic institutes are only permitted to investigate cases when requested to do so by the police or justice authorities.[87] If the defence wishes to commission evidence, it must not only (usually) bear the costs of commissioning the expertise, it is also likely to encounter difficulties when attempting to recruit willing or able experts, particularly if it intends that they challenge the findings of the experts appointed by the justice authorities.[88] Even if the defence is able to commission its own expertise, there is no guarantee that the court will afford the same weight to this evidence as to that produced by the official forensic scientists.[89]

---

[87] L. Jakobs and W. Sprangers, 'Forensic Expertise and Counter Expertise', in Nijboer and Sprangers, *Harmonisation in Forensic Expertise*, 213 and 214.

[88] This has the potential to give rise to conflict with notions of adversarial proceedings or equality of arms. For detailed consideration of these principles, see Ch. 4.2.

[89] Jakobs and Sprangers, 'Forensic Expertise', 215. The ECtHR has considered these issues in cases such as *Bönisch* v. *Austria*, 6 May 1985, Series A no. 92; *Brandstetter* v. *Austria*, 28 August 1991, Series A no. 211; and *Mantovanelli* v. *France*, 18 March 1997, Reports 1997-II, 424.

It is frequently acknowledged that while judges are required to evaluate the expert evidence, most lack scientific knowledge and training in the context of interpreting scientific evidence and in particular statistical probabilities.[90] This inevitably leads to considerable reliance on the experts and calls into question the debate about whether the judge can truly be said to take personal responsibility for the correct determination of the verdict. Such concerns are clearly analogous to *Daubert*-inspired debates and scepticism about whether judges are in fact effective gatekeepers of scientific evidence if they are not equipped to apply *Daubert*-type criteria.[91] One way of addressing such concerns is to regulate the qualifications of those entitled to act as experts.[92] While such requirements are obviously important, it is equally important for the reliability of the evidence to be adequately tested by the fact-finder. It is not sufficient for the court merely to assume that the reliability of the evidence is automatically guaranteed by the status of the expert. Increasingly, European courts have held that judges must also consider such factors as the methods used by the expert, the reasons why he or she considers the method to be reliable and the competence of the expert in applying the specified methodology.[93] Some have argued that such standards are too weak and that the criteria ought to be expanded in order to assist the court in assessing the value of the scientific evidence. Particular criticism has been focused on the tendency of scientific experts, and of forensic psychiatrists and psychologists in particular, to take on a quasi-judicial role by assessing the value of the evidence.[94]

The importance of the judge's role in assuming responsibility for the charge has also been challenged by the changing structure of the investigation phase. The nature and form of the investigation phase differs significantly across the continent, not least in relation to the institutional status of the authority – be it the police, prosecutor, judge or investigation judge – charged with its supervision.[95] The relationship between the determination of the evidence and the structure of the investigation itself is especially significant in those countries, such as the Netherlands or Switzerland, where the evidence is heard

[90] On this issue, see, e.g. S. M. Solomon and E. J. Hackett, 'Setting Boundaries between Science and Law: Lessons from Daubert v. Merrell Dow Pharmaceuticals, Inc.' (1996) 21 *Science, Technology & Human Values* 131–56.
[91] For an examination of equivalent issues in common law systems and on the importance of the *Daubert* criteria in US law, see Ch. 2.4.2.
[92] See, e.g. the Austrian Law of 19 February 1975 über den allgemein beëideten gerichtlichen Sachverständigen und Dolmetscher and Arts. 157 and 167 of the French Code of Criminal Procedure.
[93] See, e.g. the judgment of the Dutch Supreme Court of 27 January 1998, *Nederlandse Jurisprudentie* 1998, 404.
[94] For a good overview of the problems in the context of psychological expertise and for suggestions on the types of criteria which the courts ought to apply, see P. van Koppen, 'How Psychologists Should Help Courts', in Nijboer and Sprangers, *Harmonisation in Forensic Expertise*, 257.
[95] For an interesting comparison of the Dutch, Swedish and Spanish models, see W. Perron, 'Auf dem Weg zu einem europäischen Ermittlungsverfahren?' (2000) 112 *Zeitschrift für die gesamte Strafrechtswissenschaft* 202, 211 ff.

and contested during the investigation phase, and rarely (directly) re-heard during the 'principal' proceedings.[96] Several commentators have identified a trend whereby the focal point of the criminal proceedings is continually moving forward. Aspects of the proceedings which were designed to take place at a later and, from a legal perspective, more differentiated stage in the proceedings are in fact taking place earlier in the context of widely under-regulated preliminary or investigatory proceedings.[97] The effect of this has been to increase the control and influence of the prosecuting and investigating authorities in relation to the evidence, thereby calling into question the power and authority of the judge.

3.7 Conclusion

An examination of the development of the laws of evidence and procedure demonstrate that in continental European jurisdictions there is little connection between the inquisitorial procedures of the past and the doctrine of free proof. Indeed, the latter seems to have been instituted, at least in part, in an attempt to rectify the weaknesses of the system caused by the procedural rules. Contrary to some beliefs, the doctrine of free proof does not grant the judge complete discretion to determine the charge; rather it denotes freedom from the former restrictive hierarchical rules of evidence. Restrictions on the evidence which can be used in the decision-making process do exist, but these are based on the notion of inclusion rather than exclusion. Consequently, extreme care must be taken when comparing these evidential rules with 'exclusionary'-type rules in common law jurisdictions. Although the rules themselves may appear very similar, their application cannot be divorced from the general theories of evidence in the systems in which they operate.

---

[96] P. Tak, 'Das Ermittlungsverfahren in den Niederlanden' (2000) 112 *Zeitschrift für die gesamte Strafrechtswissenschaft* 170, 184 ff; and Schmid, *Handbuch*, 338 ff.

[97] A. Eser, 'Strafverfahrensrecht in Europa' (1996) 108 *Zeitschrift für die gesamte Strafrechtswissenschaft* 86, 95. See also R. Miklau and W. Szymanski, 'Strafverfahrensreform und Sicherheitsbehörden – eine Nahtstelle zwischen Justiz- und Verwaltungsrecht', in W. Melnizky and O. F. Müller (eds.), *Strafrecht, Strafprozeßrecht und Kriminologie, Festschrift für Franz Pallin zum 80. Geburtstag* (Vienna: Manz Verlag, 1989) 249 and 254, who refer to a '*Kette von Vorverlagerungen*'; and M. Mérigeau, 'Frankreich', in A. Eser and B. Huber (eds.), *Strafrechtsentwicklung in Europa: Landesberichte über Gesetzgebung, Rechtsprechung und Literatur* (Freiburg i. Br.: Max-Planck-Institut für ausländisches und internationales Strafrecht, 1989) vol. 4.1, 467 and 505.

4

The international human rights context

4.1 Introduction

The previous chapters have drawn attention to the manner in which the common law and civil law traditions have adopted different approaches towards the regulation of evidence in criminal proceedings. Although we have seen that common beliefs in the importance of reaching accurate decisions and accommodating individual rights have underpinned each tradition, there was no conscious attempt to find common ground between the various systems until the second half of the twentieth century, when in the aftermath of the Second World War efforts were made to forge closer links between nations on the basis of shared rights and values. Since then, common principles of fairness have assumed considerable importance in the regulation of the process of proof in criminal proceedings. The development in the second half of the twentieth century of a number of international fair trial provisions forced states to reconsider their national evidential principles, and the values on which these were based, in the light of the right to a fair trial.

This reliance on fairness has not met with universal acceptance. Some have questioned whether fairness is the most satisfactory basis for a theory of the criminal process,[1] while others have drawn attention to the necessary limitations of framing fairness in terms of individual rights.[2] More recently, there has been considerable philosophical debate on the justification for human rights norms, such as the right to a fair trial.[3] Although human rights can be justified on the fundamental moral premises of autonomy and personhood,[4] it can be argued that certain rights such as the right to a fair trial can only be given meaning within the development of social practices and political

---

[1] A. Duff, L. Farmer, S. Marshall and V. Tadros, *The Trial on Trial (3): Towards a Normative Theory of the Criminal Trial* (Oxford: Hart, 2007) 108.
[2] See, e.g. in the context of the 'right' to a public trial, J. Jaconelli, 'Rights Theories and Public Trial' (1997) 14 *Journal of Applied Philosophy* 169–75.
[3] See generally S. Besson and J. Tasioulas (eds.), *The Philosophy of International Law* (Oxford University Press, 2010) section 8.
[4] See, e.g. J. Griffin, *On Human Rights* (Oxford University Press, 2008). Cf. J. Raz, 'Human Rights without Foundations', in Besson and Tasioulas, *Philosophy of International Law*, 321.

institutions.[5] Hence, just as we have seen that the notion of defence participation within the context of the criminal process may be better viewed as an institutional right or safeguard within a political system heavily weighted in favour of the state apparatus, so the right to a fair trial may be similarly better viewed as an 'institutional' right. Whatever the philosophical justifications, fairness is currently the principal frame of reference for regulating criminal proceedings.[6] The international bodies responsible for interpreting and applying the fair trial principles have amassed a considerable body of case law and this provides an ideal basis on which to reassess some of the major premises of comparative evidence law.[7]

The successful application of a generalised notion of procedural fairness to a variety of procedural systems, each with its own distinctive cultural and legal tradition, has important implications. The development of an international notion of fairness as a key criterion for the regulation of criminal proceedings implicitly challenges conventional assumptions about the classification of criminal procedural systems. The truly transformative nature of the fair trials case law has, however, been obscured by the continual reliance on the dualistic understanding of criminal proceedings as either inquisitorial or adversarial.[8] Although the bodies charged with interpreting and applying the various fair trials provisions commonly refer to 'adversarial' rights and principles, these conceptions do not match existing practices within the adversarial tradition and it is misleading to consider that these are leading to a convergence in the direction of traditional adversarial processes. Although it is difficult to identify the core features of these processes, they are commonly associated with one or more of the following characteristics: party control of the proof process, concentration on a climactic trial and reliance on oral testimony, trial by jury and exclusionary rules of evidence.[9] Yet we shall see that the contracting parties have not been required to adopt any of these practices. Instead, it will be argued that they are being required to realign their processes in accordance with what is better described as a new model of proof altogether, albeit one grounded in a particular procedural or institutional understanding of criminal proceedings. In this chapter, we will explore the principle of fairness developed in the case

---

[5] J. Tasioulas, 'The Moral Reality of Human Rights', in T. Pogge (ed.), *Freedom from Poverty as a Human Right: Who Owes What to the Very Poor* (Oxford University Press, 2007) 75.

[6] See also G. Maher, 'Natural Justice as Fairness', in D. N. McCormick and P. B. H. Birks (eds.), *The Legal Mind: Essays for Tony Honoré* (Oxford University Press, 1986) 103 and 110 (noting that fairness has been 'hailed as the "new" natural justice').

[7] See J. Jackson, 'The Adversary Trial and Trial by Judge Alone', in M. McConville and G. Wilson (eds.), *The Handbook of the Criminal Justice Process* (Oxford University Press, 2002) 335, 336.

[8] Findlay, for instance, refers to 'two broad and divergent Western criminal justice traditions': see M. Findlay, 'Synthesis in Trial Procedures? The Experience of the International Criminal Tribunals' (2001) 50 *International and Comparative Law Quarterly* 26.

[9] See J. Jackson, 'The Effects of Human Rights on Criminal Evidentiary Processes: Towards Convergence, Divergence or Realignment' (2005) 68 *Modern Law Review* 737, 742–4.

law of the international bodies and the impact of this notion on the procedural systems of the member states.

4.2 The evolution of evidentiary human rights norms

4.2.1 The right to a fair trial

A number of countries have long included within their constitutions a system of fundamental rights, but after the Second World War, 'a constitutional and civil rights revolution' occurred when these rights began to be enforced through judicial machinery at a national and international level.[10] States not only began to sign up to common human rights norms, they also acceded in various treaties to certain forms of review that would be exercised by international authorities. Thus, the Inter American Court has responsibility for applying the American Convention on Human Rights, the African Commission applies the African Charter on Human and Peoples' Rights and the UN Human Rights Committee applies the International Covenant on Civil and Political Rights. The most advanced example of supranational application of human rights norms, however, has been that of the European Convention on Human Rights by the (now abolished) European Commission of Human Rights (ECommHR) and by the European Court of Human Rights (ECtHR).[11]

Over a number of years these bodies have attempted to apply common standards to legal systems within the common law and civil law traditions. Although the ECtHR was established in 1959, it took some time for its judicial machinery to exert a material impact on the national legal systems of member countries because of the delay by a number of states in granting the right of individual petition to, and in accepting the jurisdiction of, the ECtHR. Today, however, it is estimated that taken together both the text of the European Convention and the case law of the ECommHR and ECtHR have inspired several hundred national constitutional court decisions.[12] The International Covenant also affords the right of individual petition,[13] but the majority of complainants able to choose between the bodies have opted for the ECtHR, principally because its judgments are legally binding and are generally perceived to have been more effectively implemented.[14] Consequently, the Strasbourg authorities have accumulated a considerable body of case law, unrivalled by that of the other international bodies, such as the Human Rights Committee

---

[10] M. Cappelletti, *The Judicial Process in Comparative Perspective* (Oxford: Clarendon Press, 1989) 207.
[11] The Commission was abolished in 1998 under Protocol 11 and the court now has sole jurisdiction to determine applications.
[12] M. Delmas-Marty, *Towards a Truly Common Law* (Cambridge University Press, 2002) 67.
[13] Art. 1 of the Optional Protocol to the International Covenant on Civil and Political Rights 1966.
[14] Cf. C. Phuong, 'The Relationship between the European Court of Human Rights and the Human Rights Committee: Has the Same Matter Already Been Examined?' (2007) 7 *Human Rights Law Review* 385.

(HRC).[15] The ECtHR's mandate spans the civilian and common law traditions and thus provides an ideal basis for examining attempts to create a cross-jurisdictional notion of procedural fairness. It is true that the Convention and ECtHR can hardly be said to have created a truly independent legal order, as their role has been merely to correct rather than supplant national legal norms, but it can be argued that this distinction has become blurred as the jurisprudence of the ECommHR and ECtHR has come to complete and enrich the often vague text of the Convention and in this manner arrive at a set of norms that increasingly seems to be that of a true supranational legal order.[16]

The key vehicle in the development of evidentiary human rights norms has been the fair trial right in Article 6 of the European Convention. The right to a fair trial finds its roots deep in the history of human rights and is given expression in the UN Universal Declaration of Human Rights.[17] Article 6(1) of the Convention contains a general definition of the right which closely follows Article 10 of the Declaration, while Article 6(2) enshrines the presumption of innocence which is contained in Article 11 of the Declaration. But Article 6 goes further than the Declaration by enumerating a number of other specific safeguards, including in Article 6(1) the right to be brought to trial within a reasonable time and in Article 6(3) a number of defence rights for those charged with a criminal offence, including the right to have adequate time and facilities for the preparation of the defence, the right to legal assistance, the right to examine or have examined witnesses against the defence and to obtain the attendance and examination of witnesses under the same conditions as prosecution witnesses.[18]

In many respects, the inclusion of these specific rights may be seen as a triumph for those British lawyers steeped in the common law tradition who argued against their civil law counterparts in favour of a more specific set of rights in preference to a mere restatement of the principles in the Universal Declaration. In his masterly account of the formation of the Convention, Simpson has shown how the final draft of the Convention was a compromise between civil law and common law approaches towards the protection of individual rights.[19] The civil

---

[15] In the period between 1955 and 1998, the Commission received a total of 128,000 applications. Since then, the number of cases received each year has continued to rise. In 2009, for instance, the court received a staggering 57,100 applications and had in the region of 119,000 pending cases: see European Court of Human Rights, *Annual Report 2009* (Strasbourg: Registry of the European Court of Human Rights, 2010) 139.

[16] Delmas-Marty, *Towards a Truly Common Law*, 63–4.

[17] A. H. Robertson and J. G. Merrills, *Human Rights in Europe*, 3rd edn (Manchester University Press, 1993) 87.

[18] These rights are also expressly set out in Art. 14(3) ICCPR, which also expressly guarantees the right of the accused not to testify against him or herself or to confess guilt: see further S. Trechsel, *Human Rights in Criminal Proceedings* (Oxford University Press, 2005) 340 ff; and D. Weissbrodt, *The Right to a Fair Trial under the Universal Declaration of Human Rights and the International Covenant on Civil and Political Rights* (The Hague: Martinus Nijhoff, 2001).

[19] A. W. B. Simpson, *Human Rights and the End of Empire* (Oxford University Press, 2001) chs. 13 and 14.

law approach favoured setting out the enumerated rights in brief general terms, leaving the detailed working out to be done by member states with a Court of Human Rights responsible for elaborating a jurisprudence of rights. The common law approach, on the other hand, was distrustful of bills of rights and reluctant to place its trust in the evolution of a jurisprudence derivative from very general principles of law. Instead, it put its weight behind a more precise specification of the rights and limitations to the rights and in the provision of effective remedies. The resulting compromise was one which appeared to favour both sides. On the one hand, the ultimate text that was agreed appeared to favour the common law approach of a more specific delineation of the rights than that outlined in the Universal Declaration.[20] On the other hand, the establishment of the ECommHR and ECtHR to enforce the rights was a victory for the civil law approach, albeit that the Convention did not require member states to accept either the right of individual petition or the jurisdiction of the ECtHR.

Taken at face value, the specific rights incorporated in Article 6 of the ECHR, drafted as they were largely by the British, not unnaturally appeared to favour an approach which had greater resonance in the common law than in civil law tradition. Although the right to a trial within a reasonable time has not been an independently recognised right in either tradition, the emphasis in Article 6(3) on the rights of the defence and in particular the concern to buttress the role of the parties in presenting and challenging evidence appears to give the Convention a decidedly adversarial mould.[21] Any victory which the common law tradition was able to claim from the enumeration of defence rights in the Convention, however, was over time reined back by the interpretation that came to be given to these rights by the ECommHR and the ECtHR in subsequent jurisprudence. Therefore, the very development resisted by the British at the time of the drafting of the Convention, namely that the rights would come to be interpreted by an international court with binding effect on national courts, was one that came to pass. In the process, some of the adversarial purity of the written text was sacrificed.

Although the ECommHR and ECtHR have emphasised that the right to a fair trial holds a prominent place in a democratic society with the result that Article 6 must be given a broad construction,[22] a number of limiting principles have taken hold to prevent the Strasbourg authorities being overprescriptive about the evidentiary procedures that should be adopted in the member states. Firstly, from the beginning the Commission established that

---

[20] For a useful account of the drafting process of the Universal Declaration and the ICCPR, see Weissbrodt, *The Right to a Fair Trial*.

[21] B. Swart and J. Young, 'The European Convention on Human Rights and Criminal Justice in the Netherlands and the UK', in P. Fennell, C. Harding, N. Jorg and B. Swart (eds.), *Criminal Justice in Europe: A Comparative Study* (Oxford: Clarendon Press, 1995) 57 and 84; J. F. Nijboer, 'Common Law Tradition in Evidence Scholarship Observed from a Continental Perspective' (1993) 41 *American Journal of Comparative Law* 299, 311; and J. F. Nijboer, 'Vision, Abstraction and Socio-Economic Reality' (1998) 49 *Hastings Law Journal* 387, 394.

[22] *Delcourt* v. *Belgium*; and *Moreira de Azevedo* v. *Portugal*, para. 66.

the Strasbourg authorities do not constitute a further court of appeal from the national courts.[23] This fourth instance doctrine together with the doctrine of the margin of appreciation has meant that the national courts are given considerable discretion concerning the evaluation of evidence. The Strasbourg authorities will only intervene if the judgment of the national court is found to be wholly arbitrary.[24] A similar approach has been adopted by the HRC, which has held that it is generally the task of the national courts to review facts and evidence, or the application of domestic law in a particular case, 'unless it can be shown that such an evaluation or application was clearly arbitrary or amounted to a manifest error or denial of justice'.[25]

Secondly, as a general principle, the member states enjoy considerable freedom in the choice of the appropriate means of ensuring that their judicial systems comply with the requirements of Article 6.[26] The ECtHR does not require states to adopt any particular rules governing the admissibility of evidence, although we shall see that it has embraced certain evidentiary principles that have had to be translated into national systems. Instead, it has considered that it is for the competent authorities to determine the relevance of proposed evidence and that rules on the admissibility of evidence are 'primarily a matter for regulation under national law'.[27] The ECtHR's unwillingness to prescribe rules of evidence or concepts such as admissibility was a clear signal that it had no wish to impose a common law system of evidence on member states. Likewise, the HRC has held that it is 'primarily for the domestic legislatures of the States parties to determine the admissibility of evidence and how their courts assess it'.[28]

Thirdly, the ECommHR and ECtHR both said at an early stage that their task is to determine whether they can be satisfied that the proceedings taken 'as a whole' were fair.[29] On the one hand, this has enabled the ECtHR to give an expansive interpretation to Article 6, and to hold that the rights accorded to

---

[23] *X* v. *FRG* (dec.), no. 254/57, 152. See further *Kemmache* v. *France (No. 3)*, para. 44. Other transnational courts have taken a similar approach: see, e.g. Inter-American Commission on Human Rights in *Juan Santaella Telleria and others* v. *Venezuela*, para. 40; for examples of distinctions between complaints understood to violate due process and those prevented from consideration by the fourth instance formula, see IACHR Annual Report 1990–91, Report 74/90, Case 9850, *Lopez Aurelli, Argentina*, para. 20.

[24] See, e.g. *Khamidov* v. *Russia*, para. 174; *Berhani* v. *Albania*, para. 50; and *Camilleri* v. *Malta* (dec.).

[25] See inter alia *Cuartero Casado* v. *Spain*, para. 4.3; *Riedl-Riedenstein and others* v. *Germany*, para. 7.3; *Mulai* v. *Republic of Guyana*; *Smartt* v. *Republic of Guyana*; *Arutyunyan* v. *Uzbekistan*; *Svetik* v. *Belarus*; *Martínez Muñoz* v. *Spain*; *Bochaton* v. *France*; *Arenz* v. *Germany*; *Ramil Rayos* v. *The Philippines*; *Errol Simms* v. *Jamaica*, para. 6.2; and *Serguey Romanov* v. *Ukraine*, para. 6.4.

[26] *Hadjianastassiou* v. *Greece*, para. 33.

[27] *Engel and others* v. *Netherlands*, para. 46; *Schenk* v. *Switzerland*; and *Delta* v. *France*, para. 35.

[28] Human Rights Committee, General Comment No. 32 [90]: *Article 14: Right to equality before the courts and tribunals and to a fair trial*, adopted on 27 July 2007, para. 39.

[29] *Nielsen* v. *Denmark* (report), 518; *Barberà, Messegué and Jabardo* v. *Spain*; and *Delta* v. *France*, para. 35. For criticism of the 'fairness as a whole' doctrine, see Trechsel, *Human Rights in Criminal Proceedings*, 87.

defendants in Article 6(2) and (3) are 'specific aspects of the general principle stated in paragraph 1 and are to be regarded as a non-exhaustive list of "minimum rights" which form constituent elements amongst others, of the notion of a fair trial in criminal proceedings'.[30] This expansionist principle has enabled the ECtHR to read other important protective rights into Article 6, such as the privilege against self-incrimination.[31] On the other hand, however, it has given the ECtHR a certain leeway to consider that it is not essential for the special rights to be respected in every case if measures restricting the rights of the defence are 'strictly necessary' and there are adequate compensatory measures taken to protect the accused at trial.[32] This has permitted inroads to be made by domestic jurisdictions into the specific rights, provided that the trial as a whole may be considered fair.[33] Finally, the ECtHR has given the Convention an evolutionary interpretation according to which the Convention is 'a living instrument which must be interpreted in the light of present day conditions'.[34] On the one hand, this has enabled some of the rights and principles developed under Article 6 to be given an expansionist interpretation in the light of present-day conditions; on the other hand, it has also enabled these to be balanced, as we shall see, against other competing concerns that come to dominate the criminal process landscape.

4.2.2 The equality of arms principle

These limiting principles have enabled the ECtHR to be quite flexible about the evidentiary principles and processes that are to be equated with Article 6, permitting it when necessary to depart from the straitjacket of the specific rights in Article 6(2) and (3) and to develop its own distinctive principles of fairness. Instead of adopting a fully-fledged adversarial position requiring party control over the presentation of evidence, the ECommHR and ECtHR from an early stage chose to develop the principle of 'equality of arms', an old principle with roots in both common law and civil law traditions.[35] It is a principle that has been expressed as affording every party to the proceedings 'a reasonable opportunity to present his case in conditions that do not place him at substantial disadvantage *vis-à-vis* his opponent'.[36] The principle does

---

[30] *Deweer* v. *Belgium*, para. 56.   [31] See, e.g. *Funke* v. *France*.
[32] See, e.g. *Van Mechelen* v. *Netherlands*, para. 58.
[33] See, e.g. *Brown* v. *Stott* [2001] 2 All ER 97.   [34] *Tyrer* v. *United Kingdom*, para. 31.
[35] The principle is an expression of the old natural law principle, *audi alteram partem*, which was first formulated by St Augustine: see J. R. Lucas, *On Justice* (Oxford: Clarendon Press, 1980) 84. A number of commentators have questioned whether there can in fact be any room for a notion of equality of arms in criminal proceedings: see, e.g. Trechsel, *Human Rights in Criminal Proceedings*, 96; M. Wąsek-Wiaderek, *The Principle of Equality of Arms in Criminal Procedure under Article 6 of the European Convention on Human Rights and its Function in Criminal Justice of Selected European Countries: A Comparative View* (Leuven University Press, 2000) 50.
[36] *Kaufman* v. *Belgium* (dec.), 115; and *Foucher* v. *France*, para. 34. The HRC has also interpreted Art. 14(1) of the ICCPR as requiring equality of arms between the parties: see, e.g. *Robinson* v. *Jamaica*, paras. 10.4 ff; *Guesdon* v. *France*, para. 10.2: 'The Committee observes, as it has done

not guarantee specific rights or procedural opportunities as such, rather it is charged with preventing substantial procedural imbalance between the parties. Although this principle was enunciated early on in the jurisprudence of the ECommHR and ECtHR,[37] it has undergone development and refinement over the years. In 1970, for instance, the ECtHR upheld an old Belgian practice whereby the *procureur général* would retire with the court having expressed a view as to whether the appellant's appeal should be heard.[38] Over 20 years later, however, the ECtHR reached a different conclusion. Once the *procureur général* had expressed an opinion on the merits of the appeal, he became the applicant's opponent and the *procureur général*'s participation in the private deliberations of the court gave him an unfair advantage over the appellant.[39] In emphasising the importance of the appearance of justice, the ECtHR drew attention to the increased sensitivity of the public to the fair administration of justice. This emphasis on the importance of equal participation by the parties has underlined the necessity of distinguishing between those responsible for prosecuting or appearing to be prosecuting and those responsible for judging and, in doing so, has broken with the old continental practices which tended to blur the distinction. We see here a clear connection between the equality of arms principle and the requirement of judicial impartiality. The ECtHR has recently confirmed that the failure of the prosecutor to appear at trial, at which the evidence is contested, will inevitably result in some confusion between the functions of prosecuting and judging and will violate Article 6(1).[40]

It is not only equality in presenting arguments that is required, but also equality in being able to present evidence.[41] Thus, in *Bönisch* v. *Austria*, a court-appointed expert provided a report that meat prepared by the applicant contained an excessive concentration of a carcinogenic substance called bezopyrene.[42] The ECtHR considered that he was more like a witness against the accused than an impartial expert. As a court witness, he could attend the hearings, put questions to the accused and to witnesses with the leave of the court, and comment on the evidence. Since he was given much greater control over the proceedings than a defence expert witness would have been given, Bönisch had not been accorded equal treatment.[43]

In some of the case law, the principle seems to have been interpreted as going beyond ensuring that the parties are accorded a formal equality during the presentation of evidence at the trial and appeals process. In order to be able to contest on equal terms, the ECommHR and ECtHR suggested in some of the older case law that as a result of the disparity in the resources between

on a previous occasion, that article 14 is concerned with procedural equality; it enshrines *inter alia*, the principle of equality of arms in criminal proceedings'; and *Dudko* v. *Australia*, para. 7.4.

[37] See, e.g. *X* v. *FRG* (dec.), no. 254/57, 16 December 1957, 1 YB 150. [38] *Delcourt* v. *Belgium*.
[39] *Borgers* v. *Belgium*.   [40] *Ozerov* v. *Russia*, paras. 53–5.
[41] *Ruiz-Mateos* v. *Spain*, paras. 61–3.   [42] *Bönisch* v. *Austria*.
[43] See also the cases of *Brandstetter* v. *Austria*, and *Dombo Beeher BV* v. *Netherlands*.

prosecution and defence, the principle of the equality of arms requires that the facilities which everyone charged with a criminal offence should enjoy under Article 6(3)(b) include the right of the accused to have at his disposal all relevant information that has been or could be collected by the competent authorities.[44] The Strasbourg authorities have here recognised the disparity of resources between prosecution and defence. Since the prosecution enjoys considerable facilities derived from its powers of investigation, equality demands that the results of these investigations be shared with the defence.

This notion of considering whether all relevant information in the possession of the prosecution has been properly disclosed to the defence not only stretches the notion of equality away from formality towards a more substantive inquiry, it also broadens the scope of the inquiry from the trial towards pre-trial procedures. When we discuss the disclosure of evidence in Chapter 9, we shall see that this is not a notion that has been applied evenly within the common law and civil law tradition. In continental eyes, the principle of disclosure of evidence through a shared dossier which is constructed by judicial or prosecutorial officials charged with gathering evidence, in favour of as well as against the accused, is an essential condition to be met before the defence can have any chance of gaining equality of arms or indeed of the 'adversarial rights' that we shall discuss below.[45] But the notion of sharing information is not so easy to assimilate into the common law tradition, with its emphasis on each side gathering and presenting its 'own' evidence. Although the ECtHR has claimed that the requirement of fairness under Article 6 that the prosecution authorities disclose to the defence all material evidence for or against the accused is one which is recognised under English law,[46] this is not a principle that has been deeply embedded in the English tradition. It is true that the notion of inspecting the depositions on which the accused was to be committed for trial dates back to the nineteenth century,[47] but it has taken much longer for the principle of disclosure of prosecution material which does not form part of the case against the accused to be accepted.[48] Even today, the notion that evidence is used by one side or the other rather than shared is retained in the idea of two sides holding on to 'their' evidence unless required to do so by rules of disclosure. We shall see that English procedure has fallen foul of the ECtHR on issues of disclosure in a number of cases.[49] Disclosure is now governed by a statutory regime which determines what material needs to be disclosed by each side.[50] But it has been pointed out that it falls short of European jurisprudence both in failing to require the prosecution to disclose all material evidence and in failing

---

[44] *Jespers* v. *Belgium* (report).   [45] *Jespers* v. *Belgium* (report), paras. 87–8.
[46] *Edwards* v. *United Kingdom*, para. 36.
[47] P. Devlin, *The Criminal Prosecution in England* (London: Stevens, 1960) 6.
[48] See *R* v. *Ward* (1993) 1 WLR 619.
[49] See, e.g. *Rowe and Davis* v. *United Kingdom*; *Atlan* v. *United Kingdom*; and *Edwards and Lewis* v. *United Kingdom* [GC].
[50] See Criminal Procedure and Investigations Act 1996.

to provide the defence with adequate access to judicial review.[51] Besides, the disclosure obligations only come into play at the stage when a case has been investigated. There is no obligation on the prosecution to disclose information while investigations are ongoing.[52]

Despite the significance that the principle of the equality of arms attaches to party information and party presentation, however, there are limitations in regarding it as an adversarial principle.[53] Towards the end of the 1980s, the ECtHR began to develop the right to be heard and to refer not just to the principle of equality of arms, but also to the principle that 'all the evidence must be produced in the presence of the accused at a public hearing with a view to adversarial argument'.[54] The distinction between these principles is not always apparent or indeed clearly set out in the case law. The equality of arms is best understood as requiring a balance of procedural opportunities between defence and prosecution, while the adversarial proceeding requirement embodies the various elements of the right to be heard.

4.2.3 The right to an adversarial trial

In a number of decisions, the Strasbourg authorities have ruled that the right to an adversarial trial requires, in a criminal case, that the prosecution and defence be given the opportunity to have knowledge and comment on the observations filed and the evidence adduced by the other party.[55] It is important to see, however, that in developing this adversarial right, the ECtHR falls short of prescribing the kind of adversarial trial that is associated with common law jurisdictions where procedural control is largely in the hands of the parties rather than the judge. Under the label of *une procédure contradictoire*, it has long been considered important in continental procedure that the defendant should be present when procedural activities are under way and should be entitled to offer counter-proofs and counter-arguments.[56] The Commission and ECtHR sought to 'translate' the defence rights prescribed in Article 6 into a vision of adversarialism that was as compatible with the continental notion of *une procédure contradictoire* as with the common law adversary trial. Defendants

---

[51] S. D. Sharpe, 'Article 6 and the Disclosure of Evidence in Criminal Cases' [1999] *Criminal Law Review* 273. New changes to the regime enacted in the Criminal Justice Act 2003 have remedied some of these defects. See M. Redmayne, 'Criminal Justice Act 2003: Disclosure and its Discontents' [2004] *Criminal Law Review* 441, 444–5. See further Ch. 9.

[52] See J. Spencer, 'Evidence', in M. Delmas-Marty and J. Spencer (eds.), *European Criminal Procedures* (Cambridge University Press, 2002) 594, 632.

[53] See, e.g. *Feldbrugge* v. *Netherlands*; and *Monnell and Morris* v. *United Kingdom*, para. 62: no violation of the equality of arms principle, as although the defence was not permitted to attend the hearing, the prosecution was similarly absent.

[54] *Barberà, Messegué and Jabardo* v. *Spain*, para. 78.

[55] *Brandstetter* v. *Austria*, para. 67; and *Rowe and Davis* v. *United Kingdom*, para. 60.

[56] M. Damaška, 'Evidentiary Barriers to Conviction and Two Models of Criminal Procedure: A Comparative Study' (1973) 21 *University of Pennsylvania Law Review* 506, 561.

have to be guaranteed rights to legal representation, a right to be informed of all information relevant to the proceedings, a right to be present and to present arguments and evidence at trial.[57] But this does not rule out considerable participation by judges in asking questions or even calling witnesses.

The Strasbourg authorities have not self-consciously tried to squeeze the Article 6 defence rights into a continental mould and imposed this across the contracting states. The one right that would seem to stretch the notion of *une procédure contradictoire* is the right to examine witnesses, expressly safeguarded in Article 6(3)(d) of the ECHR. In a series of judgments beginning in 1986,[58] the ECtHR began to interpret Article 6(3)(d) to mean that convictions should not be substantially based upon the statements of witnesses whom the defence were unable to cross-examine. There would seem to be little doubt that these decisions, although not always consistent with one another,[59] were a major factor in some of the changes that began to take effect in a number of continental jurisdictions which were more firmly associated with the old inquisitorial tradition.[60]

As a result of the decision in *Kostovski v. Netherlands*, for example, in which the ECtHR ruled that there was a breach of Article 6 where the conviction was based to a decisive extent on the statements of two anonymous witnesses who gave evidence in the absence of the accused,[61] the Dutch Supreme Court was forced to retreat from earlier case law that had permitted the use of anonymous hearsay evidence and the Code of Criminal Procedure was amended in 1993 to restrict the use of anonymous witnesses.[62] In France, the Court of Cassation held that Article 6(3)(d) requires the trial court to grant the defendant's request to summon and question a witness unless the witness is clearly unavailable, or his testimony would be irrelevant, or the accused has had an adequate opportunity to confront and question the witness in prior proceedings, or there is a serious

---

[57] See, e.g. *Stanford* v. *United Kingdom*, para. 26; see also S. J. Summers, *Fair Trials: The European Criminal Procedural Tradition and the European Court of Human Rights* (Oxford: Hart, 2007) 112–23; and Trechsel, *Human Rights in Criminal Proceedings*, 89–94.

[58] See, e.g. *Unterpertinger* v. *Austria*, 24 November 1986, Series A no. 110; *Kostovski* v. *Netherlands*; *Windisch* v. *Austria*; and *Delta* v. *France*.

[59] Although the court has generally considered that cross-examination must be permitted where the evidence plays a substantial, decisive or main part in the conviction, on occasions it has varied this standard, narrowing it at times to apply where the evidence is the only item of evidence (see, e.g. *Asch* v. *Austria* and *Artner* v. *Austria*) and widening it in other cases to apply where the evidence has 'played a part' in the conviction (see, e.g. *Lüdi* v. *Switzerland*). See D. J. Harris, M. O'Boyle, E. P. Bates and C. M. Buckley, *Harris, O'Boyle and Warbrick: Law of the European Convention on Human Rights*, 2nd edn (Oxford University Press, 2009) 324.

[60] Nijboer has singled out Spain, France, Belgium and the Netherlands in this category: Nijboer, 'Common Law Tradition', 311. See also M. Chiavario, 'The Rights of the Defendant and the Victim', in Delmas-Marty and Spencer, *European Criminal Procedures*, 548.

[61] 20 November 1989, Series A no. 166.

[62] See P. T. C. Van Kampen, *Expert Evidence Compared: Rules and Practices in the Dutch and American Criminal Justice System* (Antwerpen and Groningen: Intersentia Rechswetenschappen, 1998) 105–6; and L. F. Zwaak, 'The Netherlands', in R. Blackburn and J. Polakiewicz (eds.), *Fundamental Rights in European Law* (Oxford University Press, 2001).

risk of witness intimidation or retaliation.[63] The adversarial defence rights in Article 6 had a strong influence upon the Delmas-Marty Commission, which proposed that a list of basic principles should be placed at the head of a new code of criminal procedure and in reforms in 2000 the principle that criminal procedure should be fair and '*contradictoire*' was given pride of place in the list of guiding principles.[64] In Italy, the new code of criminal procedure in 1988 gave expression to these principles and Article 111 of the Italian Constitution was amended to provide that every trial should be based on giving the parties the right to offer counter-proofs and counter-arguments against unfavourable evidence (including *contradittorio tra le partii*) on an equal standing in front of an impartial judge.[65]

Although the ECtHR seems to have played a significant role in prompting these changes, it again failed to prescribe the need for anything like a fully-fledged common law adversarial trial.[66] Firstly, as we have seen, the ECtHR has steered well clear of imposing any common law concepts on member states such as the notion of admissibility or hearsay. It has put much more emphasis on the *use* that is made of evidence than on the question of its admissibility as evidence. Thus, in the first major decision on Article 6(3)(d), the ECtHR stressed that in itself the reading out of statements cannot be regarded as inconsistent with Article 6, but the *use* made of the statements as evidence must nevertheless comply with the rights of the defence.[67]

Secondly, it would seem that it is not necessary for the right to examine witnesses to be exercised at the trial.[68] The Human Rights Committee has adopted a similar approach, emphasising that the defence must have the opportunity to question the witness at some stage in the proceedings.[69] This again is an illustration of accommodation of a civil law approach which has been much more receptive towards the idea of reviewing, or even contesting, evidence before the trial.[70] So long as opportunities exist for challenging witnesses before trial,

---

[63] J. Pradel, 'France', in C. van den Wyngaert (ed.), *Criminal Procedure Systems in the European Community* (London: Butterworths, 1993) 120.

[64] See V. Dervieux, 'The French System', in Delmas-Marty and Spencer, *European Criminal Procedures*, 218, 220–2.

[65] A. Perrodet, 'The Italian System', in Delmas-Marty and Spencer, *European Criminal Procedures*, 348, 368–9.

[66] J. Spencer, 'Introduction', in Delmas-Marty and Spencer, *European Criminal Procedures*, 45.

[67] *Unterpertinger* v. *Austria*, 24 November 1986, Series A no. 110, para. 31 (emphasis added). See further Ch. 10.3.2.1.

[68] *Kostovski* v. *Netherlands*, para. 41.

[69] '[Article 14(3)(e)] does not, however, provide an unlimited right to obtain the attendance of any witness requested by the accused or their counsel, but only a right to have witnesses admitted that are relevant for the defence, and to be given a proper opportunity to question and challenge witnesses against them *at some stage of the proceedings*' (emphasis added), Human Rights Committee, General Comment No. 32 [90], para. 39.

[70] In Switzerland, the defence is usually restricted to challenging witness evidence during the investigation phase: see N. Schmid, *Handbuch des schweizerischen Strafprozessrechts* (Zurich:

the absence of an opportunity to examine these witnesses at trial is not fatal to compliance with Article 6 standards. This would seem to presuppose some level of judicial supervision of the pre-trial or investigation phase, not least because the defence would seem to be put at a significant disadvantage if the prosecution authorities were to have principal responsibility for conducting the examination of the witnesses. This can pose difficulties for common law processes where there is no properly organised pre-trial phase of procedure which takes place under judicial control at which witnesses may be examined.[71] Where vital witnesses become unavailable at trial and there has been no pre-trial opportunity for cross-examination, the European jurisprudence suggests that prosecution cases may fail in the absence of other evidence against the accused. Within the common law tradition, where there is considerable attachment to the concentrated trial, any dilution of the right to an adversarial trial such as the relegation of the right to examine witnesses to the investigatory stage of the criminal process is viewed with disapproval. The examination will not then be heard in public and the trial court is deprived of the chance to observe the demeanour of the witnesses and form its own impression of their reliability.[72] From this perspective, the defence should be entitled to examine witnesses where possible at trial, although where this proves impossible the fact that the defendant had a right to challenge the witness at the investigatory stage is a relevant fact when considering whether it is fair to rely on the witness's deposition as evidence at the trial.[73]

Thirdly, not all witnesses need to be examined on the defence's request in order to meet the fair trial standards of Article 6. In some cases, the ECtHR would seem to have taken into account the difficulty in producing witnesses at the trial where they have gone missing or where the witnesses exercise their right not to testify.[74] In these instances the ECtHR will look for any compensating safeguards, which might include the fact that the witness has already been questioned by a judge or that the defence have had an opportunity to view the demeanour of the witness or an opportunity to cast doubt on the witness's credibility.[75] Another relevant factor would seem to have been the impact of the witness evidence in question upon the conviction. Even where there has been no justification for the failure to comply with the requirements of Article 6(3)(d),

---

Dike, 2009) 345 ff. Note, however, that the German immediacy principle attempts to put a fetter on the use of derivative sources at trial by restricting the use of hearsay evidence when better sources of information are easily accessible. For an explanation of this principle, see M. R. Damaška, 'Of Hearsay and its Analogues' (1992) 76 *Minnesota Law Review* 425.

[71] J. Spencer, 'French and English Criminal Procedure: A Brief Comparison', in B. S. Markesinis (ed.), *The Gradual Convergence* (Oxford: Clarendon Press, 1994) 33.

[72] See, e.g. the comments in *R* v. *Horncastle and others* [2009] UKSC 14, para. 75.   [73] Ibid.

[74] See, e.g. *Asch* v. *Austria* and *Artner* v. *Austria*; see B. Emmerson, A. Ashworth and A. Macdonald, *Human Rights and Criminal Justice*, 2nd edn (London: Sweet & Maxwell, 2007) para. 5–128.

[75] *Van Mechelen* v. *Netherlands*, para. 62.

the ECtHR has tended to emphasise the importance of the evidence being the 'main',[76] 'decisive',[77] 'only'[78] or 'sole'[79] basis for the conviction in coming to a determination that the trial has been unfair.

This suggests that the ECtHR has construed the right as much to accommodate continental systems of justice traditionally unused to giving the defence a right to examine witnesses as much as common law systems. Indeed, the emphasis on the importance of an assessment being made of the significance of the evidence suggests that it is common law judges who are being asked to change their approach towards evidence as much as their civil law counterparts. Judges in the common law tradition are used to ruling on the admissibility of evidence in a piecemeal, 'atomistic' manner, although once the prosecution case is completed, they have had a role in screening out weak cases before factual disputes are sent to the jury for decision. By contrast, the ECtHR has considered that a much more 'holistic' approach needs to be taken towards the evidence by considering how decisive or substantial the unexamined witness evidence is to the case as a whole.[80] This requires that judges are in a position to make some assessment of the strength of the other evidence against the accused and would seem to require a considerable change of perspective and practice in the English criminal process.[81] It would seem to mark a shift away from the traditional focus on deciding on the admissibility of evidence on a piece-by-piece basis towards considering whether there are sufficient grounds under Article 6 for sending a case to the jury. Judgments of sufficiency require a more probing assessment of the evidence as whole than the traditional approach taken at the end of the prosecution case, which has been to consider whether *on one possible view* of the facts there is evidence on which a jury could conclude that the defendant is guilty.[82] This in turn points towards a more active fact-finding role for the common law judge. The trial judge is there not just to referee a contest in the traditional common law mould, making atomistic rulings of evidence, but also to take a more proactive and dominant role in the proceedings in deciding whether fairness requires that particular witnesses need to be examined.[83]

The upshot of all this is that the adversarial principle of defence examination of witnesses has been accommodated by the ECtHR to meet continental processes without too much disturbance. Although the right to examine witnesses

---

[76] *Unterpertinger* v. *Austria*, 24 November 1986, Series A no. 110, para. 33.
[77] *Kostovski* v. *Netherlands*, para. 44.
[78] *Asch* v. *Austria*, para. 30; and *Artner* v. *Austria*, para. 24.   [79] *Saïdi* v. *France*, para. 44.
[80] For the contrast between 'atomistic' and 'holistic' approaches to evidence, see M. Damaška, 'Atomistic and Holistic Evaluation of Evidence', in R. Clark (ed.), *Comparative and Private International Law: Essays in Honour of John Merryman* (Berlin: Duncken and Humblot, 1990).
[81] A. Ashworth, 'Article 6 and the Fairness of Trials' [1999] *Criminal Law Review* 261, 272.
[82] *R* v. *Galbraith* [1981] 1 WLR 1039.
[83] J. Jackson, 'The Impact of Human Rights on Judicial Decision Making', in S. Doran and J. Jackson (eds.), *The Judicial Role in Criminal Proceedings* (Oxford: Hart, 2000) 109, 118. See too *Cuscani* v. *United Kingdom*, para. 39, where the judge is referred to as the 'ultimate guardian of the fairness of the proceedings'.

would seem to have stretched the continental notion of *une procédure contradictoire* beyond its traditional boundaries, this right has not required any full-scale transition towards a party-controlled trial. Indeed, so great has been the accommodation that it may be argued that traditional common law approaches, so long associated with the adversarial right of cross-examination,[84] have been as much disturbed by the ECtHR's jurisprudence as civil law traditions. So long as the need to consider the impact of the unexamined evidence on the case as a whole is restricted to determining whether an unjustified failure to permit the defence to examine witnesses makes the trial as a whole unfair, the effect on the common law tradition may not in practice be very marked, as such evidence would likely be excluded from the trial in the first place. Rules such as the hearsay rule have been developed in common law jurisdictions precisely to maintain the supremacy of oral examination of witnesses, with exceptions allowed only where admission of statements is justified out of necessity.[85] It has been suggested that in almost all of the cases where the ECtHR has held that there has been a violation of Article 6(1) taken together with Article 6(3)(d) of the ECHR on the ground of a failure to permit the defence to examine witnesses, the evidence in question would have been ruled inadmissible under common law hearsay rules.[86]

But in more recent cases, the ECtHR would seem to have given greater emphasis to the importance of determining whether unexamined evidence is the sole or decisive evidence in the case by suggesting that *even when there is a justification for not calling a witness*, because the witness is genuinely unable to give evidence orally, for example, basing a conviction solely or decisively on the evidence would be unfair.[87] In *Doorson* v. *Netherlands*,[88] the ECtHR considered that even when counterbalancing procedures were found to compensate sufficiently the handicaps under which the defence laboured, 'a conviction should not be based either solely or to a decisive extent on anonymous statements'. Later, in *Lucà* v. *Italy*,[89] the ECtHR considered that where a conviction is based solely or to a decisive degree on depositions that have been made by a person whom the accused has had no opportunity to examine or have examined, whether during the investigation or at trial, the rights of the defence are restricted to an extent that is incompatible with the guarantees provided by Article 6.

This change of approach has brought the Strasbourg jurisprudence directly into a collision course with the common law tradition, for not only does it

---

[84] J. Langbein, *The Origins of Adversary Criminal Trial* (Oxford University Press, 2003).
[85] See further Ch. 2.
[86] See *R* v. *Horncastle and others* [2009] UKSC 14, para. 93. A meticulous analysis of the cases in which the Strasbourg court has held that Art. 6(1) taken together with Art. 6(3)(d) has been violated comparing what would have been the outcome in English domestic law is provided by Lord Judge in Annex 4 of the judgment. Lord Phillips concluded that 'the cases suggest that in general our rules of admissibility provide the defendant with at least equal protection to that provided under the continental system', para. 93.
[87] See the observations of Lord Phillips in *Horncastle and others*, para. 77.
[88] Para. 76.
[89] Para. 40.

require judges to adopt a different, more holistic approach towards the assessment of evidence; it also would seem to require them in the interests of fairness to prevent juries acting on certain evidence which under domestic law might be deemed admissible in the interests of justice. In certain recent cases, the English Court of Appeal and the UK Supreme Court (UKSC) have made clear their disapproval of any absolute sole or decisive evidence rule governing the question of whether Article 6 rights have been infringed. The exchange with Strasbourg can be traced to a domestic case where it was alleged that the main witnesses in the case had been kept out of the way by fear resulting from the conduct of the defendant.[90] The Court of Appeal asked whether if the ECtHR were faced with an identified witness well known to the defendant who was the sole witness of a murder and had been kept away by the defendant, or by a person acting for him, it would hold that there were no 'counterbalancing' measures which could be taken to allow the witness's statement to be read. The Court of Appeal continued:

> If care had been taken to see that the quality of the evidence was compelling, if firm steps were taken to draw the jury's attention to aspects of that witness's credibility and if a clear direction was given to the jury to exercise caution, we cannot think that the European Court would nevertheless hold that a defendant's article 6 rights had been infringed.[91]

In the later case of *Al-Khawaja and Tahery* v. *United Kingdom*, the ECtHR conceded that there were special circumstances involved in this kind of case, but in the absence of such circumstances the court doubted whether any counterbalancing factors would be sufficient to justify the introduction in evidence of an untested statement which was the sole or decisive basis for the conviction of the applicant.[92] This judgment flatly contradicted the English Court of Appeal judgment in the *Al-Khawaja* case, which considered that where a witness who is the sole witness of a crime has made a statement to be used in prosecution and has since died, there may be a strong public interest in the admission of the statement in evidence so that the prosecution may proceed.[93] The provision in Article 6(3)(d) of the ECHR that a person charged shall be able to have the witnesses against him examined was one specific aspect of a fair trial: but if the opportunity was not provided, the question was 'whether the proceedings *as a whole*, including the way the evidence was taken, were fair'.[94] In *R*. v. *Horncastle and others*,[95] the Court of Appeal had the occasion to reflect upon the position it had adopted in *Al-Khawaja* in the light of the Strasbourg ruling in *Al-Khawaja and Tahery*, but it was unrepentant. It considered that some divergence of view as to the application of the European Convention was unavoidable, but reiterated its position that there was no breach of Article 6 if

---

[90] *R* v. *Sellick* [2005] 2 Cr App R 15.   [91] *R* v. *Sellick*, para. 52.   [92] Paras. 37–8.
[93] *R* v. *Al-Khawaja* [2005] EWCA Crim 2697.   [94] *R* v. *Al-Khawaja*, para. 26 (emphasis added).
[95] [2009] EWCA Crim 964.

a conviction was based solely or to a decisive degree on hearsay evidence that was admitted under the Criminal Justice Act 2003 which had codified the law governing the admissibility of hearsay evidence in English law.

This position was endorsed in a seven-judge ruling of the UKSC.[96] Giving the sole and unanimous judgment of the court, Lord Phillips considered that the critical question in the case of either absent or anonymous witnesses was whether the demands of fair trial require that a sole or decisive test should apply regardless of the particular circumstances and in particular regardless of the cogency of the evidence.[97] In each case the court answered with a resounding 'No'. One of the reasons why the English Court of Appeal and the UKSC in *Horncastle* were so critical of the sole or decisive evidence test was that it would give rise to a number of practical difficulties of application under the common law system. One of the difficulties was to determine what was meant by 'decisive' evidence. According to Lord Phillips, '[i]n theory any item of probative evidence may make all the difference between conviction and acquittal' as '[i]t may be the vital piece of evidence which tilts the scales enough to satisfy the tribunal beyond reasonable doubt that the defendant is guilty'.[98] Determining whether the evidence is decisive is a difficult enough task for a professionally trained judge. But in the common law context where there is a jury, 'a direction to a jury that they can have regard to a witness statement as supporting evidence but not as decisive evidence would involve them in mental gymnastics few would be equipped to perform'.[99] The only practical way to apply the sole or decisive test in a jury trial would be for the judge to rule inadmissible any statement capable of proving decisive – no easy task again, however, as any evidence may be capable of making the difference between a finding of guilt or innocence.

Apart from the difficulties of application, the UKSC considered that the test was unnecessary against the background of the code enacted in the Criminal Justice Act 2003, which was 'informed by experience accumulated over generations and represents the product of concentrated consideration by experts of how the balance should be struck between the many competing interests affected'.[100] In their lordships' view, the jurisprudence of the ECtHR in relation to Article 6(3)(d) had developed largely in cases relating to civil law rather than common law jurisdictions and this was particularly true of the sole or decisive rule. Their lordships considered that the sole or decisive evidence test was developed by the ECtHR on the premise that a conviction based solely or decisively upon the evidence of a witness who has not been subjected to cross-examination would not be safe, but it was developed without full consideration of the safeguards against an unfair trial that exist under common law procedure. Long before 1953, when the European Convention on Human Rights came into force, the common law had by the hearsay rule addressed that aspect of a fair trial that Article 6(3)(d) was designed to ensure. Both in the case of unavailable

[96] [2010] 2 WLR 47; [2009] UKSC 14. [97] Ibid., para. 50. [98] Ibid., para. 88.
[99] Ibid., para. 90. [100] Ibid., para. 29.

witnesses and in the case of apparently reliable hearsay, the Criminal Justice Act 2003 now contained a crafted code intended to ensure that evidence is admitted only when it was fair that it should be. The judgment concluded that:

> In these circumstances... it would not be right for this court to hold that the sole or decisive test should have been applied rather than the provisions of the 2003 Act, interpreted in accordance with their natural meaning... [T]hose provisions strike the right balance between the imperative that a trial must be fair and the interests of victims in particular and society in general that a criminal should not be immune from conviction where a witness, who has given critical evidence in a statement that can be shown to be reliable, dies or cannot be called to give evidence for some other reason.

We shall examine the sole or decisive evidence test in greater detail in Chapter 10 and consider the justification for it against the background of the rationalist and individual rights traditions that have dominated the development of evidence law in both common law and civil law traditions. For now, two points may be made. Firstly, it may be pointed out that this disagreement between domestic courts and the ECtHR on the application of the particular right to examine witnesses serves as an example of the difficulties faced by the ECtHR in attempting to fashion standards that are acceptable in both common law and civil law systems. A rule that is fashioned to deal with a mischief in one set of systems – namely, a tendency in the civil law tradition to depend unduly upon written depositions and to encourage important witnesses to be questioned at some point in the proceedings by the defence – may not sit easily within another set of systems that have well-established rules of evidence for encouraging the questioning of witnesses in a concentrated trial before a lay jury, while allowing their statements to be read when they are unavailable to give evidence in this forum and there are sufficient guarantees to suggest that such statements are reliable.

The second point, however, is that both the domestic courts and the ECtHR have approached this disagreement in a spirit of respectful dialogue, leaving room for a consensus to be reached in the end.[101] The UKSC emphasised that it had taken careful note of the Strasbourg jurisprudence, as indeed it was bound to do.[102] It would also be wrong to neglect the degree of consensus already achieved over the importance to be given to the right to cross-examine witnesses. In the earlier case of *R. v. Sellick*,[103] which first exposed the tensions between an absolute sole or decisive rule and UK hearsay law, the English Court

---

[101] Lord Kerr, 'The Conversation between Strasbourg and National Courts – Dialogue or Dictation?' (2009) 44 *Irish Jurist (new series)* 1.
[102] See s. 2 of the UK Human Rights Act 1998, providing that a court or tribunal determining a question which has arisen in connection with a convention right must take into account any judgment, decision, declaration or advisory opinion of the ECtHR so far as, in the opinion of the court, it is relevant to the proceedings.
[103] *R v. Sellick* [2005] 2 Cr App R 15, para. 50, per Waller LJ.

of Appeal set out a number of propositions that had been developed by the ECtHR on which it expressed no disagreement:

(1) The admissibility of evidence is primarily for the national law.
(2) Evidence must normally be produced at a public hearing and as a general rule Article 6(1) and (3)(d) of the Convention require a defendant to be given a proper and adequate opportunity to challenge and question witnesses.
(3) It is not necessarily incompatible with Article 6(1) and (3)(d) of the Convention for depositions to be read and that can be so even if there has been no opportunity to question the witness at any stage of the proceedings. Article 6(3)(d) is simply an illustration of matters to be taken into account in considering whether a fair trial has been held. The reasons for the court holding it necessary that depositions should be read and the procedures to counterbalance any handicap to the defence will all be relevant to the issue of whether, where statements have been read, the trial was fair.
(4) The quality of the evidence and its inherent reliability, plus the degree of caution exercised in relation to reliance on it, will also be relevant to the question of whether the trial was fair.

The question for the court was whether there was a fifth proposition to the effect that where the circumstances would otherwise justify the reading of the statement where the defendant has no opportunity to question the witness at any stage of the trial process, the statement must not be allowed to be read if it is the sole or decisive evidence against the defendant. The English courts have clearly disavowed such a proposition all the way up to the UKSC, which in *Horncastle* asked the ECtHR to take careful account of the reasoning that led it not to apply the sole or decisive test in this case. The Grand Chamber is to rehear the *Al-Khawaja* case and it is unlikely that the story will end in this state of impasse.

4.3 The process of proof and the regulation of the investigation/pre-trial phase

One of the biggest challenges for the human rights bodies in their attempts to elucidate a notion of fairness, which can be applied consistently across various jurisdictions, is the regulation of the pre-trial or investigation phase. Difficulties in this regard have been precipitated by the fact that the role of the trial, and by extension that of the pre-trial phase, differ significantly in common law and civilian legal systems. As Damaška notes, the common law trial, when viewed from a continental perspective, 'still stands far apart from the rest of procedural activities, overshadowing them in its critical importance as supplier of information to the court'.[104] Trials in continental countries, on the other hand, appear

---

[104] M. R. Damaška, *Evidence Law Adrift* (New Haven: Yale University Press, 1997) 59–60.

to common law observers to be 'far from the climactic events the native legal folklore proclaims them to be – especially as generators of information for the adjudicator' and seem to be 'a mere stage in a continuing procedural effort'.[105] It should come as little surprise, therefore, that the human rights bodies have, in setting out their vision of fairness in criminal proceedings, focused more on the specific rights of the defence, rather than on the procedural environment in which these should be exercised. Nevertheless, the procedural context in which the defence is afforded the opportunity to exercise its rights, and by extension the approach of the human rights bodies in this regard, is of crucial importance.

Article 6(1) of the ECHR and Article 14(1) of the ICCPR safeguard the right to a fair, public and impartially regulated 'hearing'; there is no reference in either instrument to the investigation or pre-trial phase. This seems to endorse an understanding of criminal proceedings as divided into two distinct parts: the public, judicially regulated trial hearing and the secret investigation or pre-trial phase. The ECtHR has made it clear, however, that the scope of Article 6 of the ECHR extends beyond this 'hearing'. In a series of early cases, it held that Article 6 applied from the moment that an accused was 'charged' with a criminal offence, within the meaning of the Convention.[106] In *Deweer*, it defined the charge as 'the official notification to be given to an individual by the competent authority of an allegation that he has committed a criminal offence, a definition which also corresponds to the test whether the situation of [the suspect] has been substantially affected'.[107] In subsequent cases, it has confirmed that this notification can take the form of inter alia an arrest,[108] the issuing of an arrest[109] or a search warrant[110] or the opening of a preliminary investigation.[111]

The ECtHR's broad, autonomous definition of the term 'criminal charge' acts as a counterweight to the trial-centric conception of criminal proceedings outlined in the text of Article 6(1) of the ECHR. Indeed, in extending the scope of the provision, the ECtHR has acknowledged the impact that events during the pre-trial phase can have on the fairness of the trial. In *John Murray* v. *United Kingdom*, for instance, it held that the provisions of Article 6 could be 'relevant before a case is sent for trial if and so far as the fairness of the trial is likely to be seriously prejudiced by an initial failure to comply with its provisions'.[112] The

---

[105] Damaška, *Evidence Law Adrift*, 59–60.
[106] See also the approach of the Human Rights Committee, General Comment No. 32 [90], 13 [21], A/39/40 (1984) Annex VI (pp. 143–7); CCPR/C/21/Rev.1, (pp. 12–16), para. 8: 'Art. 14, subparagraph. 3(a) applies to all cases of criminal charges, including those of persons not in detention...'
[107] *Deweer* v. *Belgium*, para. 46; see also *Eckle* v. *Germany*, para. 73.   [108] *B* v. *Austria*, para. 48.
[109] *Boddaert* v. *Belgium*, para. 35.   [110] *Eckle* v. *Germany*, paras. 73–5.
[111] e.g. *Ringeisen* v. *Austria*, para. 110. See further R. Reed and J. Murdoch, *A Guide to Human Rights Law in Scotland*, 2nd edn (Edinburgh: Tottel, 2008) 5.21; and Trechsel, *Human Rights in Criminal Proceedings*, 32.
[112] *John Murray* v. *United Kingdom* [GC], para. 62; see too *Imbrioscia* v. *Switzerland*, para. 36; and *Salduz* v. *Turkey* [GC], para. 50.

consequence of these developments is that the pre-trial phase can no longer be regarded as a distinct entity, entirely separate from the trial itself. Criminal proceedings must be seen as 'a continuum rather than as a succession of discrete episodes, with the trial as the central episode'.[113]

Acceptance of the importance of viewing criminal proceedings as a continuous process does not mean, though, that simply providing the defence with the opportunity to challenge the case against it and to present its own case at any stage in this process will automatically satisfy the fairness requirement in Article 6 of the ECHR: the context in which these rights are to be exercised are of fundamental importance. Recognition of the potential for the investigative or pre-trial phase to influence the fairness of the trial does not equate to automatic acceptance of the pre-trial phase as affording the requisite procedural environment in which the defence is afforded the opportunity to exercise its rights. It is essential, in considering the relationship between the trial and the pre-trial or investigation phase, to distinguish between two separate but related issues: firstly, the principal procedural or institutional environment in which the defence is to be afforded the opportunity to exercise its rights; and, secondly, the potential for events during the pre-trial or investigation phase to impact on the defence's opportunity to exercise these adversarial rights.

4.3.1 Defence rights and the importance of the procedural environment

We have seen that the defence is to have the opportunity to be present, to be provided with the evidence levelled against it, to be afforded the opportunity to challenge this evidence, whether it be oral or documentary, and to present its own evidence, yet the human rights bodies have proven slow to set out expressly any concrete notion of the institutional environment in which the defence is to have the opportunity to exercise these rights. According to provisions such as Article 6(1) of the ECHR and Article 14(1) of the ICCPR, a fair trial is guaranteed through the assurance that the criminal charge will be determined at a public hearing supervised by an independent and impartial judge. Such provisions are based on the premise that public hearing is the principal forum in which the evidence will be heard and challenged. If, however, the public trial resembles, in essence, a sentencing hearing and the evidence is presented and contested at an earlier stage in the proceedings, difficult issues arise. Does fairness dictate that the defence has the opportunity to exercise its rights during the public trial or is it sufficient to allow the defence to challenge witnesses and make its case during the investigation or pre-trial phase?

The transfer of hearings, such as those at which the defence is afforded the opportunity to cross-examine or confront witnesses, to the investigation stage gives rise to a number of problems.[114] Firstly, the pre-trial hearings, during

---

[113] I. H. Dennis, *The Law of Evidence*, 4th edn (London: Sweet & Maxwell, 2010) para. 5.1, 150; see also *R v. Horseferry Magistrates Court, ex p. Bennett* [1994] 1 AC 42 (HL).

[114] e.g. *Kostovski v. Netherlands*; Human Rights Committee, General Comment No. 32 [90], para. 39.

which the evidence is heard and directly challenged, are generally conducted in secret. Indeed, both the HRC and the ECtHR have held that the public hearing requirement does not apply to 'pre-trial decisions made by prosecutors and public authorities'.[115] This mirrors the consensus which emerged among European jurists in the nineteenth century that characterised trial hearings as public and investigation hearings as secret, but crucially this consensus was based on the assumption that the evidence would be heard and challenged at trial.[116] Moving the opportunity of the defence to confront witnesses to the pre-trial phase calls into question the sufficiency of the guarantee that hearings be held in public. This is particularly problematic if the public hearing requirement is viewed as integral to the fairness of the proceedings. Duff et al. argue, for instance, that the trial must be public precisely because the accused is called to answer a charge and to account for his conduct if he is criminally responsible. They suggest that in calling an accused to answer and to account:

> ... the trial purports to be acting on the basis of a public wrong, a wrong which the public are properly concerned with prosecuting and convicting, that it is alleged the defendant has perpetrated. That this is done in the name of the public particularly invites critical public scrutiny in order that the members of the public could distance themselves from recognising the defendant's alleged conduct as wrongful or from the basis on which he has been convicted of the offence.[117]

If, however, the public trials requirement is understood as necessitating that the method of determining criminal liability is able to withstand public scrutiny and engender public acceptance of the verdict, then the fact that various hearings are not held in public may be less problematic.[118]

Secondly, there can be little doubt that the defence must be afforded the opportunity to exercise its rights, including the right to challenge witness evidence, in an environment which respects the institutional requirements of Article 6(1), in particular the equality of arms principle and the guarantee of an impartial judge. The equality of arms requirement dictates that the defence has the opportunity to present its case and to challenge the case against it in surroundings which do not put it at a substantial disadvantage vis-à-vis the prosecution. While this does not necessarily rule out a substantial role for the judiciary in the presentation of the evidence, it would seem to preclude significant unilateral prosecution involvement in the construction of the facts. Scepticism about any 'impartial' role, at least in the sense of Article 6(1) of the ECHR, for the prosecuting authorities is inherent in the equality of arms doctrine[119] and would seem to disqualify prosecution authorities from

---

[115] *Kavanagh* v. *Ireland*, para. 10.4; Trechsel, *Human Rights in Criminal Proceedings*, 122; and R. Esser, *Auf dem Weg zu einem europäischen Strafverfahrensrecht* (Berlin: De Gruyter, 2002) 708.
[116] Summers, *Fair Trials*, 46. For an interesting discussion of the issue of whether the investigation ought to be public, see C. J. A. Mittermaier, *Die Gesetzgebung und Rechtsübung über Strafverfahren nach ihrer neusten Fortbildung* (Erlangen: Ferdinand Enke, 1856) 323.
[117] Duff et al., *Trial on Trial (3)*, 278. [118] Summers, *Fair Trials*, 47.
[119] As well as in the context of the impartiality of the judiciary, see, e.g. *Ozerov* v. *Russia*.

supervising hearings during the investigation, which are designed to provide the defence with its principal opportunity to challenge the evidence. It is difficult to envisage, for instance, how a system which affords the prosecution authorities the principal responsibility for conducting important evidential examination hearings either in the context of witness confrontation hearings or the questioning of the accused, which are designed to facilitate the creation of a written transcript of the evidence, could be considered compatible with Article 6(1) of the ECHR.[120]

Thirdly, the adversarial proceedings principle requires that the accused have the assistance of counsel. This suggests that if the defence's opportunity to challenge the evidence takes place during the investigation/pre-trial phase, the accused must be afforded the assistance of counsel at this stage in the proceedings. Just as the point in the proceedings at which evidence is to be disclosed necessarily depends on the point in the proceedings at which the defence has the opportunity to challenge the evidence, so too does the determination of the point in time at which counsel is required depend on the point in time in the proceedings at which the evidence is to be heard and challenged.

In view of these issues, it is essential that, in overseeing the correct application of defence rights, the human rights bodies apply a substantive test designed to distinguish between investigative and determinative aspects of the pre-trial phase. Merely accepting states' classification of the various procedural stages of their systems has the potential to interfere with the ECtHR's notion of fairness. By allowing for the examination of the evidence to take place during the pre-trial phase, the human rights bodies have emphasised the importance of affording the defence the opportunity to challenge witness evidence at the point in the proceedings at which the witness is actually giving evidence. In order to ensure the consistent application of the fair trials principle, they must also ensure that the defence is able to exercise its rights in an adversarial procedural setting equivalent to that which would be available at trial.

4.3.2 Potential for pre-trial activities to impinge on defence rights

The fact that the principal forum for presenting and challenging evidence takes the form of an adversarial hearing before an independent and impartial judge does not automatically mean that events and activities which take place during the pre-trial phase do not impact on the rights of the defence. As Twining has noted: 'The law of evidence casts a shadow over pre-trial proceedings in ways which are imperfectly understood and hardly documented.'[121] One advantage of the reluctance of the human rights bodies to insist on a characterisation

---

[120] This is the procedural arrangement, however, in the new Swiss federal code of criminal procedure, which came into force in 2011. For criticism, see S. Arquint and S. Summers, 'Konfrontationen nur vor dem Gericht' (2008) 2 *Plädoyer* 38.

[121] W. Twining, *Rethinking Evidence: Exploratory Evidence*, 2nd edn (Cambridge University Press, 2006) 212.

of criminal proceedings as comprising public trials and secret investigations is that it forces consideration of the effect that procedures carried out during the pre-trial phase can have on the fairness of the criminal charge. The 'segmental' understanding of the criminal justice process that characterises the criminal proceedings as 'divisible into three linked but independent parts: the investigative, accusative and determinative' is inherently flawed because it fails to recognise that the criminal process is 'marked by *unity* not disunity, and requires singular not separate analysis'.[122]

Of particular concern here are issues such as the right of access to counsel. Until recently, the approach of the human rights bodies can only be characterised as patchy and incoherent. We shall examine this issue in more depth in Chapter 8, where we will see that the ECtHR has only recently begun to accept the principle that as a rule access to a lawyer should be provided from the first interrogation of a suspect by the police unless there are compelling reasons to restrict this right.[123] This principle is a welcome recognition of the fact that lack of access to counsel at the pre-trial phase inevitably affects the fairness of any subsequent trial. It provides a much clearer benchmark than earlier jurisprudence, which had made a finding of unfairness in each case dependent on whether the lack of access had seriously prejudiced the trial requiring the court either to make a hypothetical assessment of the effect on future fairness or a retrospective examination of the influence of the pre-trial factors on the fairness of the trial.[124]

Ambiguity in relation to the regulation of the pre-trial is by no means confined to the issue of access to counsel; this subject is representative of the failure to establish an effective and adequate strategy for the regulation of the pre-trial investigative phases of the proceedings. This is partly due to deficiencies in the text of Article 6 of the ECHR and Article 14 of the ICCPR, although this must be seen in itself as an insufficient excuse, particularly in the light of the judicial activism in other areas such as in relation to the privilege against self-incrimination.[125] The more plausible explanation lies, not least because of the differences frequently emphasised in comparative criminal law scholarship and the underplaying of the institutional context, in the lack of coherent theorising about the connection between the form of the trial and the investigation and the consequent differences in the nature of the rights that are required in the respective phases. Concerns about the under-regulation of the pre-trial phase have existed since the origins of the modern system of European criminal procedure law.[126] This seems to suggest that the under-regulation of the pre-trial

---

[122] M. McConville, A. Sanders and R. Leng, *The Case for the Prosecution* (London: Routledge, 1991) 198–9 (emphasis in original).
[123] e.g. *Salduz* v. *Turkey* [GC]. See further Ch. 8.6.   [124] See *Imbrioscia* v. *Switzerland*, para. 36.
[125] Trechsel, *Human Rights in Criminal Proceedings*, 340–59; and R. Schlauri, *Das Verbot des Selbstbelastungszwangs im Strafverfahren: Konkretisierung eines Grundrechts durch Rechtsvergleichung* (Zurich: Schulthess, 2003), 82–4 and 357–97. See generally Ch. 8.
[126] Several nineteenth-century jurists criticised the continuing importance of the investigation phase: see, e.g. F. O. Schwarze, 'Die Verteidigung im mündlichen Verfahren' (1878) 15

is not merely an oversight, but that it is in fact representative of the systematic prioritisation of the effectiveness of prosecuting crime over the importance of the adversarial conception of fairness and the legitimacy of the criminal procedural system. The emphasis on the 'fair trial' becomes a crucial means of diverting attention away from the unfairness of the most important part of the proceedings, namely the investigation. This seems to suggest that acceptance of the 'fairness' of the modern European criminal trial is heavily dependent on the 'unfairness' of the investigation.[127] For our purposes, it is essential, therefore, to consider the ways in which the right to a fair trial might be undermined by activities in the investigative phase. If fairness is to be understood as requiring that the defence be afforded the opportunity to challenge the evidence against it and to present its own case at a hearing or hearings supervised by an impartial judge, it is essential that the investigation phase also be structured in such a way as to facilitate the defence's opportunity to exercise these adversarial rights. This will require consideration, in particular, of issues such as the role of the police in questioning the accused and the imposition of coercive measures, such as detention and access to legal advice.

4.4 Towards convergence or realignment?

It has been seen that traditional common law and civil law approaches to evidence have been challenged by some of the rulings of the Strasbourg authorities. The principle of equality of arms has required civil law countries to make a sharper differentiation between those exercising judicial functions and those exercising 'party' functions. The principle of an adversarial trial has also required such systems to give greater weight to defence rights to examine witnesses. Although some commentators have argued that this move towards adversarialism is promoting some sort of convergence between the two legal traditions, it is accepted that the ECtHR's idea of adversarial proceedings does not necessarily correspond in every respect with the notion as it is understood in common law countries. The ECtHR itself did not set out with any presumption that the common law concept of a fair trial is superior to the civil law concept, or the latter superior to the former.[128] We have seen that the common law tradition has been equally discomforted by the 'adversarial' principle of open disclosure of material evidence and by the rule that prevents convictions being based upon unexamined statements which constitute the sole or decisive evidence against the defendant. The ECtHR has steered clear of imposing any abstract model of proof on contracting parties.[129] Instead, as we have seen, it has tried to 'translate' the principles in Article 6 in such a manner as to make

Zeitschrift für Rechtspflege und Verwaltung in Sachsen 8; and J. Vargha, *Die Verteidigung in Strafsachen* (Vienna: Manz'sche k. u. k. Hof-Verlag und Univ. Buchhandlung, 1879) 391.

[127] Summers, *Fair Trials*, 91–3.
[128] Swart and Young, 'European Convention on Human Rights', 86.
[129] Chiavario, 'The Rights of the Defendant and the Victim', 542.

them amenable to accommodation within both common law and civil law traditions.

It is tempting to see in this some sort of gradual convergence of party- and court-dominated procedures towards a mixed model of proof, more party-orientated than traditional continental criminal procedure, but falling short of the party control exercised in the common law adversarial trial. But we would argue that rather than attempt to piece together the various strands of both traditions, borrowing from each tradition where possible to reach a compromise between the two, the ECtHR has developed its own distinctive brand of jurisprudence through the principles of the equality of arms and the right to an adversarial trial which is transforming rather than merely mixing together the two traditions. As explained, the notion of adversarialism is far removed from that which is evident in common law countries. Delmas-Marty has argued that the great lesson of the European jurisprudence is that *no* model of criminal procedure – accusatory, inquisitorial or mixed – has escaped censure by the Strasbourg tribunals.[130] Instead, the ECommHR and ECtHR have over the years developed a vision of participation in the decision making of the justice system which is rooted both in common law principles of natural justice and due process and in what is known on the continent as *la theorie de la procédure contradictoire*. At the heart of this vision is what Delmas-Marty has called the 'contradictory debate' – the rejection, as she has put it, 'of revealed, uncontested truth replaced by facts which are contested and only then established as truths'.[131] Her own commission in France went some way towards attempting to realise this ideal in practice when it recommended that defence lawyers be given enhanced rights of access to their clients in custody, access to the official dossier, a right of attendance at judicial hearings and the power to request investigative acts of the *juge d'instruction*.[132]

But if this vision is rooted in both common law and civil law traditions of criminal justice, the ECtHR's jurisprudence has shown that it has not always been evident in the practice and procedure of national systems. In drawing attention to shortcomings in the procedures of national systems, the ECtHR has had to develop its vision in a piecemeal fashion, case by case, proceeding on the basis, as the ECtHR has done throughout its jurisprudence, that the Convention is a living instrument that requires adaptation as circumstances change. Nevertheless, it is possible to identify four broad strands in the

---

[130] M. Delmas-Marty, 'Toward a European Model of the Criminal Trial', in M. Delmas-Marty (ed.), *The Criminal Process and Human Rights: Towards a European Consciousness* (Dordrecht: Martinus Nijhoff, 1995) 191, 196. See also Fennell et al., *Criminal Justice in Europe*, 384.
[131] Delmas-Marty, 'Toward a European Model', 197.
[132] For recent studies on how far these participatory principles are challenging and reforming pre-trial practice in France, see J. Hodgson, 'Constructing the Pre-trial Role of the Defence in French Criminal Procedure: An Adversarial Outsider in an Inquisitorial Process' (2002) 6 *International Journal of Evidence & Proof* 1; and S. Field and A. West, 'Dialogue and the Inquisitorial Tradition: French Defence Lawyers in the Pre-trial Criminal Process' (2003) 14 *Criminal Law Forum* 261.

development of its vision of defence participation in the criminal processes of proof that require to be accommodated within national systems: non-compulsion; informed involvement; an opportunity to challenge evidence; and a reasoned judgment that can be challenged.

Firstly, defendants cannot be required to participate in the proof process. Although Article 6 makes no mention of the privilege against self-incrimination, the ECtHR made it clear in 1993 that the right of anyone charged with a criminal offence to remain silent and not contribute to incriminating himself flowed directly from Article 6 of the Convention.[133] At first glance, it may seem that the principle of participation sits uneasily with a principle that permits defendants to refuse to participate. Here we see a tension that we shall encounter throughout this book and that has over-shadowed the ability of the ECtHR to develop a coherent theory of defence participation. On the one hand, there is a need to respect the autonomy of the individual defendant charged with a criminal offence. Although the criminal process is a coercive process in which individuals may be required to give up their liberty when they are arrested and their privacy when their homes and their person are searched, the principle of autonomy dictates that they should be able to choose how to conduct their defence even if this means refusing to conduct any defence at all. At the same time, the rationalist tradition of evidence suggests that in order for triers of fact to gain access to all relevant information, criminal processes should be built around requiring the full participation of the parties. If participation is viewed broadly as the right of the individual to choose to participate in the fact-finding process, then this must be compatible with a right not to choose to do so.[134] But if it is viewed as an important aid to fact finding, then everything should be done to encourage if not compel the parties to participate. We shall see that the ECtHR has mediated this tension by requiring that in situations which clearly call for an explanation from the accused, accused persons should be strongly encouraged to answer questions and to have inferences drawn against them if they do not, provided appropriate safeguards are put in place.[135]

The need to ensure that the defence assists in the fact-finding enterprise implies a second principle: that any participation must be on an informed basis. This would seem to require the assistance of counsel at pre-trial stages when the accused is being questioned, full disclosure of relevant information to the defence and the right to comment on the evidence.[136] Again, a problem arises, however, when an accused does not wish to be assisted by counsel. Should defendants have the right to refuse counsel even when their interests

---

[133] *Funke* v. *France*.
[134] Chiavario, 'The Rights of the Defendant and the Victim', 570; see also Duff et al., *Trial on Trial (3)*, 119.
[135] *John Murray* v. *United Kingdom* [GC].
[136] The precise parameters of the right of access to counsel before trial, like the right of silence, remain uncertain. Cf. *John Murray* v. *United Kingdom* [GC]; *Brennan* v. *United Kingdom*; and *Öcalan* v. *Turkey* [GC]. But see more recently *Salduz* v. *Turkey* [GC] and the discussion in Ch. 8.6.

would be better safeguarded by having one? Thirdly, the defence must be given an opportunity to challenge the evidence against it, including, as we have seen, the right to examine decisive witnesses at some stage during the proceedings. This principle requires the participation not only of the defence, but also of victims and witnesses, which raises questions about how far the autonomy of the latter should be safeguarded. There is a consensus that victims and witnesses should generally be required to answer questions, but their interests in doing so need to be protected. Finally, the national courts must indicate with sufficient clarity the grounds on which they base their decisions. This requires some form of reasoned judgment which can be challenged by the defence.[137] But, again, if this challenge is to be effective, it would seem to require that defendants are assisted by counsel.

The ECtHR has given states considerable leeway in translating these principles into national law in an attempt to accommodate established procedures within the two prevailing traditions. It may seem, for example, that jury trial offends against the principle of a reasoned judgment, but the ECtHR has accepted that one way of compensating for the lack of a reasoned judgement is by a carefully framed direction from the judge.[138] It is also true that each principle may not in isolation measure up to the degree of participation permitted in one or other of the established traditions. For example, the right to examine witnesses in the adversarial tradition has not been confined only to decisive witnesses. By contrast, however, the second principle requiring informed defence participation before trial goes much further than traditional adversarial or inquisitorial procedure. Collectively, it may be said that the principles extend the boundaries of participation beyond those that have been traditionally permitted within each of the traditions and the established procedures have had to be realigned upon a more participatory footing.

It is no longer possible for proof processes to be dominated entirely by judicial inquiry, but neither is it possible for them to be dominated entirely by a trial contest between partisan parties refereed by a passive judge. Instead, defence participation has come to enable defendants to play an active role in the proof process throughout the course of the proceedings, with access to legal advice when suspects are being questioned and material evidence disclosed to the defence well before trial. This seems to call for more than just a realignment of procedures. It requires a change in legal culture on the part of public authorities. In the common law tradition, judges have long had a responsibility to guarantee a fair trial, but what is now required is a much more protective stance towards defendants on the part of those acting on behalf of public authorities – including police officers and prosecutors, as well as judges – throughout the criminal process. It requires those responsible for examining defendants in the preparatory phase of procedure to ensure that rights to legal access are safeguarded. In the course of criminal investigations, it requires police and prosecutors to search

---

[137] *Hadjianastassiou* v. *Greece*, paras. 33–7.   [138] *Saric* v. *Denmark* (dec.).

for evidence, *à charge et à décharge*, and then to share this information with the defence.[139] Then in the course of the trial itself prosecutors must consider whether to rely on evidence that has been tainted by coercion or illegality and judges must adopt a vigilant approach to ensure that convictions are not based substantially on unexamined or otherwise suspect evidence. Although all of this requires a considerable change of culture on the part of public authorities, particularly where prosecutors and judges are unused to monitoring investigative activities,[140] it would also seem to entail a change of culture on the part of defence lawyers who have been accustomed within the common law tradition to focus their proof-gathering activities on the trial. Now they are obliged to represent their clients at earlier vital stages of the proof process and, with greater rights to disclosure, they are being encouraged to participate in this process at a much earlier stage.[141]

Finally, however, it would be wrong to see the need for gradual realignment in favour of greater participatory defence rights as an attempt to pinpoint some fixed 'ideal' position that can hold true for all time. We have seen that the ECtHR has stressed that the Convention is a living instrument which must be interpreted in the light of present-day conditions and this would seem to apply to the standards of fairness prescribed under Article 6.[142] On the one hand, this can lead to higher standards of fairness being applied to defendants than were once considered appropriate. One example is a change in perception in the way in which persons younger than 18 should be treated in the criminal justice process. In considering whether the attribution of criminal responsibility to children of the age of 10 gave rise to a violation of Article 3 of the ECHR, the Grand Chamber of the ECtHR in *T and V* v. *United Kingdom* referred explicitly to the principle that since the Convention is a living instrument, it is legitimate in considering whether a certain measure is acceptable to take account of the standards prevailing among the member states of the Council of Europe. It refrained from considering that there was a breach of the article

---

[139] This has not traditionally been a requirement on the police conducting criminal investigations in the United Kingdom. However, the Code of Practice under s. 23(1) of the Criminal Procedure and Investigations Act 1996 provides that the police are now expected 'to pursue all reasonable lines of inquiry, whether these point towards or away from the suspect' (para. 3(4)).

[140] In the United Kingdom, prosecutors have been said to occupy a quasi-judicial role, but this has fallen far short of becoming actively involved in monitoring criminal investigations: see S. Field, P. Alldridge and N. Jörg, 'Prosecutors, Examining Judges and Control of Police Investigations', in Fennell et al., *Criminal Justice in Europe*, 227; C. Brants and S. Field, 'Discretion and Accountability in Prosecution: A Comparative Perspective on Keeping Crime out of Court', in Fennell et al., *Criminal Justice in Europe*, 77; and J. Jackson, 'The Effect of Legal Culture and Proof in Decisions to Prosecute' (2004) 3 *Journal of Law, Probability and Risk* 109.

[141] For the different role played by defence lawyers in the Netherlands and England and Wales, see Field et al., 'Prosecutors', 246–7.

[142] The English Court of Appeal has said that fairness is a constantly evolving concept and that standards and perceptions of fairness may change from one century to another, but also, sometimes, from one decade to another: see *R* v. *H* [2004] 2 AC 134, para. 11.

because there did not exist at that time an international consensus on the issue of criminal responsibility. In this case, the court did not refer explicitly to the living instrument principle in considering what fair trial standards were appropriate in the case of young defendants. But its ruling in a later case that the need to ensure that children are able to participate effectively in their trial may make it essential that they be tried in a specialist tribunal which is able to give full consideration to and make allowances for the handicaps under which they labour is an illustration of the willingness of the ECtHR to take account of modern psychology which is much more sensitive to children's needs than in the past.[143] Another example is the tendency of the ECtHR to consider that when children are being questioned by the police, they are entitled to have access to a lawyer, social worker or friend to ensure that they have a broad understanding of what is stake.[144]

All of this suggests that, as the ECtHR refines and develops its vision of participatory proof in the light of modern-day conditions and takes criminal procedure beyond the traditional boundaries of adversarial/inquisitorial discourse, the European states are given considerable freedom of manoeuvre in realigning their procedures in a manner that respects the rights of the defence. This means that while countries may naturally try to hold on to procedural traditions indigenous to their system as best they can, they are encouraged to develop distinctive processes which diverge from the traditional norm for particular kinds of cases. It follows that there may be considerable divergence in the manner in which the participatory principles developed by the ECtHR are translated from one system to another and even from one category of case to another within the same system.

4.5 Conclusion

The debate on whether systems of criminal proof are converging or diverging has continued to be dominated by 'adversarial' and 'inquisitorial' models of proof, with some suggesting that European models are converging towards an 'adversarial' model. An analysis of the case law of the European Commission and ECtHR and of the HRC shows that the human rights bodies have been steadily developing a model of proof which requires none of these traditionally adversarial features to be adopted. Although the ECtHR has referred to 'adversarial' rights, the model of proof that has been developed is better characterised as 'participatory' than 'adversarial' or 'inquisitorial'. Contracting parties are being forced to realign their processes and procedures, and indeed the attitudes

---

[143] *SC* v. *United Kingdom*.
[144] *Panovits* v. *Cyprus*. It is interesting to note that in the light of modern standards of fairness, the Northern Ireland Court of Appeal has quashed convictions obtained in the Northern Irish Diplock courts in the 1970s on the basis of confessions made by young persons in the absence of an appropriate adult. See L. Elks, *Righting Miscarriages of Justice? Ten Years of the Criminal Cases Review Commission* (London: Justice, 2008).

of the professional actors concerned must adapt, to meet the standards of fairness that this model entails. The human rights case law demonstrates that there is indeed a great deal of consensus on the importance and nature of defence participation, but it has also highlighted significant institutional differences and these differences have the potential to destabilise a consistent notion of procedural fairness. We shall also see that there are tensions between notions of participation based around individual autonomy and notions of participation based around effective defence.

The human rights bodies are unable through their practice to impose any detailed evidentiary rules upon contracting parties, since they have always proceeded upon the basis that contracting parties should be given as much freedom as possible to organise their systems in order to meet the standards of fairness. It is therefore unlikely that human rights law will lead to any clear convergence of evidentiary practices. To the contrary, we may witness further fragmentation of existing processes as particular countries adapt their procedures to meet the demands of fairness laid down by the ECtHR. This is not to say that other external pressures, such as the need for transnational cooperation in the fight against crime and terrorism, will not induce greater convergence, difficult as this may be to accomplish. So long as the present machinery of human rights protection continues, however, states will have to comply with the standards of fairness laid down by these institutions. If the participatory model continues to evolve in the manner described in this chapter, this will mean that any convergence that is achieved will have to meet the participatory standards of proof required by this model.

5

Evidence in the international criminal tribunals

5.1 Towards an international system of justice

In the last chapter we discussed the attempts that have been made to fashion a common law of criminal evidence within international human rights regimes and we argued that the European Court of Human Rights in particular has been developing within its jurisprudence a participatory model of proof that is rooted in both common and civil law traditions, but may be genuinely classified as *sui generis*. These regimes marked an important turning point for international law, as they shifted the focus away from the interests of states towards the interests of individuals. The individual rights theories that developed during the Enlightenment were re-invigorated within the international arena as the treatment of individuals by states became a matter of international concern. But these regimes were still state-centred in the sense that their rulings were concerned with whether states had met their obligations towards individuals, such as the obligation to ensure a fair trial. For our purposes, we have seen that they tolerated a fair degree of divergence between states as to how fair trials could be achieved. When international law took a further step towards recognising the significance of the individual by making individuals responsible for international crimes, however, agreement had to be reached not only on the principles of fair trial, but also on detailed rules of procedure and evidence for trying persons charged with such crimes.

Although there are precedents for international crimes that hark back a number of centuries, the Nuremburg trials of the Nazi leaders after the Second World War are widely credited as marking a turning point in the evolution of international criminal justice.[1] Before the end of the war, the allies agreed that German officers responsible for atrocities, massacres and executions should be tried according to the laws of the liberated countries and in August 1945 the London Charter provided for an international military tribunal for the trial of war criminals whose offences have no particular geographical location. Although this in itself did little more than provide for the application of a customary right on the part of enemy belligerents to try war criminals, the

---

[1] G. Robertson, *Crimes against Humanity: The Struggle for Global Justice* (London: Penguin, 2002) xii and xiii.

charter went on to extend the range of crimes that could be tried beyond the traditional classification of war crimes to include crimes against peace and crimes against humanity. Even more importantly, it also enabled senior state officials to be tried without the protection of state sovereignty, thereby establishing the principle that individuals have duties which transcend the obligations that are owed to the state.[2] From our perspective, the importance of the tribunal is that it consisted of judges from the allied powers and it thereby represented the first attempt to bring judges from the common law and civil law traditions together to dispense a common form of justice.

In 1993, the international community took a further step towards the creation of an international criminal order when the Security Council used its Chapter VII powers to establish an International Criminal Tribunal to prosecute those responsible for serious violations of humanitarian law in the territory of the former Yugoslavia.[3] The tribunal, sitting in The Hague, known as the International Criminal Tribunal for the Former Yugoslavia (ICTY), may claim to be the first truly international criminal tribunal. The ICTY was followed by a number of other international or 'mixed' international and national tribunals. In 1994, the Security Council invoked its Chapter VII powers once more to establish an international tribunal to punish those responsible for international crimes in Rwanda.[4] The International Criminal Tribunal for Rwanda (ICTR) sits in Arusha, but the prosecutor for the tribunal is also the prosecutor for The Hague Tribunal and the Appeals Chamber for both courts is the same body based in The Hague. These tribunals were followed by attempts to establish hybrid international and national courts to deal with atrocities after conflicts. For example, a Special Court was established by the United Nations and Sierra Leone involving international as well as local judges and lawyers to try those guilty of crimes against humanitarian law in that country.[5] Extraordinary Chambers established under Cambodian law after an agreement with the United Nations with co-investigating judges and prosecutors appointed by Cambodia and the United Nations are putting on trial Khmer Rouge defendants for the atrocities committed during the years 1975 to 1979 in Cambodia.[6] In addition, a number of countries such as East Timor, Kosovo, Bosnia and Herzegovina and Iraq have established special tribunals to prosecute international crimes, adopting procedures that are not dissimilar from the international tribunals.[7]

---

[2] A. Cassese, *International Criminal Law* (Oxford University Press, 2003) 40. For an analysis of the historical development of international criminal jurisdiction, see C. M. Bassiouni, *Crimes against Humanity in International Criminal Law* (Amsterdam: Kluwer, 1999).

[3] Security Council Resolutions 808 (22 February 1993) and 827 (25 May 1993).

[4] Security Council Resolution 955 (8 November 1994).

[5] The Agreement between the UN and the Sierra Leone Government on the establishment of the Special Court was signed in Freetown on 16 January 2002. See J. R. W. D. Jones and S. Powles, *International Criminal Practice*, 3rd edn (Oxford University Press, 2003), 20.

[6] Jones and Powles, *International Criminal Practice*, 33–5.

[7] See P. Wald, 'Fair Trials for War Criminals' (2006) 4 *International Commentary on Evidence*, Issue 1, Art. 6, and P. Wald, 'Iraq, Cambodia and International Criminal Justice' (2006) 21 *American University International Law Review* 541.

The ICTY also provided the impetus for a renewed attempt to draft a statute for a permanent international court. The International Law Commission completed a draft in 1994 and a Preparatory Committee on the Establishment of an International Criminal Court was tasked with preparing a widely acceptable consolidated text of a convention for an international criminal court. On 17 July 1998, the Rome Statute for an International Criminal Court (ICC) was signed and was finally ratified on 11 April 2002 by the necessary sixty states with jurisdiction to take effect from 1 July 2002.[8] The United Nations no longer needs to set up ad hoc tribunals. Instead, the Security Council can directly refer a situation to the ICC prosecutor. The court's jurisdiction is less extensive than that of the ad hoc tribunals. Although paragraph 10 of the preamble to the treaty states that the court's jurisdiction shall be complementary to national criminal jurisdictions, it is better described as 'subordinate' to them.[9] Unlike the ad hoc tribunals which can assume jurisdiction as of right without having to demonstrate the failure of a domestic system, the ICC can only assume jurisdiction once a national jurisdiction is 'unwilling or unable' genuinely to carry out an investigation or prosecution.[10] The court also does not have the same freedom of manoeuvre under the ICC as in the ad hoc tribunals and the Security Council may adopt a resolution under Chapter VII of the charter requesting the court to suspend a prosecution, in which case the court may not proceed with it.[11] Nevertheless, in the words of one commentator, the ICC is perhaps the most innovative and exciting development in international law since the creation of the United Nations, establishing the principle that individuals responsible for serious violations of human rights can become criminally liable before an international forum.[12]

5.2 Problems of legitimacy

The development of international criminal tribunals presented the international community with the challenge of promulgating for the first time a set of evidentiary norms for the prosecution of crimes which could become the basis for an international law of criminal evidence and serve as a benchmark for domestic systems. Although the International Criminal Court is increasingly developing its own distinctive rules of evidence and procedure, particular attention will be given in this chapter to the evidentiary regime established within the ICTY and to a lesser extent the ICTR, as these provide the longest running and best-sourced examples of international criminal tribunals.[13] We shall see

---

[8] As of 22 June 2011, there were 116 states parties to the Rome Statute: see www.icc-cpi.int/Menus/ASP/states+parties.
[9] Robertson, *Crimes against Humanity*, 372. See also W. A. Schabas, *The International Criminal Court*, 3rd edn (Cambridge University Press, 2007) 174–5.
[10] Art. 17 ICC Statute. For full discussion of the complementary principle, see M. Politi and F. Gioia (eds.), *The International Criminal Court and National Jurisdictions* (Aldershot: Ashgate, 2008).
[11] Art. 16 ICC Statute.   [12] Schabas, *International Criminal Court*, 57.
[13] The ICTR which was established closely in its wake followed similar procedures.

that although adversarial features from the common law tradition originally had a decisive influence in determining these rules, this influence is now less pronounced and the tribunals have been characterised more as a hybrid or 'marriage' of both the common law and civil law traditions.[14] Before we come on to how these norms were created, however, we need to step back and consider that although the development of international criminal tribunals has been a notable achievement, it has presented the international community with a huge challenge of legitimacy for a number of reasons.

5.2.1 Function and purpose of international criminal trials

Firstly, there has been a lack of clarity about the precise function and purpose of international criminal trials. A number of objectives have been canvassed for international criminal tribunals that go beyond the conventional purpose of domestic criminal procedures to convict those guilty of crimes.[15] A central purpose in establishing international criminal tribunals has been to eliminate impunity of the highest civilian and military leaders in order to prevent a recurrence of war crimes and crimes against humanity.[16] This means that tribunals need to establish a policy of prioritising cases within their budgets to deal with those who are highest up the chain of the command and suggests a need to engage in active trial management to ensure that all cases are dealt with expeditiously. Where conflicts are ongoing, it may be particularly important to ensure that any allegations of war crimes and crimes against humanity are investigated and dealt with as quickly as possible so that the protagonists are deterred from committing such offences.

Wider objectives have been advanced beyond the need to deal swiftly with the perpetrators of international crimes. Since the international tribunals were established to protect the victims of international crimes,[17] it has been argued that their procedures need to allow for much greater participation of victims than conventional domestic procedures. In particular, it is claimed that giving victims a 'right to truth' can help to heal divisions and prevent future repetition of gross violations of human rights in post-conflict societies.[18] A further purpose of international criminal tribunals is that they can help to achieve national reconciliation by shedding light on the history of events that led up to the crimes that are being tried. This raises wider questions as to whether

[14] M. Fairlie, 'The Marriage of Common Law and Continental Law at the ICTY and its Progeny, Due Process Deficit' (2004) 4 *International Criminal Law Review* 243.
[15] For discussion, see M. Damaška, 'What is the Point of International Criminal Justice?' (2007) 83 *Chicago-Kent Law Review* 329; W. A. Schabas, *The UN International Criminal Tribunals: The Former Yugoslavia, Rwanda and Sierra Leone* (Cambridge University Press, 2006) 67–73; and R. Cryer, H. Friman, D. Robinson and E. Wilmshurst, *An Introduction to International Criminal Law and Procedure*, 2nd edn (Cambridge University Press, 2010) ch. 2.
[16] See C. Jorda, 'The Major Hurdles and Accomplishments of the ICTY' (2004) 2 *Journal of International Criminal Justice* 572, 579.
[17] A. Cassese, 'Opinion: The International Criminal Tribunal for the Former Yugoslavia and Human Rights' (1997) *European Human Rights Law Review* 329, 332.
[18] J. Doak, *Victims' Rights, Human Rights and Criminal Justice* (Hart: Oxford, 2008) 181.

international justice should pursue policies of retribution or policies of restorative justice.[19] Another purpose is that they can construct an historical account of the atrocities that have taken place during conflicts and thereby in the words of Justice Jackson, the principal American prosecutor at the Nuremberg trials, 'establish incredible events by credible evidence'.[20] In the more recent era of the international criminal tribunals, a number of protagonists have also spoken of the court creating a historical record of what occurred to prevent 'historical revisionism'.[21] Scholars and lawyers, however, have cast doubt on whether courts are the proper forum for constructing historical accounts of mass human rights violations.[22]

It is not surprising that there continues to be much debate about what are the proper functions of international criminal tribunals. International criminal justice is a 'fledgling discipline [which] has barely been conceptualised, or elaborated'.[23] The broader aims of victim participation, truth telling, reconciliation and establishing a historical record would seem to clash with the need to deal swiftly with perpetrators to put an end to ongoing violence and conflict.[24] But the lack of consensus on the precise objectives of the tribunals allows those brought before international tribunals to cast them as pursuing peace and other political aims at the expense of justice.

5.2.2 The evidentiary context

Even if a consensus could be reached about what international criminal justice is for, a second set of legitimacy problems is posed by the evidentiary context in which the new tribunals have to operate. At the Nuremberg and Tokyo trials, allied occupying forces had control of all of Japan and Germany and many of

---

[19] See P. Roberts, 'Restoration and Retribution in International Criminal Justice: An Exploratory Analysis', in A. von Hirsch, J. Roberts and A. E. Bottoms (eds.), *Restorative Justice and Criminal Justice* (Oxford: Hart, 2003) 115.

[20] *Report to the President by Mr Justice Jackson*, 6 June 1945 in *Report of Robert H. Jackson, US Representative to the International Conference on Military Trials, London 1945* (Washington, DC: US Government, 1949) 48. Cited in T. Taylor, *The Anatomy of the Nuremberg Trials: A Personal Memoir* (London: Bloomsbury, 1993) 54.

[21] See Address of Antonio Cassese, the first President of the ICTY to the General Assembly of the United Nations, IT/127 4 November 1997. See also the remarks of Judge Gabrielle McDonald after the conclusion of the *Tadić* trial, the first full trial at the ICTY, that the judgment established findings that 'no amount of revisionism or amnesia can erase'. Cited in R. May and M. Wierda, 'Evidence before the ICTY', in R. May, D. Tolbert and J. Hocking (eds.), *Essays on the ICTY Procedure and Evidence: In Honour of Gabrielle Kirk McDonald* (Amsterdam: Kluwer, 2001) 349, 253.

[22] See H. Arendt, *Eichmann in Jerusalem: A Report on the Banality of Evil* (London: Penguin, 1994); May and Wierda, 'Evidence before the ICTY', 253. Cf. R. A. Wilson, 'Judging History: The Historical Record of the International Criminal Tribunal for the Former Yugoslavia' (2005) 27 *Human Rights Quarterly* 908.

[23] Roberts, 'Restoration and Retribution', 336.

[24] M. Damaška, 'Problematic Features of International Criminal Procedure', in A. Cassese (ed.), *The Oxford Companion to International Criminal Justice* (Oxford University Press, 2009) 175, 178–9; and R. May and M. Wierda, *International Criminal Evidence* (Ardsley: Transnational Publishers, 2001) 15.

the high-ranking officers to be charged were already in custody. The armed forces were able to seize evidence and make further arrests anywhere within their control and the prosecution had access to a massive amount of German documents. Such are the advantages of 'victor's justice'. Things are not nearly so easy when the setting is an international tribunal where there is no international control over the territory where witnesses and suspects reside and where the evidence is held.

Prosecutors at the ICTY have pointed out how different an international criminal investigation is from a standard domestic investigation.[25] To begin with, there is often a physical distance between the location of the tribunal and the sites where the crimes occurred. The distance between the ICTY located in The Hague and the sites where the crimes occurred in the former Yugoslavia made the investigation and prosecution of crime very difficult. Then there is the problem of locating a crime scene when the majority of crimes have been unreported. Once this is found, the logistics of on-site investigation in a conflict or post-conflict environment can be difficult. Access to crime scenes may only be possible years after the crime has been committed, by which time the physical evidence may have been tampered with or deteriorated. Another problem is that finding the location of victims who can testify to the events can also be a costly and time-consuming job, and even when they can be found there are often doubts about the reliability of their evidence. In the charged atmosphere of armed conflict or post-armed conflict, witnesses from one side of the conflict may often have a considerable interest in the conviction of those associated with another party.[26] They may also be unwilling to inculpate those who may still be in positions of authority. If those implicated in international crimes continue to be in a position of authority, there is also likely to be a lack of cooperation by state officials, media and political leaders. Even when witnesses are forthcoming, there can be great difficulties for investigators and lawyers as accounts are translated from native languages into English and French and interpreted across cultural barriers.[27]

A further difficulty is that the tribunals have lacked the coercive machinery necessary for investigating and obtaining evidence.[28] The establishment of

---

[25] M. B. Harmon and F. Gaynor, 'Prosecuting Massive Crimes with Primitive Tools: Three Difficulties Encountered by Prosecutors in International Criminal Proceedings' (2004) 2 *Journal of International Criminal Justice* 403. See also Cassese, 'ICTY and Human Rights', 595.

[26] M. Scharf, *Balkan Justice* (Durham: Carolina Academic Press, 1997) 212. See also P. Murphy, 'Excluding Justice or Facilitating Justice? International Criminal Law would benefit from Rules of Evidence' (2008) 12 *International Journal of Evidence & Proof* 1.

[27] The ICTR has faced particular difficulties in translating the oral testimony of witnesses from their native language into French and then into English. *Prosecutor* v. *Akayesu*, Trial Chamber, Judgment, para. 145. See R. Cryer, 'Witness Evidence before International Criminal Tribunals' (2003) 3 *Law and Practice of International Courts and Tribunals* 411; R. Cryer, 'A Long Way From Home: Witnesses before the International Criminal Tribunals' (2006) 4 *International Commentary on Evidence*, Issue 1, Art. 8 and N. Combs, *Fact Finding Without Facts* (Cambridge University Press, 2010).

[28] G. K. McDonald, 'Problems, Obstacles and Achievements of the ICTY' (2004) 2 *Journal of International Criminal Justice* 558. See also Cassese, *International Criminal Law*, 442.

the ICTY on the basis of a Chapter VII decision created a binding obligation on states to cooperate with the international tribunal in the investigation and prosecution of persons accused of committing serious violations of international humanitarian law and to assist in requests for assistance in the gathering of evidence.[29] Although the legality of this obligation has been upheld by the Appeals Chamber,[30] certain states have chosen to be less than cooperative with the tribunal and even cooperative governments may sometimes be unwilling to furnish evidence such as intelligence information on national security grounds.[31]

Even when a sufficient amount of evidence of international crimes has been amassed and indictments are issued against the suspected perpetrators, there may be great difficulties in translating this evidence into convictions. Firstly, there is the problem of locating and arresting those indicted. When the case comes to trial, there are particular difficulties in proving international crimes not present in domestic criminal law. International criminal law requires proof of complex factual issues, such as the existence of a widespread or systematic practice for crimes against humanity or the need to establish the historical and social context of the criminal conduct.[32] This means that it is not enough to prove, as in most domestic criminal cases, one or two incidents, but rather a number of incidents over sometimes a long period of time have to be proved. In addition, international crimes are usually committed by individuals who are part of organisations, which means that is it is necessary to prove command responsibility.[33]

The inability of the international legal order to be able to assure those who have committed war crimes that they will be brought to justice deprives international tribunals of the legitimacy that can be generated by an effective domestic system. We have seen that under the terms of the original social contract, individuals agreed to obey laws that restricted their freedom of movement in return for protection from their fellow citizens and from the sovereign state. The great promise raised by international criminal justice is that the citizens of failed states will be protected by the international legal order. Without effective enforcement mechanisms, however, this promise cannot be delivered. The weakness of the international order also prevents the new order from honouring the other side of the social contract, which is to protect those charged with crimes against humanity from abuse by those who operate the machinery of justice. The lack

---

[29] Art. 29 ICTY Statute.
[30] *Prosecutor* v. *Blaškić*, Case No. IT-95-14-AR108bis, 29 October 1997, Judgment on the Request of the Republic of Croatia for Review of the Decision of Trial Chamber II of 18 July 1997, Appeals Chamber.
[31] W. A. Schabas, 'Fair Trials and National Security Evidence' (2006) 4 *International Commentary on Evidence*, Issue 1, Art. 9.
[32] Cassese, *International Criminal Law*, 442–3.
[33] Some of the difficulties of proving command responsibility are explained in G. Boas, 'Creating Laws of Evidence for International Criminal Law: The ICTY and the Principle of Flexibility' (2001) 12 *Criminal Law Forum* 41.

of effective enforcement mechanisms means that there is even more than in domestic settings considerable discretion over whom of the many individuals suspected of committing crimes in a particular conflict situation shall be chosen to be indicted.[34] The justice meted out is then highly selective rather than even-handed. In addition to this, the international order lacks the ability that domestic jurisdictions have to exercise effective supervision over the investigators, prosecutors and even the tribunals themselves.[35] This again makes it easy for individuals and their state sponsors at the receiving end of international criminal justice to claim that they have been singled out for nothing more than a political show trial.[36]

5.2.3 Reaching agreed rules of procedure and evidence

A third set of legitimacy problems relates more directly to the theme of this chapter, which is how the international community has arrived at a consensus on the rules of procedure and evidence that should govern the international tribunals and courts. It is not immediately clear that either of the traditional approaches associated with the common law and civil law systems – the 'adversarial' approach or the 'inquisitorial' approach – should be taken towards international criminal procedure as a matter of *a priori* principle. International tribunals are unable to latch on to any particular national conception of justice and there is no available international machinery of government that would dictate whether justice should be seen as pursuing an active 'policy-implementing' or a reactive 'conflict resolution' role.[37] Where, on the other hand, it is possible to locate tribunals in the regions where the crimes have been committed, albeit with international judges in support, and to latch on to indigenous procedures, some legitimacy can be attached to the process. It has been argued that in order to offset the claim by accused persons that they are being tried by 'alien' procedures, international tribunals should place a high priority on devising

---

[34] Prosecutors, of course, exercise considerable discretion over whether to prosecute individuals in domestic systems. What differentiates prosecutorial discretion in the international arena is that it is detached from the sovereign power of domestic systems to be able to prosecute effectively. Cf. A. Sarat and C. Clarke, 'Beyond Discretion: Prosecution, the Logic of Sovereignty, and the Limits of the Law' (2008) 33 *Law & Social Inquiry* 387.

[35] M. Bohlander, 'The International Criminal Judiciary – Problems of Judicial Selection, Independence and Ethics', in M. Bohlander (ed.), *International Criminal Justice: A Critical Analysis of Institutions and Procedures* (London: Cameron May, 2007) 325.

[36] G. Simpson, 'Objective Responsibility: Show Trials and War Crimes Trials' (2006) 4 *International Commentary on Evidence*, Issue 1, Art. 4. See also G. Simpson, *Law, War and Crime: War Trials and the Reinvention of International Law* (Cambridge: Polity Press, 2007), and J. Laughland, *Travesty: The Trial of Slobodan Milošević and the Corruption of Justice* (London: Pluto Press, 2007).

[37] G. Sluiter, 'Beyond the Written Law: Why International Criminal Tribunals Function the Way They Do', paper delivered at the International Law and Society Conference, Berlin, July 2007. See M. Damaška, *The Faces of Justice and State Authority* (New Haven: Yale University Press, 1986) 73 and 80.

procedural forms and practices that open effective lines of communication with local audiences.[38] It would also seem important to develop structures that accord best with the objectives that have been set by the international community for international criminal justice. But we have seen that there is not a consensus on these. The goals of eliminating impunity and prevention of further war crimes might seem to argue for an inquisitorial mode of procedure, as this gives overriding priority to truth-seeking and efficiency.[39] Other wider goals such as truth-telling, reconciliation and establishing a historical record, however, might seem to argue for the more transparent and oral models of truth-finding associated with adversarial procedure, although the scope that this mode of procedure lends to bargained outcomes between prosecution and defence can serve as much to *exclude* as to include the interests of victims and others which need to be accommodated if reconciliation is to be achieved.[40]

One of the core aims on which consensus can be reached is the need to apply fair trial norms in determining whether accused persons are guilty of international crimes and these, it will be suggested, together with the associated jurisprudence discussed in the last chapter that has grown out of them, should form the basis for devising the most appropriate rules of evidence and procedure rather than any *a priori* attachment to 'adversarial' or 'inquisitorial' procedure. Before coming to how these norms might be most effectively applied within the constraints that international criminal tribunals have to work under, we need to consider the particular procedural and evidentiary rules that were created for the first international criminal tribunals. Given the differences in legal tradition across the common law/civil law world, it is quite an achievement in itself that a consensus was able to be reached on what these should be.

5.3 Common law foundations

To understand how a consensus was able to be reached on the rules of evidence and procedure that should govern the ad hoc international criminal tribunals, we need to revisit the Nuremberg trials, which were the first attempt to impose international criminal liability on individuals. When the allied powers decided to establish an international tribunal, an immediate challenge was posed by the fact that the four powers – the United States, the United Kingdom, the Soviet Union and France – came from such different legal traditions. The Nuremberg Charter and Rules of Procedure are often depicted as a blend of elements from the continental European inquisitorial tradition and the Anglo-American

---

[38] M. Damaška, 'Problematic Features', 185.
[39] See, e.g. W. Pizzi, 'Overcoming Logistical and Structural Barriers to Fair Trials at International Tribunals' (2006) 4 *International Commentary on Evidence*, Issue 1, Art. 4.
[40] For discussion of the impact of plea bargaining on international criminal justice, see M. Damaška, 'Negotiated Justice in International Criminal Courts' (2004) 2 *Journal of International Criminal Justice* 1018; and R. Henman, *Punishment and Process in International Criminal Trials* (Aldershot: Ashgate, 2005).

adversarial system.[41] But they were in fact largely based on the American practice of military commissions, which had a decidedly adversarial structure, albeit without elaborate rules of evidence and without the safeguards that were given to military personnel tried before a courts-martial.[42] Cassese has observed that this choice of framework was based on the logic of the position in which the four powers found themselves.[43] The solution whereby prosecutors appointed by the four powers would collect the evidence against the accused through the military forces of each of them and then present it at trial was much better suited to the historical, political and military circumstances than the alternative solution of establishing an investigating judge, which would have led to difficulty in determining how such an imposing and powerful figure should be appointed.[44]

There were, nevertheless, certain features which bore some of the hallmarks of civil law procedure. Judges had the power to call and question witnesses, the accused had the right to make an unsworn statement and the tribunal was not 'bound by technical rules of evidence', but could admit any evidence it deemed to be of probative value.[45] Although these might be considered successes for the French and Soviet delegations, in truth, as Cassese points out, the American and British delegations were happy enough to adopt them. English judges have never taken the view that they must adopt a passive umpireal role in the courtroom and they retain the power to question witnesses.[46] Moreover, until recently, defendants in English trials were able to make unsworn statements from the dock.[47] The American prosecutor, Robert Jackson, justified the absence of common law rules of evidence, rather disingenuously it has been suggested, with reference to the fact that they were viewed with abhorrence by continental lawyers.[48] This suggested that the United States was somewhat reluctant to take this stance when in fact it appeared that the Americans and British were only too pleased to adopt a simplified procedure that would bring about more expeditious trials. Looking back after the trials, Jackson attributed the achievement in completing the trials within 10 months to the fact that less time was devoted to disputes over procedure and admissibility than would have occurred if the trials had been subjected to the strictures of US criminal procedure.[49]

---

[41] V. Morris and M. Scharf, *An Insider's Guide to the International Criminal Tribunal for the Former Yugoslavia: A Documentary History and Analysis* (Irvington-on-Hudson: Transnational Publishers, 1995) 7.

[42] E. J. Wallach, 'The Procedural and Evidentiary Rules of the Post World War II War Crimes Trials: Did They Provide an Outline for International Legal Procedure?' (1999) 37 *Columbia Journal of Transnational Law* 854.

[43] Cassese, *International Criminal Law*, 377–8.   [44] Cassese, *International Criminal Law*, 378.

[45] Art. 19 Charter of the International Military Tribunal. See Cassese, *International Criminal Law*, 381–2.

[46] See J. Jackson, 'Judicial Responsibility in Criminal Proceedings' (1996) 49 *Current Legal Problems* 59.

[47] This right was abolished by s. 72 Criminal Justice Act 1982.

[48] Wallach, 'War Crimes Trials', 855, n. 12.

[49] R. H. Jackson, 'Nurnberg in Retrospect' (1949) 27 *Canadian Bar Review* 761, 769 cited by Wallach, 'War Crimes Trials', 883.

There has been some division of view as to how fair this first attempt was to meld together a procedure that would be acceptable to both the common law and civil law traditions.[50] Efforts were made to incorporate fair trial standards into the charter. In Section IV, the charter made provision for a number of safeguards that would today be considered essential for a fair trial – the right to be furnished with the indictment in a language understood by the defendant at a reasonable time before trial; the right to be given an explanation relevant to the charges made against the defendant; the right to translation of proceedings before the tribunal in a language understood by the defendant; and the right to assistance of counsel and to present evidence and to cross-examine any witness called by the Prosecution.[51] Moreover, although the charter did not explicitly recognise the presumption of innocence, it was recognised in a number of judgments of the International Military Tribunal.[52]

But by the standards of the participatory principles developed by the ECtHR and discussed in the last chapter, there were a number of defects. Firstly, Article 12 of the charter permitted trials to be held in absentia, largely due to the fact that at the time the rules were drafted the allies were uncertain about the location of all of the defendants.[53] One defendant, Martin Bormann, was in fact tried and convicted *in absentia*.[54] In addition, there was no right of silence guarantee for defendants, with the result that affidavits of the accused were readily admitted into evidence. Although the accused had a right to counsel, the German counsel who were briefed were unversed in the practice of adversarial procedure and there were very limited facilities available for preparing cases. The process of disclosure of evidence was also 'rudimentary', with no requirement for early disclosure.[55] The denial of defence access to prosecution files meant that sometimes incriminating documents could be used to ambush the accused with dramatic effect in cross-examination. The absence of hearsay rules meant that the case against the defendants could rest in large measure on documentary and affidavit evidence, although there was some reluctance on the part of the Anglo-American judges who dominated, at least the Nuremberg Tribunal, to rely heavily on hearsay and affidavit evidence unless witnesses were made available for cross-examination or for counter-interrogation by the defence. There has been some debate as to the extent to which the tribunals actually used such evidence as the sole basis for convictions.[56]

---

[50] See D. Amann, 'Harmonic Convergence? Constitutional Criminal Procedure in an International Context' (2000) 75 *Indiana Law Journal* 809, 820.
[51] Art. 16 Charter of the International Military Tribunal.
[52] See R. May and M. Wierda, 'Trends in International Criminal Evidence: Nuremberg, Tokyo, The Hague, Arusha' (1999) 37 *Columbia Journal of Transnational Law* 727, 753–4.
[53] Cassese, *International Criminal Law*, 382.
[54] S. Zappalà, *Human Rights in International Criminal Proceedings* (Oxford University Press, 2003) 19.
[55] May and Wierda, 'Trends in International Criminal Evidence', 756.
[56] May and Wierda, 'Trends in International Criminal Evidence', 752. Cf. Wallach, 'War Crimes Trials', 875–6.

It is easy with the benefit of hindsight to criticise the Nuremberg procedures. It must be remembered that the trials took place in the mid 1940s before a number of protections such as the privilege against self-incrimination and the doctrine of equality of arms had become fundamental constitutional safeguards in national jurisdictions and were recognised as international standards of a fair trial. This has led commentators to take the view that while the trials were not 'fair' by contemporary standards, they were the fairest that defendants of vanquished powers might have had at that time.[57] Despite the changes that have been made in constitutional and international criminal procedure since this time, however, we shall see that from the evidentiary point of view, there are important resonances between the Nuremberg procedures and the modern-day international criminal tribunals. One of the most striking is the tendency for adversarial features of party control to be mixed with flexible rules of admissibility. In this way it may seem, as the US Prosecutor Robert Jackson argued, that a successful amalgamation was created between the Anglo-American and continental traditions accommodating both the adversarial principle of party presentation and the civil law principle of free proof.[58] There would seem to be a certain logic in this amalgamation. The interest of expediency dictated, as we have seen, that trials were not drawn out by long and tedious arguments over the admissibility of evidence. Furthermore, one of the features which we have seen has justified the exclusionary rules in common law jurisdictions – the presence of the jury – was absent from the Nuremberg trials and from the later international tribunals. With experienced judges required to evaluate the evidence and give it appropriate weight, there is arguably no need for strict admissibility rules. Judges in the tribunals have made arguments along these lines, but we shall see that such an amalgamation has not been universally acclaimed by modern commentators.

5.4 The ad hoc tribunals

The atrocities committed in the former Yugoslavia and Rwanda provided an opportunity for the international community to establish international tribunals free from the taint of victor's justice and on the basis of international standards that only came into prominence after the Nuremberg Tribunal. There were a number of reasons why it was important for the ad hoc tribunals to adhere to international fair trial standards. Firstly, as Cassese has explained, since the rationale for the tribunals was to apply international humanitarian law through the medium of criminal trials, it would have been illogical if in applying

---

[57] B. V. A. Roling and A. Cassese, *The Tokyo Trial and Beyond – Reflections of a Peacemonger* (Cambridge: Polity Press, 1993) 54. Zappalà, *Human Rights in International Criminal Proceedings*, 20–1.

[58] This view is largely endorsed by Cassese, *International Criminal Law*, 382–3. Not all agree that the amalgamation has been successful. See Fairlie, 'The Marriage of Common Law and Continental Law'.

substantive human rights law, the tribunals did not adhere to procedural human rights standards.[59] There is a specific link between substantive humanitarian law and procedural law in the Geneva Conventions which in regulating the treatment of persons during armed conflicts contain a prohibition against the carrying out of sentences and executions without previous judgment pronounced by a regularly constituted court affording all the judicial guarantees which are recognised as indispensable by civilised peoples.[60] Secondly, since the tribunals were established by the Security Council under the auspices of the United Nations, it would again be illogical if the tribunals did not adhere to the fair trial standards laid down by the United Nations, principally the Universal Declaration of Human Rights adopted and proclaimed by the General Assembly in 1948 and the more detailed International Covenant on Civil and Political Rights (ICCPR) adopted in 1966. Thirdly, as a matter of realpolitik, it would be impossible for the tribunals to achieve the ends for which they were set up by the Security Council, namely to restore international peace and security, if the tribunals did not pass some threshold of fairness, for otherwise the whole process would be represented by its opponents as a mere exercise of power – 'victor's justice' – over those unfortunate enough to be brought before the courts.[61]

The report which the Security Council requested the Secretary General to prepare on the international tribunal for the prosecution of persons relating to violations of international humanitarian law committed in the former Yugoslavia considered that it was 'axiomatic' that the international tribunal must fully respect internationally recognised standards regarding the rights of the accused at all stages of its proceedings.[62] Consequently, Article 14 of the ICCPR was incorporated, almost verbatim, into Article 21 of the draft statute approved by the Security Council for the tribunal. Article 21 entitled 'Rights of the Accused' therefore provides a basic framework for the rules and procedures that were later developed for the tribunal.

It followed from this that the rights of the accused before the international tribunals were to be more extensive than those guaranteed under the Nuremberg Charter. Article 21(3), for example, expressly states that the accused shall be presumed innocent until proved guilty according to the provisions of the statute. The accused is entitled also to the full guarantees associated with the equality of arms, not only the right to counsel, but the right to adequate time and facilities

---

[59] Cassese, 'ICTY and Human Rights'. See also Zappalà, *Human Rights in International Criminal Proceedings*, 5–6.
[60] See Common Article 3 of all four Geneva Conventions. In *Hamdan* v. *Rumsfeld*, 126 SCt 2749 (2006), the US Supreme Court considered that the article was applicable to the conflict with Al Qaeda.
[61] C. Warbrick, 'International Criminal Courts and Fair Trial' (1998) 3 *Journal of Armed Conflict Law* 45, 48–9.
[62] *Report of the Secretary General pursuant to para 2 of Security Council Resolution 808*, s/25704, para. 106. Cited in Morris and Scharf, *An Insider's Guide*, 23.

for the preparation of his defence and to communicate with counsel of his own choosing. Article 21 further states that he is not to be compelled to testify against himself or to confess guilt. While Article 21 appears limited to the rights of the accused at trial, it was clearly recognised as the International Law Commission said in its report published at approximately the same time, that the rights of the accused during the trial have little meaning in the absence of respect for the rights of the suspect during the investigation.[63] Article 18 of the Statute therefore goes beyond the International Covenant by expressly setting forth the rights of suspects during questioning, namely the right to counsel, including assigned counsel for an indigent suspect; the right to free interpretation of oral statements for a suspect who does not speak or understand the language being used; and the right to free translation of any document on which the suspect is being questioned.[64] A further extension of an accused's rights is to be found in Article 25, which gives convicted persons the right to appeal on grounds of an error of law or an error of fact which has occasioned a miscarriage of justice.

Although these specific rights are guaranteed under the statute, the overall right to a fair and public hearing is stated in Article 21 to be 'subject to Article 22 of the Statute'. Article 22 states that in the light of the particular nature of the crimes committed in the former Yugoslavia, it will be necessary for the tribunal to ensure the protection of victims and witnesses. This raises the question of balancing the rights of the accused against the rights of victims, which we shall see was the subject of some litigation once the tribunal was established. A further possible limitation on the overall right to a fair hearing is to be found in Article 20, which states that the Trial Chambers shall ensure that the trial is fair and expeditious. Article 21 itself refers to the right to be tried without undue delay. We have seen that expedition was an important consideration in the conduct of the Nuremberg trials and it was to become as we shall see no less an 'obsession' with the ad hoc tribunals and to lead to some major changes in the rules.[65]

The standards of fairness laid down in the statute did not in themselves give detailed guidance on the precise evidentiary practices to be adopted within the procedures of the tribunal and the statute as a whole gave little guidance on the approach to be adopted. Article 16 provides for a prosecutor who would be responsible for the investigation of persons responsible for serious violations of international humanitarian law and this ruled out the possibility of a continental investigating judge becoming involved in pre-trial investigation. But, contrary to what certain commentators have said,[66] this did not itself mean that a fully

---

[63] *Report of the International Law Commission*, 45th session Supp No. 10 UN Doc. A/48/10 cited in Morris and Scharf, *An Insider's Guide*, 198.
[64] For commentary, see Morris and Scharf, *An Insider's Guide*, 198–9.
[65] The word 'obsession' is used by Boas, 'Creating Laws of Evidence', 45.
[66] See, e.g. Cassese, *International Criminal Law*, 384; and *First Annual Report of the International Tribunal for the Prosecution of Persons Responsible for Serious Violations of International*

adversarial procedure had to be adopted.[67] A number of civil law countries also allocate the function of pre-trial investigation to a prosecutor, but unlike in Anglo-American countries, the prosecutor is not only conceived as a party to the proceedings, but rather as a public official whose role is to investigate the truth.[68]

The Rules of Procedure and Evidence which were drawn up by the judges of the tribunal in accordance with Article 15 of the statute, however, did adopt a decidedly adversarial approach. In his statement made on the day the rules were adopted, the President of the Court said that based on the limited precedent of the Nuremberg and Tokyo Trials and in order for the judges to remain as impartial as possible, an adversarial approach had been adopted rather than the inquisitorial approach found in continental Europe and elsewhere.[69] Apart from the precedent of Nuremberg, the judges received proposals from a number of states and organisations. By far the most comprehensive proposal came from the United States and the detailed attention given by this proposal to procedural and evidentiary matters proved to be 'particularly influential'.[70] When the judges appointed to the Rwanda Tribunal were faced with a similar task one year later, there was pressure on them to adopt a similar adversarial approach, particularly as they drew up the rules with the appeal judges from the ICTY.[71]

Although the rules did not slavishly adopt US criminal procedures, the adversarial approach adopted is clear from the manner in which the parties were made the most active actors in the proceedings, in charge of developing their own pre-trial investigations and cases at trial.[72] Judges were given the power of their own motion to issue such orders, summonses, subpoenas and warrants as may be necessary for the purpose of an investigation or for the preparation or conduct of the trial.[73] But the prosecutor was given responsibility for investigation. At the trial judges have powers to change the order in which evidence is presented and to order either party to produce additional evidence and summon

---

Humanitarian Law committed in the territory of the Former Yugoslavia Since 1991, A/49/342, S/1994/1007 (1994).

[67] M. Langer, 'The Rise of Managerial Judging in International Criminal Law' (2004) 53 *American Journal of Comparative Law* 835, 863.

[68] T. Weigend, 'Prosecution: Comparative Aspects', in J. Dressler (ed.), *Encyclopedia of Crime & Justice*, 2nd edn (New York: Macmillan, 2001) 1233–4. See also Art. 54(1)(a) ICC Statute.

[69] *Statement by the President at a briefing to members of diplomatic missions concerning the adoption of the Rules of Procedure and Evidence of the ICTY* (IT/29, 11 February 1994).

[70] Morris and Scharf, *An Insider's Guide*, 177. According to Cassese, the fact that the adversarial model was upheld, chiefly in its US version, 'was in part due to the US Government's having meritoriously provided the Tribunal with a draft that was, no doubt, well crafted and complete'. A. Cassese, 'The ICTY: A Living and Vital Reality' (2004) 2 *Journal of International Criminal Justice* 585, 594.

[71] Interview with Judge Navanethem Pillay, The Hague, 17 November 2006.

[72] M. Langer, 'The Rise of Managerial Judging in International Criminal Law' (2004) 53 *American Journal of Comparative Law* 835, 858–9.

[73] See r. 54 ICTY RPE.

witnesses, but it is clear that the bulk of the trial is dominated by the presentation of the parties' cases.[74] Apart from the clear domination of the pre-trial and trial process by the parties and their cases, the parties themselves are conceived of in the rules as competitors in a dispute or contest rather than as organs to facilitate the court.[75] This can be clearly seen from the disclosure rules, which are conceived in terms of evidence either supporting the prosecution case or as evidence supporting the defence case. Although the prosecution must provide the defence with evidence supporting the indictment and exculpatory evidence,[76] there is no requirement that all relevant evidence that has come into the hands of the prosecutor should be handed over to the defence.

As with the Nuremberg Tribunal, however, a more relaxed attitude was taken towards the rules of evidence than in common law procedures. In his statement on the adoption of the rules, the president declared that the tribunal did not need to 'shackle itself to restrictive rules of evidence which have developed out of the ancient trial by jury system'.[77] In the absence of a jury needing to be shielded from irrelevancies or given guidance as to the weight of the evidence they have heard, the judges could afford to admit all relevant evidence unless its probative value was substantially outweighed by the need to ensure a fair and expeditious trial. Thus, Rule 89(C) states that the Trial Chamber may admit any relevant evidence which it deems to have probative value and Rule 89(D) states that a chamber may exclude evidence if its probative value is substantially outweighed by the need to ensure a fair trial. The rules also make special provision for confession evidence, evidence of consistent pattern of conduct and evidence in sexual assault cases and no evidence shall be admissible if obtained by methods which cast substantial doubt on its reliability or if its admission is antithetical to, or would seriously damage, the integrity of the proceedings.[78]

Despite this tendency towards a fairly free admissibility regime, there were indications in the original rules which suggested a greater bias towards oral evidence than was evidenced in the Nuremberg Tribunal. Rule 90 originally stated that in principle witnesses shall be heard directly by the chambers unless a chamber had ordered that the witness be heard by means of a deposition provided for in Rule 71. Deposition evidence is less threatening to the fair trial principle of cross-examination, as these are taken by an officer of the tribunal and the deposed witness is subject to cross-examination.[79] Rule 71 originally provided that at the request of either party a trial chamber may in exceptional circumstances and in the interests of justice order that a deposition be taken for use at trial. Although it was not spelt out what 'exceptional circumstances'

---

[74] Morris and Scharf, *An Insider's Guide*, 256–9. See rr. 84–86 ICTY RPE.
[75] Langer, 'Managerial Judging', 861.   [76] Rr. 66, 68 ICTY, RPE.
[77] *Statement by the President.*   [78] Rr. 92, 93, 95 and 96 ICTY RPE.
[79] P. Wald, 'To "Establish Incredible Events by Credible Evidence": The Use of Affidavit Testimony in Yugoslavia War Crimes Tribunal Proceedings' (2001) 42 *Harvard International Law Journal* 535, 551.

meant, this was interpreted strictly as limited to situations when the witness was unable to be physically present at the tribunal.[80]

There appeared then to be a certain ambiguity in the attitude of the original rules towards the admissibility of evidence. On the one hand, the free admissibility approach laid down in Rule 89 gave judges considerable freedom to admit whatever relevant evidence they wished, provided it was probative. On the other hand, Rule 90 appeared to impose a greater degree of evidential restriction into the regime by its preference for oral testimony. Although the rules did not exclude the admissibility of hearsay evidence related by live witnesses, they appeared at first to express a preference for oral evidence over the kind of written affidavit evidence that was regularly presented before the Nuremberg Tribunal. Only time would tell how judges would apply these rules in practice.

5.5 Rubbing points between the common law and the civil law

At first it was reported that judges were 'scrupulous in their respect for the distribution of responsibilities implicit in the common law adversarial system and tended to refrain from intervention in the manner of presentation elected by the parties'.[81] It would seem that they also tried at first to give preference where possible to live testimony and to fit in with the adversarial approach that underlay the other rules of evidence and procedure, although they early on dismissed any notion that there should be a special rule against hearsay.[82] In the intervening years, however, the judges have made a number of changes to the rules, which most commentators have characterised as a move away from the adversarial approach of the common law in the direction of the civil law system.[83] That such an evolution could have occurred so quickly is due to the fact that under the rules adopted by the judges there was a power of amendment if agreed by judges at a plenary meeting of the ICTY.[84]

Shortly after the tribunals started work, there were anxieties expressed about the length of time it was taking to process cases which cut against the requirement for fair and expeditious trials and against the right to be tried without undue delay. The first judgment in the *Tadić* trial was not delivered until May 1997 – a full three years after the ICTY had been set up. Given the evidential

---

[80] See *Prosecutor* v. *Kupreškić*, Appeals Chamber, Decision on Appeal by Dragan Papić.
[81] *Report of the Expert Group to Conduct a Review of the Effective Operation and Functioning of the International Criminal Tribunal for the Former Yugoslavia and the ICT for Rwanda.* UN Doc. A/54/634 of 22 November 1999, paras 77–8.
[82] *Prosecutor* v. *Tadić*, Trial Chamber, Decision on Defence Motion on Hearsay.
[83] See, e.g. D. A. Mundis, 'From "Common Law" towards "Civil Law": The Evolution of the ICTY Rules of Procedure and Evidence' (2001) 14 *Leiden Journal of International Law* 287; and A. Orie, 'Accusatorial v. Inquisitorial Approach in International Criminal Proceedings Prior to the Establishment of the ICC and in the Proceedings before the ICC', in A. Cassese, P. Gaeta and J. R. W. D. Jones (eds.), *The Rome Statute of the International Criminal Court – A Commentary* (Oxford University Press, 2002) 1439.
[84] R. 6 ICTY RPE. Amendments currently need the consent of ten permanent judges.

difficulties endemic in prosecuting international criminal cases referred to above, it was perhaps inevitable that there would be such delays. But a number of prosecutors and judges began to attribute these delay problems to the adversarial system. Two main problems were posed by the system.[85] Firstly, as the system is structured around a contest, prosecutors who bear the burden of proof may obtain more evidence than is necessary to prove their case and the defence will inevitably want to stipulate as little as possible about the facts that have to be proved. Secondly, the preference for live oral testimony created a huge burden for prosecutors in ensuring that the many hundreds of witnesses who may be involved are brought to trial. Langer has suggested that two main approaches were taken to speed up the proceedings: to make judges more active managers of cases and to change the ICTY's initial preference for oral testimony.[86]

The first signs of action towards greater case management by judges may be seen as early as the first case before the Rwandan Tribunal, when the Trial Chamber ordered all available prosecution written statements to be submitted to the tribunal.[87] In order to exert more control over the case, the judges thought they needed more information about it before the trial. In the later ICTY case of *Dokmanović*, the Trial Chamber made a similar request for the purpose of 'better comprehension of the issues and more effective management of the trial'.[88] Other changes introduced over time included the appointment of a pre-trial judge who would take responsibility over pre-trial matters, including: pre-trial filings, requiring the defence to stipulate the nature of its defence;[89] greater powers at trial for judges to control the presentation of evidence, including limiting the number of witnesses and the time for examination;[90] and the issuing of a combined verdict including sentence so that there was no need for separate sentence hearings.[91] The evidentiary steps taken to reduce reliance on oral evidence included: changes permitting the Trial Chamber to take judicial notice of previously adjudicated facts even when parties wished to contest them;[92] a wider use made of depositions;[93] and the admission of documentary expert evidence and the superceding of Rule 90(A) stating a preference for live witness testimony by a new Rule 89(F), which stated that a chamber may receive the evidence of a witness orally or where the interests of justice allow, in written form. In one bare sentence the tribunal's policy appeared to change from one of preference for live testimony to a 'no-preference alternative',[94] although some

---

[85] Langer, 'Managerial Judging', 872–3.   [86] Langer, 'Managerial Judging', 59–60.
[87] *Prosecutor* v. *Akayesu*, Trial Chamber, Decision.   [88] *Prosecutor* v. *Dokmanović*.
[89] See r. 65 ICTY RPE.   [90] Rr. 90(B)(H) ICTY RPE.   [91] R. 87(C) ICTY RPE.
[92] *Prosecutor* v. *Krajišnik*, Trial Chamber.
[93] See r. 71 as amended on 17 November 1999 and *Prosecutor* v. *Naletilić and Martinović*, Trial Chamber, Decision on Prosecutor's Motion to Take Depositions for Use at Trial, for an early interpretation suggesting that the chamber would permit depositions where the witnesses were not used to implicate the accused directly.
[94] Wald, 'Incredible Events', 548. For helpful statements of the relaxed standards that now apply to the admissibility of documentary evidence, see *Prosecutor* v. *Brdjanin and Talić*, Trial Chamber; and *Prosecutor* v. *Martić*.

preference for oral evidence regarding the acts and conduct of the accused was preserved under a new Rule 92*bis*, which was directed at written statements prepared for the purposes of legal proceedings.

It would be wrong to conclude that the gradual erosion of the preference for oral testimony over the years has marked a triumph for the civil law tradition over the common law tradition and that the procedure in the ad hoc tribunals has moved towards a continental style of evidence taking. A number of commentators have considered that although the international criminal tribunals set out as a common law system, they have evolved over time into a 'hybrid' of the two major legal systems, combining a common law contest with a civil law scrutiny of evidence with active informed judges.[95] Langer has characterised this hybrid as a managerial model that does not fit into either of the two traditional systems and is closer to the managerial system adopted in US civil procedure.[96] The changes would seem to have been motivated by a managerial need to speed up proceedings rather than by any concerted desire to move the structure of the proceedings away from party competition towards a more truth-finding court. The pressure for cases to be expedited became even more pronounced with the endorsement by the Security Council of a Completion Strategy for both the ICTY and the ICTR in 2003.[97] The effect was to make judges more activist, but activist in the sense of encouraging the parties to expedite the proceedings rather than in the sense of taking over the fact-finding process. Indeed, one of the effects of the changes has been to lead to greater prominence of a traditional feature of common law rather than civil law procedure, namely plea agreements. Pressure on parties to dispose of or narrow down cases has led to a substantial increase in the number of cases that have concluded through plea agreements rather than through trials.[98]

But as Langer admits, it would be equally wrong to give the impression that there has been a consensual and effortless shift towards a managerial model of judging. He points out that just as there was gradual resistance to the adversarial system in the early years, so there has been resistance to the idea that judges should become active managers of cases from some of the judges themselves and from defence attorneys and defendants reluctant to agree on factual issues before trial.[99] Although Langer makes a persuasive case that there

---

[95] Zappalà, *Human Rights in International Criminal Proceedings*, 22; V. Tochilovsky, 'Rules of Procedure for the International Criminal Court: Problems to Address in the Light of the Experience of the Ad Hoc Tribunals' [1999] *Netherlands International Law Review* 343, 359; and M. Scharf, 'Self-Representation versus Assignment of Defence Counsel before International Criminal Tribunals' (2006) 4 *Journal of International Criminal Justice* 31, 39.

[96] Langer, 'Managerial Judging'.

[97] See Security Council Resolution 1503. The strategy called for a completion of all investigations by 2004, trials by 2008 and appeals by 2010. See S. D. Roper and L. A. Barria, *Designing Criminal Tribunals* (Aldershot: Ashgate, 2006) ch. 6.

[98] Langer states that in 2003 there were more cases concluded (8) in this manner than through trials (7): Langer, 'Managerial Judging', 922. By February 2007, there had been twenty guilty pleas before the ICTY.

[99] Langer, 'Managerial Judging', 903–4.

has been a movement in the direction of managerial judging, there would seem to be considerable scope within the rules for individual judges, influenced or not by the parties in their cases, to slide back to their traditional and more comfortable roles. There has been very little empirical research on how cases are actually conducted within the international criminal tribunals. One study has demonstrated admittedly on the very limited basis of two trials that in practice there is considerable scope for very different styles of procedure to be adopted in individual cases.[100] One trial presided over by a continental judge was said to adopt the style of the continental inquisitorial tradition and another trial presided over by an Anglo-American judge was seen to adopt the role of judge as a referee, resembling the traditional role of a judge in adversarial proceedings. These differences were discerned in the number and content of the questions asked, the extent to which the judges interrupted proceedings, and in their decision whether or not to introduce witnesses and have witnesses introduced to them or not. This was a limited survey and there is a need to caution against the generalisation suggested in the study that judges accustomed to an adversarial manner of trial proceedings will be more reactive than judges from an inquisitorial tradition.[101] The study nevertheless makes the valid point that judges who tend to work at international tribunals for a limited period of time after being in the bench in their home countries are likely to 'bring their domestic culture with them' when they sit as a judge at the tribunal and thereby to favour the domestic features with which they identify. It follows that in promoting 'their' own features, they will come up against a number of rubbing points from the opposing tradition. The demands of realpolitik require that these are resolved by negotiation or by the leverage of judicial authority, but this does not mean that there is a consensus between the two traditions as to how the procedure ought to be managed.

First of all, we have seen that whatever the movement towards managerialism, the trials continue to be adversarial in the sense that they remain dominated by party collection and presentation of evidence. The result is that the evidence is collected and presented in a partisan manner by witnesses who are called for the prosecution or defence. To a continental lawyer who considers that witnesses belong to the court and not to one side or the other, this appears as a considerable impediment to truth finding. Tochilovsky gives the example in an early trial of a civil law defence counsel reacting to a 'one-sided' investigation by the prosecutor:

> We had already, in the investigation stage, asked the investigators to come to Vitez and not to interview only one side ... You have an indictment that is absolutely one-sided. Not a single person was heard from the Croatian side ... I must say,

---

[100] F. J. Pakes, 'Styles of Trial Procedure at the International Criminal Tribunal for the Former Yugoslavia' (2003) 17 *Perspectives in Law & Psychology* 309. The two trials examined were *Prosecutor* v. *Tadić* and *Prosecutor* v. *Blaškić*.
[101] Pakes, 'Styles of Trial Procedure', 313.

unfortunately, that for the first time in my career as an attorney, before I was a Judge, it was the first time that I came across the problem of, 'My witnesses and your witnesses', because in the area in which we worked, we usually had witnesses of the court, a person who has to tell the truth regardless of whether he is speaking in favour of the Defence or the Prosecution. He conveys what he saw and what he heard.[102]

The reaction of the judge is a telling illustration of how judges may feel they have to enforce rules even if they are not wholly comfortable with them. The judge replied:

As for the point of, 'Our witnesses, their witnesses,' I'm afraid this is the procedure. And this is, of course, as you know, Mr Radović, better than me, it is the adversarial system, which is totally different from the inquisitorial system with which you are familiar in your country, and also other European persons from continental Europe are also familiar with namely the inquisitorial system where you have a totally different approach, but we have to stick to the rules.[103]

Continental judges are equally bewildered by the practices of examination in chief and cross-examination, which restrict the way in which witnesses give evidence to the court. It would seem that they sometimes try to temper these by asking witnesses to speak freely and spontaneously and encouraging the parties to ask broad-ranging questions that the witness can answer without interruption.[104] Often it seems they are tempted to interrupt cross-examinations which seem designed to confuse witnesses rather than elicit the truth.[105] An example given by a continental judge to one of the authors was where a witness was testifying that he saw a number of buildings being burned and then later in his testimony said that a mosque was burned. The witness was challenged by cross-examining counsel that this change of testimony amounted to perjury. The judge intervened and asked the witness whether when he said he saw buildings being burned he deliberately meant to exclude the mosque and the witness replied that he was not deliberately lying.

If adversarial practices can bewilder and frustrate continental judges and lawyers, common lawyers can be equally discomforted by the practices of trial chambers such as the flexible approach adopted towards the admissibility of evidence. Common law commentators have drawn attention to the dangers of admitting hearsay evidence in the adversarial context and expressed bewilderment at the ease with which judges say they can assess the weight of hearsay.[106]

---

[102] Tochilovsky, 'Rules of Procedure', 350. See *Prosecutor* v. *Kupreškić*, Transcript, 1220–1. Common law systems do not adopt an entirely proprietorial approach towards witnesses. There is no property in a witness in the sense that a party can prevent a witness from testifying. However, once a witness in criminal proceedings has given evidence for the prosecution, she cannot be called to give evidence for the defence. See A. Keane, *The Modern Law of Evidence*, 6th edn (Oxford University Press, 2006) 122.
[103] Tochilovsky, 'Rules of Procedure'. [104] Pakes, 'Styles of Trial Procedure'.
[105] Interview with Judge Stefan Trechsel, 17 November 2006.
[106] Wald, 'Incredible Events', 551; and Murphy, 'Excluding Justice', 16.

Some common lawyers have been equally frustrated by the doctrine of adjudicated facts according to which by taking judicial notice of an adjudicated fact, a chamber establishes a well-founded presumption for the accuracy of this fact with the result that it does not need to be proven again at trial, although it may be challenged. The point has been made that certain facts in earlier proceedings may not have been contested by a party or the parties at the trial because they were not central to the determination of the guilt of the particular accused; yet in later proceedings those very facts may become central to the determination of the defendant's guilt and it is inappropriate, therefore, for a court to take judicial notice of them.[107]

Another source of frustration for common lawyers occurs when judges exercise the powers they have to question witnesses and follow their own lines of inquiry as this interferes with the case that the lawyers are trying to make. To a continental judge, it makes perfect sense for judges to be able to order the production of additional evidence or new evidence. As Judge Cassese said in his address when the rules were being adopted, this enables judges to be fully satisfied with the evidence on which they have to base their final decisions and to ensure that the charge is proved beyond reasonable doubt.[108] It also minimises the possibility of a charge being dismissed for lack of evidence. In the more recent managerial era, it also enables judges to have more information about the case. From a common law perspective, however, this power can lead to judges riding roughshod over the rights of the accused, interfering with the contest that has been carefully drawn up between the prosecution and defence, causing confusion and giving an unintended advantage upon one party at the expense of the other.[109]

Cultural discordance can also be caused by the approach which is taken towards statements that are submitted to the court in advance of the trial. We have seen that parties are now required to submit to the court pre-trial briefs, including a summary of the evidence the parties intend to bring. To a civil law judge, it makes sense to read the papers before the trial so that the judge is better informed about the case and can undertake an active role in truth finding. It also enables judges to be more informed about the case so that they can be active managers.[110] A common law judge, on the other hand, is likely to be much more hesitant about reading papers before the trial that have not yet been admitted as evidence in the trial. It follows that there is likely to be a disparity of practice between judges in the degree to which they are able to be effective

---

[107] E. O'Sullivan, 'Judicial Notice', in R. May, D. Tolbert and J. Hocking (eds.), *Essays in Honour of Gabrielle Kirk McDonald* (Amsterdam: Kluwer, 2001) 329, 339. See also S. Kay, 'The Move from Oral to Written Evidence' (2004) 2 *Journal of International Criminal Justice* 495, 501.

[108] *Statement by the President*.

[109] For a classic statement of the dangers of judicial interventionism in adversary proceedings, see M. Frankel, 'The Search for Truth: An Umpireal View' (1975) 123 *University of Pennsylvania Law Review* 1031. See also J. Jackson and S. Doran, *Judge without Jury: Diplock Trials in the Adversary System* (Oxford: Clarendon, 1995).

[110] Langer, 'Managerial Judging', 898.

case managers, with civil lawyers more inclined to read the pre-trial briefs as if they were part of the dossier of the case and common lawyers more reluctant to do so.[111]

Differences have also been exposed over the accused's right of self-representation in international tribunals. One of the features of a number of international trials has been the determination of a number of accused to represent themselves, which has raised questions about the nature and scope of the right to self-representation.[112] Although the ad hoc tribunals have followed the human rights instruments in recognising the right of an accused 'to defend himself in person or through legal assistance of his own choosing',[113] there are differences between the practice of common law and civil law countries in terms of when the right to self-representation may be limited, with common law countries typically recognising the right out of respect for the individual's free will, while civil law countries have routinely provided for the imposition of defence counsel on accused.[114] This issue came to a head in the *Milošević* trial, where the Trial Chamber reversed an original ruling that Milošević had a right to represent himself in the courtroom and ruled that the right of self-representation could be qualified where self-representation threatened to disrupt the trial and undermine its integrity.[115] The Trial Chamber could then assign counsel to the conduct of the defence case. Although the Appeals Chamber affirmed the Trial Chamber's imposition of defence counsel, it considered that on the basis of the ICTY Statute defendants had a presumptive right to represent themselves before the tribunal and that when they were physically capable they should take the lead in representing their case, with assigned counsel acting in a secondary position.[116]

If civil lawyers are uncomfortable about giving such autonomy to the accused in a criminal trial, they are traditionally even more uncomfortable about plea

---

[111] In the *Dokmanović* trial, Judge Cassese was the first ICTY judge to suggest that the parties hand over certain evidentiary material including witness statements before the hearing. The American and German prosecutors agreed, as did the defence counsel from Belgrade. But when he asked the common law judges who had sat in the *Tadić* trial what they thought of the idea, he was told that he would become contaminated, polluted and could no longer be unbiased. Interview with Professor Antonio Cassese, 30 May 2008.

[112] G. Boas, *The Milošević Trial: Lessons for the Conduct of Complex International Criminal Proceedings* (Cambridge University Press, 2007) 206.

[113] Art. 21(4)(d) ICTR Statute; and Art. 20(4)(d) ICTY Statute.

[114] Boas, *Milošević Trial*, 58–61. In the United States the leading USSC decision of *US* v. *Faretta*, 422 US 806 (1975) held that the right to self-representation was a constitutional right which could not be taken away from an individual by a state or one of its courts.

[115] *Prosecutor* v. *Milošević*, Trial Chamber, Reasons for Decision on Assignment of Defence Counsel.

[116] *Prosecutor* v. *Milošević*, Appeals Chamber, Decision on Interlocutory Appeal of the Trial Chamber's Decision on the Assignment of Defence Counsel. Both the ICTR and the Special Court for Sierra Leone have by contrast considered that assignment of counsel to an unwilling defendant is permissible under international law. See *Prosecutor* v. *Barayagwiza* and *Prosecutor* v. *Norman*. For discussion, see Scharf, 'Self-Representation'.

agreements taking place between the prosecution and defence. We have seen that plea agreements have been a way of expediting proceedings, but they are a feature of common law trials much more than civil law trials and can lead to much misunderstanding on the part of civil law lawyers.[117] For them, the court should decide the level of sentence, not the parties, and the idea that the parties should be able to bargain over the outcome of a trial is fiercely contested within the civil law culture. As a result, certain judges have been reluctant to embrace plea agreements and these have proved a less effective mechanism for dealing with cases than in a 'pure' adversarial system.[118]

5.6 The need for realignment

The previous section drew attention to the tensions that have emerged within the hybrid procedure of the ad hoc tribunals, whereby the collection and presentation of evidence is party-driven and the admissibility of evidence is based on the more relaxed civilian system of 'free proof'. Lawyers from each tradition have sometimes been prepared to concede that they could work within a system other than their own and some have even advocated such an approach.[119] In order to provide guidance to judges who have to chart a way through the different legal traditions and find an accommodation that can be truly satisfying, it would seem necessary to go back to the first principles of human rights law and pay regard to the context and purpose of trials of persons charged with serious breaches of humanitarian law.[120] We have seen that Article 21 of the ICTY Statute closely mirrors Article 14 of the ICCPR.

Over the years, the tribunals have given some attention to the jurisprudence of human rights law as interpreted by other judicial bodies charged with the application of human rights standards such as the UNHRC and the ECtHR.[121] But they have not considered themselves bound by such jurisprudence. In the first case to be dealt with at the ICTY, the prosecution applied to withhold the names of certain witnesses from the defence.[122] Scope for protection of witnesses is limited in the international environment by the fact that the tribunals cannot

---

[117] Zappalà gives an example from the first guilty plea in the *Erdemović* case, where it appeared that Erdemović's defence counsel did not understand the procedure. See *Prosecutor v. Erdemović* and Zappalà, *Human Rights in International Criminal Proceedings*, 27.

[118] For discussion of the relative advantages and disadvantages of plea negotiation within international criminal tribunals, see Damaška, 'Negotiated Justice', 1018–19.

[119] See *Report of the Expert Group*, para. 82. See also G. Nice and P. Vallieres-Roland, 'Procedural Innovations in War Crimes Trials' (2005) 3 *Journal of International Criminal Justice* 354; and Pizzi, 'Overcoming Logistical Barriers'.

[120] As argued by P. Robinson, 'Rough Edges in the Alignment of Legal Systems in the Proceedings at the ICTY' (2005) 3 *Journal of International Criminal Justice* 1037, 1039.

[121] G. Sluiter, 'International Criminal Proceedings and the Protection of Human Rights' (2003) 37 *New England Law Review* 935.

[122] *Prosecutor v. Tadić*, Trial Chamber, Decision on the Prosecutor's Motion Requesting Protective Measures for Victims and Witnesses.

operate effective protection programmes for witnesses in their home territories. At this early stage of the ICTY's work, there were also no arrangements in place for the re-location of witnesses.[123] In holding that witnesses could give their evidence anonymously under certain conditions, a majority of the Trial Chamber held that the terms of Article 21 of the ICTY's Statute setting out an accused's fair trial rights had to be interpreted within the context of the '"object and purpose" and unique characteristics of the Statute', which imposed affirmative obligations on the tribunal to protect victims and witnesses.[124]

The majority decision was widely criticised and the prosecutor almost immediately abandoned the practice of using anonymous witnesses.[125] But the tribunals should not necessarily be criticised for giving their own independent interpretation to international human rights standards. The human rights principles relating to criminal trials have been developed by the international community to apply to the municipal criminal trial process and the situation within which the ad hoc tribunals operate is very different from that in which the ICCPR and the ECHR operate. The tribunals exercise their jurisdiction over individuals, while the human rights regime is concerned with the behaviour of states towards their nationals. As well as this, the human rights regime has recognised as we have seen that state parties are accorded a measure of flexibility in their adherence to the human rights standards. Departures from established norms are permissible where these can be justified by the particular circumstances of the state in question and the ECHR has developed its own form of contextual approach, with concepts such as the 'margin of appreciation'. The types of consideration therefore relevant to these human rights bodies may not be appropriate for international tribunals freed from municipal considerations and acting on behalf of the international community as a whole. It would seem from this that the tribunals are not only legally entitled to depart from the jurisprudence of the international rights bodies, but that the context in which the tribunals operate and the purposes of the tribunal may positively require them to develop different standards.

The importance of context, however, should not necessarily lead international tribunals to seek to reduce the protections that have been afforded to accused persons within the existing human rights regimes. We have seen that a variety of objectives have been suggested for international criminal justice, but the central purpose that led to the establishment of the international tribunals was to bring to justice those who had committed international crimes and if the

---

[123] J. R. W. D. Jones, 'Protection of Victims and Witnesses', in Cassese et al., *Rome Statute*, 1355, 1365.

[124] *Prosecutor v. Tadić*, para. 26.

[125] Schabas, *The UN International Criminal Tribunals*, 474. For different views on the justification for the use of witness anonymity in the international tribunals, see M. Leigh, 'The Yugoslav Tribunal: Use of Unnamed Witnesses against Accused' (1996) 90 *American Journal of International Law* 235; and C. M. Chinkin, 'Due Process and Witness Anonymity' (1997) 91 *American Journal of International Law* 75.

verdicts handed down are to have any legitimacy they must be accepted as fair and accurate. It follows that the tribunals should embrace the participatory standards that have been developed on behalf of the defence by the international human rights bodies. In the last chapter, we argued that these standards centred on the two concepts of the equality of arms and the right to an adversarial trial. Each of these concepts serve to enhance fair participation on the part of the defence and to advance a rational system of fact-finding by providing opportunities for the parties to increase the flow of relevant evidence and to test its probative value. The debate as to whether the system that has emerged fits a common law or civil model or is *sui generis* then becomes less important than the question as to how well the system conforms to each of these participatory standards.[126] We shall examine each of them in turn.[127]

5.6.1 The right to equality of arms

Article 21 of the ICTY Statute and Article 20 of the ICTR Statute provide that 'all persons shall be equal before the International Tribunal' and the tribunals have recognised that the principle of 'equality of arms' goes to the heart of the fair trial guarantee.[128] Within the context of international criminal proceedings, however, the adversarial structure that has been developed by the ad hoc tribunals raises so many obstacles to ensuring a meaningful equality of arms between prosecution and defence that one commentator has said that the principle has, in practice, been reduced to 'a melodious yet vacuous slogan, a consoling though ineffectual mantra'.[129] For one thing, by the time the defence lawyer comes into the picture, which in the ad hoc tribunals is usually after an accused has been indicted, the prosecution has had ample opportunity to select what evidence it wishes and get first sight of the pickings. By the time the defence begin their investigation with much more limited time and resources, memories may have been tainted and material documents lost. These handicaps can, of course, make it very difficult to achieve substantive equality between prosecution and defence even in established domestic adversarial settings. At least in these settings, however, defence lawyers are on a somewhat similar footing to prosecutors in terms of investigating and then compelling the presence of witnesses or the production of material evidence.[130] At the international level, however, this is often far from the case because of the inability of the

---

[126] K. Ambos, 'International Criminal Procedure: "Adversarial", "Inquisitorial" or "Mixed"?' (2003) 3 *International Criminal Law Review* 1, 35.

[127] The analysis that follows is drawn substantially from J. Jackson, 'Finding the Best Epistemic Fit for International Criminal Tribunals – Beyond the Adversarial-Inquisitorial Dichotomy' (2009) 7 *Journal of International Criminal Justice* 17.

[128] See, e.g. *Prosecutor* v. *Tadić*, Appeals Chamber, Judgment, para. 44; and *Prosecutor* v. *Orić*, para. 7.

[129] M. K. Karnavas, 'Gathering Evidence in International Criminal Trials – The View of the Defence Lawyer', in Bohlander, *International Criminal Justice*, 75, 92.

[130] Schabas, 'Fair Trials and National Security', 1.

tribunals to force states to cooperate in the production of evidence. Although this can place the prosecution as well as the defence at a disadvantage, as an official organ of the tribunal and with certain coercive powers, prosecutors are better equipped to enter the territory of even uncooperative states, while it is next to impossible for the defence to operate in states that are uncooperative with it.[131]

In *Prosecutor v. Tadić*, the ICTY Appeals Chamber recognised the difficult conditions under which parties operated in the international criminal tribunals.[132] According to the chamber, while domestic courts have the capacity through the extensive enforcement powers of the state to control matters that could materially affect the fairness of the tribunals, international tribunals must rely upon the cooperation of states without having the power to compel them to cooperate through enforcement measures.[133] To ensure equality, the tribunal had an obligation to assist the parties in the presentation of their case in every practicable way and it gave a number of examples of measures which trial chambers could take, including the power to adopt witness protection measures, to take evidence by video-link or by way of deposition, to summon witnesses and issue binding orders to states to take or produce evidence.[134] But in the course of its judgment, the chamber stated that there was nothing in the ECHR case law to suggest that the principle was applicable to conditions outside the control of a court that prevented a party from securing the attendance of a certain witness.[135] This appeared to suggest that there were limits to the principle of equality and that where tribunals have proved ineffective in their assistance, that was not a matter that affected the fairness of the trial; although the chamber did accept that there could be situations where a fair trial was not possible because witnesses central to the defence case did not appear due to the obstructionist efforts of a state and a stay of proceedings could be ordered.

Aside from the issue of state cooperation, it is impossible to ignore the considerable inequality of resources between prosecution and defence. Each prosecutorial team is invariably composed of numerous lawyers, police investigators and inspectors, analysts and in-house experts, case-managers and staff. In contrast, the defence have limited resources available for pre-trial preparation. The court's restriction of the principle of equality arms to procedural rather than substantive equality has been criticised as failing to comply with the rationale of equality.[136] While it is questionable whether it would ever be

---

[131] Ambos, 'International Criminal Procedure', 36. See also J. K. Cogan, 'International Criminal Courts and Fair Trials: Difficulties and Prospects' (2002) 27 *Yale Journal of International Law* 111.

[132] *Prosecutor v. Tadić*, Appeals Chamber, Judgment.   [133] Ibid., para. 51.

[134] Ibid. See also *Prosecutor v. Bralo*.

[135] *Prosecutor v. Tadić*, Appeals Chamber, Judgment, para. 49.

[136] G.-J. A. Koopes, *Theory and Practice of International and Internationalised Criminal Proceedings* (The Hague: Kluwer, 2005) 42. See also May and Wierda, *International Criminal Evidence*, 271.

possible to put the prosecution and defence on exactly the same footing in terms of means and resources,[137] it has been argued that the inequality suffered by the defence is not just the result of conditions outside the control of the tribunals, but is a consequence of the conditions created by them.[138] They created the Office of the Prosecutor as an institution and organ of the tribunal and made no comparative provision for the defence. They then required the parties to make their own investigations before seeking the assistance of the tribunal in circumstances where the Office of the Prosecutor had much greater institutional and resource advantages.

One way in which the human rights jurisprudence has considered that the disparity of resources between prosecution and defence can be met is by requiring the competent authorities to make available all relevant information to the defence.[139] We examine this obligation later in more detail in Chapter 9. The tribunals have made it clear that they view the prosecutor not only as a party to adversarial proceedings, but as an organ of the tribunals whose 'object is not simply to secure a conviction but to present the case for the Prosecution, which includes not only inculpatory, but also exculpatory evidence, in order to assist the Chamber to discover the truth in a judicial setting'.[140] The disclosure rules consequently form part of the prosecution's duty as 'ministers of justice assisting in the administration of justice . . . to assist an accused'.[141] But the prosecution has been given considerable discretion as to what material is to be considered exculpatory and its duty extends only to disclosing exculpatory material that it possesses rather than seeking it out.[142] There is no general right of access on the part of the defence to the prosecution's files,[143] nor is there any right to receive all prosecution material that could be useful to the defence.[144] The tribunals have operated a presumption that the prosecution is able to and will discharge its obligation faithfully,[145] despite the fact that there have been a number of cases in which materials that the prosecutor claimed not to have in its possession were subsequently shown to have been in its possession.[146] A further hurdle for the defence is that if it believes that the prosecution has not complied with its obligation, it must first establish that the requested information is indeed in

[137] May and Wierda, *International Criminal Evidence*, 271.
[138] G. McIntyre, 'Equality of Arms – Defining Human Rights in the Jurisprudence of the International Criminal Tribunal for the Former Yugoslavia' (2003) 16 *Leiden Journal of International Law* 269.
[139] See *Jespers* v. *Belgium* (report); and *Edwards* v. *United Kingdom*.
[140] *Prosecutor* v. *Kupreškić*, Trial Chamber, Decision, para. 3(ii).
[141] *Prosecutor* v. *Kordić and Čerkez*, Appeals Chamber, Decision on Second Motions to Extend Time For Filing Appellants Brief.
[142] R. 68 ICTY RPE. *Prosecutor* v. *Karemera*, Trial Chamber, Decision on Joseph Nzirorera's Notices of Rule 68 Violations, para. 5.
[143] *Prosecutor* v. *Bralo*, Appeals Chamber.
[144] *Prosecutor* v. *Blagojević*, Trial Chamber, Joint Decision, para. 26.
[145] *Prosecutor* v. *Blaškić*, Trial Chamber, Decision on the Defence Motion for Sanctions for the Prosecutor's Repeated Violations of Rule 68 of the Rules of Evidence and Procedure, para. 21.
[146] McIntyre, 'Equality of Arms'.

the possession of the prosecution and present a prima facie case which would make probable the exculpatory nature of the materials sought.[147]

More steps could have been taken to give resources to the defence, such as the creation of a Defence Office at the seat of every international tribunal to provide assistance to defence teams.[148] But even with better resources, it is difficult to see how the defence can ever operate effectively in obtaining evidence in a context where a state refuses to cooperate with it and within the adversarial system of the tribunals it is hard to see prosecutors ever sharing the fruits of their investigations even-handedly with the defence. Ultimately, of course, the prosecution bears a heavy burden of proving the defendant's guilt beyond reasonable doubt and we shall see that this is sometimes claimed in domestic adversarial settings to be adequate compensation for the inequality of resources between the prosecution and defence.[149] But this burden is made easier in the international context where the defence are unable to make effective investigations to combat the prosecution case due to the lack of cooperation by states.[150]

In summary, then, the tribunals have adhered to a basic procedural equality which satisfies the minimum requirements of the fair trial norms by entitling both parties to the same access to the powers of the court and the same right to present their cases. In some respects, they have gone further by recognising the duty to provide every practicable facility they can when faced with a request for assistance. But the international setting makes it almost impossible for an adversarial system of fact-gathering to grant the defence the substantive equality necessary to make the most effective case against the prosecution. This suggests that there needs to be greater responsibility placed upon the court for the gathering of evidence.

5.6.2 The right to an adversarial trial

Since the introduction of Rule 92*bis*, two broad categories of evidence were created by the ad hoc international tribunals: one relating to evidence of the

---

[147] *Prosecutor* v. *Bralo*, Appeals Chamber, Decision.
[148] The Defence Office at the Special Court for Sierra Leone provides an example. See G. Mettraux and A. Cengic, 'The Role of a Defence Office – Some Lessons from Recent and Not So Recent War Crimes Precedents', in Bohlander, *International Criminal Justice*, 13, 54–5; G. Higgins, 'Fair and Expeditious Pre-trial Proceedings' (2007) 5 *Journal of International Criminal Justice* 394, 396.
[149] See Ch. 7.7.2.
[150] It would be possible to address this by imposing a further burden on the prosecutor to show that any missing evidence which the defence are unable to secure is not material to the defence. See Cogen, 'International Criminal Courts', 137–8. But the defence would still assume the burden of initiating investigations and finding out what evidence is missing. Cf. Art. 72 ICC Statute, which allows the court to 'make such inference in the trial of the accused as to the existence or non-existence of a fact, as may be appropriate in the circumstances' when states refuse to produce evidence for national security reasons. For discussion of the dangers of drawing inferences in these circumstances, see Schabas, 'Fair Trials and National Security'.

acts and conduct of the accused, for which there remains a preference that it be given by live witnesses, and the second category consisting of other evidence in respect of which there is no such preference, provided certain conditions are fulfilled. At first, the chambers were cautious in applying this rule, but over time they have been prepared to admit written statements without cross-examination over the objection of the defence and the rule has been used to admit large amounts of evidence that would otherwise have had to be led in chief.[151] The prospect of even greater amounts of written evidence being admitted has been further advanced by a change which has permitted the admission of written statements even when they go to the acts and conduct of the accused, provided the witnesses who made them are tendered for cross-examination and questioning by the judges if they are available.[152]

Given the complex task of proving international crimes which often consists first in having to prove that the crimes occurred and then in having to impute responsibility for them on to political and military leaders who did not personally perform any acts of violence with their own hands, it is understandable that the tribunals have tried to expedite procedures by making a distinction between 'crime base' evidence and evidence going to the acts and conduct of the accused. Although the ICTY and ICTR Statutes have recognised the right of the defence to examine, or have examined, witnesses against them, following human rights instruments such as Article 14(3)(e) of the ICCPR and Article 6(3)(d) of the ECHR, we have seen that the ECtHR has never considered that this requires that the defence be able to examine *all* witnesses against it. Instead, it has considered that convictions should not be *substantially* based upon the statements of witnesses whom the defence were unable to cross-examine.[153] The difficulty with creating a fault line between evidence going to the acts and conduct of the accused and other evidence, however, is that, firstly, it can be difficult especially in command cases to interpret what are 'the acts and conduct' of the accused, when statements refer to the acts and conduct of the accused's immediately proximate subordinates.[154] Secondly, although such evidence can often be the crux of the prosecution case against the accused, other evidence sometimes described as 'linkage' evidence consisting of 'insider' witnesses who establish the workings of the government, army, police and paramilitary units can also be crucial in tying the 'crime base' evidence to the accused.[155]

Since the rules leave considerable discretion to the courts to decide in each particular case whether to require witnesses who have made written statements to appear for cross-examination, it is hard to make the argument that the rules act unfairly upon the accused. So long as tribunals are sensitive to the requirement that convictions are not based substantially upon untested evidence, they

---

[151] See Boas, *Milošević Trial*, 45.
[152] See rr. 92*bis*, 92*ter* and 92*quater* ICTY RPE, September 2006.
[153] See *Unterpertinger* v. *Austria*, 24 November 1986, Series A no. 110; *Kostovski* v. *Netherlands*; *Windisch* v. *Austria*; and *Delta* v. *France*.
[154] *Prosecutor* v. *Galić*, Appeals Chamber, Decision.   [155] See Boas, *Milošević Trial*, 137.

are unlikely to fall foul of human rights law. This does not, however, dispose of the question of whether the admission of large amounts of written evidence at trial which has not been subject to testing before or at trial creates the best foundation for enabling tribunals to make reliable findings of fact. One of the reasons why common law systems have been traditionally suspicious of written statements is because there are well-founded doubts about the reliability of statements taken by parties for the purpose of litigation.[156] It is true that a number of common law jurisdictions would seem to be increasingly admitting written hearsay statements despite the dangers of concoction and distortion associated with them.[157] But the conditions for taking evidence are particularly poor in the case of international crimes. There are a number of factors that point to the added difficulty in assessing written statements in this environment. Firstly, many of the witnesses coming from one side of an armed conflict may be said to be inherently biased as they have a considerable interest in the outcome of the proceedings. Secondly, there are grave dangers of errors creeping into the fact-finding process where different languages are at play. In the usual case, the witnesses give their statements orally in their native tongue. These are then translated into English, prepared in written form by investigators, read back and translated for the witnesses who then sign an English written statement. Neither the interview nor the reading back is tape-recorded to ensure the accuracy of the oral translation given at each stage.[158] A third point is that, quite apart from any errors in translation, there is considerable scope for fabrication and misrepresentation in this environment. There would appear to be an absence of ethical rules concerning the coaching of witnesses and the preparation of their statements by investigators from the Office of the Prosecutor (OTP). The ICTY has commented on the fact that questions concerning the reliability of written statements given by prospective witnesses to OTP investigators have unfortunately arisen.[159]

It may be argued that the forensic conditions of the international tribunals are more amenable to making an evaluation of written statements than in common law trials. There is a commonly held view that the international tribunals operating in a non-jury environment with experienced judges can be trusted to

---

[156] See A. Stein, *Foundations of Evidence Law* (Oxford University Press, 2005) 190–1. An expression of this suspicion is to be found in Lord Blanesburgh's dictum that 'the truth... may leak out sometimes even from an affidavit': *Ellerman Lines Ltd* v. *Murray* [1931] AC 126, 144. We are grateful to Judge Hunt for drawing this remark to our attention. Although exceptions have been created to the hearsay rule, common law jurisdictions have invariably excluded documents made in relation to pending or anticipated legal proceedings. See *Prosecutor* v. *Galić*, Appeals Chamber, Decision, para. 29. 'Testimonial statements' have been ruled inadmissible against defendants under the US Sixth Amendment confrontation clause: see *Crawford* v. *Washington*, 541 US 36 (2004).

[157] See the changes in the rules of criminal hearsay in England and Wales, for example, introduced by Part 11 Criminal Justice Act 2003.

[158] The process is described in *Prosecutor* v. *Galić*, Appeals Chamber, Decision, para. 30, n. 56.

[159] See *Galić*, para. 30.

give evidence its proper weight.[160] We have seen that this argument has not been accepted by certain common law commentators who have drawn attention to the dangers of admitting written hearsay evidence within an adversarial context. Others have been more sanguine about the ability of triers of fact to assess hearsay evidence, especially when there are independent indicia supporting the hearsay evidence.[161] Moreover, when statements go to the acts and conduct of the accused, the witnesses must be made available if possible to the court so that the defence and the court can cross-examine them. The debate over the assessment of hearsay evidence, however, tends to put too much emphasis upon the importance of cross-examination as a means of testing evidence. What can be overlooked is that when written statements are tendered as a substitute for the witness's direct evidence, the court is denied the prospect of seeing the witness first relate the evidence in question in his or her own words.[162] Common law systems have generally insisted upon witnesses being 'put to proof' and forbidden the use of prior prepared statements as substantive evidence even when the witness is available for cross-examination.[163] The purpose of putting witnesses to proof under common law procedure is to enable the court to make a full evaluation of the witness's testimony, first by a process of examination in chief (unprompted by counsel) and then by a process of cross-examination. The admission of a prepared statement as a substitute for oral testimony prevents the court from obtaining a complete picture of the witness's recollection of events.

It may be said that any weaknesses caused to the adversarial process by the admission of prepared statements in the absence of *viva voce* evidence are counter-balanced by the 'inquisitorial' features of the international tribunals. As we have seen, one of the conditions for the admission of statements which go to the acts and conduct of the accused is that the witnesses who made them are made available for any questioning by the judges. Judges are given the functional equivalent of a written dossier of the case before the trial consisting of the parties' pre-trial briefs.[164] But although this gives judges advanced knowledge of some of the evidence, it is far from being a complete account of all previous investigative activity as would be available to judges in a civil law jurisdiction and this raises the question of whether they are as fully equipped to conduct a full and effective examination of the witness.

The attempt to graft 'inquisitorial' features on to an adversarial model goes to the heart of Damaška's warning that a mixing of procedures can produce a far less satisfactory fact-finding result in practice than under either continental

---

[160] See K. Khan and R. Dixon, *Archbold International Criminal Courts*, 3rd edn (London: Sweet & Maxwell, 2009) § 9–2.
[161] Karnavas, 'Gathering Evidence', 109.
[162] This was the concern of the dissenting judge, Judge Hunt, in the *Milošević* Appeals Chamber decision to admit witness statements relating to the acts and conduct of the accused. See *Prosecutor* v. *Milošević*, Appeals Chamber, Dissenting Opinion of Judge David Hunt.
[163] See, e.g. the Advisory Committee to Notes to r. 801(d)(1) US Federal Rules of Evidence.
[164] Langer, 'Managerial Judging', 858–9.

or Anglo-American evidentiary arrangements in their unadulterated form.[165] Strict rules such as hearsay in an adversarial setting reflect suspicions about the way in which evidence is gathered and collected by the parties. Relaxing the standards for the admissibility of such evidence without the possibility of a full and effective examination of the original source runs the risk of error. Examination at trial is less necessary, on the other hand, when statements are taken before trial by a judge in a proper forensic atmosphere, especially when in such a process the defence are given an opportunity to be present and put questions in this process. The ECtHR has held that when opportunities exist for challenging witnesses before trial, the absence of an opportunity to examine these witnesses at trial is not fatal to compliance with Article 6 of the ECHR.[166] Indeed, it may be argued that the epistemic conditions for examining and cross-examining witnesses are *better* before trial than at trial because witnesses will have a fuller recollection of events at this earlier stage. A full dossier of evidence relating to the entire case can then be passed on to the trial judge. But this cannot be done under a system which is essentially party driven, with the investigation of crimes and the collection of evidence solely in the hands of the prosecutor and the defence.

5.7 Towards the future and the International Criminal Court

It has been argued that there are shortcomings in the procedures of the ad hoc tribunals so far as the principles of equality of arms and adversarial procedure are concerned. Although the tribunals have accepted that they need to comply with the minimum standards of fairness set out in the international instruments, the adversarial system of party presentation combined with the ever-increasing admission of written statements taken by the prosecution within a context in which it is difficult for the defence to make their own investigations has restricted defence access to information and its ability to challenge evidence. While the courts are able to take an 'inquisitorial' approach towards the evidence at trial, they may be hampered in doing so without a full dossier of the evidence and the conditions for questioning witnesses are less conducive to fact-finding at the trial stage than at the pre-trial phase when memories of events will be fresher in witnesses' minds. We shall see that some of these shortcomings have been addressed in the International Criminal Court, although it will be argued that there are still changes that need to be made to enable the defence to exercise a more effective challenge to the prosecution case.

Although the debates on the procedural rules of the ICC were far more extensive than those that took place for the ad hoc tribunals, in their final product it has been suggested that 'the adversary-accusatorial process prevails in

---

[165] M. Damaška, 'The Uncertain Fate of Evidentiary Transplants: Anglo-American and Continental Experiments' (1997) 45 *American Journal of Comparative Law* 839, 852.
[166] *Kostovski* v. *Netherlands*.

substance'.[167] The result is a hybrid essentially modelled on the same adversarial structure as the ad hoc tribunals, with the prosecutor retaining control over the investigation of evidence and the evidentiary regime at trial based, as in the ad hoc tribunals, to a large extent on the principle of 'free admission'.[168] Yet while the ICC retains a party structure which makes it inappropriate to describe it as 'inquisitorial', there are certain features which distinguish it quite starkly from the 'adversarial' philosophy that has tended to dominate the ad hoc tribunals. These can be seen in the more demanding truth-finding duties that have been imposed upon prosecutors and in the greater control over the pre-trial proceedings given to the pre-trial chamber than to the pre-trial judge in the ad hoc tribunals.

We have seen that although the prosecution is required to act in the ad hoc tribunals as a 'minister of justice', it is essentially concerned with preparing cases for trial in an adversarial context. Article 54(1)(a) of the ICC Statute by contrast states that 'the Prosecutor shall in order to establish the truth, extend the investigation to cover all facts and evidence relevant to an assessment of whether there is criminal responsibility under the Statute and, in doing so, shall investigate incriminating and exonerating circumstances equally'. This would seem to be an attempt to tilt the balance of prosecutorial responsibility more towards an impartial search for the truth in accordance with the civil law tradition.[169]

It is unclear to what extent this exhortation to the prosecutor to search for the truth fundamentally changes the prosecutor's role. The court has fallen short of requiring that prosecutors hand over the product of their inquiries to the court in the classic civil law tradition, but it has at least fettered any adversarial zeal on the part of prosecutors to prepare 'their' witnesses for trial case by proscribing the practice of 'witness proofing'. In a judgment which can be contrasted with the 'adversarial' attitude taken by the ad hoc tribunals towards witnesses,[170] the Pre-Trial Chamber of the court declared in its first case that witnesses are the property 'neither of the Prosecution nor of the Defence' and that they should not therefore be considered as 'witnesses of either party, but as witnesses of the Court'.[171] This judgment appeared to contradict flatly the view of the ad hoc tribunals that witness proofing is conducive to the better administration of justice, truth-finding and enhancing fairness and

---

[167] M. C. Bassiouni, 'Negotiating the Treaty of Rome on the Establishment of an International Criminal Court' (1999) 32 *Cornell International Law Journal* 443, 464. According to Boas, 'A Code of Evidence and Procedure', 32, '... the Statute and Rules of the ICC have been drafted in a similarly adversarial frame of mind.'
[168] R. 63(2) ICC RPE.
[169] G. Turone, 'Powers and Duties of the Prosecutor', in Cassese et al., *The Rome Statute*, 1137, 1165.
[170] See R. Karemaker, B. D. Taylor III and T. W. Pittman, 'A Critical Analysis of Widening Procedural Divergency in International Criminal Tribunals' (2008) 21 *Leiden Journal of International Law* 683.
[171] *Prosecutor* v. *Lubanga Dyilo, Situation in the DRC*, Pre-Trial Chamber, Decision on the Practice of Witness Familiarisation and Witness Proofing.

expedition, allowing the parties to present their cases more effectively, although they have condemned any deliberate manipulation of a witness's evidence.[172] The ICC Trial Chamber has reaffirmed the judgment of the Pre-Trial Chamber in prohibiting the practice.[173] In its view, proofing 'could lead to a distortion of the truth and come dangerously close to constituting a rehearsal of in-court testimony' and might diminish the 'natural spontaneity of testimony', which could be of 'paramount importance' to the court's ability to find the truth.[174] Although this divergence between the international tribunals may be seen as an expression of the common law/civil law divide over the respective merits of court- and party-dominated fact-finding processes, the distinction made by the ICC chambers between the permissible process of witness familiarisation and the impermissible process of witness training or coaching was actually based on an English Court of Appeal decision and the Pre-Trial Chamber drew attention to a range of jurisdictions where proofing is unethical or unlawful which span the common law/civil law divide.[175] Rather than adapting practices to one particular model of criminal procedure, the ICC chambers would seem to have been motivated more by the difficulty of transposing proofing into the procedural system of the ICC, which has a specific truth-finding mandate, and by the negative experiences of other international tribunals and national jurisdictions, where it has proved difficult to find a clear dividing line between acceptable witness preparation and the impermissible influencing of a witness.[176]

There was considerable discussion during the negotiations leading to the ICC on what role, if any, pre-trial judges should play in reviewing the work of the prosecutor. The idea that judges should intervene in certain investigative acts to protect the rights of the suspect or accused proved particularly controversial.[177] On the one hand, it was thought that if a 'pure' adversarial system were adopted during the stage of investigation or prosecution, this would leave the suspect unprotected. Some delegations were worried that an accused would be unable to collect evidence essential to the preparation of his defence without the assistance of a pre-trial judge. On the other hand, it was considered that too much

---

[172] *Prosecutor* v. *Limaj*, Trial Chamber, Decision; *Prosecutor* v. *Milutinovic*, Trial Chamber, Decision; *Prosecutor* v. *Karemera*, Trial Chamber, Decision on Defence Motions to Prohibit Witness Proofing; and *Prosecutor* v. *Sesay*, Trial Chamber, Decision on the Gbao and Sesay Joint Application for the Exclusion of the Testimony of Witness TF1–141.

[173] *Prosecutor* v. *Lubanga Dyilo, Situation in the DRC*, Trial Chamber, Decision Regarding the Practices Used to Prepare and Familiarise Witnesses for Giving Testimony at Trial.

[174] *Prosecutor* v. *Lubanga Dyilo*, ibid., paras. 51 and 52.

[175] See *R* v. *Momodou and Limani* [2005] EWCA Crim 177. The Pre-Trial Chamber referred to Brazil, Spain, France, Belgium, Germany, Scotland, Ghana, England and Wales and Australia to give 'just a few examples': para. 37.

[176] See S. Vasiliev, 'Proofing the Ban on "Witness Proofing": Did the ICC Get it Right?' (2009) 20 *Criminal Law Forum* 193, 248.

[177] S. A. Fernandez de Gurmendi, 'International Criminal Law Procedures', in R. Lee (ed.), *The International Criminal Court: The Making of the Rome Statute* (The Hague: Kluwer, 1999) 231–5.

interference by the judiciary would undermine the independence of the prosecutor. In the event, the door was opened towards some scrutiny over the prosecutor's investigations. The Pre-Trial Chamber must authorise any investigations which the prosecutor seeks to open on her own initiative, it may request the prosecutor to re-open any investigations which have been closed and it may take measures when there is a 'unique investigative opportunity' to take testimony or a statement from a witness or to examine, collect or test evidence which may not be available at the trial, on the request of the prosecutor, or on its own motion, or at the request of the defence.[178]

Different views have been expressed as to whether these measures will work effectively. The danger yet again is that a hybrid constructed to satisfy both of the dominant legal traditions will result in a skewed procedure – in the words of one commentator, 'inviting the judiciary to take over the job of prosecuting which is incompatible with the Anglo-American adversarial model upon which the Court is principally based'.[179] Viewed from another perspective, however, the changes may not go far enough in transforming the role of prosecutor from being *parti pris*. Although the ICC Statute requires the prosecutor to search for all of the evidence, incriminating and exonerating, in reality he or she still brings the case to court as an adversary and as one commentator has put it '[t]he indicia of reliability evident in an investigating judge's collection and presentation of evidence is not readily identifiable in such a structure'.[180] Some have concluded that what is necessary is a process that is from its inception 'fundamentally civilian in structure, and not adversarial', a process governed by judicial control in which 'an investigating judge is responsible for the investigation of the case, the preparation of an indictment and the collection and presentation of a dossier upon which the court proceeds with the case'.[181] The risk again, however, is that by expressing a preference for one established model over the other, the protagonists involved are asked to think only in terms of established domestic procedures. The danger here is that the choice of criminal procedure becomes a kind of 'global popularity contest' between domestic legal traditions where the most celebrated features of one tradition are transplanted into the international context in a 'one size fits all' paradigm.[182] We have seen that the boundaries between the various legal traditions are fragmenting, with the result that it is no longer accurate to think in terms of fully coherent 'adversarial' and 'inquisitorial' procedural traditions.[183] The tendency in domestic civil law

---

[178] See Arts. 15(4), 53(2)(3), 56 and 57 ICC Statute. See O. Fourmy, 'Powers of the Pre-Trial Chambers' in Cassese et al., *Rome Statute*, 1207.
[179] Robertson, *Crimes against Humanity*, 377.
[180] Boas, 'A Code of Evidence and Procedure', 26.
[181] Boas, 'A Code of Evidence and Procedure'. See also Pizzi, 'Overcoming Logistical Barriers'. Cf. Schabas, *International Criminal Court*, 238, suggesting that this is met by the ICC, which has 'wide powers under the Statute to supervise matters at the investigation stage'.
[182] P. Roberts, 'Why International Criminal Evidence?', in P. Roberts and M. Redmayne (eds.), *Innovations in Evidence and Proof* (Oxford: Hart, 2007) 347, 364.
[183] See Damaška, 'Negotiated Justice', 1019.

systems is as we have seen to move away from the concept of the investigating judge as an ideal model.[184]

The pre-trial model developed under the ICC Statute then retains an investigating prosecutor but one whose activities may be reviewed by a Pre-Trial Chamber, with an opportunity given to enable the defence to participate so that a dossier may be compiled which is more than just a prosecution case file. Although some have been sceptical about the ability of the Pre-Trial Chamber to make much impact on the pre-trial phase of evidence gathering, given that this continues to be dominated by the parties,[185] first signs are that the chambers are keen to develop an active role in the investigative stage.[186] In the first case to be brought before the International Criminal Court involving allegations of child soldiering in the Democratic Republic of Congo, the Pre-Trial Chamber made orders of its own motion to have the prosecutor report to it on developments in his investigations.[187] It has also been active in using its powers under the statute to guarantee the rights of the defence by making orders requesting that the United Nations obtain access to interview notes made by officials with witnesses which fell outside the scope of the prosecution's disclosure obligations.[188]

In truth, however, much of the time of the Pre-Trial Chamber has been spent on disclosure matters rather than on taking active investigative steps. In keeping with the more active duties imposed on prosecutors to seek exculpatory as well as inculpatory material, the chamber has considered that the prosecution is under an obligation to make its utmost effort to obtain the prior statements of those witnesses on whom it intends to rely and that the rules do not limit disclosure of prior statements only in the possession or control of the prosecutor.[189] But the disclosure obligations on the prosecution remain substantially the same as those of the prosecutors in the ad hoc tribunals.[190] The prosecutor must disclose the evidence on which it intends to rely at the confirmatory hearing held to determine whether there is sufficient evidence to establish substantial grounds that the person committed each of the crimes charged.[191] The single judge

---

[184] See, e.g. J. Hodgson, *French Criminal Justice* (Oxford: Hart, 2005).
[185] G. Sluiter, 'The Law of Domestic Criminal Procedure and Domestic War Crimes Trials' (2006) 6 *International Criminal Law Review* 605, 616.
[186] J. de Hemptinne, 'The Creation of Investigating Chambers at the ICC' (2007) 5 *Journal of International Criminal Justice* 402, 414.
[187] See M. Miraglia, 'The First Decision of the ICC Pre-Trial Chamber – International Criminal Procedure Rules Under Construction' (2006) 4 *Journal of International Criminal Justice* 188–95.
[188] *Prosecutor* v. *Lubanga Dyilo*, Pre-Trial Chamber, Decision on Defence Requests for Disclosure of Materials.
[189] *Prosecutor* v. *Lubanga Dyilo*, ibid.
[190] cf. in particular the identical language used in r. 66(B) ICTY RPE and r. 77 ICC RPE (requiring the prosecutor to permit the defence to inspect materials in its possession or control which are material to the preparation of the defence).
[191] Art. 61(3)(b) ICC Statute.

sitting in the pre-trial hearing in the case against Thomas Lubanga Dyilo ruled that the requirement upon the prosecutor to disclose exculpatory evidence 'as soon as practicable' meant that this obligation was triggered by the surrender of the accused before the confirmatory hearing, but there [is] no requirement on the prosecution to give the defence full access to the prosecutor's file.[192] But if, as we have seen, the conditions of accessing evidence relevant to international crimes invariably put the defence at a disadvantage, the defence becomes particularly reliant on the prosecution for information and the [equ]ality of arms principle is not in practice achieved by disclosing merely some of the evidence that the prosecution deems to be exculpatory or useful to the [de]fence. The defence can always seek an order of disclosure from the court, b[ut t]he Pre-Trial Chamber is also denied full access to prosecution materials, with [the] result that it is difficult for it to rule on disclosure motions.[193]

Full access to the prosecution file would enable [the] chamber to rule more effectively on these motions, but also allow it to [exer]cise greater supervisory powers over the investigation.[194] At present, the p[ower t]o take investigative steps is limited to situations where evidence may not [be av]ailable at trial. But this could be extended to situations where the condit[ion of e]vidence may deteriorate before trial, including situations where the mer[it o]f witnesses is likely to be substantially impaired by procedural delay. O[pportu]nities would be given for the defence or the new Office of Public Coun[sel for t]he Defence to be present and to cross-examine such witnesses. The ef[fect of] this would be to create a full dossier of evidence taken under more re[liable c]onditions than if the task of investigation was left entirely to the prose[cution. Su]ch a proposal would also reduce the number of witnesses who may [need to] attend trial and give oral evidence and enhance the powers under t[he RPE] for the Trial Chamber to allow previously recorded audio or video te[stimony o]f witnesses to be admitted at trial in the absence of the witness at cour[t, provide]d that the prosecution and defence had the opportunity to examine t[hem] during the recording.[195]

5.8 Conclusion

We have argued that although the arri[val of inter]national criminal tribunals marks a significant step in the developm[ent of inter]national criminal justice, the tribunals face legitimacy problems, wh[ich make i]t all the more important that their decisions can be justified to those [affected by] them and to the international

---

[192] *Prosecutor* v. *Lubanga Dyilo*, Pre-Trial Cha[mber,] on the Final System of Disclosure and the Establishment of a Timetable.
[193] Under r. 121(2)(b) ICC RPE the Pre-Trial [Chamber must] hold status conferences to ensure that disclosure takes place under satisfact[ory conditions.] R. 121(2)(c) requires that all disclosed evidence should be communica[ted to the Tr]ial Chamber, but this falls short of providing the chamber with full access t[o prosecution m]aterials.
[194] See de Hemptinne, 'Investigating Cham[ber'.] [195] See r. 68 ICC RPE.

community. In order to ensure that decisions are accepted locally in the societies from which the accused originate, it makes sense to devise procedures that deviate as little as possible from local norms. At the same time, these procedures need to measure up to the fair trial norms contained within the international instruments. The participatory model of justice that has been developed by the human rights courts in other international fora is one way of achieving judgments that can be considered fair and accurate.

In this chapter, we have mainly focused on the experience of the ICTY as one of the first international criminal tribunals in the post-Cold War era. While this tribunal and the other ad hoc tribunals which followed it have been sensitive to the need for fair trial standards, it has been argued that the hybrid of adversarial presentation combined with relatively free admission of evidence has not provided the best means of enhancing the principles of equality of arms and adversarial procedure. Within the context of international criminal trials, where endemic conditions are difficult and witnesses may be highly partisan, it is argued better to structure investigations around one dossier created by both prosecution and defence under the supervision of a pre-trial chamber than to sustain parallel party investigations.

The development of this hybrid in the ICC to include greater judicial control over the trial process would seem to be a welcome step in this direction. But there would seem to be a need for further evolution by giving the defence greater access to information and judges greater powers to take evidence under specially protected forensic conditions where there are opportunities for adversarial testing by prosecution and defence. The trial could then be reserved for those witnesses who had not been previously examined properly. With greater equality of arms guaranteed at the pre-trial phase and an 'adversarial procedure' provided for taking testimony of all significant witnesses either at the pre-trial or trial phase, the ICC would be in a stronger position to win legitimacy for international justice.

This is not to say that international criminal justice should impose a one-size-fits-all approach in all types of tribunals. Within the participatory standards argued in the last chapter, we saw that there is considerable scope in domestic law for variety in how these standards are achieved. Similarly, within the international arena, there is scope for many different kinds of approach. It would seem to make a lot of sense for international tribunals to take special care to justify those practices that deviate from local standards and practices that pertain in the societies where accused persons come from. This is important for developing the kind of internationalised tribunals that allow a combination of local and international players and it would seem to be an argument for deploying the 'global' ICC as little as possible. As the permanent international criminal court, however, it is behoven on it to ensure possible on a consensus of best practice and to act as a standard for international criminal justice as a whole. At this point, we turn to look more specifically at some of the well-established evidentiary principles that have emerged from the fair trial standards in the international instruments and consider how they have been interpreted and applied by the international human rights bodies and the international criminal courts.

Part II
Evidentiary rights

6

Fair trials and the use of improperly obtained evidence

6.1 Introduction

The manner in which evidence is collected, regulated and assessed has the potential to impact on the fairness of the criminal trial. Most legal systems, irrespective of their exclusionary or 'inclusionary' tendencies, provide for rules which prohibit in certain circumstances the use of particular types of evidence, regardless of its probative value. Explaining the nature of the relationship between fairness and improperly obtained evidence and determining when the use of such evidence will undermine the fairness of the proceedings is less than straightforward. These difficulties are reflected in the reluctance of the international bodies responsible for regulating the fairness of criminal proceedings expressly to develop principles to regulate the use of evidence. That is not to say that the potential for matters involving criminal evidence to impact on the fairness of the trial has been completely ignored, only that in many respects these international bodies have been slow to explain the connection between improperly obtained evidence and fairness and that this has necessarily had an impact on the nature of the regulation.[1]

The relationship between the treatment of criminal evidence and the fairness of criminal proceedings is expressly recognised in provisions such as Article 6(3)(d) of the ECHR and in the ECtHR's case law on the privilege against self-incrimination, which has been interpreted as lying at the heart of Article 6(1) of the ECHR.[2] The ECtHR nevertheless seems ill at ease in its role as a regulator of evidential matters. It is not uncommon to read statements in its case law to the effect that, '[w]hile Article 6 of the Convention guarantees the right to a fair trial, it does not lay down any rules on the admissibility of evidence as such, which is therefore primarily a matter for regulation under national law';[3] or that

---

[1] The ECtHR is by no means alone in struggling to explain the manner in which the use of improperly obtained evidence can serve to undermine the fairness of the proceedings: see, e.g. the judgment of the German Constitutional Court, BVerfG, NStZ 2000, 489 (490) in which the court notes that there is not yet a fixed constitutional standard for determining whether and under which conditions prohibitions on the use of evidence in criminal proceedings should be imposed. See also BVerfGE 44, 353, 370.

[2] See, e.g. *Saunders* v. *United Kingdom*, para. 68; see further Ch. 8.

[3] See, among many authorities, *Schenk* v. *Switzerland*, para. 40.

'it is not the role of the ECtHR to determine, as a matter of principle, whether particular types of evidence – for example, unlawfully obtained evidence – may be admissible, or indeed, whether the applicant was guilty or not'.[4] Such statements are often cited in the literature on the subject as substantiating the claim that the ECtHR has little to say about the regulation of criminal evidence.[5]

The ECtHR's repeated statements to the effect that evidence is primarily a matter for national legal systems might simply be seen as reflecting its reluctance to be cast in the role of a court of fourth instance.[6] Equally, however, they seem to suggest some uncertainty on the part of the ECtHR about how best to regulate criminal evidence; uncertainty which contrasts with its more confident approach in developing the equality of arms and adversarial principles in Article 6(1) of the ECHR.[7] This hesitancy might be explained as a result of awareness of the differences between the various jurisdictions in the regulation of criminal evidence. Certainly, there can be little doubt that there are substantial variations both within and between the various European legal systems in the regulation of criminal evidence. Despite differences, however, in the manner in which the exclusion or 'non-use' of evidence is regulated,[8] there is a surprising degree of agreement about the types of evidence which could compromise the fairness of the trial.[9]

Before examining the ECtHR's case law on the use in criminal proceedings of such evidence, it is useful to consider briefly the various theories, which set out to explain and justify the exclusion or non-use of evidence despite its potential probative value.

---

[4] *Khan* v. *United Kingdom*, para. 34; mutatis mutandis *PG and JH* v. *United Kingdom*, para. 76. As we shall see, however, the ECtHR has, in setting out an apparently mandatory rule prohibiting the use in criminal proceedings of evidence obtained by torture as defined by Art. 3 ECHR, created at least one category of evidence which cannot be used.

[5] K. Reid, *A Practitioner's Guide to the European Convention on Human Rights*, 3rd edn (London: Sweet & Maxwell, 2008) 119; D. J. Harris, M. O'Boyle, E. P. Bates and C. M. Buckley, *Harris, O'Boyle and Warbrick: Law of the European Convention on Human Rights*, 2nd edn (Oxford University Press, 2009) 258, referring to the ECtHR's 'hands off approach'; W. Peukert, 'Artikel 6 (Recht auf ein faires Verfahren)', in J. Frowein and W. Peukert, *Europäsiche Menschenrechtskonvention Kommentar*, 3rd edn (Kehl am Rhein: NP Engel, 2009) 207, N 165; W. Wohlers, 'Legalität und Opportunität im teilharmonisierten europäischen Strafverfahren und der Grundsatz ne bis in idem', in H. E. Müller, G. M. Sander and H. Válková, *Festschrift für Ulrich Eisenberg* (Munich: C. H. Beck, 2009) 807, 810.

[6] See, e.g. *Tengerakis* v. *Cyprus*, para. 74: 'the Court notes that it is not its task to act as a court of appeal or, as is sometimes said, as a court of fourth instance, from the decisions taken by domestic courts'; see also *Edwards* v. *United Kingdom*, para. 34 and *García Ruiz* v. *Spain* [GC], paras. 28–9.

[7] J. Jackson, 'The Effect of Human Rights on Criminal Evidentiary Processes: Towards Convergence, Divergence or Realignment' (2005) 68 *Modern Law Review* 737; see further Ch. 4.

[8] See further Chs. 2 and 3.

[9] See C. M. Bradley, 'Mapp goes Abroad' (2001) 52 *Case Western Law Review* 375 for an overview of exclusionary provisions. See also J. B. Dawson, 'The Exclusion of Unlawfully Obtained Evidence: A Comparative Study' (1982) 31 *International and Comparative Law Quarterly* 513; and U. Eisenberg, *Beweisrecht der StPO: Spezialkommentar*, 6th edn (Munich: C. H. Beck, 2008) 98 ff.

6.2 Theories explaining the exclusion of improperly obtained evidence

Not all evidence, irrespective of its character or the manner in which it has been obtained, can be used to ground a verdict. This, while generally accepted to be the prevailing view in modern times, was not always acknowledged to be the case. According to the traditional common law rule, for instance, the manner in which the evidence was obtained was deemed to be irrelevant to the question of its admissibility.[10] It was not the manner in which the evidence was obtained that was relevant, but the accuracy and reliability of the evidence. Bentham famously argued that the aim of the law of evidence and the object of adjudication was the rectitude or accuracy of the decision. Consequently, he argued that all evidence probative of the facts at issue, with some exceptions – in the event of vexation, delay or expense – ought to be admitted.[11] In other jurisdictions, meanwhile, there was resistance to the imposition of restraints on the principles of substantive truth and the freedom of proof.[12] Reliance on rectitude or accuracy alone has become to be seen as unsatisfactory not just because it 'neither takes adequate account of, nor offers a case against, the principle of wrongful conviction',[13] but also because it does not take into account the competing values which are also to be guaranteed. It is now widely recognised that not every means of obtaining evidence is acceptable.[14] There are various restraints imposed by constitutional and procedural law for the purposes of protecting other values and evidence must be obtained in accordance with these principles.[15] There is also acknowledgement of the fact that, in the event that evidence has been obtained by improper means, it might be necessary for reasons of fairness, or possibly also other grounds,[16] to prevent reliance on that evidence in securing a criminal conviction.[17] There continues to be, however,

---

[10] See, e.g. *R* v. *Warickshall* (1783) 1 Leach 263. See also *R* v. *Leatham* (1861) 8 Cox CC 498, 501, per Crompton J.: 'It matters not how you get it; if you steal it even, it would be admissible in evidence'. See also J. H. Wigmore, *A Treatise on the Anglo-American System of Evidence in Trials at Common Law*, 3rd edn (Boston: Little, Brown, 1940) vol. 8, para. 2183; and *United States* v. *Payner*, 447 US 727 (1980).

[11] J. Bentham, *A Treatise on Judicial Evidence* (London: Paget, 1825) 2–3. See also W. Twining, *Theories of Evidence: Bentham and Wigmore* (London: Weidenfeld & Nicolson, 1985). See further Ch. 2.

[12] See further Ch. 3.

[13] D. J. Galligan, 'More Scepticism about Scepticism' (1988) 8 *Oxford Journal of Legal Studies* 249, 262.

[14] e.g. Eisenberg, *Beweisrecht*, para. 329.

[15] See, for instance, the judgments of the German Federal Court: BGH 14, 365; 19, 329; 31, 308 and the judgment of the constitutional court in BVerfG NStZ-RR 04, 19.

[16] See, e.g. A. Duff, L. Farmer, S. Marshall and V. Tadros, *The Trial on Trial (3): Towards a Normative Theory of the Criminal Trial* (Oxford: Hart, 2007) 108.

[17] Good examples of provisions which require that improperly obtained evidence is not used in convicting an accused are § 136a German Criminal Procedure Code, Art. 140 Swiss Criminal Procedure Code and s. 76(2) Police and Criminal Evidence Act 1984 (England & Wales), discussed below. See also Eisenberg, *Beweisrecht*, para. 331; A. Donatsch, T. Hansjakob and V. Lieber (eds.), *Kommentar zur Schweizerischen Strafprozessordnung* (Zurich: Schulthess, 2010) 601, which includes an English translation of the Swiss Federal Code of Criminal Procedure.

considerable disagreement about the reasons underpinning the prohibition on the use of evidence obtained by way of impropriety.[18]

One rationale sometimes put forward to justify the prohibition on the use of evidence is the need to guarantee the reliability of the evidence.[19] According to this argument, the exclusion of the evidence is required as a consequence of the risk that the evidence is unreliable and that allowing the fact-finder to evaluate the evidence would result in a significant risk of error. This explanation is obviously problematic in that much of the evidence which is routinely excluded does in fact have a high degree of reliability. As Dennis notes:

> An illegal search may yield evidence of the defendant's possession of drugs or stolen goods. A bodily sample illegally taken from the defendant may yield a match with a DNA profile from the victim. If such evidence is to be excluded, this cannot be on the ground that it is unfair to use unreliable evidence.[20]

Another argument often advanced is that the prohibition on the use of evidence serves as a deterrent to investigators and prosecutors from repeating their improper conduct in the future.[21] This has become the 'dominant argument for the exclusionary rule' in US constitutional law as a result of the US Supreme Court 'repeatedly' stating that 'the rule exists solely in order to deter violations of the Fourth Amendment'.[22] Critics of this theory point to the fact, however, that in many, perhaps even the majority of, cases the exclusionary rule will have no deterrent effect. Roberts and Zuckerman refer to the exclusionary rule as 'an astonishingly inept tool for deterring official misconduct' and point out that even where policing results in a prosecution, the majority of cases are concluded by way of a guilty plea which in turn means that the police conduct is not scrutinised in court.[23] Other critics have noted that the deterrence is likely to be,

---

[18] Eisenberg, *Beweisrecht*, para. 332; I. H. Dennis, *The Law of Evidence*, 4th edn (London: Sweet & Maxwell, 2010) para. 3.42, 103; and BVerfG, NStZ 2000, 489 (490).

[19] For a good overview of the rationales for the exclusion of improperly obtained evidence, see P. Mirfield, *Silence, Confessions and Improperly Obtained Evidence* (Oxford: Clarendon Press, 1997) chs. 2 and 6.

[20] Dennis, *Law of Evidence*, para. 3.42, 104.

[21] L. T. Perrin, H. M. Caldwell, C. A. Chase and R. W. Fagan, 'If It's Broken, Fix It: Moving Beyond the Exclusionary Rule' (1998) 83 *Iowa Law Review* 669. The US Supreme Court has endorsed this theory in several cases: see, e.g. *Elkins* v. *United States*, 364 US 206 (1960), in which the court held that the purpose of the exclusionary rule was 'to deter – to compel respect for the constitutional guaranty in the only effectively available way – by removing the incentive to disregard it'; see too *Mapp* v. *Ohio*, 367 US 643 (1961).

[22] R. J. Allen, J. L. Hoffmann, D. A. Livingston and W. J. Stuntz, *Comprehensive Criminal Procedure*, 2nd edn (New York: Aspen, 2005) 346, citing *United States* v. *Leon*, 468 US 897 (1984) as an example; see also M. Orfield, 'The Exclusionary Rule and Deterrence: An Empirical Study of Chicago Narcotics Officers' (1987) 54 *University of Chicago Law Review* 1016.

[23] P. Roberts and A. Zuckerman, *Criminal Evidence*, 2nd edn (Oxford University Press, 2010) 188. See also C. Slobogin, 'Why Liberals Should Chuck the Exclusionary Rule' [1999] *University of Illinois Law Review* 363, 368; and D. A. Sklansky, 'Is the Exclusionary Rule Obsolete?' (2008) 5 *Ohio Journal of Criminal Law* 567, 582. See also *R* v. *Mason* [1988] 1 WLR 139, 144.

'at best, a weak reason for excluding evidence or staying prosecutions where there is a sufficiently strong epistemic case against the defendant to secure a conviction' and that in view of this it is 'likely to be outweighed by reasons in favour of prosecution, coupled with the deterrent effect of prosecuting the relevant official breaches'.[24]

A third theory posits that the prohibition on the use of evidence is principally concerned with the protection of the rights of the accused and that proscribing the use of evidence obtained in breach of the accused's fundamental rights is necessary to vindicate these rights.[25] According to this thesis, known as the 'rights theory' or the 'protective principle', the state has, by enshrining formal fundamental rights in law, defined the boundaries for lawful access to evidence. Consequently, the courts must ensure that the state and the citizen 'are placed in the position that they would have been in' had the fundamental rights of the accused not been violated.[26] The best way to remedy the breach is thus to exclude the evidence obtained in violation of the fundamental rights.[27] This proposition has been the subject of much criticism. Proponents of the 'separation thesis' have criticised the assumption of a connection between the actions of the investigating authorities in investigating crime and the verdict of the court.[28] They argue that the guilty verdict condemns the accused; it does not approve the conduct of the investigating authorities.[29] Acceptance of this argument, however, means that reliable improperly obtained evidence should never be excluded. Such a situation does not reflect current practice and seems in many cases to be counter-intuitive.[30] Other criticism of the rights thesis has focused on the fact that in many cases, such as in the case of entrapment, it is by no means clear that any fundamental rights have in fact been breached and further that the theory only seems to support violations of the fundamental rights of the accused, not those of third parties.[31] Roberts and Zuckerman argue meanwhile that the theory is unconvincing in view of the fact that 'time and events have marched on, and the informational status quo ante can never, in reality, be retrieved once epistemic innocence is lost' and that the state cannot

---

[24] Duff et al., *Trial on Trial (3)*, 229.
[25] See especially A. Ashworth, 'Excluding Evidence as Protecting Rights' [1977] *Criminal Law Review* 723.
[26] A. Ashworth, 'Exploring the Integrity Principle in Evidence and Procedure', in P. Mirfield and R. Smith (eds.), *Essays for Colin Tapper* (London: Reed Elsevier, 2003) 111–12.
[27] The Irish Supreme Court adopted a strongly protectionist stance towards the exclusion of evidence in *People (DPP)* v. *Kenny* [1990] 2 IR 110, where a majority of the court held that evidence obtained by invasion of the constitutional personal rights of a citizen must be excluded unless the court is satisfied that the act constituting the breach of rights was committed unintentionally or accidentally, or is satisfied that there are extraordinary, excusing circumstances which justify the admission of evidence in the court's discretion.
[28] See, e.g. Ashworth, 'Exploring the Integrity Principle', 113 referring to *R* v. *Sang* [1980] AC 402.
[29] For an overview of this argument, see M. Redmayne, 'Theorising the Criminal Trial' (2009) 12 *New Criminal Law Review* 287, 306.
[30] Redmayne, 'Theorising the Criminal Trial', 306.
[31] See, e.g. Duff et al., *Trial on Trial (3)*, 232.

simply pretend not to know of the evidence which has been obtained.[32] They claim that this approach is particularly problematic – and indeed essentially disproportionate – in cases where the violation is relatively trivial and the evidence strongly probative of serious offence.[33] Finally, Dennis suggests that despite the principle's 'undeniable attractions', 'the law of evidence is not an appropriate mechanism for protecting substantive rights: the latter are the concern of the law of tort (and the criminal law, in some cases), and they need to be vindicated by a remedy that is available in all cases and is available as a matter of right, not as a matter of exclusionary discretion'.[34]

Several commentators have argued that the need for the exclusion of improperly obtained evidence can best be understood by recourse to a theory of legitimacy or integrity.[35] According to this fourth theory, which has attracted a considerable following in recent times, the use of improperly obtained evidence endangers the moral and expressive authority of the verdict.[36] A good example of this argument is to be found in the case of *A and others (No. 2)*, in which Lord Hoffmann stated that:

> English law has developed a principle illustrated by cases like *R v. Horseferry Magistrates Court, Ex p. Bennett* [1994] 1 AC 42 that the courts will not shut their eyes to the way the accused was brought before a court or the evidence was obtained. Those methods may be such that it would compromise the integrity of the judicial process, dishonour the administration of justice, if the proceedings were to be entertained or the evidence admitted. In such a case the proceedings may be stayed or the evidence rejected on the ground that there would otherwise be an abuse of the processes of the court.[37]

This thesis is not without its detractors.[38] Ashworth questions whether it can answer criticism that the controlling principle of the trial ought to be relevance

---

[32] Roberts and Zuckerman, *Criminal Evidence*, 183.
[33] Roberts and Zuckerman, *Criminal Evidence*, 153; see also P. Duff, 'Admissibility of Improperly Obtained Physical Evidence in the Scottish Criminal Trial: The Search for Principle' (2004) 8 *Edinburgh Law Review* 152, 165; but see Duff et al., *Trial on Trial (3)*, 230–1, contending that such arguments only apply against a very extreme version of the rights thesis.
[34] Dennis, *Law of Evidence*, para. 3.44, 105–6.
[35] For a useful examination of the notion of legitimacy, see I. Dennis, 'Reconstructing the Law of Criminal Evidence' [1989] *Current Legal Problems* 21.
[36] See notably Roberts and Zuckerman, *Criminal Evidence*, 188–91; and Dennis, *Law of Evidence*, para. 3.45, 108. See also *R v. Grant* 2009 SCC 32, [2009] 2 SCR 353, para. 107, in which s. 24(2) of the Canadian Charter was interpreted as requiring that admissibility 'be determined by inquiring into the effect admission may have on the repute of the justice system, having regard to the seriousness of the police conduct, the impact of the *Charter* breach on the protected interests of the accused, and the value of the trial on the merits'; *R v. Ngai* [2010] AJ No. 96 (QL) (CA). See too Art. 69(7)(b) ICC Statute.
[37] *A and others v. Secretary of State for the Home Department (No. 2)* [2006] 2 AC 221, para. 87, per Lord Hoffmann. For an informative comment on this case, see N. Rasiah, '*A v Secretary of State for the Home Department (No 2)*: Occupying the Moral High Ground?' (2006) 69 *Modern Law Review* 995, 1002 ff.
[38] It has come under particular criticism in the United States as a result of its perceived 'fuzziness': see, e.g. *Stone v. Powell*, 428 US 465, 485 (1976).

and reliability. Further, he raises doubts that it is unable to withstand the separation thesis that pre-trial breaches of rights do not compromise the fairness of the trial itself, especially if alternative remedies are available.[39] This, he argues, is a crucial weakness of the integrity principle and strengthens his contention that it is necessary to return to the protective principle because it 'chimes better with the notion of human rights'.[40]

In the context of improperly obtained evidence, the reasons justifying the decision to exclude or not to use the evidence are of considerable importance. The belief that accused persons ought to be acquitted solely because non-important 'procedural technicalities' have not been complied with has the potential to undermine confidence in the criminal justice system. Further, from an alternative perspective, the failure to acknowledge the impact of improperly obtained evidence on the verdict calls into question the fairness principle and the legitimacy of the proceedings.[41] It is therefore important to explain why the manner in which the evidence has been obtained can impact negatively on the fairness of the proceedings. None of the theories referred to above provide an entirely satisfactory account as to why improperly obtained evidence should not be admitted to form part of the conviction against the accused if it is reliable. In particular, they fail to address directly the connection between the impropriety and the fairness of the proceedings. In this chapter, the case law of the international human rights organs will be examined to determine whether it is developing its own approach to the use of improperly obtained evidence and whether it can assist in providing a better understanding of the relationship between such evidence and the fairness of the trial.

It is not uncommon for the provisions which regulate the use of improperly obtained evidence to be broadly framed;[42] this would seem to suggest the existence of one rationale explaining the exclusion of evidence generally. The ECtHR has seemed disinclined to accept that different considerations might apply to evidence obtained by differing methods of impropriety.[43] In *Schenk v. Switzerland*, for instance, it claimed that it was not its role 'to determine, as a matter of principle, whether particular types of evidence – for example, unlawfully obtained evidence – may be admissible . . . .'.[44] In more recent times, however, it has held – albeit while continuing to cite the *Schenk* case – that evidence obtained in violation of Article 3 of the ECHR ought to be treated

---

[39] Ashworth, 'Exploring the Integrity Principle', 121.
[40] Ashworth, 'Exploring the Integrity Principle', 122.
[41] See, e.g. T. Kelly, 'Criminal Proceedings Etc (Reform) (Scotland) Bill' [2006] *Scots Law Times* 73.
[42] See, e.g. para. 136a German Code of Criminal Procedure; Art. 69(7) ICC Statute; and Rule 95 ICTY RPE.
[43] Contrast the approach of Lord Hoffmann in *A and others* v. *Secretary of State for the Home Department (No. 2)* [2006] 2 AC 221, para. 87, distinguishing 'fairly technical' illegalities from torture.
[44] *Schenk* v. *Switzerland*, para. 34.

differently from evidence obtained in violation of Article 8 of the ECHR.[45] In order to assess the various types of improperly obtained evidence and the impact of the use of such evidence on the fairness of the criminal proceeding, the various types of evidence will be divided into separate categories. By examining the case law, it should be possible to identify and evaluate the rationales advanced in support of the exclusion or non-use of evidence which was improperly obtained during the investigation.

6.3 Evidence obtained by way of torture, inhuman or degrading treatment

The use of evidence against an accused obtained by means of torture or ill-treatment has long been a concern in the context of criminal proceedings. The history of criminal procedure law in both civil law and common law jurisdictions demonstrates the potential for the use of such methods, particularly in securing a confession from the accused or a witness.[46] A number of more recent incidents and cases underline the continued relevance of such concerns in modern times. It is now widely acknowledged that the US authorities had, in the course of the 'war on terror', recourse to torture and ill-treatment, notably in the context of interrogations in Guantánamo Bay, Abu Ghraib and Bagram.[47] The United States is, however, by no means alone in being forced to confront such matters; several European countries have also had to struggle with the use in legal proceedings of evidence obtained as a result of torture or inhuman and degrading treatment. The German courts were faced with a situation in which the assistant chief of the Frankfurt police force had authorised his subordinates to use torture in an attempt to force an accused, suspected of abducting a child, to disclose the child's whereabouts.[48] Similarly, in *A and Others* v. *Secretary of State for the Home Department (No. 2)*, the House of Lords had to determine whether

---

[45] *Jalloh* v. *Germany* [GC], para. 99, citing *İçöz* v. *Turkey* (dec.) and *Koç* v. *Turkey* (dec.). See also *Gäfgen* v. *Germany*, no. 22978/05, 30 June 2008, para. 98 and *Gäfgen* v. *Germany* [GC], no. 22978/05, 1 June 2010, para. 165.

[46] J. Vargha, *Die Verteidigung in Strafsachen* (Vienna: Verlag der Manz'schen Hof- und Universitäts-Buchhandlung, 1879) 87 ff; Mirfield, *Silence, Confessions*; J. Langbein, *The Origins of the Adversary Criminal Trial* (Oxford University Press, 2003) 277 ff; see too D. Friedman, 'Torture and the Common Law' (2006) *European Human Rights Law Review* 180.

[47] See, e.g. R. Bonner, 'Forever Guantánamo', (2008) LV (6) *The New York Review of Books* 52–6.

[48] LG Frankfurt/M (first instance) judgment of 9 April 2003, (2003) 23 Strafverteidiger 325; judgment of 28 July 2003, 5/22 Ks 3490 Js 230118/02. See also the appeal court decisions: BGH, Judgment of 21 May 2004, 2 StR 35/04 (Federal Court); BVerfG 3. Kammer des Zweiten Senats (Constitutional Court), judgment of 14 December 2004: 2 BvR 1249/04 (2005) *Neue Juristische Wochenschrift* 656. For commentary, see C. Roxin, 'Kann staatliche Folter in Ausnahmefällen zulässig oder wenigstens straflos sein?', in J. Arnold, B. Burkhardt, W. Gropp, H. Koch, G. Heine, O. Lagodny, W. Perron and S. Walther, *Menschengerechtes Strafrecht: Festschrift für Albin Eser zum 70. Geburtstag* (Munich: C. H. Beck, 2005) 461; and W. Brügger, 'Vom unbedingten Verbot der Folter zum bedingten Recht auf Folter' [2000] *Juristen-Zeitung* 165. The case went all the way to the GC in Strasbourg (*Gäfgen* v. *Germany* [GC], no. 22978/05, 1 June 2010), and is discussed below.

statements obtained by acts of torture, albeit carried out by the authorities of a foreign state, could be used in proceedings before the UK Special Immigration Appeals Commission.[49]

Several international instruments, including the UN Convention Against Torture and Other Cruel, Inhuman or Degrading Treatment (UNCAT) and the International Covenant on Civil and Political Rights (ICCPR), contain provisions which regulate, be it directly or indirectly, the use of such evidence in criminal proceedings.[50] The ECHR does not contain a provision which directly prohibits the use of evidence obtained by torture or ill-treatment in criminal proceedings. Instead, the ECtHR has examined the issue by considering Article 6 of the ECHR in conjunction with the prohibition on ill-treatment as set out in Article 3 of the ECHR. According to Article 3 of the ECHR, 'no one shall be subjected to torture or to inhuman or degrading treatment or punishment'. Torture was defined in some of the earlier case law as 'deliberate inhuman treatment causing very serious and cruel suffering';[51] in more recent cases, however, the ECtHR has attached particular importance to the motive or purpose of the state in classifying the nature of the treatment. Some commentators have suggested that this implies that 'in relation to the definition of "torture" the stricter test found in the United Nations Convention against Torture is appropriate'.[52] Inhuman treatment has been defined as involving the unjustified infliction of severe pain,[53] while degrading treatment is classified as treatment 'designed to arouse in the victims feelings of fear, anguish and inferiority capable of humiliating and debasing them and possibly breaking their physical or moral resistance',[54] although the ECtHR will sometimes consider the two concepts together.[55] The definitions of these terms are not constant, but have instead continued to evolve

---

[49] [2005] UKHL 71; [2005] 3 WLR 1249. For a comment on this case, see T. Thienel, 'Foreign Acts of Torture and the Admissibility of Evidence' (2006) 4 *Journal of International Criminal Justice* 401. For a sobering analysis of the United Kingdom's approach to evidence obtained by way of torture, see G. Peirce, 'Was it Like This for the Irish?' (2008) 30/7 *London Review of Books* 3.

[50] Arts. 1(1) and 15 UNCAT; Art. 7 ICCPR – the HRC has declared in relation to Art. 7 that 'the law must prohibit the use or admissibility in judicial proceedings of statements or confessions obtained through torture', HRI/GEN/1/Rev.3, A/47/40, Annex VI, para. 12. See also *Berry* v. *Jamaica*, para. 11.7: in the context of Art. 14(3)(g), 'it is unacceptable to treat an accused person in a manner contrary to Article 7 of the Covenant in order to extract a confession'; and *Sahadeo* v. *Republic of Guyana*, para. 9.3: 'the law must exclude the admissibility in judicial proceedings of statements or confessions obtained through torture or other prohibited treatment'. Under Art. 8(2)(a)(ii) ICC Statute, Arts. 3, 17 and 130 Geneva Convention III and Arts. 3, 31 and 147 Geneva Convention IV, it is a crime to extract information from civilians or prisoners by way of torture or ill-treatment.

[51] *Ireland* v. *United Kingdom*, para. 167.

[52] R. Reed and J. Murdoch, *A Guide to Human Rights Law in Scotland*, 2nd edn (Edinburgh: Tottel, 2008) para. 4.30, 279–80. Art. 1(1) UN Convention Against Torture and Other Cruel, Inhuman or Degrading Treatment or Punishment imposes a four-part test: (i) the intentional infliction of (ii) severe mental or physical pain or suffering (iii) for any purpose (iv) by a public official or person acting in an official capacity.

[53] *The Greek Case* (report), 186.   [54] *Ireland* v. *United Kingdom*, para. 167.

[55] *Selmouni* v. *France* [GC], para. 96, where the court distinguished between 'torture' and 'inhuman and degrading treatment'.

in the ECtHR's case law. Treatment, classed in earlier times as inhuman, might now be considered in light of increased expectations to constitute torture.[56]

Applicants must provide support for their allegations of ill-treatment in the form of appropriate evidence sufficient to meet the standard of proof 'beyond reasonable doubt', although such proof 'may follow from the coexistence of sufficiently strong, clear and concordant inferences or of similar unrebutted presumptions of fact'.[57] It will often prove difficult for applicants to substantiate their claims and the test has been criticised as 'legally untenable and, in practice, unachievable'.[58] In *Labita*, eight judges subscribed to a dissenting opinion, which has been described as 'persuasive',[59] in which they argued that particularly in cases where the victim is in prison 'it may even be considered that the burden of proof is on the authorities to provide a satisfactory and convincing explanation' and that in any event the standard of proof ought to be lower if the authorities have failed to conduct an effective investigation and to make the findings available to the ECtHR.[60]

This approach is closer to that of the Human Rights Committee, which has held that 'the burden of proof cannot rest alone on the author of the communication, especially considering that the author and the State party do not always have equal access to the evidence and that frequently the State party alone has access to relevant information'.[61] Consequently, it has held that the state party has the duty to investigate in good faith all allegations of violations of the covenant made against it and its authorities and to furnish to the committee the information available to it.[62] In those cases in which the applicant has made allegations supported by some prima facie evidence and where 'further clarification of the case depends on information exclusively in the hands of the State party', the HRC has held that it is entitled to 'consider such allegations as substantiated in the absence of satisfactory evidence and explanations to the contrary submitted by the State party'.[63]

6.3.1 Evidence obtained by way of torture

The ECtHR has had the opportunity in a line of judgments to expound on the reasons for restrictions on the use in criminal proceedings of evidence obtained in violation of Article 3 of the ECHR. Of particular note is the fact that it has adopted a stricter approach to evidence obtained by way of torture than evidence

---

[56] See Reed and Murdoch, *Human Rights Law*, para. 4.27, 273.
[57] *Ireland* v. *United Kingdom*, para. 161.
[58] Judge Bonello, dissenting in *Veznedaroglu* v. *Turkey*. See also U. Erdal, 'Burden and Standard of Proof in Proceedings under the European Convention' (2001) 26 *European Law Review, Supplement (Human Rights)* 68.
[59] Reed and Murdoch, *Human Rights Law*, para. 4.34, 286.
[60] *Labita* v. *Italy* [GC], dissenting opinion attached to the judgment.
[61] *Conteris* v. *Uruguay*, para. 7.2.   [62] Ibid.
[63] Ibid. See too the cases of *Bleier* v. *Uruguay* and *Romero* v. *Uruguay*.

obtained in breach of the prohibition on inhuman and degrading treatment. This is clearly evident in the case of *Jalloh* v. *Germany*.[64] In its judgment, the ECtHR referred to the fact that Article 3 enshrined 'one of the most fundamental values of democratic societies'. It noted that 'even in circumstances, such as the fight against terrorism and organised crime, the Convention prohibits in absolute terms torture and inhuman or degrading treatment or punishment, irrespective of the victim's conduct'.[65] Although the applicant's treatment was found to constitute inhuman and degrading treatment rather than torture, the ECtHR nevertheless noted in the course of its judgment that the use in criminal proceedings of evidence obtained by torture would violate Article 6 of the ECHR, irrespective of the weight of the evidence.[66]

The ECtHR has subsequently confirmed that the use in criminal proceedings of evidence obtained by way of torture will automatically violate the right to a fair trial. In *Harutyunyan* v. *Armenia*, the applicant alleged that he and two witnesses had been subjected to torture and that the evidence had been used against him in criminal proceedings; the government accepted that the accused had been subjected to ill-treatment amounting to torture.[67] The ECtHR rejected the government's attempts to justify the use of the applicant's confession on the basis that the applicant had confessed to the investigator and not to the police officers who had ill-treated him, that the witness had confirmed his earlier confession at a confrontation hearing and that both witnesses had made similar statements at the subsequent court hearing.[68] The ECtHR noted that:

> ... where there is compelling evidence that a person has been subjected to ill-treatment, including physical violence and threats, the fact that this person confessed – or confirmed a coerced confession in his later statements – to an authority other than the one responsible for this ill-treatment should not automatically lead to the conclusion that such confession or later statements were not made as a consequence of the ill-treatment and the fear that such a person may experience thereafter.[69]

The ECtHR concluded that the 'use of evidence obtained in violation of Article 3 in criminal proceedings raises serious concerns as to the fairness of the proceedings' and that 'regardless of the impact the statements obtained under torture had on the outcome of the applicant's criminal proceedings, the use of such evidence rendered his trial as a whole unfair'.[70]

The ECtHR took a similar approach in *Levinta* v. *Moldova*, in which it found that the applicants had been subjected to ill-treatment amounting to torture in

---

[64] *Jalloh* v. *Germany* [GC].
[65] *Jalloh* v. *Germany* [GC], para. 99, citing *Chahal* v. *United Kingdom*, para. 79; and *Selmouni* v. *France* [GC], para. 95.
[66] *Jalloh* v. *Germany* [GC], para. 105.   [67] Para. 64.
[68] *Harutyunyan* v. *Armenia*, para. 65.   [69] Ibid.
[70] *Harutyunyan* v. *Armenia*, para. 66. See also *A and others* v. *Secretary of State for the Home Department (No. 2)* [2005] WLR 1249 para. 51 (HL) and para. 52. For comment on this case, see Thienel, 'Foreign Acts of Torture', 401–9.

order to extract confessions from them.[71] The applicants subsequently made a number of self-incriminating statements which were used against them in criminal proceedings. In holding that there had been a violation of Article 6, the ECtHR held that:

> ... the statements obtained from the applicants in such circumstances, following their torture and while being deprived of any support from their lawyers and faced with a total lack of reaction by the authorities to their lawyers' complaints, fall within the category of statements which should never be admissible in criminal proceedings since use of such evidence would make such proceedings unfair as a whole, regardless of whether the courts also relied on other evidence.[72]

It held that in view of the fact that the applicants had been subjected to torture it was unnecessary to determine 'the extent to which the domestic courts relied on evidence obtained as a result' and whether the evidence had been a decisive factor in their conviction. It held that the 'mere fact that the domestic courts actually relied on evidence obtained as a result of torture rendered the entire trial unfair'.[73]

These cases demonstrate that the use of evidence obtained by way of treatment which amounts to torture is prohibited, not necessarily because the evidence is in itself unreliable, although this may well be a factor, but principally because the use of such evidence is seen as fatally undermining the fairness of the proceedings and the legitimacy of the criminal justice system. In arguing for the automatic, compulsory prohibition on the use of evidence obtained through torture, the ECtHR refers to the fact that such evidence 'should never be relied on as proof of the victim's guilt, irrespective of its probative value' and that any other 'conclusion would only serve to legitimate indirectly the sort of morally reprehensible conduct which the authors of Article 3 of the Convention sought to proscribe'.[74]

The phrase 'never be relied on as proof of the victim's guilt' seems to leave open the question of whether evidence obtained by way of the ill-treatment of a witness or a co-accused could be used in evidence against an accused who had not been subjected to such ill-treatment. The legitimacy of the proceedings would presumably also be undermined by the use of any evidence obtained by way of torture, irrespective of whether this took the form of a confession or witness testimony. These cases make it clear that there is no room here for consideration of the weight of the evidence or a type of sole and decisive test resembling that applied by the ECtHR in the context of Article 6(3)(d) of the ECHR.[75] At the same time, there is no indication of support in this context for the proposition that the use of torture ought to result in a stay

---

[71] *Levinta* v. *Moldova*, paras. 71 and 92.   [72] *Levinta* v. *Moldova*, para. 104 (references omitted).
[73] *Levinta* v. *Moldova*, para. 105.
[74] *Levinta* v. *Moldova*, para. 63; and *Jalloh* v. *Germany* [GC], para. 105, citing *Rochin* v. *California*, 342 US 165 (1952).
[75] See further Ch. 10.

of the proceedings.[76] In *Harutyunyan*, the ECtHR considered at length the government's arguments that the national court had not relied on the evidence at issue, eventually concluding that the national courts had relied on the evidence in convicting the applicant. This suggests that the evidence must actually be used in criminal proceedings for there to be a violation of Article 6 of the ECHR. This in turn indicates that the ECtHR does not believe that the use of torture during a criminal investigation per se undermines the prosecution to such an extent as to make a fair trial impossible. These cases also emphasise that the ECtHR is not reading an exclusionary rule, such as that set out in Article 15 of the UNCAT, into Article 3 of the ECHR, but is rather justifying the automatic exclusion of evidence obtained by torture solely in the context of guaranteeing the right to a fair trial as set out in Article 6 of the ECHR.

6.3.2 Evidence obtained by way of inhuman or degrading treatment

In view of the fact that the ECtHR's prohibition on the use of evidence obtained by torture is based principally on legitimacy and in particular on the importance of upholding the values underpinning Article 3 of the ECHR, it would not be unreasonable to assume that the prohibition would also extend to the use of any evidence obtained by methods constituting ill-treatment not amounting to torture, but sufficient to constitute a violation of Article 3. The ECtHR has proven reluctant, however, to endorse this view and has instead introduced a distinction between evidence obtained in violation of the torture prohibition and evidence obtained by way of inhuman or degrading treatment. In *Jalloh* v. *Germany*, the ECtHR had to consider the alleged mistreatment of an applicant who had been observed by the police dealing in drugs.[77] When approached by a police officer, the applicant swallowed a small plastic bag, which was later found to contain 0.2 grams of cocaine. He was taken by the police to hospital, but refused voluntarily to take medication, which would have caused him to vomit and reproduce the drugs. He was then pinned down by four police officers, a tube was fed through his nose into his stomach and he was forced to regurgitate. He claimed that the procedure violated his rights under Article 3 of the ECHR and that the use of this evidence to convict him violated Article 6 of the ECHR.

While holding that the use of evidence obtained in violation of the Article 3 ECHR prohibition on torture would automatically violate the fair trial requirement in Article 6 of the ECHR, the ECtHR deliberately left open the question of whether this would also be the case if the evidence had been obtained through inhuman or degrading treatment. It noted that it could not be excluded that 'on the facts of a particular case the use of evidence obtained by intentional acts of

---

[76] Some commentators have argued that where the authorities have resorted to torture against an accused, any proceedings against the accused must be stayed, notwithstanding the existence of other evidence incriminating him or her, which was not obtained on the basis of, and thus was not contaminated by, the impugned evidence. See, e.g. Duff et al., *Trial on Trial (3)*, 247.

[77] *Jalloh* v. *Germany* [GC].

ill-treatment not amounting to torture will render the trial against the victim unfair irrespective of the seriousness of the offence allegedly committed, the weight attached to the evidence and the opportunities which the victim had to challenge its admission and use at his trial'. Nevertheless, in the case at issue the various pieces of evidence obtained by 'the impugned measure were the decisive element in securing the applicant's conviction' and thus although the applicant was provided with the opportunity to challenge the use of the evidence, 'any discretion on the part of the national courts to exclude that evidence could not come into play as they considered the administration of emetics to be authorised by the domestic law'.[78] The use in evidence of the drugs obtained by the forcible administration of emetics consequently rendered the applicant's trial as a whole unfair.[79]

The ECtHR's judgment turns on three aspects: the seriousness of the offence, the weight of the evidence and the opportunity to challenge the use of the evidence in court. With regard to the issue of the seriousness of the offence, the ECtHR seemed to suggest that on the facts of the case, the public interest in securing the applicant's conviction – referring to the fact that the applicant was a small-time street drug dealer, who had only been given a six months' suspended prison sentence and probation – was not sufficient to warrant allowing the use of the evidence at trial. This has been interpreted by some as implying that seriousness of the offence might be relevant to the question of whether the treatment attained the level of severity required for it to constitute inhuman and degrading treatment for the purposes of Article 3 of the ECHR. A number of commentators and indeed judges have baulked at this suggestion. Ashworth writes that 'to allow the question of the relative seriousness of the offence to dilute the protection guaranteed by the article is surely wrong'[80] and that it is 'staggering' how frequently judges repeat this argument without thinking of the consequences.[81]

The ECtHR's examination of whether the evidence was 'decisive' to the conviction mirrors its approach to the defence's opportunity to cross-examine witnesses.[82] This implies that it may be permissible for the authorities to use evidence obtained by inhuman or degrading treatment providing that it is not decisive to the conviction. Finally, in finding a violation of Article 6 of the ECHR, the ECtHR was influenced – echoing cases such as *Khan* v. *United Kingdom* – by the fact that while the applicant had had the opportunity to challenge the use of

---

[78] *Jalloh* v. *Germany* [GC], paras. 106–7.   [79] *Jalloh* v. *Germany* [GC], para. 108.
[80] A. Ashworth, 'Case Comment: Human Rights Article 3 – Article 6' [2007] *Criminal Law Review* 717–21.
[81] A. Ashworth, 'Exploring the Integrity Principle', 120: 'As has been pointed out sharply on more than one occasion, just as the greater seriousness of the crime makes it more of a social priority for the guilty to be convicted, so also the greater seriousness of the crime makes the allegation more crucial for defendants, particularly the innocent, and hence more important that all the fundamental rights are properly secured.' See also the concurring opinion of Judge Bratza attached to the judgment in *Jalloh* v. *Germany* [GC].
[82] See further Ch. 10.

the evidence obtained in violation of Article 3 of the ECHR, the national court did not have any discretion to exclude the evidence as the manner in which it had been obtained was in accordance with domestic law. Ashworth is critical of this reasoning, stating that:

> If the majority is implying that, if German law had given the court a discretion, it would have followed *Khan v. United Kingdom* and have held the trial fair if the court had given the defendant the opportunity to challenge the authenticity of the evidence, this would substantially reduce the effectiveness of Art. 3 and contradict the court's own lyrical phrases about the importance of Art. 3.[83]

In *Haci Özen* v. *Turkey*, the applicant disputed the evidence on which his conviction had been based, arguing that his statements had been made under duress.[84] The ECtHR confirmed that the applicant had been subjected to ill-treatment while in detention such as to violate the prohibition set out in Article 3 of the ECHR on inhuman and degrading treatment.[85] Initially, it seemed unreceptive to the distinction drawn between torture and other types of ill-treatment by the ECtHR in *Jalloh*, stating that it had 'already held that the use of evidence obtained *in violation of Article 3* in criminal proceedings infringed the fairness of such proceedings even if the evidence was not decisive in securing the conviction'.[86] Nevertheless, in finding that there had been a violation of Article 6 of the ECHR, it did not hold that the use of evidence obtained in violation of Article 3 of the ECHR automatically violated Article 6. As in *Jalloh*, it examined the importance of the evidence at issue, noting that the national court had used the statements 'as the main evidence in its judgment convicting the applicant, despite his denial of their accuracy'.[87] The ECtHR also referred to the fact that the trial court had not first determined 'the admissibility of the applicant's statements made in the custody of the gendarmerie before going on to examine the merits of the case'. Finally, in holding that the applicant's right to a fair trial had been violated, it referred to the fact that the applicant had not received any legal assistance during his time in custody, that he had made the impugned statements in the absence of his lawyer and that he 'denied the accuracy of those statements'. Consequently, it held that 'the use of the applicant's statements obtained during his custody period in the absence of his lawyer in the criminal proceedings brought against him rendered his trial as a whole unfair'.[88]

Similarly, in *Gladyshev* v. *Russia*, the applicant alleged that he had been beaten while in custody.[89] These allegations were supported by a forensic medical expert, who recorded various injuries to the applicant's body, including 'chest trauma with broken ribs'. He also complained that his initial confession

---

[83] Ashworth, 'Case Comment', 720.   [84] See also *Göcmen* v. *Turkey*.   [85] Paras. 56–8.
[86] *Haci Özen* v. *Turkey*, para. 101 (emphasis added), referring to *Jalloh* v. *Germany* [GC], para. 99 and *Söylemez* v. *Turkey*, para. 23; and *Örs and others* v. *Turkey*, para. 60.
[87] *Haci Özen* v. *Turkey*, para. 103.   [88] *Haci Özen* v. *Turkey*, paras. 103–4.
[89] *Gladyshev* v. *Russia*.

had been induced by the ill-treatment to which he had been subjected. The ECtHR found it proven that the applicant had been subjected to ill-treatment in violation of Article 3 of the ECHR when he made his initial confession.[90] In finding a violation of Article 6 of the ECHR, the ECtHR noted that although the confession made as a result of the ill-treatment was not the only evidence against the accused (subsequent statements by the applicant and 'other indirect evidence' were also adduced), it was uncontested that the applicant's initial statements 'formed a relevant part in his conviction'. Furthermore, the ECtHR seemed to be influenced by the fact that the trial court had not held the statements to be inadmissible and that the Supreme Court had not referred in its judgment either to the circumstances of the interrogation or to the admissibility of the statements at issue. It held that the fact that the applicant's statements obtained while the applicant was subjected to ill-treatment played a role in his conviction, coupled with the manner in which the trial court had 'dealt with the evidence before it', rendered the applicant's trial unfair. The ECtHR also held that in view of this finding it was unnecessary to examine the applicant's complaint that the use of the confession violated his right not to incriminate himself.[91]

In these judgments, the ECtHR is mainly concerned with two factors: the importance of the evidence at issue and the manner in which the national courts have approached the question of the admissibility or 'usability' of the evidence. With regard to the importance of the evidence, it seems that the court is employing a different test from that applied in the context of Article 6(3)(d) of the ECHR. The evidence need not be the sole basis for the conviction; indeed, in *Gladyshev* it is doubtful whether the evidence at issue was important at all. The fact that it played a relevant part in the applicant's conviction sufficed. The ECtHR's emphasis on the importance of the judicial role in determining the fairness of the use of the evidence is also apparent. In all of the cases at issue, the national courts failed to consider or did not have the discretion to refuse to rely on the evidence at issue. The importance of this issue is rather unclear. If the national courts considered the question of admissibility of the evidence at issue and had the discretion to exclude it, but nevertheless decided to admit or use it, would that mean that the trial was fair?

6.3.3 Fairness and evidence obtained by recourse to torture or ill-treatment

It seems to make little sense to emphasise, as the ECtHR does in *Jalloh* and *Haci Özen*, the importance of the guarantees outlined in Article 3 of the ECHR and in particular to justify the prohibition on the use of such evidence by reference to the fact that its use would 'indirectly legitimise' the 'morally reprehensible

---

[90] *Gladyshev* v. Russia, paras. 57–8.   [91] *Gladyshev* v. Russia, paras. 79–80.

conduct which the authors of Article 3 of the Convention sought to proscribe' and then to limit the prohibition on the use of evidence to evidence obtained by torture. It is unclear why evidence obtained in violation of the other aspects of Article 3 would not also indirectly legitimise this 'morally reprehensible conduct'. The ECtHR notes in *Jalloh* that evidence obtained by torture should never be used and in *Harutyunyan* that the use of evidence obtained under torture rendered the applicant's trial as a whole unfair, regardless of the impact of the evidence on the outcome of the proceedings. Equally, it seems very likely, however, that the use of evidence obtained by inhuman or degrading treatment might also undermine the legitimacy of the process.[92]

The ECtHR's reluctance to find an automatic violation of the right to a fair trial in the event of the use in criminal proceedings of evidence obtained in a violation of Article 3 of the ECHR is difficult to understand. One reason might be a perceived lack of agreement about the definition of ill-treatment not amounting to torture. In this regard, the ECtHR seems to have been influenced by the terminology employed in Article 15 of the UNCAT, which provides that statements which are established to have been made as a result of torture shall not be used in evidence in proceedings against the victim of torture. References in earlier drafts of Article 15 to ill-treatment were deleted in the course of the drafting process.[93] It is fair to assume that the decision to drop 'ill-treatment' from Article 15 was precipitated by a lack of agreement about its definition. This argument seems, however, to carry considerably less weight in the context of the ECHR, not least because the contracting states have agreed to be bound by Article 3 of the ECHR and many if not the majority have provisions designed to prohibit the use of evidence obtained by means of ill-treatment from being used to ground a criminal conviction.[94]

The German Criminal Procedure Code, for instance, prohibits the use of evidence obtained by interfering or threatening to interfere with an accused's will, by recourse to ill-treatment, sleep deprivation tactics, physical attacks, torture, deception or hypnosis.[95] According to Eisenberg, the provision reflects the principle that the 'truth' is not to be obtained at any price and that criminal proceedings must be compatible with the rule of law and serves to protect the integrity of the state and the criminal justice system.[96] Similar provisions are

---

[92] Concurring opinion of Judge Bratza in *Jalloh v. Germany* [GC]; see also Ashworth, 'Case Comment', 717–21.

[93] See further R. Pattenden, 'Admissibility in Criminal Proceedings of Third Party and Real Evidence Obtained by Methods Prohibited by UNCAT' (2006) 10 *International Journal of Evidence and Proof* 1.

[94] For a good overview, see Pattenden, 'Admissibility in Criminal Proceedings'.

[95] § 136a German Code of Criminal Procedure. In Germany, Art. 15 of the Torture Convention has legal effect: *El Motassadeq*, decision of the Higher Regional Court of Hamburg, 14 June 2005, para. 2.

[96] See, e.g. Eisenberg, *Beweisrecht*, 191, para. 625; see also BVerfG NStZ 84, 82; NJW 05, 2383; BGH 12, 358, 365.

also to be found in France,[97] the Netherlands,[98] Canada[99] and in the Swiss federal criminal procedure code, which prohibits the use of 'coercion, force, threats, promises, deception and measures which could interfere with the will of a person'.[100] In England and Wales, section 76(2) of the Police and Criminal Evidence Act 1984 (PACE)[101] makes clear that it is unacceptable to rely on evidence obtained by oppression, irrespective of whether or not the evidence is in fact true.[102] The explicit reference to the irrelevance of the truthfulness of the confession is particularly noticeable in that it offers some support to the view that 'a conviction based on a confession obtained by torture lacks moral authority and fails to fulfil the moral and expressive functions of the criminal verdict'.[103]

In view of this consensus, the attempt to restrict the prohibition on the use of evidence obtained by ill-treatment to that obtained by way of torture would seem to be unduly restrictive. Some argue that all evidence which can be 'traced back to a violation of Article 3 should be automatically inadmissible in litigation', that the exclusionary rule ought to be read into Article 3 itself and thus that 'the question whether its use will render the defendant's trial fair or unfair ought not to arise'.[104] This approach is not necessarily desirable. Evidence obtained by the state authorities in violation of Article 3 of the ECHR should never be used as evidence to found a conviction against an accused, but it is essential that the manner in which it impacts on the fairness of the proceedings is clearly elucidated.

Violations of Article 3 of the ECHR and in particular of the torture prohibition are generally agreed to be so reprehensible as to warrant forbidding the use of such evidence at trial. Nevertheless, as the manner in which the

---

[97] See, e.g. *French Republic* v. *Haramboure*, Cour de Cassation, Chambre Criminelle, 24 January 1995, No. de pourvoi 94–81254; and *Le Ministère Public* v. *Irastorza Dorronsoro*, Cour d'Appel de Pau, No. 238/2003, 16 May 2003. See also *LaFrance* v. *Bohlinger*, 499 F 2d 29 (1974), para. 6, where the court ruled that it was 'unthinkable that a statement obtained by torture or by other conduct belonging only in a police state should be admitted at the government's behest in order to bolster its case'.

[98] The Dutch Supreme Court has interpreted Art. 3 ECHR and Art. 7 ICCPR as dictating that witness statements obtained by torture cannot be used in evidence: *Pereira*, 1 October 1996, no. 103.094, para. 6.2. See also s. 359a Dutch Code of Criminal Procedure.

[99] Art. 15 of the Torture Convention is set out in the Canadian criminal code: see, e.g. *India* v. *Singh*, 108 CCC (3d) 274 (1996), para. 20.

[100] Swiss Federal Criminal Procedure Code, para. 143. In both Switzerland and Germany, the consent of the accused is irrelevant. See N. Schmid, *Handbuch des schweizerischen Strafprozessrechts* (Zurich: Dike, 2009) 327 ff, paras. 783 ff; BGE 118 Ia 31. See also para. 202 of the Austrian Code of Criminal Procedure, which is phrased in similar terms.

[101] See s. 76(2) PACE 1984.

[102] See also the Report of the Royal Commission on Criminal Procedure (London: HMSO, 1981) Cmnd. 8092, para 4.132; and *R* v. *Fulling* [1987] 2 All ER 65, 69.

[103] Dennis, *Law of Evidence*, para. 6.14, 227; see also Duff et al., *Trial on Trial (3)*, ch. 4; and Eisenberg, *Beweisrecht*, 191, para. 625.

[104] e.g. R. Pattenden, 'Case Comment: Evidence Obtained by Inhuman Treatment in Violation of Article 3 – European Court of Human Rights' (2009) 13 *International Journal of Evidence and Proof* 58, 61.

evidence has been obtained becomes less obviously outrageous, so too is there less willingness to rely on general notions of moral reprehensibility to justify the proscription on the use of the evidence. It is important, therefore, to consider how the use of such evidence might interfere with the fairness of the criminal proceedings as expressed in Article 6 of the ECHR. Fairness dictates that the accused have the opportunity to be heard in adversarial proceedings. Pressure exerted on the accused or indeed on witnesses is designed to undermine this opportunity by pre-empting the questioning of the person involved and undermining the potential for adversarial argument either at trial or in the appropriate forum for the discussion of the evidence. The ECtHR has taken some tentative steps towards setting out this notion in the context of the privilege against self-incrimination,[105] but has often seemed rather unclear on how this guarantee is itself essential to promoting the importance of the correct institutional environment for the hearing and challenging of the evidence. It is this opportunity to challenge the evidence in adversarial proceedings which lends the criminal proceedings their fairness and legitimacy and it is precisely this which is compromised by coercing or ill-treating the accused or witnesses in the preliminary proceedings.

6.4 Deception, coercion, traps and tricks

As we have seen, the ECtHR has justified the prohibition on evidence obtained by the recourse to torture principally on the basis that its use would undermine notions of humanity and the ethical principles on which the administration of justice is based, thereby rendering the proceedings unfair. In view of its hesitance in extending this reasoning to evidence obtained by way of inhuman and degrading treatment, it should come as little surprise that it has eschewed reference to this justification in the context of the use in criminal proceedings of evidence obtained by means which while improper do not infringe Article 3 of the ECHR. A number of applicants have sought, for instance, to argue that the use in criminal proceedings of evidence obtained in violation of their right to privacy as guaranteed by Article 8 of the ECHR violated their right to a fair trial.[106] The use of covert investigative techniques in the investigation of crime in particular has given rise to questions about the manner in which such devices are employed and the impact of their use on the fairness of the proceedings.

In the context of investigating crime, there is considerable room for the police to resort to deceptive or coercive tactics in order to further the investigation or gain the evidence necessary to secure a conviction.[107] Such tactics will not always be as far-fetched or ingenious as tricking a suspect into believing that

---

[105] See further Ch. 8.   [106] E.g. *Khan* v. *United Kingdom*; and *PG and JH* v. *United Kingdom*.
[107] For an interesting comparison of rules governing deception in Germany and the United States, see J. Ross, 'Do Rules of Evidence Apply Only in the Courtroom? Deceptive Interrogation in the United States and Germany' (2008) 28 *Oxford Journal of Legal Studies* 443.

a photocopier is a lie detector machine,[108] or arranging a staged killing,[109] but there are a whole host of tactics which can be used by the police and investigating authorities to convince a suspect to cooperate. These might be as simple as wrongfully suggesting that a co-accused has confessed,[110] lying about the nature or probative value of the evidence found or resorting to the use of undercover officers or informants. It is important to bear in mind that deception is not viewed as inherently problematic per se. Certainly, some deception is accepted as a legitimate – and sometimes essential – strategy in the investigation of crime. The ECtHR has acknowledged, for instance, that the challenges of investigating crime may necessitate the use of undercover operations, operations which by their very nature involve deception.[111] But equally there is awareness that resorting to deception or coercion might infringe fundamental human rights, such as property or privacy, and further that such methods have the potential to impact on the fairness of the trial. The difficulty lies in determining when deception or trickery is acceptable, in establishing the boundaries between proper and improper tactics and in developing a satisfactory regulatory structure. In order to be able to justify a decision to prohibit the use of potentially relevant information in the determination of the charge, it is essential to establish why the fairness of the trial might be affected by the use of evidence obtained by deception or coercion.

It is important to note in considering the regulation of this matter that neither the ECHR nor the ICCPR contains an 'exclusionary-type' provision comparable to the Fourth Amendment to the US Constitution,[112] which has ensured that the concept of privacy has played a substantial role in US constitutional criminal procedure law.[113] The substantive right to privacy is protected in Article 8(1) of the ECHR. Article 8(2) of the ECHR permits public authorities to interfere with the right to privacy providing that the interference is in accordance with the law, proportionate and carried out for one of the aims set out in the provision, including for the purposes of protecting public safety or national security or preventing crime and disorder.[114] As a general rule, violations of Article 8 of the ECHR in the criminal sphere have been a consequence of the absence,

---

[108] As Bunk Moreland manages to do in *The Wire*, Season 5, Episode 1.
[109] As happened in the case of *Bykov* v. *Russia* [GC], discussed below.
[110] See, e.g. the Swiss case: ZR 73 (1974) Nr. 44, 107.
[111] *Constantin and Stoian* v. *Romania*, para. 54; see also *Ramanauskas* v. *Lithuania* [GC], paras. 49–50.
[112] 'The right of the people to be secure in their persons, houses, papers, and effects, against unreasonable searches and seizures, shall not be violated, and no warrants shall issue, but upon probable cause, supported by oath or affirmation, and particularly describing the place to be searched, and the persons or things to be seized.' For a good overview of the law of the Fourth Amendment, see Allen et al., *Comprehensive Criminal Procedure*, ch. 5.
[113] See, e.g. W. Stuntz, 'Privacy's Problem and the Law of Criminal Procedure' 93 (1995) *Michigan Law Review* 1016.
[114] See further Reed and Murdoch, *Human Rights Law*, para. 6.25, 608; and S. Uglow, 'Covert Surveillance and the European Convention on Human Rights' [1999] *Criminal Law Review* 287.

or non-specific nature, of the laws regulating interferences with the right to privacy rather than because the interferences themselves were deemed to be disproportionate.[115] As we shall see, this seems to have been a factor which has influenced the ECtHR in its case law.[116] In any event, it is clear that the use in criminal proceedings of evidence obtained in violation of Article 8 of the ECHR will not automatically result in a finding of a violation of the right to a fair trial.[117]

6.4.1 Wiretapping and covert surveillance

Wiretapping and covert surveillance have become important methods of investigating crime. Despite this, there is widespread awareness of the dangers of unlimited controls on their practices. Most states have laws which control the imposition of such measures and restrict their scope. These typically include requirements that there is sufficient suspicion that a crime has been committed for an investigation to be instigated, restrictions on the types of crimes which can be investigated by way of such methods, restrictions on the period of time for which the covert surveillance may be imposed, and some form of judicial control of the imposition and extension of applications for covert surveillance.[118]

The ECtHR has had to consider a number of cases in which applicants alleged that their right to a fair trial was compromised by the use of evidence obtained by such means. In *Schenk* v. *Switzerland*, the applicant, who had been convicted of inciting another person to murder his wife, complained about the fairness of proceedings.[119] He had published an advert which stated: 'Wanted. Former member of the Foreign Legion or similar for occasional assignments; offer with telephone number, address and curriculum vitae to RTZ 81 poste restante CH Basel 2.' He then selected one of those who had responded and commissioned him to carry out various 'assignments', including killing his wife. Instead of carrying out the killing, the prospective hit man called the applicant's wife and informed her of the plan. The hit man and the applicant's wife then went together to the authorities to tell them of the plan and an investigation was

---

[115] The lack of appropriate regulation proved especially problematic in the United Kingdom. The court held on a number of occasions that the scope and manner of exercise of discretionary authority was insufficiently regulated: see, e.g. *Malone* v. *United Kingdom*; *Halford* v. *United Kingdom*; and *Khan* v. *United Kingdom*.
[116] See, e.g. *Khan* v. *United Kingdom*, para. 36.
[117] See, e.g. *Bykov* v. *Russia* [GC], para. 89; *PG and JH* v. *United Kingdom*, para. 76; and *Heglas* v. *Czech Republic*, paras. 89–92.
[118] For an interesting analysis of the US restrictions, see C. S. Fishman, 'Interception of Communications in Exigent Circumstances: The Fourth Amendment, Federal Legislation, and the United States Department of Justice' (1987) 22 *Georgia Law Review* 1. For an overview of the regulatory structure in the new Swiss federal criminal procedure code, see Schmid, *Handbuch*, 509 ff, N 1136 ff.
[119] *Schenk* v. *Switzerland*.

opened. The hit man later recorded, apparently on his own initiative, although the applicant alleged that this had been on the instigation of the police, a telephone conversation with the applicant in which they discussed the killing in abstract terms. He did this despite the fact that covert recordings of telephone conversations were prohibited by the Swiss Federal Criminal Code.

The applicant Schenk sought to argue that the use of this evidence was not compatible with his right to a fair trial as guaranteed by Article 6(1) of the ECHR. His argument was rejected by the ECtHR, which held that he had had the opportunity to challenge the authenticity and use of the evidence and that the fact that his attempts were unsuccessful 'made no difference'. It also held that it attached 'weight to the fact that the recording of the telephone conversation was not the only evidence on which the conviction was based'.[120] On the facts of the case, it seems that the ECtHR deemed the question of whether the authorities had acted unlawfully in obtaining the evidence or whether they had merely used or relied on evidence which had been unlawfully obtained by a private party to be irrelevant.[121] In this case, the ECtHR endorses a narrow reading of the adversarial proceedings requirement in Article 6(1) of the ECHR. The opportunity to challenge the use of the evidence in adversarial proceedings is sufficient to satisfy the demands of fairness, irrespective of whether the applicant has any real chance of success in having the evidence excluded.

Several judges were critical of this finding, arguing in their dissenting opinion that: 'No court can, without detriment to the proper administration of justice, rely on evidence which has been obtained not only by unfair means but, above all, unlawfully. If it does so, the trial cannot be fair within the meaning of the Convention.' They also argued that even if the judgment had been based on evidence other than the recording, the recording was nevertheless taken into account in convicting the accused and consequently the conviction was 'partly founded' on the disputed evidence.[122]

The use of wiretapping evidence which had been unlawfully obtained was again at issue in the case of *Khan* v. *United Kingdom*. In this case, the applicant and his cousin had been searched on arrival at Manchester airport and the cousin, on being found to be in possession of a large quantity of heroin, was arrested and charged.[123] The applicant was also searched, but no drugs were found and he was released without charge. The applicant later visited a friend and admitted to him that he had been involved with his cousin in importing the

---

[120] *Schenk* v. *Switzerland*, paras. 47–8.
[121] According to the prevailing opinion in Germany, for instance, evidence which has been unlawfully obtained by private persons may as a general rule be used in evidence against the accused as the prohibition on the obtaining of such evidence applies to the authorities and not to private persons: see, e.g. BGH 27, 357; BGH 36, 172; see also G. Godenzi, *Private Beweisbeschaffung im Strafprozess: Eine Studie zu strafprozessualen Beweisverboten im schweizerischen und deutschen Recht* (Zurich: Schulthess, 2008).
[122] Dissenting opinion of Judges Pettiti, Spielmann, de Meyer and Carillo Salcedo, attached to the judgment *Schenk* v. *Switzerland*.
[123] *Khan* v. *United Kingdom*.

drugs. Neither the applicant nor his friend was aware that the police had installed a covert listening device in the friend's house for the purposes of securing proof that the friend was dealing in drugs. The police had not expected or foreseen that the applicant would visit his friend's house.[124] The applicant was subsequently arrested and jointly charged with his cousin with offences under the relevant drug legislation. The applicant at no point confessed to any involvement and the only evidence against him stemmed from conversations recorded by the covert listening device. The applicant alleged that his right to private life under Article 8 of the ECHR had been violated, as there was no basis in national law for the use of such devices. The ECtHR agreed with the applicant and held that the installation of such a device, in the absence of a statutory framework regulating the use of such devices, could not be seen to be in accordance with the law and consequently violated the applicant's rights under Article 8 of the ECHR. The applicant then sought to argue that the use of such evidence to ground his criminal conviction violated his right to a fair trial.[125]

The ECtHR accepted that the contested material was 'in effect the only evidence against the applicant and that the applicant's plea of guilty was tendered only on the basis of the judge's ruling that the evidence should be admitted'. It held, however, that:

> [T]he relevance of the existence of evidence other than the contested matter depends on the circumstances of the case. In the present circumstances, where the tape recording was acknowledged to be very strong evidence, and where there was no risk of it being unreliable, the need for supporting evidence is correspondingly weaker.[126]

The ECtHR admitted that in *Schenk* it had attached some weight to the fact that the evidence at issue was not the only evidence against the accused. It then seemed, however, to reject its own interpretation in *Schenk* of the evidence at issue as 'not the only evidence on which the conviction was based',[127] referring instead to the fact that the national court had characterised the evidence as 'a perhaps decisive influence, or at the least a not inconsiderable one, on the outcome of the proceedings'.[128] Consequently, it held that it was not convinced, despite its earlier finding to the contrary, that the weight of the evidence was a 'determining factor' in its judgment in *Schenk*.[129] In rejecting any sort of sole or decisive test, the ECtHR held that the question to be determined was whether the proceedings were fair and that this was to be assessed with reference to the nature of the applicant's opportunity to challenge 'both the authenticity and the use of the recording' and to the discretion that the national court had to prevent the use of the evidence, had it deemed it to have given rise to 'substantive unfairness'.[130]

---

[124] Ibid., para. 9.   [125] Ibid., para. 22.   [126] Ibid., para. 37.
[127] Ibid., para. 48: 'The Court also attaches weight to the fact that the recording of the telephone conversation was not the only evidence on which the conviction was based.'
[128] *Schenk* v. *Switzerland*.   [129] *Khan* v. *United Kingdom*, para. 37.
[130] *Khan* v. *United Kingdom*, para. 38; see also *Chalkley* v. *United Kingdom*.

In the case at issue, the applicant had had the opportunity to challenge the evidence and the national court had not only considered the admissibility of the evidence, but would also have had the discretion to exclude it, had it so desired. The ECtHR held, as a result, that there had been no violation of Article 6 of the ECHR.[131]

The ECtHR appeared to attach weight to the fact that 'the fixing of the listening device and the recording of the applicants' conversation were not unlawful in the sense of being contrary to domestic criminal law' and that the unlawfulness related exclusively to the fact that there was 'no statutory authority for the interference with the applicants' right to respect for private life'.[132] The ECtHR's suggestion that it would have decided differently and found a violation of Article 6 of the ECHR had the evidence been obtained in a manner which was contrary to domestic law seems disingenuous, particularly in view of the fact that in *Schenk* the ECtHR refused to hold that there had been a violation, despite the government's admission that the evidence had been unlawfully obtained.[133]

In *PG and JH v. United Kingdom*, the applicants complained about the use of evidence obtained by covert surveillance devices.[134] The authorities had suspected them of planning to commit a robbery and had them placed under surveillance and subsequently arrested. The applicants refused to comment during the police interviews and refused to provide the police with speech samples. These voice samples were essential to enable a comparison to be carried out with the material obtained from the earlier surveillance. The police then obtained authorisation to install covert listening devices in the applicant's police cell, enabling voice samples to be obtained, despite the applicants' refusal to cooperate. The ECtHR held that as there was no statutory system in operation to regulate the use of covert listening devices in such a situation, the interference was not 'in accordance with the law' and there had thus been a violation of Article 8 of the ECHR.[135] The applicants then sought to argue that the use of this evidence in the criminal proceedings violated their right to a fair trial.

They attempted to distinguish their situation from that of the applicant in *Khan* on the basis that 'the evidence in relation to at least the first applicant was not particularly strong in that the forensic expert was only able to conclude that it was "likely" that his voice featured in the tape recordings'.[136] The ECtHR, however, was unconvinced by this attempt to induce it to focus on the authenticity of the evidence and determined that the applicants' right to a fair trial had not been violated. Instead, it referred to the government's contention that 'there was other evidence corroborating the involvement of the applicants in the events' and held that 'there was no unfairness in leaving it to the jury, on

---

[131] *Khan v. United Kingdom*, para. 40.   [132] *Khan v. United Kingdom*, para. 36.
[133] *Schenk v. Switzerland*, para. 43: 'The Government did not dispute that the recording in issue was obtained unlawfully... The Federal Court held that "it [could] be accepted that the ingredients of an offence under Art. 179ter CC were present as far as the disputed recording is concerned".'
[134] *PG and JH v. United Kingdom*.   [135] Ibid., para. 60.   [136] Ibid., para. 74.

the basis of a thorough summing up by the judge, to decide where the weight of the evidence lay'.[137] The reference to the other corroboratory evidence is confusing in that it seems to resurrect the sole and decisive type test, which the ECtHR appeared to reject in *Khan*. Indeed, the reference to the significance of the evidence seems especially problematic in the light of the ECtHR's suggestion in *Khan* that its reference to the importance of the evidence in *Schenk* in any case carried no weight.

6.4.2 De facto 'interrogation' of suspects in custody

The ECtHR has taken its most activist stance in the context of the use in criminal proceedings of evidence obtained by coercion or compulsion in the course of custodial interrogation. It is no coincidence in this regard that confession evidence has long been regarded as potentially unreliable and that most member states have provisions prohibiting the use of evidence obtained by compulsion.[138] The approach of the ECtHR in cases involving compulsion in the investigation phase is well illustrated by the case of *Allan* v. *United Kingdom*.[139] The applicant Allan was suspected of involvement in the murder of a store manager in the course of a robbery at a supermarket. He was arrested on suspicion of murder and informed that he had the right to remain silent; he chose to avail himself of that right. On several occasions he was interviewed by the police in the presence of his solicitor and refused to answer any questions. The police requested and received permission to bug his cell and the visiting area which he used after arguing that 'all regular methods of investigation' to identify the victim's killer had failed. A listening device with a video system was installed and recordings were made of conversations between the applicant and a co-accused who had been held for long periods in the same cell as the applicant and between the applicant and a female visitor. The surveillance of the applicant in his cell lasted for weeks.

The police then arranged for a 'long standing police informant with a criminal record' who had been arrested for unrelated offences to be placed in the same cell as the accused for the purposes of eliciting information from him. The police coached the informant, instructing him to 'push him [Allan] for what you can'.[140] The police informant subsequently produced a long witness statement detailing the confessions the applicant had allegedly made in the cell. The trial judge refused to exclude the evidence and the applicant was convicted of murder. The ECtHR held that the use of covert video- and audio-recording devices in the applicant's cell and prison visiting area and on the person of a

---

[137] Ibid., para. 79.
[138] See, e.g. D. Wolchover and A. Heaton-Armstrong, *Confession Evidence* (London: Sweet & Maxwell, 1996) 10 ff on the 'not altogether subversive strand of scepticism about the nature of confession evidence in general'.
[139] *Allan* v. *United Kingdom*.   [140] Ibid., para. 52.

fellow prisoner in the absence of a statutory system to regulate the use of covert recording devices by the police violated Article 8 of the ECHR.

In determining whether the applicant's right to a fair trial had been violated by the use of the recordings, the ECtHR held that it was necessary to examine the manner in which the evidence was obtained, in particular the '"unlawfulness" in question', and, in the event that a violation of another convention right was at issue, the nature of the violation. Various other factors were also held to be of relevance, notably whether the rights of the defence had been respected, in particular whether the applicant had been given the opportunity to challenge the authenticity of the evidence and to oppose its use, as well as the opportunity to examine any relevant witnesses; whether the admissions made by the applicant during the conversations were made voluntarily and in the absence of entrapment or inducement to make such admissions; and the quality of the evidence, including whether the circumstances in which it was obtained cast doubt on its reliability or accuracy.[141] It also referred to the importance of the evidence, noting that while 'no problem of fairness necessarily arises where the evidence obtained was unsupported by other material, it may be noted that where the evidence is very strong and there is no risk of its being unreliable, the need for supporting evidence is correspondingly weaker'.[142]

In the context of the evidence obtained from the audio- and video-recordings, the ECtHR noted that it was not unlawful according to domestic criminal law, nor was it involuntary 'in the sense that the applicant was coerced into making them or that there was any entrapment or inducement'. Indeed, the applicant had stated that 'he was aware that he was possibly being taped while in the police station'. The ECtHR noted that the applicant's counsel 'challenged the admissibility of the recordings in a voir dire, and was able to put forward arguments to exclude the evidence as unreliable, unfair or obtained in an oppressive manner'. The trial judge had, in what the ECtHR referred to as 'a careful ruling', admitted the evidence, held that it was of probative value and had not been shown to be so unreliable that it could not be left open to the jury to decide for themselves. This decision was reviewed on appeal by the appeal court, which found that the judge had taken account of all the relevant factors and that his ruling could not be faulted. At each step of the procedure, the applicant had therefore been given 'an opportunity to challenge the reliability and significance of the recording evidence'. Consequently, it concluded that the use at trial of the recordings had not infringed the applicant's right to a fair trial.[143]

It then went on to consider the evidence obtained through the use of the informant. Here, the ECtHR considered the case from the perspective of the right to silence and the privilege against self-incrimination.[144] It held that

---

[141] Ibid., para. 43 (references omitted).   [142] Ibid.
[143] Ibid., paras 46–8.   [144] See further Ch. 8.

the aim of the principles was 'to protect the freedom of a suspected person to choose whether to speak or to remain silent when questioned by the police' and noted that such freedom of choice is 'effectively undermined' in a case in which, although the suspect has elected to remain silent during questioning, 'the authorities use subterfuge to elicit, from the suspect, confessions or other statements of an incriminatory nature, which they were unable to obtain during such questioning and where the confessions or statements thereby obtained are adduced in evidence at trial'.[145]

In finding a violation of the privilege against self-incrimination, the ECtHR was particularly influenced by the fact that the accused had continually, in the formal procedural context of the police interviews, availed himself of his right to silence and that the witness had been placed in the applicant's cell for the 'specific purpose of eliciting from the applicant information implicating him in the offences of which he was suspected'.[146] Furthermore, the statements made by the accused were not 'spontaneous and unprompted statements volunteered by the applicant', but were induced by the persistent questioning of the witness in circumstances 'which can be regarded as the functional equivalent of interrogation, without any of the safeguards which would attach to a formal police interview, including the attendance of a solicitor and the issuing of the usual caution'.[147] The ECtHR noted that while there was 'no special relationship between the applicant and [the witness] and that no factors of direct coercion have been identified', the applicant 'would have been subjected to psychological pressures which impinged on the "voluntariness" of the disclosures allegedly made by the applicant to [the witness]'. Consequently, the ECtHR held that 'the information gained by the use of the witness in this way may be regarded as having been obtained in defiance of the will of the applicant and its use at trial impinged on the applicant's right to silence and privilege against self-incrimination'.[148]

This judgment contrasts markedly with the admissibility decision of the ECtHR in *Portmann* v. *Switzerland*.[149] In this case, the applicant had continually asserted his right to remain silent and had refused to make statements during the interrogation hearings. Two police officers then entered his cell and sought to engage him in conversation; he allegedly then made incriminating statements. The policemen produced a written statement from memory setting out the applicant's statements, which was then used in convicting the applicant.

---

[145] *Allan* v. *United Kingdom*, para. 50.   [146] Ibid., para. 52.
[147] On the importance of access to counsel during the police investigations, see Chs. 8 and 9.
[148] *Allan* v. *United Kingdom*, para. 52. See also *Massiah* v. *United States*, 377 US 201, 204 (1964); *United States* v. *Henry*, 447 US 264 (1980); and *Kuhlman* v. *Wilson*, 477 US 436 (1986), where the USSC distinguished between active and passive jailhouse informants in a case similar to *Allan*. The German Federal Court (BGH) also upheld a prohibition on the use of evidence obtained in similar circumstances to those in *Allan*, BGHSt 34, 362, 364 (1987). See also H.-H. Kühne, *Strafprozessrecht: Eine systematische Darstellung des deutschen und europäischen Strafverfahrensrechts*, 6th edn (Heidelberg: C. F. Müller, 2003) 459, para. 904.
[149] *Portmann* v. *Switzerland* (dec.).

The ECtHR rejected the applicant's contention that the statements were not 'voluntary', citing *Khan* for its contention that the statements were made spontaneously by the applicant and not as a result of direct pressure by the police officers. The ECtHR was not convinced by the applicant's claim that in view of the psychological pressure and the long period of time which he had spent in almost total isolation the statements could not be considered as voluntary.

The problem is that the setting in which an accused will usually find him- or herself – police custody, no or restricted access to legal assistance, repeated police questioning – generally represents an 'oppressive environment', designed precisely for the purpose of putting pressure on an accused to confess.[150] It seems implausible, therefore, to attempt to distinguish proper from improper compulsion on the basis that an accused who confesses while detained in such circumstances does so 'voluntarily'.

The reliance on 'voluntariness' also leaves the ECtHR's approach open to criticism on other grounds, in particular on the relevance of the distinction between surveillance or deception and coercion. The notion of coercion suggests that an unwilling person has been persuaded by way of force or threats to do something, while compulsion suggests that a person has been obliged to do something or his or her cooperation has been brought about by force. The facts of *Allan* do not, however, suggest that the applicant was coerced into or compelled to make a confession. Rather, it seems that he was deliberately tricked into making statements. But if this is enough to make the statements 'involuntary', it is difficult to see how the ECtHR is able to distinguish evidence obtained by covert surveillance. As Trechsel has noted, 'to record a conversation which the participants are entitled to regard as confidential is certainly the equivalent of setting a trap'; if this is accepted then such methods must also be 'hard to reconcile with the privilege against self incrimination'.[151] And yet in the wiretapping case of *Khan* v. *United Kingdom*, the ECtHR stressed that 'the admissions made by the applicant during the conversation with [the witness] were made voluntarily' and he was not under any 'inducement to make admissions'.[152] This highlights the fact that the ECtHR seems to be demanding a causal connection between the deception employed by the

---

[150] In this context it is interesting to note that the insistence of the Northern Ireland courts on adherence to the common law rules led Parliament on the recommendation of the Diplock Commission to amend the law in 1973 so that the admissibility of confessions no longer depended on the principle of voluntariness, but instead on the absence of conduct such as to violate Art. 3 ECHR: see J. Jackson, 'Human Rights, Criminal Justice and the Future of the Common Law' (2006) 57 *Northern Ireland Legal Quarterly* 357. See further D. S. Greer, 'The Admissibility of Confessions under the Northern Ireland (Emergency Provisions) Act' (1980) 31 *Northern Ireland Legal Quarterly* 205; J. Jackson, *Northern Ireland Supplement to Cross on Evidence*, 5th edn (Belfast: SLS Legal Publications, 1983) 146–7; and J. Jackson and S. Doran, *Judge without Jury: Diplock Trials in the Adversary System* (Oxford: Clarendon Press, 1995) 37–8.

[151] S. Trechsel, *Human Rights in Criminal Proceedings* (Oxford University Press, 2005) 113.

[152] *Khan* v. *United Kingdom*.

investigating authorities and the decision of the applicant to make statements.[153] But it also calls into question the usefulness of the reliance on notions of 'voluntariness' and emphasises the inherent limitations of justifying the exclusion on the basis of the privilege against self-incrimination. Just as the applicant in *Allan* claimed his right to remain silent and only broke his silence in discussions with a confidante, it could equally be argued that the applicant in *Khan* would have chosen to remain silent, as indeed he subsequently did, had he known that his conversations with his friend were being taped.

The reasoning in *Allan* which distinguishes between encouraging an informant to elicit information from the accused and installing listening devices in the cell of a prisoner who has asserted his defence rights is unsatisfactory. Further, the suggestion in *Allan* and *PG and JH* that the opportunity to challenge the wiretap evidence in an adversarial context is sufficient to satisfy the fairness requirement in Article 6(1) of the ECHR is unconvincing, particularly if the actions of the authorities, whether deliberately or unintentionally, in the pre-trial or investigative phase serve to undermine the possibility of the applicant to present his or her case in an adversarial setting. The determination of whether the statements were made voluntarily is a poor substitute for the stronger test of whether the accused waived his right to remain silent or to be questioned in the presence of a lawyer. As the ECtHR noted in finding a violation of the privilege against self-incrimination, the situation in which the accused found himself could be 'regarded as the functional equivalent of interrogation, without any of the safeguards which would attach to a formal police interview'.[154] Equally, though, it could be argued that this was also the case in the context of the audio- and video-taping of the applicant in his cell over a period of many weeks, after he asserted his right to silence and indicated quite clearly that he did not want to cooperate or make any statements.

6.4.3 De facto 'questioning' of suspects not in custody

In the investigation of crime, it is not uncommon for the authorities to seek to carry out de facto questioning of the suspect either by way of undercover officers or informants. The problems arising in such cases are well illustrated by the case of *Bykov* v. *Russia*. An investigation had been opened in respect of the applicant, the chairman of an aluminium plant and a deputy chairman in the regional parliamentary assembly, for conspiracy to murder, after a former member of his entourage informed the police that the applicant had hired him to kill a former business associate and handed over a gun which he claimed to have received from the applicant. The police decided to arrange a covert operation based on the pretence that the former business associate had in fact been murdered. They staged the discovery of two dead men at the home of

---

[153] See also the approach of the German Federal Court BGH 5 StR 409/81.
[154] *Allan* v. *United Kingdom*, para. 51.

the former associate and officially announced in the media that he had been identified as one of those killed. The man allegedly hired to carry out the killing was then fitted with a hidden radio-transmitting device and sent to see the applicant. He engaged the applicant in conversation and told him that he had carried out the assassination. The recording of the conversation was then used in criminal proceedings against the applicant.[155] There was little doubt in view of the lack of regulation that the evidence had been obtained in violation of Article 8 of the ECHR.

The ECtHR then considered whether the use of the evidence obtained in violation of Article 8 of the ECHR had violated the applicant's right to a fair trial. The ECtHR was unconvinced, noting that: 'the applicant was able to challenge the covert operation, and every piece of evidence obtained thereby, in the adversarial procedure before the first-instance court and in his grounds of appeal'.[156] Moreover, the ECtHR noted that his allegations concerning 'the alleged unlawfulness and trickery' and 'subterfuge incompatible with the notion of a fair trial' in obtaining the evidence were addressed by the courts and dismissed in reasoned decisions.[157]

It then went on to determine whether the applicant's privilege against self-incrimination could be said to have been violated by the covert operation. Distinguishing the case from *Allan*, it noted that the applicant had not been officially questioned about or charged with a criminal offence and that he had not been on remand or under pressure to speak to the former associate at his house. This was in direct contrast to the applicant in *Allan* who had been in pre-trial detention and who had expressed his wish to remain silent when questioned by the authorities investigating his case. Consequently, it held that it was 'not convinced that the obtaining of evidence was tainted with the element of coercion or oppression which in the *Allan* case the ECtHR found to amount to a breach of the applicant's right to remain silent'.[158] In his dissenting opinion, Judge Costa challenged this conclusion. He noted that 'the right to remain silent would be truly "theoretical and illusory" if it were accepted that the police had the right "to make the suspect talk" by using a covert recording of a conversation with an informer assigned the task of entrapping the suspect'.[159] In his opinion, that was exactly what had happened in the case at issue: by telling the applicant that he had carried out the killing, the former associate sought to induce the applicant to talk.[160]

The ECtHR took a similar approach in *Heglas* v. *Czech Republic*, where the applicant was suspected of involvement in an incident which involved a woman being attacked and her handbag stolen.[161] The police arrested another person, AM, who was then detained in custody and they ordered that the applicant's mobile phone be placed under surveillance. They also arranged for AM's

---

[155] *Bykov* v. *Russia* [GC], paras. 38–40.   [156] Ibid.   [157] Ibid., para. 95.
[158] Ibid., para. 102.   [159] See further Ch. 8.
[160] Ibid., dissenting opinion attached to the judgment, para. 10.   [161] *Heglas* v. *Czech Republic*.

girlfriend to be fitted with a listening device and sent her to meet the applicant. In the course of their conversation, which was recorded by the listening device, the applicant confessed to organising the robbery with AM. The applicant was subsequently convicted on the basis of the telephone records showing that the applicant and AM had called each other just before and just after the attack and the transcript of the conversation between the applicant and AM's girlfriend, which was described by the trial court as crucial evidence. The applicant was sentenced to nine years' imprisonment. As in the *Bykov* case, the applicant's Article 8 ECHR rights were held to have been violated by the insufficient legal basis for the covert operations. The ECtHR refused to find a violation of Article 6 of the ECHR, principally it would seem because the applicant had had the opportunity to contest the use of the evidence before the domestic courts.[162]

6.4.4 Fairness and the use of evidence obtained by deception and coercion

These cases demonstrate reluctance to impose any restraints on the police and investigating authorities in the context of surveillance for the purposes of ensuring fairness. A violation of Article 8 of the ECHR in the course of the criminal investigation will not automatically invalidate the evidence to such an extent as to prevent it being relied upon in convicting the accused. The cases also suggest that in determining whether the use of the evidence violates Article 6 of the ECHR, the ECtHR displays a trial-centric bias. The case law suggests that provided that the applicant had the opportunity to raise the alleged impropriety at trial and that the trial court considered the applicant's argument and had the discretion to decide not to use the evidence, the fairness of the trial will not be compromised by the decision to make use of the evidence in convicting the accused.[163] Essentially, the test for evaluating the compatibility of the use in criminal proceedings of evidence obtained in violation of laws regulating covert surveillance devices with Article 6 of the ECHR goes no further than the principle of adversarial proceedings which the ECtHR has read into Article 6(1) of the ECHR.[164] The defence must be afforded an effective and adequate opportunity to challenge the evidence levelled against it and the ECtHR must have full discretion to take into consideration any arguments and objections raised by the defence.

This approach pays insufficient attention, however, to the potential for the manner in which the evidence was collected during the investigation to impact on the fairness of the trial. In framing the test solely in terms of the defence's opportunity to challenge the evidence at trial, the ECtHR moreover fails to give any guidance as to the circumstances in which a domestic court might be compelled to refuse to use the contested evidence. Indeed, the approach

---

[162] Ibid., paras. 88–90.   [163] A good example of such exclusionary discretion is s. 78(1) PACE.
[164] On the right to adversarial proceedings, see Ch. 4.2.3; and Trechsel, *Human Rights in Criminal Proceedings*, 89 ff.

suggests that providing the domestic court has discretion to exclude, or refrain from using, the evidence, it must never actually do so: the domestic courts are thus free to set out their own conception of fairness. This approach is obviously flawed, as it fails to explain the circumstances in which the fairness of the trial could be compromised and crucially why this should be the case.

The ECtHR's insistence that the use of evidence obtained in violation of a suspect's privacy rights will not necessarily result in a violation of Article 6 of the ECHR[165] underlines the fact that it does not endorse the rights thesis in determining which evidence must not be used to ground a conviction.[166] It has not followed the suggestion that 'fairness presupposes respect for lawfulness and thus also, a fortiori, respect for the rights guaranteed by the Convention, which it is precisely the ECtHR's task to supervise',[167] or that 'the term "fairness", when examined in the context of the European Convention on Human Rights, implies observance of the rule of law and... presupposes respect of the human rights set out in the Convention'.[168] If the use in criminal proceedings of evidence obtained in violation of the constitutionally protected right to privacy does not automatically undermine the fairness of these proceedings, then it is necessary to investigate the circumstances in which the use of improperly obtained evidence might be said to violate the right to a fair trial and why this should be the case. In all of the cases discussed above, the authorities had managed to secure valuable evidence by making covert recordings of the applicant's conversations. In each of the cases considered above, with the exception of *Allan* – and even then only in the context of the privilege against self-incrimination and not in relation to the wiretap evidence – the ECtHR held that there had been no violation of the right to a fair trial. In evaluating the ECtHR's approach, it is useful therefore to consider the similarities and differences between the various cases in order to determine how *Allan* can be distinguished.

One significant difference could be the conduct of the authorities in obtaining the evidence. In this regard, it is worth recalling, for instance, that the USSC has interpreted the fact that the authorities were acting in 'good faith' as grounds permitting for an exception to be made from the Fourth Amendment exclusionary rule.[169] This might be seen as a relevant factor when comparing the cases of *Khan* and *Allan*. While the authorities in the *Khan* case had obtained the evidence against the applicant accidentally in the context of a separate

---

[165] See also Lord Hobhouse's interpretation of the court's approach in *R* v. *P* [2001] 2 Cr App R 121 at [39] and *R* v. *Sang* [1980] AC 402.

[166] In several cases a number of judges have disagreed with the court's approach and have advocated reliance on the rights thesis. Judges Pettiti, Spielmann, De Meyer and Carrillo Salcedo, dissenting, in *Schenk* v. *Switzerland*.

[167] Dissenting opinion of Judge Spielmann joined by Judges Rozakis, Tulkens, Casadevall and Mijović in *Bykov* v. *Russia* [GC], para. 7.

[168] See the dissenting opinion of Judge Loucaides in *Khan* v. *United Kingdom*; see also the dissenting opinion of Judge Tulkens in *PG and JH* v. *United Kingdom*: 'I do not think one can speak of a "fair" trial if it is conducted in breach of the law.'

[169] See, e.g. *United States* v. *Leon*, 468 US 897 (1984).

ongoing investigation, the authorities in the *Allan* case had intentionally resorted to extraordinary measures to secure evidence to assist in convicting the applicant after all the usual means of investigation had failed. And yet the ECtHR does not seem to consider the authorities' motives as especially relevant. In *Bykov*, where the authorities' actions seemed to exceed normal boundaries, the ECtHR held that there was no violation of Article 6 of the ECHR. Similarly, in *Schenk*, where the evidence had been obtained in violation of the Swiss criminal code – possibly on the instigation of the authorities – the ECtHR held that the fairness of the trial had not been compromised. These cases also seem to rule out any sort of distinction based on the active or passive conduct of the authorities.

Another possible distinguishing factor is the fact that the applicant in *Allan* was in custody. In finding a violation of the privilege against self-incrimination, the ECtHR placed considerable emphasis on the fact that the applicant was detained on remand. In the other cases (with the exception of *PG and JH*), on the other hand, the applicants were not in custody and had not, or not yet, been charged with a criminal offence. In view of the fact, however, that the ECtHR did not hold the fact that the applicant had been subjected to surveillance for a period of weeks while in custody to violate Article 6 of the ECHR, neither the detention itself nor the fact that the surveillance took place after the accused had been informed of his or her right to remain silent can be the principal distinguishing factor.

The ECtHR seems to have been influenced by the fact that there was a causal link between the statements made by the applicant and the actions of the authorities. If the authorities had not arranged for the informant to speak to the applicant, he would not have made the statements. As we have seen, the ECtHR indicates that under these circumstances the applicant's statements could not be characterised as 'voluntary'. But it is difficult to see how the statements made by the applicants in *Bykov* and *Heglas* – where there was also a clear causal link between the applicants' statements and the intervention of the authorities – were any more voluntary, let alone those of the applicant in *Portmann*, which seems impossible to reconcile with *Allan*.

The issue here is not so much that the statements were 'involuntary', but rather that they were made after the accused had been informed of his procedural rights, including the right to remain silent. In *Bykov* and *Heglas*, the suspect had not been arrested, while in *Khan* the applicant was not even considered to be a suspect at the material time. After the applicant in *Allan* had been informed of his rights, and after the police realised that they could not induce him to confess, they resorted to devising a strategy designed to circumvent the official, procedural setting for the interrogation of the accused and thus also the rights of the defence.[170] Were the domestic

---

[170] The court also makes much of this in its judgment: *Allan* v. *United Kingdom*, para. 51.

authorities allowed to circumvent these defence rights, for instance by conducting informal interrogations outwith the official procedural setting, the rights guaranteed by Article 6 of the ECHR, including the privilege against self-incrimination, could only be described as illusory rather than practical and effective.[171] Crucially, though, this will be the case irrespective of whether the authorities attempt to circumvent these rights by sending an informant or policeman into the applicant's cell or by installing listening devices for the same purposes.

It is important to consider the consequences of such an approach, not least because of its potential to discourage the investigating authorities from informing accused persons that they are the subject of investigation and informing them of their rights in this regard. The police would be well advised to refrain from arresting suspects for questioning, thereby alerting them to the fact that an investigation is underway – and of course of their procedural rights – and instead to keep them under surveillance until there is sufficient evidence for a conviction. This highlights the importance of ascertaining when the authorities must decide that they have sufficient evidence to charge the suspect or at least inform him or her that he or she is the subject of a criminal investigation. It also emphasises that a decision to delay informing a suspect of the investigation could adversely impact on his or her right to a fair trial. Article 6 of the ECHR says little about such issues and the ECtHR has been slow to elaborate on the relationship between the regulation of the investigation or pre-trial phase and the fairness of the trial. Nevertheless, it remains unclear why, if there is sufficient evidence to arrest and question an accused, it is acceptable to refrain from doing so, thereby allowing the investigating authorities to gain more evidence and sidestep the problem of the accused asserting his or her procedural rights, notably the rights to remain silent and have contact with counsel.

There are two distinct questions here: under which circumstances should the authorities be allowed to impose coercive measures such as covert surveillance, and once this initial suspicion has been established, at what point must the authorities decide that there is sufficient suspicion to cease the surveillance and inform the suspect of the criminal investigation and of his or her procedural rights? The first issue was of relevance in the *Khan* case. In *Khan*, the authorities came across the evidence implicating the accused in the course of investigation which was not related either to the applicant or to the crime. Unease about the situation in *Khan* is related not so much to the fact that the applicant's opportunity to present his defence was imperilled, but rather to the fact that he was effectively subjected to coercive measures employed by the authorities, despite a lack of reasonable suspicion that he was involved in the crime. In most domestic criminal justice systems, the imposition of coercive measures will

---

[171] e.g. *Airey* v. *Ireland*, para. 24: the ECHR 'is intended to guarantee not rights that are theoretical or illusory but rights that are practical and effective'.

usually only be permitted in the event of the existence of reasonable suspicion that the accused has committed a crime. The requirement of probable cause as set out in provisions like the Fourth Amendment to the US Constitution plays an important role in delineating the boundaries of state interference in the lives of individuals in the context of investigating crime.[172]

There is, however, little mention in the convention of a requirement equivalent to that of probable cause. In the context of deprivation of liberty, it is reflected in the language of Article 5(1)(c) of the ECHR, which states that an accused can only be detained if there is 'reasonable suspicion' that he or she has committed an offence. The ECtHR has interpreted the term 'reasonable suspicion' in this context as implying that there are 'plausible' grounds[173] which would convince an objective observer that the accused might have committed the offence. In *Fox, Campbell and Hartley*, it held that this meant that the government had to 'furnish at least some facts or information capable of satisfying the ECtHR that the arrested person was reasonably suspected of having committed the alleged offence'.[174] Article 5 of the ECHR only applies in the context of interferences with liberty and security of person and not to other interferences such as those arising in the context of wiretapping or search and seizure.[175] This lack of regulation adds to the difficulties in determining how to deal with cases such as *Khan*, where the investigation authorities discover, in the course of an investigation against an individual, evidence of crimes committed by others.[176]

The issue of the point in time at which the authorities must cease covert surveillance and inform the suspect of the investigation is not only more complicated, but also seems to have greater potential to impact on the fairness of the trial. Once the investigating authorities are aware that a crime has been committed, is it acceptable for them to wait and allow a suspect to commit more crimes before intervening? It is not uncommon for the police and investigation authorities to monitor the actions of suspects over a prolonged period of time, but this can give rise to real questions of legitimacy. In the drugs context, where the sentence will often be significantly determined by the quantity of drugs involved, such delay can have serious repercussions on the seriousness of the crime committed and the sentence imposed. In a comment on an English Court of Appeal case,[177] Ormerod and Rees write that the 'defendants' claims that the

---

[172] A. Amsterdam, 'Perspectives on the Fourth Amendment' (1979) 58 *Minnesota Law Review* 349, 410–11.
[173] e.g. *Murray* v. *United Kingdom*, para. 63; *NC* v. *Italy*, para. 45; and *K-F* v. *Germany*, para. 57.
[174] *Fox, Campbell and Hartley* v. *United Kingdom*, para. 34.
[175] The ambivalence of the ECtHR towards recognition of the potential for unlawful searches to impact on the fairness of the trial is clearly evident in cases such as *Buck* v. *Germany*, *Chappell* v. *United Kingdom*, *Narinen* v. *Finland*, *Petri Sallinen and others* v. *Finland*, and *Lee Davies* v. *Belgium*.
[176] For an analysis of the Swiss approach in such circumstances, see N. Schmid, *Handbuch des schweizerischen Strafprozessrechts* (Zurich: Dike, 2009) 521 ff, N 1156 ff.
[177] *R* v. *SL* [2001] EWCA Crim 1829.

operation was allowed to continue beyond the point at which arrest could have been made, thereby allowing the suspects more opportunity to incriminate themselves, might be described as disingenuous'.[178] Yet this is an important point. If it is accepted that the role of the police is to enforce the law, and where possible to prevent crime, allowing or enabling the continuation of criminal offences is problematic. In considering this point, it is also important to bear in mind that in the absence of regulation the authorities will generally have little incentive to put an end to covert surveillance. It is important, therefore, that restrictions are placed on such operations. In the context of the investigation of complex crimes – such as drugs offences or corruption – if the continuance of the investigation is deemed to be more important than apprehending the individuals involved, this must be taken into consideration. Fairness would seem to demand that the individuals only be held to account for conduct carried out up until the point at which the authorities would have had sufficient opportunity to intervene but chose not to do so.[179]

The main problem with the ECtHR's case law on evidence obtained by deception is the suggestion, well illustrated in *Khan*, *Jalloh* and *Allan*, that the opportunity to challenge the evidence in adversarial proceedings is sufficient to ensure compatibility with Article 6 of the ECHR. The focus is thus exclusively on the defence opportunities at trial, which has prevented development of a more coherent notion of the importance of regulation of the preliminary proceedings for the ECtHR's own notion of fairness as set out in Article 6 of the ECHR. More recent cases such as *Haci Özen* v. *Turkey* seem to provide a basis for a more satisfactory approach to determining whether the use of evidence improperly obtained during the investigation must be seen as compromising the fairness of the trial. In this case, the ECtHR acknowledged that the fact that the evidence in question had been obtained by recourse to inhuman and degrading treatment was of relevance in assessing the fairness of the trial, but it refused to hold that its use alone would automatically violate Article 6 of the ECHR. The ECtHR considered the impact of the state actions not just at the trial phase, but also during the investigative phase. It held, in relation to the accused's opportunity at trial to challenge the use of evidence alleged to have been improperly obtained, that the Turkish court had not determined 'the admissibility of the applicant's statements made in the custody of the gendarmerie before going on to examine

---

[178] D. C. Ormerod and T. Rees, 'Evidence: Disclosure – Surveillance Device' [2002] *Criminal Law Review* 584, 586–7.

[179] It is worth noting in this regard that many countries, including Denmark and Norway, have adopted legislation restricting the access of the defence to information on undercover operations. For a good overview of this issue and an analysis of the position in Norway following a Supreme Court decision ordering disclosure of such information, see A. Strandbakken, 'Disclosure of Evidence by the Prosecution', in H. Müller-Dietz, E. Müller, K.-L. Kunz, H. Radtke, G. Britz, C. Momsen and H. Koriath (eds.), *Festschrift für Heike Jung* (Baden Baden: Nomos, 2007) 945. See further Ch. 9.

the merits of the case' and that it had 'used these statements as evidence in its judgment convicting the applicant, despite his denial of their accuracy'.[180] As in the cases of *Khan* and *Allan*, it thus stressed the importance not only of the applicant being afforded an opportunity to challenge the impugned evidence at trial, but also of the fact that the domestic court actually uses its discretion to determine whether or not to make use of the evidence in convicting the accused.

However, it went further than the ECtHR had done in the earlier cases by emphasising the importance of the investigative, pre-trial phase. It seemed to be strongly influenced by the fact that the applicant had not received any legal assistance during his time in custody and that he had made the impugned statements in the absence of his lawyer.[181] Indeed, in finding a violation the ECtHR seemed to rely almost entirely on the fact that the applicant was never assisted by a lawyer during his time in custody, holding that 'the use of the applicant's statements obtained during his custody period in the absence of his lawyer in the criminal proceedings brought against him rendered his trial as a whole unfair'.[182] This implies recognition of the fact that in the determination of whether the use of improperly obtained evidence in criminal proceedings violates the fair trial requirement set out in Article 6 of the ECHR it is essential to consider not just whether the applicant had the opportunity to contest the evidence at trial, but also whether the manner in which it was obtained in the investigative phase in itself undermined the fairness of the trial.

The use of evidence obtained by way of covert surveillance after an accused has been informed of his or her defence rights, including the right to remain silent and the right to be assisted by counsel, is incompatible with the principle of adversarial proceedings and thus with the right to a fair trial. The adversarial proceedings principle protects the defence's opportunity to present its case as it sees fit. Importantly, the accused is under no compulsion to cooperate with the investigation. Traditionally this has meant protecting the accused from being compelled to confess while in custody, but the development of new surveillance measures necessitates reconsideration of the scope of the principle that the accused must not be compelled to 'cooperate' or assist in the investigation against him or her. Covert surveillance of an accused who has been informed of his or her procedural rights would seem clearly to violate this principle, regardless of whether or not the accused is in custody. This raises the question as to when in the course of an investigation an accused should be informed of these rights. In order to guarantee the fair trial rights of the defence, it is essential that consideration is given to the development of a requirement regulating the point in time at which the authorities ought to be required either to inform a suspect of his or her defence rights or to forfeit the right to use evidence

---

[180] *Haci Özen* v. *Turkey*, para. 103.
[181] Referring to *Hulki Güneş* v. *Turkey*, para. 91; and *Dikme* v. *Turkey*, para. 111.
[182] *Haci Özen* v. *Turkey*, para. 104.

subsequently obtained. Such regulation is essential to prevent the authorities usurping defence rights by delaying informing the accused that he or she is a suspect in a criminal investigation.

6.5 Entrapment

While '[a]rtifice and stratagem may be employed to catch those engaged in criminal enterprises', it is unacceptable to try a person for 'a crime where the government officials are the instigators of his conduct'.[183] This principle, articulated in 1932 by the USSC, reflects concern about governments seeking to punish individuals for actions which have been brought about as a direct result of the activities of their own officials.[184] Such concern is also reflected in the case law of the ECtHR. The extent to which investigating and prosecuting authorities should be allowed to go to obtain sufficient evidence to secure a conviction and the boundaries between acting as '*agent provocateurs*' and legitimate undercover agents has been at issue in a number of cases. The use of '*agent provocateurs*' was at issue in the case of *Teixeira de Castro* v. *Portugal*.[185] In *Teixeira*, the applicant had been approached by two undercover officers who asked him for drugs; he obtained drugs from the house of an acquaintance and was subsequently arrested and prosecuted. The ECtHR distinguished the case from *Lüdi* v. *Switzerland*[186] on the basis that in *Lüdi* 'the police officer concerned had been sworn in, the investigation judge had not been unaware of his mission and the Swiss authorities, informed by the German police, had opened a preliminary investigation'. Consequently, the role of the police officers had been 'confined to acting as an undercover agent'.[187] In *Teixeira*, on the other hand, the officers had not been acting in the context of an anti-drug-trafficking operation ordered and supervised by a judge. Some commentators, noting that the ECtHR 'did not go so far as to prescribe that pre-operation judicial supervision/authorisation was necessary', have argued that the absence of judicial supervision 'should not be a decisive factor'.[188] The ECtHR's reference to the existence of judicial supervision ought to be understood as highlighting not the existence of judicial supervision per se, but the existence of an organised investigation into the commission of a particular crime or series of criminal activity. Consequently, this is closely linked to the ECtHR's argument that it did

---

[183] *Sorrells* v. *United States*, 287 US 435, 441–52 (1932).
[184] For a useful overview of the US approach to the entrapment defence, see R. J. Allen, M. Luttrell and A. Kreeger, 'Clarifying Entrapment' (1999) 89 *Journal of Criminal Law and Criminology* 407.
[185] *Teixeira de Castro* v. *Portugal*.
[186] *Lüdi* v. *Switzerland*: here the court held that Art. 6 had been violated not by the actions of the undercover agents per se, but by the fact that the applicant had not had sufficient opportunity to challenge the witness evidence of the anonymous undercover officer.
[187] *Teixeira de Castro* v. *Portugal*, para. 37.
[188] A. Roberts and D. Ormerod, 'The Trouble with *Teixeira*: Developing a Principled Approach to Entrapment' (2002) *International Journal of Evidence and Proof* 38.

not appear that the authorities had 'good reason to suspect that Mr Teixeira de Castro was a drug dealer; on the contrary, he had no criminal record and no preliminary investigation concerning him had been opened'.[189]

The ECtHR also appeared to place weight on the fact that the applicant had only obtained precisely the quantity of drugs requested by the police officers and thus had not gone beyond what he had been incited to do by the police and that there was no evidence to support the government's argument that the applicant was predisposed to commit offences. In view of this, the police had not investigated the applicant's conduct in a passive manner, but had 'exercised an influence such as to incite the commission of the offence': 'the two police officers' actions went beyond those of an undercover agent because they instigated the offence and there is nothing to suggest that without their intervention it would have been committed'. Consequently, that intervention and the use of the evidence in the criminal proceedings 'meant that, right from the outset, the applicant was definitively deprived of a fair trial'.[190]

Similarly, in *Khudobin* v. *Russia*, the applicant alleged he had been incited by police officers, through their use of a private individual as their agent, to commit drugs offences. In finding a violation of Article 6 of the ECHR, the ECtHR held that domestic law 'should not tolerate the use of evidence obtained as a result of incitement by State agents'.[191] As in *Teixeria* the ECtHR was particularly influenced by the fact that the applicant was not a drug dealer known to the police, but had rather been implicated by a police informer, who had not known where else to obtain the drugs. Consequently, the ECtHR noted that this could reasonably be interpreted as suggesting that the police operation had not targeted the applicant personally, but rather was designed to catch any person who would agree to procure heroin for the police informant. Furthermore, the ECtHR emphasised that clear and foreseeable procedures for authorising investigative measures, as well as their proper supervision, should be put into place in order to ensure the authorities' good faith and compliance with the proper law-enforcement objectives. In the case at issue, the police operation had been authorised by a simple administrative decision of the body which later carried out the operation and 'the text of that decision contained very little information as to the reasons for and purposes of the planned "test buy"'.[192]

The reasoning behind the ECtHR's case law in cases involving entrapment focuses on the existence of reasonable suspicion and the extent to which the investigation authorities entice the accused to commit a crime. That these issues are closely connected is well illustrated by the *Eurofinacom* case. Here the ECtHR held that the incitement by police officers of offers of prostitution-related services made to them personally had not in the true sense incited the commission by the applicant company of the offence of living on immoral

---

[189] *Teixeira de Castro* v. *Portugal*, para. 38, see also *V* v. *Finland*, para. 70.
[190] *Teixeira de Castro* v. *Portugal*, paras. 38–9.   [191] *Khudobin* v. *Russia*, para. 134.   [192] Ibid.

earnings, since at the time such offers were made the police were already in possession of information suggesting that the applicant company's data-communications service was being used by prostitutes to contact potential clients.[193]

In *Ramanauskas* v. *Lithuania*, the Grand Chamber confirmed the approach taken in *Teixeira* when it held that the conviction of the applicant, who was a prosecutor, for bribery was unfair. It noted that there was no evidence that the applicant had been involved in corruption before the investigation and that all of the meetings between the applicant and the police had been initiated by the police. Consequently, the conduct of the police went beyond 'the mere passive investigation of existing criminal activity' and incited the applicant to commit the offence.[194]

The ECtHR has also connected the entrapment issue to broader procedural rights, noting that in the event that an accused alleged that he or she was incited to commit an offence, the domestic courts must carry out 'a careful examination of the material in the file, since for the trial to be fair within the meaning of Article 6 § 1 of the Convention, all evidence obtained as a result of police incitement must be excluded'.[195] Moreover, in the event that the prosecution authorities fail to disclose the information required by the court to conclude whether the applicant was subjected to police incitement, the ECtHR has held that it is 'essential that the Court examine the procedure whereby the plea of incitement was determined in each case in order to ensure that the rights of the defence were adequately protected, in particular the right to adversarial proceedings and to equality of arms'.[196] It is for the prosecution to prove that there was no incitement, 'provided that the defendant's allegations are not wholly improbable'.[197]

The unfairness at issue in the entrapment cases seems similar to that which arises in the context of the continued surveillance of an accused, despite the existence of sufficient evidence which would allow for intervention to prevent the unlawful activity. It seems counterintuitive and incoherent for state authorities charged with preventing and investigating crime to be permitted to 'instigate' criminal activities or to fail to intervene to prevent them from occurring.[198] The authorities ought only to intervene when there is reasonable suspicion[199] that

---

[193] *Eurofinacom* v. *France* (dec.). See also *Sequeira* v. *Portugal* (dec.).
[194] *Ramanauskas* v. *Lithuania* [GC].   [195] See *Khudobin* v. *Russia*, paras. 133–5.
[196] See *Edwards and Lewis* v. *United Kingdom* [GC], paras. 46–8; and *Jasper* v. *United Kingdom* [GC], paras. 50 and 58.
[197] *Ramanauskas* v. *Lithuania* [GC], para. 71.
[198] R. A. Duff, 'I Might be Guilty, But You Can't Try Me: Estoppel and Other Bars to Trial' (2005) 1 *Ohio State Journal of Criminal Law* 245.
[199] Several commentators have advocated the introduction of a principle of reasonable suspicion: see, e.g. A. Ashworth, 'Re-drawing the Boundaries of Entrapment' [2002] *Criminal Law Review* 161, 179; and M. F. J. Whelan, 'Lead Us Not into (Unwarranted) Temptation: A Proposal to Replace the Entrapment Defence with a Reasonable Suspicion Requirement' (1985) 133 *University of Pennsylvania Law Review* 1193.

the individual targeted was involved in crime, not because the individuals have a 'right' to be free from the temptations of crime,[200] but because by coercing an individual into providing evidence against him or her, the practice undermines the adversarial rights of the defence.

6.6 Fruit of the poisonous tree

Determining why the use of improperly obtained evidence violates the right to a fair trial is also essential to enabling consideration of the related issue of the treatment of derivative evidence. The use of derivative evidence obtained as a result of evidence improperly obtained, the so-called fruit of the poisonous tree, is extremely controversial.[201] The USSC has upheld a form of the doctrine, as have the Scottish courts.[202] On the other hand, many other courts, including those in England,[203] Switzerland[204] and Germany,[205] have proven disinclined to endorse the poisonous tree doctrine. Although many influential German commentators have supported the introduction of this type of doctrine on the basis that without such a doctrine it is easy to circumvent the prohibition on the use of unlawfully obtained evidence,[206] the German courts have refused to introduce the doctrine, referring instead to the importance of prosecuting crime and to the fact that 'procedural technicalities' should not be allowed to derail the criminal proceedings.[207] The German courts have frequently held that the fruit of the poisonous tree can be relied upon, providing that the authorities could have been able to obtain the evidence properly had they not resorted to employing improper methods.[208] Clearly, it could equally be argued that the fruits of the poisonous tree ought not to be relied upon as evidence in

---

[200] On the problems associated with such an approach, see D. Squires, 'The Problem with Entrapment' [2006] *Oxford Journal of Legal Studies* 351, 371.

[201] See, e.g. C. Roxin and B. Schünemann, *Strafverfahrensrecht*, 26th edn (Munich: C. H. Beck, 2009) § 24 N 59.

[202] See in the context of the United States, *Nardone* v. *US*, 308 US 338, 341 (1939); *Wong Sun* v. *United States*, 371 US 471 (1963); *Murray* v. *United States*, 487 US 533 (1988); and *Hudson* v. *Michigan*, 547 US (2006). In respect of Scotland, see *Chalmers* v. *HM Advocate*, 1954 JC 66 and *HM Advocate* v. *McLean*, 2000 SCCR 987.

[203] cf. *A and others* v. *Secretary of State for the Home Department* (*No. 2*) [2006] 2 AC 221, para. 88, per Lord Hoffmann.

[204] See the cases ZR 91/92 (1992/1993) Nr 10; BGE 109a 246; SJZ 77 (1982).

[205] See, e.g. BGHSt 34, 362; BGHSt 32, 68. See further S. Gleß, 'The Use of Illegally Gathered Evidence in the Criminal Trial', in J. Basedow, U. Ischel and U. Sieber, *German National Reports to the 18th International Congress of Comparative Law* (Tübingen: Mohr Siebeck, 2010) 692–3.

[206] See, e.g. H. Henkel, *Strafverfahrensrecht*, 2. Aufl. (Stuttgart: W. Kohlhammer, 1968) 271; and Roxin and Schünemann, *Strafverfahrensrecht*, § 24 N 47.

[207] See, e.g. the judgment of the German Federal Court in BGH 34, 364 = JZ 87, 936.

[208] This was the reasoning used by the German courts in case BGHSt 34, 364–5 (1987), involving the use of the evidence of a witness who had been traced after being mentioned in an accused's coerced confession could be used to convict the accused. See also BGHSt 27, 355, 358; 32, 68, 71; BGHSt 32, 68, 71.

such circumstances precisely because the authorities could have obtained the evidence lawfully.[209]

In *Gäfgen v. Germany*, the ECtHR had to consider the use of indirect evidence which was obtained on the basis of statements made by the accused after he had been subjected to ill-treatment. The applicant was arrested on suspicion of involvement in the kidnapping of the eleven-year-old son of a prominent German banker after he had been seen picking up the ransom. A police officer, acting on the instructions of the deputy chief of the Frankfurt police, threatened the accused with sexual abuse and told him that he would 'suffer considerable pain at the hands of a person specially trained for such purposes if he did not disclose the child's whereabouts'.[210] The officer also hit him on the chest and shook him so that his head hit the wall. The applicant then disclosed the whereabouts of the child and was driven by the police to the location where the child's body was found. The German courts in convicting and subsequently upholding the conviction of the accused held that although the statements made by the accused during the interrogation were obtained in violation of the German criminal procedure code and could not be used to ground the accused's conviction, it was permissible to use the indirect evidence obtained as a result of the statements, in particular the location of the body of the child and the autopsy reports, which established that the child had been suffocated.[211] The applicant claimed that the treatment inflicted upon him by the police violated his rights under Article 3 of the ECHR and that the use of this evidence in convicting him had infringed his right to a fair trial.

In determining that there had been no violation of Article 6 of the ECHR, the chamber placed considerable emphasis on the fact that the applicant had made a fresh confession at trial, that he was assisted by defence counsel and that he had been able to exercise his right to silence. It also noted that the applicant had had the possibility at trial to object to the use of the evidence.[212] The chamber concluded that 'in the particular circumstances of the present case, including the police observation of the applicant after he collected the ransom and the available untainted evidence, the impugned items of evidence were only accessory in securing the applicant's conviction, and that the applicant's defence rights were not compromised as a result of their admission'.[213]

The Grand Chamber confirmed that the use of indirect evidence obtained on the basis of evidence collected in violation of Article 3 of the ECHR could

---

[209] e.g. J. Wolter, 'Zur Fernwirkung von Beweisverwertungsverboten: Anmerkung zu BGHSt 32, 68' [1984] *Neue Zeitschrift für Strafrecht* 276, 277.

[210] *Gäfgen v. Germany*, para. 13; and *Gäfgen v. Germany* [GC].

[211] LG Frankfurt/M (First Instance) judgment of 9 April 2003–5/22 Ks 3490 Js 230118/02, Strafverteidiger 2003, 325; BVerfG *3. Kammer des Zweiten Senats* (Constitutional Court), judgment of 14 December 2004–2 BvR 1249/04.

[212] *Gäfgen* v. Germany, para. 108. [213] Ibid., para. 109.

impact on the fairness of the trial, but held that there had been no violation of Article 6 of the ECHR.[214] Like the chamber, the Grand Chamber held that 'the failure to exclude the impugned real evidence, secured following a statement extracted by means of inhuman treatment, did not have a bearing on the applicant's conviction and sentence'.[215] The reasoning behind its approach is not entirely clear. It refers first to the 'vital public interest in preserving the integrity of the judicial process and thus the values of civilised societies founded upon the rule of law'.[216] It then suggests that the prohibition on the use of the evidence might be based on deterrence, stating that in the absence of such a prohibition there might be 'an incentive for law-enforcement officers to use such methods' notwithstanding the provisions of Article 3 of the ECHR. Finally, after distinguishing evidence obtained by torture from that obtained as a result of inhuman or degrading treatment, it introduces a reliability-type argument and holds that in relation to the latter category of evidence the use of the fruit of the poisonous tree should only be prohibited 'if it has been shown that the breach of Article 3 had a bearing on the outcome of the proceedings against the defendant, that is, had an impact on his or her conviction or sentence'.[217] It also refers to the fact that the prohibition on the use of evidence might be necessary in order to protect individuals from conduct prohibited by Article 3 of the ECHR. In any event, neither the chamber nor the Grand Chamber endorsed this justification in the context of evidence obtained as a result of inhuman and degrading treatment, although it seems likely that the use of indirect evidence obtained after recourse to torture would violate the right to a fair trial.[218]

If evidence obtained directly by torture is deemed inadmissible on the basis that its use fatally undermines the legitimacy of the criminal process, it is difficult to see how the use of evidence obtained indirectly by way of such illegitimate means could be tolerated without similarly damaging the moral authority of the criminal justice system.[219] More broadly, if the manner in which the evidence has been obtained, be it directly or indirectly, undermines the opportunity of the accused to challenge the evidence in an adversarial forum, reliance on such evidence ought to be viewed as violating the accused's right to a fair trial. In the context of the *Gäfgen* case, there can be little doubt that the applicant's coerced confession played a major part in enabling the authorities to secure evidence which was later used to convict him of the killing and torpedoed his opportunity to present his case in an adversarial setting. It is somewhat disingenuous to suggest that the applicant was not forced to confess at trial; by this time the damage to his adversarial rights had already been done.

---

[214] *Gäfgen v. Germany* [GC], para. 178.   [215] Ibid., para. 187.
[216] Ibid., para. 175.   [217] Ibid.
[218] For criticism of this distinction, see the dissenting opinion of six judges attached to the judgment in *Gäfgen v. Germany* [GC].
[219] Duff et al., *Trial on Trial (3)*, 104.

6.7 Conclusion: improperly obtained evidence, fairness and the under-regulated pre-trial/investigative process

Criminal evidence law is commonly thought to be one of the most difficult areas to regulate at the international level. It is often assumed that a combination of different legal traditions and awareness of the dangers of usurping, or being seen to usurp, the decisions of national courts has resulted in reluctance on the part of the international bodies such as the ECtHR to play an active role in determining when the use of improperly obtained evidence will undermine the fairness of the trial. As we have seen, however, certain types of evidence are recognised in many jurisdictions as having the potential to impact on the fairness of the trial. Furthermore, the ECtHR has clearly recognised that the manner in which the evidence is obtained in the investigation phase has the potential to impact on the fairness of subsequent proceedings. The ECtHR's difficulties in regulating the use of improperly obtained evidence can be seen to be directly connected to its failure to determine not so much why the use of such evidence ought to be prohibited, but why the use of the evidence violates the fairness of the proceedings. It has not yet developed a deliberate and reasoned approach to determining why or under which circumstances evidence which has been improperly obtained during the pre-trial investigative phase will impact on the rights of the defence at trial.

There is a tendency in both the literature and in the ECtHR's case law in addressing the question of improperly obtained evidence to focus mainly on the nature of the substantive violation as a means of determining whether the right to a fair trial has been violated. This would make sense if the ECtHR were to endorse the rights thesis and to hold that the use of evidence obtained in violation of a Convention right automatically violates the right to a fair trial.[220] The ECtHR's case law clearly demonstrates, however, that it does not endorse this approach. The fact that evidence has been obtained in violation of one of the substantive rights protected by the Convention, such as privacy or even the right not to be subjected to inhuman treatment, will not necessarily result in a finding of a violation of Article 6 of the ECHR. The emphasis on substantive rights is less self-evident if the prohibition of evidence is justified in terms of legitimacy. In the context of Article 3 of the ECHR in particular, the ECtHR has explained the requirement that evidence be suppressed by reference to general notions of the importance of the integrity or legitimacy of the criminal process. The use of evidence obtained by recourse to 'morally reprehensible conduct' serves to legitimise such acts indirectly.[221] The resort to torture consequently undermines the legitimacy of the criminal trial to such an extent as to make

---

[220] An approach favoured by several judges. For criticism, see D. Ormerod, 'ECHR and the Exclusion of Evidence: Trial Remedies for Article 8 Breaches' [2003] *Criminal Law Review* 61, 71, who refers to the argument that all breaches of Art. 8 violate the right to a fair trial as 'over-simplistic and over-inclusive'.

[221] *Jalloh* v. *Germany* [GC], para. 105; and *Levinta* v. *Moldova*, para. 71.

it unfair.[222] The problem here, though, is that as the conduct becomes less 'morally reprehensible', so too does the need to exclude evidence. This has led to distinctions being made on the basis of degrees of ill-treatment. So while the use of torture will automatically violate the accused's right to a fair trial, there is room for discussion on the matter of 'mere' inhuman or degrading treatment.[223] This in turn seems to call into question the reliance on legitimacy – or at least legitimacy as understood by the ECtHR – to guarantee fairness. It seems unlikely, for instance, that evidence obtained by deception, even if it has been obtained in violation of Article 8 of the ECHR, will ever be sufficiently 'morally reprehensible' to justify the prohibition on its use. Consequently, the approach seems unduly narrow.

An alternative, preferable approach is to focus on the impact of improperly obtained evidence on the principles of fairness on which Article 6 of the ECHR is based. In determining whether the activities of the police or investigating authorities have compromised the fairness of the criminal proceedings, it is important to focus not simply on the substantive right at issue, such as freedom from torture or privacy, but to consider the manner in which these activities actually impact on the accused's right to a fair trial. It is the potential of the substantive violation to impact on the fairness of the trial and not the substantive violation per se that necessitates a finding of a violation of Article 6.[224] The only way to establish whether the accused's right to a fair trial has been violated is to focus on the way in which the violation of the substantive right has actually impacted on his or her trial rights. On this theory exclusion is linked to the arguments made in support of the need to guarantee the legitimacy of the process. Unlike the traditional legitimacy theories, however, the focus is not on the moral reprehensibility of the state authorities' conduct, but rather on the effect of the conduct on the ability of the accused (and the defence) to present its case.

In order to determine the circumstances in which the use of improperly obtained evidence could give rise to a violation of the right to a fair trial, it is essential first to consider what this notion of fairness requires. The legitimacy of the trial in Article 6 of the ECHR derives from a concrete understanding of fairness as affording those charged with a criminal offence an opportunity to challenge the evidence against them in an adversarial environment. According to the ECtHR's interpretation of Article 6 of the ECHR, fairness demands that those accused of criminal offences have the opportunity to challenge the evidence levelled against them by the prosecution and to present their own

---

[222] Dennis, *Law of Evidence*, para. 3.45, 108.
[223] Duff et al., *Trial on Trial (3)*, 251: 'The PACE exclusionary rule applies to confessions obtained not only by torture but also by inhuman and degrading treatment, but it is less clear that courts should also exclude evidence that emerged as a side-effect of a wrong comparable in seriousness to inhuman and degrading treatment.'
[224] cf. Ashworth, 'Excluding Evidence'; and J. Chalmers, 'More Fair Play for Suspects: *HM Advocate v HM Higgins*' (2007) 11 *Edinburgh Law Review* 100, 104.

evidence in adversarial proceedings, that is to say assisted by defence counsel in proceedings adjudicated by an independent and impartial judge. Only criminal proceedings which are conducted in such a manner have the sufficient integrity or legitimacy to sustain confidence in the administration of justice. If the improperly obtained evidence is to impact on the right to a fair trial it must be seen to challenge something in this understanding of fairness. Crucially, this suggests that there must be a link between the impropriety in the manner in which the evidence has been obtained and the accused's right to be heard in adversarial proceedings. Such an approach means that violations of other substantive rights will not automatically violate the right to a fair trial, but equally it highlights the fact that impropriety which does not amount to a violation of a substantive fundamental right might still give rise to a violation of Article 6 of the ECHR.[225]

In invoking the privilege against self-incrimination in cases like *Allan*, the ECtHR underlines the fact that the manner in which the evidence is obtained has the potential to impact on the fairness of the trial and thereby draws attention to the importance of the earlier pre-trial or investigative phase of the criminal proceedings for the subsequent fairness of the trial. But it does so at the expense of outlining a more coherent notion of adversarial proceedings doctrine in the earlier stages of the proceedings and thereby undermines its own adversarial conception of fairness in Article 6 of the ECHR which is based principally on defence opportunities and not just on the autonomy of the accused. The relationship between the trial and the investigative pre-trial phase is still underdeveloped in its case law and the reliance on voluntariness in its understanding of the privilege against self-incrimination is very much symptomatic of the ECtHR's reticence in acknowledging the importance of the institutional context in which the defence is to be afforded the opportunity to enforce its Article 6 ECHR procedural rights. This failure to insist on adequate safeguards in the pre-trial phase is also a failure to come to terms with the impact of unfairness in the pre-trial phase on the fairness of the trial.

Criminal proceedings must be seen as a continuous process and not as a series of compartmentalised stages.[226] Consequently, the 'fairness of a trial may be compromised by unfairness earlier in the proceedings, including impropriety in the way in which the evidence was obtained'.[227] The activities of the police and investigation authorities have the potential to affect the fairness of the subsequent proceedings. The pre-trial investigative phase requires a different regulatory structure from that of the determinative trial, which takes into account

---

[225] See, e.g. Duff et al., *Trial on Trial (3)*, 232: 'It is not clear that entrapment cases or cases of reliance on official advice involve breaches of fundamental rights. It is difficult to see how there is a breach of a fundamental right simply by giving false advice or encouraging a criminal offence to be committed.'

[226] *R v. Horseferry Road Magistrates Court Ex p. Bennett* [1994] 1 AC 42 HL; *Saunders* v. *United Kingdom* [GC]; and *Imbrioscia* v. *Switzerland*.

[227] Dennis, *Law of Evidence*, para. 5.1, 150.

the adversarial understanding of the rights of the defence at trial and which emphasises the ways in which these rights can be fatally undermined by the activities of the authorities in the investigative pre-trial phase. The proceedings must be orientated towards safeguarding the notion of adversarial proceedings. The fairness, and thus the legitimacy, of the proceedings will be undermined by any practices which serve to undercut the adversarial opportunities of the accused.

The use of torture, inhuman or degrading treatment in the investigation phase as a means to obtain evidence will necessarily undermine the opportunity of those charged with criminal offences to challenge the case against them in subsequent adversarial proceedings by undermining their procedural rights and their opportunity to present their case as they see fit in adversarial proceedings. Any use of ill-treatment to obtain evidence – whether it be real, as in *Jalloh*, or oral – undermines the defence right to answer charges in a fair, adversarial setting. In the context of deception, inducements, traps or other improper practices by the police or investigating authorities, the matter to be decided will be less the violation of constitutional-type privacy protections and more the extent to which such activities serve to compromise the principle of adversariality at any subsequent trial.[228] Knowledge of the extent of the evidence incriminating the accused is essential in order to enable the defence to prepare and present its case and deception on the part of the authorities during the investigation, for instance by wrongly providing information in an attempt to induce the accused to confess[229] or by knowingly withholding information which could assist the defence in preparing its case, ought to give rise to concerns about the impact of the use of such evidence on the fairness of the subsequent trial. Surveillance operations which undermine defence rights, and in particular the right to answer allegations once sufficient evidence comes to light, will always impact on the fairness of the trial. Consideration ought also to be given to the impact of the use of detention on remand on the fairness of the trial. Long periods of detention on remand or unfavourable conditions during detention ought to be seen as having the potential to affect adversely the opportunity of the defence to present its case and thus on the fairness of the trial. Furthermore, it is essential that there is consideration of matters such as the point in time at which the accused is to be informed of his or her defence rights in order to prevent these rights being undermined in the course of the investigative process.

The difficulties encountered by the ECtHR in dealing with the issue of improperly obtained evidence are connected to the broader issue of the lack of a satisfactory regulatory structure for the investigative pre-trial phase. Fairness in provisions such as Article 6 of the ECHR is principally understood in terms of safeguarding the rights of the accused, but in order for this to be achieved,

---

[228] In this regard it is important to note that many cases may never get to trial.
[229] See, e.g. the facts of the English case *R* v. *Mason* [1987] 3 All ER 481, CA (lie by the police to accused and counsel that defendant's fingerprints had been found on an item used during the offence, counsel advised client to confess, confession inadmissible).

it is essential that the institutional setting in which the accused is to have the opportunity to exercise these rights be carefully regulated.[230] Judgments such as *Jalloh*, *Haci Özen* and *Harutyunyan* underline the ECtHR's recognition of the fact that events in the investigation phase can adversely impact on the adversarial opportunity of the defence at trial, yet it has been slow to explain why and when this will be the case. A more coherent approach would be achieved by clarifying the relationship between improperly obtained evidence and fairness and by explaining the prohibition on the use of such evidence from the perspective of the impact on the rights of the defence.

[230] This has particularly serious repercussions in the evidential context: 'The rules and doctrines of evidence can barely be understood, or their significance appreciated, without taking proper account of the procedural environments in which they operate' (Roberts and Zuckerman, *Criminal Evidence*, 42).

7
The presumption of innocence

7.1 Introduction

Although the maxim 'presumption of innocence' can be traced in common law history as far back as the days of Bracton and in continental history as far back as three centuries later,[1] it is only in recent times that it has acquired considerable constitutional prominence. We have seen that it was enshrined in the *Déclaration des droits de l'homme et du citoyen* and in his study of human rights in national constitutions conducted some years ago Bassiouni found that it was contained in at least sixty-seven national constitutions across the common law and civil law world.[2] The presumption of innocence has also been recognised in a wide range of international instruments such as the ICCPR, the ECHR, the ACHR and the African Charter on Human and Peoples' Rights and by the international criminal tribunals and courts.[3]

Before we examine how this principle has been applied across the two dominant legal traditions and by international human rights regimes, however, it will help our analysis if we are clear about what we mean by the presumption. Despite becoming so accepted, there is often a lack of clarity about what it means and we will argue that this can serve to obscure its central importance. As we shall see, it is commonly discussed exclusively within the context of a rule of evidence requiring a high standard of proof before conviction. But it is sometimes used in terms which make it almost synonymous with the right to a fair trial encompassing the fair trial standards we have discussed so far. In broader terms, it is also used to signify the right of individuals to be protected against coercive measures by the state or the right not to be convicted for crimes of which one is 'morally' innocent. In the first section we consider three rather different fields of application which can be viewed on a sliding scale from the

---

[1] According to J. B. Thayer, *A Preliminary Treatise on Evidence at the Common Law* (Boston: Little, Brown, 1898) 553.
[2] See M. C. Bassiouni, 'Human Rights in the Context of Criminal Justice: Identifying International Procedural Protections in National Constitutions' (1992–3) 3 *Duke Journal of Comparative and International Law* 235, 266. The national constitutions are listed at n. 143.
[3] See Art. 14(2) ICCPR, Art. 6(2) ECHR, Art. 8(2) ACHR and Art. 7(1)(b) African Charter. See also Art. 21(3) ICTY, Art. 20(3) ICTR and Art. 66 ICC Statute.

particular to the general. We then go on to consider how the presumption has been regarded across the common law and civil law divide and by international human rights regimes.

7.2 The meaning of the presumption of innocence

7.2.1 The presumption as an evidentiary protection

The presumption is perhaps most commonly associated with a rule of evidence whereby it is for the prosecution to prove the guilt of the accused to a high standard. There are three different questions that arise from this meaning. First of all, what exactly is meant by proving guilt? Secondly, does the prosecution have to prove all aspects of guilt? Thirdly, what is the precise standard of proof required? It is commonly accepted in common law and continental legal systems that in order to prove guilt, each element of the offence that has been charged must be proved against the defendant.[4] These elements are sometimes referred to as the 'material' or 'ultimate' or 'dispositive' facts which lead to a determination of guilt.[5] Distinctions are often made in both common law and continental European jurisdictions between those material facts that relate to elements of the offence and those that relate to exceptions, exemptions or provisos which are not properly part of the elements of the offence, but relate to defences.[6]

Common law jurisdictions have also traditionally made a distinction between legal or persuasive and evidential burdens of proof. The legal or persuasive burden is described as the obligation of a party to meet the requirement that a fact in issue be proved or disproved, while the evidential burden is the obligation to show, if called upon to do so, that there is sufficient evidence to raise an issue as to the existence or non-existence of a fact in issue.[7] Generally speaking, the prosecution bears the legal burden of proving the elements of the offence, but also has the evidential burden in the first place of raising sufficient evidence of these elements before the defence need respond. A failure to discharge the evidential burden by raising sufficient evidence of an element of the offence may result in the entire offence being withdrawn before the court even comes

---

[4] See, e.g. *R* v. *Morin* [1988] 2 SCR 345 and *R* v. *Shepherd* (1990) 170 CLR 573, 580–1. In relation to the principle in Germany, see U. Eisenberg, *Beweisrecht der StPO*, 6th edn (Munich: C. H. Beck, 2008) para. 120 and in Switzerland see N. Schmid, *Handbuch des schweizerischen Strafprozessrechts* (Zurich: Dike, 2009) para. 216. The international criminal tribunals have endorsed this approach: see *Prosecutor* v. *Stakic*, para. 219.

[5] These are determined by considering which facts are required as a matter of substantive criminal law for a conviction. This is sometimes described as a question of materiality distinguished from questions of admissibility which come within the realm of the law of evidence. See, e.g. G. F. James, 'Relevancy, Probability and the Law' (1941) 29 *California Law Review* 689; and J. L. Montrose, 'Basic Concepts of the Law of Evidence' (1954) 70 *Law Quarterly Review* 527.

[6] See, e.g. Schmid, *Handbuch*, para. 220 (Switzerland); and C. Roxin and B. Schünemann, *Strafverfahrensrecht*, 26th edn (Munich: C. H. Beck, 2009) 356 (Germany).

[7] C. Tapper, *Cross & Tapper on Evidence*, 11th edn (Oxford University Press, 2007) 131 and 132.

to consider whether the offence has been proved. Generally speaking, the party which bears the legal burden of proof on an issue also bears the evidential burden in relation to it. But in relation to certain defences such as self-defence or provocation, the defence may bear the evidential burden of producing sufficient evidence in relation to it in the first place before it is considered by the court; once borne, it is for the prosecution then to disprove the defence.[8]

Although issues of burden of proof are of vital importance in systems of proof that are party-driven as the manner in which they are allocated can have a profound effect on the outcome of the case, questions have been raised as to how important they are in less party-driven systems. There has been some dispute as to whether it is even appropriate to use the term 'burden of proof' in continental countries where it is the obligation of the court to discover the truth.[9] Similar arguments are sometimes made in the context of 'inquisitorial' procedures within common law countries.[10] But we have seen that continental systems accept the need for an 'accusatorial' system of proof, whereby the prosecution and defence are represented as parties to the proceedings. If we set a high standard of proof for conviction, this entails that the burden of proof is on the party arguing for prosecution, for if this standard is not met the prosecution will not prevail. Therefore, so long as there is an 'accusatorial' structure, with a prosecution and defence represented as parties to the proceedings, it would seem to make sense to speak in terms of a burden of proof on whichever party stands to lose if the proof is not made out to the satisfaction of the court.

Regarding the third question as to the precise standard of proof that must be borne by the prosecution in order to prove the material facts that constitute the elements of the offence, common law systems and certain Scandinavian countries associate the standard as one of proof beyond reasonable doubt, whereas continental systems often speak instead of 'in dubio pro reo'.[11] We

---

[8] There is an important relation between the two types of burden because what may amount to sufficient evidence to discharge the evidential burden will depend upon what standard of proof is required for the legal burden to be surmounted. See Tapper, *Cross & Tapper on Evidence*, 132.

[9] C. J. M. Safferling, *Towards an International Criminal Procedure* (Oxford University Press, 2002) 257.

[10] See, in relation to prisoner release cases in the United Kingdom, *Lichniak* v. *R* [2002] UKHL 47, para. 16, *Re McClean* [2005] UKHL 46 and for comment J. Jackson, 'Evidence and Proof in Parole Hearings: Meeting a Triangulation of Interests' [2007] *Criminal Law Review* 417, 421–4.

[11] See C. Van Den Wyngaert (ed.), *Criminal Procedure Systems in the European Community* (London: Butterworths, 1992) 22, 129 and 173–4. For the position in Scandinavian countries, see K. Waaben, 'Criminal Responsibility and the Quantum of Proof' (1965) 9 *Scandinavian Studies in Law* 243, 274–9. The *in dubio pro reo* principle, which means 'in doubt you must decide for the defendant' was developed by continental jurists in the twelfth and early thirteenth centuries; however, its roots can be found in works of the early medieval Pope Gregory the Great. See, e.g. J. Q. Whitman, 'The Origins of "Reasonable Doubt"', Yale Law School Faculty Scholarship Series, Paper No. 1, 2005), http://lsr.nellco.org/yale/fss/papers/1. See also G. P. Fletcher, 'Two Kinds of Legal Rules: A Comparative Study of Burden-of-Persuasion Practices in Criminal Cases' (1968) 77 *Yale Law Journal* 880, 880–1; P. Holtappels, *Die Entwicklung des Grundsatzes 'in dubio pro reo'* (Cram: De Gruyter, 1965); and J. Zopfs, *Der Grundsatz 'in dubio pro reo'* (Baden-Baden: Nomos, 1999). Denmark, Malta and Norway, however, require the beyond reasonable doubt standard for conviction.

shall examine the meaning of these terms later, but it is important to note for now that this standard must be reached in relation to each of the material facts on which a conviction is based, but not in relation to the individual items of evidence presented at the trial.[12] Thus, the prosecution is not obliged to prove each and every individual circumstance alleged against the accused beyond a reasonable doubt. The tribunal of fact must consider the evidence as a whole and after analysis of all the relevant evidence determine whether the facts forming the elements of the crime or the responsibility alleged against the accused are proved beyond a reasonable doubt. Essentially, this seems to mean that the tribunal must find beyond a reasonable doubt only those facts upon which a finding of guilt must depend.[13]

As well as encompassing a rule of evidence directed to prosecutors and adjudicators, the requirement that the accused be 'proved' guilty is sometimes said to require that adjudicators ignore all pre-trial indications of guilt and determine guilt or innocence solely on the evidence presented in court.[14] Thayer, for example, spoke of the 'twofold' nature of the presumption: 'that an accused person is not to be prejudiced at his trial by having been charged with crime and held in custody, or by any mere suspicions, however grave; but is only to be held guilty when the government has established his guilt by legal evidence and beyond all reasonable doubt'.[15] This may be seen as an expression of the idea that the verdict must be confined to the charge and that the defendant begins the trial with a clean slate without prejudice.[16] In so far as this principle is grounded in the idea that defendants can only be judged on the offence charged, it would seem to speak to a different principle, that of *nullum crimen, nulla poena sine lege*, which the European Court of Human Rights has said is embodied within Article 7 of the ECHR.[17] But it also seems to require more than this by exhorting fact-finders to approach the evidence without prejudice and to keep an open mind on the evidence on the charge.[18]

---

[12] *Prosecutor* v. *Ntagerura*. [13] See *Prosecutor* v. *Brdjanin*, Trial Chamber, Orders to File Table.
[14] Thayer, *Preliminary Treatise on Evidence*, 559 and 565.
[15] Ibid., 565. See also J. H. Wigmore, *A Treatise on the Anglo-American System of Evidence in Trials at Common Law*, 3rd edn (Boston: Little, Brown, 1940) vol. 9, 467.
[16] See, e.g. P. Roberts and A. Zuckerman, *Criminal Evidence*, 2nd edn (Oxford University Press, 2010) 559–60.
[17] *Kokkinakas* v. *Greece*.
[18] This is said to provide a justification for certain rules of evidence which prohibit the fact-finder from relying on evidence of previous misconduct. See, e.g. Roberts and Zuckerman, *Criminal Evidence*, ch. 14. There is a difference of view, however, as to whether this aspect of the presumption of innocence requires merely that the fact-finder keeps an open mind about a person's guilt or innocence or whether it positively requires that the fact-finder actually presumes the defendant's innocence. Cf. L. Laudan, *Truth, Error and Criminal Law: An Essay in Legal Epistemology* (Cambridge University Press, 2006) 96–106; A. Duff, L. Farmer, S. Marshall and V. Tadros, *The Trial on Trial (3): Towards a Normative Theory of the Criminal Trial* (Oxford: Hart, 2007) 113; and H. L. Ho, *A Philosophy of Evidence Law* (Oxford University Press, 2008) 296. At the heart of this debate there would seem to be a question of whether this aspect of the presumption protects defendants against unwarranted temptation to be prejudiced by their criminal past or whether it imports a moral view that whatever the empirical warrant for

If we link together within the meaning of the presumption of innocence the rule of evidence that the prosecution bears the burden of proving guilt to a high standard and the principle that fact-finders must keep an open mind when evaluating the evidence, then the presumption can be seen as an evidentiary mechanism for avoiding the wrongful conviction of accused persons on the offences charged against them with all the harmful consequences that this can have for the individual and society. Although the requirement of a high standard of proof may not have originated in concerns about convicting the innocent,[19] we have seen that this was a particular concern of the social contract theorists of the seventeenth and eighteenth centuries, as it was considered a heinous breach of the social contract for the state to condemn someone who had not himself breached the social contract. We have seen that at the core of the contract was a bargain whereby individuals agreed to submit to the laws deemed necessary for the security and liberty of all provided they would be protected from others against breach of these laws and protected also from punishment for breach of these laws where this was not justified. This punishment may entail more than intrusion on one's basic liberties; it involves the censure of the whole community for breach of the laws and when one is wrongly subjected to it, one suffers a deep injustice, what Dworkin describes as a 'moral' harm.[20]

In order to guard against such a risk, we should aim to make our criminal procedures as accurate as possible, but no matter how exacting these safeguards, there is a limit to the resources, time and effort that we as a society can put into ensuring the accuracy of decisions. As Dworkin has said, we provide less than the most accurate procedures for testing guilt or innocence than we could in order to save resources, but also to secure other benefits.[21] He takes as an example the fact that the police force may be inhibited in its task of investigating crime if it had to disclose the name of its informers under the principle of equality of arms. Even if we were prepared to commit ourselves to the most accurate procedures possible – something that is not politically possible in the real world – we would still have to accept that human beings make errors in the way in which they perceive events and evaluate evidence. The possibility of error means that beyond the need to ensure accuracy, we need to have mechanisms for ensuring that any risk of error is directed or distributed in a manner that protects individuals against wrongful conviction.[22]

The high standard of proof required before there can be conviction is a supreme example of such a mechanism. In requiring a very high standard of proof before we convict, we are clearly decreasing the chances that an innocent

---

treating criminal past wrongdoing as relevant to the present offence, it is morally wrong to do so as an accused is to be tried for what he did and not for the sort of person he is.

[19] See J. Whitman, *The Origins of Reasonable Doubt: Theological Roots of the Criminal Trial* (New Haven: Yale University Press, 2008).
[20] R. Dworkin, *A Matter of Principle* (Oxford: Clarendon, 1986) 80–1.   [21] Ibid., 72.
[22] For an elaborate theory explaining many of the exclusionary rules of evidence as well as the rule of proof beyond reasonable doubt on the basis of allocating risk between the parties, see A. Stein, *Foundations of Evidence Law* (Oxford University Press, 2005).

person may be convicted. But we are also increasing the chances that the guilty escape punishment, with the risk that this poses to the community of further harm being perpetrated against it in the future. Clearly, there has to be some balance in setting the standard between the need to avoid the conviction of the innocent and the need to avoid the acquittal of the guilty, but the reason why we give particular weight to avoiding the former is as a result of the special 'moral' harm that is inflicted on individuals when they are wrongly convicted over and above the 'bare' harm that may be imposed on the community as the result of a wrongful acquittal.

Apart from the standard of proof, a number of other rules can assist in altering the balance of risk in favour of defendants. It is commonly assumed that the general principles of relevance and probative weight and the rules governing the admissibility of evidence should be the same in every context and apply symmetrically to both prosecution and defence.[23] But in practice this symmetrical aspiration may be difficult to achieve, as judges may apply different thresholds of admissibility to the prosecution and defence in accordance with their base-rate assumptions of the guilt of the accused.[24] Furthermore, certain rules may impact on one party more severely than another. Corroboration rules, for example, impact on the prosecution rather than the defence, as they prevent any conviction unless certain kinds of evidence are corroborated. A number of exclusionary rules such as the hearsay rule may appear formally to bite against both sides, but some, for example, rules excluding evidence of the accused's bad character, have a particular applicability to the prosecution. In addition, a number of rules can be specifically designed to be asymmetric in their application to the prosecution and the defence with the aim of avoiding wrongful convictions.[25] Rules allocating the burden and standard of proof on admissibility issues impact disproportionately as between the prosecution and defence. In a number of common law jurisdictions, for example, the prosecution may be required to prove beyond reasonable doubt that a confession made by the accused was voluntary before it can be admitted, whereas an accused wishing to admit the confession of a co-accused may only need to show that it was voluntary on the balance of probabilities.[26]

---

[23] For a critique of this principle, see R. Leng, 'Losing Sight of the Burden of Proof? A Challenge to Symmetrical Assumptions about Admissibility', in I. Madelin (ed.), *The Admissibility of Evidence in Criminal Cases* (Collected Papers from A Consultation held at St George House, Windsor Castle, 1999) 12. D. M. Risinger, 'Guilt vs. Guiltiness: Are the Right Rules for Trying Factual Innocence Inevitably the Wrong Rules for Trying Culpability?' (2008) 38 *Seton Hall Law Review* 885, 886–8.

[24] D. M. Risinger, 'Baserates, the Presumption of Guilt, Admissibility Rulings, and Erroneous Conviction' (2003) 4 *Michigan State Law Review* 1051, 1060.

[25] For a general critique of such rules, see Laudan, *Truth, Error and Criminal Law*.

[26] This is the position in Canada, Hong Kong, Singapore, Malaysia, Ireland and South Africa. See also *Prosecutor v. Sesay*, Trial Chamber, para. 52. In other jurisdictions such as Australia and Scotland, the prosecution only needs to prove voluntariness on the balance of probabilities. For a critique, see R. Pattenden, 'The Proof Rules of Pre-Verdict Judicial Fact-Finding in Criminal Trials by Jury' (2008) 125 *Law Quarterly Review* 79. In so far as the voluntariness doctrine

7.2.2 Treating defendants as innocent

Thus far, we have identified the presumption of innocence with evidentiary protections which have their fundamental rationale in the need to protect the innocent from conviction. But there is a second broader conception of the presumption of innocence which sees it as extending beyond the domain of procedural protections to avoid wrongful conviction into the domain of a substantive right of individuals to be treated as innocent until proved guilty. If guilt is dependent on the prosecution proving its case to a high standard, it may seem to follow logically that individuals should be treated as innocent until the prosecution has discharged this burden.[27] But there is a difference between viewing the presumption as necessary to the epistemic need to prevent wrongful convictions and viewing it as a way of treating defendants before they are found guilty. The two aspects serve different purposes: one is related to the outcome of the proceedings and the other to protecting what Trechsel has described as the reputation aspect of the presumption, protecting the image of the person concerned as 'innocent'.[28] At the same time, the two aspects may be connected as aspects of the need to protect the individual against the power of the state. On this conception the presumption of innocence is more than merely a procedural protection designed to protect individuals from wrongful conviction, but is broadly concerned to protect the dignity of the individual against the power of the state by prescribing that individuals should be treated as innocent throughout all stages of criminal proceedings.[29]

The question remains how far to take this broader principle. At one level it could be restricted to a protection from any presumption of guilt that is imputed directly to individuals before they are convicted, either by statements made to this effect or by action taken against them which in effect amounts to punishment. It may also be that certain actions taken by the state prior to guilt, such as imposing punishment on persons being detained on remand or perhaps freezing a person's assets prior to guilt, might be said to amount to conduct which presumes guilt. At the other end of the spectrum, however, the principle could prohibit the state from taking *any* intrusive action

---

underpins the reliability of confessions, it may be argued that in order to give maximum effect to the policy of avoiding convictions upon unreliable confessions the prosecution should be required to prove their voluntariness beyond reasonable doubt, but that because the exclusion of a truthful confession of a co-defendant may risk a defendant's wrongful conviction, the standard for proving the voluntariness of a co-defendant's confession which a defendant is seeking to admit should be set much lower. Civil jurisdictions are less clear in their demarcation of the respective burden and standards of proof between the parties in respect of admissibility issues. For the position in Germany, see R. Juy-Birmann, 'The German System', in M. Delmas-Marty and J. Spencer (eds.), *European Criminal Procedures* (Cambridge University Press, 2002) 292, 326–8.

[27] P. J. Schwikkard, *The Presumption of Innocence* (Cape Town: Juta, 1999) 36.
[28] S. Trechsel, *Human Rights in Criminal Proceedings* (Oxford University Press, 2005) 164 and 178.
[29] S. Stavros, *The Guarantees for Accused Persons under Article 6 of the European Convention on Human Rights* (Dordrecht: Martinus Nijhoff, 1993) 50.

against them until they have been proved guilty. It would be hard to find any criminal justice system that has ever subscribed to this degree of protection for individuals. This would suggest that a whole variety of coercive measures that are at present at the disposal of investigating authorities – wiretapping, surveillance, the taking of samples of blood or saliva, search and seizure, arrest, interrogation and detention – could not be taken by the state until it had proved that the individuals at whom they are directed were proved to be guilty.[30]

The presumption may be put another way, however, by saying that such measures should at least have to be justified before they can be taken against individuals. Put like this, the presumption of innocence then expresses the proper relationship between the state and the citizen, as Ashworth has put it, implying the need for case-by-case justification for any measure that is taken against the individual at each stage of the criminal process and not just at the stage of conviction.[31] As with the standard of proof required for conviction, there is a judgment that must be made at each stage as to what degree of evidence is required for coercive action to be justified and what institutional safeguards are necessary to determine this. We can see clear parallels here with Article 5 of the ECHR, which seeks to restrain the state's power to detain persons before trial by requiring reasonable suspicion of having committed an offence and requiring judicial authorisation for continued detention. These requirements impose a certain standard of proof before coercive measures are taken and also call for the institutional safeguard of judicial scrutiny before certain actions are taken. A number of other institutional checks can be put in place as well as judicial scrutiny. The function of investigation may be separated from that of prosecution as has been the case in a number of common law countries. Alternatively, investigations may be supervised by independent prosecutors as in certain civil law countries.[32] Finally, as we saw in the last chapter, there can be mechanisms for excluding evidence which has been obtained in breach of the standards laid down before intrusive action can be taken against the individual.

From the point of view of protecting the individual accused, there would seem to be attractions in this broader conception of the presumption of innocence. Given that the consequences for individuals caught up in pre-trial detention can be just as harmful as the consequences of conviction, we should concentrate our efforts not just in protecting the innocent from conviction, but protecting them from intrusive coercive action. It is also the case that intrusive action against the individual can itself lead to wrongful convictions. In the last

---

[30] See Trechsel, *Human Rights in Criminal Proceedings*, 179.
[31] A. Ashworth, 'Four Threats to the Presumption of Innocence' (2006) 10 *International Journal of Evidence & Proof* 241, 249.
[32] For discussion of the impact that different models of prosecutorial authority and function have had upon the accuracy of prosecutorial decision-making, see J. Jackson, 'The Effect of Legal Culture and Proof in Decisions to Prosecute' (2004) 3 *Law, Probability and Risk* 109.

chapter, we saw that we can justify the exclusion of evidence that has been obtained as a result of unlawful detention on broad integrity grounds, but also on the ground of procedural fairness as individuals are less able to rebut charges made against them when they are in detention. There are dangers, however, in conflating the presumption of innocence with a broad over-arching principle that defines the relationship between the state and the individual throughout the criminal process. For one thing, other principles that govern how we believe individuals should be treated may be squeezed out or balanced away too readily in the process.[33] One of these, examined in the next chapter, is the right of silence. As we shall see, there are independent reasons for the right of silence even when we can mount a strong case against an accused linking him or her to an offence. Similarly, after conviction, we may still want to insist that defendants be protected by, say, legal representation at the sentencing stage or on appeal, even though they have been proved guilty beyond reasonable doubt. Arguably, it is a distraction to use the presumption of innocence to justify a whole host of protections that we deem it necessary to have to prevent the state intruding on our individual privacy and autonomy.[34] These can be justified independently of the presumption and in so far as the presumption is used to justify them, they suggest that they may be balanced away once we have evidence of a person's guilt.

If this broader conception of the presumption of innocence risks overshadowing other important rights and fair trial standards in the criminal process, it can also serve, however, to overshadow the normative value of the narrower procedural protections. Both the narrow protections and the broader conception are directed at limiting the state's power to take coercive action against the individual. But as we have seen, the amount of evidence required to justify such action at each stage varies according to the interests at stake and the necessity of the action. We can require that strict proportionality tests are applied in each case, but the importance of the proof beyond reasonable doubt standard that comes into play before there can be a conviction is that it sends out a very strong and public message as to what is required before there can be a conviction. We require this particularly high standard before conviction because although coercive actions such as arrest and detention and search and seizure can have equally if not more harmful consequences for the individual, they do not carry the same opprobrium as when we convict a person for criminal conduct and consequently do not carry the same 'moral' harm as when we publicly convict an innocent person of criminal conduct.[35] It follows that any derogation from the procedural protections which support such an important principle will need to be justified in a stronger manner than other coercive action taken by the state.

---

[33] Schwikkard, *Presumption of Innocence*, 37–8.
[34] See, e.g. S. J. Summers, 'Presumption of Innocence' [2001] *Juridical Review* 37, 38.
[35] For the condemnatory aspect of convictions, see Duff et al., *Trial on Trial (3)*, 83–7.

7.2.3 Substantive innocence

The particular opprobrium attached to a conviction takes us to a third meaning that can be given to the presumption of innocence which is concerned with the circumstances under which the state may convict persons: a question of substantive guilt. Under this conception, the right not to be convicted if 'innocent' is not just addressed to the procedural means by which a defendant is convicted, but requires a scrutiny of the substantive law itself to ensure that it only penalises those who are properly 'guilty'. The distinction between these procedural and substantive aspects was well put by Regan J. in her judgment in the South African case of *S* v. *Coetzee*, when she said that the two aspects were important in a democracy:

> [T]he State may not deprive its citizens of liberty for reasons that are not acceptable, nor, when it deprives citizens of freedom for acceptable reasons, may it do so in a manner which is procedurally unfair. The two issues are related, but a constitutional finding that the reason for which the State wishes to deprive a person of his or her freedom is acceptable, does not dispense with the question of whether the procedure followed to deprive a person is fair.[36]

The substantive scrutiny of the law can take one of a number of forms. First of all, under the principle of *nullum crimen sine culpa*, it can involve scrutiny to see whether the law is penalising blameless individuals. For some, all offences which breach the 'fault principle' that criminal liability should only be imposed for wrongs that are culpably committed are a breach of the presumption of innocence.[37] This is a principle that would seem to be more honoured in certain continental legal systems than in common law systems where strict liability is imposed for a number of offences.[38] Another form of scrutiny is to consider whether the law is properly penalising only wrongful conduct.[39] It has been argued that a statute which defines 'guilt' so as to include those who are innocent of anything that could plausibly count as wrongdoing may satisfy a formal presumption of innocence, but does not satisfy the substantive presumption that a person is innocent until proved guilty of wrongdoing.[40]

---

[36] 1997 (3) SA 527 (CC), para. 159.
[37] See, e.g. A. Paizes, 'A Closer Look at the Presumption of Innocence in our Constitution: What is an Accused Presumed to be Innocent *of*?' (1998) 11 *South African Journal of Criminal Justice* 409. For discussion of the 'fault principle', see generally A. P. Simester, *Appraising Strict Liability* (Oxford University Press, 2005). See also Trechsel, *Human Rights in Criminal Proceedings*, 157.
[38] But see Canadian Charter's interpretation of the presumption of innocence, which seems to give the Supreme Court of Canada jurisdiction to assess the substance of criminal law: see, e.g. *Wholesale TravelGroup Inc.* [1991] 3 SCR 154. For comparison between English law and French and German law, see J. Spencer and A. Pedain, 'Strict Liability in Continental Criminal Law' in Simester, *Strict Liability*, 237. See also Trechsel, *Human Rights in Criminal Proceedings*, 158.
[39] For the distinction between wrongs and faults, see J. Gardner, 'Wrongs and Faults', in Simester, *Strict Liability*; and A. Duff, 'Strict Liability, Legal Presumptions and the Presumption of Innocence', in Simester, *Strict Liability*, 125, 134.
[40] Duff, 'Strict Liability', 134.

More recently, Tadros and Tierney have argued for a more limited form of substantive scrutiny, which is to ask whether the law goes beyond the reach of the mischief aimed at by the legislature to penalise those who should not properly come within its reach.[41]

These issues take us deep into difficult questions of criminal law beyond the scope of this book. But precisely because it is difficult territory in which there are contested views as to what the concept of fault means and what the criminal law should sanction – and there can even be argument as to what a legislature intended should be penalised, it would seem that these questions are better kept separate from the evidential and procedural foundations of the presumption of innocence.[42] This is not to deny that there is a connection between these foundations and more substantive inquiries. It may seem illogical to prevent legislatures imposing evidential requirements on defendants to prove certain defences in the name of the presumption of innocence when they would be permitted to prevent defendants availing of such defences in the first place.[43] From the point of view of the defendant, it can be argued that there is little point in protecting the procedural rights of defendants in the absence of fair substantive criminal law.[44] From the point of view of the legislature determining whether an offence should require the defendant's fault to be established, it would also seem relevant to consider how easy or difficult it will be to prove fault under the procedural and evidential regime at hand. It has been suggested that a major reason why French and German criminal laws have been able to dispense with offences of strict liability more readily than English law is because the rules of criminal procedure and evidence in these countries make it relatively more easy for a defendant's fault to be established.[45]

We shall compare the relative ease or difficulty experienced by the prosecution in proving guilt in civil and common law systems later. For now, the point to be made is that to concede that there are connections between procedural law and substantive law does not mean that it is sensible to use the presumption of innocence in both a procedural and substantive manner. There may be good grounds for the courts to scrutinise the substance of certain laws – status crimes may be an example, or where the effect of a particular statute is to prohibit certain conduct which the legislature did not intend to criminalise. But this scrutiny would seem to relate more to the principle of legality or 'the rule of law' than to the presumption of innocence, in that individuals here risk being

---

[41] V. Tadros and S. Tierney, 'The Presumption of Innocence and the Human Rights Act' (2004) 67 *Modern Law Review* 402.
[42] See Ashworth, 'Presumption of Innocence', 254.
[43] For arguments of this nature, see J. C. Jeffries and P. B. Stephan III, 'Defences, Presumptions and the Burden of Proof of Criminal Law' (1979) 88 *Yale Law Journal* 1325.
[44] V. Tadros, 'Rethinking the Presumption of Innocence' (2007) 1 *Criminal Law and Philosophy* 193, 194.
[45] Spencer and Pedain, 'Strict Liability', 269.

punished either for no conduct at all or for conduct which falls outside the scope of what was intended.

The view that the presumption of innocence should be restricted to its procedural and evidential foundations does not rest purely on pragmatic grounds or on grounds of conceptual clarity. As with the second meaning we ascribed to the presumption above, there is a risk that if we mix the evidential rationale with others we become distracted from the essential message that the presumption is designed to convey, namely the need to avoid convicting a person who is innocent under the terms of the substantive law.[46] So when it is argued that it is illogical to prevent legislatures from placing burdens of proof on defendants in relation to defences when there is nothing to oblige them to create the defence in the first place,[47] we lose sight of the danger that in reversing the burden of proof and requiring defendants to prove the defence we increase the risk of convicting a defendant as guilty of the offence on less than proof beyond reasonable doubt.

A further difficulty relates to whether questions of substantive law should properly come within the scope of international human rights.[48] It may be that we would wish to protect individuals from being convicted for actions which cannot by any measure be fairly attributable to them, for example making individuals vicariously liable for the acts of others.[49] But international human rights regimes have been wary about guaranteeing the particular content of substantive law. Article 6(1) of the ECHR, for example, has been said by the ECtHR to give everyone the right to have a claim relating to his or her civil rights and obligations brought before a domestic court, but it does not guarantee any substantive content for those rights.[50] In a similar fashion, as far as criminal law is concerned, the ECtHR has generally subscribed to the principle that the Convention leaves states free to designate as criminal an act or omission not constituting the normal exercise of one of the rights that it protects.[51]

Having staked out a claim for the presumption of innocence being regarded, first and foremost, as an evidentiary procedural mechanism for protecting persons against being wrongly convicted by a court, we must next consider how this aspect of the presumption of innocence relates to the common rationalist

---

[46] See P. Roberts, 'Strict Liability and the Presumption of Innocence: An Exposé of Functionalist Assumptions', in Simester, *Strict Liability*, 151.

[47] This 'greater includes the lesser test' argument has been used on occasions by the courts to uphold burdens of proof on the defence. See, e.g. *Sheldrake* v. *Director of Public Prosecutions* [2005] 1 All ER 237, per Lord Bingham.

[48] cf. G. R. Sullivan, 'Strict Liability for Criminal Offences in England and Wales Following Incorporation of the European Convention on Human Rights', in Simester, *Strict Liability*, 95.

[49] See, e.g. *AP, MP and TP* v. *Switzerland*.

[50] See, e.g. *Z and others* v. *United Kingdom*; and *Roche* v. *United Kingdom*.

[51] *Engel and others* v. *Netherlands*, para. 81. On occasions, however, the ECtHR has engaged in a scrutiny of the substantive criminal law where this impacts adversely on the exercise of Convention rights. See, e.g. *MC* v. *Bulgaria*.

and institutional procedural rights traditions that we have identified across the common law and civil law divide before coming to the international jurisprudence.

7.3 The presumption of innocence and the rationalist tradition

It is not altogether clear when precisely high standards of proof such as proof beyond reasonable doubt and *in dubio pro reo* came to be accepted standards in criminal cases. We have seen that while the abandonment of the old irrational proofs of trial by ordeal were replaced on the Continent by Roman-canon principles of full proof, in England the development of juries who were less familiar with the facts of cases led to the question of what standards they should employ in reaching decisions on the evidence. The standards of 'satisfied conscience', 'moral certainty' and 'beyond reasonable doubt' became characteristics of the late seventeenth- and eighteenth-century English criminal courts as the rationalist tradition of evidence scholarship was developed. 'Moral certainty', according to Locke, rose so near to a certainty that it governs 'our thinking as absolutely as the most evident demonstration'.[52] As decisions had to be made in conditions of uncertainty, judges began to speak more of doubts about the evidence, and in the middle of the eighteenth century it would seem that the first use was made of the familiar 'beyond reasonable doubt' standard.[53] The suggestion that any doubt about the conviction had to be reasonable might suggest that this is a lesser standard than the previous requirements of satisfied conscience or moral certainty. But it has been suggested that this standard was not introduced in order to diminish the need for a high standard of proof, but rather to clarify what was meant by a 'satisfied conscience'. Reasonable doubt was a better explanation of the satisfied conscience expressing the idea that there had to be moral certainty, but not absolute certainty.[54]

In continental Europe, the old Roman-canon system of proof came to be replaced by the notion in the Napoleonic Code of 'intime conviction', which has been described as a reasonably 'close facsimile' of proof beyond reasonable doubt.[55] In suggesting that what matters is the 'deep-seated' conviction of the fact-finder in the guilt of the accused, this concept may suggest that fact-finders are free to act according to their own beliefs and conscience without regard to the evidence in the case which would, of course, be a breach of the procedural protection to judge each case on the evidence.[56] Some of the scholars in the nineteenth century from both the common law and civil law traditions criticised

---

[52] J. Locke, *An Essay Concerning Human Understanding*, ed. Alexander Fraser (New York: Dover, 1959) bk 4, ch. 16.

[53] B. J. Shapiro, *Beyond Reasonable Doubt and Probable Cause: Historical Perspectives in the Anglo-American Law of Evidence* (Berkeley: California University Press, 1991) 21. See also Whitman, *Origins of Reasonable Doubt*.

[54] Shapiro, *Beyond Reasonable Doubt*.   [55] Ibid., 247.

[56] M. Damaška, *Evidence Law Adrift* (New Haven: Yale University Press, 1997) 21.

this standard on this basis.[57] But in accordance with the intellectual climate of the time, this was not how the principle came to be regarded. Freedom from the chains of the old system of legal proofs did not mean freedom to ignore the evidence and 'intime conviction' is no longer regarded as a sufficient condition for a guilty verdict in criminal cases.[58] A number of jurisdictions use instead the maxim 'in dubio pro reo', whereby the fact-finder must accord the defendant the benefit of any factual doubt and this has been seen as a limitation on any idea that the fact-finder is free to act according to his or her conscience.[59]

Whatever the exact phrase used across the two different legal traditions, the idea that factual doubts should be resolved in favour of the defendant came to be applied across both traditions. In certain respects, it may seem that requiring a very high standard of proof before persons can be convicted rubs against the rationalist tradition of evidence scholarship. We will recall that the tradition is associated with two sets of ideas about the purpose of adjudication and about how facts are to be found. According to the first set of ideas, the end of adjudication is rectitude of decision-making. We have made a distinction already between the error reduction and error distribution aspects of the standard of proof. There is no conflict with the rationalist tradition so far as the aim is one of reducing errors. Where it may seem there is a difficulty is when we distribute errors in such a way as to skew them heavily in favour of the defendant, for it may then be said that we are no longer maximising the number of accurate decisions in accordance with the rationalist tradition. But we have seen that the rationalist tradition acknowledges and indeed is based upon the notion that decisions are made under conditions of uncertainty with the result that some decision rule specifying the degree of certainty required for a verdict is necessary in order for decisions to be reached. As to what the standard of proof should be, the rationalist tradition is content to concede that within the legal system this is a political choice regarding what is at stake when a decision is made one way or another.[60] On this view, the epistemological considerations associated with accuracy are separated out from the moral and

---

[57] See Shapiro, *Beyond Reasonable Doubt*, 327, citing William Best's classic treatise, *The Principles of Evidence*, first published in 1844. See also C. J. A. Mittermaier, *Erfahrungen über die Wirksamkeit der Schwurgerichte in Europa und Amerika, über Ihre Mangel und Abhülfe* (Erlangen: F. Elke, 1865) 137–8.

[58] Damaška, *Evidence Law Adrift*, 40.

[59] See J. H. Langbein, *Comparative Criminal Procedure: Germany* (St Paul: West, 1977) 79 (arguing that the standard of free evaluation of evidence ('intimate conviction') does not permit German judges to convict on whim and is limited by the maxim *in dubio pro reo*). See also Eisenberg, *Beweisrecht*, para. 116; S. Seiler, *Strafprozeßrecht*, 10th edn (Vienna: WUV Universitätsverlag, 2009) para. 55 (Austria); and W. Wohlers, 'Art. 10', in A. Donatsch, T. Hansjakob and V. Lieber, *Kommentar zur Schweizerischen Strafprozessordnung* (Zurich: Schulthess, 2010) para. 11. In France, any doubt about the accused's guilt must be resolved in his or her favour: see Cass. crim., 21 March 1990, Bull. crim., No. 125; and J.-C. Soyer, *Droit pénal et procédure pénale*, 20th edn (Paris: LGDJ, 2008) 107.

[60] J. Jackson, 'Evidence: Legal Perspective', in R. Bull and D. Carson (eds.), *Handbook of Psychology in Legal Contexts* (Chichester: John Wiley, 1999) 171.

political considerations associated with the domain of allocating the risk of errors. As Stein has put it, 'morality picks up what the epistemology leaves off'.[61]

Common law systems, unlike countries such as France or Germany,[62] typically make a distinction between civil and criminal cases. In civil cases where there is an assumption of equality between the parties and a mistake affecting one side is generally regarded as serious as a mistake affecting another, a standard is applied which is known as the 'balance of probabilities', requiring claimants to tip the balance of probabilities in their favour.[63] In criminal cases, on the other hand, it is accepted that the standard of proof must be much greater than this before we can convict, in order to give greater effect to the risk of convicting the innocent than to the risk of acquitting the guilty.[64]

This may not seem to dispense entirely with the argument that the high standard of proof skews the overall aim of achieving rectitude, as the effect of such a standard is that we end up quantitatively making more errors than if we set a lower, more symmetrical standard of proof associated with that in civil cases. But we have seen that the rationalist tradition is not simply prescribing that truth should be pursued in adjudication solely for its own sake, but rather in order to implement the substantive law.[65] One of the consequences of the application of the criminal law is that those subjected to it are liable to be punished and exposed to severe censure and because of the injustice or 'moral harm' that arises when persons are wrongly subjected to this treatment, we allocate the risk of error in such a way as to guard against this consequence. It is noteworthy that even Bentham accepted the presumption of innocence, although in accordance with his utilitarian philosophy he judged the error of a conviction to be greater than the error of an acquittal because of the greater

---

[61] Stein, *Foundations of Evidence Law*, 12. See also R. J. Allen, 'Rationality and Accuracy in the Criminal Process: A Discordant Note on the Harmonizing of the Justices' Views on Burdens of Persuasion in Criminal Cases' (1983) 74 *Journal of Criminal Law and Criminology* 1147, 1155.

[62] In countries such as Germany and France, the intime conviction standard applies in both civil and criminal cases: see further C. Engel, *Preponderance of Evidence versus Intime Conviction: A Behavioural Perspective on a Conflict between American and Continental European Law* (Bonn: Working Paper Series of the Max Planck Institut for Research on Collective Goods, 2008/33), 2.

[63] Considerable confusion, however, has been caused by Lord Denning's statement in *Bater* v. *Bater* [1951] P 35, 37 that there may be degrees of probability within the civil standard depending on the seriousness of the subject matter. See M. Redmayne, 'Standards of Proof in Civil Litigation' (1999) 62 *Modern Law Review* 167. For a recent review of how the English authorities have tried to apply this apparently flexible standard, see *In re Doherty* [2008] UKHL 33.

[64] As Harlan J. put it in *In re Winship*, 397 US 358, 371(1970): 'Because the standard of proof affects the comparative frequency of these two types of erroneous outcomes, the choice of the standard to be applied in a particular kind of litigation should, in a rational world, reflect an assessment of the comparative social disutility of each.'

[65] Ch. 1.3. See also W. Twining, 'Evidence and Legal Theory' (1984) 47 *Modern Law Review* 261, 272; and D. Nance, 'Allocating the Risk of Error: Its Role in the Theory of Evidence Law' (2007) 13 *Legal Theory* 129, 132–4.

alarm prompted in the public mind by such an error.[66] The effect of the doctrine is that we may end up *quantitatively* making more errors than if we set the standard of proof lower, but because we make a *qualitative* distinction between certain kinds of truth, considering that more attention needs to be given to safeguarding against wrongful convictions than against wrongful acquittals, this does not mean that we are abandoning the rationalist tradition goal of rectitude. We are only giving greater value to certain kinds of rectitude over others.[67] Only if we were to require absolute certainty would we abandon the rationalist tradition's enterprise as we would then be insisting on an impossible standard of proof, with the result that we would be abandoning the enterprise of determining guilt at all.

Another respect in which the rationalist tradition can seem to rub against a high standard of proof lies in the way in which the standard has been articulated. The second set of ideas associated with the rationalist tradition is concerned with how accuracy is achieved. This requires a process of reasoning based on evidence. We have seen that one of the requirements of the presumption of innocence is that triers of fact act solely on evidence presented in court. When juries are being directed by judges in the common law world, they will frequently exhort juries to pay regard only to the evidence.[68] But commentators have been critical of the way in which the high standards of proof have been formulated.[69] The suggestion, for example, that fact-finders should act in accordance with their satisfied conscience or that they must be sure about a defendant's guilt arguably deflects them from the task of considering how they are to be satisfied to the required standard.

Laudan has commented upon the fact that during the last two centuries Anglo-American criminal law has assiduously avoided saying anything specific about the kind of evidence needed for a conviction. By contrast, the old methods of proof specified precisely how much and what kind of evidence was needed to convict. He makes the point that in most areas of life where inquiry after the truth is at stake, the advice offered to ensure that such an inquiry is rational specifies the kinds of evidence, tests or proofs necessary for a well-founded belief. There has, however, been considerable difficulty and some sharp disagreement in determining how the standard of proof beyond reasonable doubt should be articulated and how exactly triers of fact should go about determining when it has been met. For some time now, there has been a continuing debate between probability theorists which has centred on

---

[66] For a discussion of Bentham's treatment of the presumption of innocence, see W. Twining, *Theories of Evidence: Bentham and Wigmore* (London: Weidenfeld & Nicolson, 1985) 96–100.
[67] J. D. Jackson, 'Theories of Truth Finding in Criminal Procedure: An Evolutionary Approach' (1988) 10 *Cardozo Law Review* 475, 484–5; and A. Goldman, *Knowledge in a Social World* (Oxford University Press, 1999) 284. For the argument that moral and epistemic considerations are intertwined in judicial fact-finding, see Ho, *Philosophy of Evidence Law*.
[68] Laudan, *Truth, Error and Criminal Law*, 52.
[69] See, e.g. Roberts and Zuckerman, *Criminal Evidence*, 253–8.

whether the degree to which the evidence confirms a hypothesis, say guilt, is measured by the relative amount of evidence for or against it or by subjecting the hypothesis to a variety of tests to determine its explanatory force in relation to the evidence.[70] On the first approach, there must be a high probability of guilt based on the available evidence; on the second approach, there must be no plausible explanation consistent with innocence on the available evidence. But there is scope for debate in the first approach as to what degree of probability is required and in the second as to how plausible explanations have to be in order to raise a reasonable doubt.[71]

7.4 The presumption and fair trial standards

Given the difficulties experienced in articulating clear standards for determining proof beyond reasonable doubt, legal systems have to develop other strategies for assuring all of us, including not least those at the receiving end of decisions of guilt, that the presumption of innocence is indeed adhered to in determining questions of guilt. This involves shifting the focus away from evidentiary tests for determining guilt towards examining the accuracy of the procedures that are adopted within the criminal justice system for determining guilt. Seen in this light, then, the presumption of innocence is inextricably tied to a number of vital institutional, procedural and evidentiary protections that seek to protect the innocent from being wrongly convicted by providing accurate procedures of decision-making.

We have seen that contrary to what is sometimes claimed, there is quite a high degree of consensus on what these procedures should be across the two dominant common law and civil law traditions ever since an 'accusatorial' mode of decision-making was developed during the nineteenth century in continental Europe rather than a unilateral 'inquisitorial' procedure. Such an approach requires a separation of the functions of deciding on prosecution and of determining guilt, safeguarding independent decision-making from over-zealous decision-making on the part of those dedicated to protecting society from criminal offences. There is an important link here, of course, to the doctrine of separation of powers promoted originally by social contract theorists such as Montesquieu. The separation of the functions of those who prosecute and those who determine guilt also helps to promote a degree of impartiality of decision-making, whether the decision-makers are composed of professional

---

[70] There is a large literature. See, e.g. Boston University Law Review, 'Symposium: Probability and Inference in the Law of Evidence' (1986) 66 *Boston University Law Review* 377–952; P. Tillers and E. D. Green (eds.), *Probability and Inference in the Law of Evidence: The Use and Limits of Bayesianism* (Dordrecht: Martinus Nijhoff, 1988); P. Tillers (ed.), 'Decision and Inference in Litigation' (1991) 13 *Cardozo Law Review* 253–1079; and R. Allen and M. Redmayne, 'Bayesianism and Juridical Proof' (1997) 1 *International Journal of Evidence & Proof* 253–360.

[71] See the debate on the reference class problem in R. Allen and P. Roberts, Special Issue on the Reference Class Problem (2007) 11 *International Journal of Evidence & Proof* 243–317.

or lay judges, which is vital in order to prevent cognitive biases. The danger recognised by nineteenth-century jurists as we have seen of mixing the functions of investigation, prosecution and judgment in the hands of one person or institution is that a defendant may be pre-judged to be guilty too early in the fact-finding process. Finally, in order to ensure that individuals were able to conduct their best defence, legal assistance was gradually provided and the principles of equality of arms and adversarial procedure were developed.

These institutional safeguards tie the presumption of innocence very closely with the standards for a fair trial set out in the international instruments discussed in Chapter 4. It may be suggested that because we stack the burden and standard of proof so heavily against the prosecution, there is no need to make such a close connection between the presumption and fair trial standards. While these standards can assist in the search for accuracy, according to this argument the defence have no reason to fear a wrongful conviction if we make it evidentially so difficult to convict defendants. So it is sometimes considered in the common law world that the inequality of resources between the prosecution and defence is compensated by the requirement that the prosecution bear the burden of proof and by imposing strict rules of evidence.[72] Thus, it has been suggested that the principle of discovery which applies in civil cases whereby each party is entitled to know from the other in advance any information that would enhance his own case or destroy his adversary's case is less applicable in criminal proceedings, where the entire burden of proof rests on the prosecution.[73] More recently, it has been suggested that one way of reducing wrongful convictions in capital cases in the United States would be by statutorily excluding the known evidentiary sources of wrongful convictions such as eyewitness identification evidence, confessions, criminal informants and unvalidated forensic evidence.[74] Yet it is conceded that even this would not eradicate wrongful convictions in such cases and what is also required is adequately compensated, experienced capital defence lawyers to combat the inevitable risks of bad prosecutorial lawyering, police corruption and witness misconduct. It would seem that, however strictly certain categories of evidence are excluded, the burden on the prosecution is inevitably reduced where the defence are precluded from making effective investigations in order to combat the prosecution case.

If the prosecution's burden is eased by a lack of effective defence, might it not be said that the high standard of proof insulates defendants from such a handicap? It has been argued that the standard of proof should be viewed as

---

[72] According to Langbein, the modern rules of criminal evidence were developed by judges in order to safeguard the defendants against the risk of mistaken conviction from prosecutorial abuse: see J. H. Langbein, *The Origins of Adversary Criminal Trial* (Oxford University Press, 2003) 179–80.
[73] *People (DPP)* v. *Flinn* [1996] ILRM 317.
[74] R. Little, 'Addressing the Evidentiary Sources of Wrongful Convictions: Categorical Exclusion of Evidence in Capital Statutes' (2008) 37 *Southwestern University Law Review* 965.

an attitude of mind, an instruction to the fact-finder that she must exercise such caution when determining on the verdict as is commensurate with the seriousness of what is at stake for the party affected by the finding. In order to safeguard against the risk of wrongful conviction, this requires a 'protective attitude' to be adopted towards the defendant in deliberation.[75] Again, however, the fair trial standards are arguably necessary if anything like this degree of caution is going to be achieved. Unless triers of fact are institutionally separated from the process of investigation, it may be difficult for them to retain true impartiality and independence. Moreover, however careful triers of fact seek to be, there would seem to be a limit to the degree of caution that can be exercised without an effective defence. Triers of fact need to focus not only on the quality of the evidence that is presented by the prosecution, but also on the extent to which there are gaps in the evidence and jurors are sometimes asked to consider the lack of evidence, alerting them to consider the 'weight' or 'thinness' of the evidence adduced by the prosecution.[76] But the reality is that so long as the prosecution make a plausible case for guilt on the elements of the offence, the defendant risks conviction unless he can come up with a plausible alternative to negate one of these elements.[77] It follows that when we consider the presumption of innocence as a device for protecting against wrongful conviction, it is not enough simply to focus on the extent to which the defendant is protected from this risk by evidentiary tests such as the need for proof beyond reasonable doubt and by the exclusion of potentially unreliable evidence (error distribution). The defendant also needs an effective defence to challenge the evidence that is admitted and seek out evidence in his favour in order to reduce the risk of error happening in the first place (error reduction).[78]

7.5 The scope of the presumption of innocence under human rights law

Having argued that there are close ties between the presumption of innocence and the fair trial standards that have been associated with international human rights law, it is now time to consider how human rights regimes have interpreted the presumption of innocence and how common and civil law systems have to adapt to conform to human rights requirements. The ICCPR and ECHR state

---

[75] Ho, *Philosophy of Evidence Law*, 185–6.
[76] J. B. Weinstein and I. Dewsbury, 'Comment on the Meaning of "Proof Beyond Reasonable Doubt"' (2006) 5 *Law, Probability & Risk* 167, 169. The problem of evidential weight has been the source of considerable debate between probability theorists, with some arguing against the classical Bayesian view that proof beyond reasonable doubt may be expressed in terms of some numerical threshold. See L. J. Cohen, 'The Role of Evidential Weight in Criminal Proof' (1986) 66 *Boston University Law Review* 635; and Stein, *Foundations of Evidence Law*, ch. 3.
[77] R. J. Allen, 'The Narrative Fallacy, the Relative Plausibility Theory and a Theory of the Trial' (2006) 3 *International Commentary on Evidence*, Issue 1, Art. 5, 6.
[78] See A. Roberts, 'Pre-Trial Defence Rights and the Fair Use of Eyewitness Identification Procedures' (2008) 71 *Modern Law Review* 331 (making a conceptual distinction between a suspect's participatory rights and protective rights).

that everyone charged with a criminal offence has the right to be presumed innocent until proved guilty according to law and the ACHR states that every person has the right 'so long as his guilt has not been proved according to law'. It will be recalled that we have distinguished between narrow and broader concepts of the presumption. The narrow view would restrict its meaning to procedural protections related to the outcome of the trial, protecting the accused from wrongful conviction, and the broader meaning views it as a right to be treated as innocent by public authorities. International human rights bodies have viewed the presumption in both these senses.

In its General Comment, the Human Rights Committee has said:

> By reason of the presumption of innocence, the burden of proof of the charge is on the prosecution and the accused has the benefit of the doubt. No guilt can be presumed until the charge has been proved beyond reasonable doubt. Further, the presumption of innocence implies a right to be treated in accordance with this principle. It is therefore a duty for all public authorities to refrain from prejudging the outcome of the trial.[79]

The reference to the right to be treated as innocent takes us into the realm of the broader principle of protecting the accused's reputation, although the emphasis on not prejudicing the outcome of the trial would seem to limit the scope of the right to be treated as innocent to the instrumental purpose of a correct trial outcome.

The European organs would seem to have treated the presumption, first and foremost, as a procedural guarantee affecting the outcome of the proceedings. According to *Barberà, Messegué and Jabardo v. Spain*,[80] it 'requires, inter alia, that when carrying out their duties, the members of the court should not start with the preconceived idea that the accused has committed the offence charged; the burden of proof is on the prosecution, and any doubt should benefit the accused'. But the European organs have also recognised the reputation-related aspect of the right protecting persons from being treated by public officials as guilty of an offence before this is established by a competent court.[81]

As regards the procedural outcome-related aspect of the guarantee, some of the earlier decisions of the human rights bodies occasionally gave a very wide meaning to the presumption, making it equivalent almost to all of the fair trial protections. Two early decisions of the Human Rights Committee appeared to consider that violations of Article 14(1) and (3) of the ICCPR which deprived an accused of the safeguards of a fair trial also constitute a violation of the

---

[79] GC 13/21. Doc. A/39/40, 143–7, 12 April 1984.
[80] Para. 77. See also *Austria v. Italy (Pfunders Case)* (report), 782.
[81] Stavros, *Guarantees for Accused Persons*, 49. See *X v. Austria* (dec.), no. 9295/81; *Sekanina v. Austria* (considering that the presumption of innocence was obligatory not only for criminal courts ruling on the merits of a charge, but also for other authorities). See also *P, RH and LL v. Austria* (dec.).

presumption of innocence.[82] In subsequent cases, there has been less suggestion that these violations also constitute a violation of the presumption of innocence.[83] The ECtHR has also on occasions appeared to equate the presumption of innocence with other aspects of a fair trial. In *Barberà, Messegué and Jabardo*, for example, the court said that it followed from the presumption that it was for the prosecution to inform the accused of the case to be made against him so that 'he may prepare and present his defence accordingly'.[84] More usually, however, it has said that the presumption of innocence embodied in paragraph 2 of Article 6 and the various rights in paragraph 3 are 'constituent elements' of the notion of a fair trial in criminal proceedings.[85] We have seen that there is a very close link between the presumption and other fair trial protections, particularly the right to an independent and impartial tribunal and the rights to defence, as these give institutional support to the presumption. In the next two sections, we examine how thoroughly the human rights bodies have safeguarded the outcome-related aspects of the presumption and we shall argue that the human rights bodies could have done more to assert these links.

Turning to the reputation-related aspect of the guarantee, one of the difficulties is that the guarantee is tied to persons charged with an offence.[86] It might be argued that this restriction is significant, implying that the presumption is addressed primarily to those judging accused persons and should not be given the wider meaning we have identified of a right to be treated as innocent by public authorities whether they are charged or not. Early drafts to the Covenant were not restricted in this way and when the limitation was inserted, no significance seemed to be attached to it.[87] It has been suggested that the limitation is redundant as it simply emphasises the fact that persons who are charged with criminal proceedings are particularly vulnerable so far as the presumption is concerned because they need protection against the eagerness of prosecutors who will tend to treat the suspect as guilty.[88] It is noteworthy, however, that in one case the Human Rights Committee considered that Article 14(2) of the ICCPR only relates to individuals charged with a criminal offence. The authors had alleged that their right to be presumed innocent had been violated by not segregating or treating them separately from convicted prisoners. Since the authors had not been charged by the state party with a criminal offence, the Committee considered that this did not raise an issue under the Covenant.[89] The European organs would seem to have taken a different stance from each other on this issue. The Commission took the view that Article 6(2) should be

---

[82] *Ambrosini, de Massera and Massera* v. *Uruguay*, 124; and *Lanza and Perdomo* v. *Uruguay*, 111.
[83] D. McGoldrick, *The Human Rights Committee* (Oxford: Clarendon, 1991) 419.
[84] *Barberà, Messegué and Jabardo* v. *Spain*, para. 77.
[85] *Deweer* v. *Belgium*, para. 56; see also *Minelli* v. *Switzerland*, para. 27.
[86] cf. the wording in Art. 7 African Charter, which extends the right to every individual. See Safferling, *Towards International Criminal Procedure*, 68.
[87] See D. Weissbrodt, *The Right to a Fair Trial* (The Hague: Kluwer, 2001) 18.
[88] Trechsel, *Human Rights in Criminal Proceedings*, 155. [89] *Cabal* v. *Australia*.

read as if the presumption were not limited to a person charged with criminal proceedings and not tied to Article 6(1), which is a fair trial right limited to persons charged with criminal proceedings. The ECtHR, on the other hand, has accepted that the presumption is restricted to persons charged with criminal proceedings, which has raised a particular difficulty when, as has occurred in many cases, proceedings have been terminated, but the state has continued to impute guilt to the accused by ordering acquitted or time-barred defendants to pay costs.[90]

The human rights bodies have been more guarded about the third aspect of the presumption that we have identified concerning the right of persons not to be convicted for conduct for which they are blameless. Here, as we have seen, scrutiny is extended beyond evidence and procedure into the domain of substantive criminal law. Of course, the guarantee requires that individuals must be proved guilty according to law. Where a court lacks the jurisdiction to try an accused or tries him for crimes which are not an offence under the law, that would be a clear violation of the presumption.[91] In addition, however, it would seem that the human rights bodies are prepared to exercise some scrutiny over laws which give no opportunity for persons to have acted otherwise. In the leading case of *Salabiaku* v. *France*,[92] the ECtHR considered that 'in principle the Contracting States remain free to apply the criminal law to an act where it is not carried out in the normal exercise of one of the rights protected under the Convention . . . and, accordingly, to define the constituent elements of the resulting offence'. The words 'in principle' suggest that the states' freedom in this regard is not unqualified and the ECtHR went on to say that 'again in principle, the Contracting States may, under certain conditions, penalise a simple or objective fact as such, irrespective of whether it results from criminal intent or from negligence'.[93] The ECtHR said that examples of such offences existed in the member states, but did not illustrate this with any examples.

This is not a very helpful statement of the limits that are imposed on states in their promulgation of the criminal law. To suggest that prohibiting a simple or objective fact may under certain conditions be permissible regardless of the mental element does not indicate what the conditions are. One of the conditions mentioned later in the judgment would seem to be that there is no breach of the 'fundamental principle of the rule of law' which is enshrined by the presumption of innocence. In a later case, the ECtHR used this principle to show its concern for penalising persons on the basis of vicarious liability when a fine for tax evasion had been imposed on the heirs of someone who had failed to declare part of his income. The ECtHR considered that inheritance of the guilt of the dead was not compatible with the standards of criminal justice in a society governed by the 'rule of law'.[94] Beyond extreme cases like this, however, the ECtHR would seem to be reluctant to use the presumption of innocence to

---

[90] See *Minelli* v. *Switzerland*; and *Y* v. *Norway*. [91] See *Loayza Tamayo Case* v. *Peru*.
[92] Para. 27. [93] Ibid. [94] *AP, MP and TP* v. *Switzerland*, para. 48.

interfere with the substantive law of domestic criminal law and that it regards the principle primarily as a means of procedural protection for those charged with criminal offences.[95] Yet as we shall see in the following section, where we turn to look at the manner in which the human rights bodies have applied the procedural protection, the ECtHR has not been particularly vigilant in guarding against presumptions that appear to reverse the burden of proof.

7.6 Reversal of the burden of proof

As suggested above, there are good reasons why international human rights bodies should be reluctant to interfere with member states' delineation of substantive law. It is another matter, however, when it comes to provisions which reverse the burden of proof so as make it possible for defendants to be convicted despite the fact that there may be a reasonable doubt about their guilt relating to the charge. Whether the weakening in the requirement of proof beyond reasonable doubt applies to an element of the offence or a defence, the effect as we have seen is the same in that it increases the chances of wrongful conviction for the offence, thereby undermining the fundamental purpose of the presumption of innocence as developed in common law and civil law jurisdictions. There is, of course, a relationship between the substantive and procedural aspects of the presumption. Legislatures unable to impose reverse burdens because of the presumption may think long and hard before permitting defendants to avail of certain defences that would show their substantive innocence. If, however, the courts were to allow this consideration to govern the question of whether reverse burdens should be permitted, the procedural aspect of the presumption could be constantly held to ransom by the threat of taking away defences altogether.[96]

Although the Human Rights Committee has taken the position that 'no guilt can be presumed until the charge has been proven beyond reasonable doubt', the European organs early on considered that presumptions of fact and law could operate against the accused in certain circumstances. In an early case, the European Commission upheld a statutory provision in the United Kingdom which stated that 'a man who lives with or is habitually in the company of a prostitute ... shall be presumed to be knowingly living on earnings of prostitution unless he proves the contrary'.[97] The Commission made it clear that it retained the power to review the extent to which the reversal of proof serves a useful purpose and to ensure that presumptions are not so widely worded as to amount to a presumption of guilt. The Commission was here beginning to articulate a proportionality test whereby it would consider the reasonable limits of any presumption against the accused. In *Salabiaku* v. *France*, however,

---

[95] B. Emmerson, A. Ashworth and A. Macdonald, *Human Rights and Criminal Justice*, 2nd edn (London: Sweet & Maxwell, 2007) 348–9.
[96] Ashworth, 'Presumption of Innocence', 254.   [97] *X* v. *United Kingdom* (dec.).

it seemed to take a contrary view in suggesting that the right to be presumed innocent 'according to law' required the courts to apply the presumption in accordance with the domestic law of each state. The ECtHR, however, was critical of such an approach as it would enable the national legislature to 'strip the trial court of any genuine power of assessment'.[98] Such a situation could not be reconciled with the object and purpose of Article 6, which by protecting the right to a fair trial and in particular the right to be presumed innocent was intended to enshrine the fundamental principle of the rule of law.

The ECtHR's judgment, however, was hardly a model of clarity and it illustrates the danger of not distinguishing clearly enough between the different aspects of the presumption we have identified. The applicant had been charged with smuggling prohibited goods in accordance with a statutory provision which 'deemed' any person in possession of the goods to be liable for the offence. He was arrested outside Roissy Airport after a padlocked trunk which he took through customs in France was found to contain 10 kg of herbal and seed cannabis. The trunk had no name on it and he claimed that he thought it contained samples of African food which he had arranged to pick up at the airport. There seemed to be some substance to his claim of mistaken belief when a parcel of food with his name and address mistakenly arrived at Brussels airport two days later. He was also charged with illegally importing narcotics, but his conviction for this offence was overturned by the Paris Court of Appeal on the ground that it was not impossible that he might have believed that the trunk which he took through customs was really intended for him. The possibility of mistaken belief was not enough, however, to permit him to escape liability for the offence of smuggling prohibited goods as his mere possession of these goods was enough to deem him liable and the applicant argued that the 'almost irrebuttable' presumption on the basis of which he was convicted of this customs offence was incompatible with Article 6.

The ECtHR began its analysis by stressing that presumptions of fact or of law operate in every legal system and clearly the Convention did not prohibit such presumptions in principle. It did, however, require contracting states to remain within certain limits in this respect as regards criminal law. Having criticised the Commission's approach, it went on to say:

> Article 6 para. 2 ... does not therefore regard presumptions of fact or of law provided for in the criminal law with indifference. It requires States to confine them within reasonable limits which take into account the importance of what is at stake and maintain the rights of the defence.[99]

In proceeding to examine whether these limits were exceeded in the case before it, the ECtHR appeared to stress the substantive question of the acceptable limits to imposing strict liability upon defendants more than the procedural question of the acceptable limits to imposing burdens of proof upon defendants. The

---

[98] *Salabiaku* v. *France*, para. 28.   [99] Ibid.

ECtHR stated that even though the 'person in possession' is 'deemed liable for the offence', this did not mean that he was left entirely without a means of defence. The French courts had developed a defence of *force majeure*, whereby defendants could escape liability if they could show that their possession of the goods resulted from an event beyond their control. The ECtHR went on to say, however, that it was not called upon to consider 'in abstracto' whether the customs legislation conformed to the Convention, but rather to determine whether it had been applied to the applicant in a manner compatible with the presumption of innocence. In this case, the Paris Court of Appeal had held that the applicant could not claim unavoidable error because he had been warned by an airport official before taking possession of the trunk not to take possession of it unless he was sure the trunk belonged to him. The ECtHR considered that the French courts had been careful to avoid resorting automatically to the presumption and had exercised the freedom of assessment that they were given through the defence of *force majeure*.

Although it has been argued that the ECtHR's judgment was an important statement of the extent to which it is prepared to supervise strict liability offences,[100] its reference to the fact that it was not called upon 'in abstracto' to make judgments about whether particular legislation conformed to the presumption of innocence would appear to suggest that the ECtHR was confining its supervision to whether the domestic court exercised 'a genuine power of assessment' in relation to the presumption that was applied against the accused rather than exercising any meaningful supervision over the substantive legislation itself. Provided the presumption was able to be rebutted in some manner, as it could be through the *force majeure* exception, and the court did not automatically presume guilt, there would seem to be no violation of the presumption of innocence.

The focus on how the presumption against the accused was applied is, of course, consistent with the ECtHR's approach, which is to review the fairness of the trial as a whole after the event. But the fairness analysed by the ECtHR was aimed more at how the domestic court applied the substance of the legislation to the accused rather than on the procedural fairness of imposing burdens of proof on the defence. The result is that the judgment provides little guidance to domestic courts which have to decide on the justifiability of reverse burdens of proof in advance of the trial.[101] Furthermore, it does not dispose of the question as to what the limits should be on imposing reverse burdens on the defence, as we have seen that these inevitably increase the chances of a wrongful conviction. In referring to the fact that the Convention requires the contracting states to keep presumptions within certain limits as regards the criminal law, the ECtHR in *Salabiaku* appeared to be more concerned about ensuring that presumptions

---

[100] Stavros, *Guarantees for Accused Persons*, 224.
[101] See I. Dennis, 'Reverse Onuses and the Presumption of Innocence: In Search of Principle' [2005] *Criminal Law Review* 901, 916–17; and J. Jackson and K. Quinn, 'Evidence' [2005] *All ER Annual Review* 229.

did not place accused persons in the position of being unable to rebut them rather than on ensuring that such presumptions did not place accused persons unnecessarily in the position of having to rebut them in the first place.[102]

In a number of cases after *Salabiaku*, the Strasbourg organs rejected claims that Article 6(2) was breached on the grounds that the court retained a 'genuine freedom of assessment'.[103] In later case law, however, the ECtHR has been more prepared to consider the justification for imposing presumptions against the accused. In *Janosevic* v. *Sweden*, the applicant claimed that a tax surcharge imposed an almost insurmountable burden of proof on him when he claimed that it should not have been imposed or should have been remitted. Under Swedish tax law, a tax surcharge was imposed on taxpayers when incorrect information was furnished that was relevant to the tax assessment, but it could be remitted if the provision of incorrect information appeared excusable due to the nature of the information in question or other special circumstances or where the imposition of the surcharge would be manifestly unreasonable. While the tax authorities had to have regard to the provisions on remission even in the absence of a claim by the taxpayer to that effect, the burden of proving that there was reason to remit a surcharge was in effect on the taxpayer.

The ECtHR repeated the point made in *Salabiaku* that in principle contracting states may penalise a simple and objective fact irrespective of whether it results from criminal intent or from negligence, but then went on to make the point that, as in the case of the French customs legislation, the Swedish provisions catered for excusable acts. The ECtHR went further than *Salabiaku*, however, in analysing the procedural question as to whether the imposition of the burden of proving excuse on the taxpayer was justified, explaining that in striking a balance between the importance of what is at stake and the rights of defence, 'the means employed have to be reasonably proportionate to the legitimate aim sought to be achieved'.[104] In concluding that the presumptions applied in Swedish law with regard to tax surcharges were confined within reasonable limits, the ECtHR stressed once again the fact that there were means of defence based on subjective elements, but also made the point that an efficient system of taxation could not function properly without some form of sanction against the provision of incorrect or incomplete information and that the large number of tax returns that are processed annually, coupled with the interest in ensuring a foreseeable and uniform application of sanctions, required that they be imposed according to standardised rules.

Although the broad 'reasonable limits' doctrine enabled the ECtHR to blur the lines somewhat between the substantive justification for imposing strict liability and the procedural justification for reversing the burden of proof, the ECtHR here began to apply its proportionality doctrine more directly to

---

[102] See Trechsel, *Human Rights in Criminal Proceedings*, 170. The court applied the same approach in *Pham Hoang* v. *France*.

[103] See, e.g. *AG* v. *Malta* (dec.); and *Bates* v. *United Kingdom* (dec.).

[104] *Janosevic* v. *Sweden*, para. 101.

the procedural justification for reversing the burden of proof than it did in *Salabiaku* by considering that the 'legitimate aim' of pursuing an efficient system of taxation justified standardised rules that imposed a burden on the taxpayer. It may not be very difficult for a state to show that it is employing a presumption in order to pursue a legitimate aim. The effective collection of taxes or prosecution of crime may be reasonably considered to be a legitimate aim, although some jurisdictions have gone further in requiring that there be a pressing special need for the effective prosecution of the particular kind of offence to which the presumption applies.[105] What may be more difficult to show is that the means used were proportionate, taking account of the interests and rights of the defence. Although the ECtHR did not engage in an analysis of this question, this presumably requires showing that the presumption used bears a rational connection to the aim or purpose and how it will assist in the aim, whether for example it will lighten the prosecution's burden of proving an element of the offence that may present difficulties of proof.[106]

It is equally important here, however, to take into account the interests of the defence in the imposition of any burden and how reasonable any burden is in the circumstances.[107] Although the ECtHR did not go on to weigh the competing interests at stake, it can be argued that it is not unreasonable to require persons filling in tax returns to exercise care in doing so and to show that either the return they furnished was correct or that there is good reason for any inaccuracies. Similarly, it might be said that in a case like *Salabiaku* it is not unreasonable to expect persons taking goods through customs to exercise care to see that they are not taking through prohibited goods.[108] Taking into account the 'rights of the defence', however, also includes the right underlying the presumption of innocence not to be wrongly convicted. This would seem to require that account is taken of the connection between the basic objective facts that it is for the state to prove and any presumed fact. The greater the gap between apparently 'innocent' objective facts and 'guilty' presumed facts, the greater the risk of an accused being wrongly convicted unless he proves his innocence. It would also seem relevant to take account of the facilities at the accused's disposal in surmounting any burden. A further relevant factor to consider in relation to the rights of the defence would seem to be the seriousness of the penalties imposed as a consequence of a finding of liability. One point of contrast between the provisions in *Salabiaku* and *Janosevic* was that the French legislation imposed a sentence of imprisonment for non-payment of any fine arising out of the customs offence, whereas there was no imprisonment

---

[105] See Schwikkard, *Presumption of Innocence*, 150.
[106] See *X* v. *United Kingdom* (dec.), 266, where the Commission considered that the prosecution task might be made impossible if there were not some burden on the defence to show that when living with or in the company of a prostitute the accused was not living on the earnings of prostitution.
[107] Ashworth, 'Presumption of Innocence', 266.
[108] See Trechsel, *Human Rights in Criminal Proceedings*, 170–1.

attached to the non-payment of taxes in the Swedish legislation. This factor also militates against giving too ready weight to the seriousness of the offences in justifying placing a reverse burden on the defence, for seriousness works both ways. The public interest in protection from serious crimes may be greater than less serious crime, but the defendant equally has a greater interest in protection from wrongful conviction when charged with a serious offence.[109]

Finally, it would seem relevant to consider how necessary it is to reverse the burden of proof and whether less intrusive means might be used to circumvent any infringement of the presumption of innocence. This is a factor that arises particularly in common law jurisdictions where the courts have had to consider whether an evidential burden could have been imposed upon the defence instead of a legal burden, with the result that the accused only then has to raise a reasonable doubt in relation to the prosecution's case. Although the European Commission has upheld the imposition of a legal burden in relation to the defence of insanity and has considered manifestly unfounded a complaint based upon the legal burden of proving diminished responsibility in a murder case,[110] it has placed significance on the fact that an evidential burden places a much lesser burden on the defence as the consequence of an evidential burden is that the state still bears the legal burden of proving all the elements of the offence to the required standard of proof.[111]

Another less draconian alternative to imposing a legal burden on the defence might be to require that the defence disclose the nature of its defence to the prosecution in advance of the trial. In as much as the justification for imposing a legal burden on the defence in respect of certain defences may be due to a fear that defendants might concoct false defences which might be very difficult to disprove beyond a reasonable doubt,[112] one alternative means of preventing such a risk would be to require the defence to disclose in advance any evidence relevant to the defence that it proposes to adduce, including any expert evidence relevant to his state of mind in cases where insanity or diminished responsibility is claimed.[113] We shall see that there has been a reluctance to require the defence to undergo burdens of disclosure as sometimes it is mistakenly considered that this is an infringement of the privilege against self-incrimination.[114] But the burden of disclosing one's defence would seem to be less onerous than the burden of proving its truth on the balance of probabilities, with the inevitable incursion that this entails into the presumption of innocence.

The courts in a number of domestic jurisdictions have applied the doctrine of proportionality in a stricter manner than the Strasbourg organs by setting

---

[109] *State v. Coetzee* (1997) (3) SA 527 (CC), para. 220.
[110] *H v. United Kingdom* (dec.); and *Robinson v. United Kingdom* (dec.).
[111] *Hardy v. Ireland* (dec.). [112] See Ashworth, 'Presumption of Innocence', 263–6.
[113] For discussion of the relationship between burdens of proof on the defence and pre-trial disclosure, see C. Moisidis, *Criminal Discovery* (Sydney: Sydney Institute of Criminology, 2008) ch. 7.
[114] See Ch. 9.4.

exacting standards to be satisfied before limits on the presumption can be said to be reasonable.[115] In *R v. Oakes*,[116] for example, Dickson CJ set down four requirements that needed to be satisfied before it could be said that any limitation on the presumption came within the 'reasonable limits' test provided in the Canadian Charter: a sufficiently important objective for imposing a limitation, rational connection to the objective, minimal impairment to the presumption and proportionality between the effects of the limitation and the objective.[117] The South African Constitutional Court has been particularly reluctant to find infringements of the presumption of innocence justifiable and held that any justification for infringement must be 'clear, convincing and compelling'.[118] While the limitation clause in the 1996 Constitution does not expressly mandate an inquiry into whether any limitation on the presumption is necessary, it has been argued that such an inquiry is made inevitable by the requirement that the court consider whether the limitation is reasonable and justifiable, taking into account whether there were less restrictive means to achieve the purpose.[119]

These exacting demands have not necessarily led to a different conclusion being reached from the Strasbourg bodies in respect of similar legislative provisions.[120] It also would be wrong to consider that the 'reasonable limits' proportionality test that was applied in *Janosevic* is necessarily any less rigorous in itself. As we have suggested, it can be argued that this test entails the application of standards that are just as rigorous. We have yet to see the ECtHR apply these standards to the proportionality test, but the incorporation of the ECHR into UK law has enabled the courts there to use Article 6(2) to apply a stricter approach than the Strasbourg organs have been inclined to pursue.[121] The precise allocation of the burden of proof remained unclear in England until the famous case of *Woolmington* v. *DPP* decided that 'throughout the web of English criminal law one golden thread is always to be seen, that it is the duty of the prosecution to prove the prisoner's guilt'.[122] Despite this, however, *Woolmington* recognised that 'statutory exceptions' could be made to this principle and legislatures have increasingly created exceptions which have taken the form of imposing an express burden, sometimes known as a reverse burden, on the accused to prove an element of the offence or to establish a

---

[115] For a full analysis, see A. Stumer, *The Presumption of Innocence: Evidential and Human Rights Perspectives* (Hart: Oxford, 2010) ch. 5.
[116] (1986) 50 CR (3d) 1.   [117] See also *R* v. *Whyte* (1989) 651 DLR 481.
[118] See, e.g. *S* v. *Mbatha*; *S.* v. *Prinsloo*, 1996 (3) BCCR 293; and *S* v. *Ntsele* 1997 (11) BCLR 1543. See also Schwikkard, *Presumption of Innocence*, 162, comparing the South African Constitutional Court favourably with the approach of the Canadian Supreme Court.
[119] Schwikkard, *Presumption of Innocence*, 144.
[120] e.g. the Canadian Supreme Court has upheld the limitation requiring the defence to prove insanity in *R* v. *Chaulk* (1990) 2 CR (4th) 1.
[121] A. Ashworth, *Human Rights, Serious Crime and Criminal Procedure* (London: Sweet & Maxwell, 2002) 17, 68–9.
[122] [1935] AC 462, 481.

particular statutory defence.[123] In more recent decisions, however, the courts have given the *Woolmington* 'golden thread' a greater pull by considering that Article 6(2) requires statutory exceptions that appear to place a legal burden on the defence to be 'read down' so as to impose only an evidential burden.[124] The UK courts have had difficulty in formulating clear guidance as to how the proportionality test should be applied and this has led to some considerable uncertainty as to whether in a particular case a burden will be construed as legal or evidential.[125] Instead of setting out clear guidance as to how decisions should be structured according to strict proportionality criteria, they have strayed in certain decisions into the domain of substantive criminal law by considering whether the provision imposed a burden on defendants to prove their innocence in morally substantive terms.[126] What the UK experience demonstrates, however, is that there would seem to be a broad agreement between Strasbourg and the domestic courts that limits on the presumption of innocence may only be imposed in pursuance of a legitimate aim and when it is proportionate to the achievement of that aim.[127] The fact that the UK courts have in certain cases applied a stricter approach towards the proportionality test than the ECtHR is not an indication that there is something wrong with the proportionality test being developed by the ECtHR, but that the ECtHR has yet to refine how contracting states should apply such a test.

7.7 Avoiding prejudice

Apart from the requirement that the prosecution bear the burden of proving guilt beyond reasonable doubt, we have seen that another aspect of the presumption of innocence protecting the accused against wrongful conviction is that the tribunal of fact itself judges the case on the evidence with an open mind and free of prejudice. The human rights bodies will not as we have seen intervene as some kind of fourth-instance court to review the merits of a particular decision on the evidence. The ECtHR has said on numerous occasions that it is not the province of the ECtHR to substitute its own assessment of the facts for that of the domestic courts and, as a general rule, it is for these courts to assess the evidence before them.[128] As one commentator has put it: 'The law of human

---

[123] It has been estimated that approximately 40 per cent of indictable offences in England and Wales impose some form of reverse burden on the defence: see A. Ashworth and M. Blake, 'The Presumption of Innocence in English Criminal Law' [1996] *Criminal Law Review* 314.

[124] See, e.g. *R* v. *Lambert* [2001] UKHL 28. Cf. *R* v. *Johnstone* [2003] UKHL 28; and *Sheldrake* v. *DPP; Attorney General's Reference (No. 4 of 2002)* [2004] UKHL 43.

[125] For criticism, see A. Ashworth, 'Comment' [2005] *Criminal Law Review* 218; and Stumer, *Presumption of Innocence*, 120–32.

[126] See, e.g. Lord Bingham's argument in *Sheldrake* v. *DPP* that it was relevant to consider whether the defendant was being asked to prove his innocence in relation to conduct that could be considered blameworthy. For a critique, see Dennis, 'Reverse Onuses'.

[127] Dennis, 'Reverse Onuses'.

[128] *Edwards* v. *United Kingdom*, para. 34; and *Van Mechelen and others* v. *Netherlands*, para. 50.

rights is one thing; fact-finding in particular cases is quite another.'[129] This is appropriate for an international body whose function is to review standards of fairness rather than to deal with errors of fact or law allegedly committed by a national court.[130] Of course, if a tribunal were to indicate in the course of its judgment that it had failed to apply a high standard of proof to the evidence or that it believed in the guilt of a defendant notwithstanding the evidence, these would be grounds for a violation of the presumption.[131]

As we have seen, one manner in which common law systems have sought to prevent prejudice on the part of triers of fact is to impose exclusionary rules so that they do not become privy to particular items of evidence likely to cause prejudice such as, for example, evidence of the accused's criminal record. We have seen that the Strasbourg organs have been very unwilling to prescribe rules of evidence, in particular rules on the admissibility of evidence and on the probative value of evidence which are essentially matters for the national law.[132] In early cases, the Commission rejected a complaint that a jury was informed about an accused's criminal record, on the ground that in a number of contracting states information as to previous convictions is routinely disclosed before the court pronounces on guilt.[133] To the extent that the ECtHR has intervened to ensure that certain types of evidence are not used, its concern has been primarily based on the use of improperly obtained evidence rather than on the use of particularly prejudicial kinds of evidence.[134] The primary protection for the accused against prejudice thus lies in certain essential elements of a fair trial that we discussed in Chapter 4 and that we have identified in this chapter as closely tied to the presumption of innocence: for example, the right to an independent and impartial tribunal and the participatory rights of the defence, which include the principles of equality of arms and the right to an adversarial procedure, and the right to a reasoned judgment. We shall look at each of these in turn.

7.7.1 An independent and impartial tribunal

Although the ECtHR has not made the connection explicitly, the right to an impartial tribunal would seem to be particularly tied to that aspect of the presumption which requires that triers of fact must approach the evidence with an open mind and it has been argued that there is no difference in this

---

[129] P. Roberts, '(Un)grateful Comments on Six Commentaries' (2007) 5 *International Commentary on Evidence*, Issue 2, Art. 2, 15.
[130] See *Schenk* v. *Switzerland*, para. 45.
[131] See *Lavents* v. *Latvia* (judge declaring to the press that she did not believe the accused to be innocent).
[132] *X* v. *Belgium* (dec.), no. 7450/76; *X* v. *Belgium* (dec.), no. 8876/80; *Engel and others* v. *Netherlands*, para. 46; *Schenk* v. *Switzerland*; and *Delta* v. *France*, para. 35.
[133] *X* v. *Denmark* (dec.); *X* v. *Austria* (dec.), no. 2676/65; and *X* v. *Germany* (dec.), no. 5620/72.
[134] See Ch. 6 above.

respect between the two guarantees.[135] According to the ECtHR, a tribunal must be impartial from a subjective as well as an objective point of view.[136] Subjective bias involves the question of whether the tribunal was actually biased and objective bias involves the question of whether there are legitimate doubts as to the impartiality of the tribunal,[137] or whether the judge offered guarantees sufficient to exclude any legitimate doubt in this respect.[138] In each case, the question is approached from the standpoint of an 'objective observer'.[139] It is difficult to found an allegation on subjective bias because there is a presumption that tribunals are impartial, which can only be displaced by strong evidence to the contrary.[140] In practice, the ECtHR has been very reluctant to find subjective personal bias and has tended to focus more on the question of objective bias.[141] The objective test has been justified by the ECtHR on the ground that what is at stake is 'the confidence which the courts in a democratic society must inspire in the public and above all, as far as criminal proceedings are concerned, in the accused'.[142] It can be argued, however, that given the difficulty of proving personal bias, the objective test is the only means of mounting an effective challenge on the basis of bias and a failure to approach the case with an open mind in accordance with the presumption of innocence.

It has been claimed that the standards adopted in Strasbourg have strengthened over the years due to the court's emphasis on the increasing sensitivity of the public to an appearance of fairness.[143] The ECtHR has made it clear that any confusion of roles between the functions of prosecutor and judge will lead to doubts as to impartiality under the objective test. In *Ozerov v. Russia*,[144] the Moscow Savelovsky District Court convicted the applicant of traffic offences and burglary after a trial which it held in the absence of the prosecutor. Having heard the applicant, the court proceeded to hear the evidence of the victims and other witnesses, including the evidence of a police officer whom it called of its own motion and who gave evidence incriminating the applicant. Preparatory work had been done for the trial by the prosecutor, but the ECtHR took the view that the court had done much more than examine the evidence prepared for the trial by taking new incriminating evidence of its own motion and in addition by removing certain evidence submitted by the prosecutor's office in support of the charges. Although the applicant had not aired any objection to his trial proceeding in the absence of the prosecutor, any waiver of rights guaranteed by Article 6 could not depend on the parties alone where a right of such

---

[135] Trechsel, *Human Rights in Criminal Proceedings*, 174.
[136] *Piersack* v. *Belgium*, para. 30; *Hauschildt* v. *Denmark*, para. 46; and *Sander* v. *United Kingdom*, para. 22.
[137] *Hauschildt* v. *Denmark*, para. 48; and *Ferrantelli and Santangelo* v. *Italy*, para. 58.
[138] *Incal* v. *Turkey*, para. 65.   [139] *Pullar* v. *United Kingdom*, para. 39.
[140] See, e.g. *Le Compte, Van Leuven and De Meyere* v. *Belgium*, para 58; *Piersack* v. *Belgium*, para. 30; and *De Cubber* v. *Belgium*, para. 25.
[141] Trechsel, *Human Rights in Criminal Proceedings*, 64; but see *Kyprianou* v. *Cyprus*.
[142] *Incal* v. *Turkey*, para. 71.   [143] Emmerson et al., *Human Rights and Criminal Justice*, 529.
[144] *Ozerov* v. *Russia*.

fundamental importance as the right to an independent and impartial tribunal had been breached. The ECtHR contrasted the case with *Thorgeirson* v. *Iceland*, where the applicant complained that the prosecutor had been absent from certain sittings during his trial, but the court had not assumed any functions that might have been fulfilled by the prosecution had it been present.

There has been an absence of clear guidelines as to how the objective test should be applied. Generally speaking, it would seem that the mere fact that judges or jurors have occupied positions as police or prosecutors does not itself give rise to any justified fears of impartiality,[145] although it may be different where they are continuing to serve in these positions.[146] But if members of the tribunal have previously had some association with the defendant, his case or a witness in the case, this can give rise to greater doubts.[147] This would seem to be justified. 'Generic prejudice', which arises when a person's pre-existing opinions or position cause bias, may creep into a tribunal consciously or subconsciously, but in the absence of evidence to the contrary a fair-minded person may be entitled to take the view that when properly directed, a tribunal as a whole should be capable of guarding against this kind of bias.[148] It is different when a member of the tribunal actually has knowledge of persons involved or circumstances in the case which can give rise to what has been called 'interest prejudice'.[149] In this event, there is a real possibility that the tribunal will be tainted by an interested member bringing in outside information which does not constitute part of the evidence in the case, with the possible risk to the principle that the accused should only be tried on the evidence in the case.

The question remains as to what steps should be taken by states to try to dispel prejudice in particular cases. With a presumption that tribunals will be impartial, it is left for allegations of bias to be made by the parties or by other members of the tribunal. The ECtHR has held that Article 6 of the Convention imposes an obligation on every national court to check whether, as constituted, there is an 'impartial tribunal' within the meaning of that provision where this is disputed on a ground that does not immediately appear to be manifestly void of merit.[150] Where the allegations are confirmed, it would seem that a judicial direction to a jury to disregard any bias will not be enough to dismiss any objectively justified or legitimate doubts as to the impartiality of the jury.[151]

The requirement to investigate allegations of bias poses problems for common law systems which go to considerable lengths to protect the secrecy of

---

[145] *Piersack* v. *Belgium*.   [146] *R* v. *Abdroikov* [2007] UKHL 37.
[147] See *Piersack* v. *Belgium*; and *Holm* v. *Sweden*. Cf. *Pullar* v. *United Kingdom*. See also *R* v. *Pintori* [2007] EWCA Crim 1700; and *R* v. *Alan I* [2007] EWCA Crim 2999.
[148] *R* v. *Abdroikov* [2007] UKHL 37, paras. 37–8, per Lord Rodger. See also *R* v. *Khan* [2008] EWCA Crim 531.
[149] For distinctions between different kinds of bias that may impact upon the jury, see N. Vidmar, 'Pretrial Publicity in Canada: A Comparative Perspective on the Criminal Jury' (1996) 79 *Judicature* 49. See also generally N. Vidmar, *World Jury Systems* (Oxford University Press, 2000).
[150] *Remli* v. *France*, para. 48.   [151] *Sander* v. *United Kingdom*. Cf. *Gregory* v. *United Kingdom*.

the jury deliberation room. The rationales that are most commonly given for this are that they encourage candour between jurors and promote finality in the verdict.[152] The ECtHR has endorsed the former reason, considering that secrecy is a legitimate feature of English jury trial law which serves to reinforce the jury's role as the ultimate arbiter of fact and to guarantee open and frank deliberations among jurors on the evidence which they have heard.[153] While judges are not generally prohibited from investigating allegations of bias,[154] a number of common law systems have limited the evidence that can be received in such investigations. A distinction is commonly made between facts, statements and events *extrinsic* to the deliberation process which are admissible as evidence and statements made, arguments advanced or votes cast in the course of deliberations which are *intrinsic* to the deliberation process and are not admissible.[155] This does not exclude evidence about a juror having knowledge about the case or characteristics that make it inappropriate for him to serve on the jury.[156] But it would seem to prevent evidence of so-called 'generic prejudice', such as was alleged in one case in the United Kingdom where a juror had written to defence counsel after a defendant had been convicted, complaining that during deliberations certain jurors had taken a racist attitude towards the defendant.[157] A majority of the House of Lords held that the secrecy rule was compatible with Article 6, but the better view is surely that of Lord Steyn, the sole dissentient in the case, who considered that it would be astonishing for the ECtHR to hold, when the point arises before it, that miscarriages of justice may be ignored in the interest of the general efficiency of the jury system.[158]

If common law systems have had some difficulty adapting their tradition of jury secrecy to the demands of effective scrutiny of allegations of bias, continental systems would seem to have a difficulty in ensuring that their tradition of court experts conforms to the standards of an impartial tribunal. In a number of systems, experts are appointed by the court as independent advisers on scientific matters. But in practice the prosecution can exercise considerable control over their appointment.[159] In *Bönisch* v. *Austria*, the applicant was prosecuted for preparing meat which contained an excessive concentration of benzopyrene

---

[152] See C. M. Quinn, 'Jury Bias and the European Convention on Human Rights: A Well Kept Secret?' [2004] *Criminal Law Review* 998, 1007–8.
[153] *Gregory* v. *United Kingdom*, para. 44.
[154] See *R* v. *Smith (Patrick); R* v. *Mercieca* [2005] 1 WLR 704A.
[155] *R* v. *Pan; R* v. *Sawyer* (2001) 200 DLR (4th) 577, para. 77. See also Advisory Committee Note to Rule 606(b) of the US Federal Rules of Evidence.
[156] See, e.g. *Pintori* [2007] EWCA Crim 1700, para. 19.
[157] *R* v. *Mitza; R* v. *Connor and Rollick* [2004] AC 1118.   [158] Ibid., para. 19.
[159] For the position in Germany, see K. Volk, 'Forensic Expertise and the Law of Evidence in Germany', in J. F. Nijboer, C. R. Callen and N. Kwak (eds.), *Forensic Expertise and the Law of Evidence* (Amsterdam: Royal Netherlands Academy of Arts and Sciences, 1993) 37. For the position in the Netherlands, see P. T. C. van Kampen, *Expert Evidence Compared: Rules and Practices in the Dutch and American Criminal Justice System* (Antwerpen and Groningen: Intersentia Rechswetenschappen, 1998) 6–76.

on the basis of a report prepared by the director of the Federal Food Control Institute, who was appointed later as an expert by the court. The ECtHR considered that as it was his report that had led to the charges being brought, he was more like a witness against the accused, and considered that although he could be heard by the court, the principle of equality of arms inherent in the concept of a fair trial required equal treatment as between the hearing of the director and the hearing of persons who were or could be called in whatever capacity by the defence. Since the director had been heard as an 'expert', his statements must have carried greater weight than those of an 'expert witness' called by the accused and he exercised a privileged position in being allowed to attend throughout the hearings, put questions to the accused and witnesses with the leave of the court and comment on their evidence. It followed that there had been a violation of the right to a fair trial.

The case is commonly compared to *Brandstetter* v. *Austria*, where the applicant was charged with mixing wine with water and sugar. On this occasion, however, the expert whom the court appointed was not the person who filed the report leading to the applicant's prosecution, but was employed by the same institute as the expert who had filed the report. The ECtHR held that in this case doubts about the neutrality of the expert could not be objectively justified and the Austrian courts had not breached the principle of equality of arms in refusing the applicant's request to appoint another expert. It follows from the judgment that a court does not have to appoint further experts at the request of the defence just because the opinion of the court-appointed expert supports the prosecution case. Even accepting the ECtHR's view that there is no ground for objective bias when the court appoints an expert from the same institute as the one that prepared the initial report against the applicant, the case arguably gives undue deference to the status of a 'neutral' expert, as experience shows that even when there are no objective fears to question an expert's objective neutrality, the expert can nevertheless be wrong.[160] Of course, giving the defence recourse to additional experts is no guarantee that the tribunal of fact will come to an accurate result. The ECtHR has yet to insist that courts adopt *Daubert*-style criteria to forensic criminal evidence. But at least it gives a meaningful opportunity for the defence to challenge the conclusions of the expert supporting the prosecution case and offset any possible error.

7.7.2 Participatory rights

The possibility of challenging the evidence and arguments against one is, of course, at the heart of the principle of adversarial procedure, which along with the principle of equality of arms has been central to the notion of defence participation and a fair trial. In Chapter 9, we look in more detail at how the

---

[160] J. D. den Hartog, 'The Case Law of the European Court of Human Rights Regarding the Use of Expert Statements in Criminal Procedures', in Nijboer et al., *Forensic Expertise*, 156.

ECtHR has developed the notion of defence participation. For now, it is enough to reiterate the point already made that the exercise of these rights can be vital in protecting the presumption of innocence. In the absence of rules governing the admission of unreliable evidence, it is particularly important to give the defence the opportunity to make an effective challenge to the evidence against him either by examination of witnesses or by evidence in rebuttal. Of course, this is no guarantee against a biased tribunal, which is pre-disposed against the accused. But the right of challenge can help to guard a fair-minded tribunal against the tendency to put too much weight upon unreliable prosecution evidence. The ECtHR has on occasions recognised this. In *Kostovski v. Netherlands*, for example, where an accused was faced with the evidence of anonymous witnesses, the ECtHR stressed the importance of effective challenge when it said that if the defence is unaware of the identity of the person it seeks to question, it may be deprived of the very particulars enabling it to demonstrate that he or she is prejudiced, hostile or unreliable. According to the ECtHR:

> Testimony or other declarations inculpating an accused may well be designedly untruthful or simply erroneous and the defence will scarcely be able to bring this to light if it lacks the information permitting it to test the author's reliability or cast doubt on his credibility.[161]

This does not mean that the interests of victims and witnesses need to be disregarded. Balancing the rights of the defence against witnesses does not need to result in a kind of zero sum game, but it does call for the application of strict proportionality tests towards any encroachment on the rights of the defence to challenge evidence against it. We discuss the right to examine witnesses in Chapter 10.

The ECtHR has been somewhat less robust in reviewing the right of the defence to adduce evidence in rebuttal.[162] The European organs have repeatedly stressed that there is not an unlimited right for the accused to call evidence on his or her behalf and that Article 6 leaves it to the competent authorities to decide upon the relevance of proposed evidence.[163] The Human Rights Committee has also stated that Article 14(3)(c) of the ICCPR does not provide an unlimited right to obtain the attendance of any witness requested by the defence.[164] The reluctance to become involved in expressing an opinion on the relevance of particular evidence is understandable, but in reviewing whether a trial has been fair the human rights bodies do have a duty to see that the relevant principles have been applied properly. We have seen that the right of the defence to obtain

---

[161] *Kostovski* v. *Netherlands*, para. 42.
[162] Trechsel refers to the 'great reluctance' of the Strasbourg authorities to intervene in this area: see Trechsel, *Human Rights in Criminal Proceedings*, 324. Harris, Boyle and Warbrick refer to their 'hands off' approach: see D. J. Harris, M. O'Boyle, E. P. Bates and C. M. Buckley, *Harris, O'Boyle & Warbrick: Law of the European Convention on Human Rights*, 2nd edn (Oxford University Press, 2009) 326.
[163] *X* v. *Austria* (dec.), no. 753/60; *Austria* v. *Italy (Pfunders Case)* (report); *X* v. *Germany* (dec.), no. 4119/69; *Engel and others* v. *Netherlands*; *Bricmont* v. *Belgium*; and *Vidal* v. *Belgium*.
[164] *Gordon* v. *Jamaica*.

the attendance and examination of witnesses is linked expressly to the principle of equality of arms by the qualification, 'under the same conditions' as their opponent.[165] The danger with this approach is that it can focus attention on matters of form more than substance, such as how many witnesses and how much time each party is given to present its evidence, rather than whether the defence can mount an effective challenge to the prosecution case in order to safeguard the presumption of innocence. The European Commission and Court have at times recognised that the equality of arms is not the only principle at stake here. In an early opinion, the Commission recognised that the principle of the presumption of innocence imposes an obligation on the national court to permit the accused to produce evidence to rebut the charges made.[166] Later, in *Vidal* v. *Belgium*,[167] the ECtHR recognised that the concept of equality of arms does not 'exhaust the content' of Article 6(3)(d) in a case on appeal against the applicant's acquittal where the Brussels Court of Appeal did not hear any witness, whether for the prosecution or the defence, before giving judgment on the basis of the case file. The ECtHR considered that the failure to give reasons for not calling witnesses whom the defence had proposed was not consistent with a fair trial. We shall also see that the ECtHR has developed strong disclosure rights for the purposes of accused persons being able to exonerate themselves.[168]

Certain national courts have been more robust than the ECtHR in recognising the importance of the defence right to present evidence and have sought to link it with the presumption of innocence. In the United States, for instance, there is a considerable line of authority holding that in an extreme case, an accused has a constitutional right to introduce critical, demonstrably reliable testimony even when there are other evidentiary rules that would otherwise preclude its admission.[169] The Canadian Charter of Rights and Freedoms guarantees the right to 'make full answer and defence' as one of the fundamental principles of justice and the Supreme Court has recognised that the right of the innocent not to be convicted is dependent on this right, which in turn depends on being able to call the evidence necessary to establish a defence and to challenge the evidence called by the prosecution.[170]

It is sometimes suggested that the requirement that the prosecution bears a heavy burden of proof compensates adequately for any restriction put on the defence to admit evidence. In *Holmes* v. *South Carolina*,[171] the petitioner who had been convicted of the murder of an 86-year-old woman was prevented at his trial from introducing evidence that another man had attacked the victim

---

[165] See Ch. 4.2.2.   [166] *Austria* v. *Italy (Pfunders Case)* (report), 784.
[167] Para. 33.   [168] See Ch. 9.3.
[169] The landmark cases are: *Washington* v. *Texas*, 388 US 14 (1967); *Chambers* v. *Mississippi*, 410 US 284 (1973); and *Davis* v. *Alaska*, 415 US 308 (1974). For an analysis arguing that 'the Supreme Court mandated the admission of the excluded evidence in these cases in large part because the exclusion created a grave risk of miscarriage of justice, namely the conviction of an innocent accused', see L. Heffernan and E. J. Imwinkelried, 'The Accused's Constitutional Right to Introduce Critical, Demonstrably Reliable Exculpatory Evidence' (2006) 40 *Irish Jurist* 111, 136.
[170] *R* v. *Seaboyer* [1991] 2 SCR 577, 630, per McLachlin J.   [171] 547 US 319 (2006).

on the basis of a ruling of the South Carolina Supreme Court that where there is strong evidence of an appellant's guilt, especially where there is forensic evidence, evidence of third-party guilt did not raise a reasonable inference as to the appellant's own innocence. The USSC held that whether rooted in the due process clause of the Fourteenth Amendment or the compulsory process clause of the Sixth Amendment, the Constitution guaranteed criminal defendants 'a meaningful opportunity to present a complete defense'. State and federal rule-makers had a broad latitude to exclude evidence in criminal trials and this could include the exclusion of evidence of third-party guilt where this did no more than raise suspicion. However, the rule applied in this case did not focus on the probative value or the potential adverse effects of admitting evidence of third-party guilt, but instead the critical inquiry concerned the strength of the prosecution case. By evaluating the strength of only one party's evidence, no logical conclusion could be reached regarding the strength of the contrary evidence and the rule did not therefore rationally serve the end that other rules on third-party guilt were designed to further.

The decision is a useful reminder of the dangers of putting too much credence on the strength of the prosecution's case without inquiry into the defence case.[172] It has been hailed as a strong affirmation of the USSC's commitment to protecting the affirmative evidentiary right to present a defence even where the state is pursuing a legitimate aim in permitting the exclusion of defence evidence.[173] A contemporary example of such a legitimate aim is to be seen in the number of rape shield statutes which have sought to limit the sexual history evidence that the defence may wish to adduce.[174] The courts across a number of jurisdictions have recognised that such evidence may cloud the issues rather than illuminate them by perpetuating what has been described as the twin myths, that because a woman has had sexual intercourse in the past she is more likely to have consented to intercourse on the occasion in question and that by reason of her sexual behaviour in the past she is less worthy of belief as a witness.[175] But ultimately, as the House of Lords held in a case where in accordance with the United Kingdom's rape shield laws the defence had been denied leave to cross-examine the complainant and lead evidence relating to her alleged sexual relationship with the defendant, 'the right of a defendant to call

---

[172] 'There can be few practising lawyers who have not had the experience of resuming their seat in a state of hubristic satisfaction, having called a respectable witness to give apparently cast-iron evidence, only to see it reduced to wreckage by ten minutes of well-informed cross-examination or convincingly explained away by the other side's testimony. Some have appeared in cases in which everybody was sure of the defendant's guilt, only for fresh evidence to emerge which makes it clear they were wrong. As Mark Twain said, the difference between reality and fiction is that fiction has to be credible ... [Y]ou cannot be sure of anything until all the evidence has been heard, and even then you may be wrong.' *Secretary of State for the Home Department v. A.F. (No. 3)* [2009] 2 WLR 423, 468, para. 113, per Sedley LJ.

[173] Heffernan and Imwinkelried, 'Accused's Constitutional Right to Introduce Evidence', 111, 135.

[174] For a survey of the US experience, see M. S. Raeder, 'Litigating Sex Crimes in the United States: Has the Last Decade made any Difference?' (2009) 6 *International Commentary on Evidence*, Issue 2, Art. 6.

[175] *R v. Seaboyer* [1991] 2 SCR 577, 630, per McLachlin J.

relevant evidence where the absence of such evidence may give rise to an unjust conviction is an absolute right which cannot be qualified by considerations of public interest no matter how well founded that public interest may be'.[176]

7.7.3 The right to a reasoned judgment

Finally, we have seen that the Strasbourg bodies have held that there is a right to a reasoned judgment. This is a right that extends to civil proceedings as well as criminal proceedings and can be justified on a number of grounds, such as transparency, acceptability and legitimacy of the verdict.[177] It can also be regarded as helping to reinforce the presumption of innocence in so far as it assists defendants to identify for the purposes of appeal what types of evidence were relied upon by the tribunal and whether there were any weaknesses in the reasoning that led it to be convinced beyond reasonable doubt of the defendant's guilt.[178] Although the Strasbourg organs have not connected the right to a reasoned judgment expressly with the presumption of innocence, they have stated that a reasoned judgment makes it possible for the accused to exercise effective rights of appeal.[179] We have seen that this can be particularly important in civil law systems where tribunals have access to all kinds of evidence, some of which may be unreliable. A reasoned judgment can be an important mechanism for ensuring that the tribunal has not relied upon any unlawful or 'suspect' kinds of evidence.[180] The ECtHR has recognised this is in relation to the question of drawing inferences from silence. In the next chapter, we examine this question in detail, but for now it is worth observing that although the ECtHR considered that Article 6 did not exclude the drawing of such inferences, it would not be compatible with the immunities afforded by the Convention if a defendant were convicted mainly or solely on the strength of his or her silence.[181] The ECtHR went on to consider that certain safeguards had to be put in place before inferences could be drawn and in this respect it emphasised the importance of the availability of reasons for conviction. Where there is a reasoned judgment setting out the reasons for conviction, it is then possible to scrutinise what reliance was placed on the defendant's silence in arriving at a decision of guilt.

The ECtHR has not been particularly rigorous in setting out what is required for a reasoned judgment.[182] Much would seem to depend on the submissions made by the parties and the ECtHR is prepared to take into account the

---

[176] *R* v. *S (No. 2)* [2001] UKHL 25, para 161, per Lord Hutton.
[177] Trechsel, *Human Rights in Criminal Proceedings*, 102–6.
[178] Stavros, *Guarantees for Accused Persons*, 259.
[179] *X* v. *FRG* (dec.), no. 1035/61; and *Hadjianastassiou* v. *Greece*, para. 33. For more on the argument that a reasoned judgment enhances a defendant's right of appeal, see J. Jackson and S. Doran, *Judge without Jury: Diplock Trials in the Adversary System* (Oxford: Clarendon, 1995), ch. 9.
[180] Stavros, *Guarantees for Accused Persons*, 258.
[181] *John Murray* v. *United Kingdom* [GC], para. 47.
[182] Trechsel, *Human Rights in Criminal Proceedings*, 106–7.

differences existing in the contracting states with regard to statutory provisions, customary rules, legal opinion and the presentation and drafting of judgments.[183] The requirement does not oblige national tribunals to file a detailed answer to every argument.[184] But it would seem that it is necessary for there to be a 'specific and express reply' to every submission that, if accepted, is decisive for the outcome of the case.[185] In *Taxquet* v. *Belgium* the applicant had been convicted, along with seven others, by a jury of murdering a government minister without any reasons given to him. The jury had answered four questions in the affirmative confirming the main elements of the charge, but the ECtHR considered that such 'laconic answers to vague and general questions' could have left the applicant with an impression of arbitrary justice lacking in transparency.[186] The ECtHR continued as follows:

> Not having been given so much as a summary of the main reasons why the Assize Court was satisfied that he was guilty, he was unable to understand – and therefore to accept – the court's decision. This is particularly significant because the jury does not reach its verdict on the basis of the case file but on the basis of the evidence it has heard at the trial. It is therefore important, for the purpose of explaining the verdict both to the accused and to the public at large – the 'people' in whose name the decision is given – to highlight the considerations that have persuaded the jury of the accused's guilt or innocence and to indicate the precise reasons why each of the questions has been answered in the affirmative or the negative.[187]

This requirement would seem to pose some difficulty for common law and civil law systems, which do not require juries to give reasons for their verdicts.[188] The ECtHR has accepted that one way of compensating for a reasoned judgment is a carefully framed direction from the judge.[189] This can impose an onerous duty on the trial judge. In *Condron* v. *United Kingdom*, for example, which was concerned with the directions which the judge had given the jury on drawing inferences from silence, the ECtHR considered that the direction had not been careful enough. Pointing out that it was impossible to ascertain what weight if any was given to the defendant's silence as the safeguard of a reasoned judgment was absent in the case, the ECtHR said that it was even more compelling in these circumstances to ensure that the jury was properly advised on how to address the issue of the applicant's silence.

---

[183] See, e.g. *Hiro Balani* v. *Spain*, para. 27.   [184] *Van de Hurk* v. *Netherlands*, para. 61.
[185] *Hiro Balani* v. *Spain*, para. 28; and *Ruiz Torija* v. *Spain*. See Harris et al., *Law of the European Convention*, 268.
[186] *Taxquet* v. *Belgium*, para. 48.   [187] Ibid.
[188] Certain continental jury systems do require explanations to be given: see S. Thaman, 'Europe's New Jury Systems: The Case of Spain and Russia', in Vidmar, *World Jury Systems*, 338–47. The court in *Taxquet* referred to the fact that certain states such as France had made provision for the publication of a statement of reasons in assize court decisions: see *Taxquet* v. *Belgium*, para. 43.
[189] *Saric* v. *Denmark*.

A judicial direction, however, can never fully compensate for a reasoned judgment, as it can only set out how the facts *should* be reached, not how they *were* reached.[190] Furthermore, to be satisfied of guilt a jury must simply reach a consensus that each element of the offence has been proved beyond reasonable doubt, but does not have to agree collectively on the weight of all the items of proof that make up the evidence for each element.[191] When a reasoned judgment is required, on the other hand, the need for reasoning requires that a consensus is reached on the grounds for guilt. The greater restraints imposed by a reasoned judgment were recently recognised by the ICTR Appeals Chamber when it made the point that in the case of a jury, the one question that has to be answered is the question of guilty or not guilty and the factual findings supporting this conclusion are neither spelled out nor can they be challenged by the parties. It continued:

> The instruction given to the jury concentrates on this 'ultimate issue' of the case. In this Tribunal, on the other hand, Trial Chambers cannot restrict themselves to the ultimate issue of guilty or not; they have an obligation . . . to give a reasoned opinion.[192]

Of course, looked at another way it can be argued that the requirement of a reasoned judgment is merely a compensation for other aspects of the decision-making process that are not as demanding as that imposed on the jury – the fact, for example, that most continental systems and indeed the international criminal systems as well operate on the theory that if a majority of the tribunal are satisfied of guilt, that suffices for proof beyond reasonable doubt, whereas in most common law systems unanimity or at least a heavily weighted majority is necessary before there can be a verdict of guilty. This serves to emphasise the complexity of trying to ascertain which system is more protective of the presumption of innocence. The international human rights bodies have been understandably flexible about the particular decision rules and processes that national systems should adopt. But the insistence upon a reasoned judgment or a careful direction helps to give some assurance that guilt is determined in accordance with the principles governing the presumption of innocence and not on the basis of prejudicial and unreliable forms of evidence.

7.8 Conclusion

Although we have identified various meanings that can be attached to the presumption of innocence, we have argued that the importance of the presumption

---

[190] This point was well made in the context of drawing inferences from silence by Nicolas Bratza QC in his opinion for the European Commission in *John Murray* v. *United Kingdom* [GC], para. 37.
[191] See J. C. Smith, 'Satisfying the Jury' [1988] *Criminal Law Review* 335.
[192] *Prosecutor* v. *Ntagerura*, para. 169.

of innocence lies primarily in the protection that it offers against wrongful convictions and have argued that this outcome-related aspect of the presumption is to be seen in two principles: that the prosecution prove guilt beyond reasonable doubt and that accused persons are protected against prejudicial judgments. The human rights bodies have recognised the procedural importance of the presumption of innocence as a means of protecting against wrongful conviction and have been less clear about the scope of the broader right to be treated as innocent. But they have not been as vigilant in protecting against the risk of wrongful conviction as they might have been. They have recognised the importance of the prosecution bearing the burden of proof, but have given states a wide margin as to the 'reasonable limits' that may be placed on this principle, although there are signs that they are edging towards requiring national states to permit exceptions only where they pursue a legitimate aim and these can be justified as proportionate. As regards the importance of avoiding prejudice, it is not of course their function to review the evidence in particular cases in accordance with the tradition of leaving matters of assessing evidence to national states. But in eschewing the need for admissibility rules to regulate potentially prejudicial or unreliable pieces of evidence, they could have done more to emphasise the important connection between the presumption and other aspects of a fair trial such as the need for an independent and impartial tribunal and defence rights to adduce and challenge evidence. It is now time to turn to look in more detail at these defence rights. In Chapter 4 we centred these around the notion of defence participation in the fact-finding exercise. But one of the important rights which we come to first is the right *not* to participate in proof processes, the so-called privilege against self-incrimination.

8

Silence and the privilege against self-incrimination

8.1 The historical and transnational importance of the right of silence

In Chapter 4 we noted that one of the strands developed by the European Court of Human Rights in its vision of defence participation is the right to choose not to participate in the proof process. In this chapter, we explore this principle which the court has referred to as 'the right to remain silent and not to contribute to incriminating oneself.[1] The principle is commonly believed to have its origins in the common law and is generally traced back to 1641 when the Star Chamber and the High Commission were abolished in England along with the ex officio oath procedure under which accused persons were required to take an oath to answer all questions.[2] The precise origins of the privilege remains obscure, with some tracing it back to ancient Christian writings and to Talmudic law.[3] The maxim 'nemo teneter prodere se ipsum', which served as a guarantee that no one would be required to become the source of their own prosecution, has been traced back to medieval canon law and the European *ius commune*.[4]

The growing consensus that the privilege has a broader and older ancestry than the English common law may explain why it has gained acceptance not only in the English speaking world, but around the globe, as well as in various human rights instruments.[5] Although the privilege was not part of the charters that established the Nuremberg or the Tokyo tribunals, it is expressly recognised, as we shall see, in the ICCPR and the ACHR. It has been estimated that

---

[1] *Funke* v. *France*.
[2] J. H. Wigmore, *A Treatise on the Anglo-American System of Evidence in Trials at Common Law*, 3rd edn (Boston: Little, Brown, 1940) vol. 8, § 2250; and P. Levy, *The Origins of the Fifth Amendment: The Right against Self-Incrimination* (Oxford University Press, 1968). For a description of the *ex officio* procedure, see R. H. Helmolz, 'The Privilege and the *Ius Commune*: The Middle Ages to the Seventeenth Century', in R. H. Helmolz, C. M. Gray, J. H. Langbein, E. Moglen, H. E. Smith and A. W. Alschuler (eds.), *The Privilege against Self-Incrimination: Its Origins and Development* (University of Chicago Press, 1997) 17.
[3] See, e.g. R. Schlauri, *Das Verbot des Selbstbelastungszwangs im Strafverfahren: Konkretisierung eines Grundrechts durch Rechtsvergleichung* (Zurich: Schulthess, 2003) 39.
[4] Helmolz, 'The Privilege and the *Ius Commune*'.
[5] S. Sedley, 'Wringing out the Fault: Self-Incrimination in the 21st Century' (2002) 52 *Northern Ireland Legal Quarterly* 107, 117–18.

no less than forty-eight national constitutions provide for a privilege against self-incrimination, although over half of these instruments expressly limit it to testimony at trial, many in former British colonies with common law roots.[6] Although the right is not expressly mentioned in the ECHR, the ECtHR has described the privilege and the right of silence as 'generally recognised international standards which lie at the heart of the notion of a fair trial procedure'.[7]

At first glance, the principle would seem to be a supreme example of the tension between the rationalist tradition's emphasis on rectitude of decision-making and the emphasis on individual liberty and freedom of the individual to be left alone by the state. Certainly, Bentham reserved perhaps his most trenchant criticism for the privilege against self-incrimination on the ground that it was a considerable impediment towards convicting the guilty. In one of the most famous passages attributed to him, he claimed that 'if all the criminals of every class had assembled, and framed a system after their own wishes, is not this rule the very first which they would have established for their security? Innocence never takes advantage of it; innocence claims the right of speaking, as guilt invokes the privilege of silence.'[8] Bentham acknowledged that the historical legacy of the privilege arose out of a system of interrogation practised in England under the ecclesiastical courts of the High Commission and the Star Chamber which proved to be extremely averse to rectitude of outcome, involving as it did the use of torture to obtain confessions.[9] What Bentham objected to, however, was elevating the principle to one of importance in a modern reformed criminal justice system. Just because questioning accused persons could lead to abuse, and even torture, did not mean that questioning itself was wrong and that persons should not be compelled to answer questions in certain circumstances.

It is important to be clear, however, that the privilege against self-incrimination has rarely extended to immunity from being questioned.[10] Although in the reaction against the Star Chamber accused persons were no longer put on oath, there was no prohibition against them being questioned at trial. Indeed, the essential purpose of the criminal trial from the middle of the sixteenth century until the late eighteenth century was to afford the accused the opportunity to speak to the charges against him.[11] Ironically, it was only at the time when Bentham was inveighing against the privilege that it was

---

[6] See M. C. Bassiouni, 'Human Rights in the Context of Criminal Justice: Identifying International Procedural Protections in National Constitutions' (1992–3) 3 *Duke Journal of Comparative and International Law* 235, 265, n. 138.
[7] *Saunders* v. *United Kingdom* [GC], para. 68.
[8] J. Bentham, *A Treatise on Judicial Evidence*, ed. E. Dumont (London: Baldwin, Craddock and Joy, 1825) 241.
[9] J. Bentham, *Rationale of Judicial Evidence*, ed. J. S. Mill (London: Hunt and Clarke, 1827) vol. 5, 250 ff.
[10] For the distinction between the right of silence and the right not to be questioned, see G. Williams, *The Proof of Guilt*, 3rd edn (London: Stevens, 1963) ch. 3.
[11] J. H. Langbein, 'The Privilege and Common Law Criminal Procedure: The Sixteenth to the Eighteenth Centuries', in Helmolz et al., *Privilege against Self-Incrimination*, 82.

beginning to emerge in its modern form as a protection not only for sworn witnesses, but also for defendants at trial.[12] The practice of questioning defendants did not cease until the early nineteenth century, when lawyers appeared more in criminal trials and an adversarial procedure came to be developed.[13] Justices of peace continued to question accused persons before trial until 1848, when justices were required to warn the accused that they were not bound to say anything in answer to the charge and the practice of conducting interrogations ceased. By this time, however, the police came to take over investigative functions before trial and they too were permitted to question suspects until they were charged. In the twentieth century, Judges' Rules and later Codes of Practice were developed requiring officers to caution suspects at various stages of questioning, warning them that they did not have to answer questions, but provided the cautions were delivered, questions could still be put to them before they were charged and any confessions made were admissible against them at trial provided they were voluntary.[14]

This brief foray into English history explains why it has been said that the privilege against self-incrimination has crept into English life rather than being seen as a major constitutional landmark.[15] Given that interrogation procedures put enormous pressure on persons to speak, the most effective way of enforcing the privilege would be to prohibit the questioning of those suspected of crime altogether, yet there has been a consistent reluctance to do this up to the point of charge. Even at trial where defendants remain free to refuse to testify the compromise worked out in 1898 under the Criminal Evidence Act whereby defendants became competent to testify but retained the right not to testify with the protection that their silence could not be commented upon by the prosecution may be seen as much as a recognition that there was no longer any need to protect accused persons from giving evidence on oath in the changed adversarial climate of the late nineteenth century as any victory for the autonomy of the accused.[16] In the late twentieth century, further steps were taken to weaken the privilege by amending this legislation so as to enable prosecutors to comment upon a failure to testify along with other provisions permitting courts and juries to draw inferences from silence in certain circumstances.[17]

---

[12] H. E. Smith, 'The Modern Privilege: Its Nineteenth Century Origins' in Helmolz et al., *Privilege against Self-Incrimination*, 145.
[13] See J. H. Langbein, *The Origins of the Adversary Criminal Trial* (Oxford University Press, 2003).
[14] See Code of Practice for the Detention, Treatment and Questioning of Persons by Police Officers issued under the Police and Criminal Evidence Act 1984 (known as PACE), Notes for Guidance 1K.
[15] Wigmore, *Treatise on Evidence*, vol. 8, § 2250.
[16] S. J. Summers, *Fair Trials: The European Criminal Procedural Tradition and the European Court of Human Rights* (Oxford: Hart, 2007) 77–8.
[17] For background to these changes, see M. Berger, 'Reforming Confessions Law British Style: A Decade of Experience in England and Wales' (2000) 2 *Columbia Human Rights Law Review* 243, 248–66; and J. D. Jackson, 'Silence and Proof: Extending the Boundaries of Criminal Proceedings in the UK' (2001) 5 *International Journal of Evidence & Proof* 145.

The emphasis given to the privilege has been greater in the United States, where in the words of the Fifth Amendment to the Constitution 'no one can be compelled to be a witness against himself'. Even here, however, the privilege had little practical significance throughout the nineteenth century, since virtually all defendants answered questions before trial and testified at trial. This changed in the twentieth century, when defendants came to be represented by counsel and in the landmark decision of *Miranda* v. *Arizona*[18] the USSC laid down a number of safeguards to secure the privilege against self-incrimination which had to be complied with before statements stemming from custodial interrogation could be admitted. Prior to any questioning, suspects must be warned that they have a right to remain silent, that any statement they do make may be used as evidence against them and that they have a right to the presence of an attorney. Although suspects may waive these rights, if at any time they indicate that they wish to speak with an attorney or that they do not wish to be questioned, the police may not question them. This is a significant variation from the regime in England, which permits the police to continue questioning suspects even when they indicate an unwillingness to be questioned.[19] Since *Miranda*, however, the USSC has subsequently cut back in a number of ways from this position by developing exceptions to the exclusionary rule.[20] The rule remains intact, but it has been upheld by the USSC more for reasons of *stare decisis* than it would seem out of any deep-seated commitment to uphold it on its merits.[21] Despite *Miranda*, considerable numbers of suspects waive their rights and speak.[22] At trial, a rather different picture appears and it has been suggested that the extent of refusals to testify is 'considerable', from one-third to over one-half in some jurisdictions.[23] A growing acceptance of the notion that the accused is not expected to testify is aided by rules of evidence which discourage defendants from testifying, such as the threat that they may be impeached on their previous criminal record and the requirement, unlike England, that no adverse inferences may be drawn from silence.[24]

---

[18] 384 US 436 (1966).

[19] G. Van Kessel, 'European Perspectives on the Accused as a Source of Testimonial Evidence' (1998) 100 *West Virginia Law Review* 800.

[20] On the retreat from Miranda, see W. Stuntz, 'The American Exclusionary Rule and Defendants' Changing Rights' [1989] *Criminal Law Review* 117; and P. Roberts and A. Zuckerman, *Criminal Evidence*, 2nd edn (Oxford University Press, 2010) 546–7.

[21] *United States* v. *Dickerson*, 120 S. Ct 2326 (2000). See D. J. Seidmann and A. Stein, 'The Right to Silence Helps the Innocent: A Game Theoretic Analysis of the Fifth Amendment Privilege' (2000) 114 *Harvard Law Review* 431. See also P. Mirfield, 'Miranda Rule Re-affirmed: US v Dickerson' (2001) 6 *International Journal of Evidence & Proof* 61.

[22] In two US studies, cited by Seidmann and Stein, 'The Right to Silence Helps the Innocent', the numbers of suspects who exercise their right of silence varied from between 9.55% and 20.9%. It has been suggested that the numbers of suspects who make damaging statements though is less than in the United Kingdom: see G. Van Kessel, 'The Suspect as a Source of Testimonial Evidence, A Comparison of the English and American Approaches' (1986) 38 *Hastings Law Journal* 1. See also S. Easton, *The Case for the Right of Silence*, 2nd edn (Vermont: Ashgate, 1998).

[23] Van Kessel, 'European Perspectives', 841.   [24] Ibid., 839–40.

By contrast, the experience in continental Europe is that silence is a 'rare event'.[25] Despite the introduction of the privilege against self-incrimination in many European countries, requiring that at different stages accused persons be told of their right to silence,[26] most countries allow questioning of suspects to continue even when they refuse to make a statement or assert a desire to remain silent. There are particular differences between common law and civil countries when it comes to trial. The continental defendant is frequently put into the more vulnerable position of being the first person to answer questions, rather than as in common law systems enjoying the advantage of waiting until the prosecution establishes a prima facie case against them. Unlike the common law defendant, continental defendants are also not free to decide whether or not to take the stand and questions can always be asked of them, as at the pre-trial phases.[27] Suspects and accused persons are encouraged in various ways to participate in the proceedings. At the pre-trial stage, a lack of cooperation can sometimes be used as an argument for detaining the accused.[28] Although as we shall see prosecutors and magistrates have to search for exculpatory as well as inculpatory evidence, in practice it is up to the defence to point to exculpatory evidence and sometimes it would seem that interrogators can point out the advantages in suspects making a statement.[29] These inducements to speak carry on into the trial stage. In most continental countries, the accused does not take an oath and therefore can lie without fearing a subsequent prosecution for perjury. The unitary trial in which guilt and punishment issues are decided in the one proceeding means that a defendant who refuses to speak forfeits the opportunity to give a mitigating account of his or her actions. Furthermore, there are not the same disadvantages caused by rules of evidence as in the United States, for example the use of prior convictions does not turn on whether the accused testifies. In addition, the informality of the proceedings at the trial which stands in contrast to the formal system of examination

---

[25] Ibid., 833. See also M. R. Damaška, 'Evidentiary Barriers to Conviction and Two Models of Criminal Procedure: Comparative Study' (1973) 121 *University of Pennsylvania Law Review* 511, 527 ('almost all continental defendants choose to testify').

[26] But not all. In Belgium, the police are under no obligation to inform persons who are about to be interviewed that they have a right of silence: H. D. Bosly and D. Vandermeersch, *Droit de la Procédure Pénale*, 4th edn (Bruges: La Charte, 2005) 617. By contrast, in Germany and Italy, police and prosecutor must inform suspects of their right to silence before questioning them. See Germany, CCP §136 §1; Italy, Art. 64 § 3 CCP. After the reforms of June 2000, police in France were obliged to inform persons in custody of their right of silence, but this requirement was repealed in March 2003: see J. Hodgson, *French Criminal Justice* (Oxford: Hart, 2005) 120. In France, only suspects appearing before the *juge d'instruction* are informed of the right.

[27] Damaška, 'Evidentiary Barriers', 527–30.

[28] See J. Fermon, F. Verbruggen and S. de Decker, 'The Investigative Stage of the Criminal Process in Belgium', in E. Cape, J. Hodgson, T. Prakken and T. Spronken (eds.), *Suspects in Europe* (Antwerp: Intersentia, 2007) 29, 44.

[29] T. Weigend and F. Saditt, 'The Investigative Stage of the Criminal Process in Germany' in Cape et al., *Suspects in Europe*, 79, 84.

and cross-examination in Anglo-American trials arguably encourages participation by all, including questioning of the accused by professional and lay judges.[30]

Despite the wide recognition given to the principle that one should not be required to testify against oneself, there would appear to be some differences between the dominant legal traditions in the extent to which defendants are encouraged to invoke this right. Even where it has been given the most constitutional significance as in the United States, however, it would not seem to be exercised frequently in the pre-trial phase of proceedings. Against this background, in this chapter we examine how the international human rights bodies have applied the privilege against self-incrimination. In the following sections, we examine the jurisprudence that has developed by looking at how these bodies have determined the scope and limitations of the privilege. In Chapter 4, we saw that the international bodies have interpreted the fair trial provisions in a manner that gives institutional support to the defence at trial. In considering that the privilege should be at the centre of a fair trial procedure, the ECtHR had an opportunity to apply it and the right of silence in a manner that might help to achieve equality of arms in the pre-trial phase. Instead, however, it has linked the privilege very closely to the suspect's freedom to choose whether or not to speak without regard to the inherently coercive atmosphere of police questioning and without regarding what institutional support is necessary for suspects to be able to mount an effective defence in such circumstances. As a result, the privilege does not enable the defence to play the kind of participatory role in the vital pre-trial phase of criminal proceedings that it envisages for the trial stage. At a time when increasing numbers of cases are being disposed of by various means in order to avoid trial, this is detrimental to the rights of the defence.

8.2 The scope of the privilege in international law

8.2.1 The international instruments

Although there is no explicit mention of the privilege against self-incrimination in the text of Article 6 of the ECHR, Article 14(3)(g) of the ICCPR states that everyone shall be entitled to the right '[n]ot to be compelled to testify against himself or to confess guilt' and Article 8(2)(g) of the ACHR refers in similar terms to 'the right not to be compelled to be a witness against himself or to plead guilty'. Article 8(3) of the ACHR also states that a confession of guilt by the accused shall be valid only 'if it is made without coercion of any kind'. It has been argued that the ACHR does not add any substance to the ICCPR text except that it demonstrates the particular attention given to the problem

---

[30] Van Kessel, 'European Perspectives', 834.

of forced confessions.[31] Indeed, it is this confessional aspect and in particular the need to protect persons from physical and verbal abuse when authorities attempt to obtain confessions from them that has consumed a large part of case law of the ACHR and the Human Rights Committee on Article 14.[32] Of course, as we have seen, the Convention Against Torture prohibits the use of evidence obtained by torture and in its general observations regarding the Torture Convention the committee has made the point that one of the essential means of preventing torture is the existence in procedural legislation of detailed provisions on the inadmissibility of unlawfully obtained confessions.[33] The committee has stressed, however, that Article 14 imposes wider duties on states than simply prohibiting evidence obtained by torture. In its General Comment, it has said that when considering Article 14(3)(g) of the Covenant, Article 7 (prohibiting the use of torture or cruel, inhuman or degrading treatment or punishment) and Article 10(1) (stating that all persons deprived of their liberty shall be treated with humanity and with respect for the inherent dignity of the individual) must be borne in mind, as methods violating these articles are frequently used to compel the accused to confess or to testify against himself.[34] Consequently, laws should require that evidence provided through such means *or any form of compulsion* should be entirely unacceptable.[35] In its case law, it has held that Article 14 should be understood in terms of the absence of any direct or indirect physical or psychological pressure from the investigating authorities on the accused with a view to obtaining a confession of guilt.[36] The committee has also considered that it is implicit in this principle that the prosecution prove that the confession was made without duress.[37]

It would seem that the Human Rights Committee has therefore considered that the privilege is primarily useful as a means of preventing states from using coercive means in their attempt to obtain confessions. This doctrine of

---

[31] S. Trechsel, *Human Rights in Criminal Proceedings* (Oxford University Press, 2005) 340.

[32] See, e.g. *Cantoral-Benavides* v. *Peru*, where the IACtHR concluded that by subjecting the applicant to torture to break down his psychological resistance and force him to incriminate himself or confess to certain illegal activities, the respondent state had violated Art. 8(2)(g) and 8(3) ACHR. The HRC has constantly expressed concern in its general observations about the systematic use of torture in order to extract confessions. See, e.g. ICCPR, A/52/40 vol. I (1997) paras. 241–2, 357; ICCPR, A/56/40 vol. I (2001) 59 para. 79(8), 70 para. 81(8); ICCPR, A 59/40 vol. I (2003) 15 para. 63(12); ICCPR, A/60/40 vol. I (2004) 25 para. 82(13); and ICCPR, A/60/40 vol. I (2005) 70 para. 92(10).

[33] Yugoslavia, CAT, A54/44 (1999) 6 at para. 45. The committee has constantly recommended that states expressly legislate to make inadmissible evidence obtained through torture. (See its reports for Slovakia, Brazil, Togo, Russian Federation, Sweden, Uzbekistan, Cambodia and Belgium.)

[34] HRC, General Comment 13, Art. 14 (Twenty-first session, 1984), para. 14, Compilation of General Comments and General Recommendations Adopted by Human Rights Treaty Bodies, UN Doc. HRI\GEN\I\Rev 1 at 14 (1994).

[35] Emphasis added.   [36] *Berry* v. *Jamaica*.

[37] *Nallaratnam* v. *Sri Lanka*, para. 7.4; and *Ganga* v. *Guyana*, para. 5.1.

non-compulsion is reminiscent of the voluntariness doctrine at common law and can lead to problems in assessing whether the applicant was really compelled to speak.[38] It is clear that mere moral exhortation is not enough to amount to compulsion.[39] It is different, however, where suspects or accused persons are legally required to provide information or to testify. These situations have been the focus of much of the jurisprudence of the ECtHR on the subject.

8.2.2 *Funke* v. *France*

Despite the absence of any reference to the privilege in Article 6 of the ECHR, the Committee of Experts which reported to the Committee of Ministers of the Council of Europe on the differences between the ICCPR and the ECHR considered that the prohibition of self-indictment was of the 'very essence' of a fair trial.[40] It was not until 1993 in *Funke* v. *France* that the ECtHR made its first pronouncement on the privilege, although the European Court of Justice had recognised in an earlier case the right of a company not to incriminate itself.[41] In *Funke*, customs officers who suspected the applicant of breaching exchange control regulations issued orders to the applicant to produce details of foreign bank accounts, which he was required to do under French customs law. In the space of a few lines and with little explanation, the ECtHR upheld the applicant's argument that the authorities had violated Article 6 in bringing proceedings to compel the applicant to cooperate in a prosecution mounted against him. The ECtHR considered that the special features of customs law could not justify 'such an infringement of the right of anyone "charged with a criminal offence", within the autonomous meaning of this expression in Article 6 to remain silent and not to contribute to incriminating himself'.[42]

There are two preliminary points that are worth emphasising about this rather elliptical statement. Firstly, it is to be noted that here and elsewhere in its jurisprudence the ECtHR referred to the privilege against self-incrimination and the right of silence together, suggesting that they are one and the same thing.

---

[38] See discussion in Ch. 6.4.2.   [39] *Castillo Petruzzi and others* v. *Peru*, 30 May 1999.
[40] Council of Europe, *Report of the Committee of Experts on Human Rights to the Committee of Ministers* (1970) para. 141(vi).
[41] See Case C-374/87, *Orkem* v. *Commission* [1989] ECR 3283. Interestingly, however, the court held, contrary it would appear to the ruling in *Funke*, that while the European Commission could not compel an undertaking to provide it with answers which might involve an admission, it could be required to disclose documents even if they are then used to establish against it the existence of anti-competitive conduct. See M. O'Boyle, 'Freedom from Self-Incrimination and the Right of Silence: A Pandora's Box?', in P. Mahoney, F. Matscher, H. Petzold and L. Wildhaber (eds.), *Protecting Human Rights: The European Perspective: Studies in memory of Rolv Ryssdal* (Cologne: Carl Heymanns Verlag KG, 2000) 1021.
[42] Para. 44.

In fact, as has been helpfully pointed out, they are better seen as represented by two partly overlapping circles.[43] On the one hand, the right to silence is narrower in that it refers to acoustic communication, whereas in *Funke* the subject matter concerned documents. On the other hand, the right of silence is commonly considered to be much wider as it refers not just to self-incriminating statements, but any statements at all.[44] In this wider sense, the right can refer to a general immunity from being compelled to answer questions by other persons or bodies, including the state.[45] This immunity reflects the idea that persons should be free from any inquiry made of them, but it takes only a moment's reflection to realise how difficult it would be for any legal system to operate if this immunity were truly enforced. If this were the case, citizens could avoid giving evidence in legal proceedings, with the result that it could prove impossible to prove anything.

The second point is that the ECtHR appeared to confine the immunities to persons who had been charged within the autonomous meaning which the ECtHR has attached to 'charged'. We shall come to this meaning later. For the moment, however, it may be noted that the ECtHR did not have to restrict these immunities to such persons. Indeed, in a case which predated *Funke* but which never got to the ECtHR because of a friendly settlement, the European Commission recognised a general right of silence as the negative counterpart of the right to freedom of expression enshrined in Article 10 of the ECHR.[46] The Commission here appeared to build into this broader right of silence a recognition of the fact that when individuals are required to incriminate themselves out of their own mouth (whether or not they are actually charged), this involves a particular intrusion on individuals by forcing them to act against their own interest which is entitled to particular weighting, although the more likely that criminal proceedings will be taken against them as a result, arguably, the more powerful this weighting should be.[47] This broader right of silence giving weighting to a general privilege against self-incrimination has not, however, been developed in the later jurisprudence of the Commission and the ECtHR,[48] although as we shall see, the rationale behind it, the liberty of the individual to withhold information from the state, is arguably a sounder one than that provided by the ECtHR for the more specific privilege against self-incrimination recognised in Article 6 of the ECHR, which is confined to situations where an accused has been charged. Before coming to the rationale, let us examine the specific requirements that trigger the protection of the privilege.

---

[43] Trechsel, *Human Rights in Criminal Proceedings*, 342.
[44] Roberts and Zuckerman, *Criminal Evidence*, 540.
[45] See *Smith* v. *Director of Serious Fraud Office* [1993] AC 1, 30, per Lord Mustill.
[46] *K* v. *Austria*.
[47] See also *Ferreira* v. *Levin and others*, 1996 (1) BCLR 1, 123, para. 258, per Sachs J.
[48] See, e.g. *Serves* v. *France*.

8.2.3 Charged with a criminal offence

The confinement of the privilege and the right to silence under Article 6 of the ECHR to persons charged with criminal proceedings was emphasised in the later case of *Saunders* v. *United Kingdom*, which did more than *Funke* to clarify the scope of these protections. In this case, Inspectors of the Department of Trade and Industry in England and Wales had a power under section 434 of the Companies Act 1985 to question individuals with a penalty of up to two years' imprisonment for failure to answer questions. The court held that the admission of the answers in the applicant's subsequent trial breached Article 6. But what was objectionable was the *use* of compelled answers in criminal proceedings and not the original compulsory questioning under the inspection, which was a purely administrative investigation.[49]

This was an important clarification regarding the scope of the privilege which made it clear that the privilege could only have a reach in criminal proceedings, but at the same time within these proceedings the privilege extends not just directly to protect suspects from incriminating themselves, but also indirectly to the use made of any self-incriminating information against them at their trial. Clearly, as we have seen, there would be little point prohibiting torture if government authorities were able to use information obtained by torture at their trial. We saw above that the Human Rights Committee has commented that legislation ought to exclude the admissibility as evidence of all statements obtained in violation of the privilege.[50] At the same time, it is not so obvious that statements should be immune from use in criminal proceedings where these were obtained in the course of procedures where it is considered legitimate to place a legal obligation to answer questions such as in the administrative proceedings with which Saunders was faced. If compulsory questioning in an administrative setting is justified and it furnishes evidence of criminal activity, why should evidence of that criminal activity not be able to be used in a criminal trial?[51]

Another difficulty arising from the *Saunders* case is to determine the dividing line between administrative and criminal proceedings in situations where one may be under suspicion of criminal activity in the administrative proceedings. The ECtHR has taken a broad view of criminal proceedings, extending it to early stages where the applicant may not have been technically charged within the national law.[52] In *Funke* itself, no proceedings had been brought against the applicant when he was asked to produce documents, although he was aware that he was suspected of criminal activity. Similarly, in *Heaney and McGuinness* v. *Ireland*, the prosecution of two applicants for withholding information which

---

[49] See also *Fayed* v. *United Kingdom*; *Abas* v. *Netherlands* (dec.); and *IJL, GMR and AKP* v. *United Kingdom*, where the European organs made it clear that compulsory powers to answer questions outside criminal investigations did not infringe Art. 6.
[50] See General Comment No. 13 1984, para. 14.   [51] See Sedley, 'Wringing out the Fault', 120.
[52] cf. *Shannon* v. *United Kingdom*.

they were compulsorily required to give about their whereabouts when they were arrested on suspicion of terrorist acts was held to be a breach of the privilege. As in *Funke*, the applicants were faced with criminal sanctions because they had failed to supply information to the authorities investigating them for criminal offences. These cases make it clear that a breach can occur at these early stages even when the state does not go on to prosecute the applicants for the offences they were suspected of, thereby illustrating in contrast to what occurred in *Saunders* that the incriminated material does not have to be used at trial for the protection to come into play. By contrast, a requirement to disclose assets for tax purposes when there were no pending or anticipated proceedings has fallen outside the protection of the privilege.[53] Sometimes, however, there would seem to be fine distinctions made on the question of whether proceedings were pending. In *Weh* v. *Austria*, the applicant's car was seen to break the city speed limit and when criminal proceedings were opened against unknown offenders, he was ordered as the registered car owner to disclose who had been driving his car and was subsequently fined for submitting insufficient and vague information. By a close majority of four votes to three, the ECtHR considered that this case fell outside the scope of the privilege as criminal proceedings were not pending against him and there was nothing to show that he was 'substantially affected' so as to consider him charged with the offence of speeding within the autonomous meaning of Article 6.[54]

8.2.4 Incrimination

Where an applicant is effectively 'charged' within the autonomous meaning given to the Convention and comes within the protection of Article 6, there would seem generally to be three conditions to be satisfied before the protection of the privilege comes into play: firstly, incrimination; secondly, compulsion; and, thirdly, defiance of the will of the accused.[55] Again, however, the boundaries have not always been clearly determined by the ECtHR. As regards incrimination, the ECtHR does not limit the privilege merely to statements detrimental to the applicant, vindicating perhaps its equation of the privilege with a right of silence. In the *Saunders* case, the applicant had not made any incriminating statements and the government sought to argue that only incriminating

---

[53] *Abas* v. *Netherlands* (dec.); *IJL, GMR and AKP* v. *United Kingdom*; and *Allan* v. *United Kingdom* (dec.). Cf. *JB* v. *Switzerland*, where proceedings had already been opened against the applicant when he was requested to provide information on investments made by him.

[54] *Weh* v. *Austria*, para. 54. But see the dissenting opinion of Judges Lorenzen, Levits and Hajiyev.

[55] In a number of judgments, the court has consistently stated that the right not to incriminate oneself presupposes that 'the prosecution in a criminal case seek to prove their case against the accused without resort to evidence obtained through methods of coercion or oppression in defiance of the will of the accused'. See, e.g. *Saunders* v. *United Kingdom* [GC], para. 68; *Heaney and McGuinness* v. *Ireland*, para. 40; and *JB* v. *Switzerland*, para. 64. By analogy, the USSC has said that the Self-Incrimination Clause contains three elements: compulsion, incrimination and testimony. *Fisher* v. *United States*, 425 US 391, 408 (1976).

statements fell within the scope of the privilege. But the ECtHR considered that the right not to incriminate oneself could not be confined in this way, for testimony obtained under compulsion which appears on its face to be of an non-incriminating nature – such as exculpatory remarks or mere information on questions of fact – may later be deployed in support of the prosecution case.[56] *Saunders* can be contrasted with *Weh* v. *Austria*, where one of the reasons why the ECtHR did not consider that the applicant was 'substantially affected' so as to be charged was because he was being asked questions in his capacity as a car owner and only had to state who had been driving his car at the time when it was seen to break the speed limit, which was not in itself incriminating.[57] Instead of incriminating himself, the applicant gave the name of a third party. But the minority took the view that he could have been the driver and there was therefore a risk that he might incriminate himself. Only if the owner of the car could not have been the driver would there be no risk of incrimination by being compelled to identify the driver.[58]

8.2.5 Compulsion

The second condition requires that there is compulsion. While we have seen that the ICCPR and ACHR expressly refer to compulsion, the ECtHR has at various times referred to 'compulsion', 'coercion' and 'oppression'.[59] On occasions, it has referred to 'improper compulsion', which is tautological as it does not tell us what types of coercion are proper.[60] Although the ECtHR has veered away from giving an 'abstract analysis' of what constitutes 'improper compulsion',[61] its approach has been to consider whether the degree of compulsion imposed on the accused destroyed the 'very essence' of the privilege against self-incrimination and the right to remain silent.[62] As we have seen, there is clearly a spectrum of pressure that can be put on a person to speak from the infliction of torture, cruel and inhuman treatment at one end, through to requiring answers under pain of penalty through to applying moral pressure and simply directing questions to the person. The ECtHR has not always been clear about the boundary lines and on occasions it has suggested that even the pain of a financial penalty need not encompass compulsion.[63] As soon as we stray beyond using the concept of compulsion as a legal duty to provide information and extend it to

---

[56] Para. 71. [57] Para. 54.
[58] *Weh* v. *Austria*, dissenting opinion of Judges Lorenzen, Levits and Hajiyev, para. 2.
[59] See, e.g. *Saunders* v. *United Kingdom* [GC], para. 68; *Heaney and McGuinness* v. *Ireland*, para. 40; and *JB* v. *Switzerland*, para. 64.
[60] Trechsel, *Human Rights in Criminal Proceedings*, 347.
[61] *John Murray* v. *United Kingdom* [GC], para. 46.
[62] The term 'very essence' of the privilege seems to have first appeared in *John Murray* v. *United Kingdom*, para. 49. It was extensively used in *Heaney and McGuinness* v. *Ireland*, paras. 48, 55 and 58.
[63] In *King* v. *United Kingdom (No. 2)* (dec.), limited fines of up to £300 were held not to be 'coercion'; a fine of £700, however, was held to be coercion in *JB* v. *Switzerland*. See also the discussion in *Lückhof and Spanner* v. *Austria*, para. 54.

cover conduct used to induce or incriminate, there are bound to be difficult dividing lines. We have seen that the Human Rights Committee has considered that direct or indirect physical or psychological pressure comes within the scope of the privilege, but that the Inter-American Court of Human Rights has considered that being urged to tell the truth does not come within its scope. This presumably rules out the need for any warning to suspects that they need not answer questions.[64]

The ECtHR has not addressed these questions very clearly, but it has ruled that warning suspects that adverse inferences may be drawn at their trial from a decision to remain silent during police questioning does not amount to improper compulsion.[65] The ECtHR has emphasised the difference between direct compulsion of the threat of criminal sanctions, such as that with which the applicant was faced in *Funke*, and a certain level of 'indirect compulsion', which is acceptable.[66] It has accepted that a system which warns the accused who is possibly without legal assistance that adverse inferences may be drawn from a refusal to provide an explanation to the police for his presence at the scene of the crime or to testify during his trial, when taken in conjunction with the weight of the case against him, involves a certain amount of 'indirect compulsion'. But since this does not compel the suspect to speak or to testify, this fact on its own cannot be decisive.[67] It is not surprising that the ECtHR has preferred not to be drawn into an abstract analysis of what amounts to improper compulsion or how much 'indirect compulsion' may be used. But the result is a degree of uncertainty about where the dividing line should be.

8.2.6 Defiance of the will of the suspect

The third condition – the need for defiance of the will of the suspect – has caused even greater problems of interpretation. In *Funke*, as we have seen, the documents relating to the accounts that the applicant was required to hand over were considered to come within the privilege. But in *Saunders*, the ECtHR considered that the right not to incriminate oneself is primarily concerned with respecting the will of an accused person to remain silent and did not extend to the use in criminal proceedings of material which may be obtained from the accused through the use of compulsory powers, but which 'has an existence independent of the will of the suspect such as documents pursuant to a warrant, breath, blood and urine samples, and bodily tissues for the purpose of DNA testing'.[68]

The ECtHR made the point that this distinction conforms with the laws of many contracting parties of the Convention and elsewhere.[69] But it did

---

[64] See Trechsel, *Human Rights in Criminal Proceedings*, 352–3.
[65] *John Murray* v. *United Kingdom* [GC].   [66] Ibid., paras. 49 and 50.
[67] Ibid., para. 50.   [68] Para. 69.
[69] Ibid. In the United States, for example, the Fifth Amendment protects only against compelled testimonial communications: see *Schmerber* v. *California*, 384 US 757 (1966), excluding the taking of blood samples from the scope of the privilege. See R. J. Allen and M. K. Mace, 'The

not offer any principled justification for the distinction between testimonial and real evidence and critics have claimed that the distinction was little more than a pragmatic attempt to rein back the scope of the privilege.[70] In his dissenting judgment, Judge Martens raised the question of why a suspect should be free from coercion to make incriminating statements, but not from coercion to cooperate to furnish incriminating data.[71] It can be argued that, strictly speaking, the court was referring to compulsory powers to obtain evidence such as breath, blood or urine samples which can be taken by force without any cooperation from the suspect and therefore without any coercion of his will.[72] This does something to explain the decision in *Funke*, where the applicant's documents were obtained by requiring him to hand them over rather than by a warrant. Although such documents had 'an existence independent of the will', their production depended on the applicant's cooperation in handing them over. But some of the other examples of the ECtHR, such as breath and urine samples, do seem to require some cooperation on the part of the suspect if they are to be taken effectively and therefore on this distinction would seem to come within the scope of the privilege.

The distinction between testimonial evidence and real evidence came into focus again in *Jalloh* v. *Germany*, where it will be recalled that emetics were forcibly administered to the applicant after he was seen to swallow a tiny plastic bag or bubble thought to contain drugs when he was approached by police officers. In a majority decision, the Grand Chamber of the ECtHR considered that in addition to breaching Articles 3 and 8 of the Convention, the German authorities had also undermined the applicant's privilege against self-incrimination. The court repeated its statement in *Saunders* that the privilege is commonly understood in the contracting states to be concerned with respecting the will of the defendant to remain silent in the face of questioning and not to be compelled to provide a statement.[73] Referring to *Funke* and *JB* v. *Switzerland*, however, it stated that it had on occasion given the privilege a broader meaning so as to encompass cases in which coercion to hand over real evidence to the

---

Self-Incrimination Clause Explained and its Future Predicted' (2004) 94 *Journal of Criminal Law & Criminology* 243. English law permits compulsory powers to be used to obtain non-intimate samples and inferences to be drawn from a refusal without good cause to consent to the taking of intimate samples: see ss. 62(10) and 63 Police and Criminal Evidence Act 1984. See generally I. H. Dennis, 'Instrumental Protection, Human Right or Functional Necessity: Reassessing the Privilege against Self-Incrimination' (1995) 54 *Cambridge Law Journal* 342; and Easton, *The Case for the Right of Silence*. In Canada, however, it is now settled that the principle of self-incrimination applies to compulsion relating to products of the mind and of the body: see *R* v. *B (SA)* [2003] 2 SCR 678. See D. M. Paciocco and L. Stuesser, *The Law of Evidence* (Toronto: Irwin Law, 2005).

[70] B. Emmerson, A. Ashworth and A. MacDonald, *Human Rights and Criminal Justice*, 2nd edn (London: Sweet & Maxwell, 2007) 620–1.

[71] Para. 12.

[72] M. Redmayne, 'Rethinking the Privilege against Self-Incrimination' (2007) 27 *Oxford Journal of Legal Studies* 209, 214–15.

[73] *Jalloh* v. *Germany* [GC], para. 110.

authorities was at issue.[74] In the ECtHR's view, the evidence in the present case, namely, drugs hidden in the applicant's body which were obtained by the forcible administration of emetics, could be considered to fall into the category of material having an existence independent of the will of the suspect, the use of which was generally not prohibited in criminal proceedings.[75] However, there were several elements which distinguished the present case from the examples listed in *Saunders*.[76] Firstly, as in the *Funke* and *JB* cases, the administration of emetics was used to retrieve real evidence in defiance of the applicant's will. Conversely, the bodily material listed in *Saunders* concerned material obtained by coercion for forensic examination with a view to detecting, for example, the presence of alcohol or drugs. Secondly, the degree of force differed significantly from the degree of compulsion required to obtain the types of materials referred to in *Saunders* and, thirdly, the evidence in the present case was obtained by means of a procedure which violated Article 3 of the ECHR.

It is suggested that these distinctions hardly mark out a clear distinction between this case and the examples given in *Saunders*. With regard to the first distinction, there is a difference between forcibly retrieving real evidence, which in itself incriminates the suspect, and using coercion to obtain material, which requires further forensic examination, but in each case the suspect's will is surely defied. The second and third distinctions relating to the degree of force and to the violation of Article 3 may be valid distinctions in so far as how the actions impacted on the suspect's bodily integrity, but it is difficult to see how they are relevant to the issue of incrimination. In each case, the effect of the authorities' actions is to incriminate the suspect. It is hard to escape the view that the court wanted to include the authorities' actions in *Jalloh* within the scope of the privilege because of the extreme degree of force and coercion that was used in obtaining the incriminating material. But the court was able to use other articles in the Convention to hold these actions in breach without having to rely upon the privilege against self-incrimination. In failing to distinguish satisfactorily the *Saunders* examples, the ECtHR only added to the uncertainty as to its proper scope.[77]

Although the decision in *Jalloh* seemed to be affected by the extreme degree of compulsion and force used, we have seen that the ECtHR has also extended the privilege to situations where there was no direct compulsion and defiance of will, but where the suspect was tricked into making admissions, with the result that his freedom of choice whether to speak or remain silent was effectively undermined.[78] In *Allan* v. *United Kingdom*, the ECtHR held that there was a violation of the right to silence and a violation of Article 6 when an accused had chosen to remain silent and was then led to make a confession by an informant who was put into his cell. The ECtHR drew on Canadian jurisprudence, however,

---

[74] Ibid., para. 111.   [75] Ibid., para. 113.   [76] Ibid., paras. 113–15.
[77] See also the concurring opinion of Judge Bratza attached to the judgment in *Jalloh*.
[78] See Ch. 6.4.2.

to hold that the right would only be infringed where the informant was acting as an agent of the state at the time the accused made the statement.[79]

The use of informants to question suspects in custody has also been contrasted with using informants to question suspects out of custody in a situation where the suspect is free to speak to the informant or to refuse to do so, which the ECtHR in *Bykov* v. *Russia* considered did not contain the same degree of coercion or oppression.[80] But although the circumstances in which the statements were made in *Allan* and *Bykov* were somewhat different, it is hard to say in either case that the applicant was compelled to make a confession.[81] If attention is directed less upon the suspect's freedom of choice and more upon the conduct of the authorities in inducing an informant to in effect play the role of an interrogator without providing the safeguards available to a suspect during questioning, then the decision in *Allan* may be justified not so much because it violated the privilege against self-incrimination, but rather because the suspect was not given the institutional safeguards available for informed participation. The suspect in *Bykov* was equally deprived of these safeguards and this raises questions as to whether Bykov was not similarly deprived of his right to a fair trial.[82] For present purposes, it may be doubted whether the privilege against self-incrimination with its focus on will and compulsion provides a sufficiently clear ground for making a distinction between the outcome in *Allan* and *Bykov*, and this raises questions as to how strong a contribution the privilege can play in protecting fair trial standards. Before we come to the rationale for the privilege, however, we must consider whether the ECtHR was prepared to make exceptions to the application of the privilege in certain instances.

8.3 Exception to the rights against self-incrimination and of silence

8.3.1 The public interest

Although the ECtHR in *Saunders* did not find it necessary to decide whether the right not to incriminate oneself is absolute or whether infringements may be justified in particular circumstances,[83] in subsequent cases the ECtHR has stated that neither the right of silence nor the right not to incriminate oneself are absolute rights.[84] In the earlier cases, however, there would appear to have been a reluctance to allow the rights to be balanced against the pursuit of legitimate aims in the public interest. In *Saunders*, the ECtHR did not accept

---

[79] *Allan* v. *United Kingdom*, para. 51. See *R* v. *Hebert* [1990] 2 SCR 151. Cf. also *R* v. *McKeown* [2003] NICC 3.
[80] *Bykov* v. *Russia* [GC], para. 102.
[81] See, e.g. Dennis, 'Reassessing the Privilege against Self-Incrimination', 366.
[82] cf. *R* v. *Bryce* (1992) 95 Cr App R 320 (incriminating answers to questions put by a police officer acting under cover excluded by English Court of Appeal on the ground that the questions amounted to an interrogation which circumvented the formal framework for questioning suspects and adversely affected the fairness of the proceedings).
[83] Paras. 69 and 74.   [84] *O'Halloran and Francis* v. *United Kingdom*, para. 53.

the government's argument that 'the complexity of corporate fraud and the vital public interest in the investigation of such fraud and the punishment of those responsible could justify such a marked departure as that which occurred in the present case from one of the basic principles of a fair procedure'.[85] In the ECtHR's view, both the fairness requirement of Article 6 and the privilege itself applied to criminal proceedings in respect of all types of criminal offences without distinction, from the most simple to the most complex. As a result, the public interest could not be invoked to justify the use of answers compulsorily obtained in a non-judicial investigation to incriminate the accused during the trial proceedings.[86]

This suggests that the ECtHR was not prepared to engage in a balancing act such as is required in respect of other rights in the Convention, for example, the right of freedom of expression, whereby a legitimate aim such as the need to provide for public safety may justify an infringement of the right provided it is in accordance with law and necessary to achieve this aim. This was precisely the kind of approach taken by the Irish Supreme Court in the *Heaney and McGuinness* case to justify the constitutionality of the provision in the Offences Against the State Act, which required persons to give a full account of their movements during a specified period.[87] Reserving its opinion on whether the case affected the fair trial right guaranteed by the Constitution, the court preferred to base its decision on the proposition that the right to silence was but a corollary to the freedom of expression conferred by Article 40 of the Constitution. It went on to specify that the qualifying language of Article 40, which states that the guarantee is subject to public order and morality, meant that a proportionality test had to be applied and in applying this test it considered that the prima facie entitlement of citizens to exercise their right of silence had to yield to the right of the state to protect itself.[88] The ECtHR, on the other hand, took the view as we have seen that the conviction of the applicants for failing to comply with the provision constituted a breach of their fair trial right. In the ECtHR's view, the 'degree of compulsion' imposed on the applicants by the application of the Offences Against the State Act with a view to compelling them to provide information relating to charges against them under the Act in effect destroyed the very essence of the privilege and the security and public order concerns of the government could not justify a provision which extinguished this essence.[89]

This approach suggests that when an infringement goes to the 'essence of the privilege', it can never be justified whatever the countervailing public interest considerations. But in *Jalloh* v. *Germany*, the ECtHR seemed to cast doubt

---

[85] Para. 74.
[86] This was also the view of the Commission: 'The right of silence must apply as equally to alleged company fraudsters as to those accused of other types of fraud, rape, murder or terrorist offences' (paras. 329–30).
[87] *Heaney and McGuinness* v. *Ireland*.
[88] For a full discussion, see D. McGrath, *Evidence* (Dublin: Thomson Round Hall, 2005), 634–7.
[89] Para. 55.

on this by stating that in determining whether there has been a violation of the privilege, the ECtHR *will* consider the weight of the public interest in the investigation and punishment of the offence.[90] In this case, the impugned measure targeted a street dealer who was offering drugs for sale on a comparably small scale and was finally given a six-month suspended prison sentence and probation. As a result, the public interest in securing the applicant's conviction could not justify recourse to such a grave interference with his physical and mental integrity. But in applying this balancing test, the ECtHR left open the possibility that the privilege could be infringed in the public interest, something that seemed to be precluded in *Saunders* and *Heaney and McGuinness*. Not only content with adding uncertainty to the scope of the privilege, this judgment compounds this uncertainty by suggesting that a certain degree of balancing of the privilege against the public interest may be appropriate.

8.3.2 Other factors

Apart from the question of the weight of the public interest in the investigation and punishment of the offence, the ECtHR in *Jalloh* mentioned a number of other factors to be taken into account in determining whether the applicant's right not to incriminate himself has been violated: the nature and degree of the compulsion, the existence of relevant safeguards in the procedure and the use to which any material so obtained is put.[91] We have seen that the ECtHR had already accepted that not all forms of compulsion infringe the privilege, although this opens the door to further uncertainty. There is also the suggestion here that if there are relevant safeguards in the procedure, these may be enough to offset a finding that there has been a violation of the privilege. The ECtHR observed that section 81a of the German Code of Criminal Procedure provided that bodily intrusions had to be carried out *lege artis* by a doctor in a hospital and only if there was no risk of damage to the defendant's health. In this case, however, the applicant refused to submit to a prior medical examination. He could only communicate in broken English, which meant that he was subjected to the procedure without a full examination of his physical aptitude to withstand it. This, however, raises the question of whether the ECtHR might have been prepared to consider that there was no violation of the privilege if he had been subjected to a proper medical examination. It is hard to see how safeguards to protect the applicant's *physical* health could affect the essence of the privilege with which the court has said it is primarily concerned respecting the will of the accused. The suggestion that there may be compensating safeguards which may be enough to offset the privilege raises questions, which we shall see, about how significant the privilege is in the first place as a protection for accused persons.

---

[90] Para. 117 [GC].
[91] See also *Tirado Ortiz and Lozano Martin* v. *Spain*; *Heaney and McGuinness* v. *Ireland*, paras. 51–5; and *Allan* v. *United Kingdom*, para. 44.

Finally, the ECtHR's reference to the use to which any material obtained is put as a factor in determining whether the right against self-incrimination has been violated suggests that there may be circumstances when the court may consider that incriminating material may be used against the accused at trial. Unlike Judge Morenilla, who expressed the view in his concurring opinion in *Saunders* that the very fact that the applicant's statements were admitted in evidence against him undermined the very essence of his right not to incriminate himself, the ECtHR did not go so far as to rule out the possibility that some use could be made of the statements.[92] In *Jalloh*, the ECtHR stated that the drugs obtained following the administration of the emetics were the decisive evidence in the applicant's conviction for drugs-trafficking, thereby suggesting an analogy with the approach taken by the ECtHR towards the testimony of witnesses whom the defence has had no opportunity of examining.[93] In cases involving the issue of self-incrimination, the ECtHR has not as frequently resorted to asking itself whether the proceedings as a whole were unfair, notwithstanding the breach of the privilege, but there are suggestions here that the privilege is less than absolute. It is to be noted that the question here is not a legal question requiring some judgment be made about the importance of the privilege against other principles or public interests. It is more a factual question of whether in the light of other evidence in the trial, the self-incriminating aspect could not be considered significant and therefore to have affected the overall fairness of the trial. Other questions that are raised by this approach are whether the use of derivative evidence obtained as a result of the information provided under compulsion can be used against the accused or whether the use of the incriminating material to impeach the accused's evidence or another witness might be acceptable as an alternative to using the evidence directly against the accused.[94]

Instead of re-affirming an approach that would justify certain infringements of the privilege only where they do not go to the 'essence of the privilege', *Jalloh* seemed to embark on a 'wholly new approach' whereby a wide range of factors may be considered in deciding whether a particular instance of self-incrimination constitutes a violation.[95] This approach was re-affirmed by the Grand Chamber in *O'Halloran and Francis* v. *United Kingdom*,[96] where the ECtHR held it could not accept that any direct compulsion requiring an accused person to make incriminatory statements automatically violated the privilege against self-incrimination. The central issue in each of the cases was whether the privilege was violated when the registered keeper of a car was required under

[92] O'Boyle, 'Freedom from Self-Incrimination', 1029.
[93] See discussion of witnesses in Ch. 4.2.3.
[94] O'Boyle, 'Freedom from Self-Incrimination', 1029–30.
[95] This was the view of the dissenting judge, Judge Pavlovschi, in *O'Halloran and Francis* v. *United Kingdom*. See also A. Ashworth, 'Commentary' [2007] *Criminal Law Review* 897.
[96] For comment, see S. Summers, 'Das Recht sich nicht selbst belasten zu müssen, Verkehrsdelikte und der Fall O'Halloran und Francis gegen Vereinigtes Königreich', in R. Schaffhauser (ed.), *Jahrbuch zum Strassenverkehrsrecht* (St Gallen: Schriftenreihe des IRP-HSG, 2009) 639.

UK road traffic law to furnish the name and address of the driver of the car when it was caught speeding on camera. The ECtHR followed *Jalloh* by referring to the factors mentioned in that case in order to determine that the privilege had not been infringed. As regards the nature and degree of the compulsion used to obtain the evidence, the ECtHR referred to Lord Bingham's opinion in the Privy Council case of *Brown* v. *Stott*[97] that all who own or drive motor cars know that they are subject to a regulatory regime which requires them to disclose certain information in the interest of public safety.

8.3.3 Inferences from silence

Aside from the uncertainty created by recent decisions as to whether particular instances of direct compulsion to incriminate will constitute a violation of the privilege, one question that the ECtHR did make clear at a comparatively early stage of its exposition of the right of silence was that an accused is not entitled to absolute immunity from his silence being used against him at trial. In *John Murray* v. *United Kingdom*, the applicant was arrested during a raid on a house in which a man had been kidnapped and pursuant to legislation permitting the courts to draw inferences in certain circumstances was asked to account for his presence in the house on pain of adverse silences being drawn against him if he refused to answer. The applicant remained silent throughout the period he was in police custody and the trial judge drew strong inferences against him for his refusal to account for his presence and for his refusal to testify at his trial. In a passage making it clear that there is no absolute immunity from a failure to answer questions, the ECtHR declared:

> On the one hand, it is self-evident that it is incompatible with the immunities under consideration to base a conviction solely or mainly on the accused's silence or on a refusal to answer questions or to give evidence himself. On the other hand, the court deems it equally obvious that these immunities cannot and should not prevent that the accused's silence, in situations which clearly call for an explanation from him, be taken into account in assessing the persuasiveness of the evidence adduced by the prosecution.[98]

Having licensed the 'indirect' compulsion of warning suspects that inferences may be used against them, it seems logical that the court should then permit courts to draw such inferences where the facts justify it, provided adequate safeguards are put in place. The ECtHR, however, made it clear in this and subsequent judgments that it would scrutinise very carefully the kinds of inferences that can be drawn in these circumstances. If courts were seen to be allowed to use silence too easily as a springboard for finding guilt, then this could indeed affect the fairness of the trial and also turn acceptable 'indirect compulsion' at the level of warning accused persons about the consequences of silence into

---

[97] [2001] 2 WLR 817.   [98] *John Murray* v. *United Kingdom* [GC], para. 47.

unacceptable compulsion. It is one thing to warn suspects that in the course of its fact-finding courts may give their silence some weight in evaluating the case against them. It is quite another for courts to penalise defendants for exercising their right of silence by making it count against the defendant come what may.[99] This would seem to raise the level of compulsion into a more direct category, while also offending the principles of rational fact-finding and of the need for proof beyond reasonable doubt.

Somewhat against its approach towards other areas of potentially unreliable evidence where we have seen national courts have been given considerable leeway in their evaluation of the evidence, the ECtHR has therefore been vigilant to see that silence has not been given greater weight in the decision of the national court than was appropriate. In the *John Murray* case, for example, the ECtHR went on to say in respect of the approach to be taken to the Northern Ireland Order permitting the drawing of inferences:

> The question in each particular case is whether the evidence adduced by the prosecution is sufficiently strong to require an answer. The national court cannot conclude that the accused is guilty merely because he chooses to remain silent. It is only if the evidence against the accused 'calls' for an explanation which the accused ought to be in a position to give that a failure to give any explanation 'may as a matter of common sense allow the drawing of an inference that there is no explanation and the accused is guilty'. Conversely if the case presented by the prosecution has so little evidential value that it called for no answer, a failure to provide one could not justify an inference of guilt. In sum, it is only common sense inferences which the judge considers proper, in the light of the evidence against the accused, that can be drawn under the Order.[100]

On the facts before it, the ECtHR considered that having regard to the weight of the evidence – the accused was arrested in the house where the kidnapped man was being held – the drawing of inferences from his refusal, at arrest, during police questioning and at trial to provide an explanation for his presence in the house was a matter of common sense and could not be regarded as unfair or unreasonable in the circumstances.[101]

This case – described by one commentator as the 'paradigm case for the drawing of "common sense" inferences'[102] – can be contrasted with others where the ECtHR was less convinced that inferences had been drawn appropriately. One of the ways in which the ECtHR can be satisfied that inferences have been drawn properly is by looking at the reasoned judgment of the court. The applicant in *John Murray* was tried by an 'experienced judge' and he was provided on his conviction with a reasoned judgment explaining the reasons for his decision to draw inferences and the weight attached to them.[103] No such

---

[99] Redmayne, 'Rethinking the Privilege against Self-Incrimination', 217–18.
[100] *John Murray* v. *United Kingdom* [GC], para. 51. [101] Ibid., para. 54.
[102] O'Boyle, 'Freedom from Self-Incrimination', 1035.
[103] *John Murray* v. *United Kingdom* [GC], para. 51.

safeguard was available in a jury trial and in a number of cases the ECtHR stressed how important it is therefore to scrutinise the directions that were given to the jury by the trial judge. In certain cases, the ECtHR has held that the trial judge did not give proper weight to the applicant's explanation for silence that he acted on the advice of his solicitor and did not emphasise that it must be consistent only with guilt before inferences could be drawn.[104] When an accused person remains silent after being advised to do so, it may be difficult for triers of fact to decide whether the accused was genuinely acting under legal advice or out of a fear that they have no answer to the charge.[105] The ECtHR in *Averill* v. *United Kingdom* reiterated its cautious approach by stating that the extent to which inferences can be drawn from an accused's failure to respond to questioning must necessarily be limited. While it may be expected that an innocent person would be willing to cooperate with the police in explaining that they were not involved in suspected crime, there may be reasons why in a specific case an innocent person would not be prepared to do so and the ECtHR considered that following a lawyer's advice will usually be an acceptable reason for silence.[106] In *Averill*, however, there appeared to be strong evidence against the accused in the form of fibres of hair and clothing matching fibres of clothing found at the scene of the crime. The accused explained his silence on the ground that it was his policy not to cooperate with the police, but the ECtHR considered that it was fair to draw inferences against him when such incriminating evidence was put to him.

Whatever the fairness in terms of the privilege against self-incrimination of drawing inferences from silence, the ECtHR's careful limitation on the circumstances when inferences can be drawn and its requirement that this may only be done where the failure to answer questions is consistent with guilt illustrates how limited the scope for drawing inferences is as a matter of logic. Of course, there may be cases where a court or jury may conclude that the reasons put forward for an accused's silence do not seem plausible and this may help them to decide that, say, a particular defence that is being run is not credible. Without an evidential basis on which to judge why an accused was silent other than the strength of the evidence against him, however, it would seem to be safe to conclude from the accused's silence that the accused has no explanation for the charge only when the court has already formed a view of the accused's guilt. But

---

[104] *Condron* v. *United Kingdom*; and *Beckles* v. *United Kingdom*.

[105] Matters have not been made easier for judges directing juries on this question or for juries as a result of a series of conflicting rulings of the Court of Appeal in England, some of which would seem to have crossed the line between directing juries on the logical inferences to be drawn in these circumstances and encouraging them to draw adverse inferences when they consider the defendants' silence was unreasonable. Cf. *R* v. *Betts and Hall* [2001] EWCA Crim 224; *R* v. *Howell* [2003] EWCA Crim 1; *R* v. *Knight* [2003] EWCA Crim 1977; *R* v. *Hoare* [2004] EWCA Crim 784; and *R* v. *Beckles* [2004] EWCA Crim 2766. For commentary, see Emmerson et al., *Human Rights and Criminal Justice*, 637–8; and M. Redmayne, 'English Warnings' (2008) 30 *Cardozo Law Review* 1047, 1066–71 (arguing that the case law is a 'sad mess').

[106] *Averill* v. *United Kingdom*, para. 47.

the inference then becomes merely an *ex post facto* rationalisation of what the court or jury is already convinced of and the legislation becomes redundant.[107] Domestic courts interpreting legislation which permits inferences to be drawn against defendants when they fail to mention facts under questioning have accepted that the legislation cannot apply when the fact that the defendant fails to mention becomes the central issue in the case.[108] In such cases, the jury cannot reject the accused's reason for not mentioning the fact without rejecting the truth of the fact itself and drawing an adverse inference cannot independently help to determine whether the defendant is guilty. If, on the other hand, the jury is using silence, in the words of one commentator, as 'evidential poly-filler' for cracks in the prosecution evidence,[109] then it will be doing so on the basis of pure speculation about the reasons for silence and not on the basis of evidence. Of course, one can understand how a failure to mention a defence earlier may enable a jury to be suspicious about a particular defence and this may warrant an inference that the defence is untrue, but this does not *in itself* justify an inference of guilt from silence.[110]

In permitting adverse inferences to be drawn from silence, the ECtHR would seem to have weakened the right of silence more than has been tolerated in a number of national jurisdictions across the common law/civil law divide where there is a general prohibition against the drawing of inferences from silence, although some jurisdictions have gone to greater lengths to prevent inferences being drawn than others.[111] Other international bodies have recognised the importance of not drawing inferences from the exercise of the right of silence. The Human Rights Committee has taken the view that the legislation in the United Kingdom permitting inferences to be drawn from the silence of accused persons violates various provisions of Article 14 of the ICCPR despite the range

---

[107] See J. Jackson, 'Interpreting the Silence Provisions: The Northern Ireland Cases' [1995] *Criminal Law Review* 587.

[108] See, e.g. *R* v. *Mountford* [1999] Crim LR 575; *R* v. *Gill* [2001] 1 Cr App R 160.

[109] R. Pattenden, 'Inferences from Silence' [1995] *Criminal Law Review* 602, 607.

[110] For a helpful discussion of the proper inferences to be drawn from a failure to mention facts, see Redmayne, 'English Warnings', 1055–8.

[111] In the United States, an extreme position is taken whereby the jury are not allowed even to be informed as to whether a defendant refused to answer questions by the police as the prosecution may not use at trial the fact that 'he stood mute or claimed his privilege in the face of accusation': *Miranda* v. *Arizona*, 384 US 436, 468 (1966); and *Doyle* v. *Ohio*, 426 US 610 (1976). There is also a total prohibition on any comment on the defendant's refusal to testify: *California* v. *Griffin*, 380 US 609 (1965). Moreover, lest jurors are tempted to draw their own inferences from silence, defence counsel may request that the judge instruct jurors that they are to attach no significance to the defendant's silence: *Carter* v. *Kentucky*, 450 US 288 (1981). Most states in Australia have enacted statutory provisions prohibiting comment by the prosecutor on the accused's failure to testify: see also s. 20 of the Uniform Evidence Act 1994. See also in Canada *R* v. *Noble* [1977] 1 SCR 874. There are now prohibitions on the use of silence to draw inferences in most continental European jurisdictions (Norway appears to be an exception), but they have been described as 'rather anemic', largely it would seem because of the strong cultural expectation that defendants will respond to questions. See Van Kessel, 'European Perspectives', 823, 833–5.

of safeguards built into the legislation.[112] The ICC Statute explicitly states that silence shall not be a consideration in the determination of guilt or innocence of the accused and the international criminal tribunals have chosen not to draw adverse inferences from the accused's exercise of the right to remain silent and not to testify at trial.[113]

The ECtHR has made the point that whatever the formal position, the courts in a considerable number of countries where evidence is freely assessed may have regard to all relevant circumstances, including the manner in which the accused has behaved or has conducted his defence, when evaluating the evidence in the case.[114] What distinguished the drawing of inferences under legislation permitting inferences was that in addition to the existence of the specific safeguards, it instituted as the Commission had said a 'formalised system which aims at allowing common-sense implications to play an open role in the assessment of evidence'.[115] The ECtHR here was making the important point that in many cases it is open to courts to draw inferences from silence as part of the process of determining guilt even when this is not openly acknowledged. The result is that, as Damaška has reminded us, even where formal doctrine forbids the drawing of unfavourable inferences from silence, the defendant's quite realistic concern that such inferences will, consciously or unconsciously, in fact be drawn acts in a typical case as a psychological pressure to speak and respond to questions.[116]

This comment was made in the context of discussing continental prohibitions on adverse inferences from a defendant's silence at trial. Earlier examinations will be revealed to the triers of fact. In the common law context, more can be done to shield juries from the defendant's conduct before trial. At trial, however, it is impossible to shield them from a defendant's refusal to testify. We have seen that there is a difference even here in that defendants do not have to expose themselves to questioning at trial and it may be that the pressure to speak is greater in the continental context where more immediate inferences can be drawn from a refusal to answer specific questions than from a general refusal to submit to questioning.[117] Nevertheless, it is very difficult to predict what effect a refusal to testify has on juries. Steps can be taken to warn juries not to attach significance to this, but who knows what effect such warnings have on the inner workings of jurors' minds.[118]

---

[112] HRC, ICCPR, A/50/40 vol. I (1995) 72, para. 424.
[113] Art. 55(2)(b) ICC Statute. See *Prosecutor* v. *Niyitegeka*, Trial Chamber, para. 46 (expressly stating that the chamber did not draw any adverse inference from the accused's failure to testify).
[114] *John Murray* v. *United Kingdom* [GC], para. 54.   [115] Ibid.
[116] Damaška, 'Evidentiary Barriers', 527.
[117] Ibid. On the difficulties in drawing inferences from a failure to testify, see Redmayne, 'English Warnings', 1071–80.
[118] For a summary of the general effect of warnings to disregard evidence on juries, see J. D. Lieberman, J. Arndt and M. Vess, 'Inadmissible Evidence and Pretrial Publicity: The Effects (and Ineffectiveness) of Admonitions to Disregard', in J. D. Lieberman and D. A. Krauss (eds.), *Jury Psychology: Social Aspects of Trial Processes* (Farnham: Ashgate, 2009) 67.

There is a further point that raises questions about the strategy of exercising the right of silence, which is that even if it were possible to prevent triers of fact drawing inferences from silence, triers of fact are left in the end with no countervailing explanation of the facts which appear to incriminate the accused. The exercise of the right may, in other words, protect the accused from self-incrimination, but it cannot obviously protect the accused from the incriminating effect of the evidence against him and the absence of any exculpatory explanation may harm his defence. The ECtHR has limited the drawing of inferences to situations where the evidence calls for an explanation. Although we have seen that the actual adverse inferences that can be drawn against an accused from his silence in such circumstances are limited, the failure to provide the court with an exculpatory explanation in such circumstances inevitably prevents it from being able to find a reasonable doubt. Of course, various innocent explanations may be put forward by counsel for the accused's behaviour, but in the absence of an evidentiary foundation for them, which may only be able to be provided by the accused, these are inevitably speculative. A distinction has been made in some jurisprudence between legal compulsion and tactical compulsion, holding that the privilege only protects legal and not tactical compulsion.[119] But in so far as defendants are encouraged by the privilege not to provide an explanation or not to testify, it may not serve the best interests of the defence.

This suggests that the interests of the defence may be better served by focusing on rights and safeguards enabling defendants to participate fairly in the forensic process than on encouraging defendants not to participate at all. In *John Murray*, the ECtHR attached weight to the fact that there were important safeguards in place designed to respect the rights of the defence, in particular that appropriate warnings were given to him about the legal effects of maintaining silence, that the prosecution had not established a prima facie case against the accused before inferences could be drawn, that the judge had a discretion as to whether inferences should be drawn and that he had to explain the reasons for the decision to draw inferences and the weight attached to them and that the exercise of his discretion was reviewable on appeal.[120]

These safeguards were concerned with ensuring that proper weight is attached to any inferences that are drawn from the defendant's silence. But the ECtHR also addressed the question of the degree of compulsion inherent in the situation in which the accused found himself when warned about the legal effects of maintaining silence. The applicant had asked to consult a lawyer when he was arrested, but access was delayed for 48 hours. The ECtHR considered that notwithstanding this, there was no indication that the applicant had failed to understand the significance of the warning given to him by the police prior to

---

[119] See, e.g. *R v. Darrach* (2000) 148 CCC (3d) 97, 121–4; and *R v. Warsing* (2002) 167 CCC (3d) 569. See Paciocco and Stuesser, *Law of Evidence*, 283–4.
[120] Para. 51.

seeing his solicitor. Consequently, the refusal of access did not detract from its conclusion that the drawing of inferences was not unfair or unreasonable. Nevertheless, although there was no breach of the privilege against self-incrimination under Article 6(1), the ECtHR considered that the denial of access for the first 48 hours was a breach of Article 6(3)(c) of the Convention, which guarantees a right to legal assistance. In particular, the ECtHR considered that since the Northern Ireland legislation permitted inferences to be drawn from silence, it was 'of paramount importance' for the rights of the defence that an accused had access to a lawyer at the initial stages of police interrogation. Accused persons were confronted with a fundamental dilemma relating to their defence: if they chose to remain silent, adverse inferences could be drawn against them, but if they chose to answer police questions, they might prejudice their defence. It followed that inferences should not be drawn against defendants until such time as they have been given the opportunity to obtain access to legal advice.

8.4 Rationale of the privilege and the right of silence[121]

The ECtHR first set out its rationale for the privilege in *Saunders* and it has restated this or parts of it in a number of subsequent judgments.[122] After reciting the claim made in *Funke* that the right to silence and the right not to incriminate oneself are generally recognised international standards which lie at the heart of the notion of a fair procedure, the ECtHR in *Saunders* continued:

> Their rationale lies, *inter alia*, in the protection of the accused against improper compulsion by the authorities thereby contributing to the avoidance of miscarriages of justice and to the fulfilment of the aims of Article 6 . . . The right not to incriminate oneself, in particular, presupposes that the prosecution in a criminal case seek to prove their case against the accused without resort to evidence obtained through methods of coercion or oppression in defiance of the will of the accused. In this sense the right is closely linked to the presumption of innocence contained in Article 6.2 of the Convention.

The right not to incriminate oneself is primarily concerned, however, with respecting the will of an accused person to remain silent.[123]

The first observation to make is that this statement links the rights very closely to the aims of a fair trial, putting them at the heart of a fair procedure. This takes them out of the realm of the general right of silence, which as we have seen is a principle that individuals generally should not have to account to the state for their actions or activities but one that may need to be balanced

---

[121] The following sections are derived from J. D. Jackson, 'Re-Conceptualising the Right of Silence as an Effective Fair Trial Standard' (2009) 58 *International and Comparative Law Quarterly* 835.
[122] See *John Murray* v. *United Kingdom* [GC], para. 45; *Serves* v. *France*, para. 46; *Quinn* v. *Ireland*, para. 40; *Heaney and McGuinness* v. *Ireland*, para. 40; *Allan* v. *United Kingdom*, para. 44; *JB* v. *Switzerland*, para. 64; and *Jalloh* v. *Germany* [GC], para. 100.
[123] *Saunders* v. *United Kingdom* [GC], paras. 68–9.

against other interests and principles and into the specific situation where an accused is charged with an offence where we have seen the ECtHR has not been so willing to engage in a balancing exercise. In this situation, the two rights come together to give an accused immunity not only from saying anything that might incriminate himself, but from saying anything at all.

At first sight it seems strange to say that the rights lie at the heart of a fair procedure as they prescribe negatively what constitutes an unfair procedure without positively setting out what is a fair procedure.[124] Perhaps the ECtHR here has fallen into the trap of relying upon the 'tyranny of slogans',[125] resorting to 'stirring rhetoric that may move the heart but leaves the intellect unconvinced'.[126] There is, however, a more charitable explanation for the ECtHR's statement. We have argued that the rights that lie at the heart of a fair procedure in Article 6 are best viewed as positive rights of participation for the accused, but that there is an important relationship between the negative right of non-participation and the positive right of participation, which is predicated on the principle that any positive participation by the accused must be on a voluntary basis[127] – hence the statement that the rights are 'primarily' concerned to respect the will of the accused. There is a difficulty, however, as we shall see in speaking of the voluntariness of an accused's will when he or she is being questioned by the police in their custody. Arguably, indeed anyone facing criminal charges is placed in a position where their freedom to choose whether or not to speak is extremely limited. The coercive situation of facing criminal charges also suggests why someone who is charged or suspected of an offence should be entitled to special protections over and above the general right to silence.

The ECtHR appears to provide two kinds of rationales: an intrinsic substantive rationale that it is in principle unfair to require accused persons to do anything that might incriminate themselves; and non-substantive rationales which claim that the requirement offends other basic rights and principles associated with a fair trial, such as the presumption of innocence and the need to avoid miscarriages of justice.[128] Looking first at the intrinsic rationale, a number of commentators taking their cue from Bentham have found it difficult to justify why there should be a special right to protect accused persons from being required to incriminate themselves. We have seen that accused persons

---

[124] Trechsel, *Human Rights in Criminal Proceedings*, 247–8.
[125] A. A. W. Alschuler, 'A Peculiar Privilege in Historical Perspective', in Helmolz et al., *Privilege against Self-Incrimination*, 200–1.
[126] Allen and Mace, 'The Self-Incrimination Clause Explained', 244. Treschel suggests that the statement is an unfortunate rhetorical turn which contributes little to the understanding of the provision: *Human Rights in Criminal Proceedings*, 348.
[127] See Ch. 4.4.
[128] This useful distinction has been made by McGrath, *Evidence*, 623. See also Dennis, 'Reassessing the Privilege against Self-Incrimination', 348 (making a distinction between theories concerned with 'accusatorial process norms' and theories concerned with upholding 'substantive values'). Roberts and Zuckerman, *Criminal Evidence*, 548 (making a distinction between intrinsic, conceptualist and instrumental rationales).

are already protected under the ICCPR, the ACHR and the ECHR in an absolute way from being forced to confess by the requirement that they are not to be subjected to torture, cruel, inhuman or degrading treatment.[129] In addition, persons are protected in the criminal process, although not in an absolute way, by a right to privacy and as we have seen arguably under Article 10 by a general right of silence. So what is it that justifies the additional protection from being required to incriminate oneself within the criminal process?

According to critics, we have to fall back here on the 'old woman's reason' given by Bentham that it is harsh to subject accused persons to the burden of self-incrimination or as the USSC has put it, to the 'cruel trilemma of self-accusation, perjury or contempt'.[130] Of course, in the reality of modern criminal justice systems, this trilemma is not as painful as is suggested here. As a general rule, defendants are not prosecuted for refusing to answer questions before trial and at trial are never prosecuted for contempt for failing to testify. The modern debate in many jurisdictions is instead directed to whether adverse evidential consequences should attach to silence.[131] In most continental jurisdictions, defendants are not sworn as witnesses, so no question of perjury arises and in common law jurisdictions there is no serious sanction for perjury when accused persons tell lies in their defence.[132] Of course, in telling lies, there is the risk that one might be caught out, but this takes us to the nub of the point made by many critics that the trilemma, if trilemma it be, is only faced by guilty persons.[133] Martens J. made this point forcibly in his dissenting opinion in *Saunders*,[134] when he said that this rationale cannot justify the immunities under discussion since they presuppose that the suspect is guilty, 'for an innocent person would not be subjected to such choices nor bring about his own ruin by answering questions truthfully'. Consequently, innocent suspects are not treated 'cruelly or unethically, whilst guilty suspects should not complain that society does not allow them to escape conviction by refusing to answer questions or otherwise hiding evidence'.

It has been suggested that we should not be too quick to accept these counter-arguments.[135] Distinctions based on the guilty and the innocent imply that there is *no* value in protecting a guilty person from self-incrimination. Yet under the general rubric of the right of silence already discussed, we should arguably give some weighting to situations when individuals are forced to act against their own interests.[136] Furthermore, there may be some justification for giving this additional weighting to defendants in the criminal process as there is then

---

[129] See Ch. 6.4.
[130] *Murphy v. Waterfront Commission*, 378 US 52, 55 (1964), per Goldberg J. For a critique of the old woman's reason, see Bentham, *Rationale of Judicial Evidence*, 230.
[131] Roberts and Zuckerman, *Criminal Evidence*, 541.   [132] Ibid., 550.
[133] R. J. Allen, 'The Simpson Affair, Reform of the Criminal Justice Process and Magic Bullets' (1996) 67 *University of Colorado Law Review* 989, 1021.
[134] Para. 9, n. 74.   [135] Redmayne, 'Rethinking the Privilege against Self-Incrimination', 221.
[136] See R. K. Greenawalt, 'Silence as a Moral and Constitutional Right' (1981) *William and Mary Law Review* 15, 39.

a stronger reason to believe that any self-incrimination will be acted upon. Conversely, the argument that the innocent are never subjected to cruel choices is also over-stated. As Redmayne has pointed out, imposing a duty to co-operate may sometimes confront innocent persons with difficult choices as where one may be compelled to incriminate others who are close to us.[137] He gives the example of the applicant in *Weh* who was asked to disclose the identity of the person driving his car. If he was not driving, then it was another person, presumably a friend. As Redmayne recognises, the same dilemma, however, confronts witnesses who are compelled to testify against an intimate person. We ought not lightly to impose requirements on a person to testify, but ultimately we consider that such arguments are counterbalanced by the need for the criminal justice system to have access to relevant information. Domestic and international systems rarely give absolute protection to confidential relationships. These arguments suggest that we should place *some* weight on the privilege against self-incrimination, but do not go so far as to make the case for it to be given the special status of a fair trial right entitling suspects and defendants to a special immunity from being compelled to provide self-incriminating information being used against them.

Another problem with a rationale based on respecting the will of the accused is that it is difficult to find a clear and coherent dividing line between what state conduct may be said to respect the will and what does not. We have seen that Judge Martens questioned the distinction between the use of material obtained by legal compulsion such as blood and urine samples and the use of material obtained in defiance of the will.[138] In both cases, the will of the suspect is not respected in that he is forced to bring about his own conviction. We have seen that the best interpretation of the distinction made by the ECtHR is to be found by equating the privilege with immunity from *wilfully* participating in one's own incrimination. This would include the handing over of documents, but would not include submitting to blood tests, although certain decisions such as *Jalloh* do not seem to square with this. There is still a problem, however, in finding a rationale which would justify handing over documents coming within the privilege, but not submitting to a blood test outside the privilege. In each case, there is compulsion in terms of restricting personal autonomy: in the one case by requiring the accused to act against his will; and in the other by requiring that he submit to interference with his body. Thus, the Supreme Court of Canada has recognised that the principle against self-incrimination applies to 'products of the mind and products of the body'.[139]

As the court recognised, some jurisdictions have tried to limit the compulsion to condemn oneself to testimonial rather than real evidence. This may seem an easier line to draw, although it can still lead to fine distinctions such as

---

[137] Redmayne, 'Rethinking the Privilege against Self-Incrimination', 222.
[138] Para. 12. [139] *R* v. *B (SA)* [2003] 2 SCR 678, para. 34.

what to do about lie detection tests.[140] But the difficulty remains that one can incriminate oneself in other ways than condemning oneself out of one's own mouth, and if the rationale for the principle is to be found in respecting the will of the suspect, why should these other forms of self-incrimination be excluded? One reason that has been given is that there is something inherently worse about the state invading the 'sanctum of the mind' for the purpose of incriminating an individual.[141] Another point of difference is that real evidence is frequently more 'objective' and reliable, with the result that it can be of considerable assistance in a criminal investigation.[142] But these would seem to be arguments better made in the context of considering whether the privilege should be given more or less force to specific situations rather than for making hard and fast distinctions based on what should be included or excluded within the privilege. Thus, although the Supreme Court of Canada has considered that body samples may come within the privilege, the key question is whether in each case the search for truth outweighs self-incrimination concerns about the abuse of state power.[143] This is reminiscent of the kind of balancing exercise required in respect of a number of qualified rights under the Convention, such as the right of privacy under Article 8 and the freedom of expression under Article 10. But it is not as we have seen an approach that the ECtHR has developed in relation to the privilege against self-incrimination. Although the court could go down this road,[144] it raises the question again, however, as to whether a special right against self-incrimination has any particular rationale that could not be served by the rights to privacy and silence that we have seen already exist or may be deduced under the Convention.[145]

It is difficult, then, to justify the privilege against self-incrimination in terms of a self-standing right that should exist over and above the absolute right not to be subjected to cruel, inhuman and degrading treatment and the qualified rights to privacy and the general right of silence. If it is difficult to make out a convincing case for such a substantive right on its own ground; it is equally difficult to make a convincing case for the need for such a privilege in order to safeguard other principles. In the statement quoted above, the court links the privilege with the presumption of innocence. We have seen that this presumption carries with it an evidentiary obligation on the state to prove the ingredients of the offence charged against the accused, but that it has also been used to express more diffusely the idea that individuals in the criminal process should be treated as innocent and that intrusive actions should not be taken

---

[140] See Allen and Mace, 'The Privilege against Self-Incrimination Explained'.
[141] *R v. S (R)* (1995) 121 DLR (4th) 589, 702–3, per L'Heureux-Dube J. See P. Arenella, '*Schmerber* and the Privilege against Self-Incrimination: A Reappraisal' (1982) 20 *American Criminal Law Review* 31.
[142] *Ferreira v. Levin and others* 1996 (1) BCLR 1, 123, para. 259, per Sachs J.
[143] [2003] 2 SCR 678.
[144] This seems to be the view favoured by Martens J. in *Saunders*, para. 10.
[145] For arguments basing the privilege against self-incrimination on the protection of privacy, see D. J. Galligan, 'The Right to Silence Reconsidered' [1988] *Current Legal Problems* 69.

against them unless there are good reasons to do so.[146] This can include such actions as searching and seizing their property, stop and search, their arrest and questioning. But it is difficult to link the privilege conceptually with these principles.[147] Clearly, requiring a person to incriminate himself can constitute evidence for the prosecution's case, but it does nothing to diminish the high standard of proof required for guilt. Clearly, also we should limit the state's ability to take action against us in the criminal process without good reason, but the privilege extends beyond these situations entitling individuals to refuse to cooperate with an investigation even where there is reasonable suspicion against them. We might try to link the privilege more closely to the presumption by saying that it expresses the idea that an accused should not have to contribute in any way to the prosecution case at least until there is a prima facie case against him. In a case brought under Article 6(2) of the ECHR, the ECtHR held that drawing inferences against an accused before there was a convincing prima facie case against him was not permissible, for the effect was then to shift the burden of proof to the defendant.[148] But the problem again here is that the privilege purports to extend to protecting persons from direct compulsion to incriminate themselves, even when there is strong evidence against them.

Another argument made by the court which is closely tied to the presumption of innocence is that the privilege can help to avoid miscarriages of justice. An obvious first problem with this claim is that there is not an exact fit between protection from self-incrimination and protection from wrongful conviction. Much argument has been generated over claims about whether innocent suspects or defendants need the right, with Bentham claiming as we have seen that the rule can never be useful to the innocent.[149] Bentham was primarily concerned about bars to questioning witnesses in court rather than with the private interrogation of suspects in custody which had not been developed in his day and even he may have conceded that there is a danger of vulnerable innocent suspects making incriminating statements in the coercive atmosphere of the police station.[150] But according to the ECtHR, the privilege extends beyond giving immunity to making incriminating statements to the handing over of documents that were in existence before any criminal charge. Clearly, these may be of considerable assistance to the court in determining guilt without any risk of them being used to convict the innocent.

When the argument is confined to the making of incriminating statements in the criminal process, another problem is that as an instrumentalist rationale it risks more than arguments based on intrinsic merit counter-arguments being

---

[146] See Ch. 7.2. [147] Roberts and Zuckerman, *Criminal Evidence*, 554–6.
[148] *Telfner* v. *Austria*.
[149] Even in his own day, these claims were hotly contested: see, e.g. Lord Denman's arguments in the *Edinburgh Review* in 1824, recounted by Twining, *Theories of Evidence*, 105.
[150] Ibid., 209, n. 83. For discussion of how Bentham's views have been misused by modern advocates of the abrogation of the right of silence in the police station, see W. Twining, 'The Way of the Baffled Medic' (1973) 12 *Journal of Society of Public Teachers of Law (NS)* 348.

made that far from providing a protection to the innocent, the right jeopardises the conviction of the guilty. In the absence of the empirical data either way, the arguments and counter-arguments tend to consist of grossly inflated claims about the effect of the right of silence on the guilty and the innocent without enough attention being given to the procedural context in which the right operates. Taking their cue from Bentham, many critics, for example, point to the debilitating effect on the prosecution of allowing the guilty to remain silent when they erect a 'wall of silence' upon being called to account for their actions. Even when it appears that suspects are hiding behind a 'wall of silence', however, there is little evidence to suggest that removal of the right of silence will make much difference to the prosecution's prospects of success. When legislation was introduced in Northern Ireland to permit the courts to draw adverse inferences from silence in certain circumstances, there is some evidence to suggest that this encouraged more to speak to the police and testify, but no evidence that this did anything to improve the conviction rates.[151] Conversely, however, when advocates of the right of silence point to the role that it plays in protecting the innocent, it is almost impossible to provide data on the numbers of innocent persons who might be convicted in the absence of the privilege.[152]

The reality in most jurisdictions as we have seen is that most suspects and defendants do speak to the police or testify, irrespective of whether or not there is a right of silence. Within the context of custodial interrogation, the pressure to speak notwithstanding the right is immense, because silence can be seen as an act of non-cooperation with the authorities, which can do the suspect little good in terms of decisions that affect his or her liberty or that affect the level of the charge brought. Certainly, where policing is organised around interrogation and confession, the failure to speak can be interpreted as a challenge to authority.[153] As regards silence at trial, there is the risk as we have seen that whatever comments are made exhorting juries to disregard the accused's failure to testify, juries may penalise defendants for not testifying. If the right of silence does not affect behaviour that much, then it is hard to see it as a great buttress for the innocent. So, whichever form the argument for the right of silence as a safeguard for the innocent takes – either that it encourages innocent persons to be silent (and thereby saves them from falsely incriminating

---

[151] See J. Jackson, M. Wolfe and K. Quinn, *Legislating against Silence: The Northern Ireland Experience* (Belfast: Northern Ireland Office, 2000).

[152] Greenawalt, 'Silence as a Moral and Constitutional Right', 44. A sophisticated version of the argument that abolition risks convicting the innocent on the ground that it would encourage the guilty as well as the innocent to speak, with the net result that fact-finders would find it harder to distinguish the guilty who would tell lies from the innocent who would speak the truth, also falls short of providing data on how many innocent persons would be detrimentally affected by such a change. See Seidmann and Stein, 'The Right to Silence Helps the Innocent', 431.

[153] See D. Dixon, 'Politics, Research and Symbolism in Criminal Justice: The Right of Silence and the Police and Criminal Evidence Act 1984' (1991) 20 *Anglo-American Law Review* 27, 38.

themselves) or that it encourages the guilty to be silent (and thereby marks them out from being pooled with the innocent) – in reality it appears to affect very few people in their decision about whether or not to speak.

Another problem with basing arguments for the privilege against self-incrimination and the right of silence upon the protection of the innocent is that again as an instrumentalist rationale they are vulnerable to counter-arguments that offer compensating mechanisms in exchange for these immunities.[154] We have seen that the ECtHR itself has endorsed such arguments in permitting adverse inferences to be drawn from silence in certain circumstances. Although the ECtHR has conceded that warning suspects about inferences may amount to indirect compulsion, it has been prepared to justify this degree of compulsion provided safeguards are built into the system, such as providing access to legal advice and at court ensuring that any inferences that are drawn can be justified. These were exactly the arguments that were used to justify the extension of the Northern Ireland legislation permitting inferences to be drawn from silence to England and Wales, where it was argued that as a result of the statutory right of access to legal advice introduced under the Police and Criminal Evidence Act 1984, sufficient safeguards had already been put in place to protect suspects in the police station.

8.5 The right of silence as a necessary condition for active defence participation

We have reached the point where it would seem difficult to argue for a distinctive privilege against self-incrimination linked to the right to a fair trial over and above the other protections provided for by human rights instruments. It is hard to see why we should give specific priority to respecting the voluntariness of an accused's decision to hand over or reveal incriminating information over and above respecting an individual's general personal autonomy and freedom of action. Other rationales linked conceptually or instrumentally to principles and objectives associated with a fair trial fail to mark out a close enough connection to these principles and objectives.

This is not to say that there should not be a general right of silence deduced from the right to freedom of expression or linked with other rights such as the right of privacy by the need to prevent undue government restrictions on our personal autonomy. We may also want to give special protection against interferences which compel us to incriminate ourselves and others in the course of a criminal prosecution. But these rights need to be weighed against other interests, in particular the need for citizens to account for their actions in certain circumstances. It has been argued, for example, that it is perfectly legitimate to require people who engage in regulatory activities to account for themselves

---

[154] See S. Greer, 'The Right to Silence: A Review of the Current Debate' (1990) 53 *Modern Law Review* 58.

either to public officials or to opponents in litigation.[155] Within the criminal justice process, there may also be a legitimate aim in requiring persons to account for themselves in order to reach a conclusion as to whether a criminal offence has been committed. Applying a strict proportionality test, we should only require persons to account for themselves when certain proportionality conditions are fulfilled, such as rationality and necessity.[156] Just as the right of silence can be grossly exaggerated as a mechanism for protecting the innocent, we have seen that it can also be grossly exaggerated as an obstacle for convicting the guilty. Irrespective of whether or not there is a right of silence, there are good prudential reasons why suspects and defendants would want to provide an account of themselves. Of the few who would be affected by an abrogation of the right and change their behaviour by providing an account, it is unclear how advantageous their speaking is to the police or the prosecution.

Hence, in general terms we should not require suspects to account for themselves. Exceptions might be made in cases where it might otherwise be difficult to find the necessary evidence, such as in road traffic cases of the kind that arose in the *Weh* case, where a driver was required to name who had been driving his car at a particular time when it was seen to be exceeding the speed limit.[157] But it is not enough in these situations, arguably, just to claim that the right of silence can be 'balanced away' by a general public interest such as the need to subject more vehicles and their owners to a strict regulatory regime.[158] There would in addition have to be specific reason to show why requiring motor owners to name drivers was necessary in order to achieve this aim. On this reasoning, *pace* the ruling in the *Saunders* case, there may also be circumstances where enforced answers made outside the criminal context should be allowed to be presented as part of the prosecution case. But again these would need to be strictly justified on the bases of rationality and necessity, taking account of all reasonable alternatives.[159]

Short of compelling a person to give evidence or answer questions in the criminal process, however, once there is a basis in evidence for suspecting that a person has been engaged in criminal conduct, it would seem reasonable to call for an answer not out of necessity in order for the prosecution to make out its case (the need for the prosecution to obtain answers from a suspect can, as we have seen, be greatly exaggerated), but rather to advance the general interests of truth-finding within the 'adversarial' rationalist tradition that we

---

[155] Sedley, 'Wringing out the Fault', 107.
[156] See, e.g. R. Alexy, 'The Structure of Constitutional Rights Norms' in *A Theory of Constitutional Rights* (Oxford University Press, 2002).
[157] Redmayne, 'Rethinking the Privilege against Self-Incrimination', 230.
[158] A. Ashworth, *Human Rights, Serious Crime and Criminal Procedure* (London: Sweet & Maxwell, 2002) 65 (criticising the *Brown* decision for putting the privilege against self-incrimination second to the general public interest).
[159] *Ferreira* v. *Levin and others* 1996 (1) BCLR 1, 23, para. 265, per Sachs J. (doubting whether these conditions were met where examinees' compelled answers to questions in an inquiry into a company's affairs could be used against them in subsequent criminal proceedings).

have explained. Although we have seen that traditionally this mode of fact-finding has been reserved for the trial, states are increasingly 'front-loading' the forensic enterprise into the pre-trial phase in order to expedite proceedings and there is no reason why this should not be done provided suitable safeguards are put in place. Safeguards are necessary to ensure that suspects are not put under improper physical or psychological pressure and that they are able to put forward any defence as effectively as they can. As this is the point where suspects are effectively 'charged' with allegations, they ought arguably to be given the same or equivalent defence rights available to them at trial. If this is accepted, then these safeguards would include, most importantly, access to legal advice, disclosure of the evidence against them and an authenticated record of any interview either by audio or video tape. Rather like the *Miranda* rules, there should be a ban on questioning until these safeguards are able to be offered to suspects. But again, because as we have seen suspects are inevitably put under pressure when faced with criminal allegations, especially when they are in custodial interrogation, it is questionable whether suspects in custody should be given an opportunity to waive these conditions 'voluntarily', at least until they have had an opportunity to speak to a lawyer.

Once then there is sufficient evidence of a person's involvement in a criminal offence, the right of silence should arguably be given greater salience than in other encounters between the state and the citizen by preventing any questioning until safeguards are put in place to enable him to mount an effective defence. When these are in place, the right of silence would still be respected in the sense that suspects would not be compelled to answer police questions, but as at trial they would be given the opportunity to respond to the allegations against them. It is doubtful also whether at this stage there is any need to apply the 'indirect compulsion' of warning suspects that adverse inferences may be drawn against them. Suspects would be made aware, however, that they have an opportunity to respond to certain allegations that have arisen against them and that a record will be made of any answers for the purposes of trial. In recognition of the growth in non-judicial and non-court disposals across a number of jurisdictions,[160] they would also be made aware through access to a lawyer of any informal disposals or decisions that may be made if they are prepared to make an admission to the allegations.

On this analysis, the right of silence would be maintained throughout the stage of police investigation because it is not generally necessary for the investigation for suspects to be compelled to give evidence. At a point when there are allegations based on evidence that call for an answer, suspects should, however, be given an opportunity to respond under conditions that allow for informed and fair participation. These conditions which would still caution suspects that

---

[160] See S. Thaman, 'Plea-Bargaining, Negotiated Confessions and Consensual Resolution of Criminal Cases', in K. Boele-Woelki and S. van Erp (eds.), *General Reports of the XVII Congress of the International Academy of Comparative Law* (Utrecht: Eleven International, 2007).

they have a right not to respond are required not out of any sentimental desire to see 'fair play' or to give suspects a 'sporting chance' to avoid conviction, but out of a need to enable suspects to participate effectively in the proceedings that have in effect been mounted against them. Of course, under legal advice suspects may decide as at trial not to answer questions. But this decision will be an informed one after they have been told, for example, that there may be costs attached to such a strategy in terms of delayed disposal of the case.[161] It will also be a decision made with the full participation of an active defence. The decision not to answer questions would be a negative one, but again as at trial it would be made as part of an active defence strategy on the basis of equality of arms.

We have reached the point then where it would seem justified to give the right of silence a special weighting for suspects in the criminal process and for this to be considered part of the right to a fair trial. It is not helpful, however, to link such a right with the privilege against self-incrimination in so far as this suggests that just because they are suspects, they should be given some special or absolute immunity from disclosing information that may indicate their guilt. A better ground for justifying a 'weighted' right of silence for suspects is that there needs to be a recognition, especially where suspects are in custodial interrogation, of their vulnerable position and of the need, therefore, to avoid the risk of false confession.[162] When persons such as the applicant in the *Saunders* case are required to provide information to non-criminal investigators, they are often given advanced notice in writing of what is required of them and positively advised to have a legal adviser present. A police interview with a person in custody may take a very different form.[163] It is certainly arguable that in this situation the potential for systemic abuse of law enforcement powers is at its greatest.

Our argument for a right of silence at this stage, however, goes beyond simply an instrumentalist need to avoid persons falsely incriminating themselves. In this book, we have been arguing for a distinction between protective and participative defence rights.[164] As well as providing a protection for the innocent, it may be argued that the right is justified as a necessary procedural part of the general rights of the defence to enable the suspect to mount an effective

---

[161] The ICTY Chamber has held that the lack of cooperation of an accused should not as a rule be taken into consideration as a factor that might justify denial of an application for provisional release. See *Prosecutor* v. *Jokic*, Trial Chamber. But cooperation with the prosecution can be cited as a mitigating factor at the sentencing stage: see W. Schabas, *The UN International Criminal Tribunals* (Cambridge University Press, 2006) 532–3.

[162] See A. Ashworth and M. Redmayne, *The Criminal Process*, 4th edn (Oxford University Press, 2010) ch. 4; and P. J. Schwikkard, 'The Muddle of Silence' (2009) 6 *International Commentary on Evidence*, Issue 2, Art. 4.

[163] See J. Jackson, 'The Right of Silence: Judicial Responses to Parliamentary Encroachment' (1993) 57 *Modern Law Review* 270, 274; and Dennis, 'Reassessing the Privilege against Self-Incrimination', 370.

[164] See also A. Roberts, 'Pre-Trial Defence Rights and the Fair Use of Eyewitness Identification Procedures' (2008) 71 *Modern Law Review* 331.

defence. Once under criminal suspicion, the accused is entitled to be given the opportunity to defend him- or herself, but in order to do this effectively, the rights of the defence need to be put into place *before* he or she is asked to provide a defence. Just as at trial, so in the pre-trial phase, suspects should be given an opportunity to mount their most effective defence and this requires that there should be no questioning of suspects until such time as the conditions for this are put in place, principally by giving access to legal advice which is necessary so that decisions as to how to mount the defence are, just as at trial, taken on an informed basis. Various options as at trial are available at this stage. One may simply admit to the allegations that are being put. One may answer police questions or, depending on the procedure, submit to judicial inquiry. Another option may be to offer a detailed written explanation of one's conduct or to suggest certain lines of exculpatory inquiry.

8.6 Incorporating fair trials standards from the point of being called to account

Since on our argument proceedings have effectively begun against suspects as soon as they are called to account for evidence against them, they should be entitled at this point to all of the fair trial safeguards that are provided under the ECHR and other international standards. International instruments and bodies have been increasingly recognising the importance of the presence of counsel during interrogations. The UN *Basic Principles on the Role of Lawyers* make it clear that the right of access to a lawyer extends to all stages of criminal proceedings, which presumably include interrogations before arrest and charge.[165] The Human Rights Committee has recognised the importance of the presence of counsel at the pre-trial phase of criminal proceedings, most recently during police interrogation.[166]

The international criminal tribunals also recognise that defence rights come into play at this stage. We have seen that Article 14 of the ICCPR, which includes a right not to be compelled to give evidence, was expressly incorporated into the statutes of the ad hoc bodies. In addition, the statutes require that if questioned by the prosecutor, the suspect has a right to the assistance of legal counsel provided for free if he or she does not have the means to pay and the right to any necessary translation.[167] The rules go further by requiring that suspects are

---

[165] *United Nations Principles on the Role of Lawyers, relative to the special safeguards in criminal justice matters*, approved by the Eighth United Nations Congress on the Prevention of Crime and the Treatment of Offenders at its meeting in Havana, Cuba, from 27 August to 7 September 1990, no. 1.

[166] HRC, *Aliev* v. *Ukraine*; and see Concluding Observations of the Human Rights Committee: South Korea, UN Doc. CCPR/C/KOR/CO/3, 28 November 2006, para. 14.

[167] See Art. 18(3) ICTY Statute; and Art. 17(3) ICTR Statute. The inclusion of this latter right was added to the rules in 1995 out of recognition of its importance: see J. R. W. D. Jones and S. Powles, *International Criminal Practice*, 3rd edn (Oxford University Press, 2003) 502. See also Art. 55(2)(c) ICC Statute.

informed of these rights before being questioned and in addition are informed of the right to remain silent, and to be cautioned that any statement that is made shall be recorded and may be used in evidence.[168] Somewhat akin to the *Miranda* rules,[169] the rules further require that questioning of a suspect should not proceed without the presence of counsel unless the suspect has voluntarily waived his right to counsel.[170] In addition, all interviews must be recorded by audio- or video-tape.[171] The ICTY Trial Chamber has also recognised the principle that where statements have been obtained by national authorities in breach of these safeguards, they may not be able to be admitted.[172]

The ICC Statute goes further by granting certain basic safeguards to any persons who are subject to questioning at *any* time during an investigation under the statute, including the privilege against self-incrimination, the right not to be subjected to any form of coercion, duress or threat, to torture or to any other form of cruel, inhuman or degrading treatment or punishment and rights to translation.[173] Then where there are grounds to believe that such persons have committed a crime within the jurisdiction of the court and they are about to be questioned either by the prosecutor or by national authorities conducting an investigation under the statute, they shall be informed of their defence rights, which in addition to the rights under the ad hoc tribunals require that they be informed prior to being questioned about which crimes they are suspected of.[174] Although these rights do not go quite as far as the optimum rights granted to accused persons at trial, they establish an important basis for an equality of arms in the pre-trial phase of proceedings at the stage when accusations are made against suspects.

The ECtHR has been somewhat unclear as to when defendants are 'charged' for the purposes of Article 6 of the ECHR so as to enable their defence rights to come into play. It has considered that defendants are engaged within the

---

[168] R. 42(A) ICTY, ICTR RPE. Cf. Art. 55(2)(b)(c) ICC Statute.

[169] Note though the difference in that the *Miranda* rights only extend to a right to the presence of an attorney *prior to* questioning, whereas the international criminal tribunals extend this right to the presence of counsel *during* questioning. This marks an important difference of perception in the way in which the right to counsel is exercised. Once suspects exercise their *Miranda* rights, it would seem that American defence lawyers virtually always advise them not to talk to the police. See Van Kessel, 'European Perspectives', 837. The way in which the right is expressed in the international criminal tribunals' statutes and rules, however, suggests that defence lawyers have at this stage a more positive role to play in participating in the defence.

[170] R. 42(B) ICTY, ICTR RPE. The prosecution bears a heavy burden of proof to show convincingly and beyond reasonable doubt that the waiver is voluntary: *Prosecutor* v. *Delalić*, Trial Chamber, Decision on Mucić's Motion for the Exclusion of Evidence, paras. 42 and 48. The waiver must also be 'express and unequivocal': *Prosecutor* v. *Bagosora*, Trial Chamber, Decision, para. 18.

[171] R. 43 ICTY, ICTR RPE, 43.

[172] *Prosecutor* v. *Delalić*, Trial Chamber, Decision on Mucić's Motion for the Exclusion of Evidence (excluding statements obtained by Austrian police in circumstances where the accused was not offered counsel or informed adequately of his rights). See R. May and M. Wierda, *International Criminal Evidence* (Ardsley: Transnational Publishers, 2002) 277–8.

[173] Art. 55(1) ICC Statute.   [174] Art. 55(2) ICC Statute.

meaning of Article 6 when they have been officially notified of an allegation or 'substantially affected' by the steps taken against them.[175] It has been argued elsewhere that the mere exercise of investigatory powers against a suspect should not in itself trigger the initiation of proceedings, but that proceedings do commence when defendants are held to account for allegations.[176] If this is the point at which defendants are charged, their defence rights under Article 6 are then triggered and they should be entitled to the full panoply of equality of arms, including the presence of a legal adviser when being questioned and – something that is not presently provided as of right – disclosure of the case against them as well.[177]

If the ECtHR has been less than clear as to when exactly a person is charged for the purposes triggering Article 6 rights, it has also been less than unequivocal about the importance of defence rights in the pre-trial phase of proceedings. It would seem that the court has accepted that suspects should be informed of their right to silence before they are questioned by the police.[178] The court has also recognised the importance of having the assistance of counsel in connection with appearances before an investigating judge and accepted the principle that a defendant should have a right to assistance by counsel during police interrogations.[179] But in *Imbrioscia v. Switzerland*, the ECtHR held that there had been no breach of Article 6 because the applicant's lawyer had not asked to be present. This makes it clear that it is up to the defence to activate the right to be present at the examinations of the accused.[180] Moreover, the principle is somewhat weakened by the fact that the ECtHR considered that there is no breach of Article 6 unless the fairness of the trial is seriously prejudiced by an initial failure to comply with its provisions. In its own words, 'the manner in which Article 6(3)(c) was applied during the preliminary investigation depended on the special features of the proceedings involved and on the circumstances of the case'.[181]

These observations were repeated in *John Murray v. United Kingdom*, where as we have seen the ECtHR recognised the importance of legal advice being made available to suspects when warned about the possibility of adverse inferences being drawn against them. But it qualified the right to legal assistance in the pre-trial phase of criminal proceedings in a number of respects. First of all, it appeared to link the right instrumentally with the consequences that may later attach to suspects at their trial from decisions made at the pre-trial phase.

[175] *Deweer v. Belgium*, para. 46; and *Eckle v. Germany*. The UK courts have been similarly unclear on this point. Cf. *Attorney General's Reference (No. 2 of 2001)* [2003] UKHL 68 with *R (on the application of R) v. Durham Constabulary and Another* [2005] UKHL 21.
[176] J. Jackson, 'The Reasonable Time Requirement: An Independent and Meaningful Right?' [2005] *Criminal Law Review* 3, 19. See *Howarth v. United Kingdom*; and *Quinn v. Ireland*.
[177] See, e.g. R. J. Toney, 'Disclosure of Evidence and Legal Assistance at Custodial Interrogation: What Does the European Convention on Human Rights Require?' (2001) 5 *International Journal of Evidence & Proof* 39.
[178] *Brusco v. France*.   [179] *Quaranta v. Switzerland*; and *Imbrioscia v. Switzerland*.
[180] Trechsel, *Human Rights in Criminal Proceedings*, 267.   [181] Para. 38.

Where consequences attach to the attitude of an accused at the stages of police interrogation which are decisive for the prospects of the defence in later proceedings, Article 6 will normally require that an accused be allowed to benefit from the assistance of a lawyer. But it has been suggested that the behaviour of the suspect immediately after arrest will *always* have consequences.[182] Whatever use is made of the suspect's responses or lack of them at a later trial, the suspect's reaction may have a considerable effect on the way in which the case is investigated, whether it is prosecuted or disposed of by other means.

Even in circumstances when decisions are made at the pre-trial stage which have consequences at trial, the ECtHR has considered that restrictions may be placed on access to legal advice 'for good cause'. Under the Northern Ireland legislation, access could be denied to terrorist suspects for 48 hours if there was a risk of alerting persons suspected of involvement in the offence who were not yet arrested. In *Magee* v. *United Kingdom*,[183] it was considered that whatever the justification, the restriction in this case could not be compatible with Article 6 given the fact that the rights of the defence were so irretrievably prejudiced. In this case, the applicant had confessed while being held in custody in a coercive atmosphere specifically devised to sap his will and make him confess. But the ECtHR left it open in other cases to consider that there may be just cause to restrict access, perhaps where the coercive atmosphere of the interrogation was less pronounced or where the defendant was not facing such serious charges.[184]

Thirdly, the ECtHR has looked at the proceedings as a whole before deciding whether there has been a breach of Article 6. Thus, the fairness of trials has been upheld even where there has been a systemic denial of access to a lawyer at the pre-trial phases. In one case, the applicants had been in custody for 20 days without seeing a lawyer; the ECtHR took note of the fact that at trial he had the benefit of legal assistance and that he had enjoyed, 'overall', a fair trial.[185]

In its latest decisions, however, the ECtHR would seem to have given stronger expression to the need for suspects to avail of legal advice before being questioned, although it has repeated the qualifications made by it in *John Murray*. In *Salduz* v. *Turkey*, the applicant had been interrogated in the absence of a lawyer after signing a form reminding him of the charges against him and of his right to silence. He made various admissions to the police of being involved in an unlawful organisation and hanging an illegal banner from a bridge. He later retracted his statement to the police, alleging that it had been extracted under duress. His statement was used for the purpose of his conviction and in concluding that there had been a breach of Article 6 of the ECHR, the ECtHR held that he had been undoubtedly affected by the restrictions on his access to

---

[182] Trechsel, *Human Rights in Criminal Proceedings*, 283.   [183] Para. 63.
[184] Cf. *Brennan* v. *United Kingdom*, where the court considered that deferral was in good faith and on reasonable grounds, but in any event the admission was made after the deferral of access and could not be linked to it.
[185] *Sarikaya* v. *Turkey*. See also *Mamaç and others* v. *Turkey*. Cf. *Öcalan* v. *Turkey* [GC].

a lawyer. The ECtHR expressly linked the right of access not only to the need to protect the accused against abusive conduct on the part of the authorities and the prevention of miscarriages of justice, but also to fulfilment of the aims of Article 6, notably 'equality of arms between the investigating or prosecuting authorities and the accused'.[186] The court underlined the importance of the investigation stage for the preparation of the criminal proceedings as the evidence obtained during this stage determines the framework in which the offence charged will be considered at the trial. At the same time, the ECtHR continued, 'an accused often finds himself in a particularly vulnerable position at that stage of the proceedings, the effect of which is amplified by the fact that legislation on criminal procedure tends to become increasingly complex, notably with respect to the gathering and use of evidence'.[187] Against this background, the court found that in order for the right to a fair trial to remain sufficiently 'practical and effective', Article 6(1) required that, as a rule, access to a lawyer should be provided as from the first interrogation of a suspect by the police, unless it is demonstrated that in the light of the particular circumstances of each case there are compelling reasons to restrict this right.[188] Even then, the rights of the defence must not be unduly prejudiced and the ECtHR went on to say more unequivocally than it did in *Magee* that the rights of the defence will in principle be irretrievably prejudiced when incriminating statements made during police interrogations without access to a lawyer are used for a conviction.

This judgment is to be welcomed for putting the right of access to a lawyer on a firmer footing, emphasising not only the protective role that the lawyer can play in ensuring that detained persons are not coerced into making a confession in breach of the privilege against self-incrimination, but also the positive participative role that is required in advising on the complexities of gathering and using evidence.[189] This is emphasised particularly in the concurring opinions of Judge Zagrebelsky (with Judges Casadevall and Turmen) and of Judge Bratza, who would have preferred the ECtHR to have emphasised that detained persons should be entitled to access to legal assistance not just from the point of interrogation, but as soon as they are imprisoned, so that from that stage they can give their lawyer instructions in order to prepare their defence. The ECtHR rightly emphasises here the important impact which the investigation stage may have for the trial, but the reality is that increasing numbers of cases in many jurisdictions do not reach trial at all. This makes it all the more important, however, that accused persons are given access to a lawyer before the first stages of interrogation, as in many cases it is this first encounter with the police that may determine whether the case is advanced to trial or is otherwise diverted out of the court process.

There was some ambiguity in *Salduz* as to whether 'access to a lawyer' from the point of interrogation included a right of assistance during the questioning

---

[186] *Salduz* v. *Turkey* [GC], para. 53.   [187] Ibid., para. 54.   [188] Ibid., para. 55.
[189] See also to similar effect *Amutgan* v. *Turkey*; *Cimen* v. *Turkey*; and *Tagac and others* v. *Turkey*.

of the suspect. In *John Murray*, the ECtHR had emphasised the importance of the assistance of a lawyer *at the initial stages of police interrogation*. The ECtHR in *Panovits* v. *Cyprus* repeated this, but went on to state that 'the lack of legal assistance *during* an applicant's interrogation would constitute a restriction of his defence rights in the absence of compelling reasons that do not prejudice the overall fairness of the proceedings'.[190] This would seem to entitle suspects to have their lawyer present during police questioning and poses a challenge to a number of domestic common law and civil law systems that do not recognise the right to have the assistance of counsel during questioning.[191]

In *Salduz*, the applicant was denied access to legal advice. In *Panovits*, the authorities were willing to allow the applicant to be assisted by a lawyer, but the applicant, a 17 year old who was cautioned about his right of silence, was not made aware of his right of access to a lawyer and he confessed to murder in the absence of a legal adviser and his guardian. The ECtHR considered that the right of an accused who is a minor to effective participation in his or her criminal trial required that he be dealt with with due regard to his vulnerability and capacities from the first stages of his involvement in a criminal investigation and in particular during any questioning by the police. In order that a minor has a broad understanding of the nature of the investigation, of what is at stake, including the significance of any penalty which may be imposed as well of his rights, the assistance of an interpreter, lawyer, social worker or friend may be called for. Furthermore, any waiver of such assistance could only be accepted where it was expressed in an unequivocal manner after all reasonable steps had been taken to ensure that he was fully informed of his rights of defence and could appreciate the consequences of his conduct. In view of what happened in this case, it was unlikely given his age that he was aware he was entitled to legal representation before making any statement to the police or what the consequences of proceeding without a lawyer would be. Despite the domestic court's ruling that the applicant's statement was voluntary, there had been a violation of Article 6(3)(c) of the ECHR in conjunction with Article 6(1) on account of the lack of assistance to the applicant in the initial stages of police questioning and the subsequent use of the statement obtained in circumstances which breached his rights was a further violation of Article 6(1). This is another welcome decision stressing once again the need for the authorities to take a proactive stance to ensure that applicants are made fully aware of their rights and the consequences of failing to take advantage of them. Although it falls short of requiring that vulnerable accused persons be encouraged to seek legal advice,

---

[190] *Panovits* v. *Cyprus*, para. 66 (emphasis added).

[191] Such a right is not recognised in Ireland, Germany or the Netherlands. In Scotland, the UKSC has reversed a Scottish Appeal Court decision which considered that the principle of access to a lawyer from the first interrogation of a suspect by the police should not be applied without qualification: see *Cadder* v. *HM Advocate* [2010] UKSC 43, reversing *Mclean* v. *HM Advocate* [2009] HCJAC 97, and for comment F. Leverick, 'The Right to Legal Advice During Detention' (2010) 14 *Edinburgh Law Review* 300.

it does require a full explanation of the consequences of not doing so which is understood by the applicant if needs be with the assistance of an interpreter, lawyer or social worker.

8.7 Conclusion

In this chapter, we have argued that although human rights standards and jurisprudence have linked the privilege against self-incrimination with the right of silence as an essential ingredient of a fair trial, it would be better in this context to make a distinction between the two. While in general terms these rights may be viewed as part of the need for states to respect the individual dignity and autonomy of the individual, it is indisputable that there are circumstances when they may have to give way to other considerations when states need access to information. We have argued, however, that within the criminal process the right of silence is entitled to be given a special weighting not specifically for reasons to do with upholding substantive rights such as the dignity and respect of the individual, but in order to uphold the procedural rights of the defence which it has been argued come into play not just at the trial phase of criminal proceedings, but at the stage of pre-trial proceedings when a suspect is called upon to answer allegations against him.

We have seen that human rights jurisprudence has developed special protections for the defence such as equality of arms and adversarial proceedings at the trial phase of proceedings. It would seem only logical that these principles are applied at the pre-trial phase when the defendant is equally affected by the proceedings by being asked to participate in them. If it is important for a defendant to be given full access to the rights of the defence at the stage when he or she is asked to account for allegations in order that he or she can mount the most effective defence, then it is important that these rights are in place at this stage and that a defendant is not asked to account for him- or herself *until* they are in place. The right of silence is thereby transformed at this stage of the criminal process from a right which is inextricably linked to the exercise of an individual's will, but which we have seen is extraordinarily difficult to assert in the coercive atmosphere of a police station and becomes instead a procedural right inextricably linked to the participatory rights of the defence by requiring that there can be no participation by the accused until such rights are put in place.

In its recent decisions, the ECtHR has come close to recognising the importance of providing defendants with access to a lawyer before they are questioned and has stressed that any waiver of such a right must be made in a voluntary and unequivocal manner. Once the right is invoked, any waiver must not only be voluntary, but must also constitute a knowing and intelligent relinquishment of the right.[192] As an institutional right, however, rather than a right exercised by

---

[192] See *Pishchalnikov v. Russia.*

choice, it may be argued that it should no more be able to be waived than other rights of the defence which we shall examine in the next chapter. The rights are there arguably not just out of respect for the dignity of the individual, but to safeguard institutional values that are held dear in the criminal process, such as the need for accurate findings of fact and the protection of the innocent. Once the institutional rights of the defence are put in place, however, the right of silence reverts to an exercise of will or choice on the part of the individual accused, but a choice that is made on an informed basis as part of a defence strategy which is taken in full recognition of the costs and benefits of its exercise. Having established that the right of silence is a necessary condition for the effective exercise of the participatory rights of the defence, we must now go on and examine in more detail what the scope of these rights is in human rights law and how they are applied both in human rights jurisprudence and within the common law and civil law traditions.

9

Defence participation

9.1 Introduction: legal representation and self-representation[1]

We have seen how through concepts such as the equality of arms and the right to an adversarial procedure, human rights jurisprudence has been developing a theory of effective defence participation which not only allows for the participation of the accused in the criminal proceedings, but also gives institutional rights to the defence as a party entitled to be treated on an equal basis as the prosecution. These institutional rights have their foundation in what the ECtHR has described as the 'minimum' rights laid down in Article 6(3) of the ECHR and also set out in the other human rights instruments[2] – the right to be informed of the charges, to have adequate time and facilities to prepare the defence, the right to defend oneself or to have the assistance of counsel, the right to test witness evidence and, finally, the right to the free assistance of an interpreter.

At the core of the right to defence participation lies the right to defend oneself in person or through legal assistance of one's own choosing. This right has been described as 'practically absolute',[3] although as we saw in the last chapter there has been some uncertainty about the stage in the criminal process at which legal assistance can come to the aid of defendants. Built into the wording is a strong notion of individual participation by the accused. Defendants can choose to defend themselves or through legal assistance of their own choosing. The suggestion is that counsel is there at the personal choice and as the personal representative of the accused. In this sense, the right to legal assistance can be depicted as an expression of the principles of individual dignity and autonomy that have overlain so many of the individual rights in human rights instruments. Legal assistance serves to promote individual dignity by helping to alleviate the stress of facing charges and helping to supervise and control the activities of the law enforcement officers, ensuring that accused persons are treated

---

[1] This section is distilled in part from J. Jackson, 'Autonomy and Accuracy in the Development of Fair Trial Rights', University College Dublin Law Research Paper No. 09/2009. Available at SSRN: http://ssrn.com/abstract=1407968.
[2] Art. 14(3) ICCPR; and Art. 8(3) ACHR.
[3] S. Trechsel, *Human Rights in Criminal Proceedings* (Oxford University Press, 2005) 266.

properly.[4] As well as acting in a protective capacity, counsel can also give expression to defendants' participation more effectively than defendants themselves, provided they faithfully adhere to carrying out their clients' instructions and act in accordance with their wishes.[5] The old adage that a defendant who tries to represent him- or herself has a 'fool for a client' is an expression of the fact that even the most sophisticated defendants – even lawyers who are specialists in criminal law – can lose sight of the objectivity needed to put their defence effectively.

However, seen through the lens of an institutional 'party' right, counsel not only act as the defendant's own effective 'voice', but also ensure that the most effective case is mounted against the prosecution, providing the 'key' which opens the door to all of the rights and possibilities of defence in the substantive sense.[6] Counsel not only act as a conduit for the defendant, they provide advice and assistance on how to mount the best case against the prosecution. This is why lawyers are often accused of shielding guilty defendants. But the other side of the coin is that defendants are not often in the best position to judge their legal guilt and they have a right to legal assistance in order to clarify whether indeed they have a legal case to mount against the prosecution and then to have that defence presented as effectively as possible. In this manner, it can be argued that far from undermining the rationalist tradition of truth-finding, legal assistance actually helps to promote it.[7]

Legal assistance then helps support both the individual rights tradition and the rationalist tradition of evidence that we have argued underlie the common evidentiary framework emerging across national boundaries. In many cases, defendants will be happy to permit counsel to put their most effective defence on their behalf. Tensions can occur, however, between the need for autonomy and the need for effective defence when as we saw in some of the international criminal tribunals accused persons insist on representing themselves. The risk in permitting self-representation is that the defendant's defence may not be conducted as effectively as it might otherwise be. The right to self-representation is specifically referred to in human rights instruments as an alternative to the right of legal assistance,[8] although there was little mention of its importance in the official drafting records of Article 14(3)(d) of the ICCPR, where the right first

---

[4] Ibid., 245.
[5] A. Duff, L. Farmer, S. Marshall and V. Tadros, *The Trial on Trial (3): Towards a Normative Theory of the Criminal Trial* (Oxford: Hart, 2007) 211.
[6] Trechsel, *Human Rights in Criminal Proceedings*, 245.
[7] cf. R. J. Allen, 'Rationality and Accuracy in the Criminal Process: A Discordant Note on the Harmonizing of the Justices' Views on Burdens of Persuasion in Criminal Cases' (1983) 74 *Journal of Criminal Law and Criminology* 1147, 1153 (arguing that the primary function of the right to counsel is to advance the rationality of the criminal justice process rather than its ultimate accuracy).
[8] The instruments require that an accused person shall be entitled 'to defend himself in person or through legal assistance of his own choosing': Art. 14(3)(d) ICCPR; Art. 6(3)(c) ECHR; and Art. 8(2)(d) AHRC.

Introduction

surfaced.[9] The discussion on representation centred instead upon the right of access to counsel, the choice of counsel and the problem of indigent defendants.

It has been argued that the debate as to whether counsel may be imposed on an accused reflects different attitudes about the relationship between the authorities and the individual. A liberal approach places emphasis on the preferences of the accused, while a more 'social' approach obliges states to take positive action to protect the rights of the defendant.[10] Harking back to the different rationales for defence participation discussed in Chapter 1, these attitudes also arguably reflect different rationales of the criminal trial. A liberal communicative theory which stresses the importance of the defendant being able to respond to the case against her would indicate that the accused should be free to respond in any manner she wishes. A theory that stresses the need for effective defence in order to try to reach an accurate outcome would override the wishes of an individual accused where she is unwilling or unable to represent herself effectively.

One can discern a greater emphasis in common law systems on respecting an accused's autonomous right to decide whether and how to participate in defending herself, while civilian systems have put greater emphasis on a more 'social' approach which obliges states to take positive action to protect the rights of the accused.[11] This difference of approach would seem to be reflected in different political ideologies underpinning the two systems – classical laissez faire versus a more paternalist attitude.[12] So common law systems have tended to put a high premium on accused persons deciding themselves how the proceedings against them should be presented. Defendants may be compelled to attend their trial and are required to plead guilty or not guilty, but provided they have the capacity to enter a plea and understand its implications, they can prevent the need for the case to be proved against them beyond reasonable doubt. At their trial they can then refuse to be sworn to answer questions. By contrast, civilian systems have given accused persons less opportunity to exercise choice over the course of procedural action. The idea that defendants should be able to refuse to be subjected to questioning at their trial or that they should be able to waive their right to a trial or dispense with counsel is considered an extravagant manifestation of respect for the individual's free will out of sync with the requirement that all accused persons must be provided with a fair trial.

Some see in this difference of approach a fundamental dichotomy between common law and civil law systems. It may be better, however, to view it in terms

---

[9] See M. Scharf, 'Self-Representation versus Assignment of Defence Counsel before International Criminal Tribunals' (2006) 4 *Journal of International Criminal Justice* 31, 34. See also D. Weissbrodt, *The Right to a Fair Trial under the Universal Declaration of Human Rights and the International Covenant on Civil and Political Rights* (The Hague: Martinus Nijhoff, 2001) 57.
[10] Trechsel, *Human Rights in Criminal Proceedings*, 263.
[11] Trechsel, *Human Rights in Criminal Proceedings*, 263–4.
[12] M. Damaška, 'Assignment of Counsel and Perceptions of Fairness' (2005) 3 *Journal of International Criminal Justice* 3, 5.

of competing tendencies *within* different common law and civil law systems, one emphasising individual rights and the other the need for accurate outcomes. This can be illustrated by the different attitudes taken by US justices towards the right to self-representation. In the USSC decision of *Faretta* v. *California*,[13] the majority upheld the right to self-representation as a constitutional right which could not be taken away by a state or one of its courts, although it is a right that could be forfeited when a defendant acts in a disruptive manner. In his dissenting opinion in *Faretta*, however, Justice Blackmun brought out the stark implication of an extreme attachment to the right of self-representation when he drew attention to the obvious dangers of unjust convictions that could result. The right to self-representation took away from the importance of the right to counsel and just as the right to counsel ensures a fair trial, the right to waive representation brought with it a direct undermining of the right to a fair trial. Common law systems are increasingly recognising the need for limitations and qualifications to the right of self-representation, one example being the restrictions that are put upon accused persons cross-examining complainants in sexual cases and other categories of protected witnesses.[14]

Human rights law has also given mixed signals about the importance to be attached to the right to self-representation. The HRC has held that was a breach of the Covenant when the applicant claimed that the court had denied his request to defend himself through an interpreter.[15] The ECommHR and ECtHR, however, have stated that the requirement that a defendant be assisted by counsel at all stages of the proceedings cannot be deemed incompatible with the ECHR.[16] It has been suggested that the steps taken in domestic countries to prevent accused persons personally cross-examining rape complainants and to provide in circumstances where the accused refuses to be legally represented for a legal representative appointed by the court to conduct the cross-examination on behalf of the accused, would be unlikely to breach human rights law.[17] The ECtHR would seem to have left a 'proper margin of appreciation' to states to determine whether the appointment of counsel contrary to the wishes of the accused is justified.[18]

In Chapter 5, we saw that the issue of self-representation created great difficulty in the Milošević trial and the international criminal tribunals have been unable to reach a consistent position. It is important to take account of the particular context in which courts and tribunals are operating. Damaška has argued that an adolescent criminal justice system with fragile legitimacy must

---

[13] 422 US 806 (1975).
[14] See, e.g. ss. 34–6 Youth Justice and Criminal Evidence Act 1999 (England and Wales); s. 486(2.3) Criminal Code, RS 1985 (Canada); ss. 15YF and 15 YG Crimes Act 1914 (Australian Commonwealth); s. 294A Criminal Procedure Act (NSW); ss. 21M and 21N Evidence Act 1977 (Queensland); and s. 23 F Evidence Act 1908 (New Zealand). In Scotland, accused persons are prevented from representing themselves altogether in sexual cases: see s. 288C(1) Criminal Procedure (Scotland) Act 1995.
[15] *Michael and Brian Hill* v. *Spain*.   [16] *Croissant* v. *Germany*; and *Lagerblom* v. *Sweden*.
[17] I. H. Dennis, *The Law of Evidence*, 4th edn (London: Sweet & Maxwell, 2010) para. 15.19, 641.
[18] Trechsel, *Human Rights in Criminal Proceedings*, 265–6.

be sensitive to the demand that individual accused persons are given a voice in the proceedings.[19] Where at all possible, opportunities should be given to accused persons to address the court and whether they wish to protest against the political regime and justice system that has put them on trial.[20] But the personal right to be present and address the court can be de-coupled from the institutional right to effective defence, which we have argued is integral to the overall legitimacy of the criminal trial process.[21] We next turn to the evidentiary issues that arise in the context of this institutional right. Firstly, there is the question as to when effective legal assistance should be exercised and what degree of access, communication and confidentiality should be permitted between legal counsel and their clients. Secondly, there is the question of the degree of disclosure that should be made to the defence by the prosecution. Thirdly, there is the question of what access there should be to evidence outside the possession and control of the prosecution. Finally, there is the question of how state claims of public interest immunity should be handled. We shall examine each of these issues in turn.

9.2 The right to effective legal assistance

9.2.1 Early legal assistance

In the previous chapter, it was argued that the right of silence which has tended to be associated with the individual accused's freedom *from* participation is better reconceptualised as a positive right *to* participate once the conditions for the exercise of defence rights have been put in place. A vital condition is the need for effective legal assistance at the point at which accused persons are called upon to participate. The ECtHR has slowly recognised the need for legal assistance not only at the trial stage, but at pre-trial stages as well,[22] and we saw that in *Salduz* v. *Turkey*[23] it considered that in order for the right to a fair trial to remain sufficiently 'practical and effective', Article 6(1) required that, as a rule, access to a lawyer should be provided as from the first interrogation of a suspect by the police.

9.2.2 Communication with counsel

The need for early legal assistance is recognition of the important connection between the right to legal assistance and another commonly recognised defence

---

[19] Damaška, 'Assignment of Counsel'.
[20] One of the most effective examples of this is Nelson Mandela's statement from the dock in the Rivonia trial, where Mandela was also represented by counsel: see N. Mandela, *Long Walk to Freedom* (Boston: Little, Brown, 1994) 432–8.
[21] Trechsel argues that it is important to distinguish between the right of the accused to act in his or her own defence, which is 'relatively absolute', and the right *not* to be assisted by counsel, which is much more debatable: see *Human Rights in Criminal Proceedings*, 251–2 and 263–6.
[22] *Quaranta* v. *Switzerland* (legal assistance required in connection with appearances before an investigating judge).
[23] Discussed in Ch. 8.6.

right: the right to have adequate time and facilities for the preparation of the defence.[24] Article 14 of the ICCPR indeed expressly provides in paragraph (3)(b) that 'everyone shall have adequate time and facilities for the preparation of the defence *and to communicate with counsel of his own choosing*'.[25] The HRC considered that adequate facilities must include the opportunity to engage and communicate with counsel and the European Committee of Experts has pointed out that the right to communicate with counsel is a natural corollary of the right to have adequate time and facilities for the preparation of the defence.[26] In a number of European decisions, the right of access to and free communication with counsel has also been considered a 'facility' within the meaning of Article 6(3)(b) of the ECHR.[27]

The emphasis on the right of access and communication is obviously vital if counsel are able to give effective assistance and in a number of cases where defendants have been held incommunicado the importance of the right of access to a lawyer has been stressed.[28] The ECtHR has also held that limiting lawyers' access to an applicant to 2 hours per week was insufficient in a case involving complex charges as the rights guaranteed under Article 6 had to be enjoyed in an effective manner.[29] In addition to providing effective access to the accused, it is clear that counsel as well as the accused must be given adequate times and facilities to do this.[30] Determination of what is adequate depends on an assessment of the particular circumstances of each case.[31] In *Castillo Petruzzi and others v. Peru*,[32] the ACtHR found that there was a violation of both the right to counsel and the right to have adequate time and facilities for the preparation of the defence when counsel was only able to obtain access to the case file a day before the ruling of the court of first instance. The court quoted from the *Basic Principles of the Role of Lawyers*, which sets out the proper standards for an adequate defence in criminal cases:

> All arrested, detained or imprisoned persons shall be provided with adequate opportunities, time and facilities to be visited by and to communicate and consult with a lawyer, without delay, interception or censorship and in full confidentiality.

---

[24] See Art. 14(3)(b) ICCPR, Art. 6(3)(a) ECHR and Art. 8(2)(b) ACHR. [25] Emphasis added.
[26] HRC, *General Comment*, para. 13, Art. 14 (Twenty-first session, 1984) para. 9. Report of the Committee of Experts on Human Rights to the Committee of Ministers, *Problems arising from the co-existence of the UNCHR and the ECHR* (1970) para. 141ii.
[27] *Can v. Austria*.
[28] *Perdomo v. Uruguay*; *Weinberger v. Uruguay*; *Tourón v. Uruguay*; *Conteris v. Uruguay*; *Marais v. Madagascar*; *Caldas v. Uruguay*; and *Lluberas v. Uruguay*.
[29] *Öcalan v. Turkey*; and *Öcalan v. Turkey* [GC].
[30] 'Sufficient time and facilities must be granted to accused and counsel to prepare the defence for the trial': *Thomas v. Jamaica*.
[31] HRC, *General Comment*, para. 13. See *Little v. Jamaica* (half-an-hour consultation with counsel before trial insufficient in a capital case); *Smith v. Jamaica* (four-hour adjournment insufficient time to prepare in a capital case); and *Phillip v. Trinidad and Tobago* (capital case request for adjournment case file only delivered 3 days before trial insufficient time to prepare).
[32] 17 September 1997, Series C no. 33.

Such consultations may be within sight, but not within the hearing, of law enforcement officials.[33]

In this case, the presence and participation of the defence attorneys were mere formalities and it could hardly be argued that the victims had an adequate means of defence.

9.2.3 Right to private communication and legal professional privilege

The *Basic Principles* refer to the right to consult with a lawyer without delay, interception or censorship and in full confidentiality. Of the human rights treaties, only the ACHR specifically refers to the right to communicate privately with counsel.[34] But this principle has become widely accepted in the human rights jurisprudence. In *Can* v. *Austria*, the ECommHR referred to a number of European resolutions and standards as evidence of the importance attached by legal systems to the right of the accused to communicate with his or her lawyer in private.[35] As an explanation for the importance of this right in the context of the right to a fair trial, the commission considered that several of the functions of defence counsel in criminal proceedings – including not only the assistance in the preparation for trial, but also control over the lawfulness of any measures taken against the accused during the criminal proceedings – would be interfered with or made impossible if counsel could not communicate with his client in private.[36] In later jurisprudence, the ECtHR repeated that if lawyers were unable to confer with their clients and receive confidential instructions from them without surveillance, their assistance would lose much of its usefulness, whereas the Convention is intended to guarantee rights that are practical and effective.[37]

The ECtHR's jurisprudence, however, also indicates that there are circumstances when the right of access may be restricted for good cause and the question in each case is whether the restriction in the light of the entirety of the proceedings has deprived the accused of a fair hearing. The applicant must

---

[33] *United Nations Basic Principles on the Role of Lawyers, relative to the special safeguards in criminal justice matters*, approved by the Eighth United Nations Congress on the Prevention of Crime and the Treatment of Offenders at its meeting in Havana, Cuba, from 27 August to 7 September 1990, no. 8.

[34] Art. 8(2)(d).

[35] 12 July 1984, Series B no. 79 (report). Rule 93 of the Standard Minimum Rules for the Treatment of Prisoners states that 'an untried prisoner shall be entitled as soon as he is imprisoned to choose his legal representative or shall be allowed to apply for free legal aid where such aid is available, and to receive visits from his legal adviser with a view to his defence and to receive confidential instructions'. Art. 3(2)(c) European Agreement Relating to Persons Participating in Proceedings of the European Court states that a 'person under detention shall have a right to correspond and consult out of hearing of other persons with a lawyer qualified to appear before the courts'.

[36] *Can* v. *Austria* (report), paras. 55–8.

[37] *S* v. *Switzerland*, para. 48; *Brennan* v. *United Kingdom*, para. 58; and *Öcalan* v. *Turkey*, para. 146.

be able to claim to have been directly affected by the restriction in the exercise of the rights of the defence. In *Brennan* v. *United Kingdom*,[38] the ECtHR found that the presence of the police officer during the first consultation with the applicant's solicitor prevented the applicant from speaking frankly to his solicitor, and this infringed his right to an effective exercise of his defence rights. But the requirement that in order to constitute a breach of the right to a fair trial in criminal proceedings any intrusion on communications between counsel and client must affect the exercise of the client's defence rights makes the right of access less absolute than it might be. While it is not necessary to prove that the restriction had a prejudicial effect on the course of the trial such that the accused cannot have a fair trial,[39] there would appear to be an onus on the applicant to show that he or she has been directly affected rather than rely simply on the right of confidentiality per se.

The European jurisprudence has also recognised that the nature of the lawyer–client relationship is protected under Article 8 of the ECHR, which protects the right to privacy.[40] As the ECtHR put it in *Campbell and Fell* v. *United Kingdom*,[41] it is in the general interest that any person who wishes to consult a lawyer should be free to do so under conditions which favour full and uninhibited discussion. Under Article 8(2), however, there is an explicit qualification that allows interference where necessary in a democratic society for a variety of purposes, including the prevention of disorder and crime and for the protection of the rights and freedoms of others. There are suggestions in the jurisprudence that where there is evidence that the confidential relationship is being abused, that would be a ground for restricting the protection afforded to legal professional privilege. Thus, in *Schonenberger and Durmaz* v. *Switzerland*, a letter by a lawyer to his client was withheld by the public prosecutor on the ground that the advice given in the letter not to answer questions would jeopardise the conduct of the pending criminal proceedings. The ECtHR rejected the suggestion that the lawyer's conduct was improper as the applicant had a right to silence. In *Brennan* itself, the police officer's presence at the first interview was justified by the government on the ground that there was a risk of prejudice to the ongoing search for two other suspected persons, but the court could find no compelling reasons for the imposition of the restriction. At most, the presence of the police officer would have had some effect in inhibiting any improper communication of information, assuming there was a risk that such might take place, and there was no allegation that the solicitor was in fact likely to collaborate in such an attempt. In each of these cases, the suggestion is that if the confidential relationship were being abused for unlawful or criminal purposes, restrictions on the privilege would be justified provided they were proportionate.[42]

---

[38] *Brennan* v. *United Kingdom*, para 58.
[39] *Grant* v. *R* [2005] EWCA Crim 1089, para. 54. Cf. *R (on the application of La Rose)* v. *Commissioner of the Police of the Metropolis* [2002] Crim LR 215.
[40] See *Campbell and Fell* v. *United Kingdom*; and *Niemietz* v. *Germany*.
[41] Paras. 46–48.   [42] On proportionality, see *Kopp* v. *Switzerland*.

9.2.4 Balancing away the privilege

The idea that legal professional privilege may be balanced against some other public interest would seem to conflict with the classic common law tradition, which has tended to view the privilege as 'absolute'.[43] Legal professional privilege has a long pedigree in common law jurisdictions where there has been a rule of evidence that lawyers and their clients are protected from disclosing confidential communications between them.[44] This is an exception to the general principle that the interests of justice may if necessary require information to be disclosed, even where this interferes with well-recognised confidential relationships. It is true that where communications are made for the purpose of furthering crime or fraud they are no longer privileged, although it may be argued that this is not so much an exception to the privilege as an argument that if communications are made for this purpose they are no longer privileged in the first place.[45] But that aside, there has been considerable reluctance to admit that there should be any balancing of the privilege against any public interest and this is because there has been a tendency to view the privilege as an individual right pertaining to the client, so that documents protected by the privilege continue to be protected so long as the privilege is not waived by the client. In the words of Lindley MR, 'once privileged, always privileged'.[46]

The point can be illustrated by reference to the House of Lords case of *R v. Derby Magistrates' Court Ex p. B*,[47] where the appellant was acquitted of murder on the basis of a defence that he took some part in the killing, but only under the duress of his stepfather. On being arrested, he had first made a confession which he later retracted that he alone was responsible for the murder. His stepfather who was later also charged with the murder wanted to cross-examine him about instructions he had given to his solicitors between his initial confession and his subsequent statement implicating his stepfather. Lord Taylor considered that the rule that a man must be able to consult his lawyer in defence was much more than an ordinary rule of evidence: it was a fundamental condition on which the administration of justice rests and there could be no exceptions to it, as once any exception was made the client's confidence was lost.[48] Even if the client no longer has a recognisable interest in preserving the confidentiality of the communications, it must still be preserved unless it is

---

[43] *R v. Derby Magistrates' Court Ex p. B* [1995] 4 All ER 526, 542: 'no exception should be allowed to the absolute nature of legal professional privilege, once established', per Lord Taylor, upheld by the Privy Council in *Auckland District Law Society* [2003] UKPC 38, para. 54.

[44] See *Anderson v. Bank of British Columbia* (1876) 2 Ch D 644, 658. Lord Taylor in *R v. Derby Magistrates' Court Ex p. B* [1995] 4 All ER 526 traced the rule back to the sixteenth century and considered that it was well established by the end of the eighteenth century (537–8).

[45] See *R v. Cox and Railton* (1994) 14 QBD 153, per Stephen J.

[46] *Calcraft v. Guest* [1898] 1 QB 759, 761.   [47] [1995] 4 All ER 526.

[48] See also *Anderson v. Bank of British Columbia* (1876) 2 Ch D 644, 649, per Jessel MR; and *Grants v. Downs* (1976) 135 CLR 674, 685.

waived.[49] When it is considered that the countervailing interest in this case was that of the stepfather who was seeking access to highly material evidence which might help to prove his innocence, it is questionable whether the decision accords with human rights law, which as we shall see gives considerable recognition to the importance of access to evidence.[50]

From the point of view of the participatory theory of defence rights argued in this book, it is suggested that the privilege is better viewed as a facility to assist in the effective defence of the accused than as a 'personal' right 'belonging' to an individual who seeks legal advice and more. The privilege has historically been given most prominence in common law systems. Although it has also been recognised in civil law systems, it is not expressly protected in the constitution of any member state of the Council of Europe.[51] It is well enshrined in the law and jurisprudence of the international criminal tribunals.[52] Damaška has argued that the principle deserves a serious hearing even in an activist state characterised by a tendency to favour the smooth implementation of state policy as it may help to promote the accuracy of overall outcomes.[53] Any system of justice that gives a role to lawyers to gather evidence and present cases on behalf of their client would seem to have to rely upon some principle of professional legal privilege if such a role is to be effective from an evidentiary point of view. Nor need the privilege be restricted to communications that take place when litigation is contemplated. Frank and uninhibited disclosure can be just as important when persons are seeking any kind of legal advice, as legal advice which can lead on to litigation can be adversely affected if it is not based upon as wide an informational pool as possible.[54] Damaška has argued that it would seem prudent to provide a safety valve for those instances

---

[49] Lord Nicholls was less emphatic on this point. See [1995] 4 All ER 526, 546. Cf. *R* v. *Dunbar and Logan* (1982) 138 DLR (3d) 221, 252.

[50] For criticism, see Dennis, *Law of Evidence*, para. 10.26, 436; C. Tapper, 'Prosecution and Privilege' (1996) 1 *International Journal of Evidence & Proof* 5; P. Roberts and A. Zuckerman, *Criminal Evidence*, 2nd edn (Oxford University Press, 2010) 319–20; and A. Choo, *Evidence*, 3rd edn (Oxford University Press, 2009) 239.

[51] See, e.g. Germany, where the principle of professional secrecy is guaranteed under the German Federal Lawyers Act: see *Niemietz* v. *Germany* and Art. 43 of the Criminal Code. See further J. Fish, *Regulated Legal Professionals and Professional Privilege within the European Union, the European Economic Area and Switzerland and Certain Other Jurisdictions* (Brussels: CCBE, 2004). On the differences in the various European regulatory approaches and on the distinction between professional secrecy and professional privilege, see T. Spronken and J. Fermon, 'Protection of Attorney-Client Privilege in Europe' (2008) 27 *Penn State International Law Review* 439.

[52] See r. 73(1) ICC RPE, r. 97 ICTY RPE and r. 121 ICTR RPE. See also J. P. W. Temmnick Tuinstra, *Defence Counsel in International Criminal Law* (The Hague: T. M. C. Asser, 2009) 209 ff.

[53] M. R. Damaška, *The Faces of Justice and State Authority* (New Haven: Yale University Press, 1986) 175.

[54] The extension of the privilege to cover legal advice has also been defended on the ground that it can help to avoid litigation: see *Greenough* v. *Gaskell* (1833) 1 Myl & K 98, 103, per Lord Brougham; and *Smurfit Paribas Bank Ltd* v. *AAB Export Finance Ltd* [1990] 1 IR 469.

in which the competing interest in accurate adjudication of a particular case clearly outweighs the more 'remote, speculative damage to the general accuracy of outcomes' which the privilege seeks to promote.[55] In criminal proceedings, however, where so much weight is attached to protecting the innocent accused, it may be argued that the privilege cannot be easily balanced away in the interest simply of accurate outcomes. Frank communication with counsel is arguably such an essential basis for establishing an effective defence that accused persons are entitled to be assured that it will be respected so long as they have any interest in defending the charge against them.

Although certain common law jurisdictions have elevated legal professional privilege almost to the status of a constitutional principle,[56] some have been re-considering its ambit and have been regarding it as subject to a balancing exercise with other rights and principles. The particular emphasis given in both common law and civil law systems to the presumption of innocence and the need to avoid the conviction of the innocent, for example, suggests that priority should be given to any defendant seeking access to material evidence even where it comes within the ambit of legal professional privilege.[57] In Canada, the Supreme Court has considered that the right may be required to yield to the accused's constitutional right to make full answer and defence to a criminal charge provided he can show that the information he seeks from the privileged communication is necessary to raise a reasonable doubt.[58] This approach gives due weight to the over-arching need to prevent miscarriages of justice and brings us to the need to examine the whole question of the defence right to disclosure of evidence.

9.3 The right to full disclosure of evidence

9.3.1 The case against the accused

It is obvious that effective defence participation is dependent on the defendant being made aware of the case against him or her. It is frequently claimed that

---

[55] Damaška, *Faces of Justice*, 175.
[56] For Canada, see *Solosky* v. *Canada* (1980) 105 DLR (3d) 745; *Smith* v. *Jones* [1999] 1 SCR 455; Australia, *ESSO Australia Resources Ltd* v. *Dawson* [1999] FCA 363; New Zealand, *Rosenberg* v. *Jaine* [1983] NZLR 1; and Ireland, *Duncan* v. *Governor of Portlaoise Prison* [1997] 1 IR 558.
[57] See s. 123 Australian Evidence Act 1995.
[58] See *R* v. *Seaboyer* [1991] 2 SCR 577, 607; *A (LL)* v. *B(A)* [1995] 4 SCR 536, 577; *Smith* v. *Jones* [1999] 1 SCR 455, 477–8; *R* v. *Campbell* [1999] 1 SCR 565, 610–11; and *R* v. *Brown* [2002] 2 SCR 185. For discussion, see B. Sheldrick, 'Administering Public Safety: Solicitor-Client Privilege, Medical Experts and the Adversarial Process' (2000) 4 *International Journal of Evidence & Proof* 119; G. Murphy, 'The Innocence at Stake Test and Legal Professional Privilege: A Logical Progression for the Law . . . But Not in England' [2001] *Criminal Law Review* 728; R. Pattenden, *The Law of Professional-Client Confidentiality: Regulating The Disclosure of Confidential Personal Information* (Oxford University Press, 2003) 552–3; and Choo, *Evidence*, 239–40.

if accused persons are unaware of what they are accused of, they are in the 'Kafkaesque situation' of being unable to meet those allegations.[59] Without such knowledge, the defence is so handicapped that it hardly makes sense to speak of there being any meaningful role for the defence at all.[60] At its most basic level, such a right may be linked to the right to be present at one's hearing, which is expressly guaranteed under Article 14(3)(d) of the ICCPR and has been considered to be inherent in the very notion of 'fair trial' or 'fair hearing'.[61]

The right to know the evidence against one reaches far back into the annals of basic fair procedure and has become an essential part of customary international law and the laws of war.[62] In 2004, the USSC held that the failure to afford persons detained at Guantánamo Bay, after the terrorist attacks of 11 September 2001, the right to learn of the evidence against them at closed hearings of the military commission established to put them on trial constituted a failure to comply with the rules of the Uniform Code of Military Justice and the Manual for Courts-Martial, which required that all evidence supporting a conviction be disclosed to the accused and his counsel.[63] In his opinion, Stevens J., joined by a number of other justices, referred to Common Article 3 of the Geneva Conventions, which specifies that before passing sentences on individuals captured during armed conflicts for war crimes, they had to be tried before a 'regularly constituted court affording all the judicial guarantees which are recognised as indispensable by civilised peoples'.[64] Although the conventions did not define what these guarantees were, it was considered that they must be understood to incorporate at least the barest of trial protections that have been recognised by customary international law. Many of these were described in Article 75 of Protocol I to the Geneva Conventions of 1949 and they included the principles that an

---

[59] *Roberts v. Parole Board* [2005] UKHL 45, para. 126, per Lord Carswell. The situation is described in Franz Kafka's 1925 classic masterpiece, *The Trial* (London: Secker and Warburg, 1976) 69 as follows: '... the legal records of the case, and above all the actual charge sheets, were inaccessible to the accused and his counsel, consequently one did not know in general, or least did not know with any precision, what charges to meet in the first plea; accordingly, it could only be pure chance that it contained really relevant matter.' Cited by Lord Steyn in *Roberts* (para. 95).

[60] 'In such circumstances the defence was naturally in a very ticklish and difficult position. Yet that, too, was intentional. For the Defence was not actually countenanced by the Law, but only tolerated, and there were differences of opinion even on that point, whether the Law could be interpreted to admit such tolerance at all. Strictly speaking, therefore, none of the advocates was recognised by the court; all who appeared before the Court as Advocates being in reality merely in the position of hole-and-corner Advocates' (*The Trial*, 69–70).

[61] *Colozza v. Italy*, para. 27: 'Although this is not expressly mentioned in paragraph 1 of Article 6, the object and purpose of the Article taken as a whole shows that a person "charged with a criminal offence" is entitled to take part in the hearing.'

[62] 5 UN War Crimes Commission 30 (trial of Sergeant Major Ahigerau Ohasshi), 745 (trial of Gerbna Tanklaa Hisaku).

[63] *Hamdan v. Rumsfeld*, 126 S Ct 2749 (2006).

[64] Common Art. 3 of the 1949 Geneva Conventions sets out the minimum protections and humanitarian treatment for the victims of civil or internal conflicts. See O. Gross and F. Ni Aoláin, *Law in Times of Crisis: Emergency Powers in Theory and Practice* (Cambridge University Press, 2006) 355–6.

accused must absent disruptive conduct or consent be present for his trial and be privy to the evidence against him. In its Military Commission Act revising the procedures for trying these detainees, Congress rectified these failures by requiring full disclosure of the case against the accused.[65]

The need for the accused to be made privy at trial to the evidence against him or her as a fundamental requirement of any fair hearing was also recently emphasised by the ECtHR in reviewing the procedures adopted by the United Kingdom to determine whether foreign nationals could be detained where they are considered to be a risk to national security.[66] The United Kingdom had established a scheme under which closed material that was considered too sensitive to disclose to the detainees could be disclosed instead to special advocates appointed to act on their behalf. The ECtHR ruled that the core irreducible minimum required under Article 5(4) of the ECHR in situations where a detained person faced lengthy deprivation of liberty must import substantially the same fair trial guarantees as contained in Article 6(1) of the ECHR in its criminal aspect and this required that the detained person must be given sufficient information about the allegations against him to enable him to give effective instructions to the special advocate. Where, therefore, the material disclosed consisted purely of general assertions and a decision to uphold detention is based solely or to a decisive degree on closed material, the procedural requirements of Article 5(4) of the ECHR would not be satisfied.[67]

9.3.2 The scope of the right to disclosure: *Jespers* and *Edwards*

The international human rights instruments do not specifically require that evidence be disclosed to the defence before trial. They require that accused persons be informed promptly of the nature and cause of the charge or accusation against them in a language which they understand and in detail.[68] This means that timely notice must be given of the charges before trial, but it falls short of requiring that notice be given of the evidence on which the facts of the accusation are based. It appears to be sufficient to satisfy this requirement for the information to list the offences against the accused, stating the place and date thereof and the name of the victim.[69] Much greater scope for disclosure has, however, been developed under the requirement that the accused be given adequate facilities for the preparation of his defence.[70] The Human

---

[65] P. Wald, 'Fair Trials for War Criminals' (2006) 4 *International Commentary on Evidence*, Issue 1, Art. 6.

[66] *A and others* v. *United Kingdom* [GC].

[67] See also *Secretary of State for Home Dept* v. *AF and another* [2009] UKHL 28. Cf. *Secretary of State for Home Dept* v. *MB and AF* [2007] UKHL 46.

[68] Art. 14 (3)(a) ICCPR, Art. 6(3)(a) ECHR and Art. 8(2)(b) ACHR using somewhat different language entitles the accused to prior notification in detail of the charges against him.

[69] *Brozicek* v. *Italy*.

[70] Art. 14(3)(b) ICCPR, Art. 6(3)(b) ECHR and Art. 8(c) ACHR. The ACHR uses the term 'means' instead of 'facilities'.

Rights Committee has considered that 'adequate facilities' must include access to documents and other evidence which the accused requires to prepare his or her case.[71]

Quite how extensive this right to disclosure need be has been the subject of some jurisprudence within the ECommHR and ECtHR. In its early jurisprudence, the Commission considered that Article 6(3)(b) of the ECHR did not require that the prosecuting authorities should give accused persons notice of all of the evidence which may be given during their trial.[72] But we have seen that the Strasbourg organs have used the concepts of the 'equality of arms' and 'adversarial rights' to develop a theory of effective defence rights and in *Jespers v. Belgium*[73] the ECommHR applied these concepts to the specific right of the defence to be given adequate facilities for the preparation of his defence. The Commission first made the point that in any criminal proceedings brought by a state authority, the prosecution has at its disposal, to back the accusation, facilities deriving from its powers of investigation supported by judicial and police machinery with considerable technical resources and means of coercion. In order to establish equality of arms with the prosecution, the defence had to have access to these facilities, which included the opportunity of the accused 'to acquaint himself, for the purpose of preparing his defence, with the results of investigations carried out throughout the proceedings'.[74] It held that 'although a right of access to the prosecution file was not expressly guaranteed by the Convention, such a right could be inferred from Article 6 paragraph 3(b)' and that this provision entitled the accused to have at his disposal, for the purposes of exonerating himself or of obtaining a reduction in his sentence, all relevant elements that have been or could be collected by the competent authorities.[75]

The first point to make about this interpretation of what the equality of arms principle requires the state to do in terms of pre-trial disclosure is that it would seem to require more than just disclosure of the prosecution 'case' or the prosecution 'evidence' to the defence. A distinction is sometimes made in common law jurisdictions between 'used' and 'unused' material, the former constituting only that which is used by the prosecution in support of its case and the latter constituting all other material evidence gathered during an investigation.[76] *Jespers*, however, concerned an application against Belgium, a continental jurisdiction which does not lend itself easily to distinguishing information on the basis of the prosecution case. In continental jurisdictions, the preliminary investigation is entrusted traditionally to a member of the judiciary or an independent prosecutor who gathers all the relevant evidence in favour of as well as against the accused. The file into which this evidence is

---

[71] *General Comment*, para. 9.b.   [72] *X v. United Kingdom* (dec.).
[73] *Jespers v. Belgium* (report).   [74] Ibid., para. 55.   [75] Ibid., para. 56.
[76] The term 'unused material' was first used in England and Wales with the introduction of the Attorney General's Guidelines for the Disclosure of 'Unused' Material to the Defence (1982) 74 Cr App R 302. See C. W. Taylor, *Criminal Investigation and Pre-Trial Disclosure in the United Kingdom* (Lewiston, Queenston, Lampeter: Edwin Mellen, 2006) 28.

put then contains the transcripts of the interrogations of the defendant and the witnesses by the police, the investigating authority, or the public prosecutor's office, expert opinions, pictures of the crime scene, maps and plans, reports on searches and other documents and pieces of evidence.[77] It is nevertheless important to bear in mind that in many continental European jurisdictions the prosecution and police are permitted to maintain a file for retaining personal notes and internal correspondence. In *Jespers*, the Commission ruled that this practice was legitimate and that the authorities were entitled to withhold these separate files from the defence.[78] However, the potential for abuse is clear; the investigating authorities are afforded the opportunity to withhold evidence, which they believe to be immaterial, from the defence, which has no opportunity of assessing the relevance of the evidence itself.[79] Furthermore, many systems have developed rules which restrict the prosecution's duty to disclose evidence, particularly in relation to undercover operations undertaken early on in the investigation.[80]

It might be possible to separate out in this process the evidence in the file pointing to guilt and the other evidence collected, but the equality of arms principle applied in *Jespers* appears to require that since the prosecution or a judicial figure is entrusted with the task of investigation, it is necessary that the defence see the fruits of all the investigations carried out in the course of the proceedings. Furthermore, it would seem that the obligation to disclose the fruits of the investigation is not restricted to particular state authorities or to selected stages of the proceedings. The suggestion appears to be that any investigations carried out must be disclosed to the defence. Given that the context in which the defence's opportunity to carry out meaningful investigations is limited, moreover it would appear that the prosecutor must do more than simply hand over the fruits of the investigation; he or she must also disclose 'all relevant elements that have been or could be collected by the competent authorities'. This would seem to imply that the prosecutor must disclose not only the file which contains the fruits of the investigation, but also other relevant elements that could be collected, whether they are contained in the file or not. These duties appear to be quite extensive. What is less clear, however, as we shall see, is precisely *when* disclosure of all the relevant elements should be made.

---

[77] Trechsel, *Human Rights in Criminal Proceedings*, 224.
[78] See *Jespers* v. *Belgium* (report), para. 59. See also D. Krauss, 'Der Umfang der Strafakte' (1983) *Basler Juristische Mitteilungen* 49; and S. Trechsel, 'Akteneinsicht: Information als Grundlage des fairen Verfahrens', in R. J. Schweizer, H. Burkert and U. Gasser (eds.), *Festschrift für Jean Nicolas Drury zum 65. Geburtstag* (Zurich: Schulthess, 2002) 993, 998.
[79] See Trechsel, *Human Rights in Criminal Proceedings*, 225; and S. Stavros, *The Guarantees for Accused Persons under Article 6 of the European Convention on Human Rights* (Dordrecht: Martinus Nijhoff, 1993) 179.
[80] For discussion of this issue in Norway, see A. Strandbakken, 'Disclosure of Evidence by the Prosecution', in H. Müller-Dietz, E. Müller, K.-L. Kunz, H. Radtke, G. Brutz, C. Momsen and H. Koriath (eds.), *Festschrift für Heike Jung zum 65. Geburtstag* (Baden-Baden: Nomos, 2007) 945, 948 ff.

The requirements in *Jespers* are modelled upon a continental system of justice where an impartial judge or prosecutor creates a file containing all of the material evidence in the case. These are not so easily translated into a common law context, where there is not a file that neatly encapsulates all of the evidence in the case before trial. Indeed, the information accumulated by the prosecution prior to trial is not strictly speaking 'evidence' at all, in the sense that it can be used directly at trial. This raises the question of whether the equality of arms principle should require the prosecution to hand over the fruits of its investigation in a more adversarial context where the defence as well as the prosecution is supposed to carry out its own investigations. We shall see that this adversary context has made it difficult to instill a culture whereby the prosecution is supposed to act in the interests of the defence. Nevertheless, the reality of common law investigations is that the prosecution here too has at its disposal far greater resources and power to carry out investigations than the defence and this suggests that there should be corresponding obligations on the prosecution to disclose not only its own case against the defence, but also all material information to which it has been privy.

The ECtHR clarified its position so far as common law countries are concerned in *Edwards v. United Kingdom*. Here, the prosecution had failed to disclose the fact that two fingerprints had been found at the scene of a robbery which later turned out to be those of the next-door neighbour who was a regular visitor to the house where the robbery took place. In addition, there had been a failure to disclose the fact that the victim had not picked the applicant out of a photo album. Although these were not pieces of evidence that constituted part of the prosecution case, the applicant claimed that these failures of disclosure amounted to a breach of his fair trial right under paragraph (1) to a fair hearing and, interestingly, under paragraph 6(3)(d) (not paragraph 6(3)(b)), which provides that the defence shall have the right to examine witnesses under the same conditions as the prosecution. The failure to disclose the evidence meant that when it came to examining the police witnesses, the defence were not on as equal footing as the prosecution. The court declined to examine the relevance of paragraph (3)(d) to the non-disclosure, but held that it is a requirement under Article 6(1) that the prosecution authorities disclose to the defence all material evidence for or against the accused and the failure to do so constituted a defect in the trial proceedings.[81] Later cases, however, would seem to have added a little noticed gloss to this obligation by restricting it to an obligation to disclose to the defence all material evidence for or against the accused *in their possession*, which seems to fall short of the *Jespers* obligation to disclose all relevant elements that *could* be collected by the competent authorities.[82]

---

[81] See also *Atlan v. United Kingdom*.
[82] It is not clear whether this was an intentional restriction. We shall see that the common law has fallen short of imposing legal obligations on prosecutors to seek out exculpatory evidence.

9.3.3 Uncertainties as to scope

The European jurisprudence would seem to give a fairly expansive interpretation of what is required to be disclosed in the interests of equality of arms and takes due account of the disparity of resources between the parties. There are, however, a number of uncertainties about the scope and application of these obligations. The first point to make is that while they seem to go a long way to ensuring that both prosecution and defence are able to make their arguments on the basis of a common pool of relevant evidence, they do not entitle the defence to access to *all* of the information in the hands of the prosecuting authority. This was made clear in a more recent admissibility decision of the ECtHR where during the course of a criminal investigation into the supply of drugs, the accused and his co-defendants had been subjected to intensive police observations.[83] The applicant claimed that the refusal to disclose the many covertly obtained tapes of conversations and the details of all the observations not already in evidence was a violation of Article 6(1) of the Convention. But the ECtHR held that this case was different from other cases in that it turned not on the non-disclosure of relevant (but unused) material, but on the non-disclosure of unused material, which – according to the prosecution – was not at all relevant to the defence. The ECtHR considered that the application was manifestly ill-founded. The applicant had not made any submissions which could cast doubt on the validity either of the prosecution's conclusion that the unused material was not relevant or of the domestic court's acceptance of that conclusion.

This means that judgments are left for prosecutors to make in the first instance as to what are 'relevant elements' and it is then for the defence to show that there is relevant evidence that has not been disclosed. It is questionable whether this is in true accordance with an equality of arms principle, which would seem to require that both sides should be able to make arguments from the same pool of evidence. Permitting the prosecution to make initial decisions as to the materiality of the evidence narrows the availability of this pool to the defence. The difficulty is that prosecutors may have a different view from the defence as to what constitutes material evidence.

A good example of this is to be found in the English case of *Laszlo Virag*, where the accused was wrongly convicted of the theft of parking meter coin boxes on the basis of a number of false identifications made of him. During the course of the police inquiry, certain fingerprints were discovered on the stolen cash containers and on a hand lamp that were not the prints of Virag, but these were never disclosed to the defence. At the time of the inquiry, it was inconceivable to the police that all of the identifications made of Virag were false and the police proceeded on the assumption that there was an associate working with Virag. If this information had been disclosed to the defence, however, it would have been

---

[83] *Glover v. United Kingdom* (dec.).

used to raise a reasonable doubt as to Virag's involvement in the theft, despite the strong identification evidence against him. The Devlin Committee, which reviewed the case, commented that it showed that the prosecution and defence might very easily take a different view of what may be 'material evidence'.[84] The point can also be illustrated in the *Edwards* case itself where the failure of the victim of the robbery to identify a suspect from certain photographs may not have appeared to be relevant from the point of view of the investigation targeting the suspect, but may in fact be a very significant piece of information from the point of view of the defence.[85]

A second point is that although the disclosure requirements laid down in *Jespers* and *Edwards* would seem to be quite demanding, they have been diluted by a reluctance to hold that there has been a breach of Article 6 unless there was some material that was not disclosed that was of some use to the defence.[86] In *Jespers*, the applicant complained that a special folder containing relevant evidence had been withheld from the defence, but the Commission considered that it contained nothing that would have helped the preparation of the defence. This can only be judged after the event and does little to create an incentive on prosecutors to comply with their obligations at the time that the information becomes available. It is again arguable that this approach does not comply fully with the principle of equality of arms, which as we have seen is not only designed to address procedural inequality between the prosecution and defence, but is also designed to ensure an appearance of equality.[87] Even if in a particular case the defence cannot show that it was adversely affected in some manner by the absence of disclosure, the mere lack of disclosure of aspects of the file may be considered a breach of the prosecution's disclosure obligations as it gives an appearance of inequality.[88]

A further restriction has also been placed on the principle of full disclosure by requiring defendants to cooperate in producing elements in their defence. In *Edwards* v. *United Kingdom*, there was an argument that the prosecution should have disclosed the report of an independent police investigation that was ordered when complaints were made by the applicant into the police investigation of his case. Although the report appeared to be relevant and should have been disclosed, the defence did not apply for the production of the report when it came to light before the defendant's appeal hearing and the court held by a majority that there had been no unfairness. This raises an important question that we shall see is central to disclosure obligations and that is the role of the court in seeing that they are fulfilled. The majority judgment in *Edwards* would

---

[84] *Report to the Secretary of State for the Home Department of the Departmental Committee on Identification in Criminal Cases* (1976) HC 338, para. 5.3.
[85] See Trechsel, *Human Rights in Criminal Proceedings*, 225.
[86] Ibid., 229.   [87] See further Ch. 4.2.2.
[88] Trechsel argues that the 'appearances matter' maxim could have been applied to the requirement under Art. 6(3)(b) that the defence be given adequate facilities in the same manner as it has applied the maxim to the need for judges to be regarded as impartial: see *Human Rights in Criminal Proceedings*, 229.

seem to put the onus on the defence to enforce disclosure without the court itself taking on the task of ensuring it has been met. One of the minority judges considered that when the court becomes aware of any lack of disclosure it is for it to raise the matter. As he said, 'one cannot leave to a possibly inexperienced defence alone the burden of ensuring respect for the fundamental procedural rule which prohibits the concealment of documents or evidence'.[89] This goes to the heart of an argument in this book that in order to ensure effective defence participation, it is not enough to facilitate defence participation. Steps must be taken to see that it is exercised effectively and the court has an important role to play in this regard.

It would seem that there is also some uncertainty as to when precisely disclosure should be made. *Jespers* suggests that the police as well as prosecutors may be required to disclose the fruits of their investigations as soon as they are completed. In *Lamy* v. *Belgium*, the ECtHR found that there had been a violation of Article 5(4) of the ECHR when the applicant who had been arrested on charges relating to his bankruptcy and detained on remand was not allowed access to the official file in his case when applying for bail. In rejecting his appeal, the Indictments Chamber of the Court of Appeal in Belgium relied on two material documents which were not communicated to him and the ECtHR invoked the principle of equality of arms and the adversarial principle that all evidence must be produced before the parties with a view to adversarial argument. The judgment led to pressure in Belgium to change the restrictive disclosure rules, but it was by no means clear how widely the adversarial principle advanced by the ECtHR was to be practised in other cases. The reason why access was so important in this case was because the information was essential for an assessment of the lawfulness of the applicant's detention. No doubt an applicant can argue that access is important in order to make representations on the evidence against her for the purposes of a fair trial under Article 6. If as is the case in many common law and civil law jurisdictions disclosure of the prosecution evidence is delayed until the trial stage, the defence are disadvantaged in challenging evidence at crucial pre-trial phases of the proceedings. This can be particularly detrimental to the defence in continental jurisdictions, where the examination and challenging of the evidence takes place at the investigation stage. In Switzerland, for example, many cantons prevented the defence from accessing the file until the conclusion of the pre-trial phase.[90] This situation has been significantly improved by the introduction of the new procedural code. The defence now has the right of access to the file once the first examination hearing with the accused has been conducted and any other important evidence has been taken.[91]

---

[89] Dissenting Opinion of Judge Pettiti attached to the judgment.
[90] See N. Schmid, *Handbuch des Schweizerischen Strafprozessrechts* (Zurich: Dike, 2009) para. 624, who describes these earlier provisions as no longer in keeping with the times.
[91] See Art. 101 of the Swiss Federal Code of Criminal Procedure, in A. Donatsch, T. Hansjakob and V. Lieber (eds.), *Kommentar zur Schweizerischen Strafprozessordnung* (Zürich: Schulthess, 2010), which contains an English translation of the code.

The lack of clarity as to when disclosure should be made is further compounded by the ECtHR's tendency to look retrospectively at the proceedings as a whole and to consider whether despite any failings the trial was unfair. In *Edwards*, the defect was remedied by the discovery of the undisclosed evidence by a subsequent independent police investigation so that when the case was referred to the Court of Appeal the ECtHR was then able to take into account the whole of the evidence for and against the accused and the defects in the original trial were remedied by the subsequent appeal. We have seen that this approach is consistent with the general approach of the ECtHR, but it hardly sets a very onerous requirement on the authorities if they may remedy defects in disclosure that should have taken place at earlier stages of the proceedings.

9.3.4 An absolute right?

A final gloss on the expansive interpretation given to the disclosure requirements in *Jespers* is that subsequent jurisprudence has accepted that the entitlement to disclosure of relevant evidence is not an absolute right. In *Rowe and Davis* v. *United Kingdom*, the prosecution decided without consulting the trial judge to withhold certain information relating to the role of an informer in the case. At the outset of the appeal, the defence were notified that the information had been withheld. The Court of Appeal reviewed the evidence at two ex parte hearings and upheld the decision of the Crown to withhold it. The ECtHR held that while Article 6 of the ECHR generally requires the prosecution to disclose to the defence all material evidence for or against an accused, in any criminal proceedings there may be competing interests such as national security or the need to protect witnesses at risk of reprisal or keep secret police methods of investigation of crime which must be weighed against the rights of the accused. The ECtHR noted that it may in some cases be necessary to withhold certain evidence so as to preserve the fundamental rights of another individual or to safeguard an important public interest, but it identified two constraints on state authorities wishing to withhold disclosable evidence from the defence. Firstly, any restrictions must be 'strictly necessary' and, secondly, any restrictions must be 'strictly counterbalanced' by the procedures followed by the judicial authorities.[92]

As regards the 'strictly necessary' requirement, the ECtHR has considered that it is not its role to decide whether or not any non-disclosure was strictly necessary, as it is for the national courts to assess the evidence before them.[93] While it is reasonable for the ECtHR to emphasise this fourth instance doctrine, questions remain about how exactly the competing interests should be

---

[92] *Rowe and Davis* v. *United Kingdom*, para. 61. See also *Atlan* v. *United Kingdom*, para. 40; *Fitt* v. *United Kingdom* [GC], para. 45; and *Jasper* v. *United Kingdom* [GC], para. 52.

[93] *Rowe and Davis* v. *United Kingdom*, para. 62. See also *Atlan* v. *United Kingdom*, para. 41; *Fitt* v. *United Kingdom* [GC], para. 46; and *Jasper* v. *United Kingdom* [GC], para. 53.

weighed. We have seen that a fundamental requirement of a fair hearing is that the accused is made aware of the case against him or her and it would seem to follow that disclosure of the prosecution evidence to be used in the case is not something that can be ever outweighed by some other competing interest if the case is going to proceed. It is true that domestic courts have over the years protected information divulged in the course of a number of confidential relationships, including as we have seen the relationship between lawyer and client. International law has also recognised that sources can be protected in certain situations, for example by journalists and human rights monitors.[94] But there are few relationships outside the confidential relationship between lawyers and their clients already discussed that have been considered to be absolutely protected from privilege.[95] Witnesses may be required to disclose information given to them in confidence as part of the prosecution case and in this event such information will have to be disclosed to the defence.

In addition, any evidence pointing to the innocence of the accused may also be thought to require disclosure. We have already mentioned the importance that is attached to the prevention of any wrongful convictions. While in a civil case the public interest in the administration of justice, which underpins, of course, the private interest of the litigant who wants the documents, may sometimes have to give way to the greater weight of the public interest against disclosure, it is inappropriate to use the language of balancing where there are interests such as the innocence of the accused at stake in a criminal trial.[96] There is old common law authority to the effect that if the judge should be of the opinion that the disclosure of the name of an informant is necessary or right in order to show the prisoner's innocence, then one public policy is in conflict with another public policy, and that which says that an innocent man is not to be condemned when his innocence can be proved is the policy that must prevail.[97] More recently, it has been said that 'if the disputed material may prove the defendant's innocence or avoid a miscarriage of justice, then the balance comes down resoundingly in favour of disclosing it'.[98] Assuming that evidence of assistance to the defence would help to prove the defendant's innocence or avoid a miscarriage of justice, then this suggests that any evidence of assistance

---

[94] For the position of journalists, see *Goodwin* v. *United Kingdom*; and *Prosecutor* v. *Brdjanin and Talić*, Appeals Chamber, Decision on Interlocutory Appeal. For the position of human rights monitors, see *Prosecutor* v. *Brima*, Appeals Chamber, Decision.
[95] See, however, the majority decision of the ICTY Trial Chamber in *Prosecutor* v. *Simić and others*, Trial Chamber [Public version], *Prosecutor* v. *Stakic*, Appeals Chamber, Judgment, that because of its unique position under the Geneva Conventions, International Red Cross employees were entitled under customary international law to an absolute privilege to prevent them from giving evidence of observations made while on Red Cross work.
[96] R. Scott, 'The Use of Public Interest Immunity Claims in Criminal Cases' [1996] *Web Journal of Current Legal Issues*, issue 2.
[97] *Marks* v. *Beyfus* (1890) 25 QBD 494, 498, per Lord Esher.
[98] *R* v. *Keane* [1994] 1 WLR 746, 751–2, per Lord Taylor CJ.

to the defence must be disclosed and that should be the end of any claim that the public interest requires withholding the evidence.[99]

As for the requirement that any limitations on disclosure rights be 'sufficiently counterbalanced' by other procedures, the ECtHR in *Rowe* went on to say that it would consider whether the decision-making procedure applied in each case complied, as far as possible, with the requirements of adversarial proceedings and the equality of arms and incorporate adequate safeguards to protect the interests of the accused.[100] The words 'as far as possible' would seem to give states leeway to dilute the strict requirements of adversarial procedure and the equality of arms. In this case, however, the ECtHR considered that the failure of the prosecution to notify the judge to withhold certain relevant evidence on the ground of public interest fell foul of the requirements of Article 6.

This establishes the important principle that the prosecution cannot itself attempt to assess the importance of concealed information to the defence and weigh this against the public interest in keeping the information secret. The ECtHR did not consider that the procedure was remedied at the appeal stage by an ex parte hearing by the court as the Court of Appeal was dependent for its understanding of the possible relevance of the undisclosed material on transcripts of the Crown Court hearings and did not have the opportunity of seeing the witnesses give their evidence. This principle of independent scrutiny by a judge is an important statement of the responsibility to ensure that disclosure obligations are properly abided by. However, we shall see that as objections to disclosure are increasingly made on grounds of national security, there have been difficult questions as to what is sufficient to satisfy the principles of adversarial procedure and the equality of arms when these decisions are being made.

To conclude, it would seem that although disclosure requirements are based on the principle of equality of arms and the need for effective defence participation, there is considerable uncertainty as to their scope and timing in individual cases. Instead of insisting that the defence share in the fruits of all the criminal investigation, too much discretion is left in the hands of individual prosecutors in individual cases as to whether particular material is of assistance to the defence and the courts are not required to take on enough responsibility in policing disclosure. Even when there appear to have been breaches of the obligations, these will not result in a breach of the Convention unless taken as a whole the lack of disclosure resulted in an unfair trial. Finally, the right to disclosure is not an absolute right, although the principle at least has been

---

[99] For discussion, see D. Ormerod, 'Improving the Disclosure Regime' (2003) 7 *International Journal of Evidence & Proof* 102, 123–4; and M. Redmayne, 'Criminal Justice Act 2003 – Disclosure and Its Discontents' [2004] *Criminal Law Review* 441, 457–8. This has been recognised internationally in a decision holding that the qualified privilege human rights monitors have to protect the identity of their sources must yield where the identification of the source is necessary to prove a reasonable doubt about guilt. See *Prosecutor* v. *Brima*, Appeals Chamber, Opinion of Justice Robertson, para. 33.

[100] Para. 62.

established that it is for the courts and not for the prosecution to make decisions on when the public interest may deny disclosure from the defence.

9.4 Common law shortcomings

Uncertainty as to the scope of the disclosure requirements does not help to enforce a culture of compliance. Although we have seen that the principle of effective defence participation has been accepted in Europe since the nineteenth century, the idea that the defence should be entitled in principle to full disclosure of the fruits of the investigation which has led accused persons to be charged is not one that has proved easy to inculcate. While a number of European countries accepted the principle of full disclosure of the file some time ago,[101] there are others which appear to remain attached to the inquisitorial principle of the secrecy of the file, which is incompatible with imposing disclosure obligations on the police, the prosecutor or the investigating judge.[102] A number of jurisdictions have been influenced by the ECHR and the discourse of defence rights and equality of arms. In France, lawyers have been gaining better and earlier access to the dossier.[103] Under a law in January 1993, French defence lawyers were given an unlimited right to consult the dossier four working days before any judicial questioning of the accused, although this was modified by a further reform that year which provided that its exercise should not interfere with the proper working of the *cabinet d'instruction*.[104] In the Netherlands, suspects and lawyers now have a right of access to the file during the preliminary investigation from the moment the prosecutor becomes involved in the case, which means in practice after the period of police custody of a maximum of 3 days and 15 hours.[105] There is also a variation in practice over who should make the final decisions on what gets into the file. Following the decision in *Edwards*, the Supreme Court ruled that everything that was 'relevant' for the trial judge to reach a decision should be added to the file.[106] The final decision as to what should be added to the file lies with the trial judge.

---

[101] According to §147 §1 CCP, in Germany, the defence lawyer has a right to inspect the file as well as pieces of real evidence which the prosecutor will have to give to the court. This right exists in principle at any time during the investigation subject to refusal on the ground that disclosure could jeopardise the investigation. See T. Weigend and F. Salditt, 'The Investigative Stage of the Criminal Process in Germany', in E. Cape, J. Hodgson, T. Prakken and T. Spronken (eds.), *Suspects in Europe* (Antwerp: Intersentia, 2007) 79, 93.

[102] See in relation to Belgium, J. Fermon, F. Verbruggen and S. de Decker, 'The Investigative Stage of the Criminal Process in Belgium', in Cape et al., *Suspects in Europe*, 29, 49.

[103] V. Dervieux, 'The French System', in M. Delmas-Marty and J. Spencer (eds.), *European Criminal Procedures* (Cambridge University Press, 2002) 218, 266.

[104] J. Spencer, 'Evidence', in Delmas-Marty and Spencer, *European Criminal Procedures*, 594, 632. See also S. Field and A. West, 'Dialogue and the Inquisitorial Tradition: French Defence Lawyers in the Pre-Trial Criminal Process' (2003) 14 *Criminal Law Forum* 261, 265.

[105] See T. Prakken and T. Spronken, 'The Investigative Stage of the Criminal Process in the Netherlands', in Cape et al., *Suspects in Europe*, 155, 170.

[106] HR 7 May 1996, NJ 1996, 687.

Where there is an impartial investigating judge dedicated at least in theory to the ascertainment of the truth rather than to the presentation of a case, however, it is not so difficult to accept that the defence should be entitled to share the fruits of the inquiry. The inclusion of the defence on this theory may be seen as a necessary further step in ensuring that an accurate outcome will prevail at the end of the day. Where, on the other hand, the parties are genuine adversaries and the procedure is perceived as a contest between parties advancing different cases, it is more difficult to inculcate a culture of sharing information. It is true that as an ideal mode of proof adversarialism would seem to have to ensure that there is a full equality of arms which must include the defence being given access to relevant information.[107] As Justice Traynor once put it, 'truth is most likely to emerge when each side seeks to take the other by reason rather than by surprise'.[108] Discovery rules have come into operation in civil cases where it is realised that there are considerable advantages to be obtained for resolving conflict in the case if the parties have knowledge of each other's documents and evidence.[109] But it has taken longer for this idea to take hold in criminal cases, where there is still resistance to the notion of reciprocal disclosure. The idea that the defence should be required to disclose any of its case has been resisted on the ground that this conflicts with constitutional guarantees such as the privilege against self-incrimination and the right of silence,[110] and in the absence of reciprocal disclosure duties on the defence, it has been particularly difficult to inculcate in the prosecution any notion that they should make disclosure.[111] Within this culture, indeed, there has been an attitude that discovery can impede the ascertainment of the truth. Surprise and ambush are regarded as a legitimate weapon to use in the contest, since they can force the truth out of reluctant witnesses who would otherwise be able to conceal the truth if given full disclosure of the evidence against them.[112] By contrast, criminal discovery can open the door to perjury, the suppression of evidence and threats against prosecution witnesses.[113]

Slowly, however, during the twentieth century it came to be accepted that in the more serious trials on indictment, the prosecution should disclose the evidence they intended to use at trial, although there was a greater reluctance to disclose information that would undermine the prosecution case. Part of this

---

[107] See J. Jackson and S. Doran, *Judge without Jury: Diplock Trials in the Adversary System* (Oxford: Clarendon, 1995) 61–2, and P. Duff, 'Disclosure in Scottish Criminal Procedure: Another Step in an Inquisitorial Direction?' (2007) 11 *International Journal of Evidence & Proof* 153, 172–3.

[108] R. J. Traynor, 'Ground Lost and Found in Criminal Discovery' (1962) 39 *New York University Law Review* 228, 249.

[109] See Damaška, *Faces of Justice*, 131.

[110] See Redmayne, 'Disclosure and Its Discontents', 445–6. For a critique of this position, see C. Moisidis, *Criminal Discovery: From Truth to Proof and Back Again* (Sydney: Sydney Institute of Criminology, 2008).

[111] Damaška, *Faces of Justice*, 132. [112] Spencer, 'Evidence', 630–1.

[113] See the arguments summarised in the Law Reform Commission of Canada Study Report, *Discovery in Criminal Cases* (1974) part III and in *R* v. *Stinchcombe* [1991] 3 SCR 326.

change of attitude sprang from an acknowledgement that the prosecution was not there as in civil litigation to represent a purely private party, an agent so to speak of the state or the Crown, but to act in the public interest, as a 'minister of justice' to see that justice was done.[114] In 1935, the USSC declared that the public prosecutor is the 'representative not of an ordinary party to a controversy, but of a sovereignty... whose interest... in a criminal prosecution is not that it shall win a case, but that justice shall be done'.[115] Twenty years later, the Canadian Supreme Court declared that the purpose of a criminal prosecution was not to obtain a conviction, but to 'lay before a jury what the Crown considers to be credible evidence relative to what is alleged to be a crime'.[116] Only gradually, however, did the common law courts come to link disclosure with defence rights and consider that a failure to disclose material evidence violated constitutional safeguards such as due process, the right to make full answer and defence to the charge and the right to a fair trial.[117] Yet the common law world has continued to be plagued by miscarriages caused by a lack of prosecution disclosure. The adversary culture which encourages police and prosecutors to secure convictions can still too easily lead to a wilful disregard of disclosure rules for the greater good of obtaining a conviction which is believed to be justified.

To instill a culture of compliance on the part of police and prosecutors, it has been argued by many commentators that there needs to be far greater sanctions for those who commit violations.[118] Yet the accountability mechanisms in place where there has been a breach of the rules are very weak. We have seen that the very notion of a strong prosecution system able to be held to account for its actions is not one that has been developed in most common law jurisdictions. In certain systems, it is even unclear what the prosecution actually consists of. Instead of prosecution systems being organised as in many continental systems in a hierarchical manner under the control of a public prosecutor, in common law systems specific tasks such as investigation, the decision to prosecute and the actual presentation of the prosecution evidence in court are parcelled out

---

[114] Prosecuting counsel should regard themselves rather as 'ministers of justice assisting in its administration than as advocates', *R* v. *Puddick* (1865) 4 F & F 497, per Crompton J. quoted approvingly by Avory J. in *R* v. *Banks* [1916] 2 KB 621. In England, Lord Devlin commented in 1956 that in the last half-century there had been a 'welcome transition in the role of prosecuting counsel from a prosecuting advocate into a minister of justice'. See P. Devlin, *Trial by Jury* (London: Stevens, 1956) 122. See generally J. Niblett, *Disclosure in Criminal Proceedings* (London: Blackstone, 1997) 12–13.

[115] *United States* v. *Berger*, 95 US 78, 88 (1935).

[116] *Boucher* v. *The Queen* [1955] SCR 16, 23–4, per Rand J.

[117] See, e.g. *Brady* v. *Maryland*, 373 US 83 (1963); *R* v. *Stinchcombe* [1991] 3 SCR 326; and *R* v. *Ward* [1993] 2 All ER 577, 626.

[118] J. A. Epp, 'Achieving the Aims of the Disclosure Scheme in England and Wales' (2001) 5 *International Journal of Evidence & Proof* 188; E. Yaroshefsky, 'Wrongful Convictions: Is it Time to Take Prosecution Discipline Seriously?' (2004) 8 *University of the District of Columbia Law Review* 275; and S. S. Kuo and C. W. Taylor, 'In Prosecutors We Trust: UK Lessons for Illinois Disclosure' (2007) 38 *Loyola University Chicago Law Journal* 695.

to various organisations and professional groups who operate as independent 'fiefdoms' and exercise considerable discretion in decision-making.[119]

Even if prosecutors did have the power to access relevant information, however, a further obstacle to ensuring effective disclosure in common law countries is that the defence has traditionally had very little input into the disclosure system. Disclosure obligations only generally come into effect once the criminal investigation has been completed and the entire prosecution case has been assembled and sent for trial, although it may be necessary in certain situations to disclose material at an earlier stage of the process, for example where there is significant information that might affect a bail decision.[120] By contrast, as we have seen, in almost all civil law jurisdictions the defence have certain rights of access to the file or dossier that has been built up by the police and prosecutors during the investigation, although the extent of this right varies from place to place.[121] The traditional view in common law jurisdictions is that the accused can wait until trial before having to answer the charges. This means that there is little dialogue between the prosecution and defence until the prosecution case is completed and the case is sent to court for trial.

9.5 Beyond disclosure: access to evidence outside the possession of the prosecutor

If the defence are going to be truly participative, it would seem that they must be more than the passive recipients of information that is disclosed to them and have the ability to shape the investigation as it is proceeding in order to have access to all material information in the case. This not only requires early disclosure by the prosecution. There may be information outside the possession of the prosecution which is highly relevant to the case. There may also be further procedures or expert investigations to be carried out to extend the range of relevant information. We saw that the Strasbourg authorities originally imposed an obligation on the competent authorities to ensure that the defence have access to all relevant evidence that has been collected or *could be* collected in the case. Later authorities, however, in the context of proceedings brought against common law countries appeared to require that the prosecuting authorities only disclose all material evidence in its possession. This raises the question about how member states fulfil the wider obligation of ensuring that the defence has access to all relevant evidence outside the possession of the prosecutor.

9.5.1 Defence investigations

One response is to permit the defence to make active investigations on its own behalf. Effective participation by the defence would seem to require that the

---

[119] The term 'fiefdom' is derived from J. Shapland, 'Fiefs and Peasants: Accomplishing Change for Victims in the Criminal Justice System', in M. Maguire and J. Pointing (eds.), *Victims of Crime: A New Deal?* (Milton Keynes: Open University Press, 1988) 187.
[120] See *R v. DPP Ex p. Lee* [1999] 1 WLR 1950.   [121] Spencer, 'Evidence', 631.

defence is able to make investigations for itself as well as simply relying on the information given to it by the prosecution. If the police and prosecutors have powers to undertake inquiries and investigations, the principle of equality of arms would seem to suggest that the defence be granted equal powers. The Strasbourg authorities, however, have never gone so far as to recognise such a wide-ranging principle, although we have seen that they have recognised that where the defence have the capacity to undertake inquiries, they should do so with due diligence. Quite apart from the difficulties in resourcing defence investigations, the defence is severely handicapped by the absence of powers to obtain search warrants, to make arrests or to intercept correspondence and it has never been suggested that the defence should be given such powers.

A number of continental systems also discourage the defence from making their own inquiries. This is particularly the case in countries steeped in the inquisitorial tradition, where investigations are judicially supervised. Within this culture, the role of the defence is to assist the investigation and not to engage in proactive independent defence. Certain countries such as Belgium appear to prohibit the defence from participating actively in investigations, such as contacting witnesses or interviewing them.[122] By contrast, in countries such as Italy, where a more accusatorial ethos is being cultivated, it is now possible for counsel, paralegals and investigators acting on behalf of the defence to carry out their own investigations.[123] They can interview witnesses, they have the power to authenticate statements and they can even be authorised by the judge to enter private places where the public is not allowed and seize evidence.[124] All evidence found by the defence is then collected in a specific dossier called the 'defence counsel's dossier'.[125] As a result, a stronger culture of proactive defence would seem to be developing.[126] By contrast, within a more 'inquisitorial' culture, even where the defence does engage in proactive activities, the reliability of any evidence that is produced such as witness statements is treated with suspicion by the judicial authorities.[127] Contacting witnesses before the trial consequently risks their testimony being regarded as tainted.[128]

It may be argued that the principle of equality is preserved in these countries by having a judicial investigation to which both prosecution and defence have access or entrusting the investigation to the public prosecutor's department which is instructed to gather evidence in favour of the accused as well as

---

[122] Fermon, Verbruggen and de Decker, 'Criminal Process in Belgium', 55.
[123] Arts. 327bis, 391bis–decies Italian Criminal Procedure Code. See L. Marafioti, 'Italian Criminal Procedure: A System Caught between Two Traditions', in J. Jackson, M. Langer and P. Tillers, *Crime, Procedure and Evidence in a Comparative and International Context: Essays in Honour of Mirjan Damaška* (Oxford: Hart, 2008) 81, 83.
[124] A. Perrodet, 'The Italian System', in Delmas-Marty and Spencer, *European Criminal Procedures*, 360.
[125] Ibid.
[126] G. Illuminati and M. Caianiello, 'The Investigative Stage of the Criminal Process in Italy', in Cape et al., *Suspects in Europe*, 129.
[127] J. Hodgson, *French Criminal Justice* (Oxford: Hart, 2005) 127.
[128] Field and West, 'Dialogue and the Inquisitorial Tradition', 296–7.

evidence against him or her.[129] But given the tendency we have already seen for investigators, whether judicially trained or not, to follow those inquiries which lead in the direction of the particular theory which is being tested, much would seem to depend here on how far the defence can insist on certain inquiries being carried out. The picture here is patchy. In certain countries such as the Netherlands, it appears that the defence routinely ask the prosecutor to investigate ambiguities in the police file which is disclosed to them or for it to be referred to an investigating judge.[130] Prosecutors would seem to take such requests seriously because if such a request has been refused and the defence can show the existence of unexplained, ambiguous or incomplete information in the file when the case gets to trial, the court will have to stop the trial, to the embarrassment of the prosecutor.[131] In France, by contrast, it has been suggested that the defence lawyers do not generally ask prosecutors to make further pre-trial investigations and prosecutors have complete freedom to refuse any request.[132] There are a number of reasons for this, including the fact that there was often not the time to give the dossier a detailed pre-trial reading, but also the fact that both prosecutors and defence lawyers were often suspicious of each other: the defence of prosecutors' impartiality and prosecutors of defence lawyers being too close to their clients.

9.5.2 Application to the court

When the defence are unable to make effective investigations on their own behalf and are unable to rely on the prosecution to carry out such investigations, it would seem that there can only be effective compliance with the *Jespers* obligation that the defence have access to all relevant evidence in the case if the defence is provided with an opportunity to apply to the court to enable such investigations to be carried out or have the results of these produced. Human rights instruments require that everyone charged with a crime has the right to obtain the attendance and examination of witnesses under the same conditions as witnesses against him or her.[133] This is arguably a special aspect of the right to present evidence which we have seen has been linked in certain national court decisions to the presumption of innocence.[134] There is no right under the

---

[129] *Jespers* v. *Belgium* (report), 87.
[130] See S. Field, P. Alldridge and N. Jorg, 'Prosecutors, Examining Judges and Control of Police Investigations', in P. Fennell, C. Harding, N. Jorg and B. Swart (eds.), *Criminal Justice in Europe* (Oxford University Press, 1995) 235–6.
[131] It would seem, however, that the defence may have a hard time convincing the court that the dossier is incomplete or one-sided. See C. Brants, 'The Vulnerability of Dutch Criminal Procedure to Wrongful Conviction', in C. R. Huff and M. Killias (eds.), *Wrongful Convictions: International Perspectives on Miscarriages of Justice* (Philadelphia: Temple University Press, 2008) 157.
[132] Field and West, 'Dialogue and the Inquisitorial Tradition', 294–6.
[133] See Art. 14(3)(e) ICCPR and Art. 6(3)(d) ECHR.
[134] Trechsel, *Human Rights in Criminal Proceedings*, 323. See Ch. 7.7.2.

instruments to call any witness whom the defence wish.[135] The defence may only call witnesses under the same conditions as the prosecution and in the civil law tradition in particular it is the court which decides whether witnesses or evidence shall be called.

The international decision-making bodies have generally operated under the principle that it is for the domestic courts to decide whether it is necessary to call a witness. Although there has been an inevitable deference to the national courts to make decisions on just how significant particular evidence is, there would seem to be an obligation on courts to do what they can to secure crucial evidence. In *Fuenzalida* v. *Ecuador*, the defendant, who had been convicted of raping a Peace Corps volunteer, complained that the court had denied him an examination of his own blood and semen which he contended proved he was not a rapist. The HRC considered that the refusal of the court to order expert testimony of crucial importance to the case constituted a violation of Article 14(3)(e) and (5) of the ICCPR.[136] In *Georgios Papageorgiou* v. *Greece*, the applicant, who was a bank clerk, had been convicted of fraudulently using false cheques to withdraw large sums of money from the account of one of the bank's clients. The ECtHR found a violation of Article 6(1) and (3)(d) when the applicant was unable to obtain extracts from the log file of the bank's computer and the original cheques. At his trial, the court had ordered the destruction of the original cheques, yet it was vital for the defence to have access to these documents to show that the instructions for the payments had been given by other employees and not him. In this case, the defence had been gravely disadvantaged by being unable to obtain access to essential pieces of evidence to which the prosecution had access before they were destroyed. The case can be contrasted with *Sofri and others* v. *Italy*, where items of evidence relating to charges of murder were not available for the defence at the time of the trial, including the dead man's clothing and bullets retrieved from his body. The ECtHR held that a complaint under Article 6 was inadmissible on the ground that although certain of the missing items were relevant to the case, in particular to challenging the key prosecution witness who confessed that he had carried out the killing on the orders of the applicants, the defence were able to challenge his testimony on other grounds and the prosecution were equally disadvantaged by the absence of evidence.

While the Strasbourg authorities then accept that the defence should be given access to relevant evidence, they are only prepared to declare cases admissible where it can be shown that the absence or destruction of the evidence caused a clear detriment to the accused. A number of common law countries have considered that there are certain situations where a failure to preserve evidence may give rise to a stay of proceedings.[137] Where the police or prosecutors

---

[135] *Gordon* v. *Jamaica*.   [136] See also *Grant* v. *Jamaica*.
[137] See *Carosella* v. *R* [1997] 2 BHRC 23; *R (Ebrahim)* v. *Feltham Magistrates' Court*, *Mouat* v. *DPP* [2001] EWHC Admin. 30. For a full list of the English authorities, see C. Wells, *Abuse of*

deliberately destroy evidence, it would seem that a stay of proceedings would be justified. The courts have also upheld stays where the negligent failure to preserve certain vital evidence may make it impossible for there to be a fair trial.[138] The onus is generally on the defence to show that there is a real risk that the accused cannot obtain a fair trial as a result of the lost or destroyed evidence.[139]

When evidence has disappeared, there is much greater difficulty in assessing what difference it would have made to the defence than when courts are asked to assess what difference the non-disclosure of existing information would have made.[140] Rather than requiring courts to make these judgments at trial or on appeal after the evidence has disappeared, it would seem better to provide mechanisms for the defence to have evidence produced or inquiries made before the trial. Indeed, this would seem to be required if there is to be proper adherence to the *Jespers* principle that the defence is given access to all relevant information that could be collected. Where the defence lacks the resources or the power to obtain such evidence for itself, the courts again have an important role in assisting the defence, which as we saw in our discussion of the international criminal tribunals would seem to lead to greater supervisory powers over the investigation.

There is old common law authority permitting an accused to use the court's compulsory process to secure the attendance of witnesses and common law countries have permitted the defence to apply to the courts for the production of evidence before trial.[141] It would seem reasonable to impose some proportionality requirement on the defence to show that the evidence is some assistance to the defence case rather than put the authorities to the effort of conducting all manner of speculative inquiries that may or may not be relevant to the case. The Australian courts, however, have held that before access is granted, the defence must identify a legitimate forensic purpose for which access is sought and that it is 'on the cards' that the documents will materially assist its case.[142] The language of 'legitimate forensic purpose' has been adopted by the ICTY Appeals Chamber in determining whether the tribunal should issue a summons

---

Process: A Practical Approach (London: Legal Action Group, 2006) ch. 7; and S. Martin, 'Lost and Destroyed Evidence: The Search for a Principled Approach to Abuse of Process' (2005) 9 *International Journal of Evidence & Proof* 158. For a discussion of the Irish authorities, see L. Heffernan, 'The Duty to Preserve Evidence', in I. Bacik and L. Heffernan (eds.), *Criminal Law and Procedure: Current Issues and Emerging Trends* (Dublin: First Law, 2009) 53.

[138] See the guidance given in *R (Ebrahim)* v. *Feltham Magistrates' Court, Mouat* v. *DPP* [2001] EWHC Admin 30.

[139] An alternative approach would be to establish a presumption of prejudice in such circumstances. Cf. Stavros, *Guarantees for Accused Persons*, 46; and A. Roberts, 'Pre-Trial Defence Rights and the Fair Use of Eyewitness Identification Procedures' (2008) 71 *Modern Law Review* 331, 348–9.

[140] See J. C. Smith, 'Commentary' [2000] *Criminal Law Review* 415.

[141] See W. Hawkins, *Pleas of the Crown*, 8th edn, J. Curwood ed. (London: Butterworth, 1824) Book 2, ch. 46.

[142] See *Alister* v. *R* (1984) 154 CLR 404; and *R* v. *Saleam* (1999) NSWCCA 86.

to subpoena or warrant to obtain relevant evidence under Rule 54 of the Rules of Procedure and Evidence. In an appeal judgment in an early case, an Australian judge, Judge Hunt, stated the test as follows:

> A party is not entitled to have an order made to produce material so that he may have access to it simply because he says that the material is relevant to an issue in the trial or appeal. He is not entitled to conduct a fishing expedition – in the sense that he wishes to inspect the material in order to discover whether he has any case at all to make. An order to produce is not the same as obtaining discovery against a party. Before obtaining an order for access to material where his right to access is not conceded, the party must identify expressly and precisely the legitimate forensic purpose for which access is sought.[143]

In Canada, the Supreme Court has held that in applications for third-party disclosure the defence must first satisfy the judge that the evidence will be relevant to the defendant's case and it drew a distinction between this standard and fishing expeditions which would allow the defence to engage in 'speculative, fanciful, disruptive, unmeritorious, obstructive and time-consuming requests for production'.[144]

As well as this, matters relating to the rights of third parties may need to be considered before the material is ordered to be disclosed. These may affect the defence somewhat differently from the prosecution. Third parties, for example, may be more disposed to hand over material to state prosecuting authorities than they are to private parties. Many third-party applications, for example, arise in cases of alleged sexual or physical abuse where the defence are seeking access to documents relating to contact which the complainant may have had with doctors. In such cases, the prosecution may have obtained these documents because the complainant will have given it the authority to do so, but this does mean that she is happy for such documents to be handed over to the defence. The court here must be alive to the privacy rights of complainants and balance the fair trial rights of the defendant against the privacy and other interest of the third parties affected by the disclosure.[145] It would seem that precisely because there are difficult balancing judgments to be made here involving the defence and third parties that it should be for the court and not the prosecution to make these judgments.[146] Third parties themselves should be given an

---

[143] *Prosecutor* v. *Delalic*, Trial Chamber, Separate Opinion of Judge David Hunt on motion by Esad Landzo to Preserve and Provide Evidence, para. 4.

[144] *R* v. *O'Connor* (1995) 103 CCC(3d) 1. In England and Wales and Northern Ireland, the third-party disclosure test has been considered to be the same as that which is imposed on the prosecution under the statutory disclosure regime, namely whether the material being considered might assist the defendant by undermining the prosecution case or strengthening the defence case. See *R* v. *Hume* [2005] NICC 30 and *Disclosure Protocol*, paras. 52–62.

[145] Just how strong the privacy interests of third parties can be is illustrated by a special statutory scheme which has been introduced in Canada for sexual offences. See s. 278.1–278.91 Canadian Criminal Code.

[146] See *R* v. *Brushett* [2001] Crim LR 471.

opportunity of addressing the court.[147] Where there is any doubt about the likely relevance of the records, judges should, however, arguably err on the side of disclosure in order to give particular weight to the fundamental principle that the innocent must not be convicted.[148]

9.6 Public interest immunity

As the defence have sought to make use of their rights of access to evidence, so the prosecution have sought to make greater use of claims for immunity from disclosure on grounds of public interest. The increasing use of 'proactive' methods of criminal investigation such as the use of undercover agents conducting covert surveillance, intelligence-gathering operations and co-opted civil informants would seem to have fuelled the need to protect those caught up in such activities and conceal the precise *modus operandi* of such activities.[149] The growing threat of terrorism and the consequent terrorist trials have also caused an increase in attempts to prevent sensitive national security information from being disclosed in the trial of persons accused of terrorist offences.[150] The Council of Europe has accepted that the imperatives of the fight against terrorism may justify certain restrictions on the rights of the defence, in particular with regard to the arrangements for access to the case file.[151] Within the international criminal tribunals, prosecutors are permitted in certain circumstances to enter into confidentiality agreements with states, by which the prosecutor guarantees that information will not be disclosed without their consent and that the information's sources will be protected.[152]

No matter how compelling these public interests may be, however, we have seen that disclosure of the prosecution case against the accused and any

---

[147] See *R (on the application of B)* v. *the Combined Court at Stafford* [2006] EWHC 1645 (Admin), requiring that an application for a third party's medical records affected her right of privacy under Art. 8 of the ECHR and should have been served on the third party.

[148] See *R* v. *Mills* [1999] 3 SCR 608, para. 134; and *R* v. *Leipert* [1997] 1 SCR 287, para. 24. In *Mills*, the Supreme Court took the view that the right to make full answer and defence is crucial to ensuring that the innocent are not convicted, but this does not automatically entitle the accused to gain access to information contained in the private records of complainants and witnesses. For a critique, see L. Gotell, 'When Privacy Is Not Enough: Sexual Assault Complaints, Sexual History Evidence and Disclosure of Personal Records' (2006) 43 *Alberta Law Review* 743.

[149] Roberts and Zuckerman, *Criminal Evidence*, 323. Cf. Zuckerman's comment in 1989 that issues concerning public interest immunity were a 'rare occurrence' in criminal litigation. A. A. S. Zuckerman, *The Principles of Criminal Evidence* (Oxford: Clarendon, 1989) 300–1.

[150] See National Security Information (Criminal and Civil) Proceedings Act 2004 (Aus) and the amendments to the Canada Evidence Act set out in the Anti-Terrorism Act, SC 2001, c. 41 (Can). See generally A. Lynch and G. Williams, *What Price Security? Taking Stock of Australia's Anti-Terror Laws* (Sydney: UNSW Press, 2006).

[151] *Council of Ministers: Guidelines of the Committee of Ministers of the Council of Europe on Human Rights and the Fight against Terrorism* (2003) 35 EHRR CD 232.

[152] See Art. 54(3)(e) ICC Statute, r.82(1) ICC RPE; r. 70(B) ICTY, ICTR, SCSL RPE. For the importance of prosecutors gaining access to evidence on a confidential basis, see R. Goldstone, 'A View from the Prosecution' (2004) 2 *Journal of International Criminal Justice* 380.

information pointing to the innocence of the accused are fundamental aspects of a fair trial. We have also seen that the ECtHR has established certain principles regarding the manner in which these competing interests are to be resolved in individual cases. Firstly, it is for the courts and not the prosecution to make the necessary balancing judgments as to whether the public interest in withholding disclosure outweighs the interests of disclosure. Secondly, there must, as far as possible, be compliance with the requirements of adversarial procedures and equality of arms. In this final section, we need to probe how these principles are applied in the domestic and international tribunals.

9.6.1 The principle of judicial scrutiny

Any legislative attempts to interfere with the principle of the primacy of the courts would seem to violate the right to a fair trial. Recent legislation in Australia has restricted the disclosure of information that would prejudice national security by giving the Attorney General a power to issue a certificate ordering the prosecution or defence not to disclose such information.[153] The legislation does not exclude judicial review, but at any closed hearing to determine whether to uphold the certificate, the court must give greatest weight to the risk of prejudice to national security.[154] In a challenge to the legislation, it was argued that this prioritisation of the interests of national security over the right to a fair trial exceeded the powers of the Commonwealth Parliament, but the New South Wales Supreme Court considered that the legislation did no more than give the court guidance and did not intrude on the court's task to ensure that the accused is not dealt with unfairly.[155]

The importance of judicial scrutiny of disclosable material has been stressed in the international tribunals. Where such information is in the possession of the prosecutor, the disclosure of which may prejudice further or ongoing investigations, or for any other reasons may be contrary to the public interest or affect the security interests of any state, the prosecutor may apply to the Trial Chamber sitting in camera to be relieved from the obligation to disclose the information.[156] It is particularly important that any exculpatory material in the possession of the prosecutor is brought to the attention of the tribunal if the prosecution wishes to be relieved of its disclosure responsibilities.[157]

The importance of the principle that the court must be able to review any disclosable material in the possession of the prosecutor was demonstrated by the Trial Chamber in the proceedings against the International Criminal Court's first defendant, Thomas Lubanga Dyilo, who was accused of the war crimes of

---

[153] Pt 3 of the National Security Information (Criminal and Civil Proceedings) Act 2004.
[154] See s. 31(8) of the Act.   [155] *R v. Lodhi* [2006] NSWSC 571, para. 108.
[156] R. 66(C) ICTY, ICTR RPE, r. 66 (B) SCSL RPE. Cf. r. 81 (2) ICC RPE.
[157] R. 68(iv) ICTY, ICTR RPE, r. 83 ICC RPE.

conscripting and enlisting children under the age of 15.[158] The prosecutor had collected more than half of its evidence by way of confidentiality agreements and this included considerable amounts of exculpatory or mitigating evidence indicating that the accused may have been acting under duress or had had insufficient command over the people who had committed the crimes he was charged with. When the prosecution refused the judges' offer to review the evidence ex parte and in camera and offered only to provide them with evidence excerpts or summaries, the Trial Chamber decided to suspend the proceedings.[159] The Trial Chamber could not accept a scheme under which the chamber would be denied access to the confidential evidence in its original form. The chamber further concluded that the prosecution had abused its power to obtain confidential information only on an exceptional basis and only for the purposes of it generating new evidence. Instead, it had obtained a large amount of material under the cloak of confidentiality in order to identify from it which evidence it could then use at trial having obtained the information provider's consent. As a result of this ruling, the prosecutor offered to provide the chamber with all of its confidential documents in unredacted form for review.

The ICC's scrutiny of the prosecutor's use of confidentiality agreements illustrates the importance of the court being able to supervise disclosure regimes. There remains a difficulty for the prosecution if under a confidentiality agreement it has been provided with information which points to the innocence of the accused. The ad hoc tribunal rules were amended in 2004 to stipulate that the obligation under Rule 68 to disclose any material suggesting the innocence or mitigating the guilt of the accused was 'subject to the provisions of Rule 70', which permits prosecutors to enter into confidentiality agreements.[160] But this cannot absolve the prosecutor from its fair trial obligations. The ICC Trial Chamber has indicated that if the prosecution has in its possession any exculpatory material which it is unable to disclose and which may materially impact on the court's determination of guilt or innocence, it will be under an obligation to withdraw any charges which are affected by it and if it is in doubt as to whether or not the material falls into this category, this should be put before the bench for the Trial Chamber's determination.[161]

The need for judicial supervision over the question of whether any disclosable material can be withheld from the defence, however, raises a further question, which is how is the court to make such a determination without knowing what the defence case is. This leads on to the second principle, which is that there

---

[158] For discussion, see S. Swoboda, 'The ICC Disclosure Regime – A Defence Perspective' (2008) 19 *Criminal Law Forum* 449.

[159] *Prosecutor* v. *Lubanga Dyilo*, Trial Chamber, Decision on the consequences of non-disclosure of exculpatory materials.

[160] R. 70 ICTY, ICTR RPE, amended 28 July 2004.

[161] *Prosecutor* v. *Lubanga Dyilo*, Trial Chamber, Decision Regarding the Timing and Manner of Disclosure. See also *Prosecutor* v. *Karadžić*, Trial Chamber, Decision on Accused's Application for Certification to Appeal Decision on Rule 70(B).

needs to be compliance so far as possible with the principles of adversarial procedure and the equality of arms in adjudicating on matters of public interest immunity.

9.6.2 Adversarial argument

Although the principle of judicial supremacy is well established, there has been less consensus over the extent to which, in addition to the need for judicial control, there needs to be adversarial argument when matters of disclosure are being decided. One of the difficulties with permitting the defence to make arguments on the question of disclosure is that they may in the course of argument become aware of the very information which the prosecution seek to withhold.[162] In *Fitt* v. *United Kingdom* and *Jasper* v. *United Kingdom*, the prosecution made an ex parte application to the trial judge to withhold material in its possession on the grounds of public interest immunity, notified the defence that the application was to be made, but did not inform it of the kind of material which it sought to withhold. The applicants contended that while in certain circumstances it might be necessary in the public interest to exclude the accused and his representatives from the disclosure procedure, this procedure violated Article 6 of the ECHR because it afforded no safeguards against judicial bias or error and no opportunity to address arguments on behalf of the accused. In order to counterbalance the exclusion of the defence from the procedure, it was argued that some adversarial element was necessary, such as the appointment of an independent counsel who could advance argument on behalf of the defence as to the relevance of the undisclosed evidence, test the strength of the prosecution claim to public interest immunity and act as an independent safeguard against the risk of judicial error or bias. The ECtHR, however, by the narrowest of margins held that the procedure proposed did comply with the requirements of Article 6. Great stress was placed on the fact that the defence were kept sufficiently informed and permitted to make submissions and participate in the decision-making process as far as possible without revealing to them the material which the prosecution sought to keep secret. The minority, on the other hand, considered that the failure to inform the defence even of the nature of the material being withheld meant they were not – by definition – involved in the ex parte proceedings and they were not informed of the reason for the judge's subsequent decision. The opportunity to outline their case before the judge did not improve their position, as they were unaware of the nature of the matters they needed to address and it was purely a matter of chance whether they made any relevant points.

In the later case of *Edwards and Lewis* v. *United Kingdom*, however, the ECtHR took a different view and considered that the ex parte procedure adopted by

---

[162] See *R* v. *Davis, Johnson and Rowe* [1993] 1 WLR 613, proposing various procedures for circumventing this difficulty.

the prosecution did fall foul of Article 6 of the ECHR. These cases shared in common with the others the fact that the applicants were being kept under surveillance prior to their alleged commission of offences. The difference was that the applicants at their trial had argued unsuccessfully that the proceedings against them should be stayed because they had been incited to commit the offences by *agents provocateurs*. The applicants argued that the proceedings were fundamentally unfair because the trial judge who had to decide the question of whether the accused had been the victim of entrapment and abuse of process was the same person who had to review the material for which the prosecution claimed public interest immunity. In holding that there had been a violation of Article 6 of the ECHR, the ECtHR distinguished this situation from that in *Jasper* and *Fitt* on the ground that the material which was withheld in these cases from the defence formed no part of the prosecution case whatever and was never put to the jury. In the present cases, however, the undisclosed evidence related or may have related to the issue of entrapment which the judge had to decide. In one of the cases, moreover, it was revealed that the evidence produced to the trial judge in the ex parte hearing included material suggesting that the applicant had been involved in drug dealing prior to the event leading to his arrest. The applicants were not informed of this allegation during the criminal proceedings and were denied the opportunity of countering it. Yet it might have been directly relevant to the judge's conclusions that the applicants had not been entrapped into committing the offences charged against them.

One way of countering the unfairness in this case might have been to appoint a special disclosure judge to deal with the disclosure issues in addition to the trial judge. This procedure has been adopted in other common law jurisdictions where there is no jury and without a second judge there would always be a risk of the tribunal of fact being tainted by evidence undisclosed to the defence.[163] This would not completely eradicate the difficulties, however, as it would not deal with the problem that the defence would still be deprived of making any adversarial argument with regard to the material the prosecution seek to have undisclosed. Moreover, some weight was put in the *Jasper* and *Fitt* cases on the fact that it was an important safeguard that the trial judge had been able to keep the need for disclosure under continuous review in that it was his duty to monitor throughout the trial the fairness or otherwise of the evidence being withheld.[164] Clearly, a judge going into the trial who is not privy to the undisclosed information cannot keep the need for disclosure under review, something that may be particularly important when it becomes clear what the defence actually is.

The other compensating safeguard referred to favourably by the minority in *Jasper* would be to appoint a special counsel to represent the interests of the

---

[163] This is the procedure that has been recommended for Diplock (or non-jury) trials in Northern Ireland: see *R* v. *Harper and anothe*r [1994] NI 199; and *R* v. *McKeown* [2005] NI 301. For discussion of the experience of disclosure in Diplock trials, see J. Jackson, 'Many Years On in Northern Ireland: The Diplock Legacy' (2009) 60 *Northern Ireland Legal Quarterly* 213.
[164] Para. 56.

defence at disclosure hearings. This is a procedure that would appear to have its origin in Canada where a Security Intelligence Review was established to investigate whether non-citizens posed a threat to national security.[165] The procedure was followed in the United Kingdom after the ECtHR found that the system for reviewing deportation decisions in immigration and asylum cases involving national security was in breach of Article 5(4).[166] The court referred to the special advocate system in Canada as a means of cross-examining witnesses and inviting the court to test the strength of the state's case, but it fell short of endorsing the system. Since then, it has been provided for in a number of contexts in the United Kingdom, including since *Edwards and Lewis* ex parte disclosure hearings in criminal cases prior to trial where the prosecution claims public interest immunity. The system permits advocates to make submissions on information at closed hearings and to cross-examine any witnesses at such hearings.

But the system is not free from difficulties.[167] In the United Kingdom special advocates may communicate with and take instructions from the party they are representing or from the parties' ordinary legal representatives before they have sight of any sensitive information, but once they have sight of it, they cannot take instructions, nor do they have the resources afforded to an ordinary legal team, nor can they call witnesses. The inability to take instructions can mean that the judge is not particularly helped in the task of deciding whether the evidence for which public interest immunity is sought is likely to be of assistance to the defence. In *R* v. *H and C*, the House of Lords gave cautious endorsement to the use of special advocates in criminal trials as a means of securing the accused's right to a fair trial, but it referred to the ethical problem that a lawyer who cannot take full instructions from her client, nor report to her client, who is not responsible to her client and whose relationship with the client lacks the capacity of confidence inherent in any ordinary lawyer–client relationship, is acting in a way hitherto unknown to the legal profession.[168]

Another solution would be to put some fetter on the principle of confidentiality between lawyer and client so as to enable counsel but not their clients to have access to sensitive information. There is precedent for this in a number of common law countries. In Australia and the United States, security-cleared defence counsel may appear in closed hearings to determine a matter of disclosure involving national security.[169] In Canada, the Supreme Court has upheld

---

[165] See Canadian Security Intelligence Service Act, SC 1984, c. 21 (now RSC 1985, c. C-23).
[166] *Chahal* v. *United Kingdom*.
[167] See Constitutional Affairs Committee, *The Operation of the Special Appeals Commission (SIAC) and the Use of Special Advocates* (2005) HC 323–1. Para. 52. See also Butterfield, *Review of Criminal Investigations and Prosecutions Conducted by HM Customs and Excise*, November 2002, para. 12.57, Justice, *Secret Evidence* (London, 2009), D. Jenkins, 'There and Back Again: The Strange Journey of Special Advocates and Comparative Law Methodology' (2011) 42 *Columbia Human Rights Law Review* 279.
[168] [2004] UKHL 3, para. 22. For discussion of the ethical issues, see A. Boon and S. Nash, 'Special Advocacy: Political Expediency and Legal Roles in Modern Judicial Systems' (2006) 9 *Legal Ethics* 101.
[169] See s. 29 National Security Information (Criminal and Civil Proceedings) Act 2004 (Australia). See also Classified Information Procedures Act 1980 (US).

the constitutionality of a procedure whereby witnesses were questioned under oath and in private in terrorist trials and defence counsel were permitted to be present on condition that no information acquired during the examination was to be given to the accused.[170] The Canadian Supreme Court has held that the procedures for reviewing the detention of foreign nationals under the Immigration and Refugee Protection Act were in breach of section 7 of the Charter, as they did not allow the persons involved to know the case against them.[171] The court referred approvingly to a procedure that was adopted in the *Air India* trial involving the terrorist bombing of a passenger aircraft in Japan, whereby Crown and defence counsel came to an agreement under which defence counsel obtained consents from their clients to conduct a preliminary review of national security material on the written undertaking that they would not disclose the material to their clients. These procedures suggested that a search should be made for a less intrusive solution than that provided under the Immigration and Refugee Protection Act.

The idea that counsel should be able to hold information back from their clients runs against the grain of the common law tradition, which has held firmly to the notion of confidentiality between lawyer and client. In *R v. Botmeh*,[172] the English Court of Appeal asked counsel whether he would be willing to give an undertaking that if he were permitted to look at the matter in relation to which public immunity was claimed, he would not disclose its contents to his lay clients. Having consulted his professional body, counsel declined to give this and gave six reasons to the court: a substantial risk of undermining public confidence and the clients' confidence in the profession; the inability of counsel to perform his duty advising his clients as to their best interests; proper instructions from a client not in a position to appreciate the significance of the material would be precluded; counsel might receive material adverse to his clients about which he could not obtain proper instructions; counsel would have serious practical difficulties in conducting the case without accidentally disclosing confidential material; and, if the material could not be disclosed to counsel's instructing solicitors, the matter could be compounded because of the solicitor's unrivalled knowledge of the case and professional duty of disclosure to the lay clients. The Professional Practice Committee of the Bar of England and Wales has also specifically advised against the practice of limited counsel-to-counsel disclosure in public interest immunity hearings.[173] The Professional Practice Committee noted first that neither the law nor the Code of Conduct recognised any concept of 'counsel to counsel' confidentiality and that when told something on this basis which would be to his client's advantage, counsel should inform his client and use it.[174]

---

[170] *Re Art 83.28 of the Canadian Criminal Code* [2004] 2 SCR 248.
[171] *Charkaoui v. Minister of Citizenship and Immigration and Minister of Public Safety and Emergency Preparedness* [2007] SCC 9.
[172] [2002] 1 WLR 531.
[173] See Public Interest Immunity Hearings and Disclosure, available at www.barcouncil.org.uk.
[174] See also *Attorney General's Guidelines*, para. 46: 'There is no basis in law or practice for dislcosure on a "counsel to counsel" basis.'

Although it is undoubtedly difficult for advocates when they cannot communicate freely with their clients, the question has to be asked whether the failure to permit any relaxation of the principle of confidentiality between lawyer and client is advancing the cause of effective defence when the effect is to exclude lawyers entirely from certain disclosure hearings. A move towards counsel-to-counsel confidentiality would be a break from tradition in criminal cases, although it would not appear to breach the absolute doctrine of legal professional privilege, which only protects information that is disclosed between lawyer and client. It is noteworthy that before disclosure obligations became subject to clear rules binding on the prosecution, there appeared to be a practice in England whereby disclosure took place on a counsel-to-counsel basis of confidentiality.[175] It would also seem that outside the criminal sphere there is more scope for flexibility in protecting the rights of parties in respect of material for which a claim for immunity is made and that in an appropriate case, disclosure may be made on a limited basis to solicitors and counsel.[176] If such a process can be made to work in civil cases, the question to be asked is whether they may not also be made to work in criminal cases.

9.7 Conclusion

We have seen that there has been almost universal recognition of the principle that counsel should be provided to enable defendants to confide confidentially with defendants and to conduct an effective defence. Recent case law has also determined that this should be provided at the stage at which defendants are first questioned by the police. But there has been much greater difficulty in establishing the principle that the defence should be provided with all relevant evidence in the case so as to conduct such a defence. The ECtHR has used the principle of equality of arms to give recognition to the principle of full disclosure, and although it has recognised that this principle is not absolute, it has recognised the need for the courts to supervise disclosure issues where these matters are contested. We have argued that a full expression of the principle of equality of arms in the interests of an effective defence would require not only full disclosure of what the prosecution possesses, but an ability to influence at an early stage the way in which inquiries are conducted so that relevant evidence can be discovered and retained for use by either party.

There are cultural impediments within both traditions to ensuring compliance with this principle. In common law countries, there is still a prevalent

---

[175] See *Report of the Inquiry into the Circumstances leading to the trial of three persons on charges arising out of the death of Maxwell Confait and the fire at 27 Doggett Road, London SE 6* (1977), HC 90, para. 29.26.
[176] See *Science Research Council* v. *Nassé* [1980] AC 1028, 1077. Lord Edmund Davies approved a comment made by Lord Denning (in the Court of Appeal [1979] QB 144, 173) to the effect that the chair of an industrial tribunal could in appropriate circumstances limit the sight of material received in confidence 'to counsel and solicitors on their undertaking that it should go no further'. See also Pattenden, *Law of Professional-Client Confidentiality*, para. 17.02.

attitude that provided counsel is available for the defence, it is up to the defence to search and bring forward evidence in its favour. The theory that there should be two parallel investigations operating side by side until trial, however, in practice means that the defence are severely disadvantaged. Effective participation requires that the defence engage meaningfully with the prosecution and the courts at an early stage and this requires a change of culture whereby both sides contribute to one single investigation and treat the information they possess or any information sought not as 'belonging' to their side, but, as Justice Sopinka said, as 'the property of the public to be used to ensure justice is done'.[177] In civil law countries, the attitude that it is for the competent judicial or prosecution authorities to bring forward all relevant information in the case has made it difficult for the defence to play a participatory role. Here, the principle of one single investigation is accepted, but it has tended to have the effect of excluding the defence. Although the ECtHR has established the principle that the court has a responsibility to rule on matters of disclosure, it has been less clear about the parameters of the court's role in relation to granting the defence access to evidence outside the possession of the prosecution. It would seem that there is a long way to go before there can be confidence that the principle of full disclosure and investigation is fully complied with.

[177] *R v. Stinchcombe* [1991] 3 SCR 326.

10

Challenging witness evidence

10.1 Introduction

Witnesses, famously said to be the eyes and ears of justice,[1] play a special role in criminal proceedings. Their significance transcends legal systems and is not restricted to a particular type of procedural system or period in the development of a legal system.[2] Although acknowledged across different jurisdictions and times as an important and legitimate basis on which to found a criminal conviction, witness evidence has also traditionally been viewed with suspicion.[3] Witnesses may lie, forget important points, remember things wrongly or simply misinterpret a situation. Witnesses may also be manipulated and their evidence may depend on the questions which they are asked. This explains why witness evidence is not only much discussed, but also separately regulated in the various conventions and constitutional provisions which guarantee the right to a fair trial.[4]

The principal means of regulating witness evidence in modern times is to control the manner in which the evidence is heard and challenged. Notions such as confrontation and cross-examination are thus often characterised in terms of procedural stipulations and defence opportunities: the authorities are required to ensure that the accused is afforded the procedural opportunity to cross-examine, or 'confront', witnesses who make incriminating statements. These principles also have a significant evidential dimension. If an accused is

---

[1] The statement is often attributed to Jeremy Bentham, although is not referred to in the English edition of the *Rationale of Judicial Evidence*: see P. Wall, *Eye-Witness Identification in Criminal Cases* (Springfield: Charles C. Thomas, 1965) 9. The quote does exist in the French edition: J. Bentham, *Traité des preuves judiciaires*, trans. É. Dumont (Paris: Bossange Frères, 1823) vol. II, 93, '[l]es témoins sont les yeux et les oreilles de la justice'.
[2] J. Glaser, *Beiträge zur Lehre vom Beweis im Strafprozess* (Leipzig: Duncker & Humblot, 1883) 194.
[3] C. J. A. Mittermaier, *Die Lehre vom Beweis im deutschen Strafprozesse nach der Fortbildung durch Gerichtsgebrauch und deutsche Gesetzbücher in Vergleichung mit den Ansichten des englischen und französischen Strafverfahrens* (Darmstadt: Johann Wilhelm Heyer, 1834) 290. See too J. Bentham, *Rationale of Judicial Evidence*, ed. J. S. Mill (London: Hunt and Clarke, 1827) vol. I.
[4] See, e.g. Art. 6(3)(d) ECHR; Art. 14(3)(f) ICCPR; Art. 8(2)(f) ACHR; and the Sixth Amendment to the US Constitution. See too the relevant provisions in the statutes of the various international courts and tribunals: Art. 21(4)(e) ICTY; Art. 20(4)(e) ICTR; Art. 67(1)(e) ICC Statute; and Art. 17(4)(d) Statute of the Special Court of Sierra Leone.

not, or is not sufficiently, afforded the opportunity to challenge the witness evidence, the question arises as to what extent, if at all, that evidence can be used in the determination of the verdict. In some circumstances, it may be necessary to refrain from basing a conviction on untested witness evidence.

Article 6(3)(d) of the ECHR, which guarantees those charged with a criminal offence the opportunity to challenge witness evidence against them, is one of the most important modern procedural rules for regulating witness evidence. Its significance lies largely in its European-wide application, which seems at odds with a considerable body of legal thought, both academic and judicial, which insists on an understanding of Western criminal procedure systems as belonging either to the continental European or Anglo-American traditions.[5] This makes the scope of Article 6(3)(d) of the ECHR and other similar provisions such as Article 14(3)(e) of the ICCPR of considerable interest. How, in view of the purported cultural and legal differences in the regulation of witness evidence, have the international human rights bodies developed a common notion of the right to challenge witness evidence capable of transcending these national boundaries and traditions? This chapter will examine the case law on witness evidence in order to assess its success and to ascertain the values on which it is based.

As we shall see, the principal task of the international human rights organs has not been to 'reconcile' two broad and competing traditions, but rather to address specific differences in the manner in which evidence is treated in the various jurisdictions. There is considerable variety in the nature of the regulation of criminal evidence law not just between the various legal systems of the member states, but also within individual legal systems. There is also substantial variation in the point in the proceedings at which the evidence is challenged. While some systems employ a presumption in favour of immediacy, in many others witness confrontation or examination hearings take place during the preliminary proceedings and protocols or verbatim written records are produced for the file, which is then passed on to the judge or judges responsible for determining the case. The hearing and examination of the evidence might be supervised or carried out by the police, a prosecutor or an investigating judge. Although most systems allow for witnesses to be re-heard at trial, this might occur usually, occasionally or only very rarely depending on the legal system and previous statements made by the witness might well be available to

---

[5] See, e.g. the judgment of Justice Scalia in *Crawford* v. *Washington*, 124 S Ct 1354 (2004); R. D. Friedman, 'The Confrontation Right across the Systemic Divide', in J. Jackson, M. Langer and P. Tillers (eds.), *Crime, Procedure and Evidence in Comparative and International Context: Essays in Honour of Mirjan Damaška* (Oxford: Hart, 2008) 261, 271: 'The American and continental traditions are very different, not only in the institutional aspects emphasised by Damaška but also in their constitutional styles, and particularly in their treatment of individual rights.' See too M. Findlay, 'Synthesis in Trial Procedures? The Experience of the International Criminal Tribunals' (2001) 50 *International and Comparative Law Quarterly* 26, 26, who refers to 'two broad and divergent Western criminal justice traditions'. See further P. Roberts, 'On Method: The Ascent of Comparative Criminal Justice' (2002) 22 *Oxford Journal of Legal Studies* 539.

the fact-finder, even though he or she might not be permitted to rely on them in grounding the conviction.

The international human rights organs have also had to ensure that their approach is capable of being applied in those systems that rely on 'exclusionary'-type rules and in those that insist on all available evidence being presented to the fact-finder. Whereas in several legal systems, notably in England and Wales or in Scotland, inadmissible evidence is often excluded from the fact-finder, in many other European legal systems there is a strong presumption in favour of the fact-finder being provided with all available evidence, even though he or she may be prohibited from relying on various pieces of evidence in grounding the conviction.[6] There is thus little room for notions of exclusion or admissibility precisely because witness statements gathered in the preliminary proceedings will always be available to the fact-finder. The ECtHR has sought to avoid becoming entangled in such controversy by refusing to express a preference for the principle of free proof or the exclusion of evidence.[7] These factors have complicated the ECtHR's interpretation of Article 6(3)(d) of the ECHR and must be borne in mind when evaluating its case law.

Before considering the ECtHR's approach and that of the other international human rights organs in detail, it is instructive to consider firstly the requirement that an accused person be afforded the opportunity to test adverse witness evidence in some of the European criminal justice systems and the various rationales provided for the right. It is also useful to consider the manner in which the US Supreme Court (USSC) has defined and justified the right to confrontation as set out in the Sixth Amendment. This overview of the various theories underpinning the right to challenge witness evidence will enable consideration of underlying differences and similarities in its regulation, thereby providing assistance in assessing the approach of the ECtHR and the development of a supra-national concept of the right to challenge witness evidence.

10.2 Justifying the right to challenge incriminatory witness evidence

The standard account of the cross-examination of witnesses in common law systems is rooted in an accusatorial understanding of the truth-finding process. Cross-examination was famously referred to by Wigmore as 'beyond any doubt

---

[6] For a useful overview of the distinction between evidential rules excluding evidence and those governing the decision-making process, see J. F. Nijboer, 'Common Law Tradition in Evidence Scholarship Observed from a Continental Perspective' (1993) 41 *American Journal of Comparative Law* 299.

[7] It is notable that even in common law jurisdictions exclusionary rules have had many detractors through the years: see, e.g. W. G. Dickson, *A Treatise on the Law of Evidence in Scotland*, 3rd edn (Edinburgh: T. & T. Clark, 1887) vol. I, 6: '[t]here is a much greater risk of injustice from excluding than from admitting evidence objected to as irrelevant; and the Court can always caution the jury against being misled by it, if it should turn out objectionable'; Bentham, *Rationale of Judicial Evidence*, vol. 5, 1: 'Evidence is the basis of justice: you exclude evidence, you exclude justice.'

the greatest legal engine ever invented for the discovery of truth'[8] and has been characterised as a powerful 'weapon', which can be employed to test the veracity of a witness and the accuracy and completeness of his or her story.[9] The aim of cross-examination is said to be 'to complete and correct the story told by the witness during evidence in chief'[10] by testing the evidence given by a witness for the prosecution.[11] A crucial aspect of cross-examination in common law systems is its depiction as 'an essential feature of adversarial procedure' and as closely tied to a procedural context.[12]

This exposition of the procedural setting in which the cross-examination is to take place and in particular the reliance on the principle of oral proceedings is still relevant today. As a general rule, the cross-examination of witnesses in most common law systems takes place before a judge, or perhaps before a judge and jury, and is dominated – unless the accused chooses and is permitted to conduct his or her own defence – by counsel for the defence. The judge is expected to adopt a passive role, while the prosecution is not involved in the cross-examination at all. The requirement that witnesses be cross-examined in open court was never absolute,[13] however, and there are a number of exceptions to the rule.[14] Nevertheless, the procedural setting (notably the principal role afforded to the defence, the correspondingly negligible role of the prosecution and the limited role of the judiciary) must be regarded as a crucial part of the institution of cross-examination in common law countries and one which is closely connected generally to the aims of cross-examination and specifically to a particular idea of how best to establish the facts in criminal proceedings.[15]

Traditionally, in common law jurisdictions, the prohibition on the use of hearsay evidence played an important role in restricting the use of statements made by a person other than the witness giving evidence in the proceedings.[16]

---

[8] J. H. Wigmore, *A Treatise on the Anglo-American System of Evidence in Trials at Common Law*, rev. J. H. Chadbourn (Boston: Little, Brown, 1974) vol. V, § 1367, 32.

[9] See notably Viscount Sankey in *Mechanical and General Inventions Co and Lehwess v. Austin and Austin Motor Co* [1935] AC 346, 359 (HL).

[10] C. Allen, *Practical Guide to Evidence*, 3rd edn (London: Routledge-Cavendish, 2004) 82.

[11] See, e.g. *Hartley v. HM Advocate*, 1979 SLT 26, 28, per Lord Avonside: '[Cross-examination] consists in questioning an adverse witness in an effort to break down his evidence, to weaken or prejudice his evidence, or to elicit statements damaging to him and aiding the case of the cross-examiner'.

[12] I. H. Dennis, *The Law of Evidence*, 4th edn (London: Sweet & Maxwell, 2010) para. 14.24, 597; see also Dickson, *Law of Evidence in Scotland*, vol. II, 940, para. 1716.

[13] See also Dickson, *Law of Evidence in Scotland*, 958, paras. 1754 ff; see too Lord Justice-Clerk Hope in the Scottish case *Isabella Brodie* (HC) 12 March 1846, Arkley 45.

[14] Dennis, *Law of Evidence*, para. 16.2, 661.

[15] For a good overview of cross-examination of witnesses in England and Wales, see Dennis, *Law of Evidence*, ch. 14.

[16] The hearsay rule can be defined as follows: 'a statement other than one made by a person while giving oral evidence in the proceedings [is] inadmissible as evidence of any fact stated' (R. Cross and C. Tapper, *Cross on Evidence*, 11th edn (London: Butterworths, 2007) 588). See also A. L.-T. Choo, *Hearsay and Confrontation in Criminal Trials* (Oxford: Clarendon Press, 1996).

Various rationales have been provided to justify the hearsay rule,[17] which is closely connected to the oral testimony requirement and to the requirement that witnesses give evidence on the basis of their own knowledge of the facts at issue.[18] These include the fact that hearsay is not the best evidence, that it is not given on oath, that it is potentially unreliable and might even be fabricated, that in the absence of cross-examination it is difficult to assess and that the judge and jury are not afforded the opportunity to observe the demeanour of the person making the statement at the time that he or she made the statement.[19]

In recent times, most common law jurisdictions have been steadily increasing the number of exceptions to the rule.[20] In England and Wales, for instance, statutory provisions have replaced the common law hearsay rule,[21] but there remains a general presumption in favour of the exclusion of statements not made in oral evidence which are provided as evidence of any matter stated.[22] Such evidence may, however, be admitted if this is provided for by one of the four stated exceptions.[23] An important exception to the rule against hearsay relates to unavailable witnesses.[24] According to this provision, hearsay evidence is admissible if oral evidence given in the proceedings by the person who made the statement would have been admissible, the person who made the statement has been identified to the court's satisfaction and one of the following five conditions are met: the relevant person is dead, is unfit to be a witness, is outside of the United Kingdom and it is not reasonably practicable to secure his or her attendance, cannot be found – although such steps as are reasonably practicable have been taken to find him or her, or he or she through fear does not give or does not continue to give oral evidence in the proceedings. Cross-examination is thus principally justified in terms of reliability and guaranteeing

---

[17] For a comprehensive overview, see Dennis, *Law of Evidence*, 687 ff.
[18] E. M. Morgan, 'Hearsay Dangers and the Application of the Hearsay Concept' (1948) 62 *Harvard Law Review* 177.
[19] Pt 3 ch. 2 Criminal Justice Act 2003 (England & Wales). See, e.g. *Teper* v. *R* [1952] AC 480, 486, per Lord Normand; see too Choo, *Hearsay*, ch. 2. The Law Commission considered abolishing the hearsay rule in criminal cases, but decided in favour of its retention: Law Commission No. 245 *Evidence in Criminal Proceedings: Hearsay and Related Topics* (1997) Cm. 3670. Important changes to the hearsay rule were introduced in Scotland following the Law Commission's Report: Scottish Law Commission, *Report on Hearsay Evidence in Criminal Proceedings* (1995) No. 149.
[20] For an overview of the hearsay exceptions in various jurisdictions, see Irish Law Reform Commission, *Hearsay in Civil and Criminal Cases* (2010) Consultation paper 60, ch. 3.
[21] Pt 11, ch. 2 Criminal Justice Act 2003; see further Dennis, *Law of Evidence*, para. 17.1, 717–18.
[22] See s. 114(1) Criminal Justice Act 2003.
[23] See s. 114(1): 'In criminal proceedings a statement not made in oral evidence in the proceedings is admissible as evidence of any matter stated if, but only if: (a) any provision of this Chapter or any other statutory provision makes it admissible, (b) any rule of law preserved by s. 118 makes it admissible, (c) all parties to the proceedings agree to it being admissible, or (d) the court is satisfied that it is in the interests of justice for it to be admissible.'
[24] See s.116 Criminal Justice Act 2003.

the safety of the conviction.[25] The defence ought to be afforded the opportunity to cross-examine witnesses, but if this is not possible, other measures (such as those set out in Criminal Justice Act 2003) may well be sufficient to guarantee the reliability of the evidence.[26] This approach, as we have seen and will see further, differs markedly from that of Strasbourg and has given rise to conflict with the right to challenge witnesses as guaranteed by Article 6(3)(d) of the ECHR.[27]

An alternative approach has been developed in the United States. Prior to its landmark judgment in *Crawford v. Washington*, the USSC had ruled that the purpose of confrontation was to promote the accuracy of the verdict by providing the defence with an adequate opportunity to test adverse evidence.[28] In *Crawford*, the USSC altered its stance, severing the 'operational link between hearsay and confrontation',[29] and holding that: 'Where testimonial statements are at issue, the only indicium of reliability sufficient to satisfy constitutional demands is the one the Constitution actually prescribes: confrontation.'[30] It expressly rejected the earlier reliance on reliability, holding that: 'Dispensing with confrontation because testimony is obviously reliable is akin to dispensing with jury trial because a defendant is obviously guilty.'[31] Crucially, though, it did not provide a right to confront every witness. It restricted the right of confrontation to 'testimonial statements' deemed to be 'the primary object' of the Sixth Amendment,[32] thereby introducing a distinction between testimonial statements, which fall within the scope of the clause, and non-testimonial statements, which quite possibly do not.[33] The USSC has proven reluctant to define what constitutes a 'testimonial statement', but has held that while statements such as those made to the police immediately after an attack[34] and a laboratory analyst's report prepared for the proceedings are testimonial,[35] business records not prepared for such proceedings or statements made to a telephone operator in the course of an emergency call are not.[36] The focus on protecting an accused against untested 'testimonial' evidence underlines the fact that the

---

[25] *R v. Horncastle and others* [2009] UKSC 14, [2010] 2 WLR 2; see too D. Ormerod, 'Case Comment: *R v. Horncastle and others*' [2010] *Criminal Law Review* 496, 501, who notes that cross-examination is 'of course . . . designed primarily to check reliability'.
[26] See also Ormerod, 'Case Comment', 500.
[27] See, e.g. the cases of *Al-Khawaja and Tahery v. United Kingdom* (referred to the GC). See Ch. 4.2.3.
[28] See notably *Ohio v. Roberts*, 448 US 56 (1980).
[29] D. A. Sklansky, 'Hearsay's Last Hurrah' [2009] *Supreme Court Review* 1, 4.
[30] *Crawford v. Washington*, 124 S. Ct. 1354 (2004).   [31] *Crawford v. Washington*, para. 62.
[32] *Crawford v. Washington*, 1365.
[33] As Friedman notes both this and the definition of 'testimonial' remains unclear: Friedman, 'The Confrontation Right', 261. The Supreme Court has since had to consider the notion of testimonial in a number of important cases: see, e.g. *Davis v. Washington*, 126 S Ct 2266 (2006); and *Giles v. California*, 128 S Ct 2678 (2008).
[34] *Davis v. Washington*, 547 US 813 (2006).
[35] *Melendez-Diaz v. Massachusetts*, 129 S Ct 2527 (2009).
[36] *Davis v. Washington*, 547 US 813 (2006), 822.

USSC's principal concern is with out-of-court statements made to government officials. The explanation that the 'involvement of government officers in the production of testimonial evidence presents the same risk, whether the officers are police or justices of the peace' reflects the influence of the mistrust of prosecution and investigation authorities on the scope of the clause.[37] It is unclear, however, why it is the fact that the statement is testimonial, rather than say the effect the statement is likely to have, which is critical to the scope of the right to confrontation.[38]

The USSC clearly rejects reliability as the basis for defining the scope of the confrontation principle, although as Redmayne notes this does not mean that the right is not justified on reliability grounds.[39] The rationale for the right to confrontation is largely masked, however, by the USSC's 'originalist' approach[40] and its anti-inquisitorialism[41] and some have suggested that its failure to justify the importance of confrontation can be interpreted as suggesting that 'the purpose of confrontation is confrontation'[42] or even that confrontation is necessary simply because it is one of the aspects of criminal procedure which is 'socially and historically and culturally situated' in the US justice system.[43]

Both the UKSC and the USSC have recently sought to distinguish their conception of the law of evidence from that in continental Europe. In *Horncastle*, the UKSC suggested that continental European jurisdictions do not have the same volume of literature on criminal evidence law and that the sole and decisive test was principally directed towards civil law systems, noting that 'the continental procedure had not addressed that aspect of a fair trial that Article 6(3)(d) was designed to ensure'.[44] Meanwhile, in *Crawford*, the USSC held that civil law mode of procedure was the 'principal evil' against which the confrontation clause was directed.[45] It is useful to consider briefly the regulation of the right to challenge witness evidence in some continental European jurisdictions. Some writers have suggested that the right to confrontation was transplanted

---

[37] See further S. J. Summers, 'The Right to Confrontation after *Crawford v. Washington*: "A Continental European Perspective"' (2004) 2 *International Commentary on Evidence*, Issue 1, Art. 3.

[38] See H. L. Ho, 'Confrontation and Hearsay: A Critique of Crawford' (2004) 8 *Evidence & Proof* 147; and I. Dennis, 'The Right to Confront Witnesses: Meanings, Myths and Human Rights' [2010] *Criminal Law Review* 255, 264.

[39] M. Redmayne, 'Confronting Confrontation' (2010) 10 *LSE Law, Society and Economy Working Papers* 12.

[40] Redmayne, 'Confronting Confrontation', 11.

[41] D. A. Sklansky, 'Anti-Inquisitorialism' (2008) 122 *Harvard Law Review* 1634.

[42] R. Park, 'Is Confrontation the Bottom Line?' (2006–7) 19 *Regent University Law Review* 459, 467.

[43] S. Clark, 'Who Do You Think You Are? The Criminal Trial and Community Character', in A. Duff, L. Farmer, S. Marshall and V. Tadros (eds.), *The Trial on Trial (2): Judgment and Calling to Account* (Oxford: Hart, 2006) 83, 86. See also Redmayne, 'Confronting Confrontation', 13, citing R. D. Friedman, 'Confrontation: The Search for Basic Principles' (1998) *Georgetown Law Journal* 1011, 1028.

[44] *R* v. *Horncastle and others* [2009] UKSC 14, [14], [2010] 2 WLR 2.

[45] *Crawford* v. *Washington*, 541 US 36 (2004); see further Sklansky, 'Anti-Inquisitorialism', 163.

into the criminal procedure systems of continental European countries by the ECHR and that a comprehensive discourse only developed several decades later.[46] While it is certainly true that the application of Article 6(3)(d) ECHR has resulted in considerable developments in many member states,[47] it would be wrong to think that it heralded the introduction of the right to challenge witness evidence altogether. It would certainly be incorrect to portray continental criminal procedure law as having been regulated by the principles of the inquisition until notions of fairness and defence rights were introduced by Article 6 of the ECHR. This ignores the fact that the regulation of defence rights, including the right to challenge witness evidence, was the subject of sustained academic discussion during the nineteenth century by lawyers from many continental European countries[48] and the right to challenge witness evidence was guaranteed by many jurisdictions long before the introduction of the ECHR.

The right to confront witnesses is regarded in modern times as an important procedural safeguard in most continental European legal systems. At the same time, though, it is not considered to be an absolute guarantee, nor does it protect against the use of hearsay evidence. Many, if not the majority of, jurisdictions require, for instance, that hearsay evidence be treated with considerable care,[49] but there is no general presumption against the use of such evidence and some writers have noted that this requirement is not to be found either in the text of, or in the rationale underpinning, Article 6(3)(d) of the ECHR and have counselled the ECtHR against interpreting the provision in such a way as to require continental European countries to introduce the 'English rule against hearsay evidence'.[50]

The defence's right to examine witnesses is considered in Germany to be an important aspect of the right to be heard and of the principle that the accused

---

[46] See, e.g. S. Maffei, *The European Right to Confrontation in Criminal Proceedings: Absent, Anonymous and Vulnerable Witnesses* (Groningen: Europa Law Publishing, 2006) 16.

[47] See, e.g. V. Bück, 'Le Conseil constitutionnel et les réformes pénales récentes' (2001) 10 *Les Cahiers du Conseil Constitutionnel* 191, 192; and B. Swart, 'The European Convention as an Invigorator of Domestic Law in the Netherlands' (1999) 26 *Journal of Law and Society* 38. See also Ch. 4.2.3.

[48] S. J. Summers, *Fair Trials: The European Criminal Procedural Tradition and the European Court of Human Rights* (Oxford: Hart, 2007) chs. 2 and 3.

[49] See, e.g. the decisions of the German courts: BGH NStZ 88, 144; and BGHSt 36, 166; see further C. Roxin and B. Schünemann, *Strafverfahrensrecht*, 26th edn (Munich: C. H. Beck, 2009) § 46, N 33. A conviction must not be based on hearsay evidence alone: BGHSt 44, 153, 158 ('Die Aussage eines "Zeugen vom Hörensagen" vermag für sich genommen ohne zusätzliche Indizien einen Schuldspruch nicht zu tragen').

[50] V. Krey, *Deutsches Strafverfahrensrecht* (Stuttgart: Kolhammer, 2007) vol. 2, 118. It is also interesting to note in German law that hearsay evidence is seen as compatible with the immediacy requirement, as the witness gives evidence in person in court albeit in relation to indirect evidence: see, e.g. BGHSt 6, 209 (210); 22, 268; and NStZ 1999, 578. See further H.-H. Kühne, *Strafprozessrecht: Eine Systematische Darstellung des deutschen und europäischen Strafrechts*, 7th edn (Heidelberg: C. F. Müller, 2010) paras. 915 ff.

is to be treated as a subject and not as an object of the proceedings.[51] There is a clear preference in favour of immediacy,[52] but the defence may waive the right to challenge witnesses in court[53] and there are numerous exceptions which allow for the statements made during the investigation phase of a witness who has since become 'unavoidably' unavailable – including in cases where the witness has died, fears for his or her life or safety, or cannot be traced – to be considered by the court.[54]

The German federal and constitutional courts have not always followed the ECtHR in prohibiting reliance on the 'decisive' testimony of a witness who could not be challenged by the defence. In several cases involving hearsay evidence, they have rejected claims that the fact that the defence was unable to question the immediate witness violated Article 6(3)(d) of the ECHR, holding instead that there will be no violation providing that the witness's failure to appear was based on objective reasons, not connected to the criminal justice authorities, the proceedings as a whole can be characterised as fair and there was also other evidence available to the court.[55] Particular problems have arisen in the context of undercover investigators and police informants. The German courts have, for instance, held that it is acceptable for a conviction to be based mainly on indirect hearsay evidence such as that provided by a police informant, even though the actual witness was not available to be challenged by the defence,[56] providing that the court was aware of the inherent problematic nature of such evidence and there was other evidence which served to support the indirect evidence.[57] The implication is that in such cases, the court is able to take the unreliable nature of the evidence into account and this judicial discretion is sufficient to guarantee the reliability of the conviction.

Similarly, in France, a prior witness statement, which will usually have been provided during the investigation to a prosecutor or investigating judge, can be introduced as evidence in cases where it is impossible to ensure the presence

---

[51] See the decisions of the German constitutional court in: BVerfGE 7, 275 (279); and BVerfGE 7, 35 (58).

[52] § 250 German Criminal Procedure Code.

[53] Kühne, *Strafprozessrecht*, para. 931; and R. Esser, *Auf dem Weg zu einem europäischen Strafverfahrensrecht* (Berlin: De Gruyter, 2002) 627.

[54] § 251 German Criminal Procedure Code. See further U. Eisenberg, *Beweisrecht der StPO: Spezialkommentar* (Munich: C. H. Beck, 2008) paras. 2099 ff; and Roxin and Schünemann, *Strafverfahrensrecht*, § 46 N 11 ff.

[55] See, e.g. BGH NStZ- TT 2005, 321 f; and BVerfG, NJW 2007, 206. See for instance the decision NStZ 2005, 225, involving a witness who had died; for criticism, see R. Esser, 'Anmerkung zu BGH, Urteil vom 03.12.2004' [2005] *Juristische Rundschau* 248 ff.

[56] See, e.g. the decisions of the German federal and constitutional courts in BGHSt 42, 15, 25; BGH NJW 2001, 2245; and BVerfGE 57, 250, 292.

[57] See, e.g. BGH St 17, 382; 34, 159; and BVerfGE 57, 250, 292f. See further Esser, *Auf dem Weg*, 677–81; T. Weigend, 'Spricht Europa mit zwei Zungen?' (2001) 21 *Strafverteidiger* 63, 64; Esser, 'Anmerkung zu BGH', 248 ff; J. Eisele, 'Die einzelnen Beschuldigtenrechte der Europäischen Menschenrechtskonvention' [2005] *Juristische Arbeitsblätter* 901, 905 f; and C. Safferling, 'Verdeckte Ermittler im Strafverfahren – deutsche und europäische Rechtsprechung im Konflikt?' [2006] *Neue Zeitschrift für Strafrecht* 75 ff.

of the witness in court.[58] The unavailability of the witness can be a result of illness, death or unlawful pressure,[59] but also of the fact that the witness is detained abroad, has absconded or simply cannot be found.[60] Furthermore, it is notable that the courts do not appear to require that the untested evidence be corroborated in any way or that there is other evidence in support of the conviction which does seem to lead to the conclusion that 'this area of law appears to be a good candidate for successful challenges before the Strasbourg Court'.[61] Maffei suggests that the French approach to untested witness evidence highlights the fact that reliability is deemed to be guaranteed by the role and function of the person to whom the statements are made.[62] This reliance on the 'testimonial' nature of the evidence to guarantee reliability is in direct contrast to the US approach, according to which the 'testimonial' nature of the evidence is the primary reason for affording the defence to challenge it.

There are obviously considerable differences in the treatment of witness evidence in Europe (particularly in relation to the procedural context in which the opportunity to challenge the evidence is to occur), but there are also some similarities. In relation to the issue of unavailable witnesses, many legal systems allow evidence to be used to convict the accused, even if the defence was not afforded the opportunity to challenge the evidence in person. If there is clearly a general consensus that it is helpful to question witnesses in order to assist in establishing the facts on which to base a criminal conviction, there is less agreement about the reasons justifying this opportunity or the limitations on the right. In view of the fact that the ECtHR has responsibility for regulating the right to challenge incriminatory witness evidence across Europe, it is useful to consider in detail the manner in which it has set about regulating the right to challenge witness evidence.

10.3 The regulation of the right to challenge witness evidence: the human rights perspective

The ECHR guarantees to those accused of criminal offences the right to 'examine or have examined' witnesses against them, while the ICCPR provides that they have the right to obtain the attendance and examination of witnesses on their behalf under the same conditions as the witnesses against them.[63] These provisions differ, for instance, from the right to 'confrontation' as guaranteed by the Sixth Amendment to the US Constitution. Confrontation implies a face-to-face meeting between the accused and the witness[64] and is generally

---

[58] See, e.g. the Dobbertin case: Cass. crim. 6 March 1991, Bull. crim. No. 115, *Dobbertin*.
[59] Cass. crim. 26 October 1994, Bull. crim. No. 343, *Manhallah*.
[60] Maffei, *The European Right to Confrontation*, 183.   [61] Ibid., 184.   [62] Ibid.
[63] See also General Comment No. 13: equality before the courts and the right to a fair and public hearing by an independent court established by law (Art. 14): 13.04.1984 (Twenty First Session, 1984), para. 12, A/39/40 (1984) Annex VI, 143–7.
[64] See, e.g. *Kamasinski* v. *Austria*, para. 91. Contrast *Coy* v. *Iowa* (1988) 487 US 1012, 1016. For justifications for this, see Clark, 'Who Do You Think You Are?', 83 ff. This requirement has not

perceived to be broader than the right to cross-examination.[65] The ECtHR has not always been consistent, however, in its use of terminology and has referred to the right to confront,[66] challenge and question,[67] examine[68] and cross-examine[69] witnesses seemingly interchangeably.[70] The right to confrontation as set out in the Sixth Amendment differs substantially from the right to examine witnesses in the ECHR, but it also differs from the right to confrontation as understood in the case law of the English, Australian or Italian courts.[71] As Dennis has noted, while confrontation is a 'convenient and evocative' term, there is little agreement about its scope.[72] There are a variety of ways in which the opportunity to cross-examine or confront witnesses about their evidence can be regulated and the manner of the regulation will often reflect the preoccupations and procedural traditions of the legal system. It is important, therefore, to note that the guarantee set out in Article 6(3)(d) of the ECHR is not a right to cross-examination in the English sense, nor is it the same as the right to confrontation as guaranteed by the Sixth Amendment.

All European procedural systems have rules regulating the accused's opportunity to challenge or confront witnesses about incriminatory testimony, but equally all systems provide for exceptions to this rule in various circumstances. There are, on the one hand, an abundance of reasons why important witnesses might be unable to testify in person – such as death,[73] ill health,[74] residence abroad,[75] detention in a foreign prison[76] – while, on the other, a requirement that all witnesses have to be cross-examined in person, irrespective of the fact that the relevance or importance of their evidence might be regarded as inefficient and impractical. A mandatory rule requiring that the defence be afforded the opportunity to challenge, in person, all witnesses whose evidence is produced by the prosecution, irrespective of its importance, would be too extreme. It would be difficult to justify abandoning prosecutions simply on the basis of the accused's lack of opportunity to question witnesses whose evidence is not important. In those legal systems that provide for the evidence to be heard at trial and require evidence to be admitted, it is relatively straightforward for the prosecution to withhold, or refrain from relying on, untested, unimportant evidence without unnecessarily compromising either the prosecution itself or

---

been endorsed by the ECtHR: see, e.g. S. Trechsel, *Human Rights in Criminal Proceedings* (Oxford University Press, 2005) 310.

[65] Dennis, 'The Right to Confront Witnesses', 260.   [66] *Saïdi* v. *France*, para. 44.
[67] *Bocos-Cuesta* v. *Netherlands*, para. 68.   [68] *Taxquet* v. *Belgium*, para. 58.
[69] *Solakov* v. *Former Yugoslav Republic of Macedonia*, para. 58.
[70] See, e.g. *Caka* v. *Albania*, paras. 102, 105 and 114.
[71] Contrast, e.g. *R* v. *Davis* [2008] 3 All ER 461, 5 with the position in Italy and France as described by Maffei, *The European Right to Confrontation*, 143 ff.
[72] Dennis, 'The Right to Confront Witnesses', 256.
[73] *Garner* v. *United Kingdom* (dec.); and *Ferrantelli and Santangelo* v. *Italy*, paras. 51–2.
[74] *Håkan Wester* v. *Sweden* (dec.).
[75] *Klimentyev* v. *Russia*, para. 125; and *Mirilashvili* v. *Russia*, para. 214: 'The problem of non-appearance of witnesses living abroad is well known by the Court.'
[76] *HK* v. *Netherlands* (dec.).

the rights of the defence. In those systems, however, in which all of the evidence collected during the preliminary proceedings is available to the fact-finder, and where there is no opportunity for evidence to be withheld or excluded, it would necessarily compel the abandonment of prosecutions even if the evidence was entirely irrelevant to the decision to convict. It is unsurprising, therefore, that most legal systems have rules restricting the right of the accused to confront or cross-examine witnesses. Equally inevitable, though, is the fact that the determination of the criteria for establishing those witnesses whose evidence has to be challenged in person will likely be controversial.

According to Article 6(3)(d) of the ECHR, everyone 'charged with a criminal offence' is entitled to 'examine or have examined witnesses against him'. The ECtHR has substantially restricted the remit of the provision, however, by ruling that an accused will only have the right to challenge witness evidence which was the sole or decisive basis for his or her conviction:

> ...where a conviction is based solely or to a decisive degree on depositions that have been made by a person whom the accused has had no opportunity to examine or have examined, whether during the investigation or at trial, the rights of the defence are restricted to an extent that is incompatible with the guarantees provided by Article 6.[77]

Furthermore, although the ECtHR has held that Article 6(3)(d) 'is an aspect of the right to a fair trial guaranteed by Article 6(1) which, in principle, requires that all evidence must be produced in the presence of the accused in a public hearing with a view to adversarial argument',[78] it has continually held that the right to question witnesses need not occur at the public hearing, provided that the accused has had the opportunity at some stage in the proceedings to question the witness.[79]

The ECtHR has not offered much indication in its case law about whether the importance of the evidence or the adequacy of the opportunity ought to be assessed first. In some cases, it begins by assessing whether the applicant has had a sufficient procedural opportunity to question the witness and only then goes on to consider whether the witness evidence was decisive. In other cases, it begins by considering first whether the evidence was the sole or decisive basis for the conviction. In *Van Mechelen and others* v. *Netherlands,* for instance, the fact that the authorities failed to assess whether the witness really ought to have been provided with anonymity or to ensure that the defence was afforded a sufficient alternative to a 'normal' confrontation hearing seems to have been

---

[77] *Lucà* v. *Italy,* para. 40; see too *Solakov* v. *Former Yugoslav Republic of Macedonia,* para. 58.
[78] See, e.g. *Al-Khawaja and Tahery* v. *United Kingdom,* para. 34 (referred to the GC); and *Krasnikiu* v. *Czech Republic,* para. 75.
[79] *Lucà* v. *Italy,* para. 40: 'If the defendant has been given an adequate and proper opportunity to challenge the depositions either when they are made or at a later stage, their admission in evidence will not in itself contravene Article 6(1) and 6(3).' The HRC has adopted a similar approach: see, e.g. *Compass* v. *Jamaica.*

an essential element in the finding of a violation, while the determination of whether the evidence was sole or decisive seems to have been a secondary concern. After deciding that 'the handicaps under which the defence laboured' were not sufficiently counterbalanced by the measures taken by the authorities, the ECtHR held, almost in a throwaway statement: 'Moreover, the only evidence relied upon by the Court of Appeal which provided positive identification of the applicants as the perpetrators of the crimes were the statements of the anonymous police officers. That being so the conviction was based "to a decisive extent" on these anonymous statements.'[80] In *Gossa* v. *Poland*, the ECtHR discussed at some length the efforts made by the authorities to secure the presence of the witness, only to come to the conclusion right at the end of the judgment that the provision had not been violated, as the applicant's conviction was 'in any event' not based solely or to a decisive degree on the witness's statements.[81]

The inevitable uncertainty of this approach has resulted in unnecessary confusion both in the court's case law and the interpretation of its cases by commentators and the courts.[82] In *Horncastle*, the UKSC identified *Doorson* v. *Netherlands*[83] as a turning point in the case law, noting that the ECtHR held in that case for the first time that even if the authorities were justified in not calling a witness, it would be unfair to rely on the evidence if it represented the sole or decisive basis for the accused's conviction.[84] It went on to argue that in certain cases the existence of counterbalancing factors might be such as to justify reliance on an untested statement which was the sole or decisive basis for the conviction.[85] The case law of the ECtHR does not appear to support this conclusion, however, and it is to be expected that the Grand Chamber of the ECtHR will reaffirm that there is no way to counterbalance the use of untested decisive evidence which is capable of sufficiently guaranteeing the rights of the defence.[86] If the evidence represents the sole or decisive basis for the conviction, then the accused must have the right to confront the witness, subject to the various legitimate limitations that have been developed by the ECtHR. If, on the other hand, the witness evidence is not decisive, then he or she will have no right to do so, and the reason for the witness's unavailability (bad faith on the part of the authorities, negligence, no fault on the part of the authorities) would

---

[80] *Van Mechelen and others* v. *Netherlands*, paras. 62 and 63.
[81] *Gossa* v. *Poland*, para. 63.
[82] See, e.g. Friedman, who cites the case of *Gossa* v. *Poland* in support of the contention that 'in some circumstances unavailability of the witness through the fault of neither party is deemed enough to excuse the absence of an opportunity for confrontation': Friedman, 'The Confrontation Right', 268. This will only be the case if the witness evidence is not the sole basis for or decisive to the applicant's conviction.
[83] *Doorson* v. *Netherlands*.
[84] *R* v. *Horncastle and others* [2009] USKC 14, [77], [2010] 2 WLR 2. See the discussion at Ch. 4.2.3 above.
[85] *Horncastle*, paras. 106–7.
[86] *Al-Khawaja and Tahery* v. *United Kingdom* (referred to the GC).

seem to be irrelevant. It is difficult to understand, therefore, why in its case law the ECtHR does not focus first on determining whether the evidence is the sole basis for, or decisive to, the conviction. Only once this has been positively established would it then have to consider the adequacy of the accused's opportunity to question the witness. The approach may simply be a result of the piecemeal development of the court's principles. The ambiguity in the manner in which the ECtHR has approached this issue suggests, however, some unwillingness to admit the emphasis which it places on the sole and decisive test. This in turn strengthens the impression that its determination of whether there has been a violation turns principally on notions of reliability, whether it believes that there is sufficient evidence to prove the applicant committed the alleged crime, and makes the values underlying its approach, as we shall see, difficult to ascertain.

10.3.1 The importance of the witness evidence: the sole or decisive test

The restriction of the right to challenge witness evidence which is decisive to, or the sole basis for, the conviction is one of the defining factors in the ECtHR's interpretation of Article 6(3)(d) of the ECHR. Although in some of its early cases it occasionally used other, potentially more restrictive formulations such as the 'only evidence'[87] or the 'sole basis'[88] for the conviction, the terms 'sole' and 'decisive' are now usually cited together.[89] Indeed, in some of its more recent cases the ECtHR has sometimes dropped the reference to 'sole', referring simply to the fact that where the conviction is based 'to decisive degree on such depositions the rights of the defence are restricted to an extent which is incompatible with the guarantees provided by Article 6'.[90] This is preferable as when paired with the broader adjective 'decisive', the word 'sole' in any case loses any significant meaning and only serves to contribute to the already existing uncertainty 'associated with ascertaining the weight, which is attached to untested evidence'.[91]

There are admittedly some cases, notably *SN* v. *Sweden*, in which the ECtHR seems almost to have ignored the sole and decisive test. In *SN*, the defence had not had the opportunity to cross-examine the victim in a case involved in the sexual abuse of a minor. The ECtHR held, despite finding that the untested witness statements on which the accused was convicted were in fact 'virtually the sole evidence on which the courts' findings of guilt were based', that Article 6(3)(d) of the ECHR had not been violated.[92] Such cases ought

---

[87] *Asch* v. *Austria*, para. 30; and *Artner* v. *Austria*, para. 24. [88] e.g. *Saïdi* v. *France*, para. 44.
[89] See, e.g. *Lucà* v. *Italy*, para. 43; and *Solakov* v. *Former Yugoslav Republic of Macedonia*, para. 57.
[90] *Mirilashvili* v. *Russia*, para. 216.
[91] S. Stavros, *The Guarantees for Accused Persons under Article 6 of the European Convention on Human Rights* (Dordrecht: Martinus Nijhoff, 1993) 236, n. 742. See also Trechsel, *Human Rights in Criminal Proceedings*, 297; and Esser, *Auf dem Weg*, 632.
[92] *SN* v. *Sweden*, para. 46.

to be seen, however, as isolated examples rather than as indicative of a more general approach. In *Al-Khawaja and Tahery* v. *United Kingdom*, the ECtHR directly addressed and rejected the UK Government's assertions, which were based on *SN*, that there was no absolute rule prohibiting the use of untested statements. It held instead that it did not 'regard the *SN* case as authority for any general proposition that untested statements can be admitted consistently with Article 6 when they are the sole or decisive evidence against a defendant'.[93]

The sole and decisive test stands in obvious contradiction to the ECtHR's commonly repeated claim that it is for the national courts to assess the evidence and that it is not its task to rule on whether the statements were properly used as evidence.[94] In order to determine whether the evidence at issue was decisive to the conviction, the ECtHR has no choice but to examine all of the evidence.[95] In some cases, it will be assisted by the findings of the national courts. In *Al-Khawaja*, for instance, it noted that the court of appeal had held that the 'evidence against the applicant was very strong, that it had ruled out the possibility of collusion between the complainants and that it had found that the prosecution was able to rely on similar evidence of other women'; nevertheless, it held that the trial judge's comment 'no statement, no count one' could not be ignored. In *Tahery*, the ECtHR referred to the court of appeal's findings that 'there was no reason to doubt the safety of the conviction and that the other evidence in the case was compelling', but held that it could not overlook the fact that the appeal court had referred to the witness's statement as 'both important and probative of a major issue in the case'. In each case it determined, regardless of the national court's classification of the witness evidence, that it was in fact 'the sole or, at least, the decisive basis' for the applicants' convictions.[96] Such cases emphasise that in those cases in which the national courts do not accept that the evidence was decisive, the ECtHR cannot simply rely on their assessment of the evidence. The definition of decisive evidence is essentially an autonomous one: even if the national court believes that the evidence is not decisive, the ECtHR is entitled to hold a different opinion.

Despite the ECtHR's claim that it is not its place to assess the evidence on which the criminal conviction is based, there can be little doubt that its principal means of regulating the scope of Article 6(3)(d) of the ECHR has involved precisely that. This seems to present something of a conundrum: why, if the ECtHR does not see itself as best placed to evaluate the evidence, has it developed a test which compels it to do just that? The ECtHR's approach can best be explained in the context of the significant differences in the regulation of evidence in the various member states. The importance of the sole and decisive test has essentially come about as a result of the lack of exclusionary-type rules in many European legal systems. Whereas in common law jurisdictions

---

[93] *Al-Khawaja and Tahery* v. *United Kingdom*, para. 38.   [94] e.g. *Visser* v. *Netherlands*, para. 43.
[95] See also Trechsel, *Human Rights in Criminal Proceedings*, 294.
[96] *Al-Khawaja and Tahery* v. *United Kingdom* (referred to the GC).

insignificant untested witness evidence can simply be excluded or withheld from the fact-finder, in those systems in which there is a presumption in favour of the fact-finder having access to all of the evidence obtained during the investigation, rules have to be created to determine which witnesses the defence ought to have the opportunity to challenge in person. Seen in this light, the sole and decisive test can be seen as enabling the ECtHR to develop European-wide regulation of witness evidence, without it having to enter into a discussion about the merits of exclusionary[97] or inclusionary[98] approaches to the criminal evidence. The inevitable consequence of the sole and decisive test, however, is that it requires the judge to take an active role in determining the importance of the evidence and assessing its relevance in convicting an accused.[99]

Determining which evidence is in fact 'decisive' is obviously not a simple task. In several cases involving allegations of the sexual abuse of minors, the ECtHR referred to the fact that the evidence at issue (statements of the victims, often video-taped) was decisive because it formed the 'only direct evidence against the accused'.[100] The fact that the convictions were supported by other indirect evidence, such as expert psychiatric opinions on the credibility of the victims' statements, the evidence of family members and the opinions of doctors treating the victims, was not sufficient to interfere with the assessment of the victims' statements as decisive to the convictions. These cases appear to deviate from some of the earlier case law[101] and suggest that 'decisive evidence' cannot be defined in terms of evidence which is 'unsupported'. The evidence in all of these cases was 'supported' by other evidence, but importantly this evidence was not from a separate, 'independent' source. The existence of a confession, incriminating real evidence or other witness evidence will as a general rule prevent the uncontested witness evidence from being considered decisive. In many cases, the ECtHR lists the other evidence, almost as if to stress that the fairness of the trial was not compromised.[102]

It is difficult to ascertain the ECtHR's approach, but the more recent case law seems to suggest that decisive evidence is defined as evidence which is not supported by other independent evidence and which is therefore considered to be determinative to the conviction. If the evidence is not decisive to the conviction, that is to say irrelevant to the verdict, the procedural violation is also

---

[97] Neither the refusal to admit hearsay evidence nor its admission will automatically violate Art. 6(3)(d): see *Blastland* v. *United Kingdom* (dec.); and *Trivedi* v. *United Kingdom* (dec.).

[98] The Strasbourg authorities have held that the principle of the free evaluation of evidence does not as such run counter to Art. 6(3)(d) ECHR: *Hayward* v. *Sweden* (dec.); and *MA and BS* v. *Norway* (dec.).

[99] See, for an examination of the different roles and responsibilities of the judge in Europe, S. Doran and J. Jackson (eds.), *The Judicial Role in Criminal Proceedings* (Oxford: Hart, 2000).

[100] *PS* v. *Germany*, para. 30; *AM* v. *Italy*, paras. 26 and 28; *W* v. *Finland*, para. 47; *AH* v. *Finland*, para. § 44; *AL* v. *Finland*, para. 44; and *AS* v. *Finland*, para. 67.

[101] See especially the judgment in *Asch* v. *Austria*, paras. 28–31, which Trechsel refers to as an 'unfortunate mistake': Trechsel, *Human Rights in Criminal Proceedings*, 295.

[102] See, e.g. *Robert and Gerhard Lorich* v. *Austria* (dec.); and *MK* v. *Austria*.

treated as immaterial. The fact that the accused, or more accurately the defence, has not had the opportunity to question the witness is deemed unproblematic. The implication is that the existence of other evidence provides a fair basis on which to found the applicant's conviction. Only if the evidence is decisive can the procedural violation be characterised as actually impacting on, or at least having the potential to impact on, the right of the defence to challenge the prosecution's case and thus on the accuracy of the verdict. This suggests that the ECtHR sees fairness not as external to the search for truth, but rather as internal to it, promoting the aim of truth-finding or accuracy.[103]

When compared, for instance, to the confrontation principle applied by the USSC, the sole and decisive test might be criticised as too restrictive, as denying the defence the right to challenge witnesses whose evidence while important is not decisive.[104] Even bad faith on the part of the authorities in preventing the defence from challenging witness evidence seems from an Article 6(3)(d) ECHR perspective to be irrelevant, providing the evidence at issue was not decisive. In this sense, the sole and decisive test might be seen as representative of the persistent tension alluded to by Dennis which exists between the strict application of formal rules and the desire of the judge to admit evidence which seems relevant and reliable.[105] It highlights the general unease about overturning convictions on procedural grounds which do not necessarily or obviously impact on the accuracy of the verdict.[106]

The sole and decisive test has also been criticised, though, for being too broad and some have questioned whether such a 'strong confrontation right',[107] which gives 'uncritical priority to defence interests',[108] can be justified. We have seen that the UKSC recently issued a direct challenge to the Strasbourg Court in the case of *R* v. *Horncastle and others* by rejecting the 'sole and decisive' test, casting doubt on the theoretical basis underpinning its approach and inviting it to

---

[103] Duff et al. present a considerably more sophisticated account of accuracy than that of the court arguing that 'many of what the instrumentalist portrays as side-constraints should rather be seen as internal, not merely to the trial process, but to the truth-seeking aim itself, properly understood': A. Duff, L. Farmer, S. Marshall and V. Tadros, *The Trial on Trial (3): Towards a Normative Theory of the Trial* (Oxford: Hart, 2007) 64. Contrast A. Ashworth and M. Redmayne, *The Criminal Process*, 4th edn (Oxford University Press, 2010) 23, who refer to 'the twin objects of the criminal trial' as being 'accurately to determine whether or not a person has committed a particular criminal offence and to do so fairly'.

[104] Friedman, 'The Confrontation Right', 261 ff.

[105] '[T]here is a persistent tension between the strict application of the formal rules and the desire of the judges to admit evidence which appears to be both relevant and reliable': Dennis, *Law of Evidence*, para. 3.24, 87.

[106] Such concerns are also evident in relation to other aspects of the court's Art. 6 case law: see, e.g. in the context of entrapment, *Khan* v. *United Kingdom*. The court has adopted a notably different approach in the context of violations of Art. 3: see, e.g. *Jalloh* v. *Germany*. On the theoretical considerations underpinning the different approaches to the use of evidence obtained in violation of Arts. 3 and 6, see Duff et al., *Trial on Trial (3)*, 247 ff.

[107] See Redmayne, 'Confronting Confrontation', 30; and Dennis, 'The Right to Confront Witnesses', 255.

[108] Dennis, 'The Right to Confront Witnesses', 273.

reconsider its case law.[109] The case clearly illustrates the differences between the approaches of the ECtHR and the UKSC. In its judgment, the UKSC held that in the absence of 'a convincing alternative rationale', the position of the Strasbourg Court could only be understood as stating that 'a conviction based solely or decisively upon the evidence of a witness... who has not been subjected to cross-examination... will not be safe'.[110] Having determined that the aim of the Strasbourg test was essentially the same as that of the statutory hearsay regime, namely reliability and ensuring the safety of the conviction, the UKSC was able to reject the 'impractical' sole and decisive test while claiming to uphold the fairness requirement in Article 6. The UKSC criticised the test, noting that 'the more cogent the evidence the less it can be relied upon',[111] but in doing so it appeared to be making assumptions about cogency in the absence of adversarial testing. While this might be acceptable in relation to certain types of evidence, the nature of witness evidence is such as to require that particular care be taken in making such assumptions.[112] We will consider these issues later on in this chapter. For now, it is sufficient to note that the UKSC seems to assume, perhaps too readily, not just that it is possible to make judgments about reliability in the absence of the opportunity to challenge the evidence in an adversarial environment, but also that the main rationale underpinning Article 6(3)(d) is in fact reliability.[113] Before considering these issues in more detail, it is necessary to consider the second aspect of the ECtHR's right to challenge witness evidence, namely the procedural context in which the defence should have the opportunity to exercise this right.

10.3.2 An adequate and proper opportunity to challenge the witness

10.3.2.1 The significance of the procedural environment: principal versus preliminary proceedings

In determining whether Article 6(3)(d) of the ECHR has been upheld, the ECtHR has to evaluate the adequacy of the accused's opportunity to confront the witness. One of the primary factors with the potential to impact on the sufficiency of the accused's opportunity to question a witness is the point in the proceedings at which this confrontation occurs. In view of the ECtHR's frequent statements that it regards Article 6 principally in procedural terms, it might have been to be expected that in interpreting Article 6(3)(d) of the ECHR it would have been mainly concerned with regulating the environment in which the opportunity to challenge the witness is to take place. In fact, the ECtHR has seemed reluctant to set out strict rules regulating the procedural setting for the examination of witness evidence. Unlike the USSC, which has, admittedly unsurprisingly, expressed a definite preference for the trial hearing

---

[109] *R v. Horncastle and others* [2009] 2 Cr App R 15 (CA), [2009] UKSC 14, para. 50. See Ch. 4.2.3.
[110] *Horncastle*, para. 86. [111] *Horncastle*, para. 91.
[112] See also the comments of Sedley LJ in *Secretary of State for the Home Department v AF* [2009] 2 WLR 423, para. 113.
[113] *R v. Horncastle and others* [2009] 2 Cr App R 15 (CA), [2009] UKSC 14, esp. para. 91.

as the principal forum for the defence's opportunity to confront witnesses about their incriminatory evidence,[114] the ECtHR has not insisted that the defence have the opportunity to challenge witnesses directly at trial or at the main hearing at which the question of guilt or innocence is decided.[115]

The ECtHR's approach to this matter can be summarised in the following manner. It usually begins by stating that 'all the evidence must in principle be produced in the presence of the accused at a public hearing with a view to adversarial argument'.[116] This could be interpreted as situating the right to question witnesses and challenge their testimony firmly in the context of adversarial proceedings before an independent and impartial judge and at a public hearing as required by Article 6(1) of the ECHR and as endorsing the principle of immediacy.[117] Crucially, though, the ECtHR has not outlined a preference for immediate proceedings. The words 'in principle' provide significant scope for exceptions and in its case law the ECtHR has endorsed a considerably less demanding interpretation of Article 6(3)(d) of the ECHR. After mentioning in passing the importance of the trial setting outlined in Article 6(1), it has then gone on to qualify its opening statement by noting that it is not necessarily essential 'that in order to be used as evidence statements of witnesses should always be made at a public hearing in court: to use as evidence such statements obtained at the pre-trial stage is not in itself inconsistent with paragraphs 3(d) and 1 of Article 6 provided the rights of the defence have been respected'.[118] Similarly, it has held that 'the reading out at trial of statements made by witnesses at the investigating stage of criminal proceedings' is not 'in itself inconsistent' with Article 6(1) or Article 6(3)(d) ECHR.[119] In order to ensure that 'the rights of the defence have been respected', it has held that it is essential that it have the opportunity to challenge 'the depositions either when they are made or at a later stage'.[120] The right in Article 6(3)(d) of the ECHR is thus a right to challenge the witness evidence when the witness is making the statement (either at some point during the investigation or at trial); the opportunity to challenge a written statement at trial will not suffice.

The manner in which the ECtHR has framed this issue is of particular importance. Instead of proceeding from the assumption that the defence's opportunity to challenge the witness must occur at the trial or the principal hearing at which the guilt or innocence of the accused is adjudicated and then considering exceptional circumstances in which a prior opportunity might prove sufficient, it refers first to the opportunity to challenge the witness statements 'when they

---

[114] e.g. *Barber* v. *Page*, 390 US 719, 725–6 (1968): 'The right to confrontation is basically a trial right.'

[115] In a few decisions the court has referred to the importance of immediacy, but such statements remain the exception rather than the rule. See, e.g. *PK* v. *Finland* (dec.); and *Mellors* v. *United Kingdom* (dec.).

[116] *Barberà, Messegué and Jabardo* v. *Spain*, para. 78.

[117] An excellent analysis of the contours of the immediacy principle can be found in S. Maas, *Der Grundsatz der Unmittelbarkeit in der Reichsstrafprozessordnung* (Breslau: Schletter, 1907).

[118] See, e.g. *Kostovski* v. *Netherlands*, para. 41; and *Delta* v. *France*, paras. 36–7.

[119] *Håkan Wester* v. *Sweden* (dec.). [120] e.g. *Kostovski* v. *Netherlands*, para. 41.

are made' and only after this does it refer to the trial forum indirectly through the term 'or at a later stage'. The right to challenge the evidence directly at trial therefore becomes the exception rather than the rule. And yet this seems difficult to reconcile with the text of Article 6(1) of the ECHR and the ECtHR's recurring assertion that the evidence should, as a general rule, be produced at a public hearing in the presence of the accused in order to enable adversarial argument. One explanation for this seemingly contradictory approach could be the perceived need to take account of those procedural systems in Europe which do not normally provide for witness confrontation hearings to take place at the hearing at which the guilt or innocence of the accused is judicially determined. If witness confrontation hearings need not automatically take place during the principal hearing or trial, those hearings that take place during the preliminary stages of the proceedings still have the potential to be compatible with Article 6(3)(d) of the ECHR.[121] In *Unterpertinger* v. *Austria*, a number of members of the Commission argued on their dissenting opinion that the decisive factor was that the accused had the opportunity 'at least at one stage of the proceedings, to examine or have examined witnesses whose testimony is to be relied upon for his conviction'.[122]

This was subsequently confirmed by the ECtHR, which noted that the applicant had not had the chance 'at any stage in the earlier proceedings' to question the persons whose statements had been read out in the hearing,[123] a position which quite clearly lays the foundation for arguments that a prior opportunity to question witnesses during the investigation phase might suffice. Nevertheless, it is important to note that the stage in the proceedings at which the accused is afforded the opportunity to question the witness might well define the extent of this opportunity. The preliminary proceedings might not be structured in such a way as to allow for 'adversarial' argument, which by its nature can only take place if both the defence and the prosecution have the opportunity to challenge the evidence before an impartial judicial authority.[124] This was confirmed by the Commission in a number of early cases in which it held that Article 6(3)(d) of the ECHR 'does not grant the accused an unlimited right to secure the appearance of witnesses in court. Its purpose is rather to ensure equality between the defence and the prosecution as regards the summoning and examining of witnesses'.[125]

The term 'adversarial argument' cannot simply be interpreted as a requirement that the defence have the opportunity to challenge incriminatory written

---

[121] *Unterguggenberger* v. *Austria* (dec.).
[122] See the dissenting opinions to the Commission's report in *Unterpertinger* v. *Austria* (report), no. 9120/80.
[123] *Unterpertinger* v. *Austria*, 24 November 1986, Series A no. 110, para. 31.
[124] See, e.g. J. Vargha, *Die Verteidigung in Strafsachen: Historisch und Dogmatisch Dargestellt* (Vienna: Manz'sche Hof- und Universitäts-Buchhandlung, 1879) 288: 'The decisive characteristic of criminal proceedings is the accusatorial trinity which is made up of the judge, the prosecution and the defence.'
[125] e.g. *PV* v. *Germany* (dec.); *X* v. *Austria* (dec.), no. 4428/70, 8; and *X* v. *Belgium* (dec.), no. 8417/78, 207.

witness statements in subsequent adversarial proceedings.[126] The opportunity of the accused to challenge the prosecution's evidence against it in proceedings before an impartial judge cannot be classified as adversarial irrespective of the manner in which the evidence was taken or collected. Parallel issues have arisen in the context of the interrogation of suspects in the pre-trial.[127] Can a subsequent opportunity – for instance at trial – to challenge a confession obtained during the preliminary proceedings after an accused has been subjected to prolonged detention without access to legal assistance be characterised as truly adversarial?[128] Even if one accepts, as most criminal justice systems and courts, the USSC included,[129] have done, that an adequate and proper prior opportunity to question a witness may satisfy the right to challenge witnesses, this does not detract from the fact that based on the structure of Article 6(1) of the ECHR, the ECtHR ought to be clear about asserting an unambiguous preference for the confrontation to take place in an adversarial forum, irrespective of whether this occurs during the principal or the preliminary proceedings. A prior opportunity to challenge the adverse witness evidence may well satisfy the requirements of Article 6(3)(d) of the ECHR, but this ought only to be the case if the evidence has been obtained or heard during the preliminary proceedings under conditions which can be said to be adversarial. In order to determine whether the accused's opportunity to question witness evidence at stages in the proceedings other than the trial can be characterised as adequate, it is important to consider the nature of the procedural environment at trial as guaranteed by Article 6(1) of the ECHR. Article 6(1) requires not only that the hearing is adjudicated by an independent and impartial judge, but also that the principles of equality of arms and adversarial procedure are guaranteed. This suggests that an adequate and proper opportunity to question the witness is one which is supervised by an independent and impartial judicial authority and at which the accused is assisted by defence counsel.

10.3.2.2 The circumstances of witness hearing: the importance of an impartial judge and the right to counsel

The ECtHR has interpreted Article 6(1) of the ECHR as guaranteeing the accused the right to challenge the evidence in adversarial proceedings before an

---

[126] *Al-Khawaja and Tahery* v. *United Kingdom* (referred to the GC).
[127] *Salduz* v. *Turkey* [GC], para. 55.
[128] Even where the domestic court has subsequently considered that the statements were voluntary after challenge in court, access to legal advice would seem now to be required at the questioning stage: see *Panovits* v. *Cyprus*, discussed in Ch. 8.6.
[129] The Supreme Court has held, at least since its decision in *Mattox* v. *United States*, 156 US 237 (1895), that prior-recorded testimony may be admissible in appropriate cases. In several cases it has held that this could be the case if the accused had previously had the opportunity to confront the witness in earlier proceedings: see, e.g. *Mancusi* v. *Stubbs*, 408 US 204, 213–16 (1972). See too *Crawford* v. *Washington*, 124 S Ct 1354 (2004), where the court noted the exception from the general requirement that confrontations take place at trial in the case of statements made by a witness who, despite reasonable efforts on the part of the government to ensure his or her attendance, was unavailable, provided that the accused had had a 'prior-opportunity' to confront the witness.

independent and impartial judicial authority. In the context of witness evidence, this will automatically be the case if the confrontation hearing occurs at trial. It is reasonable to assume, therefore, that an adequate prior opportunity to question a witness would require to be conducted in a similarly adversarial environment, at a hearing supervised by an impartial authority at which both the prosecution and defence are present.

The Strasbourg authorities have had little opportunity to consider the importance of impartial judicial supervision of confrontation hearings in the preliminary proceedings. In *Cardot*, the Commission held that 'the requirements of a fair trial and equality of arms generally makes it necessary for all prosecution witnesses to be heard before the trial courts and during adversarial proceedings' and emphasised that it was 'of the utmost importance that those courts should be able to observe the witnesses' demeanour under questioning and to form their own impression of their reliability'.[130] The application was, however, settled before it reached the ECtHR stage. This approach is similar to that adopted by the USSC. In *Barber* v. *Page*, it examined the difference between the opportunity to confront a witness at a preliminary hearing and at trial and held:

> It [the confrontation] includes both the opportunity to cross-examine and the occasion for the jury to weigh the demeanor of the witness. A preliminary hearing is ordinarily a much less searching exploration into the merits of a case than a trial, simply because its function is the more limited one of determining whether probable cause exists to hold the accused for trial.[131]

This leaves open the possibility of a different approach were the preliminary hearing to assume a different character. The issue of demeanour evidence while often mentioned is of limited relevance.[132] If the importance of enabling the judge responsible for determining the case to consider the demeanour of the witness were to be viewed as a significant aspect of the need for confrontation supervised by a judge responsible for determining the charge, then the routine confrontation of witnesses in the preliminary proceedings would not satisfy this requirement. On the ECtHR's own terms, however, and despite the decision in *Cardot*, this is not the main point; the issue is rather ensuring that the accused has an adequate opportunity to confront the witness in the context of an adversarial hearing. This means that it is unavoidable not only that the defence and the prosecutor are present, but also that an impartial judicial authority conduct the hearing.

---

[130] *Cardot* v. *France* (report).   [131] 390 US 719, 725–6 (1968).
[132] On the difficulties of assessing demeanour, see M. Minzner, 'Detecting Lies Using Demeanor, Bias and Context' (2008) 29 *Cardozo Law Review* 2557, 2559–66; J. A. Blumenthal, 'A Wipe of the Hands, a Lick of the Lips: The Validity of Demeanor Evidence in Assessing Witness Credibility' (1993) 72 *Nebraska Law Review* 1157. See too R. C. Park, 'Empirical Evidence for the Hearsay Rule', in P. Mirfield and R. Smith (eds.), *Essays for Colin Tapper* (London: LexisNexis, 2003) 91, 91–3.

The fact that the ECtHR has not had much of an opportunity to consider such issues is surprising, not least because there are several European procedural systems and codes, which provide that evidential hearings take place, exclusively or principally, during the preliminary proceedings. A good example is the new Swiss federal code of criminal procedure, which entrusts the supervision of the principal confrontation hearings during the preliminary proceedings to the prosecution authorities.[133] Counsel for the accused is permitted to be present during these hearings, but does not have the right to insist on putting its questions directly to the witness. Counsel may have to put the question first to the prosecutor, who will then ask the witness, sometimes using an alternative formulation. It is difficult, if not impossible, to see how this could constitute an adequate and proper 'adversarial' opportunity to question the witness such as to meet the requirements set out in Article 6(3)(d) and Article 6(1) ECHR.[134] The opportunity to confront witnesses whose evidence is decisive in the preliminary proceedings will, as a general rule, only be adequate if an impartial authority has the responsibility for conducting or overseeing these hearings.

The ECtHR seems further to have taken a somewhat equivocal approach to the issue of defence participation. As a general rule, the principles of equality of arms and adversarial proceedings taken together with the right to counsel as guaranteed by Article 6(3)(c) of the ECHR would strongly indicate that an adequate prior opportunity to confront a witness will only be guaranteed if the accused is entitled to insist on the assistance of counsel. Consequently, it might be to be expected that the ECtHR would have taken a similar approach to that of the Human Rights Committee in *Simpson* v. *Jamaica*[135] or that of the USSC in *Pointer* v. *Texas*.[136] In *Simpson*, the HRC, in interpreting Article 14(3)(d) of the ICCPR, held that 'a magistrate should not proceed with the deposition of witnesses during a preliminary hearing without allowing the author an opportunity to ensure the presence of his lawyer.'[137]

In a number of cases, however, the ECtHR has shown itself to be somewhat less willing to impose such a strict rule and has not always held that the absence of counsel during the accused's opportunity to question a witness whose evidence is decisive will breach Article 6(3)(d) of the ECHR. In *Isgrò* v. *Italy*, for instance, it held that there had been no violation of the provision despite the fact that the applicant's lawyer had been prevented by a provision of the Italian Code of Criminal Procedure from attending the confrontation hearing.[138] It held that in this case 'the purpose of the confrontation did not render the presence

---

[133] Art. 147 Swiss Criminal Procedure Code: see A. Donatsch, T. Hansjakob and V. Lieber (eds.), *Kommentar zur Schweizerischen Strafprozessordnung* (Zurich: Schulthess, 2010), which includes an English translation of the code.
[134] S. Arquint and S. Summers, 'Konfrontationen nur vor dem Gericht' (2008) 2 *Plädoyer* 38; and P. Albrecht, 'Was bleibt von der Unmittelbarkeit?' (2010) 128 *Schweizerische Zeitschrift für Strafrecht* 180.
[135] *Simpson* v. *Jamaica*, para. 7.3.   [136] *Pointer* v. *Texas*, 380 US 400 (1965).
[137] *Simpson* v. *Jamaica*.   [138] Para. 36.

of Mr. Isgrò's lawyer indispensable; since it was open to the applicant to put questions and to make comments himself, he enjoyed the guarantees secured under Article 6(3)(d) to a sufficient extent'.[139] This seems rather perplexing, but care must be taken in interpreting such judgments to factor in the importance of the evidence. Crucially, in *Isgrò*, the court held that the evidence in question was not decisive to the conviction.[140] If the evidence had been decisive in grounding the applicant's conviction, it is likely that the ECtHR would have insisted on the lawyer's presence and found a violation of Article 6 of the ECHR.

Another important issue which arises in the context of the assistance of counsel is the question of whether Article 6(3)(d) of the ECHR affords, as a general rule, the defence with the principal role of questioning the witness or whether other authorities, such as the judge, investigating judge or even a prosecutor could be permitted to play a role. The text of Article 6(3)(d) provides little guidance in this regard in that it refers, broadly, to the right of those charged with a criminal offence to 'examine or have examined' witnesses against them.[141] In common law systems, cross-examination of the witness is usually undertaken by counsel for the defence, unless the accused has chosen to represent him- or herself. The prosecution is not involved in the cross-examination process, while the role of the judiciary is substantially restricted. Indeed, significant judicial intervention may even suggest bias such as to provide grounds for appeal. In many European systems, though, the investigating and judicial authorities play a more active role in confronting witnesses, while the defence is often relegated to a more subsidiary role – often in the form of asking supplementary questions following the principal confrontation of the witness by the investigatory or judicial authority.[142] The manner in which the witness is questioned would seem to go to the heart of the notion of adversarial proceedings.

The interpretation of Article 6(3)(d) as requiring 'equality between the defence and the prosecution as regards the ... examining of witnesses'[143] would seem to preclude any role for the prosecution in cross-examining witnesses. The position with regard to judicial involvement in cross-examination is less clear. In the case of *PV* v. *Germany*, the Commission held that the requirement in Article 6(3)(d) did not always require that the defence have the opportunity to examine a witness directly. Here it stated that the provision 'is not only complied with if the accused or his defence counsel have the opportunity of putting questions to the witnesses themselves, but also if they can request that certain questions are put to the witness by the court'.[144] This was confirmed by the ECtHR in *SN*, where it held that having regard to the special features

---

[139] *Isgrò* v. Italy, para. 36. [140] *Isgrò* v. Italy, para. 35. See also *Verdam* v. *Netherlands*.
[141] See, e.g. *Solakov* v. *Former Yugoslav Republic of Macedonia*, para. 57, where the ECtHR held that 'the rights of the defence are restricted to an extent that is incompatible with the requirements of Article 6 if the conviction is based solely or in a decisive manner on the depositions of a witness whom the accused has had no opportunity to examine or have examined'.
[142] See further Doran and Jackson, *Judicial Role*.   [143] e.g. *PV* v. *Germany* (dec.).
[144] *PV* v. *Germany* (dec.); see also *Dankovsky* v. *Germany* (dec.).

of criminal proceedings concerning sexual offences, this provision cannot be interpreted as requiring in all cases that questions be put directly by the accused or his or her defence counsel, through cross-examination or by other means.[145] Even if judicial involvement in the cross-examination of witnesses is acceptable in certain circumstances (particularly in the context of vulnerable witnesses), judges who become involved in the cross-examination of witnesses will have to take particular care to maintain their objectivity and impartiality as required by Article 6(1) of the ECHR.[146] Furthermore, in this regard it is also important to consider the nature of the defence's opportunity. It is questionable whether affording the defence the opportunity to ask a few additional questions, after a witness has been examined at length by the court, in fact meets the requirement of adversariality. Finally, it is important to note that the human rights case law does not impose any restraints on the manner of questioning or the type of questions. There is no prohibition, for instance, on the use of leading questions during the examination or the recourse to character or hearsay evidence during the cross-examination.

10.3.2.3 Obligation to organise the witness examination hearing

It is the responsibility of the authorities to ensure that the defence have the opportunity to challenge witnesses who have made incriminating statements and whose evidence is decisive to the matter at issue.[147] The first element here is the obligation on the authorities to ensure that the witness attends the hearing at which the cross-examination or confrontation is to take place. The ECtHR will often examine whether the authorities took sufficient steps to ensure the attendance of the witness at the hearing or whether the failure of the witness to appear was due to circumstances outwith their control, such as illness,[148] death,[149] detention in a foreign prison,[150] residence at an unknown address abroad,[151] or to the fact that he or she relied on a legal privilege to avoid testifying.[152] In *AS* v. *Poland*, it noted that there was 'no appearance of negligence on the part of the domestic authorities in their attempts to ensure the attendance of [the witness] before the trial court'. Similarly, in *Garner* v.

---

[145] *SN* v. *Sweden*, para. 52.
[146] See, e.g. *CG* v. *United Kingdom*, where the applicant (unsuccessfully) contended that the trial judge's constant interventions and hectoring of her counsel, together with the Court of Appeal's decision that the conviction was safe, deprived her of a fair trial, in breach of Art. 6(1) ECHR.
[147] *Mirilashvili* v. *Russia*, para. 163; *Sadak and others* v. *Turkey*, para. 67; *Rachdad* v. *France*, para. 25; *Bonev* v. *Bulgaria*, para. 43; *Sheper* v. *Netherlands* (dec.); *Mayali* v. *France*, para. 32; and *Haas* v. *Germany* (dec.).
[148] *Håkan Wester* v. *Sweden* (dec.): 'The Commission is of the opinion that [the witness's] illness could not be allowed to block the prosecution.'
[149] *Garner* v. *United Kingdom* (dec.).   [150] *HK* v. *Netherlands* (dec.).
[151] *Pavletić* v. *Slovakia* (dec.).
[152] *Pobozny* v. *Slovak Republic* (dec.): 'The Commission considers that the right on which the applicant's father-in-law relied in order to avoid giving evidence could not be allowed to block the prosecution.'

United Kingdom, it referred to the fact that '[t]here is no indication that the State had any responsibility for the death of the witness',[153] while in *Verdam* it noted that the 'judicial authorities were not negligent in their efforts to bring these witnesses before the Court of Appeal'.[154] The appeal court had adjourned the trial on numerous occasions and had made several attempts to ensure the presence of the witnesses. Both were summoned and one of the witnesses was served with an order requiring that she attend. Consequently, 'in view of their efforts' the failure of the witnesses to appear 'did not make it necessary to halt the prosecution' and it was 'open to the national courts, subject to the rights of the defence being respected, to have regard to [the witnesses'] statements before the police'.[155] In *HK* v. *Netherlands*, where the witnesses were arrested in France, the Dutch authorities were deemed to have done everything in their power to make it possible for the defence to attend a hearing of the witnesses either in France or in the Netherlands; consequently, they were not to be held responsible for the reluctant attitude displayed by the French authorities.[156]

Crucially, the relevant witness evidence was not deemed in any of these cases to be the sole or decisive basis for the conviction. The relevance of the assessment of the conduct of the authorities seems thus to be necessarily limited by the strength of the sole and decisive test. Consequently, the conduct of the authorities seems rather beside the point: either the witness evidence is decisive, in which case the authorities must arrange a confrontation hearing or violate Article 6(3)(d) of the ECHR, or it is not decisive, in which case the question of whether they attempted to secure the presence of the witnesses or whether they exhibited bad faith or negligence in this regard is irrelevant. This seems to be confirmed by the case of *Mild and Virtanen* v. *Finland*, in which the evidence of the relevant witnesses was held by the ECtHR to constitute 'an important part of evidence'.[157] The accused was never given the opportunity to confront the witnesses who had been repeatedly summoned by the district court but who had refused to participate. The witnesses knew that the authorities had no way of compelling them to attend, a fact which prompted the ECtHR to note that 'law was inadequate on this point' and to find a violation of Article 6(3)(d) of the ECHR.[158]

In interpreting Article 6(3)(d) of the ECHR, the ECtHR has also had to consider not just whether the authorities have ensured that a confrontation hearing can take place, but also whether the nature of the hearing is such as to afford the defence an adequate opportunity to exercise its rights. The authorities' obligations do not necessarily extend to imposing coercive measures, such as fines or even detention, on witnesses who refuse to cooperate. In *KJ* v. *Denmark*, the Commission rejected the applicant's contention that the national authorities' failure to use coercive measures in order to make the witness give

---

[153] Citing *Ferrantelli and Santangelo* v. *Italy*, paras. 51–2.   [154] *Verdam* v. *Netherlands* (dec.).
[155] Ibid.   [156] See too *Nemet* v. *Sweden* (dec).
[157] *Mild and Virtanen* v. *Finland*, para. 47.   [158] Ibid., paras. 46–8.

evidence violated Article 6(3)(d), as it held that they 'would most likely have been to no avail'.[159] Similarly, it has remained indifferent in the face of arguments that witnesses should be required to give evidence under oath. In *I* v. *Switzerland*, it rejected the applicant's contention that the opportunity to question a witness under oath and under the threat of punishment to tell the truth had to be considered as integral to the guarantee in Article 6(3)(d) and declared the complaint inadmissible.

10.3.2.4 Restrictions on the defence's opportunity to challenge the witness

As a general rule, the opportunity to challenge a witness can be understood as conferring on the defence the opportunity to question directly the witness in person. The principle is not absolute, however, and there may be situations in which competing interests, particularly those of witnesses or victims, fall to be considered.[160] There are a whole host of reasons justifying interferences with an accused's right to confront vital witnesses, including the witness's fear of reprisal, the interests of vulnerable witnesses (in particular victims of sexual offences and children) and in the context of undercover agents, the public interest in the prosecution of crime. The nature of the interferences will necessarily depend on the reasons which have been put forward to justify them. Two of the principal interferences which the ECtHR has had to consider have concerned the accused's right to be present and put questions to the witness in person and the concealment of the identity of the witness.

The Strasbourg authorities have frequently held that respect must also be had for the 'private life of the perceived victim' and it has accepted, for example, that 'in criminal proceedings concerning sexual abuse certain measures may be taken for the purpose of protecting the victim'.[161] The most famous enunciation of this need for some sort of 'balancing exercise' to be carried out between the interests of the defence and those of witnesses was in *Doorson* v. *Netherlands*, where the ECtHR held that the 'principles of fair trial also require that in appropriate cases the interests of the defence are balanced against those of witnesses or victims called upon to testify'.[162]

The ECtHR has noted that the authorities must ensure that any procedural restrictions on the defence's right to confront witnesses are 'strictly necessary'. Consequently, the authorities must examine whether 'less restrictive measures' would suffice and if this is the case to ensure that such measures be applied.[163] In *Visser* v. *Netherlands*, for instance, the ECtHR was not satisfied that restrictions on the defence's right to confront the witness 'could reasonably be considered justified'.[164] In particular, not only had the investigation judge failed to assess the reasonableness of the fear of the witness, but the Court of Appeal had also failed

---

[159] *KJ* v. *Denmark* (dec.).   [160] See Maffei, *The European Right to Confrontation*.
[161] *Baegen* v. *Netherlands* (report), attached to the judgment, para. 77.
[162] *Doorson* v. *Netherlands*, para. 70; see also *SE* v. *Switzerland* (dec.).
[163] *Van Mechelen and others* v. *Netherlands*, para. 58.   [164] *Visser* v. *Netherlands*, para. 47.

to carry out 'an examination into the seriousness and well-foundedness of the reasons for the anonymity of the witness when it decided to use the statement made before the investigating judge in evidence against the applicant'.[165] As the witness evidence was held to be 'decisive', the ECtHR considered that there had been a violation of Article 6(3)(d) of the ECHR and that it was not necessary 'to examine further whether the procedures put in place by the judicial authorities could have sufficiently counterbalanced the difficulties faced by the defence as a result of the anonymity of the witness'.[166] This case demonstrates quite clearly the obligation on the authorities to assess carefully the reasonableness of restrictions on the defence's right to question witnesses and underlines the fact that a failure to do so in the context of a witness whose evidence is deemed to be decisive will automatically violate Article 6(3)(d).

In some circumstances, the measures taken to protect witnesses, such as those restricting the opportunity to question victims to defence counsel,[167] may not seem to be particularly intrusive, especially if the fair trial provisions are seen as applying to the accused in the context of the defence and not as an individual.[168] This was expressly stated by the ECtHR in *Dankovsky* v. *Germany*, where it held that 'generally a defendant, for the purposes of Article 6(3)(d), must be identified with the counsel who acted on his behalf'.[169] Furthermore, the Strasbourg authorities have held that Article 6(3)(d) does not necessarily guarantee the accused the right to question witnesses directly: the fact that the defence lawyer is able to put the questions to the witness may in certain circumstances be sufficient to ensure that the provision is upheld.[170]

The ECtHR has had to consider a number of cases where the interference has constituted a considerably more significant obstacle to the defence's opportunity to challenge witnesses. Determining how best to treat vulnerable witnesses or those who wish to remain anonymous has proven particularly problematic.[171] With regard to vulnerable witnesses, particularly children or those who have been the victims of sexual offences, the ECtHR has recognised that the proceedings are 'often conceived of as an ordeal by the victim, in particular when the latter is unwillingly confronted with the defendant'.[172] Consequently, it has accepted that the member states may place certain restrictions on the defence's opportunity to question such witnesses, provided that these measures

---

[165] Ibid.   [166] Ibid., para. 51.
[167] For discussion of such restrictions see, e.g. P. Roberts and A. Zuckerman, *Criminal Evidence*, 2nd edn (Oxford University Press, 2010) ch. 10; and F. Raitt, *Evidence: Principles, Policy and Practice* (Edinburgh: W. Green, 2008) para. 12.29.
[168] Summers, *Fair Trials*, ch. 3.
[169] The failure of the court-appointed defence lawyer to ask the co-accused certain questions which the applicant wished counsel to put to the co-accused did not amount to the counsel's failure to provide effective representation.
[170] *CPH* v. *Sweden* (dec.).
[171] For a detailed examination, see Trechsel, *Human Rights in Criminal Proceedings*, 314 ff.
[172] *SN* v. *Sweden*, para. 47; see also the opinion of the Commission in *Baegen* v. *Netherlands* (report), attached to the judgment, para. 77.

are 'strictly necessary' and that 'any difficulties caused to the defence by a limitation on its rights' are 'sufficiently counterbalanced by the procedures followed by the judicial authorities'.[173]

Typically, such restrictions will concern the use of close circuit television or other methods of ensuring that while the victim does not have to see the accused, the defence and the judges or fact-finders are able to see the victim. As a general rule, these limitations have been deemed compatible with Article 6.[174] But the ECtHR has been faced with a number of cases in which the interferences were considerably more significant. In *PS v. Germany*, which concerned the sexual abuse of a young child, neither the court nor the accused had had the opportunity to question the child. In convicting the applicant, the court relied on the child's statements, the evidence of the child's mother and the evidence of a police officer, who had questioned the child. In this case, the ECtHR held that the 'use of the evidence involved such limitations on the rights of the defence that the applicant cannot be said to have received a fair trial'.[175]

In *SN v. Sweden*, both the applicant and his counsel had been prevented from putting questions directly to the victim. The victim was interviewed by the police and the interview was video-taped. On the request of defence counsel, the police carried out a second interview with the victim, which was audio-taped. The legal counsel of the victim had not been informed of the hearing and opposed the presence of the accused's counsel. As a result, the applicant's counsel consented to the hearing taking place in his absence. The video-taped evidence of the witness's first police interview was shown and the recording of the second interview read out before the Court of First Instance. The ECtHR held that there had been no violation of the provision and seems to have been influenced, in particular, by the fact that the actions of the defence counsel amounted to waiver of the right to be present and that he was able to have questions put to the witness by the police officer conducting the interview. Furthermore, having 'subsequently listened to the audiotape and read the transcript of the interview, counsel for the applicant was apparently satisfied that the questions he had indicated to the police officer had actually been put to [the witness]'.[176] In view of this and 'having regard to the special features of criminal proceedings concerning sexual offences', the ECtHR found the measures taken by the authorities to be 'sufficient to have enabled the applicant to challenge [the witness's] statements and his credibility in the course of the criminal proceedings'.[177]

In *Bocos-Cuesta v. Netherlands*, however, which involved proceedings against the accused for the sexual abuse of several children, the rights of the defence were found to have been insufficiently protected.[178] Statements made by the children to the police were held to be the only direct evidence of the facts

---

[173] *PS v. Germany*, para. 23.   [174] See, e.g. *Hols v. Netherlands* (dec.).
[175] *PS v. Germany*, para. 31; see also *AM v. Italy*.   [176] *SN v. Sweden*, paras. 47 and 49–50.
[177] Ibid., para. 52.   [178] *Bocos-Cuesta v. Netherlands*.

held against the applicant and thus had to be regarded as 'having been of decisive importance for the courts' finding of the applicant's guilt' despite the fact that the applicant had not been given the opportunity to examine or have the victims examined. The ECtHR refers in particular to the fact that the applicant 'was not provided with an opportunity to follow the manner in which the children were heard by the police, for instance by watching this in another room via technical devices, nor was he then or later provided with an opportunity to have questions put to them'.[179] It referred to the fact that there was no video tape of the children giving evidence, that the trial courts had undertaken 'a careful examination of the statements taken from the children' and given the applicant 'ample opportunity to contest them', but held that this could 'scarcely be regarded as a proper substitute for a personal observation of a witness giving oral evidence'.[180] The ECtHR was also troubled by the fact that while the authorities referred to the fact that the applicant's interests were outweighed by those of 'four still very young children in not being forced to relive a possibly very traumatic experience', the authorities had not provided any expert evidence substantiating these claims.[181] Consequently, it held that the applicant's Article 6(3)(d) ECHR rights had been violated. Similarly, in *AS v. Finland*, where the child's video-taped account of alleged abuse 'formed the only direct evidence' incriminating the accused and 'thus must have had a decisive influence on his conviction on appeal', the ECtHR found a violation of the provision. The applicant had not been able to follow the interview (which had been conducted early on in the investigation, before the accused was even aware that he was a suspect) and although the trial court 'made a careful assessment of the evidence as a whole', the applicant was never afforded an opportunity to 'contest effectively' the victim's account by 'having questions put to him'.[182] The ECtHR is here quite clear: it is legitimate to take into consideration the rights of the victim, particularly in the context of the manner in which the confrontation takes place, but the defence must nevertheless have the opportunity to challenge the evidence directly by putting questions to the victim.

A number of cases have involved witnesses who have been exempted from participating in confrontation hearings or in cross-examination as a result of a fear of reprisals. In *Tahery*, the witness whose statement was adduced in evidence was not present, but not anonymous: 'Although the trial judge found the witness to have a genuine fear of giving evidence, no attempt was made to conceal his identity: he was known not only by the applicant but by all the others present at the scene of the crime.'[183] The ECtHR rejected the government's submissions that adequate counterbalancing factors, notably 'that the accused was in a position to challenge or rebut the statement by giving evidence himself and by calling other witnesses; that the trial judge warned the jury that it was necessary to approach the evidence given by the absent witness with care; and that the

---

[179] Ibid., para. 71.   [180] Ibid.   [181] Ibid., para. 72.   [182] *AS v. Finland*, para. 63.
[183] *Al-Khawaja and Tahery v. United Kingdom*, para. 44 (referred to the GC).

judge told the jury that the applicant was not responsible for [the witness's] fear' had ensured the fairness of the proceedings. It held instead that: 'The right of an accused to give evidence in his defence cannot be said to counterbalance the loss of opportunity to see and have examined and cross-examined the only prosecution eye-witness against him.'[184] The importance attached to the weight of the evidence is evident if the judgment in *Tahery* is compared with that in *Pavletić v. Slovakia*, where, in contrast to the position in *Tahery*, the witness evidence was not sole or decisive. In *Pavletić*, the ECtHR referred to the fact that the applicant had not challenged 'the relevant part of the statements of the two women and that at the main hearing he restricted himself to pointing out that he was under no duty to make any comments in that respect'. It then held that the statement which had been read out 'corresponded with the statement of [the witness's] sister who had attended the hearing and whose statements the applicant could have challenged directly in the course of the trial', thus the use of the statements was not 'inconsistent' with the applicant's rights under Article 6(3)(d).[185]

The use of anonymous witnesses has posed even greater difficulties.[186] Although the ECtHR has frequently noted that the Convention does not preclude reliance at the investigation stage on sources such as anonymous witnesses, the 'subsequent use of their statements by the trial court to found a conviction is however capable of raising issues under the Convention'.[187] In *Kostovski*, the anonymous witnesses were not present in court and thus the judges were unable to observe the witnesses' demeanour under questioning and form their own impression of the witnesses' reliability. Although one of the witnesses had been heard by an examining magistrate, the ECtHR observed that 'in addition to the fact that neither the applicant nor his counsel was present at the interviews – the examining magistrates themselves were unaware of the person's identity, a situation which cannot have been without implications for the testing of his/her reliability'.[188] This was also the conclusion in *Lüdi v. Switzerland* and in *Van Mechelen*, which differed from *Kostovski* in that both concerned undercover police officers whose function was known to the investigation judge. In *Lüdi*, the ECtHR was particularly influenced by the fact that it would have been possible to arrange a confrontation 'in a way which took into account the legitimate interests of the police authorities in a drug trafficking case in preserving the anonymity of their agent, so that they could protect him and also make use of him again in the future'.[189] In *Van Mechelen*, the investigating judge questioned the undercover police officers in a separate room, from which the accused and

---

[184] Ibid., 46.   [185] *Pavletić v. Slovakia* (dec.).
[186] See, e.g. *Kostovski v. Netherlands*, para. 42.   [187] *Doorson v. Netherlands*, para. 69.
[188] *Kostovski v. Netherlands*, para. 43.
[189] *Lüdi v. Switzerland*, para. 49. See *SE v. Switzerland* (dec.), where the procedures followed were deemed to be sufficient; see also *Kok v. Netherlands* (dec.), in which the court, in declaring the complaint inadmissible, held that 'the procedure followed approximated, as closely as possible in the circumstances, the hearing of a witness in open court'.

their counsel were excluded. Although the defence could follow the questioning via a sound link, they were 'not only unaware of the identity of the police witnesses but were also prevented from observing their demeanour under direct questioning, and thus from testing their reliability'. Thus, they could not be considered to constitute 'a proper substitute for the possibility of the defence to question the witnesses in their presence and make their own judgment as to their demeanour and reliability'.[190] In relation to anonymous evidence, at least, the ECtHR's position is clear: even if such counterbalancing measures are found sufficient to compensate for the handicaps under which the defence is labouring, a conviction should not be based either solely or to a decisive extent on anonymous statements.[191]

10.3.2.5 The substantive sufficiency of the opportunity to challenge the witness

In a number of cases, applicants have sought to argue that while the witness appeared for cross-examination or at the confrontation hearing, the defence was unable to question the witness in any true sense, as the witness either refused or was unable to answer the questions put by the defence. Some national courts have interpreted the confrontation principle as requiring not just that the defence have the opportunity to question the witness, but also that it is able to engage substantively with the substance of the witness's evidence.[192] In a line of cases, the Zurich Court of Cassation, for instance, has held that the right to confront a witness implies not just that the confrontation hearing takes place, but also that the defence have a real opportunity to elicit a response from the witness. In one case, it expressly rejected the Court of First Instance's reasoning that the fact that the defence had failed to persist in its attempt to procure a response from the witness, after the witness had refused to answer questions, was to be seen as constituting waiver:

> In light of the circumstances of the case, there can be no question of the defence having waived the right to put additional questions to the witness, rather the appellant was unable to exercise his substantive right to ask additional questions.[193]

In this case, the principal question to be determined was whether the accused had acted in self-defence when he fired the shot that killed the victim. In deciding that the accused had not acted in self-defence, the court had relied 'almost exclusively' on the evidence of a witness who had been present at the crime scene and who had previously contradicted the accused's account, but who refused to repeat his accusations in the presence of the accused, claiming that he was afraid

---

[190] *Van Mechelen and others v. Netherlands*, para. 62.   [191] *Doorson v. Netherlands*, para. 76.
[192] e.g. Kass Nr. 2003/014 (judgment of the Court of Cassation of the Canton of Zurich, Switzerland).
[193] Ibid., para. II.2.e. See also Kass.-Nr. 2002/076 S II.1.d.bb (judgment of the Court of Cassation of the Canton of Zurich, Switzerland).

of the accused. The Court of Cassation held that this violated the defence's right to confrontation: the procedural possibility to question the witness was not enough; the defence had to be afforded an effective opportunity to question the witness, so as to be able to challenge his or her version of events, otherwise it would not be possible for the defence to challenge contradictions in the witness's account and to follow the reaction of the witness to the confrontation.[194]

It is fair to say, however, that the ECtHR has, on the whole, been rather unreceptive to such arguments. In *FK v. Austria*, the applicant complained that by the time the matter came to trial, the proceedings had already lasted so long that the witnesses could no longer remember what happened and witness statements were used to fill in the gaps in the witnesses' memories. In holding the application inadmissible, the ECtHR held that: 'The applicant was not prevented from questioning the witnesses about the events, nor would he have been prevented from putting inconsistencies to them.'[195] Applicants have proved similarly unsuccessful in arguing that there ought to be a violation of the right to confrontation where a witness insists on using his or her right to remain silent. In *Bayer v. Austria*, the applicant complained that a witness refused at trial to reply in substance to his question. The Commission remained unmoved and held that: 'Insofar as the applicant complains of this reading out although he could not put questions to [the witness], the Commission considers that [the witness] was actually present at the trial and that it cannot be held against the authorities concerned if [the witness] then refused to give evidence.'[196] Consequently, the reading out at trial of statements made by the witness before the police, even though the witness refused to repeat these allegations in the presence of the accused and despite the fact that the accused was unable to 'confront' the witness in any true sense of the word, was not incompatible with Article 6(3)(d). Crucially, in both of these cases, the witness evidence at issue was not deemed to be the sole basis for or decisive to the conviction.

In *Peltonen v. Finland*, the ECtHR held that there had been no violation even though the witness indicated that she intended to remain silent and it appeared to class the defence counsel's decision not to put further questions to the witness 'even though she had the opportunity to do so' as constituting waiver. It held that while the witness's 'persistence to remain silent may have made further questioning futile, in the circumstances of the present case this neither discloses a lack of equality of arms nor justified the conclusion that the judicial authorities denied the applicant the possibility of examining witnesses in conformity with

---

[194] Kass.-Nr. 2003/014 S, para. II.4.b: 'The defence was not able to ask questions about the circumstances of the criminal offence and it was therefore not possible for any contradictions in the statements of the witness to be pointed out and for the witness's reaction to be observed. The statements of the witness remained just as he had made them. If the evidence at issue is decisive, as it is in this case, it is not acceptable, irrespective of whether the witness (or person with information) was entitled to refuse to give evidence or had good reasons for doing so, to use this evidence to the detriment of the accused.'

[195] *FK v. Austria* (dec.).   [196] *Bayer v. Austria* (dec.).

Article 6(1) and Article 6(3)(d)'.[197] The ECtHR came to the same conclusion in *Huikko v. Finland*, where it noted that the 'applicant's counsel did not put any questions to [the witness] even though she had the opportunity on several occasions' to do so. It held that even though the fact that the witness insisted on remaining silent may have 'made the questioning futile', this could not 'justify the conclusion that the judicial authorities denied the applicant the possibility of examining witnesses in conformity with Article 6(1) and Article 6(3)(d)'.[198] These cases are of particular relevance as the court held the witness evidence in both cases to be sole and decisive to the conviction. It is notable that in both cases the ECtHR explains the inadmissibility of the application in terms of waiver and while this seems to stretch the boundaries of plausibility, this reasoning nevertheless suggests, albeit indirectly, that the ECtHR recognises the importance of the accused having a substantive opportunity to question witnesses whose evidence is decisive. By dismissing the cases on the basis of waiver, it leaves open the possibility that Article 6(3)(d) requires that the defence be afforded an adequate opportunity to question witnesses whose evidence is decisive in respect of the substance of their allegations.[199]

In several cases, applicants have argued that where a witness refutes previously incriminating statements, this violates the right to confrontation on the basis that they have not had an opportunity to cross-examine the witness as to the incriminating evidence. In *Håkan Wester v. Sweden*, the applicant complained that the witness, when heard in the District Court, retracted the allegations previously made by him against the applicant and later refused to give evidence before the appeal court. In declaring the application inadmissible, the Commission held that the evidence was not the sole or decisive basis for the Conviction, and that the District Court was able to 'observe [the witness's] demeanour during questioning and to form its own impression of the nature of his retraction'.[200]

In *Camilleri v. Malta*, the applicant complained that he had been convicted solely on the basis of a statement made by a witness in his absence, which the witness had later retracted and refuted in open court and thus that his right to cross-examine the witness had been 'rendered illusory'. The ECtHR held that it could not hold 'in the abstract that evidence given by a witness in open court and on oath should always be relied on in preference to other statements made by the same witness in the course of criminal proceedings, not even when the two are in conflict'.[201] It stated that the applicant was able to call the witness and

---

[197] *Peltonen v. Finland* (dec.); see also *Vilhunen v. Finland* (dec.); and *Hopia v. Finland* (dec.).
[198] *Huikko v. Finland* (dec.).
[199] For an interesting discussion of this issue, see S. Trechsel and R. Schlauri, 'Die Praxis des Kassationsgerichts zur EMRK', in A. Donatsch, T. Fingerhuth, V. Lieber, J. Rehberg and H. U. Walder-Richli (eds.), *Festschrift 125 Jahre Kassationsgericht des Kantons Zürich* (Zurich: Schulthess, 2000) 423, 438.
[200] *Håkan Wester v. Sweden* (dec.).
[201] *Camilleri v. Malta* (dec.), citing *Doorson v. Netherlands*, para. 78.

to cross-examine him as to the reasons which led him to make the incriminating statement. This 'opportunity allowed the applicant to undermine the probative value of the statement' and was thus deemed to have 'more than compensated for any alleged disadvantage which may have resulted from the fact that the statement was made in circumstances in which he was unable to challenge its veracity'.[202] These cases demonstrate clearly that prior statements and hearsay evidence is routinely introduced in evidence in many legal systems and is not prohibited by the human rights provisions.

If confrontation is to be seen in the context of the Article 6(1) ECHR fairness guarantee, as expressed in notions of equality of arms and adversarial procedure, as a means of ensuring that the defence has the right to be heard and, by exposing inconsistencies in the witness's evidence, to contradict his or her version of events, then merely demanding that the authorities ensure the presence of the witness cannot be seen to go far enough to ensure that the defence's participation and indeed its exercise of the Article 6(3)(d) right is practical and effective.[203] The ECtHR's case law and particularly those cases which concern allegations that an applicant did not actually have the opportunity to question the witness in substance as to his or her evidence seem to suggest an understanding of fairness which is based more on restricting the state authorities than on ensuring that the defence can challenge the evidence levelled against it by the prosecution. The argument that the state authorities were not responsible for the witness's refusal to participate in the confrontation seems if not immaterial, then certainly of limited relevance in the context of the ECtHR's approach to witness evidence which is framed not in terms of restraining state authorities, but of providing an adversarial forum for the evidence to be heard and contested. A consistent reading of Article 6(3)(d) would seem to require that the accused be afforded an opportunity to challenge witnesses whose evidence is decisive about the substance of their allegations; merely providing an adequate procedural setting for this to occur is insufficient to meet aims of the confrontation provision.

10.3.3 Defence obligations, waiver and forfeiture

While much of the case law is aimed at ensuring that the domestic authorities comply with the obligation to ensure that witness confrontations can take place, the defence is also subject to various obligations. It must make use of the opportunities provided to cross-examine the witness or run the risk that its inactivity is deemed to constitute waiver.[204] It goes without saying that the defence is not entitled to use unlawful means in an attempt to prevent a witness from testifying. Some writers have suggested that the ECtHR's approach 'could

---

[202] Ibid.
[203] e.g. *Artico* v. *Italy*, para. 33: 'the Convention is intended to guarantee not rights which are theoretical or illusory but rights that are practical and effective'.
[204] See, e.g. *Pratt and Morgan* v. *Jamaica*, para. 13.2.

almost encourage accused persons to intimidate witnesses', thereby ensuring that the evidence (assuming it is decisive) cannot be used.[205] This argument fails to take into account the notion of waiver. It is highly likely that attempts to intimidate or even harm witnesses in order to prevent them from giving evidence would constitute waiver of the defence right to examine the witnesses.[206]

In *SN* v. *Sweden*, the defence counsel was not permitted to participate in the confrontation hearing with the witness, who was the victim in the case, as the witness's lawyer was unable to attend. The ECtHR appeared to treat the defence counsel's failure to request a new appointment which would suit both him and the lawyer of the victim, and thereby allow both of them to participate in the hearing, as constituting waiver: 'It was open to the applicant's counsel to ask for a postponement of the interview until such time as the witness's counsel was free to attend. However, he chose not to do so.'[207] This is important as it clearly mitigates the authorities' obligations in this regard by imposing strict obligations on the defence counsel to ensure that the procedural opportunity to cross-examine or confront the witness is in conformity with Article 6.

In *M* v. *Norway*, the Commission held that the failure of the defence to request that the police officer be heard as a witness constituted a waiver of the rights guaranteed in Article 6(3)(d) of the ECHR; nevertheless, it considered and rejected the applicant's argument that the use of the evidence violated his rights under the provision.[208] In *Lindqvist*, the witness, who was the victim in a case involving sexual offences, never appeared before the court. Instead, her evidence, which was taken by the police at four interviews, was recorded on video and played during the court hearings. The applicant complained that his request that the witness be re-examined by the appeal court had been rejected. In declaring the application inadmissible, the Commission was particularly influenced by the fact that 'the applicant failed to avail himself of the opportunity to request that additional questions be put to [the witness] . . . about a month after the last police interview and thus at a time when a further interview was likely to be less disturbing to [the witness] than during the proceedings several months later'. The Commission also referred to the fact that the applicant had failed to make such a request before the first instance court.[209]

Similarly, in *Slobodan* v. *Netherlands*, the fact that the applicant's defence counsel was able to attend the hearing by the investigating judge of the alleged rape victim and chose not to do so meant that there was no violation of

---

[205] See, e.g. S. Wallace, 'The Empire Strikes Back: Hearsay Rules in Common Law Legal Systems and the Jurisprudence of the European Court of Human Rights' (2010) *European Human Rights Law Review* 408, 413.

[206] See the statements of the ECtHR concerning the English Court of Appeal's judgment in *R* v. *Sellick* in *Al-Khawaja and Tahery* v. *United Kingdom*, para. 37 (referred to the GC), discussed at Ch. 4.2.3 above. See also the approach of the USSC according to which the defendant can lose his or her right to confrontation as a result of wrongful behaviour designed to prevent a witness from giving evidence: see, e.g. *Giles* v. *California*, 128 S Ct 2678 (2008).

[207] *SN* v. *Sweden*, para. 49.   [208] *M* v. *Norway* (dec.); see also *O and T* v. *Netherlands* (dec.).

[209] *Lindqvist* v. *Sweden* (dec.).

Article 6(3)(d) of the ECHR.[210] In an even more extreme case, the applicant's lawyer had been informed of the hearing before the investigating judge and afforded the opportunity to participate in the hearing, but had stopped acting for the accused and had failed to pass on the information to the accused's new lawyer. The Commission held that there had been no violation, as the government could not be held responsible for the failures of the initial defence counsel.[211] It is questionable whether this conclusion would still be reached today. In view of more recent case law on the importance of the effectiveness of legal representation and the obligation on the authorities, and indeed the judiciary,[212] to intervene if the legal representation is manifestly inadequate, such a situation is likely now to be viewed as constituting a violation of Article 6(3)(c) of the ECHR.[213]

10.3.4 Challenging expert witnesses

The defence also has the right to challenge the evidence of expert witnesses.[214] The extent of the opportunity to challenge the witness will depend on whether expert witnesses are appointed by the court as impartial authorities or whether the parties are responsible for employing their own experts.[215] The regulation of the right to challenge expert evidence presents several challenges. There is some indication in the case law that the sole and decisive test does not apply in the context of expert evidence. On several occasions, the ECtHR has held that while the relevance and necessity of the expert evidence are matters for the domestic courts,[216] 'if the court decides that an expert examination is needed... the defence should have an opportunity to formulate questions to the experts, to challenge them and to examine them directly at the trial'.[217] This gives rise to important issues about the type of assistance which the defence might need from experts in order for it to be able to exercise its rights properly to challenge witness evidence. In order to challenge expert evidence effectively, it is very likely that the defence will have to appoint its own expertise.[218] Here, the ECtHR has proven unwilling to provide much guidance as to when this will be the case and has often referred to the fact that it will usually be for the 'domestic judge to decide whether an expert proposed by the defence is qualified, and whether his inclusion in the expert team would contribute to the

---

[210] *Slobodan* v. *Netherlands* (dec.). [211] *RAG* v. *Netherlands* (dec.).
[212] *Cuscani* v. *United Kingdom*. [213] See Ch. 9.2.
[214] The ECtHR has held on many occasions that expert witnesses constitute witnesses for the purposes of Art. 6(3)(d) ECHR: see, e.g. *Doorson* v. *Netherlands*, paras. 81–2.
[215] See further Ch. 7.7.1; and Summers, *Fair Trials*, 125. In certain circumstances, the refusal to allow an alternative expert examination of material evidence may be regarded as a breach of Art. 6(1): see, e.g. *Stoimenov* v. *Former Yugoslav Republic of Macedonia*, paras. 38 ff.
[216] See, e.g. *H* v. *France*, paras. 60–1. [217] See, e.g. *Mirilashvili* v. *Russia*, para. 190.
[218] For an interesting discussion of these issues in the US context, see Sklansky, 'Hearsay's Last Hurrah', 71.

resolution of the case'.[219] Where the prosecution relies on expert evidence, the defence must be afforded the opportunity to challenge this evidence effectively. This means that it is essential both that the defence has sufficient resources to be able to challenge the evidence and is provided with the opportunity to put questions to the expert directly in an adversarial environment.

10.4 Conclusion

The scope of the right to challenge witness evidence is determined by the reasons justifying and values underlying the principle. The right is often interpreted in instrumental terms as providing a means for the defence to test the reliability of the evidence and thereby promoting the accuracy of the verdict,[220] but it can also be understood as furthering other rationales which are better described as non-consequentialist. Dennis has argued that the right to cross-examine witnesses provides the accused with the opportunity to participate in the presentation of evidence in the proceedings, thereby allowing for his or her autonomy and dignity to be acknowledged.[221] In this sense, the accused's opportunity to participate in the proceedings is characterised as a process value, independent of the instrumental value of the testing of the evidence. Justifying the right in such terms, however, gives rise to certain problems. If it is accepted that the accused is not the only participant in the proceedings whose process values and autonomy ought to be protected, it is not clear why his or her autonomy should 'always be preferred to the interests of other participants in the process, whose interests are founded on the same principle, when the evidence reaches a certain level of importance'. This in turn leads him to suggest that the sole and decisive evidence standard might simply be 'a value preference, a bright line rule which gives an uncritical priority to defence interests'.[222]

There are, however, alternative ways of considering the right to challenge witness evidence, beyond viewing it as having developed in order to improve the position or increase the autonomy of the accused person. Acknowledgment of the importance of defence rights in the nineteenth century reflected recognition of an understanding of fairness based on the importance of the separation of judicial and prosecutorial functions.[223] Acceptance of the separation of the roles of judging and prosecuting necessarily led to the defence being provided with more effective procedural opportunities in order to allow it to challenge the prosecution's case. The fairness and legitimacy of the proceedings was to be guaranteed not so much by promoting the autonomy of the accused, but rather by protecting the institutional rights of the defence and providing the accused

---

[219] *Mirilashvili* v. *Russia*, para. 190.
[220] This was the UKSC's interpretation, for instance, of the right in *R* v. *Horncastle and others* [2009] UKSC 14, [2010] 2 WLR 2.
[221] See further Dennis, 'The Right to Confront Witnesses', 266.   [222] Ibid., 273.
[223] For an overview of the academic discussion in the nineteenth century, see Summers, *Fair Trials*, chs. 2 and 3.

with the opportunity to mount an effective defence. We have seen that these principles are clearly represented in the ECtHR's case law on equality of arms and adversarial proceedings.[224] By re-conceptualising the right of the accused to challenge witness evidence less as a personal right of the accused and more as an institutional right of the defence, it becomes clear that unlike the personal rights of the accused, which might be balanced against other participants, especially victims and witnesses, the rights of the defence must be balanced against the procedural opportunities and power of the prosecution. The rights and interests of witnesses and victims ought to be taken into consideration, but it is incorrect to consider them in terms of being 'balanced' against the rights of the defence and they should not be permitted to hinder the right to an effective defence.

The right to challenge witness evidence in Article 6(3)(d) of the ECHR is closely connected to the understanding of fairness developed by the ECtHR, which demands that the evidence be heard and contested in a specific procedural context. The defence must be provided with the opportunity to challenge the prosecution's evidence in an adversarial setting. The sole and decisive rule was developed to rein in the broad defence right to challenge witness evidence in Article 6(3)(d) by limiting it to witnesses whose evidence is decisive to the accused person's conviction. Assuming that the rights of the defence developed in order to enable the defence to challenge the prosecution's case effectively, this restriction makes sense: the lack of an opportunity to challenge unimportant evidence will obviously impact less on the prospect of mounting an effective defence than the lack of opportunity to challenge important witness evidence. The opportunity to challenge and expose inconsistencies in the evidence clearly has the potential to promote the reliability of the evidence, but reliability is not the only or even the principal aim. As Ho notes in the context of cross-examination, 'cross-examination is an option and we do not expunge the evidence of a witness just because a party chooses not to cross-examine her'.[225] It is widely acknowledged that the defence is entitled to waive the right to challenge the witness. Were reliability the principal concern, the ECtHR would have to ensure that the witness was actually challenged, which in turn would necessarily require some sort of judicial involvement in questioning the witness, were the defence to refuse to do so. This is obviously not the case. This suggests that it is not so much the cross-examination itself, but the opportunity to conduct a cross-examination that is important.[226] The guarantee that the defence be afforded the opportunity to challenge witnesses directly about their evidence is part of an understanding of fairness expressed in terms of the opportunity to challenge the evidence in a specific procedural context in order

---

[224] See Ch. 4.2.
[225] H. L. Ho, *A Philosophy of Evidence Law* (Oxford University Press, 2008) 237.
[226] This opportunity must of course be effective, which gives rise to important issues about the type of assistance which the defence might need from experts in order for it to be able to exercise properly its rights to challenge witness evidence. For an interesting discussion of these issues in the US context, see Sklansky, 'Hearsay's Last Hurrah', 71.

to ensure an accurate verdict, while at the same time safeguarding the legitimacy of the proceedings by affording the defence procedural opportunities intended to offset the powers of the prosecutor. In this light, the right to challenge witness evidence can be seen not as operating as a restraint on the accuracy of the verdict, but as integral to the truth-finding process.[227]

If the opportunity to challenge the evidence in an adversarial environment is the essence of the ECtHR's approach, then it is legitimate to ask whether it will always be necessary for a witness to be challenged directly. Why is the opportunity to challenge written statements in an adversarial setting, which is deemed sufficient in the context of evidence obtained in violation of the right to privacy,[228] not adequate in the context of witness evidence? The special treatment of witness evidence is connected to the inherently unreliable and unpredictable character of witness evidence. The defence ought to have the opportunity to participate in the examination of the witness, rather than merely challenge the witness evidence after it has been taken. It is not just the fact that witnesses themselves are potentially unreliable, but rather that witness evidence is clearly susceptible to external influences. This might be particularly problematic in the context of statements made when 'litigation is anticipated or underway'[229] as the interviews may be biased towards confirming the view of the case taken by the prosecution or the police.[230] But *res gestae* or unsolicited statements may also be biased for other reasons linked to the circumstances in which they were made, not connected to the prosecution's actions.[231] The point here is that witness evidence will very often be significantly influenced by the questions asked or by the context in which the statement was made and in such circumstances the defence must be afforded the opportunity to influence the evidence by asking its own questions or requiring that the witness comment on its version of events. The suggestion that the prosecution is also disadvantaged by its inability to challenge the evidence might provide a response to allegations of a violation of the equality of arms principle, but it does not address the fact that the defence is deprived of the opportunity to challenge the evidence against it in an adversarial context. If it is accepted that the content of witness evidence is influenced by the questions posed or the context in which it was made, then it becomes clear that an opportunity to challenge written statements cannot be equated to the opportunity to ask different questions or to put a different

---

[227] Contrast Dennis, 'The Right to Confront Witnesses', who distinguishes truth-finding from moral legitimacy.
[228] See, e.g. *Khan v. United Kingdom*, discussed in Ch. 6.5.1.
[229] See W. E. O'Brian, 'The Right of Confrontation: US and European Perspectives' (2005) 121 *Law Quarterly Review* 481, 500 ff.
[230] See further M. Berger, 'The Deconstitutionalization of the Confrontation Clause: A Proposal for a Prosecutorial Restraint Model' (1992) 76 *Minnesota Law Review* 557; and C. Clarke and R. Milne, *National Evaluation of the PACE Investigative Interviewing Course* (London: Home Office, 2001) 58 ff.
[231] See, e.g. A. Ashworth and R. Pattenden, 'Reliability, Hearsay Evidence and the English Criminal Trial' (1986) 102 *Law Quarterly Review* 292.

context to the witness in order to elicit alternative responses or to question the manner in which the statements came to be made.

The ECtHR's case law on witness evidence can be criticised on several fronts, but there are two issues in particular, which serve to undermine its approach. The first relates not so much to the sole and decisive rule itself, but to the ECtHR's failure to explain the essence of the rule and to define what constitutes decisive evidence. The rule might sometimes prove difficult to apply in practice, particularly in relation to jury trials, but as Ormerod has pointed out this does not seem to be a compelling argument 'when we are unsure of precisely what juries do with cautionary warnings'.[232] Similarly, the fact that the rule introduces some 'fuzziness' by requiring some judicial consideration of the importance of the evidence does not in itself seem problematic.[233] There can be little doubt, however, that the ECtHR must do more to define just what evidence should be considered to be 'sole and decisive'. There is very little indication in the case law of the principles which are being applied in order to determine the importance of the evidence. Decisive evidence ought to be interpreted as evidence which is 'determinative' to the issue of guilt or innocence[234] and the ECtHR must do more to explain in which circumstances this is likely to be the case and to adopt a more coherent approach in its case law.[235]

The second main issue relates to the ECtHR's apparently laissez-faire attitude to the question of whether the defence has actually had the opportunity to challenge the evidence in an adversarial environment. In view of the fact that the ECtHR's approach to witness evidence seems to be firmly based on enabling defence participation in the context of adversarial proceedings, it would seem to be essential that witness hearings are supervised by an impartial authority. The ECtHR is correct to note that this opportunity need not necessarily occur at trial, but if the defence's only opportunity to challenge witnesses about their evidence is at an examination hearing supervised by the prosecution or the police, this will not satisfy the requirements of adversariality and equality of arms inherent in Article 6(1) of the ECHR.

The ECtHR's repeated claim that it defers to the member states in evidential matters seems disingenuous. It obviously does play an active role in regulating criminal evidence and this is especially evident in its case law on Article 6(3)(d) of the ECHR. There can be little doubt that the ECtHR has not done enough to justify adequately its approach to the right to challenge witness evidence. The failure to explain the theory underpinning its case law on the right to challenge witness evidence not only serves to undermine the enforcement of a consistent standard across the Continent, but also makes it less likely, as is well illustrated by *Horncastle*, that the judicial organs of the member

---

[232] Ormerod, 'Case Comment', 500.
[233] For an alternative view, see Friedman, 'The Confrontation Right', 269.
[234] See also the judgment of the Court of Appeal in *R* v. *Alireza Tahery* [2006] EWCA Crim 529.
[235] For criticism of considerable inconsistency in many of the early cases, see Trechsel, *Human Rights in Criminal Proceedings*, 295 ff.

states will be convinced of the merits of altering their domestic laws and following its approach. It can be argued that the ECtHR has in its case law on Article 6(3)(d) developed an understanding of the right to challenge witness evidence which, as a general rule, has been able, despite differences in the regulation of criminal evidence in the legal systems of the member states, to transcend national borders. Nevertheless, its reluctance to acknowledge its role in relation to criminal evidence has contributed to uncertainty and inconsistency in some of its case law. Such reticence is unnecessary and the ECtHR ought to be bolder about setting out in a more structured fashion the boundaries of the right to challenge witness evidence. It would be well advised to engage more with the principles underlying the rights of the defence in order to provide a more coherent basis for the right to a fair trial generally and the right to challenge witness evidence in particular.

11

Towards a theory of evidentiary defence rights

11.1 Beyond tradition

This book has sketched a theory of positive evidentiary rights around the notion of effective defence participation which it has been argued is emerging, not always coherently, from international human rights law and within domestic and international criminal processes. The theory does not require systems to model their evidentiary processes upon any particular legal tradition. It has been argued that the principles of equality of arms and the right to adversarial procedure developed in particular by the ECtHR can be accommodated across the common law and civil law traditions. The development of these principles is better portrayed in terms of realigning and transforming the established procedural traditions of the common law and the civil law than as representing a convergence of the two traditions. So the notion of 'adversarial procedure' developed by the ECtHR does not require systems to organise procedural control entirely around the prosecution and defence with a passive judge or jury deciding cases purely upon the facts and arguments adduced by the parties. Indeed, one of the themes that emerges in the human rights jurisprudence is the importance of judicial activism in ensuring the fairness of the proceedings.[1] At the same time, the notion of an active defence which has been increasingly stressed in the jurisprudence as important in the pre-trial process, as well as at trial, rubs against any old 'inquisitorial' notion of the court exclusively dominating the procedural action. In this final chapter, we assess the impact that a theory of evidentiary defence rights has on the established common law and civil law traditions and what prospects there are for such a theory taking hold in the future.

In this book we have not only argued that human rights law leans towards a positive theory of evidentiary rights, but also that such a theory underpins the rationalist and social contract values that have informed post-Enlightenment thought within both the common law and civil law traditions. Although

---

[1] See, e.g. *Cuscani* v. *United Kingdom*, para. 39 (describing the trial judge as the 'ultimate guardian of the fairness of the proceedings' when apprised of the real difficulties which the absence of interpretation might create for the applicant). See also *Chadwick* v. *United Kingdom*; and *Timergaliyev* v. *Russia*, para. 59.

principles such as the 'equality of arms' and the right to 'adversarial procedure' can be accommodated within these traditions, however, there are certain respects in which they also pose a challenge to them. We have seen that common law systems continue to be characterised by an exclusionary approach to evidence which is designed to prevent triers of fact becoming contaminated by unduly prejudicial evidence. This is a somewhat crude mechanism for trying to eradicate risks of error which inevitably leads to the exclusion of relevant evidence that does not sit easily with a rationalist theory of evidence.

Human rights law has avoided the need for any notion of exclusionary rules by refusing to endorse the concept of 'admissibility' of evidence. This does not eschew the notion of exclusion altogether. The ECtHR has considered that there are times when triers of fact must refuse to act on particular kinds of evidence when these constitute the sole or decisive evidence in the case against the defence. Although the ECtHR has not been as clear about the rationale for refusing to base convictions on such kinds of evidence as it might have been, it would seem that it is based more upon the need to prevent prosecutors relying upon evidence that has been obtained by morally reprehensible means or in circumstances that have prevented any 'adversarial' testing by the defence than upon purely epistemic grounds such as the unreliability of the evidence.[2] The ECtHR has in particular failed to endorse any notion of the tribunal of fact excluding certain kinds of prejudicial evidence on the ground that their probative value is outweighed by their prejudicial effect, which we have seen is anathema to the civil law notion of 'free proof'. The solution to the notion of prejudicial evidence adduced by the prosecution is to ensure that the evidence is heard in an 'adversarial' environment. This requires a process of full pre-trial disclosure and access to relevant evidence before trial so that the defence is able to have any countervailing evidence adduced and to exercise rights to examination of evidence. In this way, it can be claimed that human rights law has prioritised what might be called 'positive evidentiary rights' around the notion of an effective defence over 'negative evidentiary rights', or, put another way, the optimisation of evidence over the exclusion of evidence.

If common law systems are still dominated by exclusionary approaches to evidence, civil law systems continue to be dominated by the ideal of 'free proof' centred around the notion of a powerful investigator, prosecutor or judge. Without the participation of an active defence, however, this can lead to hypotheses being formed too early and to a narrowing of the pool of evidence. It is sometimes assumed that a heavy burden of proof on the prosecution or a strong 'intime conviction' on the part of the judge at least assures the citizen against the risk of wrongful conviction. But this is to confuse the issue of gathering as much relevant information about the case as possible with the

---

[2] The court does, however, sometimes take into account whether there were doubts about the reliability of the evidence. See *Lee Davies* v. *Belgium*.

making of decisions under conditions of uncertainty or, as it has been put, to confuse error reduction with error distribution. The imposition of a heavy burden of proof on the prosecution allocates any risk of error in favour of the defence, but we have seen that no matter how cautious they are, decision-makers are guided by the weight of the evidence to hand and it is better to try to eradicate error in the first place.

A system that encourages active defence participation before trial, on the other hand, can both add to the pool of evidence and ensure that any evidence presented is properly tested. In requiring that every party to the proceedings be given 'a reasonable opportunity to present his case in conditions that do not place him at a substantial disadvantage vis-à-vis his opponent',[3] the principle of equality of arms not only provides an opportunity for equal participation by the parties, it also helps to advance accuracy by ensuring that the sources of information brought to the attention of the tribunal are not overly skewed by one party. Similarly, in requiring that 'all the evidence must be produced in the presence of the accused with a view to adversarial argument',[4] the principle of adversarial procedure not only helps to ensure defence participation in the process, but also gives some epistemic assurance that the sources of evidence brought before the court can be tested. These principles do not require that common law procedures are fully adopted; rather they provide a means of transcending the limitations of traditional adversarial and inquisitorial procedure that can become overly dependent in the case of common law 'adversarial' procedure on the information provided by the strongest party – normally the prosecution – or in the case of civil law 'inquisitorial' procedure upon the cognitive shortcomings of an investigative or presiding judge.[5]

There remain questions as to what remedies are open to the defence when there have been failings to guarantee positive evidentiary rights. This is not an issue that has been well treated by the human rights bodies. Their understandable reluctance to act as a fourth instance court and the need to make an assessment as to whether the trial as a whole was fair has meant that they have not focused particularly on the remedies that ought to be available in domestic fora. We saw in the last chapter that a failure to permit the defence to examine witnesses whose testimony constitutes the sole or decisive evidence against the accused may require that this evidence is not acted upon, although we argued that this approach is in need of further refinement. It may also be argued, as would seem to be the case in the international criminal tribunals,[6] that statements obtained from suspects before they have been able to activate defence rights such as a right to counsel should not be able to be acted upon.

---

[3] *Kaufman* v. *Belgium* (dec.), para. 115.   [4] *Barberà, Messegué and Jabardo* v. *Spain*, para. 78.
[5] For discussion of the cognitive shortcomings of both adversarial and inquisitorial models of procedure, see M. Damaška, *Evidence Law Adrift* (New Haven: Yale University Press, 1997) 92–6.
[6] See Ch. 8.6.

A further unanswered question is what should happen when there has been a failure to disclose or adduce relevant evidence. It can be hard to assess the probative value of missing evidence.[7] One remedy sometimes used in common law jurisdictions for a failure on the part of one party to adduce evidence has been to permit the jury to draw adverse inferences against the party for the failure. We have seen that when triers of fact are permitted to draw inferences from silence against accused persons, there are difficulties in determining what inferences are to be drawn.[8] Similar difficulties beset triers of fact when they are asked to draw inferences from missing evidence. It has been argued that they face a stark dilemma: they are being asked to very roughly assess, or more accurately speculate about, the potential impact of the lost evidence which is epistemologically inferior to the opportunity to consider the evidence that has been lost.[9] Faced with this difficulty, they are likely to get drawn into making judgments about the litigative conduct of the party that has failed to adduce the evidence which is not the responsibility of the trial trier of fact whose job it is to adjudicate upon the evidence that is presented. In this situation, they may alter the burden of proof to the detriment of the party which has failed to produce the evidence, but in a manner that does not do justice to the evidence that is presented.

It would seem much better in such situations to provide opportunities before the trial for the defence to argue that evidence be produced and we have seen that increasingly jurisdictions do provide opportunities for criminal discovery. There are problems in determining how the onus should be determined in these situations. We have seen that the courts have tended to impose heavy burdens on the defence to show how important the evidence is to the defence.[10] The defence should certainly be encouraged to reveal the nature of their defence as part of the process of active defence, but where there has been a failure by the prosecution to obtain significant evidence or undertake various tests to establish the accused's guilt, the burden ought arguably to be placed on it to show why this has not prejudiced the defence.[11]

Even when emphasis is placed on making evidence available before trial rather than on how to respond at trial when such evidence is unavailable, there will remain situations where the evidence will have been lost or is unavailable at an early stage. A decision must then be made as to whether or not to go ahead and try the case. We have again seen that the common law courts put a heavy burden on the defence before they are prepared to stay proceedings, but if the defence

---

[7] See A. Roberts, 'Pre-Trial Defence Rights and the Fair Use of Eyewitness Identification Procedures' (2008) 71 *Modern Law Review* 331, 355.
[8] See Ch. 8.3.3.
[9] See D. Nance, 'Evidentiary Foul Play: The Roles of Judge and Jury in Responding to Evidence Tampering' (2009) 7 *International Commentary on Evidence*, Issue 1, Art. 5.
[10] See Ch. 9.5.2.
[11] See S. Stavros, *The Guarantees for Accused Persons under Article 6 of the European Convention on Human Rights* (Dordrecht: Martinus Nijhoff, 1993) 46; and Roberts, 'Pre-Trial Defence Rights', 348–9.

can show that the lost evidence is significant, it would seem that the onus ought again to be on prosecutors to show that this does not prejudice the defence. Where the defence can point to deliberate tampering or destruction of evidence, the focus shifts away from prejudicing the defence case towards the conduct of the prosecution as it is arguable that the prosecution has so fundamentally broken the terms of the social contract by engaging in such conduct that it has jettisoned any claim to prosecute the accused. After prima facie evidence of bad faith is produced, the prosecution should bear the burden of showing that it comes to its task of prosecution with a clean sheet.

11.2 Prospects for evidentiary defence rights

With the internationalisation of 'fair trial' standards, we are witnessing a consensus across domestic and international systems on how trial processes should be conducted. Whatever the status of these standards in international law,[12] they are playing an increasingly important role in relations between states. Although traditionally states have tended to be cautious in extradition cases about making any inquiries about the standards of justice in requesting states,[13] states are now refusing to extradite suspects in cases where the requesting state does not guarantee fair trial rights in accordance with international human rights treaty obligations.[14] Fair trial standards are certainly playing an important role in international criminal tribunals. References to the rights of the accused appear in every act providing for the establishment of international criminal tribunals and the ICC Statute gives 'generally recognised human rights' pride of place over any conflicting rule in the ICC legal system.[15]

In their application of fair trial standards, we have seen that international human rights bodies have placed considerable importance on concepts such as the presumption of innocence, the equality of arms and the right to adversarial procedure, which give the defence a genuine role in proof processes both before and at trials. Such jurisprudence has relevance beyond the particular treaty context in which it is applied. International human rights courts appear to be playing an increasing role in influencing domestic as well as international courts and tribunals.[16] This is perhaps most evident in Europe, where we have seen

---

[12] It has been argued that certain human rights norms have a higher status in international law based on the notion of *ius cogens*, but this is controversial. See R. Cryer, H. Friman, D. Robinson and E. Wilmshurst, *An Introduction to International Criminal Law and Procedure*, 2nd edn (Cambridge University Press, 2010) 93.
[13] See, e.g. J. Dugard and C. Van den Wyngaert, 'Reconciling Extradition with Human Rights' (1998) 92 *American Journal of International Law* 187.
[14] See, e.g. *Soering* v. *United Kingdom*, para. 113; *Ng* v. *Canada*; and Art. 3(f) of the UN Model Treaty on Extradition. See also the discussion in *Dudko* v. *The Government of the Russian Federation* [2010] EWHC 1125 (Admin) and in *M. Kozirev, Conseil d'Etat*, 13 October 2000, 2001 PL 190.
[15] See Art. 21(3) ICC Statute.
[16] See C. McCrudden, 'A Common Law of Human Rights? Transnational Judicial Conversations on Constitutional Rights' (2000) 20 *Oxford Journal of Legal Studies* 499.

that the ECtHR has encouraged a number of states from the civil law tradition to give the defence a greater role in the pre-trial phase.[17] The endorsement of these principles at the international level by the international criminal tribunals may also in time have an influence on domestic courts.[18] Even those national constitutional courts which have appeared most impervious to international developments would seem more willing to apply international standards in certain circumstances.[19]

There would appear, however, to be a number of obstacles that may beset human rights bodies, states and the international community in attempting to align evidentiary practices in accordance with active defence participation. It is not proposed to make a full analysis of all of these. The degree to which active defence participation is made meaningful depends heavily on a range of broad political, socio-economic and cultural forces within specific contexts which cannot be measured purely by the formal evidential rules in force.[20] We conclude, however, by considering four examples of various phenomena which may pose as threats to the realisation of positive evidentiary defence rights: victims' rights and participation, security and terrorism, cost and expedition, and legal culture and tradition.

11.3 Victims' rights and participation

Within the last 30 years there has been a transformation in the way in which criminal justice debates have been conducted in many jurisdictions away from

---

[17] For the influence of the ECtHR in enhancing the procedural rights of participants in European Continental criminal procedure, see K. Ambos, 'Der Europäische Gerichtshof für Menschenrechte und die Verfahrensrechte' (2003) 115 *Zeitschrift für die gesamte Strafrechtswissenschaft* 583. For the influence of fair trial principles on 'transitional' countries of the former Yugoslavia, see D. Krapac, 'Some Trends in Continental Criminal Procedure in Transition Countries of South-Eastern Europe', in J. Jackson, M. Langer and P. Tillers (eds.), *Crime, Procedure and Evidence in a Comparative and International Context: Essays in Honour of Professor Mirjan Damaška* (Hart: Oxford, 2008) 119. For the continuing influence of the case law of the ECHR on the Netherlands, see J. F. Nijboer, 'Current Issues in Evidence and Procedure: Comparative Comments from a Continental Perspective' (2009) 6 *International Commentary on Evidence*, Issue 2, Art. 7.

[18] For comments on the 'spill-over' effects of international criminal procedure on domestic war crime proceedings, see G. Sluiter, 'The Effects of the Law of International Criminal Procedure on Domestic Proceedings Concerning International Crimes', in G. Sluiter and S. Vasiliev (eds.), *International Criminal Procedure: Towards a Coherent Body of Law* (London: Cameron May, 2009) 459.

[19] See F. Ní Aoláin, '*Hamdan* and Common Article 3: Did the Supreme Court Get It Right?' (2007) 91 *Minnesota Law Review* 1523, 1525 (arguing that international legal norms were at the 'analytical core' of the USSC's decision in *Hamdan* v. *Rumsfeld*, 126 S Ct 2749 (2006)). The court's willingness to apply international humanitarian law norms has not, however, extended to international human rights law: see F. de Londras, 'What Human Rights Could Do: Lamenting the Absence of an International Human Rights Law Approach in *Boumediene Al Odah*' (2008) 41 *Israel Law Review* 562.

[20] P. J. Schwikkard, 'Convergence, Appropriate Fit and Values in Criminal Process', in P. Roberts and M. Redmayne, *Innovations in Evidence and Proof* (Oxford: Hart, 2007) 331.

viewing the interests at stake purely in terms of the prosecution and defence towards concern for the victims of crime.[21] An international consensus has emerged on the importance of victims' rights as reflected in international instruments such as the UN Declaration of Basic Principles of Justice for Victims of Crime and Abuse of Power and the Council of Europe Recommendation on the Position of the Victim in the Framework of Criminal Law and Procedure.[22] The emergence of victims' rights has had a significant impact across the criminal justice systems of both common and civil law jurisdictions forcing criminal justice professionals to pay more regard to victims in their interaction with them and to give victims a greater voice in the system.

A striking convergence of evidential measures designed to protect and empower witnesses is to be seen across many common law jurisdictions.[23] These include measures designed to protect vulnerable witnesses from the glare of trial publicity and from exposure to defendants and to enable them to give evidence more effectively unhindered by arcane corroboration rules and by the lax admission of sexual history evidence which serves to perpetuate 'rape myths'. Although there is considerable variation in the practical application of these rules across jurisdictions,[24] they amount to an important affirmation of victims' rights to security and privacy. Less evidential reform has been evident in civil law jurisdictions, where the less bipolar structure of criminal processes has traditionally given victims a greater voice and greater protection.[25] But here too concern has been raised at the treatment of vulnerable witnesses and certain witnesses are allowed to give evidence via a live television link, avoiding direct confrontation with the accused.[26]

The international criminal tribunals have also given considerable emphasis to the need to protect witnesses.[27] The statutes and rules of procedure and evidence of all the international tribunals allow for the adoption of protective measures to protect the security and privacy interests of witnesses.[28] These

---

[21] There is a large literature. For a helpful discussion of the debates, see J. Doak, *Victims' Rights, Human Rights and Criminal Justice* (Oxford: Hart, 2008). See also M. D. Dubber, *Victims in the War on Crime: The Use and Abuse of Victims' Rights* (New York University Press, 2002).

[22] GA Resolution 40/34 of 29 November 1985 and Recommendation (85)11 of 28 June 1985.

[23] For a comparative discussion of these measures across common law jurisdictions, see L. Ellison, *The Adversarial Process and the Vulnerable Witness* (Oxford University Press, 2001).

[24] See Schwikkard, 'Convergence, Appropriate Fit and Values in Criminal Process', 331, 339–40 (reporting the under use of provisions regulating the use of complainants' sexual history evidence in South Africa). For an analysis of the use of special measures for vulnerable witnesses in England and Wales, see D. Cooper and P. Roberts, *Special Measures for Vulnerable and Intimidated Witnesses: An Analysis of Crown Prosecution Service Monitoring Data* (London: Crown Prosecution Service, 2005).

[25] See, e.g. W. Pizzi and W. Perron, 'Crime Victims in German Courtrooms: A Comparative Perspective on American Problems' (1996) 32 *Stanford Journal of International Law* 37.

[26] Ellison, *Adversarial Process and the Vulnerable Witness*, 149 (discussing the position in the Netherlands).

[27] See O. Abo Youssef, *Die Stellung des Opfers im Völkerstrafrecht* (Zurich: Schulthess, 2008).

[28] Arts. 20(1) and 22 ICTY Statute; Arts. 19(1) and 21 ICTR Statute; rr. 39(ii), 75 and 79 ICTY ICTR RPE; Arts. 54(1)(b) and 3(f), 57(3), 64(6)(e) and 68 ICC Statute; rr. 87–88 ICC RPE.

include measures to prevent disclosure to the public (for example, screening, voice or image distortion, pseudonyms and photo prohibition), postponements in the disclosure of evidence to the defence, closed sessions held in camera and testimony by video-link. Victims' and witnesses' units have also been set up in the respective registries of these tribunals to implement protective measures and to provide counselling and support to victims and witnesses.[29] The tribunals have attached particular importance to the protection of victims of sexual violence, with provisions prohibiting the need for corroboration of the victim's testimony and restricting the admission of evidence of prior or subsequent sexual conduct or of consent except in very limited circumstances.[30]

Increasingly, victims' rights to participate in criminal proceedings include more than simply being able to act as effective witnesses. In many jurisdictions now, victims are given rights to be informed and consulted about the nature and progress of the case.[31] In a number of civil law jurisdictions less wedded to the notion of criminal proceedings being centred around the idea of bipolar dispute, victims have for some time been permitted to become parties to the case, enjoying rights of legal representation and access to documents.[32] Victims are also playing an increasingly important role in international criminal proceedings. Although the ad hoc international criminal tribunals have put considerable emphasis on the need to protect victims, they were not given any personal right to intervene in the case and were not able to obtain reparation from their harm. By contrast, victims in proceedings before the ICC may take a much more active part in the proceedings. They enjoy a right to make recommendations to the Pre-Trial Chamber when the prosecutor is requesting authorisation to proceed with an investigation and a right to be informed of the closure of that investigation.[33] They may also submit observations in proceedings with regard to jurisdiction or admissibility.[34] Most significantly,

---

[29] See r. 34 ICTY ICTR RPE; Arts. 43(6) and 68(4) ICC Statute; and rr. 16–19 ICC RPE.

[30] See rr. 63(4), 71 and 72 ICC RPE. See F. Ni Aoláin, 'Radical Rules: The Effects of Evidential and Procedural Rules on the Regulation of Sexual Violence in War' (1997) 60 *Albany Law Review* 883.

[31] Prosecutors across a range of different jurisdictions are increasingly required to pay attention to the interests of victims. See B. Hancock and J. Jackson, *Standards for Prosecutors: An Analysis of the United Kingdom Prosecuting Agencies* (Nijmegen: Wolf, 2006) 189–90; and B. Hancock and J. Jackson, *Standards for Prosecutors: An Analysis of the National Prosecuting Agencies in Ireland, New South Wales, the Netherlands and Denmark* (Nijmegen: Wolf, 2009) 178.

[32] See M. Chiavario, 'The Rights of the Defendant and the Victim', in M. Delmas-Marty and J. Spencer (eds.), *European Criminal Procedures* (Cambridge University Press, 2005) 543–4 and 567–8 (discussing France, Belgium, Germany and Italy). S. Walther, 'Victims' Rights in the German Court System' (2006) 19 *Federal Sentencing Reporter* 113; and F. Bommer, *Offensive Verletztenrechte im Strafprozess* (Bern: Stämpfli, 2006) (discussing the position in Switzerland); see also Arts. 116–17 Swiss Criminal Procedure Code setting out the role and rights of the victim in A. Donatsch, T. Hansjakob and V. Lieber, *Kommentar zur Schweizerischen Strafprozessordnung* (Zürich: Schulthess, 2010) (which includes an English translation of the code).

[33] Art. 15(3)(6) ICC Statute.   [34] Art. 19(3) ICC Statute.

the ICC Statute provides that where their 'personal interests' are affected, the court shall permit their 'views and concerns' to be presented and considered at appropriate stages of the proceedings in a manner which is not prejudicial to or inconsistent with the rights of the accused.[35] This includes a right to make representations on reparations.[36] Victims do not become a 'true' party to the proceedings in the sense of having the same rights and powers as the prosecution and defence.[37] The statute does not permit them to participate in investigations or to have access to the evidence gathered by the parties, and they cannot call witnesses to testify at the hearing. But their views and concerns may be presented by legal representatives who may examine witnesses, experts and the accused.

The measures that have been taken to aid victims and witnesses in the criminal process should not be viewed as at variance with the rationalist tradition of evidence and with the individual rights tradition discussed in this book. Within the rationalist tradition of evidence, steps should be taken to ensure that victims as well as defendants are able to present their evidence effectively and have it accurately assessed and within the individual rights tradition they are entitled to have their security, dignity and privacy protected. There has been a tendency to portray victims' rights in terms of a 'zero-sum' game, whereby advancing the rights of victims can only lead to losses for defendants.[38] In fact, a number of the measures designed to protect witnesses from trial publicity, for example, do not involve any significant intrusion on defendants' interests. It is true that sometimes balancing decisions have to be made between victims' and defendants' interests. In this book, we have argued for an important distinction between the identification of a defendant's personal right to dignity and autonomy and the institutional right of the defence to challenge the prosecution charges which go to the fundamental legitimacy of the trial process. Although defendants are entitled to be treated with dignity and respect throughout the pre-trial and trial process, victims and witnesses are entitled to similar dignity and respect. So when in the course of representing himself a defendant wishes to confront and cross-examine witnesses against him, the defendant's right to participate fully in his case has to be balanced against the equally important rights of the complainant to privacy and to be protected from degrading and humiliating treatment at the hands of the defendant.[39] To protect the personal rights of the complainant, a number of countries have refused to permit defendants to cross-examine child witnesses, adult complainants in rape cases and other types

---

[35] Art. 68(3) ICC Statute. [36] Art. 75(3) ICC Statute.
[37] C. Jorda and J. de Hemptinne, 'The Status and Role of the Victim', in A. Cassese, P. Gaeta and J. R. D. Jones (eds.), *The Rome Statute of the International Criminal Court* (Oxford University Press, 2002) vol. 2, 1387, 1405.
[38] D. Garland, *The Culture of Control* (Oxford University Press, 2001) 11. For a critique of the use of balancing metaphors in discourse about victims' rights, see J. Jackson, 'Justice for All: Putting Victims at the Heart of Criminal Justice' (2003) 30 *Journal of Law and Society* 309.
[39] See I. H. Dennis, 'The Right to Confront Witnesses: Meanings, Myths and Human Rights' [2010] *Criminal Law Review* 255, 263–4.

of witnesses and we have seen that these restrictions are unlikely to fall foul of the ECHR jurisprudence.[40]

The personal right of the defendant to confront witnesses, however, has to be distinguished from the more fundamental institutional right of the defence to examine important witnesses through the defendant's lawyer, having taken full instructions from the defendant. Any restrictions on this right need to be considered very carefully. We have seen that the ECtHR has recognised that the principles of fair trial require that in appropriate cases the interests of the defence are balanced against those of witnesses called upon to testify.[41] Some of the ECtHR's decisions have been criticised on the ground that the court has succumbed to a zero-sum calculation according to which safeguarding the interests of witnesses must mean diminishing the rights of the defence.[42] But in the last chapter we saw that although the manner in which the court has approached the question of confrontation can be faulted, it has required member states to apply strict proportionality standards in considering whether restrictions on the defence right to examine witnesses are justified. Special measures to protect witnesses such as the use of pre-recorded video evidence and live-link television alter the traditional means of giving oral evidence in the criminal trial and can prevent the defence from conducting face-to-face examination.[43] Applying the proportionality standard utilised by the ECtHR,[44] however, the legitimate aim of enabling a vulnerable witness to give evidence in better epistemic conditions would appear to support the use of these measures provided they are proportionate to the aim and any restrictions on defence rights are sufficiently counterbalanced.[45]

When restrictions are placed upon the identity of witnesses, the measures can impact much more severely on defence interests. For here knowledge of the identity of the witness may be necessary to make a defence case that, for example, the defendant has been framed by the witness. We have seen that the ECtHR in *Doorson* v. *Netherlands*[46] advanced the proposition that a conviction should not be based wholly or to a decisive extent on anonymous witnesses and this principle has in the main been applied in domestic and international

---

[40] See, e.g. ss. 34–6 Youth Justice and Criminal Evidence Act 1999 (UK). For the ECHR jurisprudence, see Ch. 10.3.2.4.
[41] *Doorson* v. *Netherlands*, para. 70.
[42] R. K. Kirst, 'Hearsay and the Right of Confrontation in the European Court of Human Rights' (2003) 21 *Quinnipiac Law Review* 777, 806–7.
[43] P. Roberts and A. Zuckerman, *Criminal Evidence*, 2nd edn (Oxford University Press, 2010) 285–6.
[44] See, e.g. *Van Mechelen and others* v. *Netherlands*, para. 58.
[45] I. Dennis, *The Law of Evidence*, 4th edn (London: Sweet & Maxwell, 2010) para. 15.30. See Ch. 10.3.2.4. See also *R (D)* v. *Camberwell Green Youth Court* [2005] UKHL 4. For a full discussion, see L. C. H. Hoyano, 'Striking a Balance between the Rights of Defendants and Vulnerable Witnesses: Will Special Measures Directions Contravene Guarantees of a Fair Trial?' [2001] *Criminal Law Review* 948.
[46] *Doorson* v. *Netherlands*. See Chs. 4.2.3 and 10.3.1.

tribunals.[47] The sole and decisive principle has since been applied by the ECtHR as we have seen in relation to all witness statements and has proved controversial. But if the prosecution has been given an opportunity to present important witness evidence in favour of its case, it may be argued that this institutional advantage needs to be balanced against the right of the defence to examine these witnesses directly. If, on the other hand, the court has played a greater role in eliciting the witness evidence, it may be that the prosecution and defence's rights can justifiably be restricted to making adversarial arguments in relation to the evidence. Measures taken to protect complainants from revelations about their sexual history have also proved controversial, as arguments have raged over the relevance of sexual history to issues of consent and rape shield statutes have often given rape complainants less protection than they were designed to provide.[48]

All of this puts a heavy onus on public authorities to arbitrate fairly between the interests of witnesses and the interests of the defence. Strict proportionality tests require to be applied before there can be encroachments on the rights of the defence. At the same time, public authorities must guarantee the rights of witnesses and victims to security, dignity and privacy. In accordance with its general approach, the ECtHR has refused to prescribe any common procedure. On the contrary, the flexibility given by the court to states to organise their procedures to meet the standards of fairness in Article 6 means that states are encouraged to think imaginatively of the various ways in which the rights of witnesses and the defence may be respected in their indigenous systems. This may require some significant modification to traditional approaches. The attendance of defence lawyers at pre-trial witness interviews in the absence of defendants, the pre-trial questioning of witnesses by a judge and the involvement of court-appointed or

---

[47] Discussed in *R* v. *Davis* [2008] UKHL 38, but cf. dicta in *R* v. *Horncastle and others* [2009] UKSC 14, discussed in Ch. 4.2.3. Within the international criminal tribunals, the rules have not been clear on this issue. In an early ICTY case, anonymous evidence was used, but the practice has not been repeated. See Ch. 5.7 and *Prosecutor* v. *Haradinaj and others*, Trial Chamber, Decision. The ICC system appears to permit the identity of witnesses to be withheld 'prior to the commencement of the trial', which suggests that it may not be withheld at trial. See Art. 68(5) ICC Statute, r. 81(4) ICC RPE and for commentary, Cryer et al., *International Criminal Law and Procedure*, 483–4.

[48] For contributions to the debate about the relevance of sexual history evidence, see A. McColgan, 'Common Law and the Relevance of Sexual History Evidence' (1996) 16 *Oxford Journal of Legal Studies* 275; C. Boyle and M. MacCrimmon, 'The Constitutionality of Bill C-49: Analysing Assault as if Equality Really Mattered' (1998) 4 *Criminal Law Quarterly* 198; M. Redmayne, 'Myths, Relationships and Coincidences: The New Problems of Sexual History' (2003) 7 *International Journal of Evidence and Proof* 75; and C. Boyle, 'A Principled Approach to Relevance: the Cheshire Cat in Canada', in Roberts and Redmayne, *Innovations in Evidence and Proof*, 87. It is to be noted that some of the international criminal tribunals ban evidence of the sexual conduct of the victim altogether: see r. 96(iv) ICTY, ICTR RPE. Cf. r. 71 ICC RPE: 'subject to Art. 69(4) a Chamber shall not admit evidence of the prior or subsequent sexual conduct of a victim or witness'. Art. 69(4) gives the chamber an overriding discretion to make rulings on the admissibility of evidence in the interests of a fair trial.

independent forensic psychology experts are all procedures that may be considered as compensating safeguards for direct examination, but are alien to the common law tradition. Similarly, we have seen that in order to do justice to the privacy rights of complainants in sexual cases, the defence may be required to give specific details of their defence in order to secure third-party disclosure and heavier burdens may need to be placed on it to show the relevance of their defence to any sexual history evidence they wish to be admitted.[49]

Where victims' rights extend to active participation in the proceedings, the task of balancing interests can become even more demanding. The ECtHR has yet to develop more than minimal rights for the involvement of victims in terms of rights to information and procedural rights.[50] The ICC, on the other hand, has enthusiastically endorsed the notion of victim participation, in some cases apparently going beyond what the negotiating parties envisaged.[51] The Pre-Trial Chamber has determined that victims should be given procedural status at the investigation phase of proceedings, including confirmation hearings.[52] As well as this, the chamber has held that non-anonymous victims should have extensive rights to participation at confirmation hearings, including the right to have access to the record of the case kept by the registrar, a right to make submissions on evidence, to examine witnesses, and to make oral and written interventions.[53] The Trial Chamber has also announced extensive forms of participation at the trial stage, including the right to disclosure of materials in the possession of the prosecution, and the right to introduce and examine evidence during the trial if in the view of the chamber it will assist it in the determination of the truth.[54]

These decisions would seem to go beyond the limitations imposed by the ICC Statute, which confines the presentation of victims' views and concerns to their 'personal interests' and would seem to point in the direction of giving victims institutional party rights. The Appeals Chamber has taken

---

[49] M. S. Raeder, 'Litigating Sex Crimes in the United States: Has the Last Decade Made Any Difference?' (2009) 6 *International Commentary on Evidence*, Issue 2, Art. 6 (arguing for a clear and convincing evidence standard to be borne by the defence for proof of preliminary facts for admission of sexual history evidence).

[50] See J. Doak, 'The Victim and the Criminal Process: An Analysis of Recent Trends in Regional and International Tribunals' (2003) 23 *Legal Studies* 1; and F. Leverick, 'What has the ECHR Done for Victims? A United Kingdom Perspective' (2004) *International Review of Victimology* 177.

[51] For discussion, see H. Friman, 'Participation of Victims in the ICC Criminal Proceedings and the Early Jurisprudence of the Court', in Sluiter and Vasiliev, *International Criminal Procedure*, 205.

[52] See, e.g. *Situation in the Democratic Republic of Congo*, Decision on the Applications for Participation in the Proceedings of VPRS 1, VPRS 2, VPRS 3, VPRS 4, VPRS 5 and VPRS 6, ICC-01/04. 17 January 2006. See also J. de Hemptienne and F. Rindi, 'ICC Pre-Trial Chamber Allows Victims to Participate in the Investigation Phase of Proceedings' (2006) 4 *Journal of International Criminal Justice* 342.

[53] *Prosecutor* v. *Katanga and Ngudjolo Chui*, *Situation in the DRC*, Decision.

[54] *Prosecutor* v. *Lubanga Dyilo*, *Situation in the DRC*, Trial Chamber, Decision on victims' participation.

the view that personal interests extend to raising matters concerning protection and reparations, but has considered that there must be an assessment of whether the interests asserted by the victims do not in fact fall outside their personal interests and belong instead to the role assigned to the prosecutor.[55] As soon as victims are allowed to make representations on issues relating to guilt, they would seem to be intruding seriously on the role of the prosecutor.

Expanded notions of victim participation raise difficult procedural challenges for the court, which must balance victim interests with those of the accused. The injection of strong participation rights for victims in the course of the pre-trial and trial hearings can slow down the day-to-day workings of the court in a manner that impacts on the right of accused persons to be tried without undue delay.[56] Strong participation rights may also damage the equilibrium of interests between the prosecution and defence and give rise to a perception that the defence has to fight on two fronts against the prosecution and the victims. On top of this, there are questions about whether the Pre-Trial Chamber can rule effectively on issues of investigation and can exercise effective control over victims' claims.[57] It will be recalled that the Pre-Trial Chamber does not have the investigatory powers of an investigating judge and that it does not have access to all of the documents gathered by the prosecution and defence in the course of their investigations. Giving victims access to evidence in the case also raises questions about the protection of confidential information and whether this may deter any investigations the defence might make.[58] Finally, difficult questions are raised about the different roles of victims and witnesses.[59] A number of national systems prevent witnesses from being present prior to giving testimony and the ad hoc tribunals also adhere to this rule.[60] Does this mean that when victims are to act as witnesses their participation rights are to be curtailed until they have given evidence?

Leaving aside these practical difficulties, there are more theoretical questions about the purposes of victim participation. Restorative and reconciliatory aims have been claimed for international criminal tribunals which would give victims a central role in the proceedings, but it may be doubted whether these require victims to be given institutional rights alongside prosecutors in the process of guilt determination. If, on the other hand, victims are to be given substantive rights to have crimes against them vigorously pursued and to have those responsible punished, as has been suggested in certain decisions of the

---

[55] *Prosecutor* v. *Lubanga Dyilo, Situation in the DRC*, Appeals Chamber, Decision of the Appeals Chamber on the Joint Application of Victims a/0001/06 to a/0003/06 and a/0005/06 concerning the 'Directions and Decision of the Appeal Chamber' of 2 February 2007.
[56] Art. 67(1)(c) ICC Statute.
[57] C. Jorda and J. de Hemptienne, 'The Status and Role of the Victim', in A. Cassese, P. Gaeta and J. R. D. Jones (eds.), *The Rome Statute of the International Criminal Court* (Oxford University Press, 2002) vol. 2, 1387, 1412.
[58] Ibid.   [59] Friman, 'Participation of Victims', 220–1.
[60] See r. 90(C) ICTY RPE; and r. 90(D) ICTR RPE.

IACtHR,[61] logic would seem to require that they may insist on participating in the process of guilt determination. Their interests would then collide directly with the interests of the defence. The right to have someone punished is difficult in particular to reconcile with the presumption of innocence and the right not to be wrongfully convicted.[62] Such a right arguably returns us to the 'state of nature' before we assigned our right to punish to the state on condition that we were given rights to be protected by the state from the criminal acts and the false accusations of others.

11.4 State security and terrorism

Another obstacle to the practice of active evidentiary rights lies in national and international responses to the global threat of terrorism, which has become particularly acute since the events of 9/11. Many social contract theorists have accepted that threats to security justify emergency powers which shift the nature of the relationship of power between the citizen and the state,[63] although they have disagreed on whether these powers should be solely within the discretion of the executive or should be prescribed within the Constitution.[64] States have responded to threats to their security in a variety of ways and a number of theorists have advanced several distinct models for dealing with these threats, ranging from modifying the ordinary law, enacting special emergency legislation within the rule of law, to taking extra-legal measures whereby individuals are thrown into a legal 'black hole'.[65] The more such models vary from the ordinary law, the greater the risk of individuals' rights being violated. From an evidential point of view, there is an increased risk of innocent persons being wrongly convicted as a result of a significant dilution of the fair trial guarantees offered to the defence or when the criminal process is by-passed altogether of being deprived of their liberty by detention without trial with limited opportunity for judicial review.[66]

National constitutions and the legislative and judicial branches of governments have often proved ineffective in checking violations to the individual

[61] See, e.g. *Bulacio* v. *Argentina*; and *Alban-Cornejo* v. *Ecuador*.
[62] M. Sorochinsky, 'Prosecuting Torturers, Protecting "Child Molesters": Toward a Power Balance Model of Criminal Process of International Human Rights Law' (2009) 31 *Michigan Journal of International Law* 158, 214.
[63] cf. Hobbes, who made no distinction between states of normalcy and states of emergency: see T. Hobbes, *Leviathan* (Harmondsworth: Penguin, 1651, 1968) ch. XXX.
[64] See A. Keller, 'Constitutionalising Emergency Powers in Modern Europe', in A. Biachi and A. Keller, *Counter-Terrorism: Democracy's Challenge* (Oxford: Hart, 2009) ch. 2.
[65] O. Gross and F. Ni Aoláin, *Law in Times of Crisis: Emergency Powers in Theory and Practice* (Cambridge University Press, 2006) chs. 1–3. The regime established by the Bush Administration at Guantánamo Bay where foreign nationals have been held in detention indefinitely without any constitutional protections has been characterised as a 'legal black hole': see J. Steyn, 'Guantanamo Bay: The Legal Black Hole' (2004) 53 *International and Comparative Law Quarterly* 1.
[66] See D. Dyzenhaus, *The Constitution of Law – Legality in a Time of Emergency* (Cambridge University Press, 2006).

rights and rationalist evidence traditions.[67] There has also been criticism of the failings of the international system to provide robust oversight of states' recourse to emergency powers.[68] Most of the human rights regimes have recognised that while certain rights are non-derogable,[69] derogations may be made to a number of other rights in situations of 'war or other public emergency'.[70] Both the UNHRC and the IACtHR have concluded that the fair trial guarantees cannot be suspended in times of emergency.[71] The HRC has also said that state parties to the ICCPR may not invoke Article 4 of the Covenant as justification for acting in violation of humanitarian law or peremptory norms in international law by 'deviating from the fundamental principles of fair trial including the presumption of innocence'.[72]

Despite this unambiguous position, the human rights bodies have accepted that different contexts may call for different standards of application within the fair trial guarantees. It has been suggested that the IACtHR has taken a more robust approach in its determination of both substantive and procedural questions about emergencies than its European or UN counterparts, as the court has operated in a region where emergency powers have frequently been the resort of non-democratic states.[73] The ECtHR by contrast has said that there is a 'need, inherent in the Convention system, for a proper balance between the defence of the institutions of democracy in the common interest and the protection of individual rights'.[74] The court would therefore take into account 'the special nature of terrorist crime and the exigencies of dealing with it, as far as is compatible with the applicable provisions of the Convention in the light of their particular wording and its overall object and purpose'. Although this statement was made in the context of an alleged breach of Article 5 rather than Article 6 of the ECHR, it is a clear expression of the extent to which the ECtHR may be prepared to take a contextualised approach to fair trial rights when democratic states face terrorist violence.[75] While it has been reluctant to condone the use of military officers in civilian courts,[76] it has not opposed the

---

[67] See Gross and Ni Aoláin, *Law in Times of Crisis*, 63–4. Cf. F. De Londras, 'Controlling the Executive in Times of Terrorism: Competing Perspectives on Effective Oversight Mechanisms' (2009) 30 *Oxford Journal of Legal Studies* 19.

[68] Gross and Ni Aoláin, *Law in Times of Crisis*, 247. See also S. Forster, *Freiheitsbeschränkungen für mutmaßliche Terroristen* (Berlin: Duncker & Humblot, 2010).

[69] Under Art. 15 ECHR, for example, non-derogable rights include the right to life, freedom from torture, inhuman and degrading treatment, freedom from slavery and the right not to be subject to ex post facto application of law.

[70] Art. 15 ECHR. Cf. Art. 4 ICCPR and Art. 27 of ACHR. The African Charter has no express derogation provision.

[71] HRC, General Comment 29, States of Emergency (Art. 4). UN Doc. CCPR/C/21/Rev. 1/Ass. 11 (2001), para. 16, *Judicial Guarantees in a State of Emergency*, 9 Inter-American Ct HR (ser. A) para. 24, OEA/ser.L/VI/111.9 doc. 13 (1987).

[72] HRC, General Comment 29, para. 11.   [73] Gross and Ni Aoláin, *Law in Times of Crisis*, 291.

[74] *Fox, Campbell and Hartley* v. *United Kingdom*, para. 28.

[75] See also *John Murray* v. *United Kingdom*, para. 58 (acknowledging that the investigation of terrorist offences undoubtedly presents the authorities with special problems).

[76] *Incal* v. *Turkey*.

use of special civilian courts on the grounds that they offer less protection than ordinary rules elsewhere in the contracting state, provided they comply with the minimum fair trial guarantees.[77] Similarly, it would appear that the human rights bodies do not insist that the same rules of evidence be applied to cases involving terrorists as are applied to other criminal trials.[78] The international criminal tribunals have also considered it relevant to take into account the imperfect circumstances in which they are operating, which may include a near state of emergency in the states where the crimes took place and a lack of proper enforcement mechanisms.[79]

At the same time, there are clearly limits to the extent to which a terrorist context can dilute the objective fair trial guarantees. This has led state officials to argue that these norms make the prosecution of terrorist suspects very difficult and it can provide an excuse for dealing with them outside the criminal process altogether.[80] Another type of zero-sum argument that can be made in this context is the assertion that security and a fair trial are not compatible with one another.[81] The obstacles in the way of obtaining convictions in terrorist trials which adhere to the participatory principles associated with a fair trial were well explained over 35 years ago in the report of the Diplock Commission in Northern Ireland, which was established to consider what changes should be made to deal effectively with terrorism without resort to detention without trial.[82] The difficulty in obtaining witnesses who were prepared to testify openly against defendants meant that prosecuting authorities had to fall back on the oral evidence of non-civilian witnesses whose protection could be ensured, physical evidence such as fingerprints and an admissible confession. But there were problems with using these sources. Non-civilian witnesses could not easily be the direct source of paramilitary activity. Physical evidence was not always available and confessions under the common law were inadmissible unless they were made voluntarily by suspects. The Commission recommended that

---

[77] See *Magee* v. *United Kingdom*. For argument that the existence of two different trial systems – one for ordinary offences and another for the same offences connected with an emergency – constitutes a violation of the equal protection guarantee in Art. 26 ICCPR, see B. Dickson, 'Northern Ireland's Emergency Legislation' [1992] *Public Law* 592, 607–8.

[78] C. Warbrick, 'The European Convention on Human Rights and the Prevention of Terrorism' (1983) 32 *International and Comparative Law Quarterly* 82.

[79] See, e.g. A. Cassese, 'Opinion: The International Criminal Tribunal for the Former Yugoslavia and Human Rights' [1997] *European Human Rights Law Review* 329; and G. McIntyre, 'Defining Human Rights in the Arena of International Humanitarian Law', in G. Boas and W. Schabas (eds.), *International Criminal Law Developments in the Case Law of the ICTY* (Leiden: Martinus Nijhoff, 2002).

[80] International Commission of Jurists, *Assessing Damage, Urging Action: Report of the Eminent Jurists Panel on Terrorism, Counter-Terrorism and Human Rights* (Geneva: ICJ, 2009), 144.

[81] Analogous arguments have been made as regards security and liberty in the context of the 'war against terror'. See, e.g. E. Posner and A. Vermeule, *Terror in the Balance: Security, Liberty and Courts* (Oxford University Press, 2007).

[82] *Report of the Commission to Consider Legal Procedures to Deal with Terrorist Activities in Northern Ireland* (London: HMSO, 1972) Cmnd 5185.

a number of modifications be made to ordinary trials, notably a relaxation of the voluntariness standard for the admissibility of confessions, a reversal of the burden of proof in firearms cases, provision for the admissibility of witness statements in certain situations and the replacement of the jury with a single trial judge.

In the context of the contemporary debate on terrorism, what is significant about these recommendations is that the Commission considered that they could be implemented without encroaching on the minimum requirements of Article 6 of the ECHR. Experience indeed has shown that it is possible to prosecute terrorist suspects successfully within the confines of the fair trial guarantees, the Diplock courts established on foot of the recommendations of the Commission being a prominent example.[83] As the evidentiary standards promoting defence participation have evolved in the human rights jurisprudence over the years, however, it may be argued that the balance between a fair trial and security is harder to achieve. Intelligence agencies have played an increasingly central role in identifying suspects and obtaining evidence against them and states need to ensure that the sources of information on which this evidence is based are not compromised in order to combat terrorism effectively. Yet the evidentiary standards that have been developed require that accusers are able to answer the charges against them effectively.[84] The human rights bodies have accepted that in order to protect witnesses inroads may be made into open cross-examination in court. The issues of disclosure are more difficult, but again we have seen that they are not insurmountable when resort is had to special advocates or restrictions are placed upon the information that counsel can give to the accused.

A further difficulty connected with the intelligence agencies that has arisen in the context of global terrorism is that intelligence sharing between states often results in the use of information that has been obtained by unlawful methods, including the use of ill-treatment and torture.[85] The result is that often the evidence against the accused is tainted and cannot surmount the evidentiary bars required for a fair trial. This suggests that the real obstacle to bringing successful prosecutions is not the fair trial guarantees, but the culture within the security services in both democratic and non-democratic regimes, which continues to flout international standards of human rights. This raises a wider question of the accountability of such services for their actions. The danger from a fair trial perspective is not only that the information obtained may be

---

[83] See J. Jackson, 'Many Years On in Northern Ireland: The Diplock Legacy' (2009) 60 *Northern Ireland Legal Quarterly* 213. It is also to be noted that despite the establishment of the Guantánamo regime, the US authorities have successfully convicted a large number of defendants on terrorism-related offences through the ordinary courts: see International Commission of Jurists, *Assessing Damage*, 144.
[84] See T. Brooks (ed.), *The Right to a Fair Trial* (Farnham: Ashgate, 2009) xv.
[85] International Commission of Jurists, *Assessing Damage*, ch. 4.

of such poor quality that successful prosecutions cannot be mounted, but also that such information is not fully disclosed to the prosecuting authorities, with the danger of miscarriages of justice when prosecutions are brought.

11.5 Cost and expedition

A further obstacle to the promotion of positive evidentiary defence rights lies in the increasing tendency for legal systems to seek to reduce the cost of criminal proceedings by having cases negotiated or diverted out of the criminal process. The growing volume of cases passing through the system has meant that jurisdictions have developed means of processing certain kinds of cases more quickly. The traditional method of doing this in common law jurisdictions has been by means of the guilty plea. But various forms of negotiated justice are becoming prevalent not only in common law jurisdictions, but across civil law jurisdictions as well, despite as we have seen their traditional aversion to allowing the parties to dictate the outcome of cases.[86] In addition to this, increasing numbers of cases are being diverted out of the criminal justice system altogether by offering fixed penalties or a non-criminal disposition such as a civil penalty or a conditional caution or a 'transaction' to those accused of criminal offences.[87] Many of these dispositions require the consent of the accused, but where the accused does not receive legal advice, there is an obvious risk that cases are disposed of without any proper scrutiny of the evidence.

Even where accused persons are represented, the incentives offered for a guilty plea or 'consent' may compromise any effective defence. In many common law systems, the economic pressure to avert trial has led to increasing inducements being offered to accused persons to plead guilty in the form of reductions in the charge brought, sentence discounts and indications of sentence by the judge.[88] This raises questions over the degree to which incentives to plead guilty may be compatible with Article 6.[89] There is an obvious danger in these

---

[86] M. Langer, 'From Legal Transplants to Legal Translations: The Globalisation of Plea Bargaining and the Americanization Thesis in Criminal Process' (2004) 45 *Harvard International Law Journal* 1. See the arguments in T. Weigend, 'The Decay of the Inquisitorial Ideal: Plea Bargaining Invades German Criminal Procedure', in Jackson et al., *Crime, Procedure and Evidence*, 39.

[87] For the growing use of such diversionary measures in the United Kingdom, see R. M. White, '"Civil Penalties": Oxymoron, Chimera and Stealth Sanction' (2010) 126 *Law Quarterly Review* 593; I. Brownlee, 'Conditional Cautions and Fair Trial Rights in England and Wales: Form versus Substance in the Diversionary Agenda' [2007] *Criminal Law Review* 129; and J. Jackson, 'Police and Prosecutors after PACE: The Road from Case Construction to Case Disposition', in E. Cape and R. Young (eds.), *Regulating Policing* (Oxford: Hart, 2008) 256. For the various consensual procedures in the Netherlands, see C. H. Brants-Langeraar, 'Consensual Criminal Procedures: Plea and Confession Bargaining and Abbreviated Procedures to Simplify Criminal Procedure', in J. H. M. van Erp and L. P. W. van Vliet (eds.), *Netherlands Reports to the Seventeenth International Congress of Comparative Law* (Utrecht: Intersentia, 2006).

[88] For the position in England, see A. Ashworth and M. Redmayne, *The Criminal Process*, 3rd edn (Oxford University Press, 2010) ch. 10.

[89] Ashworth and Redmayne, *Criminal Process*, 288–9.

circumstances that innocent accused persons may be persuaded to plead guilty, leading to a wrongful conviction. Defence lawyers face ethical dilemmas where the inducements offered to plead guilty can lead counsel into compromising their role to present an effective defence. Legal counsel can become drawn into 'plea bargaining' situations by seeking to reduce a charge or obtain some indication of sentence without giving due attention to the evidence against the accused.[90] Ethical rules often attempt to safeguard defendants against this by requiring that counsel do not put clients under pressure to plead guilty.[91] There has been less attention given, however, to the situation where defendants genuinely want to plead guilty even though they may have indicated they are innocent.[92] An approach which emphasises client autonomy would suggest that counsel must do as his or her client wishes.[93] But this can conflict with the theory of effective evidentiary defence, which would bear in mind that considerations of accuracy need to prevail over considerations of the accused's autonomy. Or put another way, 'the defence advocate represents more than the client – she or he is simultaneously responsible for maintaining fundamental guarantees central to the justice system'.[94]

It is tempting to be pessimistic about the slide towards the 'brave new world of consensual criminal procedure'.[95] Given the economic benefits in avoiding full trials, it would seem that such a slide is inevitable and with it the individual rights and the rationalist traditions would seem to be compromised. To obviate this drift towards consensual justice, some have advocated simplified abbreviated trials as a 'middle ground' between a full-scale trial and a merely formal assent of the parties to the court's decision.[96] At the very least, it would seem necessary to ensure that there is some meaningful scrutiny of the evidence by authorities other than the police and prosecutors before any bargaining between the prosecution and defence gets under way if there is to be any proper respect for accuracy of the decision. We have seen that the human rights bodies have belatedly begun to recognise that the right to a fair trial requires that suspects who are interviewed by the police should have a right to legal advice at the beginning of the interview.[97] An opportunity for legal advice on the evidential

---

[90] M. McConville, 'Plea Bargaining: Ethics and Politics' (1998) 25 *Journal of Law and Society* 572; and S. Doran and J. Jackson (eds.), *The Judicial Role in Criminal Proceedings* (Oxford: Hart, 2000) 67.
[91] M. Blake and A. Ashworth, 'Ethics and the Criminal Defence Lawyer' (2004) 7 *Legal Ethics* 168.
[92] See L. Bridges, 'The Ethics of Representation on Guilty Pleas' (2006) 9 *Legal Ethics* 80.
[93] M. Freedman, 'Professional Responsibility of the Criminal Defense Lawyer: The Three Hardest Questions' (1966) 64 *Michigan Law Review* 1480–1.
[94] Blake and Ashworth, 'Ethics and the Criminal Defence Lawyer', 189. Certain ethical codes suggest that there may be circumstances in which it would be improper to continue to represent a client who privately asserts innocence but intends to plead guilty, just as there are circumstances when a lawyer may not continue to represent a client who insists on denying guilt in court after having privately admitted his guilt. See English Bar Council, *Written Standards for the Conduct of Professional Work*, paras. 11.5.1–3.
[95] Weigend, 'Decay of the Inquisitorial Ideal', 53.   [96] Ibid., 62.
[97] *Salduz* v. *Turkey* [GC], discussed in Ch. 8.6 above.

aspects of the case accompanied by early disclosure would not be a full substitute for the right at trial to an independent and impartial tribunal. But if it were accompanied by an early right of access to the court to seek undisclosed material, there would at least be an opportunity for evidentiary rights to be exercised.

There remains the question as to how the theory of an effective evidentiary defence can be translated into meaningful practice in those jurisdictions which are unable to afford the kind of defence services that are needed to give the accused persons effective representation. As Schwikkard has put it, a country with a low-economic base may have constitutional guarantees protecting individual autonomy and dignity and it may subscribe to participatory values, 'yet economic reality may dictate that the state cannot afford to pay for legal representation or muster the professional skills or resources to meet disclosure requirements'.[98]

One way of compensating for the lack of legal representation may be to put greater emphasis upon exclusionary rules to offset the danger of abuse of power on the part of the authorities. Another approach would be to maintain a rigorous defence of the right of silence. In a young democracy like South Africa, preceded, as Schwikkard puts it, by 'astonishing abuses of state power and in which constitutional values are not necessarily firmly rooted', these evidentiary approaches may be necessary in order to give meaning to individual constitutional rights of autonomy and dignity.[99] The difficulty as we saw in our discussion of the right of silence is that in the absence of appropriate safeguards in place for regulating the pre-trial evidentiary process, it is difficult to protect suspects from speaking and to give meaning to the concept of effective defence. In the absence of 'an enforceable right to full legal representation', Schwikkard argues that participatory and equality values may be better pursued by 'a proactive inquisitorial judge' than by 'adversarial procedures which are dependent on approximating "equality of arms"'.[100] She points to the fact that although South African proceedings are predominantly driven by the parties, the inequality of the parties, usually due to indigence and the absence of legal representation, has led to an increasing duty on presiding officers of the court to assist the unrepresented accused by ensuring that they are aware of their rights and the appropriate procedures. Whether this duty is viewed as introducing an inquisitorial element into the judicial process or as being essential for the functionality of the adversarial system to compensate for the inequality of arms is largely irrelevant. What is important from our point of view is that this compensatory mechanism is a means, albeit an imperfect one, of pursuing more effective defence participation than if the unrepresented defendant were

---

[98] Schwikkard, 'Convergence, Appropriate Fit and Values in Criminal Process', 336.
[99] P. J. Schwikkard, 'The Muddle of Silence' (2008) 6 *International Commentary on Evidence*, Issue 2, Art. 6, 13.
[100] P. J. Schwikkard, *Possibilities of Convergence: An Outside Perspective on the Convergence of Criminal Procedures in Europe* (Deventer: Kluwer, 2008) 39.

left alone to cater for him- or herself. In a similar fashion, we have seen that although the international criminal tribunals began by being modelled on 'adversarial' party principles, the inequality of arms between prosecution and defence in the context of international investigations would seem to argue for considerably greater judicial domination, especially at the pre-trial phase. The Pre-Trial Chamber in the ICC is exhibiting some of this activism, although as we have seen the proceedings are still largely governed by the kind of 'bipolar tension' that has been more typical of international criminal proceedings to date.[101]

The important point to be made is that in developing optimum participatory defence standards attention needs to focus not upon whether the standards measure up to a particular ideal procedural form, but upon whether the procedures chosen are the best means available to meet these standards in the prevailing political, social and economic climate. This takes us on to a final obstacle in meeting these standards, which is that their development may be impeded by legal culture and tradition.

11.6 Legal culture and tradition

Nijboer has recently commented on the increasing generality in theory and practice with regard to the international, inter-professional and interdisciplinary dimensions of evidence and proof.[102] The scope for greater communication across geographical, professional and disciplinary boundaries has made the exchange of insights easier to accomplish. This has not led to a homogenous convergence of evidentiary law and practice. On the contrary, there has been a countervailing tendency to treat particular issues of evidence in a particularised manner. Examples include the special rules that are to be seen for eliciting children's evidence, the special rules governing the use of DNA evidence and the different standards of relevance that apply in sex crimes. But the different rules and procedures being employed for specific cases are being applied commonly across jurisdictions and this would appear to lend support to Nijboer's thesis that traditional national and disciplinary boundaries are being overcome.

At the same time, it would be wrong to underestimate the capacity of entrenched legal and cultural traditions to resist demands for change. Although we have argued that universally accepted human rights norms can provide a foundation for a 'common grammar' of discourse between the common law and civil law traditions, reaching a consensus on the meaning of such basic building blocks has proved difficult as we look beyond the common law and civil law traditions towards the non-Western legal traditions of Islamic states

---

[101] M. Damaška, 'Problematic Features of International Criminal Procedure', in A. Cassese (ed.), *The Oxford Companion to International Criminal Justice* (Oxford University Press, 2009) 175, 175.
[102] Nijboer, 'Current Issues in Evidence and Procedure'.

and China.[103] Even within the common law and civil law traditions which have formed the subject of this book, commentators have pointed to the genuine difficulty in introducing meaningful defence participation into systems that have long been associated with a dominating prosecution or judicial hierarchy. A number of reasons can be given for this. Some have attributed the difficulties in introducing strong defence norms into the Italian system to a failure of procedural design, the lack, for instance, of a bifurcated jury system able to break up the monopoly of the judge at the trial phase of proceedings.[104] The presence of a jury would appear to encourage higher acquittal rates suggesting a greater focus on the merits of the defence case.[105] Yet as the experience of the importation of the jury into post-Soviet systems shows, prosecutorial and judicial hierarchies are adept at finding means of neutralising changes such as these, entrenching their hold on the system as they lightly wear the new clothes of reform.[106] One commentator has concluded that it is the role of the prosecutor, the *pubblico ministero* and in particular the failure to separate the careers of judges and prosecutors which poses the most difficult institutional challenge to the attempts of the new Italian Code of Criminal Procedure to introduce an 'adversarial' system.[107]

There is likely to be opposition or clever accommodation when change threatens vested legal interests. One tactic that is often resorted to in such situations is to 'play the culture card', defying 'foreign' change on the ground that it would conflict with traditional legal values.[108] Here, we return to the much-used adversarial-inquisitorial dichotomy. We have argued against the idea that the respective 'adversarial' and 'inquisitorial' traditions represent clearly defined prescriptions on how legal proceedings should be conducted. But jurists and practitioners within common law and civil law systems tend to identify strongly with them as idealised contrasting models expressing very different values.[109]

---

[103] D. M. Amann, 'Harmonic Convergence? Constitutional Criminal Procedures in an International Context' (2000) 75 *Indiana Law Journal* 809, 851–62; and R. Vogler, *A World View of Criminal Justice* (Aldershot: Ashgate, 2005) chs. 5 and 6.

[104] E. Grande, 'Italian Criminal Justice: Borrowing and Resistance' (2000) 48 *American Journal of Comparative Law* 227.

[105] See J. Jackson and S. Doran, *Judge without Jury: Diplock Trials within the Adversary System* (Oxford: Clarendon Press, 1995).

[106] S. Thaman, 'The Two Faces of Justice in the Post-Soviet Legal Sphere: Adversarial Procedure, Jury Trial, Plea-Bargaining and the Inquisitorial Legacy' in Jackson et al., *Crime, Procedure and Evidence*, 99, 117 (conjuring up the image of 'the "two-faced" smirk of the entrenched bureaucrats dressed in their new democratic clothes').

[107] L. Marafioti, 'Italian Criminal Procedure: A System Caught Between Two Traditions', in Jackson et al., *Crime, Procedure and Evidence*, 81, 95.

[108] J. Jackson, 'Playing the Culture Card in Resisting Cross-Jurisdictional Transplants' (1997) 5 *Cardozo Journal of International and Comparative Law* 51.

[109] For the notion that the terms 'adversarial' and 'inquisitorial' are used as 'signifiers' through which the identities of the actors of the common law and civil law traditions have been defined, see Langer, 'From Legal Transplants to Legal Translations'. For an analysis of legal traditions in normative terms, see also P. H. Glenn, *Legal Traditions of the World* (Oxford University Press, 2000); P. H. Glenn, 'Comparative Legal Families and Comparative Legal

Sklansky has illustrated how there is a long-standing anti-inquisitorialism tradition in American law which has acted as a kind of 'negative polestar' for American criminal procedure.[110] In a different context, Hodgson has illustrated how 'anti-adversarialism' has tended to dominate debates on many criminal justice reforms within France, such as those strengthening defence rights, the movement towards plea bargaining and the role and function of the *juge d'instruction*.[111] Even though both authors consider that it is inaccurate to describe the US and French systems as reflecting any clear organic integrity to an 'adversarial' or 'inquisitorial' system, these terms continue to have considerable purchase as procedural traditions and cultures guiding at least in negative terms what systems should try *not* to emulate.

Views differ on the general merits of viewing traditions in these terms. From the perspective of trying to promote the participatory evidentiary principles discussed in this book, however, this approach has a number of dangers. Sklansky considers that anti-inquisitorialism in the United States has served to obfuscate the rationale for certain constitutional principles such as confrontation and self-incrimination, the scope and application of which have come under question. At times, anti-inquisitorialism can even point in the wrong direction as it seeks to drive us away from certain 'inquisitorial' systems that also recognise these protections. As well as blinding us to the fact that these principles are recognised across different legal traditions, anti-inquisitorialism also obscures the tensions we have seen are present in the application of these principles. Are they as common law systems have tended to see them – illustrations of the importance of the individual's right to exercise autonomy – or, as we prefer to portray them, are they better seen as institutional rights linked to the importance of mounting an effective defence? Seen in this light, the privilege against self-incrimination is less a protection against 'involuntary' confessions as a means of safeguarding the need for legal assistance when answering questions.

A further danger with undue emphasis on anti-inquisitorialism or anti-adversarialism is that it can obscure the need for changes in one's own system in order to promote effective defence participation. Thus, to associate anti-inquisitorialism with court domination is to give an exaggerated importance to party control when a party may not have the means and resources to mount its own defence. Common law judges have tended to give less than whole-hearted support to the notion of full disclosure on the ground that the parties themselves should be able to present their defence unaided by the prosecution. But without

---

Traditions', in M. Reimann and R. Zimmerman (eds.), *The Oxford Handbook of Comparative Law* (Oxford University Press, 2006); and S. Field, 'Fair Trials and Procedural Tradition in Europe' (2009) 29 *Oxford Journal of Legal Studies* 365.

[110] D. Sklansky, 'Anti-Inquisitorialism' (2009) 122 *Harvard Law Review* 1634. See also S. J. Summers, 'The Right to Confrontation after *Crawford v. Washington*: A "Continental European" Perspective' [2005] *International Commentary on Evidence*, Issue 1, Art. 3.

[111] J. Hodgson, *French Criminal Justice* (Oxford: Hart, 2005) 26–32 and 135–41.

court assistance to enforce full disclosure, the defence may never become privy to exculpatory material.

When it comes to promoting evidentiary principles in jurisdictions that have not cultivated a strong culture of defence participation, anti-inquisitorialism or anti-adversarialism can also serve to distract reformers from what would work best within the local legal tradition. Thus, efforts to promote effective defence and lay participation have arguably been hampered in certain post-Soviet systems by adversarial and inquisitorial ideologies insisting on foisting US-style juries or plea-bargaining or German-style lay participation on to systems without thought as to how such reforms would function in the indigenous legal culture.[112] Conversely, when reforms are proposed from within the region as opposed to outside it, as in many Latin American countries, it would seem that they have a stronger chance of success as reformers can adapt any changes to meet the demands of the indigenous legal and political culture.[113]

A final way in which anti-inquisitorialism or anti-adversarialism can hinder the progress of evidentiary participatory principles is by encouraging procedures which do little more than effect a compromise between the two opposing traditions. When actors from each tradition are forced to work together rather than in competition, as is the case in the international criminal tribunals, critics of each tradition have worked to keep the most objectionable aspects of each tradition out of the proposed procedures, with the result that a pragmatic blend of different practices has been meshed together which have little coherent unity. Thus, civil law critics have been able to hold out against exclusionary rules of evidence anathema to the principle of 'free proof' and common law critics have held out against judicial control of prosecutors. The result in many cases, however, has been a combination of adversarial party presentation and free admission of evidence within a context in which the defence have been unable to gain full disclosure of evidence and to challenge the evidence against it.

It would be wrong to end on too pessimistic a note. One of the features of legal traditions is that they are not fixed historically, but are creative interpretations of the past constantly changing over time in order to meet the demands of society.[114] The adversarial and inquisitorial traditions associated with common law and civil law traditions 'are moving targets' and the modern mixed criminal procedure systems of continental Europe and more recently Latin America are more a testament to 'frequent and often successful borrowing of procedural

---

[112] J. Jackson and N. Kovalev, 'Lay Adjudication and Human Rights in Europe' (2006) 13 *Columbia Journal of European Law* 83.

[113] M. Langer, 'Revolution in Latin American Criminal Procedure: Diffusion of Legal Ideas from the Periphery' (2007) 55 *American Journal of Criminal Law* 617.

[114] cf. R. Lempert, 'Anglo-American and Continental Systems: Marsupials and Mammals of the Law', in Jackson et al., *Crime, Procedure and Evidence*, 395 (arguing that Anglo-American and continental systems are not pure manifestations of ideal types, but are constantly evolving to meet similar challenges and post-Enlightenment constraints).

features across the adversarial-inquisitorial divide' than a sign of entrenched legal traditions holding out against change.[115] Through concepts such as the equality of arms and adversarial procedure, this book has argued that a new theory of evidentiary rights based on defence participation is developing which is leading to a realignment of the old 'adversarial' and 'inquisitorial' traditions. It may be too early to say that a new evidentiary tradition has arrived. But it is not too early to see a broad agreement on the principles that would form the foundation of such a tradition and to see these being argued for across large parts of the globe. To get a sense of how far we have already come, we can contrast the context in which international procedures are being developed today with that in which the Nuremberg procedures were conceived after the Second World War. At that time, according to Telford Taylor, the task of meshing the adversarial and inquisitorial methods was considered a nearly 'intractable' problem.[116] The 'common grammar' of human rights was in its infancy and the agreement that was reached was more the product of pragmatic compromise than any shared understanding of the different traditions. Today, there are still differences between the common law and civil law traditions, but the increased opportunities for global communication in the ensuing years has improved our understanding of the differences and the will to overcome them.

[115] Sklansky, 'Anti-Inquisitorialism', 1683.
[116] T. Taylor, *The Anatomy of the Nuremberg Trials: A Personal Memoir* (London: Bloomsbury, 1993) 63.

Index

accusatorial systems *see* adversarial or accusatorial systems
adversarial or accusatorial systems
   common law tradition *see* common law tradition
   development of the safeguarding of individual rights of the accused 20–7
   development of exclusionary rules of evidence 21
   impartiality 23
   party participation in the criminal process 21–7
   differences between common law and civil law systems *see under* inquisitorial or non-adversarial systems
   ensuring defence participation by adversarial procedure 369
   evidence and procedure 12
   flaws in 10, 17–18
   inquisitorial/adversarial dichotomy *see* inquisitorial/adversarial dichotomy
   and rationalist tradition of adjudication evaluating testimony 15–16
   and tradition of individual human rights 13–14
   traditional approach falling short of individual rights norms 17–18
adversarial trial, right to 86–95
   examining witnesses 87–8, 101, 104, 139–40
   not necessary for right to be exercised at trial 88–9, 140
   not all witnesses need to be examined on defence's request 89–90, 137
   whether unexamined evidence is sole or decisive evidence 91–5, 101
   international criminal tribunals 136–40
African Charter on Human and Peoples' Rights 79, 199

African Commission 79
American Convention on Human Rights 79, 199, 218
   legal representation and advice 291
   silence and the privilege against self-incrimination 246–7, 252–3, 267–8
anti-nomian thesis 35, 36, 37, 44
Australia
   challenging witness evidence 334–5
   public interest immunity 317, 321
   securing evidence 314–15

Bacon, Francis 34, 44
Basic Principles on the Role of Lawyers (UN) 277, 290–1
Beccaria, Cesare 13, 16, 17, 19, 61
Belgium 66, 84, 303, 311
Bentham, Jeremy 14, 15, 17, 30, 31, 33, 35–6, 44, 213–14
   anti-nomian thesis *see* anti-nomian thesis
   free proof 11, 32, 36, 55, 153
   right of silence and privilege against self-incrimination 242, 268, 271–2
best evidence principle 34–6, 45, 55
bias 229–33
burden of proof 368–9
   development of 21
   directions to juries 39
   evidence obtained by torture or inhuman/degrading treatment 160
   failure to produce evidence and altering the burden of proof 370
   legal and evidential burdens 200–1, 226, 227–8
   and presumption of innocence 200–1, 204, 210, 216, 221–8, 240
   reversal of the burden of proof 210, 221–8

Index

Cambodia, Extraordinary Chambers for 109
Canada 167–8, 269–70
    Canadian Charter and fair trial rights 51, 53, 227, 235, 321–2
    legal professional privilege 295
    public interest 308–9
    public interest immunity and national security 321–2
    securing relevant evidence 315
    special counsel representing defence interests at disclosure hearings 321
challenging witness evidence 325–66
    adequate and proper opportunity to challenge the witness 342–59, 365–6
    circumstances of hearing: importance of impartial judge and of counsel 345–9
    obligation to organise witness examination hearing 349–51
    restrictions on defence's opportunity to challenge witness 351–6
    significance of procedural environment: principal v preliminary steps 342–5
    substantive sufficiency of opportunity to challenge witness 356–9
    criticisms of ECtHR's case law 365–6
    defence participation in the examination of witnesses 364–5
    fairness and the right to challenge 363–6
    importance of witness evidence: the sole or decisive test 338–42, 365
        criticisms of test 341–2
        determining decisive evidence 340–1
        need to assess the evidence 339–40
    justifying the right to challenge incriminatory witness evidence 327–34
    methods of regulating witness evidence 325–7
    reasons why witness evidence separately regulated 325
    regulation of right to challenge witness evidence: the human rights perspective 334–62
        adequate and proper opportunity to challenge the witness 342–59
        approach of ECtHR 336–8
        challenging expert witnesses 361–2
        defence obligations, waiver and forfeiture 359–61, 363–4
        importance of witness evidence: the sole or decisive test 338–42

children
    age of criminal responsibility 105–6
    approach to the evidence of children 46, 66, 387, 388
    challenging witness evidence and vulnerable victims/witnesses 352–4, 375–6
civil law tradition 57–76
    development of criminal evidence law and movement towards freedom of proof 58–66
    excluding or prohibiting the use of evidence 72–4
    freedom of proof and restrictions on doctrine in modern evidence law 69–71
    impartial search for truth 141
    importance of nineteenth-century procedural reforms 58, 66–9
    as a 'moving target' 390–1
    prosecutors giving product of their inquiries to the court 141
    recent developments in evidence law 74–6
        changing structure of the investigation phase 75–6
        judges' ability to deal with expert/scientific evidence 74–5
    witnesses
        court deciding whether witnesses are called 312–13
        questioning witnesses 348–9
        written depositions, dependence on 94, 126
coercion
    coercive power of the state and presumption of innocence 205–7
    compelling witness attendance 350–1
    in interrogation *see under* fair trials and use of improperly obtained evidence
    see also right of silence and the privilege against self-incrimination
common law tradition 30–56
    challenges to free proof *see under* free proof
    common law conceptions of the law of evidence 34–8
        best evidence principle 34–6, 45, 55
        broadening of judicial discretion and flexibility 37–8
        inclusionary principle of probative or relevant evidence unless forbidden 36–8

common law tradition (*cont.*)
   knowledge of facts resting on authority and rules of proof 34
   common law shortcomings and disclosure 307–10
   evidence law adrift? 38–40
   free proof and the common law 30–3
     exclusion of evidence 32–3, 36
   as a 'moving target' 390–1
   questioning witnesses 348–9
compulsion
   in interrogation *see under* fair trials and use of improperly obtained evidence
   and right of silence *see under* silence and the privilege against self-incrimination
confessions
   ad hoc tribunals
     accused not to be compelled to confess guilt 121
     special provision for confession evidence 123
   admissibility and burden of proof 204
   canon law 16
   challenging confessions obtained during preliminary proceedings 345
   co-accused confessions
     admissibility and burden of proof 204
     retraction and legal professional privilege 293–4
   de facto 'interrogation' of suspects in custody, confessions from 175–9, 255–6
   de facto 'questioning' of suspects not in custody, confessions from 179–81
   deception and coercion, confessions obtained by 183–4, 187–8, 197, 280, 281
     confessions in breach of privilege against self-incrimination 281
   existence of confession supporting uncontested witness evidence 340
   failure to speak as challenge to authority 272
   false confessions 53, 216, 276
   forensic science exposing weaknesses of confession evidence 46–7
   international instruments 246–8
     ACHR 246–7, 268
     ECHR 267–8
     ICCPR 246, 267–8
     statutes of ad hoc tribunals 121, 123
   as a main type of evidence in France and Germany 60–1
   obtained by torture 60–1, 158, 160–2, 165–6, 242, 247–8
     fruit of the poisonous tree 191–3
     inadmissibility of confessions as means of preventing torture 247–8
     irrelevance of truthfulness of the confession 167–8
   voluntary nature, admissibility dependent upon 243
     ACHR 246–7
     Human Rights Committee 247
     and privilege against self-incrimination 281, 389
     relaxation of voluntariness standard in terrorist trials 382–3
     requirement to prove the confession was voluntary 204, 247
   wrongful convictions based on 46–7, 53, 216
     calls for exclusion in US cases 53, 216
   see also evidence
constitutional challenge to free proof 50–5
   fair trial rights *see* fair trial rights
   individual rights and the criminal evidence law 51
Convention against Torture, UN *see under* torture
convergence debate 3–9
   debate fixated on whether systems moving in inquisitorial or adversarial direction 6–7
   unintended effects of transplanting processes 7
   whether convergence towards a middle position 6–7
   problems of national legal systems 3
   resistance to change among national legal systems 4–6
cost and expedition *see under* negotiated justice
Council of Europe 105, 248, 294, 316
   Recommendation on the Position of the Victim in the Framework of Criminal Law and Procedure 373
counsel *see* legal representation and advice
covert surveillance *see under* fair trials and use of improperly obtained evidence
crimes against humanity
   international criminal tribunals for 4, 111
   Nuremberg trials 108–9

Index

cross-examination 35, 46, 327–8
   defence obligations, waiver and forfeiture 359–61, 363–4
   and hearsay evidence 328–34
   opportunity to cross-examine important 363–4
   right to cross examine 24, 39, 45, 52–3, 54–5
   role of counsel and judges 348–9, 352
   witnesses refuting previously incriminating statements 358–9
   see also challenging witness evidence

De l'Esprit des Lois (Montesquieu) 17
deception, coercion, traps, tricks see under fair trials and use of improperly obtained evidence
Declaration of Basic Principles of Justice for Victims of Crime and Abuse of Power, UN 373
defence participation 21–7, 111, 112, 233–7, 285–324
   active defence participation adding to the pool of evidence 369
   beyond disclosure: access to evidence outside the possession of the prosecutor 310–16
      application to the court 312–16
      defence investigations 310–12
   challenging witness evidence 347–8
   common law shortcomings 307–10
   equality of arms 298–300, 301–3, 306–7, 311–12, 323–4, 347–8, 369
   legal representation and self-representation 285–9
      right to self-representation 286–9
      role of legal advisers 285–7
   participation in the examination of witnesses 364–5
   public interest immunity see public interest immunity
   right to effective legal assistance 289–95
      balancing away the privilege 293–5
      communication with counsel 289–91
      early legal assistance 289
      right to private communication and legal professional privilege 291–2
   right to full disclosure of evidence 295–307
      an absolute right? 304
      case against the accused 295–7
      scope of right to disclosure: *Jespers* and *Edwards* 297–300
      uncertainties as to scope 301–4

   silence and the privilege against self-incrimination 246, 266–7, 273–7, 283–4, 289
   witnesses' attendance 359
Delmas-Marty, M. 87–8, 102
Descartes, René 15, 34
Diplock Commission 382–3
disclosure/discovery 118, 389–90
   access to evidence outside the prosecutor's possession see under defence participation
   assuming greater significance 40
   common law shortcomings 307–10
   criminal discovery 370
   and defence participation see under defence participation
   ECHR 85–6, 101
   international criminal tribunals 135–6, 144–5
   right to full disclosure of evidence see under defence participation
   see also evidence
DNA testing 46–7, 387, 388
drug trafficking 3

England see United Kingdom
Enlightenment and Enlightenment thinkers 13, 15, 16–17, 20, 21, 27–8, 108–47
entrapment 188–91
epistemic challenge to free proof 41–5
   probability theory 41–2, 214–15
   reasoning processes of juries 42, 43–4
   whether biases should be regulated by exclusionary rules 44–5
equality of arms principle see under defence participation; European Convention on Human Rights (ECHR); evidence in international criminal tribunals
Eurojust 4–5
European Arrest Warrant 5
European Commission of Human Rights 79
   see European Court of Human Rights (ECtHR)
European Convention on Human Rights (ECHR) 79–83, 132–3
   challenging witness evidence 326, 327, 329–30, 331–5
      human rights perspective see under challenging witness evidence
   disclosure 297–300, 301–4
   fair trial rights 80–3

European Convention on Human Rights
(ECHR) (*cont.*)
applying from moment of charge 96–7
discretion of national courts and margin
of appreciation 81–2
equality of arms 83–6, 98–9, 101, 119,
134
member states determining means of
compliance 82, 88
whether proceedings were 'as a whole' fair
82–3
whether rights can be exercised during
the pre-trial phase 97–8
incentives for a guilty plea 384–5
legal representation and advice 99, 100,
103–4, 278–84, 289, 290–1
as living instrument 83, 102, 105
presumption of innocence 199, 217–21
public interest immunity and adversarial
argument 319–20
right to an adversarial trial 86–95, 137
right of silence 83, 100, 103, 151–2, 176–9,
180, 182–4, 196, 246, 248–9, 250–2,
267–8, 278–83
unfair evidence *see* fair trials and the use of
improperly obtained evidence
European Court of Human Rights (ECtHR) 14
case against the accused 297
challenging witness evidence 327, 336–8
criticisms of case law 365–6
regulation of right to challenge *see under*
challenging witness evidence
sole or decisive test 338–42, 365
disclosure 297–300, 301–4
equality of arms principle 83–6, 134
ECHR as living instrument 83, 102, 105
fair trials
evidence *see* fair trials and the use of
improperly obtained evidence
rights *see under* European Convention on
Human Rights (ECHR)
independent and impartial tribunals 229–33
challenging witness evidence and
importance of impartial judges 345–9,
365–6
legal representation and advice 100, 278–83,
289, 290–2
participatory rights 233–5
presumption of innocence 210, 219–21
public hearing requirement not applying to
pre-trial decisions 98

public interest immunity and adversarial
argument 319–20
reversal of burden of proof 221–8
right to an adversarial trial *see* adversarial
trial, right to
right to a reasoned judgment 237–8
right to self-representation 288
silence and privilege against
self-incrimination 241–2, 246–73,
278–83
terrorism and individual rights 381–2
European Evidence Warrant 5
European Union
competence in area of criminal justice 4–5
evidence and arrest warrants 5
mutual recognition principle replacing
mutual assistance 5
slow progress in criminal justice
cooperation 4–5
Europol 4–5
evidence 12–13, 27–8
across traditions *see* evidence across
traditions
challenging witness evidence *see* challenging
witness evidence
civil law tradition *see* civil law tradition
common law tradition *see* common law
tradition
confessions *see* confessions
criminal discovery 370
derivative 191–3, 259
development of exclusionary rules of
evidence 21
evidentiary defence rights *see* towards a
theory of evidentiary defence rights
expert *see* expert evidence
failure to disclose 370
improperly obtained *see* fair trials and the
use of improperly obtained evidence
informers *see* informer evidence
lost evidence 370–1
right of silence *see* silence and the privilege
against self-incrimination
securing crucial evidence 313–16
self-incrimination *see* silence and the
privilege against self-incrimination
third-party rights 315–16
see also disclosure/discovery
evidence across traditions 3–29
beyond the civil and common law traditions
27–9

comparative evidence scholarship 9–14
    evidence and proof 11–13
        rationalist tradition of adjudication and tradition of individual rights 13–14
        whether common principles of evidence exist 13
    convergence debate *see* convergence debate
    rationalist tradition and the rights tradition 14–19
    towards shared evidentiary principles 19–27
evidence in international criminal tribunals 108–47
    ad hoc tribunals 119–24
    common law foundations 116–19
    need for realignment 131–40, 146
        and jurisprudence of other international rights bodies 132–3
        right to an adversarial trial 136–40
        right to equality of arms 133–6
    problems of legitimacy 110–16
        evidentiary context 112–15
        function and purpose of international criminal trials 111–12
        reaching agreed rules of procedure and evidence 115–16
    rubbing points between common law and civil law 124–31
        differences between civil and common law approaches 128–31
        movement towards managerialism 124–7, 387
        trials remaining adversarial 127–8
    towards the future and the International Criminal Court 140–5, 146–7
    towards an international system of justice 108–10
Evidence Law Adrift (Damaška) 40
evidential traditions in continental European jurisdictions *see* civil law tradition
evidentiary defence rights 367–91
    beyond tradition 367–71
        ensuring defence participation by adversarial procedure 368–9
        failure to disclose evidence 370
        lost evidence 370–1
        positive evidentiary rights 367–8
        production of evidence/criminal discovery 370
        remedies for failure to guarantee positive evidentiary rights 369, 370

cost and expedition *see under* negotiated justice
legal culture and tradition 387–91
prospects for evidentiary defence rights 371–2
state security and terrorism *see under* terrorism
victims' right and participation *see under* victims
expert evidence
    bias 233
    challenging expert witnesses 361–2
    and free proof *see* scientific challenge to free proof
    judges' ability to deal with expert/scientific evidence 74–5
extradition 371

fair trial rights 52, 53–6, 108
    contexts calling for different standards of application within fair trial guarantee 381–2
    in emergencies 380–1, 382
    incorporating fair trial standards from point of view of being called to account 277–83
    international context
        human rights *see under* international human rights
        internationalisation of fair trial standards 371–2
    presumption of innocence and fair trial standards 215–17
fair trials and use of improperly obtained evidence 27, 31, 151–98, 229
    confessions *see* confessions
    criminal proceedings as a continuous process 196–7
    impact of improperly obtained evidence on principles of fairness 195–8
    lack of satisfactory regulatory structure for pre-trial phase 197–8
    deception, coercion, traps and tricks 169–88, 255–6
    de facto 'interrogation' of suspects in custody and coercion/compulsion 175–9
    de facto 'questioning' of suspects not in custody 179–81
    fairness and use of evidence obtained by deception and coercion 181–8

fair trials and use of improperly obtained evidence (*cont.*)
  wiretapping and covert surveillance 171–5, 181–2, 184–8, 190–1
  ECtHR's general approach 151–2, 157–8
    evidence obtained by torture or ill-treatment distinguished 163–9, 194–5
    evidence obtained by torture undermining legitimacy of system 162–3, 169, 194–5
  entrapment 188–91
  evidence obtained by torture or inhuman/degrading treatment 60–1, 158–66
    evidence obtained by inhuman or degrading treatment 163–6, 194–5
    evidence obtained by torture 12–13, 20, 53, 54–5, 160–3, 193, 194–5
    fairness and evidence obtained by torture or ill-treatment 166–9
    international instruments relating to torture 159–60, 162–3
    standard and burden of proof 160
    terrorism cases 383–4
  fruit of the poisoned tree 191–3
  theories explaining the exclusion of improperly obtained evidence 153–8
    deterrent to improper conduct 154–5, 193
    guaranteeing reliability of evidence 154, 193
    rights theory/protective principle 155–6, 194
    theory of legitimacy or integrity 156–7, 193, 194–5
    under-regulated pre-trial/investigative process 194–8
Feuerbach, P. J. A. von 67
France
  anti-adversarialism 389
  challenging witness evidence 333–4
  Déclaration des Droits de L' Homme et du Citoyen 17, 199
  defence participation 307, 312
  disclosure 307
  evidence and procedure 59–61, 62, 66, 67, 68, 87–8, 209
  exclusion of evidence 167–8
  French Enlightenment *see* Enlightenment
  French Revolution 18, 20, 58, 67
  impartiality 23
  Napoleonic *Code d'instruction criminelle* 21–2, 62
  Nuremberg trials 116–17
  torture abolished 20
free proof 11, 21, 27–8, 119, 368–9
  challenges to free proof 40–56
    constitutional challenge *see* constitutional challenge to free proof
    epistemic challenge *see* epistemic challenge to free proof
    reform of exclusionary rules slow 41
    scientific challenge *see* scientific challenge to free proof
  and the common law 30–3
  development of criminal evidence law and movement towards freedom of proof 58–66
  exclusionary rules intruding on 37
  meaning of free proof 30–1
  presumption in favour of 33
  and restrictions on doctrine in modern evidence law 69–71

Geneva Conventions 119–20, 296–7
Germany 19, 112–13
  challenging witness evidence 332–3
  evidence and procedure 59–61, 63–5, 66, 68, 70–1, 209
  exclusion of evidence 158, 167–8, 191
  impartiality 23
Gilbert, Geoffrey 34–5, 36, 55
globalisation and internationalisation 3, 371–2

hearsay evidence 33, 71, 118, 128, 138, 139–40, 204
  and cross-examination 328–34
  discretion to admit hearsay in interests of justice 38
  and ECHR 91, 92–5
  hearsay rule 35–6, 37
    ensuring evidentiary sources of a party's case can be tested 39, 54, 328–34
    increasing exceptions to hearsay rule 329–30
    and juries 38
    justification for hearsay rule 329
    witnesses refuting previously incriminating statements 358–9
Hegel, Georg 44
Helié, F. 62

Hobbes, Thomas 13, 17, 19
human rights
  challenging witness evidence *see under* challenging witness evidence
  international human rights *see* international human rights
Human Rights Committee, UN 14
  challenging witness evidence 347
  disclosure 297–8
  evidence 81–2, 167
  fair trial rights 79, 98
    fair trial guarantees not able to be suspended in emergencies 380–1
  legal representation and advice 288, 290
  presumption of innocence 218–19, 221
  right of silence and the privilege against self-incrimination 247–8, 250, 252–3, 263–4, 277
  witnesses 88, 234
Hume, David 13, 15

impartiality
  and bias 229–33
  challenging witness evidence and importance of impartial judges 345–9, 365–6
  safeguarding of individual rights of the accused 23
individual rights 16–17, 19, 20–7
  and the criminal evidence law 51
  development of the safeguarding of individual rights of the accused 20–7
  fair trial rights and individual rights
    in adversarial systems *see under* adversarial or accusatorial systems
    in inquisitorial systems *see under* inquisitorial or non-adversarial systems
    in the UK 52, 53–4, 236–7
    in the US 51, 53–4
  and instrumental objectives of the criminal process 19
  state security and terrorism
    need to balance defence of democracy and individual rights 381–2
    risks of individuals' rights being violated 380–1
  tradition of 13–14, 51–2
  see also international human rights
inductive generalisation 15–16, 41, 43–4

informer evidence
  convictions based on informer evidence shown to be false 46–7, 53
  entrapment 180
  incitement 189
  withholding evidence relating to informers 304–6
    crime investigation inhibited by disclosure of informers' names 203, 304
    disclosure necessary to prove innocence 305–6
inhuman/degrading treatment *see under* fair trials and use of improperly obtained evidence
inner conviction 69–70, 74, 368–9
inquisitorial/adversarial dichotomy debate as to merits of different systems 10–11
  effect on evidence scholarship 9–10
  systems classified into adversarial or inquisitorial 5–9
  dichotomy increasingly unhelpful in describing actual justice systems 8–9
inquisitorial or non-adversarial systems
  agreement between prosecution and defence 9
  civil law tradition *see* civil law tradition
  defence investigations 311
  development of the safeguarding of individual rights of the accused 20–7
  impartiality 23
  party participation in the criminal process 21–7
  reasoned judgments for decisions 21
  differences between common law and civil law systems 9, 11
  disclosure requirements 307–10
  in international criminal tribunals 127–31
  legal professional privilege 294
  preliminary investigations and disclosure 298–300
  right to self-representation 287–8
  evidential traditions *see* evidential traditions in continental European jurisdictions
  flaws in 10, 17–18
  free proof *see* free proof
  inquisitorial/adversarial dichotomy *see* inquisitorial/adversarial dichotomy
  judicial investigations 311–12

inquisitorial or non-adversarial systems (*cont.*)
rationalist tradition of adjudication
exposing deficiencies of inquisitorial system 16
and tradition of individual rights 13–14
right of silence and the privilege against self-incrimination 245–6
Roman canon procedure 16, 20, 58, 59
traditional approach falling short of individual rights norms 17–18
Inter-American Court of Human Rights 79, 252–3
emergencies 380–1
fair trial guarantees not able to be suspended in emergencies 380–1
victims' participation 379–80
International Covenant on Civil and Political Rights (ICCPR) 79, 83, 132
challenging witness evidence 326, 334
fair trial rights 96, 97, 100, 120, 137, 234, 296
non-derogable 380–1
legal representation and advice 286–7, 290
presumption of innocence 199, 217–21
right of silence and the privilege against self-incrimination 246–8, 252–3, 263–4, 267–8, 277–8
International Criminal Court (ICC) 4, 110, 140–5, 146–7
judicial activism 387
principle of judicial scrutiny 317–18
rules of evidence and procedure 110, 140–5, 263–4, 278
and human rights 371
witness proofing 141–2
victims in proceedings 374–5, 378–9
International Criminal Tribunal for the Former Yugoslavia 109–10, 119–20, 124–5, 126, 146
problems in pursuing cases 113–15
right to an adversarial trial 136–40
right to equality of arms 133–6
right of silence and privilege against self-incrimination 241–2
rules of evidence and procedure 110, 120–4, 125–6, 130, 131–2, 277–8
securing legitimate forensic evidence 314–15
International Criminal Tribunal for Rwanda 109, 119–20, 126
right to an adversarial trial 136–40
right to equality of arms 133–6
right to a reasoned judgment 239

right of silence and privilege against self-incrimination 241–2
rules of evidence and procedure 110, 122, 125, 277–8
international criminal tribunals
evidence in *see* evidence in international criminal tribunals
fair trial standards 371–2
legal professional privilege 294
taking circumstances of states into account 382
victims *see under* victims
witnesses *see under* witnesses
international human rights 77–107
derogation from human rights 380–1
evolution of evidentiary human rights norms 79–95
equality of arms principle 83–6
right to an adversarial trial *see* adversarial trial, right to
right to a fair trial 79–83, 97–8
exclusion of evidence obtained in breach of human rights 31
fair trial rights and regulating criminal proceedings 77–9
and presumption of innocence 217–21
process of proof and regulation of the investigation/pre-trial phase 95–101
defence rights and importance of procedural environment 97–9
potential for pre-trial activities to impinge on defence rights 99–101
right to cross-examine accepted in human rights treaties 24
right to self-representation 288
and terrorism 382
towards convergence or realignment? 101–6
informed involvement 103–4
need for change in legal culture 104–5
non-compulsion of defendants in proof process 103
opportunity to challenge evidence 104
reasoned judgment required 104
tradition of individual rights 13–14, 51–2, 77
International Law Commission 110, 121
international terrorism *see* terrorism
interrogation of suspects *see under* fair trials and use of improperly obtained evidence

Italy 7
  challenging witness evidence 334–5, 347–8
  defence participation 311
  difficulties in introducing strong defence norms 387, 388
  evidence and procedure 61, 88

Jackson, Justice Robert 112, 117, 119
juries 18, 387, 388
  bias 231–2
  cognitive psychology questioning how juries reason 42–3
  in continental systems 72
  decline in use of 40, 51, 55
  enabling greater use of exclusionary rules and directions 21
  evaluation of evidence 15–16, 31
    ability of juries to process evidence 38, 39
    adverse inferences from failure to adduce evidence 370
    directions as to evidence 31, 39, 261–2
    directions as to standard and burden of proof 39, 214
    silence of defendants 261–2, 264, 272
  excluding evidence from juries 32, 39–40, 41–2
  lack of reasoned judgement 104, 261–2
  reasoning prejudice and moral prejudice 42
  right to a jury 52–3

Kant, Immanuel 13, 24, 44
Kries, A. von 64

legal culture and tradition 387–91
legal professional privilege 291–2, 305
  balancing away the privilege 293–5
legal representation and advice 118
  challenging witness evidence and importance of right to counsel 345–9
  confidentiality between lawyer and client
    public interest immunity and fettering principle of confidentiality 321–3
    reasons for maintaining confidentiality 322
  defence obligations, waiver and forfeiture 359–61, 363–4
  and defence participation *see* defence participation
  development of representation by counsel 22–3
  and ECHR 99, 100, 103–4, 278–84, 289, 290–1

  importance of counsel in defence participation 26–7
  incentives for a guilty plea and role of counsel 384–5
  in low-economic base countries 386–7
  questioning role 348–9, 352
  right to effective legal assistance *see under* defence participation
  right of silence and representation during interrogations 277–84
  self-representation
    in international criminal tribunals 130, 286–7, 288–9
  see also under defence participation
  special counsel representing defence interests at disclosure hearings 320–1
Leibniz, Gottfried 34
Locke, John 13, 15–16, 17, 34, 44, 211

Mill, J. S. 44
miscarriages of justice *see* wrongful convictions and miscarriages of justice
Mittermaier, C. A. 62, 67
Montesquieu, M. de 13, 15, 17, 61, 215

negotiated justice 28–9
  cost and expedition 384–7
    abbreviated simplified trials 385–6
    aim to reduce costs 384
    defences in countries with low-economic bases 386–7
    diversion out of criminal justice system 384
    greater judicial activism 386–7
    incentives for a guilty plea and compatibility with ECHR 384–5
  negotiated settlements 41
  plea bargaining 41, 130–1, 384–5
Netherlands 167–8
  defence participation 307, 312
  evidence 74, 75–6, 87
Newton, Isaac 15
non-adversarial systems *see* inquisitorial or non-adversarial systems
Nuremberg trials 108–9, 112–13, 116–19, 120, 121, 122, 123, 241–2, 391

On Crimes and Punishments (Beccaria) 16
organised crime 3, 28

participatory rights *see* defence participation
Plato 15
plea bargaining *see under* negotiated justice
prejudice
  avoiding prejudice *see under* presumption of innocence
  prejudicial evidence 239–40
    exclusion of bad character evidence 33, 44, 53, 204
    and juries 38, 229
    probative value of evidence outweighed 38
presumption of innocence 23, 25, 52, 53, 199–240, 270–1
  avoiding prejudice 228–39
    independent and impartial tribunal 229–33
    participatory rights 233–7
    right to a reasoned judgment 237–9
  in emergencies 380–1
  and legal professional privilege 295
  meaning of presumption of innocence 200–11
    presumption as an evidentiary protection 200–4
    substantive innocence 208–11
    treating defendants as innocent 205–7
  presumption of innocence and fair trial standards 215–17
  presumption of innocence and the rationalist tradition 211–15
  reversal of the burden of proof 210, 221–8
  scope of the presumption of innocence under human rights law 217–21
privacy, right to 170–1, 267–8, 269–70
  challenging witness evidence and private life of perceived victim 351
  evidence and third-party rights 315–16
  giving up privacy 103
  invasion of privacy and excluding evidence 27, 53, 169, 181–2, 194
  lawyer/client relationship 292
  protecting privacy 66
    protecting victims' rights to privacy 373, 377–8
  right to private communication and legal professional privilege 291–2
privilege against self-incrimination *see* silence and the privilege against self-incrimination

probability theory *see under* epistemic challenge to free proof
proportionality, principle of 19
  evidence and witnesses 19, 376, 377–8
  national courts 226–8, 240
  restrictions on confidential lawyer/client relationship 292
  reversing burden of proof 224–5
  right of silence 257, 274
public interest 256–8, 305–7, 308–9
  see also legal professional privilege
public interest immunity 316–23
  adversarial argument 319–23
    special counsel representing interests of the defence 320–1
    special disclosure judges 320
  principle of judicial scrutiny 317–19

questioning suspects *see under* fair trials and use of improperly obtained evidence

rationalist tradition 13–14, 20, 22–3, 66
  core tenets of the tradition 15–16
  exclusion of prejudicial evidence 33
  inductive generalisations *see* inductive generalisations
  and presumption of innocence 211–15
  and rights tradition 14–19
  theories of probability 41–2
  victims and witnesses 375
reasoned judgments 21, 104, 237–9, 261–2
reasoning and cognitive processes *see* epistemic challenge to free proof
Recommendation on the Position of the Victim in the Framework of Criminal Law and Procedure (Council of Europe) 373
rights
  African Charter on Human and Peoples' Rights 79, 199
  American Convention on Human Rights *see* American Convention on Human Rights
  Bill of Rights, US 17
  ECHR *see* European Convention on Human Rights (ECHR)
  evidentiary *see* evidentiary defence rights
  fair trial rights *see* fair trial rights
  human rights *see* international human rights
  ICCPR *see* International Covenant on Civil and Political Rights (ICCPR)

individual rights *see* individual rights
participatory rights *see* defence participation
Universal Declaration of Human Rights, UN 80, 81, 120
victims' rights *see under* victims
Rousseau, Jean-Jacques 14, 17
Rwanda *see* International Criminal Tribunal for Rwanda

Schwarze, F. O. 65
scientific challenge to free proof 45–50
  common law courts and expert evidence 48–50
  disagreements among scientists 47
  DNA testing 46–7, 387, 388
  new forms of psychological evidence 46
  non-scientists handling scientific evidence 47–50
Security Council, UN 109–10, 120, 126
self-incrimination, privilege against *see* silence and the privilege against self-incrimination
Sierra Leone, Special Court for 109
silence and the privilege against self-incrimination 241–84, 389
  compensating for lack of representation in low-economic countries 386
  compulsion/coercion 246–8, 252–6, 257, 258–61, 265–7, 269–70, 272–3, 274–5
  confessions *see* confessions
  exception to rights against self-incrimination and right of silence 256–66
    inferences from silence 260–6, 370
    other factors 258–60
    public interest 256–8
  historical and transnational importance of right to silence 241–6
  incorporating fair trial standards from viewpoint of being called to account 277–83
  representation during interrogations 277–84
  privilege against self-incrimination 19, 27, 52, 53, 119, 226
  rationale of the privilege and the right of silence 266–73
  right of silence 25, 118, 207
    nature of right to silence/privilege against self-incrimination 248–9, 283

right of silence as necessary condition for active defence participation 273–7, 283–4
scope of the privilege in international law 246–56
  charged with a criminal offence 250–1
  compulsion 252–3
  defiance of the will of the suspect 253–6
  Funke v France 248–9
  incrimination 251–2
  international instruments 246–8
witnesses remaining silent 357–8
social contract 17, 19, 27–8, 52
  and international criminal justice 114
  protecting the individual by requiring strong proof of breach 20, 23, 25, 203
  social contract vision of participation 26–7
  and terrorism 380
  use of illegally obtained evidence breaching contract 27
South Africa 227
  defence representation 386–7
Spinoza, Baruch 34
standards of proof 12, 53, 70, 207
  before coercive action is taken 206
  directions to juries 39, 214
  evidence obtained by torture or inhuman/degrading treatment 160
  historically 21, 211–12
  and presumption of innocence 201–2, 203–4, 213–14, 216–17
Switzerland 8–9, 68, 75–6, 303
  challenging witness evidence 347, 356–7
  exclusion of evidence 167–8, 191

terrorism 316–17
  approaches to resolving 3–4, 107
  and Guantánamo Bay hearings 53–4, 158, 296–7
  state security and terrorism 380–4
    accountability of security services 383–4
    evidence obtained unlawfully 383–4
    need to balance defence of democracy and individual rights 381–2
    prosecuting terrorist cases 382–3
    risks of individuals' rights being violated 380–1
  states' response to terrorism 380
Thayer, J. B. 32, 36–8, 39, 202
Tokyo trials 112–13, 122, 241–2

torture 16, 18
  abolition 61
  Convention against Torture, UN 159–60, 163, 167, 247–8
  evidence obtained by *see under* fair trials and use of improperly obtained evidence
  silence and the privilege against self-incrimination 247–8, 250, 267–8

United Kingdom (UK)
  adversarial system *see* adversarial or accusatorial systems
  burden of proof 227–8
  case against the accused 297
  challenging witness evidence 327, 331, 334–5, 341–2
  development of representation by counsel 22–3
  Diplock Commission 382–3
  disclosure 85–6
  exclusion of evidence 158–9, 167–8, 191
  expert witnesses 48
  fair trial rights and individual rights 52, 53–4, 236–7
  hearsay rule 329–30
  miscarriages of justice 47
  Nuremberg trials 116–18
  prejudicial evidence 38
  right of silence and the privilege against self-incrimination 241–3
  special counsel representing defence interests at disclosure hearings 321
  witnesses historically 16
United Nations (UN) 110, 120
  Convention against Torture *see under* torture
  Declaration of Basic Principles of Justice for Victims of Crime and Abuse of Power 373
  Security Council *see* Security Council, UN
United States (US) 122, 126
  anti-inquisitorial tradition 389
  Bill of Rights 17
  challenging witness evidence 330–1, 334–5, 342–3, 345, 346, 347
  exclusion of evidence 38, 154–5, 158, 170–1, 182, 185, 188, 191, 235–6
    confession evidence in death penalty cases 53, 216
  expert witnesses and scientific evidence 48–50

fair trial rights and individual rights 51, 53–4
Guantánamo Bay hearings 53–4, 158, 296–7
hearsay/testimonial evidence 330–1, 334
Nuremberg trials 116–18
public interest 308–9
public interest immunity and national security 321
right to privacy 170–1
right to self-representation 288
right of silence and the privilege against self-incrimination 244, 245–6, 268
wrongful convictions 53, 216
Universal Declaration of Human Rights, UN 80, 81, 120

victims 104
  balancing interests of victims and defence 352–4, 363, 375–6, 377–8
  challenging witness evidence
    respect for private life of perceived victim 351, 373
    rights of victim and of defence 352–4, 363
  victims' rights and participation 372–80
    emergence of victims' rights 372–3
    participation in international tribunals 111, 112, 374
    protecting victims in international criminal tribunals 373–4
    purposes of victim participation 379–80
    rights including more than being witnesses 374
    victims in the ICC 374–5, 378–9
  vulnerable witnesses 46, 352–4, 373, 375–6
Voltaire 15, 61
Von Kries, J. 23

Wächter, C. G. von 66–7
waiver and forfeiture 359–61, 363–4
Walther, F. 65
war crimes 28
  international criminal tribunals for 4, 111
Wigmore, J. H. 37, 327–8
wiretapping *see under* fair trials and use of improperly obtained evidence
witnesses
  anonymity 87, 91, 131–2, 351–2, 355–6, 376–7

balancing interests of witnesses and defence 351, 363, 375–6, 377–8
challenging witness evidence *see* challenging witness evidence
children *see under* children
cross-examination requirement 35
evaluating testimony based on their evidence 15–16
experts
  bias 233
  challenging expert witnesses 361–2
  and free proof *see* scientific challenge to free proof
fear of reprisals 354–5
incompetent 34
oaths 35, 350–1
protecting witnesses in international criminal tribunals 373–4
refuting previously incriminating statements 358–9
and right to an adversarial trial *see under* adversarial trial, right to
securing attendance 312–13, 314
  coercive measures 350–1
  inability to secure attendance 134
  insufficient merely to provide adequate procedural setting 359
  obligation to organise witness examination hearing 349–51
silence of witnesses 357–8
vulnerable witnesses 46, 352–4, 373, 375–6
witness proofing 141–2
wrongful convictions and miscarriages of justice 25, 47, 53
  avoiding 204, 206, 213–14, 216, 271–2
  avoiding prejudice 235
  disclosure 305–6, 309
  and legal professional privilege 295
  presumption of innocence 203, 205, 239–40
  non-disclosure of evidence in terrorism cases 383–4

Yugoslavia, Former *see* International Criminal Tribunal for the Former Yugoslavia

Zachariäe, H. A. 68